Constitutional Amendments

**Encyclopedia of the
People · Procedures · Politics · Primary Documents
Relating to the 27 Amendments to the U.S. Constitution**

Constitutional Amendments

Encyclopedia of the
People · Procedures · Politics · Primary Documents
Relating to the 27 Amendments to the U.S. Constitution

VOLUME 2

Second Edition

Mark Grossman

Grey House
Publishing

PUBLISHER:	Leslie Mackenzie
EDITORIAL DIRECTOR:	Laura Mars
PRODUCTION MANAGER:	Kristen Hayes
MARKETING DIRECTOR:	Jessica Moody
AUTHOR:	Mark Grossman
CONTRIBUTING AUTHORS:	Scott Derks; Schlager Group Inc.
COMPOSITION:	David Garoogian

Grey House Publishing, Inc.
4919 Route 22
Amenia, NY 12501
518.789.8700 · FAX 845.373.6390
www.greyhouse.com
e-mail: books@greyhouse.com

Publisher's Cataloging-In-Publication Data
(Prepared by The Donohue Group, Inc.)

Names: Grossman, Mark. | Derks, Scott. | Schlager Group.
Title: Constitutional amendments : an encyclopedia of the people, procedures, politics, primary documents, campaigns for the 27 amendments to the Constitution of the United States / Mark Grossman ; contributing authors: Scott Derks; Schlager Group Inc.
Description: Second edition. | Amenia, NY : Grey House Publishing, [2016] | Includes bibliographical references and index.
Identifiers: ISBN 978-1-68217-176-9 (hardcover)
Subjects: LCSH: Constitutional amendments—United States—Encyclopedias. | Constitutional history—United States—Encyclopedias.
Classification: LCC KF4557 .G76 2016 | DDC 342.73/03—dc23

Table of Contents

Volume 1

Volume 2

Introduction and User's Guide

This second edition of *Constitutional Amendments* is unlike any encyclopedia or reference work on the subject. In two volumes, it not only defines the 27 amendments in comprehensive chapters with detailed narratives on the process behind each amendment, but includes in each chapter a valuable collection of supportive material designed to help students and researchers more fully grasp the rationale behind the amendments, their opposition, votes, and public sentiment.

This material includes biographies of individuals significant to the amendment's passage, reprints of actual political debates, newspaper articles, government reports, and Supreme Court cases. In addition, each amendment chapter includes a unique section called *America At That Time*, that offers a look at what was happening in America at the time the amendment was being proposed, debated and voted on. What did things cost? What were important "firsts"? What was in the news?

NEW to each chapter in this edition is a brief summary and timeline of the amendment. In addition, researchers will find 10 new primary documents, and 54 new Supreme Court cases extending the coverage of this edition up to the minute in regard to the controversial issues before the court in recent years. Also **NEW** to this edition is Appendix D – a list of the 100 Supreme Court cases included in this edition. In addition to new material, other chapter elements have been updated to bring the work up to date.

CHAPTER ARRANGEMENT

Each of the 18 chapters covers one amendment, except Chapter 1 which covers the first 10 amendments known as the Bill of Rights, and includes the following sections:

Section One: Amendment
- The *Amendment* reprinted as it appears in the official record.
- **NEW** *Summary* offers a clear explanation of the amendment and its ramifications in a few succinct sentences.
- **NEW** *Timeline* allows the reader to follow the proposal and ratification process.
- *Introduction* provides the historical framework surrounding the reasons behind the amendment as it was proposed, and follows its path through to ratification.
- *Debate in Congress* offers actual transcripts of the back and forth from both advocates and opponents.
- *Historical Background Documents* are reprints of official documents, relevant to the amendment's passage, including first drafts of the amendment, letters and speeches from politicians who support or oppose the amendment, and Congressional reports, all designed to give the details necessary to fully comprehend the driving force behind each amendment's progress.
- *As Submitted to the States* offers a look at how and when the states voted.

Section Two: Original Primary Documents
This section includes newspaper articles that show how public opinion differed in different regions of the country, and Supreme Court cases that ruled based on their interpretation at the time.

Section Three: Supreme Court Cases
Each case chosen represents individuals or entities who feel that their rights, under the amendment, have been violated. The analysis opens with the case's official docket data, date, decision, and ruling justice, and includes a clear definition of the case.

Section Four: Who's Who
This section offers biographies and photographs of those individuals who either played a significant role in getting the amendment ratified, or worked to block it. These comprehensive biographies combine personal and professional details, designed to offer a better understanding of why an individual acted as he or she did.

Section Five: Footnotes, Sources, Further Reading
These exhaustive and detailed lists by chapter section make it easy to pick up with research where these volumes leave off. Whether it's more information on specific amendments, the amendment process, or the individuals responsible for the amendment, this section provides hundreds of ways to find it.

Section Six: America At That Time
This section sets *Constitutional Amendments* apart from other exclusively historical reference works. Pulling from Grey House Publishing's acclaimed *Working Americans* series, here is where you will find what was happening in America at the time each amendment was progressing through the steps toward ratification. Beginning with a snapshot of significant political, cultural, and social "firsts," this section goes on to include advertisements, selected prices (with currency conversion charts), newspaper articles and many fun images. There is nothing dry about this history lesson!

APPENDICES

Appendix A: *The Constitutional Amendment Process* describes the legal channels taken by each amendment, and whose job it is to administer that process.

Appendix B: *Ratification of Amendments to the U.S. Constitution* offers details on the process and deadlines for the amendment process, and includes timetables of the 27 amendments and average times to ratify.

Appendix C: *Proposed Amendments to the Constitution* details six amendments that made it either through the House, the Senate, or both, but were not ratified by the states. Each of these proposed amendments is detailed in depth – who, what, when, where, and why – and supplemented by relevant original documents.

Appendix D: *List of Supreme Court Cases by Amendment* includes a list of all 100 Supreme Court cases included in this edition, arranged by the amendment that the case claims is being violated.

Ending this two-volume set is a comprehensive *Index*.

Foreword

❝T❞he government of the Union, like that of each State, must be able to address itself immediately to the hopes and fears of individuals; and to attract to its support those passions which have the strongest influence upon the human heart. It must, in short, possess all the means and have a right to resort to all the methods of executing the powers with which it is entrusted that are possessed and exercised by the gov ern ments of the particular States."

—Alexander Hamilton, *The Federalist*, No. XVI, 4 December 1787.

The Founding Fathers realized even as they were writing the original Constitution that it could not be ratified without specific promises that a Bill of Rights, additional amendments giving the people a specific set of rights such as the freedom of speech and of worship, would quickly follow. And to make sure that future generations could amend the Constitution – not with ease, but through a process that demanded a widespread national consensus for such amending – they inserted the ability to change the founding document through either a Congressional action or through a convention held by the states. This power is embodied in Article V of the Constitution itself, which is simple and straightforward in its language:

> *The Congress, whenever two thirds of both Houses shall deem it necessary, shall propose Amendments to this Constitution, or, on the Application of the Legislatures of two thirds of the several States, shall call a Convention for proposing Amendments, which, in either Case, shall be valid to all Intents and Purposes, as Part of this Constitution, when ratified by the Legislatures of three fourths of the several States, or by Conventions in three fourths thereof, as the one or the other Mode of Ratification may be proposed by the Congress; Provided that no Amendment which may be made prior to the Year One thousand eight hundred and eight shall in any Manner affect the first and fourth Clauses in the Ninth Section of the first Article; and that no State, without its Consent, shall be deprived of it's equal Suffrage in the Senate.*

Leaders from all political parties and ideologies have relied on, and cheered, the built-in ability to amend the Constitution. In his first inaugural address on 4 March 1861, President Abraham Lincoln said, "This country, with its institutions, belongs to the people who inhabit it. Whenever they shall grow weary of the existing Government, they can exercise their 'constitutional' right of amending it or their 'revolutionary' right to dismember or overthrow it."[1]

Likewise, a century later, Senator (and later Vice President) Hubert Humphrey spoke about the Second Amendment's right to own guns: "Certainly one of the chief guarantees of freedom under any government, no matter how popular and respected, is the right of the citizen to keep and bear arms. This is not to say that firearms should not be very carefully used and that definite rules of precaution should not be taught and enforced. But the right of the citizen to bear arms is just one more safeguard against a tyranny which now appears remote in America, but which historically has proved to be always possible."[2]

Congress has had literally thousands of proposed amendments brought before it; few are ever voted on, and even fewer receive the coveted two-thirds of each house needed to send it to the states to begin the ratification process. Since the First Congress in 1789, only 33 proposed amendments have been sent to the states, and of these, only 27, counting the 10 amendments in the Bill of Rights, received enough state support for ratification. It is not an easy road to hew, which is just the way the Founders wanted it.

The following graph documents the attempts since the First Congress to amend the Constitution:

Congress	Date	Number of Amendments Proposed
1st-101st	1789-1990	10,431
102nd	1991-1992	153
103nd	1993-1994	155
104th	1995-1996	152
105th	1997-1998	118
106th	1999-2000	71
107th	2001-2002	77
108th	2003-2004	77
109th	2005-2006	72
110th	2007-2008	66
111th	2009-2010	75
112th	2011-2012	92
113th	2013-2014	84

Source: "Measures Proposed to Amend the Constitution," courtesy of The US Senate Reference Home, online at http://www.senate.gov/reference/measures_proposed_to_amend_constitution.htm.

Clearly, the desire to amend the Constitution through the amendment process continues unabated. As long as the American people wish to be governed by that document fashioned in the summer of 1787, the process to change it, to make it better, and to make it more relevant to today's world will continue.

Years ago, I purchased a copy of the US Constitution, which I still have, now worn and ragged, taped and stapled together. When I was beginning the research for this book I read it once again, and felt its majesty and imposing sense of value. My faded copy is a reminder of the original document, created in the minds of men whose values continue to shine and empower mankind. Imagine that a document formed by a group of men nearly two and a half centuries ago still governs our lives, our system of government, the way our laws are interpreted. But what is most fascinating is that in that span of time – more than 225 years – the hundreds of millions of people who have lived and died as Americans have seen fit to amend that precious document a mere 27 times.

But what is more important than the fact that changes have been made is the fact that changes had to be made. Under the original document, black people were slaves and could be sold as property, women could not vote, Senators were elected not by the people but by state legislatures, and the President and Vice President were elected separately...these flaws have been remedied. It took not only a document with the ability and prescription to change it built into its language, but a change of mind of the people who elected their representatives in Congress and in state legislatures, and a civil war that pitted American against American, to change those minds and hearts. Change takes time, it takes respect for both sides, and it takes debate and answers to arguments made by those sides.

Constitutional Amendments is not a dry history – it is a comprehensive work that includes how the amendments to the US Constitution came about, who was behind them, the arguments made for and against their enactment, the US Supreme Court cases which arose from them, and correspondence and contemporary news articles and opinion pieces that highlight the thoughts and feelings of those who lived through such tumultuous periods in our nation's history. As Chief Justice Marshall said in the famous case of *M'Culloch v. Maryland*:

A constitution, to contain an accurate detail of all the subdivisions of which its great powers will admit, and of all the means by which they may be carried into execution, would partake of the prolixity of a legal code, and could scarcely be embraced by the human mind. It would probably never be understood by the public. Its nature, therefore, requires, that only its great outlines should be marked, its important objects designated, and the minor ingredients which compose those objects be deduced from the nature of the objects themselves.

The theory of the Constitution has been in the consciousness of people since the beginning of time. One of the earliest persons to speak out for the need of such a governing document was Henry of Bratton, whose real name was Henricus de Brattona, or Bractona. He was an English judge, sitting on the court known as Coram Rege, or, the King's Bench, from 1247 to 1250, and then again from 1253 to 1257. In his work on the English legal system, "Bracton: De Legibus Et Consuetudinibus Angliæ" ("Bracton on the Laws and Customs of England"), written between 1210 and his death in 1268, he wrote:

Now we must explain how the dominion and possession of incorporeal things, as of rights, are acquired by express consent, by way of gift and by the creation of a servitude. Rights, being incorporeal, cannot be seen or touched, and thus do not admit of livery as corporeal things do. The gift must therefore be effected by the intention of the contracting parties, simply by the intention and will to transfer and accept and the view of the corporeal thing in which these rights inhere, and in that way, by means of a legal fiction, they are quasi-possessed; he who is thus in possession by a legal fiction always quasi-uses until he is disseised by force or without force by non-use, and if he does not use in his lifetime, being unwilling or unable to do so, his heir may use if the servitude was given 'to him and his heirs,' and so from heir to heir, near and remote, by force of the modus of the gift. If it is constituted 'to such a one and his heirs or to whomsoever he may wish to give or assign,' all such are admitted successively to its use by force of the modus of the constitution or gift, and, since they are in quasi-possession, all others are entirely excluded from using it. Rights of this sort, such as servitudes, may be called the appurtenances of some corporeal thing and are [owed] from one corporeal thing to another, as from another's estate or tenement to one's own estate or tenement, in many ways, as will be explained more fully below [in the portion] on the assises. [Such rights are transferred from one person to another by use and quasi-use before real use, as said above.] And as one has rights in another's estate, so he has them in his own, as where he has an estate to which the advows on of a church belongs...[3]

Many historians see the blueprint of the US Constitution in English and British law. But the US Constitution is a document unheard and unseen prior to 1787, when it was formulated by a convention of leading American citizens. That amendments have been made to it should not come as a surprise. An examination of newspapers and congressional documents show the wide history of attempts to amend the Constitution on a various number of subjects.

For instance, on 14 December 1882, during a rather dull debate over Post Office appropriations for the next fiscal year, Representative Roswell P. Flower, Democrat of New York, rose to challenge the members of the House to push for what is now called a line-item veto power for the President of the United States. Speaking on the subject of amending the Constitution, Flower said, "A copy of it was given [to] me when a youth. Its tattered remnants are in my pocket now." He then introduced, to be included as part of the Congressional Record, the entire US Constitution as it stood at that time. As the *New York Tribune* wrote several years later, "all around him in the House the buzz of conversation went on; members went in and out of the cloak-rooms...and doubtless at this very moment [Rep.] Leopold Morse [of Massachusetts] was walking up and down in front of the Speaker's desk, chewing an unlighted cigar, and appearing to the admiring galleries every inch a statesman." Flower was asked if he wanted to "attach" the Constitution to the postal bill, which he said he might do later. The confused members of the House then debated whether or not to adjourn for the day. The *Tribune*, a conservative paper, labeled Flower's actions as "a class act."[4]

But while there is a historical record as to what is in the Constitution – and what is not – and what the amending process has done to make the document stronger and more relevant to the lives of the American people, there is still confusion surrounding the document. Journalist Ezra Klein of *The Washington Post* in December 2010 denounced members of the US House who wished to "adhere strictly" to the precepts of the Constitution. Mocking these members, Klein said, "The issue of the Constitution is that the text is confusing because it was written more than 100 years ago and what people believe it says differs from person to person and differs depending on what they want to get done."

Unfortunately, Klein's timing was wrong (the Constitution was written 223 years prior to his statement), and he did not elaborate on what parts confused him. But the fact that such a statement was made by a member of the nation's press demonstrates how important the study of the original Constitution, as well as its amendments and the amending process, truly is.

The history of the amendments is one that historians have long sought to explain. In the pages of this work, I hope that I have aided somewhat towards this goal of making the Constitution a document not to be "confusing" or feared, but to be celebrated.

—*Mark Grossman*

---

[1] Jaffa, Harry V., "A New Birth of Freedom: Abraham Lincoln and the Coming of the Civil War" (Lanham, Maryland: Rowman & Littlefield Publishers, Inc., 2000), 346.

[2] Statement by Humphrey in Robert Cottrol, "A Liberal's Lament," online at http://www.constitution.org/2ll/2ndschol/104ali.htm.

[3] Bracton, Henry de (George E. Woodbine, ed.), "Bracton De Legibus Et Consuetudinibus Angliae" (New Haven: Yale University Press, four volumes, 1915-42), II:159.

[4] "The Constitution in the Congressional Record," courtesy of the Office of the Clerk of the US House of Representatives, online at http://artandhistory.house.gov/highlights.aspx?action=view&intID=517.

The Nineteenth Amendment

Chapter 10

H. J. Res. 1.

5

Sixty-sixth Congress of the United States of America;

At the First Session,

Begun and held at the City of Washington on Monday, the nineteenth day of May,
one thousand nine hundred and nineteen.

JOINT RESOLUTION

Proposing an amendment to the Constitution extending the right of suffrage
to women.

---

*Resolved by the Senate and House of Representatives of the United States
of America in Congress assembled (two-thirds of each House concurring therein),*
That the following article is proposed as an amendment to the Constitution,
which shall be valid to all intents and purposes as part of the Constitution when
ratified by the legislatures of three-fourths of the several States.

"ARTICLE ————.

"The right of citizens of the United States to vote shall not be denied or
abridged by the United States or by any State on account of sex.

"Congress shall have power to enforce this article by appropriate
legislation."

F. H. Gillett

Speaker of the House of Representatives.

Thos. R. Marshall

Vice President of the United States and
President of the Senate.

```
Proposed in Congress:      4 June 1919

        Sent to States:    4 June 1919

              Ratified:    18 August 1920
```

Chapter 10

THE NINETEENTH AMENDMENT

The right of citizens of the United States to vote shall not be denied or abridged by the United States or by any State on account of sex.

Congress shall have power to enforce this article by appropriate legislation.

Brief Summary

In a single sentence, the Nineteenth Amendment swept away the historical denial of the right of women to vote. The amendment, sometimes called the Susan B. Anthony Amendment after the famed women's suffragist, represented the culmination of decades of efforts on the part of women suffragists to gain access to the ballot box.

Timeline

1869	Wyoming Territory extends the right to vote to women in state and local elections. When it became a state in 1890, it was the only state with full female suffrage.
16 March 1869	Representative George Washington Julian introduces a constitutional amendment that would give women the right to vote.
January 1878	Senator Aaron A. Sargent introduces a women's suffrage amendment in Congress.
1893	Colorado extends the right to vote to women.
January 1896	Utah extends the right to vote to women when the state is admitted to the Union.
8 November 1910	The state of Washington extends the right to vote to women after a statewide referendum.
1911-1917	California, Arizona, Kansas, Oregon, Illinois, Ohio, Indiana, Rhode Island, Nebraska, Michigan, New York, and North Dakota extend the right to vote to women.
10 January 1918	The US House of Representatives passes the Nineteenth Amendment.

30 September 1918	The Nineteenth Amendment fails in the US Senate.
21 May 1919	The House of Representatives again passes the Nineteenth Amendment.
4 June 1919	The Senate passes the Nineteenth Amendment.
18 August 1920	The Nineteenth Amendment is ratified when the state legislature of Tennessee ratifies it; the wording of the amendment is the same as that of the 1878 proposal.

Introduction

❝**H**ow shall we answer the challenge, gentlemen? How shall we explain to them the meaning of democracy if the same Congress that voted to make the world safe for democracy refuses to give this small measure of democracy to the women of our country?" – Rep. Jeannette Rankin (R-Montana), arguing for the US House of Representatives to pass the Female Suffrage Amendment, 10 January 1918.

Perhaps the greatest flaw in the US Constitution when it was first drafted, aside from denying that blacks were human and allowing them to be bought and sold as slaves, was its denying women the right to vote. Until the 20th century, women were seen as being the lesser of the two sexes, not allowed the responsibility of the right to vote. In this section, we demonstrate some of the arguments used by those who opposed a constitutional amendment giving women the right to vote from the late Nineteenth century until the amendment's actual ratification in 1920. Most of these comments sound so sexist that, today, those who made them would be written off as radicals, or considered out of the mainstream of modern political thought. These arguments should be seen, however, not as *modern* political thought, but as the ideals of their time. It would be a mistake to judge those in 1918 based on our standards in 2012. We will examine the words and deeds of those who advocated for female suffrage, from the earliest days in the middle of the nineteenth century to the culmination of the movement, and final ratification of the Nineteenth Amendment to the US Constitution in 1920.

This constitutional flaw was apparent as early as 1776, as members of the Continental Congress were meeting in Philadelphia. Abigail Adams, wife of John Adams, destined to be the first Vice President of the new United States and its 2nd President, wrote to her husband, asking that as they penned the Declaration of Independence to "remember the Ladies." The men never did – the declaration begins with the clarion call that "all men are created equal." Not all men – or women – were created equal in this new land.

During the first decades of the 18th century, several women around the nation stood up, albeit in a limited fashion, to agitate for increased female rights. Such figures as Emma Hart Willard, who founded the first school for girls, the Troy Female Seminary in Troy, New York, in 1821, and Sarah Grimké, of the famed Grimké sisters, who made a speaking tour of the nation in 1836 calling for equal rights before she was shouted down by men, dared to challenge the status quo. State action would be far, far behind; however, in a landmark decision in 1838, Kentucky allowed women to vote in school elections, and the following year Mississippi enacted the Married Woman's Property Act, during a time when blacks in these two states were bought and sold as property.

In 1848, the first Women's Rights Convention was held in Seneca Falls, New York. A magnificent history of the movement up to that time is encapsulated in Sally McMillen's *Seneca Falls and the Origins of the Women's Rights Movement:*

"Standing before a crowd packed into Wesleyan Chapel in Seneca Falls, New York, thirty-two year old Elizabeth Cady Stanton proclaimed: ' We hold these truths to self-evident: That all men and women are created equal.'... This was a momentous assertion, a momentous event. The July 1848 Seneca Falls Convention and its Declaration of Rights and Sentiments formally initiated the struggle for women's equality and justice."[1]

Reporting on the meeting appeared in Frederick Douglass' famed antislavery newspaper, *The North Star:*

"A Convention to discuss the Social, Civil and Religious Condition and Rights of Women, will be held in the Wesleyan Chapel at Seneca Falls, New York, on Wednesday and Thursday, the Nineteenth and 20th of July instant...During the first day the meetings will be exclusively for women, which all are earnestly invited to attend. The public generally are invited to be present on the second day, when Lucretia Mott, of Philadelphia, and others, both ladies and gentlemen, will address the Convention."[2]

Footnotes, Sources and Further Reading for this chapter appears on page 667

In 1902, just four years before her death, Susan B. Anthony wrote of that 1848 meeting, "Women could neither fight nor vote; they were not sustained even by those of their own sex; and, while they incurred no physical risk, they imperilled their reputation and subjected themselves to mental and spiritual crucifixion. Therefore I hold that the calling of that first Woman's Rights convention in 1848 by Mrs. Stanton, Lucretia Mott and two or three other brave Quaker women, was one of the most courageous acts on record."[3]

A convention apparently was also held in Rochester, New York, on 24 August 1848, "to consider the Rights of Women: politically, socially, religiously, and industriously." Such notables as Elizabeth Cady Stanton attended; after one day, the group that assembled offered a series of resolutions, the first of which was "that we petition our State Legislature for our right to the elective franchise, every year, until our prayer be granted."[4]

Considering that these meetings happened at a time when women were often thought of as second-class citizens at best, and blacks were bought and sold like property, it's hard to imagine this movement taking hold. But these women were serious, with many spending most of their lives fighting for the cause, and take hold it did.

The Civil War may have advanced that cause; war often has unintended consequences. Women, left at home as their husbands, fathers, and sons went off to fight, took their places in helping to sustain their families, through whatever kind of work they could find. As "Rosie the Riveter" would mean so much during the Second World War, in the time of such a national emergency as the Civil War women not only did the house work and other tasks, but they also served as nurses and in other medical fields (one female doctor, Marry Edwards Walker, earned a Congressional Medal of Honor – the only woman to be so honored), in horrendous conditions, giving them more of a foothold in society. And while battlefield warriors eventually came home, the women that they came back to had changed. In 1866, the year following the war, as the nation was grappling with the passage and ratification of the Thirteenth Amendment, which ended slavery, Susan B. Anthony and Elizabeth Cady Stanton, two leading advocates for female rights and equality, formed the American Equal Rights Association (AERA) to push for additional rights not just for women but for freed slaves. Anthony and Stanton realized that if women were to ever gain equality, it would have to be in the same form that it had taken to give the same rights to former slaves and freed blacks. While these two women would come to dominate the push to get women's suffrage into legislative language throughout the remainder of the nineteenth century, neither was there when the ultimate victory came with the ratification of the Nineteenth Amendment in 1920. Their work, however, paved the way for others.

Just a few years after the end of the Civil War, women in America found a legislative champion. Rep. George Washington Julian, a Republican of Indiana, introduced on 16 March 1869, for the first time in the US Congress, specific language that proposed a constitutional amendment giving women the right to vote. His proposed amendment read:

"The Right of Suffrage in the United States shall be based on citizenship, and shall be regulated by Congress, and all citizens of the United States, whether native or naturalized shall enjoy this right equally without any distinction or discrimination whatever founded on sex."[5]

That same year, Wyoming Territory gave women the full right to vote as men did, but only in state and local elections; 11 years later, in 1890, when Wyoming became a state, it was the only state in the Union with full female suffrage. In an age when women had few if any rights and were considered subservient to their husbands, these were both landmark moves. The following year, the states ratified the Fifteenth Amendment, one of the triad of so-called "Reconstruction Amendments," which ended slavery and guaranteed black people the right to vote. Ironically, all black *males* now had the right to vote – black females, like their white counterparts, could not. It was a glaring flaw in an otherwise magnificent moment in American constitutional and legislative history.

In 1872, nearly half a century before women would get the right to vote in national elections, a woman ran for President of the United States. The woman was Victoria Claflin Woodhull, who was considered a rabble-rouser even by her supporters in the suffragist movement. One biographer, Kathleen Feeney, wrote of Woodhull, "Her brief dominance of two suffrage conventions both energized and divided the movement. Nevertheless...she offered to both her contemporaries and posterity a foil to conventional models of nineteenth-century womanhood."

[6] On 2 April 1870, Woodhull penned a letter to the *New York Herald*, specifically announcing that she would enter the presidential race two years hence. *The Boston Daily Advertiser*, two days later, reported on the announcement:

"Mrs. Victoria C. Woodhull follows the example of Mr. George Francis Train and announces herself a candidate for the Presidency. The important information is contained in a column letter published in Saturday's *New York Herald*, and signed by the distinguished broker herself. From her office on Broad Street the document comes forth, and as an advertisement of her business it is a happy device. Mrs. W asserts that while other women are clamoring for their rights, she has boldly assumed hers. Speaking in behalf of the disenfranchised sex she then reviews the political situation, discussing home and foreign affairs, the administration and the condition of parties, winding up with the conclusion that the times are out of joint and a woman President is needed to straighten them. With a rare modesty, however, she is in no hurry to reach the White House, but is willing to bide her time."[7]

Her trying to campaign for President when she didn't even have the right to vote led authorities to jail Woodhull – ironically, on election day, Susan B. Anthony tried to enter a voting precinct to vote for Woodhull and was arrested herself for trying to cast a ballot. This quickly put an end to any hopes women had of gaining the franchise, at least for the time being.

Mere months after that election, the US Supreme Court held in the first of two cases that appeared to solidify in concrete the death knell of any chances women had to gain the suffrage. The first of these is simply known as "The Bradwell Case," but is officially known as *Bradwell v. Illinois* (83 US {16 Wallace} 130 {1873}). Decided on 15 April 1873, it followed an Illinois woman, Myra Bradwell, who applied to the Illinois state bar for admission as an attorney. However, simply because she was a woman, the state bar denied her application, and the Illinois state Supreme Court upheld the decision. Bradwell sued to the US Supreme Court; the court held, 8-1 (Chief Justice Salmon P. Chase was the lone dissenter) that the Privileges or Immunities Clause of the Fourteenth Amendment had no specific right to practice a specified profession, and that a state bar, or any entity, could deny someone the right to so practice without violating the US Constitution.[8]

A little more than two years later, the US Supreme Court put their imprimatur on leaving the Constitution bereft of any enfranchisement for women when it decided the landmark case of *Minor v. Happersett* (88 US {21 Wallace} 162 {1875}). On 15 October 1872, Mrs. Virginia Minor, a white woman, tried to register to vote for the upcoming election, referenced above. In Missouri, her home state, the only requirement to voting was to be over the age of twenty-one years and to desire to vote. Minor fit this description. However, Reese Happersett, the state registrar of voters, refused to register her, stating that, according to the US Constitution, "every male citizen of the United States shall be entitled to vote." Minor then sued Happersett in the district court of Missouri for violating her rights by refusing to put her name on the register of voters. Happersett defended himself in court, and the court held that, simply because Minor was a female, she was constitutionally barred from voting. Minor appealed to the Missouri State Supreme Court; when she lost there, she then sued directly to the US Supreme Court, which heard the case. On 29 March 1875, the court held unanimously that under both the US Constitution as well as the Fourteenth Amendment, which granted voting and citizenship rights to blacks and freed slaves, women were to be considered as "citizens" but that all citizens did not necessarily have the right to vote, and that the provision of the Missouri state Constitution which narrowed the right of voting to "male citizens of the United States" was not a violation of the US Constitution, and that Minor was legally denied the right to vote.[9] Norma Basch wrote, "What more is there to say? One could say that the very presence of her case on the Supreme Court docket in the October 1874 term constitutes a turning point in the role of gender in the Constitution. The historical dimensions of *Minor* are misconstrued from the start if we conceive of it only as relegating women to second-class citizenship; women were second-class citizens before and after the decision. The case's importance lies in the fact that it drew the inferiority of women's status out of the grooves of common-law assumptions and state provisions and thrust it into the maelstrom of constitutional conflict. The demands for woman suffrage did not die when the decision was rendered; they acquired a contentious national life."[10]

In 1878, refusing to give up, Susan B. Anthony and Elizabeth Cady Stanton drafted a potential Female Suffrage amendment which they persuaded US Senator Aaron Augustis Sargent, Republican of California, to introduce as an amendment. Anthony and Sargent had been friends for years, and he had tried several times to introduce such an amendment in the US Senate. His first successful opportunity came in January 1878; Stanton and several other supporters testified before Congress calling for support for the measure. It remained in committee for eight full years, until 1887, when a full Senate vote was allowed, but it was defeated, 16 ayes to 34 nays.[11]

It's important to note that Senator Sargent, along with the aforementioned Rep. George Washington Julian, were quiet heroes of the suffrage movement, pushing for laws and legal protections that, for them, had no personal impact and offered little political gain. Of Sargent, historian Rebecca Mead wrote in 2004, "As a consistent supporter of women's rights, Aaron Sargent introduced woman suffrage into congressional debates whenever possible, and he used every argument he could muster. In 1871 and 1876, he tried to attach it to District of Columbia government bills. In a territorial debate in 1874, Sargent tried to include ' sex' as a protected suffrage category. He acknowledged the dedicated activists, numerous petitions, and ' large and popular conventions... making strong efforts,' and warned, ' There is as much agitation on this point as there was for the abolition of slavery before the war broke out.' Sargent discussed the Reconstruction amendments, the example of Wyoming, ' good government' issues, and he also included an ' appeal' for ' the great class of laboring women in the country.' He reiterated the... claim that large classes of people should not be excluded from the vote under the Reconstruction Amendments, but this was the weak spot in his argument. When an opponent observed that California included a very large class of disenfranchised ' Asiatics,' Sargent was unable to resolve the contradiction between his support for female enfranchisement and Chinese exclusion and dropped the point."[12]

In 1887, Kansas bestowed on women in its state the right to vote in state and local elections. Three years later, in 1890, the National American Woman Suffrage Association (NAWSA) was established exclusively to push for a constitutional amendment for female suffrage. The association was the amalgamation of two disparate groups – the National Woman Suffrage Association (NWSA), headed up by Susan B. Anthony and Elizabeth Cady Stanton, and its direct rival, the American Woman Suffrage Association (AWSA), led by such women as Julia Ward Howe and Lucy Stone and even including men, like Henry Brown Blackwell (1825-1909), a British-born reformer who demanded both the abolition of slavery and civil rights for blacks as well as female suffrage. The two groups had gone in divergent directions after their founding – the NWSA favored an all-encompassing constitutional amendment enacted by Congress, while the AWSA fought for specific state-by-state increases, however small they might be. (Note: Blackwell and Stone married in 1855, and had one daughter.) With the groups merged, they began a twotrack approach, pushing for the constitutional amendment while also calling for state action to move forward on equal rights for women. NAWSA grew from approximately 13,000 members in 1893 to more than two million in 1917. Elizabeth Cady Stanton was now the leader of this all-encompassing organization. In 1890, Wyoming became the first state in the Union to allow women to vote in state and local elections, although not in federal elections, such as for Congress or for President. Three years later, Colorado became the first state to ratify a state amendment to its own constitution calling for females to have the suffrage. Thus, the tactics of the former AWSA began to pay off. Between 1882 and 1898, nine different states saw eleven different ballot measures calling for female suffrage went to the voters. Of these, only two – in Colorado in 1893 and Idaho in 1896 – were passed by the voters.[13]

In 1892, Elizabeth Cady Stanton, was forced to resign as the head of NWSA. Three years later she penned the first volume of the two-volume work "The Woman's Bible" (a second volume appeared in 1898), in which she denounced the Church for its views on women as held in the Bible, and she mocked the teachings of Jesus Christ. She wrote, "Does the New Testament bring promises of new dignity and of larger liberties for woman? When thinking women make any criticisms on their degraded position in the Bible, Christian's point to her exaltation in the New Testament, as if, under their religion, woman really does occupy a higher position than under the Jewish dispensation. While there are grand types of women presented under both religions, there is no difference in the general estimate of the sex. In fact, her inferior position is more clearly and emphatically set forth by the Apostles than by the Prophets and the Patriarchs." The criticism earned her more enmity from outside and even inside the woman's suffrage movement, and mainstream suffragists distanced themselves from her even more strongly and forcefully.

The first years of the 20th century saw a new impetus toward getting a Suffrage Amendment passed through both houses of the US Congress. At the same time, so-called "anti-suffragist" movements sprang up. Led by Mrs. Arthur Dodge, who in 1911 formed the National Association Opposed to Woman Suffrage (NAOWS), they allied themselves with other movements that felt themselves under fire: liquor brewers and distillers; members of the US Congress from the American South; railroad companies; meatpackers, and others. The NAOWS was funded heavily from all of these groups, and they lobbied Congress to ignore the suffragist movement.

In 1912, former President Theodore Roosevelt boldly broke away from the Republican Party he had been a member of for decades and formed his own loose-knit group of reformers known as the Progressive Party, or the "Bull Moose" Party. At their 1912 presidential nominating convention, held in Chicago, the party placed in its platform a plank calling for a Female Suffrage Amendment to the US Constitution – the first major electoral party to call for such legislation. Although Roosevelt was not elected President, the effort of his party pushed the nation closer to having the amendment at least voted on in the Congress.

In 1914, for the second time in its history, a vote was held in the US Senate on a proposed Suffrage Amendment to the US Constitution, but again it was defeated. The vote this time, however, was 35 yeas and 34 nays – while short of the three-fourths needed to send it to the states, it was a vast turnaround from 27 years earlier, when it only got 16 yea votes. Things were moving in the direction of eventual passage of an amendment.

In 1915, the US House followed its brethren in the Senate and voted on the Suffrage Amendment (the first time ever an actual floor vote was held), with 204 yeas and 174 nays. Again, a positive step, but still short of the three-fourths needed.

In 1916, in the midst of a presidential election, the National American Woman Suffrage Association met in convention in Atlantic City, New Hampshire, where organization president Carrie Chapman Catt called for a "winning plan" to get those last votes for a constitutional amendment. At the same time, Republicans in Montana were nominating a woman named Jeannette Rankin for a seat in the US House of Representatives. In November, Rankin was elected, the first time in American history that a female had been elected to national office, even though her female constituents could not vote for her as she was running for a federal, and not a state, office. Nevertheless, when Rankin took her seat in Congress in March 1917, it marked a turning point in American politics. Although Rankin rankled many with her lone vote against American entry into the First World War, she argued from the House floor that President Woodrow Wilson could not send American boys to fight "a war for democracy" while denying that democracy to American citizens at home who happened to be female. (Rankin later voted against American entry into the Second World War, the only person to so vote against both conflicts.) Wilson continued to oppose an amendment, even as women suffragists marched in front of the White House and denounced the President by name. Many of these women were imprisoned in harsh jails for speaking out.

As women's groups struggled to get a three-fourths vote through both houses of Congress, they were making faster headway in the states. In the American West, such states as Wyoming and Colorado saw grand suffrage advancements. In fact, prior to the passage in Congress of the Nineteenth Amendment in 1919, fifteen American states gave women full suffrage rights; of these 13 were west of the Mississippi River. In 1917, two years prior to that action, New York State granted women the right to vote in state elections; in 1918, this was followed by Michigan, Oklahoma, and South Dakota.

Finally, as the war turned in America's favor in mid-1918, Wilson changed his mind and called for a vote for a Female Suffrage Amendment. Backed by both Speaker of the House Champ Clark, Democrat of Missouri, as well as House Minority Leader Robert J. Mann, Republican of Illinois, the movement began for another vote. On 10 January 1918; it passed with a vote of 274 to 136, eclipsing the three-fourths vote needed by a single yea vote. Two of the amendment's supporters, Rep. Mann and Rep. Thetus Sims, Democrat of Tennessee, came to the House from sickbeds (Mann was in a hospital in Baltimore and his doctors warned him that he was putting his life in jeopardy by going back to Washington to vote) to cast their support. The vote then moved on to the Senate, where, on 30 September 1918, the vote fell two votes shy of approval. A follow-up vote was held on 10 February 1919, but again fell two votes shy of the required three-fourths.

The Democrats lost control of the US House of Representatives in the 1918 midterm elections, and Rep. Mann, too ill to become Speaker, made it a point that the GOP in the new Congress would push for another vote. On 21 May 1919, the House voted 304-89 in favor of the resolution, with 42 votes more than necessary to send the amendment again to the US Senate, which opened debate in June 1919. Finally, on 4 June 1919, the US Senate voted 56-25 to approve the measure, giving it the requisite three-fourths vote. Speaker of the House Frederick Gillett signed it, and it was sent to the states for ratification.

The rush in the states to ratify the amendment soon turned into a deluge. As seen in the table below, by the end of June 1919 48 states, including Texas and New York, had ratified the amendment.

By August 1920, a little more than a year after being sent to the states, the amendment neared having 38 states ratify it. Tennessee was the state that pushed the amendment over the line. After long debate and arguments, involving not only residents of that state but outsiders both pro and con, on 18 August 1920, the Tennessee legislature voted by a count of 50-49 in favor of ratification. On 26 August, Secretary of State Bainbridge Colby officially proclaimed the requisite number of states had ratified the amendment, and he said that it was now a part of the US Constitution. That year, women voted for the Republican candidate for President, Warren G. Harding, in record numbers.

Since then, only one major case involving the constitutionality of the Nineteenth Amendment has ever come before the US Supreme Court. In 1922, in *Leser v. Garnet* (258 US 130), the Court held that the amendment itself was constitutional. Nothing further was added, and to this day no other case has come before the Court that has challenged that 1922 view. However, other cases dealing with voting rights and the equal protection of women have been heard, as recently as 1976.

While it is virtually unimaginable that direct constitutional challenges to the Nineteenth Amendment in the late twentieth century and beyond would be taken seriously, a ripple effect of the amendment, which essentially added women to a constitution that had excluded them, was to underpin litigation having to do with equal rights for women and for due process under the law for women. Particularly in the 1970s, during an era when numerous segments of the population fought for and won legislation and court decisions to enforce their rights, several Supreme Court cases mandated the equal treatment of women in various contexts. *Reed v. Reed* (404 U.S. 71 {1971}) was a landmark case that overturned a probate law in Idaho that gave preference to men over women in the administration of a decedent's estate. *Frontiero v. Richardson* (411 U.S. 677 {1973}) declared unconstitutional a federal law that treated men and women members of the military disparately in the assignment of benefits for dependent spouses. In *Cleveland Board of Education v. LaFleur* (414 U.S. 632 {1974}), the Court declared unconstitutional onerous regulations surrounding maternity leave in public schools for pregnant women. And in *Stanton v. Stanton* (421 U.S. 7 {1975}), the Court struck down a Utah statute that established different definitions of adulthood for men and women. In these cases, the Court took the position that in virtually all circumstances, distinctions based solely on gender were repugnant to the Constitution.

Today, we think of female voters in relation to a "gender gap" among parties, although women from both parties have served in both houses of Congress, as state governors, and as members of the President's cabinet, including three female Secretaries of State (Madeleine Albright, Condoleezza Rice, Hillary Clinton). Two women – Geraldine Ferraro in 1984 and Sarah Palin in 2008 – were selected by their parties as Vice Presidential candidates. In 2006, Nancy Pelosi became speaker of the US House of Representatives. And while a few women have run for President, none has yet broken that final "glass ceiling" of American politics. However, in 2016, Hillary Clinton became the first woman presidential nominee of a major political party. Despite her failure to win the election, it is surely only a matter of time before a woman is elected President of the United States, seated at the pinnacle of power of the nation that once withheld from all women the right to vote.

Debate in Congress

On 21 May 1919, the House voted 304-89 in favor of the resolution, with 42 votes more than necessary to send the amendment again to the US Senate, which opened debate in June 1919. Finally, on 4 June 1919, the US Senate voted 56-25 to approve the measure, giving it the requisite three-fourths vote.

Debate in the US House of Representatives, 21 May 1919.

WOMAN SUFFRAGE.

The SPEAKER. This is Calendar Wednesday, and the Clerk will call the committees in their order.

The Clerk called the committees, and when the Committee on Woman Suffrage was reached,

Mr. MANN. Mr. Speaker, by direction of the Committee on Woman Suffrage, I call up House joint resolution No. 1, proposing an amendment to the Constitution extending the right of suffrage to women, and ask that the resolution be reported.

The SPEAKER. The Clerk will report the resolution.

The Clerk read as follows:

Joint resolution (H.J. Res. 1) proposing an amendment to the Constitution extending the right of suffrage to women.

Resolved, etc., That the following article is proposed as an amendment to the Constitution, which shall be valid in all intents and purposes as part of the Constitution when ratified by the legislatures of three-fourths of the several States:

"ARTICLE ____.

"The right of citizens of the United States to vote shall not be denied or abridged by the United States or by any State on account of sex.

"Congress shall have power to enforce this article by appropriate legislation."

[...]

Mr. MANN. Mr. Speaker, hearings have been had on this resolution for more than 50 years. [Applause.] Hearings have been had on similar resolutions in the House of Representatives for a number of Congresses. There has been no hearing had on House joint resolution No. 1 in this Congress, nor is there anything new to be said in a hearing.

Mr. MOORE[14] of Pennsylvania. Mr. Speaker, I wish to ask the gentleman this question: In view of the fact that women opposed to woman suffrage have indicated, yesterday and to-day, that they are surprised by this action – and I give full credit to the gentleman from Illinois for his parliamentary cleverness in bring it up at this time – whether he thinks it would be fair to let this matter stand over for a few days until those opposed to the resolution may be heard upon it?

Mr. MANN. I do not think it would be fair to the rest of us.

Mr. MOORE of Pennsylvania. I am willing that the gentleman shall have the credit for the passage of the resolution, if it goes through, but I think it fair to have what has been said go into the RECORD.

Mr. GARNER.[15] Mr. Speaker, reserving the right to object, I want to ask the gentleman from Illinois a question about the parliamentary status. If unanimous consent is agreed to and the previous question shall be considered ordered, will that give an opportunity of reading the resolution under the five-minute rule?

Mr. MANN. There is no opportunity for reading a House Calendar resolution or bill under the five-minute rule.
Mr. GARNER. Would there be any opportunity to offer an amendment unless the one offering the amendment should get recognition for that purpose?

Mr. MANN. There would not be, unless the Member offering the amendment should get recognition for that purpose.

[...]

The SPEAKER. The gentlemen is recognized for an hour.

Mr. MANN. I yield 15 minutes to the gentleman from Kansas [Mr. LITTLE], the ranking Republican member of the Committee on Woman Suffrage. [Applause.]

Mr. LITTLE.[16] Mr. Speaker, the gentlemen from Pennsylvania [Mr. Moore] suggests that the ladies who are not in favor of woman suffrage are taken unawares. To register surprise at the appearance of propositions of a certain welcome, friendly, complimentary, and anticipated tenor is one of the most highly valued privileges of that charming sex, which no gentleman, even in the heat of debate, would ask them to surrender for any political right, however important. The ladies are certainly no more surprised than I am, because it is a scarce 30 minutes since notification from the gentleman from Illinois [Mr. MANN], chairman of the Woman Suffrage Committee and author of the resolution at issue, whose rare parliamentary sagacity and unrivaled parliamentary leadership made this day's work possible, that I was to open this debate. This is a good time to bring it up.

Five years ago Julius Caesar, after 19 centuries, challenged Jesus Christ to a final contest. The Kaiser threw down the gantlet [sic] and the friends of Christian civilization took it up. The tide of war turned in favor of the Son of Bethlehem and against the Prussian; and, if anything has been decided, it has been decided that now right, not might, shall rule the world. [Applause.] Unless our sons and our billions have been sacrificed in vain, the world is about ready to substitute the rule of reason for the rule of force in the government of reasoning creatures. What better expression of that could there be than to say now that the mothers who risked their lives to bring into the world the four millions of soldiers we mustered shall have some word to say about the destinies of their sons? [Applause.] The British House of Commons voted, I think, 7 to 1, and recently, I believe, the French Chamber of Deputies voted 7 to 1, for woman suffrage. The time is opportune for marking an era's close. Civilization has reached a stage, a period, a moment, when we can ring the liberty bell again and announce that this great step forward has been taken.

They tell us that woman [sic] should not vote merely because she is a female. No other reason has been advanced except that form which says that she can not bear arms. Every mother who bears a son to fight for the Republic takes the same chance of death that the son takes when he goes to arms. The fact that she is a woman is a reason for, not against, the utilization of every force for the advancement of society. Ninety-nine per cent of the murderers in the world are men. Ninety-nine per cent of the burglars are men. Ninety-nine per cent of the counterfeiters are men. Ninety-nine per cent of all the thieves, outlaws, forgers, pickpockets, bank robbers, train robbers, pirates, and drunkards in the world are men. Ninety-nine per cent of all criminals are men.

[...]

In the last analysis those who oppose woman suffrage imply ignore everything except brute force. They discard brains, scholarship, character, and simply seek to enforce the law of the herd, that the biggest bull is the boss. Under their theories Napoleon Bonaparte was a greater man than Abraham Lincoln; John L. Sullivan a more useful citizen than Thomas Edison. I challenge all such claims as unworthy of the citizens of a Christian and cultured land. Carried to their logical conclusion those theories have dominated and guided and wrecked and ruined the great Empire of Germany perhaps for centuries to come, and at the very moment when they had attained the rounded summit of a successful, brutal, despotic development of brute force. If during the last 40 years the women had held absolute control of Germany, that might State would now be rich, happy, contented, and yet there are still those who will tell you woman should not vote because she can not fight.

[...]

Mr. KITCHIN.[17] Mr. Speaker and gentlemen of the House, I shall vote against this resolution. I do not rise, however, to make an argument against it, but rather for the purpose of an explanation and expression of some congratulations. It appeared in the RECORD yesterday, though not intentionally, that the Democratic organization of the House had been a little amiss in nominating the membership of he Woman Suffrage Committee. I want to say that that is simply apparent. This morning was the first opportunity which the Democrats had to present the names of the Democratic membership of the Woman Suffrage Committee, though the identical Members that meet this morning elected as minority members of that committee were notified and invited by Mr. MANN, the chairman of the Woman Suffrage Committee, to meet in his committee room yesterday along with the majority members elected on Monday and participate in the consideration of this resolution. They did meet and consider this resolution, and they did vote, with the exception, I think of one, for its favorable report.

[...]

The SPEAKER. The gentleman from Florida [Mr. CLARK] is recognized.

Mr. CLARK of Florida.[18] Mr. Speaker, I yield five minutes to the gentleman from Texas [Mr. HARDY]. The SPEAKER. The gentleman from Texas is recognized for five minutes.

Mr. HARDY.[19] Mr. Speaker, this is a curious exhibition to me. I have watched the chasing of the band wagon on many occasions during all my life, but I never saw such a band-wagon chasing as there was yesterday and is to-day. I just left my home in Texas, where an amendment to our State constitution giving our women the vote is pending. It is to be voted on May 24. I have written a letter, and authorized its publication, urging the great State of Texas to adopt for itself this amendment giving to her women the same right to vote as her men now have. I earnestly hope and believe the amendment will be adopted.

But, Mr. Speaker, I believe that the very foundation of the original agreement under which the thirteen sovereign States formed the Union that constitutes this Nation is undermined and the agreement itself violated in spirit and in principle by the attempt to incorporate in the Federal Constitution a provision fixing or affecting the qualification of electors in the several States, and giving to Congress or to the Federal Government the right to enforce that provision.

The very first reservation in the Constitution of the United States when it was made by our fathers was a reservation reserving to the States the right to determine the qualifications of electors for electing Members of Congress. Article I, section 2, of the Constitution reads:

The House of Representatives shall be composed of Members chosen every second year by the people of the several States * * * and the electors in each State shall have the qualifications requisite for electors of the most numerous branch of the State legislature.

This joint resolution violates that section by providing that Congress shall determine who may vote or who shall not vote, or who may be permitted to vote or who shall not be excluded from voting by the several States, and it goes further and provides that Congress shall have the power to enforce this article by appropriate legislation.

When the States of this Union find Federal supervisors and inspectors attending all our elections, and perhaps Federal appointees holding all our elections under this provision, which violates the principle and destroys the rock of local self-government, they may rue the day when they refused to let each State decide for itself this great fundamental question.

We first violated this principle when we adopted the fifteenth amendment. Under the fifteenth amendment, not only the negro, for whom it was adopted, but the sons of every other race under the sun made vote in any State in the Union, provided they or their ancestors have once been naturalized. Our immigration and naturalization laws are in the jurisdiction and control of the Federal Government. What evils may yet come of the fifteenth amendment only the future may unfold. Under it the old force bill was introduced, and defeated only after a long and bitter fight. When a new force bill shall be introduced under the fifteenth amendment and this proposed amendment, it will not be defeated.

[...]

Mr. MANN. Mr. Speaker, I yield 10 minutes to the gentleman from California [Mr. RAKER].

Mr. RAKER.[20] Mr. Speaker and Members of the House, I am sorry that we are unable to have the time extended, so that more Members may have an opportunity to express their views to the membership of this House and to the country at large. They have been in favor of the resolution, and they feel as though a few words would give them the opportunity to express what has been in our mind for many years. This is one of the great fundamental questions confronting the American Nation to-day. We have settled many of the other questions ahead of the civilized world, but we have been behind when it comes to treating half our population and giving them the same right the other half has had with respect to participation in the Government. We are behind the other nations of the world in that respect. There are some things that I would like to adopt from the Old World and add to ours, but a great big majority of the things that our people have and that this country has the Old World has not. This country has stood for the right of the individual to express his opinion, for the doctrine that he is responsible only to himself and to his God, and up to this date, so far as the Federal Government is concerned, we have said that one-half only of our population should express their views, give their sentiment, and have a voice in our Government. But the time is coming, and it is coming fast, when there will be a change in this respect, and to-day we will see this resolution passed by a good substantial vote over and above the two-thirds majority necessary. I expect that within the next week or 10 days the resolution will have passed the Senate and will then go to the States for ratification, as it ought to.

When we come to look back is somewhat remarkable to see what the States have done. We find that there are 15 States which have full woman suffrage. There are 29 States where women can vote for President. These 29 States control 306 electoral votes, but still you do not permit these women to vote for Members of this House; you do not permit them to vote for Members of the United States Senate, and in many other instances you fail to allow them to vote for State officers. Before the last Congress adjourned, and after it had passed this resolution by a two-thirds vote on 10 January, 1919, it is remarkable to find what the countries of the Old World had done with respect to woman suffrage...

[...]

I want to congratulate the gentleman from Illinois [Mr. MANN], as I think I am entitled to, upon his insisting that this resolution be brought up the first thing when this Congress met in extraordinary session. The House by a large vote expressed its desire in the last Congress that it should pass. The Senate by one vote failed to give it passage. The President of the United States, not only yesterday but some three months ago, appeared before the Senate urging that body, with all its conservatism and its rules, because of the work women had done, because of the advantage they have been to America in winning the war, because of their loyalty and unselfishness and their ability to cope with all the vicissitudes of war, be given the same right to participate in their Government as the men have. So with propriety, with justice, with fairness, this proposition was placed on the calendar yesterday and comes up to-day as House joint resolution No. 1. It is now up for consideration by the House and within the next hour and a half the vote will have been taken and America will have taken her place with the civilized nations of the world in extending this God-given right, this thing that makes America worth while, this thing that men have died for, even within the last year, to the women of the country in order that they may exercise their individual right; that they may participate in the affairs of their country; that they may say that the laws under which they are living shall be such as human beings should live under – to the advantage of this country and of the children that are to come, so that we might have a stronger, a more virile, and a better race.

[...]

Mr. MANN. I yield five minutes to the gentleman from New York [Mr. MACCRATE].

Mr. MacCRATE.[21] Mr. Speaker and gentlemen, I realized thoroughly that a man only three days in Congress should hold his tongue, but coming as I do from a district which has equal suffrage, and being a member of the Committee on Woman Suffrage, I felt it obligatory to say why we from our section believe this national resolution or amendment should be submitted to the States for the States to decide in the constitutional way whether it shall be adopted. Now, whether you consider the franchise a right or a privilege, the women of America deserve the right, what they have earned the privilege. Everywhere you went during the past two years you saw women in uniform. You saw them in the Salvation Army, the Red Cross, the Knights of Columbus, the Young Men's Christian Association, Young Men's Hebrew Association, and other allied war activities. Whether you are at home or whether you were abroad, and like myself had the privilege of seeing the streets of London and Liverpool in January of this year, you realized that American womanhood had met the last argument that men have given for denying them the suffrage privilege, namely, that no one who is not a potential soldier is entitled to the franchise. I submit to your fairness and judgment that the women of America have been as potential soldiers during the past year as have been the men of America. [Applause.] And if potentiality for military service is the last objection, then certainly with the men who avoided the draft, or with the slackers, the women of America ought never be compared; and more certainly if men who continued in agricultural pursuits to win the war, if men who continued in shipyards to win the war, if men who continued in other branches of activities to win the war are entitled to the franchise, the women who maintained equal industrial and agricultural burdens and high moral burdens to win the war are entitled to the franchise. [Applause.] Not only that, but this resolution seems to me in perfect harmony with the Constitution itself. The preamble of the Constitution declares its purpose to be "to form a more perfect Union." This amendment will help us perfect the Union. It does not go into the homes of the country and tell the people what they shall put on or what they shall eat or what they shall drink. It does not say to the men and women of America they shall not do this or they shall not do that, but it does recognize a fundamental of our Government that rights and privileges shall be equal, and declares that sex alone shall not deprive women of the right or privilege of voting. I submit to you that this resolution is in harmony with the spirit of the Constitution itself. [Applause.]

The US Senate debated the House-approved Female Suffrage Amendment for a single day, 4 June 1919, and then passed it that same day by a vote of 56-25, more than the three-fourths needed to send it on to the states for ratification.

Debate in the US Senate, 4 June 1919.

WOMAN SUFFRAGE

The Senate, as in Committee of the Whole, resumed the consideration of the joint resolution (H.J. Res. 1) proposing an amendment to the Constitution extending the right of suffrage to women.

The PRESIDENT pro tempore. The pending question is on the amendment proposed by the Senator from Alabama [Mr. Underwood].[22]

Mr. WADSWORTH[23] obtained the floor.

Mr. BRANDEGEE.[24] I should like to have the amendment read.

Mr. WADSWORTH. Let the amendment be read.

The PRESIDENT pro tempore. The Secretary will read the amendment proposed by the Senator from Alabama.

The SECRETARY. On page 1, line 6, strike out the words "the legislatures of" and in lieu thereof insert the words "conventions in," so that the paragraph will read:

That the following article is proposed as an amendment to the Constitution, which shall be valid to all intents and purposes as part of the Constitution when ratified by conventions in three-fourths of the several States.

Mr. WADSWORTH. Mr. President, like the Senator from Idaho [Mr. BORAH],[25] I represent in part a State which has extended the franchise to women residing within its borders. In view of that fact and my decision to vote against the proposed amendment to the Constitution, as I have done upon two prior occasions, I desire to make my attitude clear before the Senate.

No vote of mine cast upon this amendment will deprive any of the electors of the State of New York of any privilege which they now enjoy. The people of that State, as the people of several other States, have decided for themselves, in an orderly and constitutional manner, to extend the franchise to the women. I feel so strongly on this question that the people of the several States should be permitted to decide this matter for themselves that I desire to say that were this amendment, instead of being drafted for the purpose of extending woman suffrage all over the country, drafted for the purpose of forbidding the extension of the franchise to women, I would vote against it.

The Senator from Idaho yesterday discussed the right of the people to settle their own affairs, particularly in matters which were local and intimate. My feelings upon that question are somewhat like his. The people of the several States when they organized their governments and adopted their constitutions delegated certain powers to their legislatures and to their executives. Then they set up their judiciary to see to it that both their legislative and executive departments should keep faith and should not transgress the limits set by the people.

[...]

Even though one might be opposed on general principles to the extension of the franchise to women, one can not logical he object to the people of a great Commonwealth voting upon that question, settling it for themselves, and if they settle it in the affirmative with respect to woman suffrage one can not then logically object, even though one may have voted against it as a citizen of the State. Nor can I see how one can logically object to the application of the principle, even though in its application the people, voting freely and openly, decide that they shall not extend the franchise in this way.

Something has been said in the debate which has thus far taken place upon this amendment as to the popular demand in favor of it all over the country. Some criticism has been uttered by one or more of its advocates against Senators who are opposing it and who have consistently opposed it in times past. An examination of the record of the different States which have voted upon this question does not, I venture to say, indicate that there is any overwhelming popular demand thus far evidenced in the elections.

[...]

Mr. President, it may seem somewhat old-fashioned for a Senator to express his reverence for the Constitution of the United States, his reverence and his devotion not only to its letter but to its spirit. When one views modern tendencies and the influences that are at work in this country to-day, one is tempted to suggest that now is an appropriate time to rededicate and reconsecrate ourselves to a proper understanding of the letter and spirit of our Constitution and to a better understanding of its meaning. The tendencies of the day, without any question, are traveling fast along the road which, if followed to its ultimate goal, will mean its destruction or its alteration to such a degree in spirit, if not in letter, that it will be scarcely recognizable. It is now proposed in this amendment, as a part of this tendency which has been so evident in recent years, to take away from the people some of that sense of responsibility the exercise of which is the only safeguard for the intelligent conduct of a democracy and to assume that responsibility at the seat of government.

[...]

Mr. SMITH[26] of South Carolina. Mr. President, as others have said before me, nothing that I can say, perhaps, can change a vote; but in view of the pending amendment and the vital issues that are now at stake, I should be derelict to duty if I did not enter my protest against the passage of this amendment, which to all intents and purposes is exactly similar to one that has already been passed, the result of which is an illustration of the point that has been made so splendidly by the Senator from Idaho [Mr. BORAH] and emphasized this morning by the Senator from New York [Mr. WADSWORTH].

In our dual form of government the principle of its duality is the one that makes it possible for every part of this vast domain of ours to progress as conditions justify. Were we a homogeneous people, were the local conditions, both social, commercial, and industrial, the same, it might be less destructive of the spirit of democracy for us to take the principle that underlies democracy and emasculate it as this will emasculate it. But when the conditions are so divergent, one local condition throughout the United States are so different, the splendid people incorporated into the Constitution finds its sanction.

I referred a moment ago to another amendment, incorporating exactly the same principle as this, that was made into our organic law. The fifteenth amendment – but who does not know and realize that the fifteenth amendment, when it was passed, was passed in a moment of heat, passion, sectional strife, and bitterness? There is not a man in America to-day capable of exercising the functions of citizenship but that recognizes that that amendment, passed when and how it was passed, jeopardized the civilization that you and I represent in a section of our country. The alien population amongst us was not like it was in other States. Even if the franchise had been granted to them in other States, their fewness of number made it possible for those States to absorb them without danger to their civilization.

But unlimited franchise in certain other States would have deluged and destroyed with a horde of ignorance and incompetency this civilization that it had taken all of these years to build up and perfect.

[...]

That was your reason, founded as it was in justice and in righteousness. Those men from the South who are sitting here to-day, who are going to vote for the ratification of this amendment or vote to submit this amendment to the people, by that vote ratify and confirm the fifteenth amendment, because I maintain to-day that there is no difference whatever between the fifteenth amendment and the proposed Susan B. Anthony amendment. The Susan B. Anthony amendment is the fifteenth amendment with the insertion of one word alone, namely:

The right of a citizen of the United States to vote shall not be denied or abridged by the United States or by any State on account of race, color, previous condition of servitude, or sex.

Those of us from the South, where the preponderance of the Negro vote jeopardized our civilization, have maintained that the fifteenth amendment was a crime against our civilization. Now, when a southern man votes for the Susan B. Anthony amendment, he votes to enfranchise the other half of that race, and ratifies, not in a moment of heat and passion, what we have claimed was a crime, but in a moment of profound calmness and sectional amity he votes to ratify the fifteenth amendment and give the lie to every protestation that we heretofore have made that the enfranchisement of the Negro men, unlimited, was a crime against white civilization. When Senators and others of the North, East, and West viewed conditions calmly the fifteenth amendment did become a dead letter, and infinitely better that it should become a dead letter than that the civilization of the South should be destroyed and in its destruction jeopardize the civilization of America.

Here is exactly the identical same amendment applied to the other half of the Negro race. The southern man who votes for the Susan B. Anthony amendment votes to ratify the fifteenth amendment. Senators on the other side have acquiesced in silence when in desperation we passed such laws as would nullify the disastrous effect of the fifteenth amendment. Southern Senators voting for this amendment puts them without excuse still further to withhold their hands.

I can understand how a man from the West or a man from the East, viewing it strictly from his own local impression, might get the idea that we ought to extend it to all, but those of us from the South who have seen the evil effect upon our section of country from this menace – worse then poverty, worse than be retarded commercial and industrial growth – those of us who have seen the very sanctity of the fireside and the sacredness of womanhood jeopardized, can not vote for this amendment without once again making possible all these evils that we have for weary years combated and overcome. How southern Senators can vote to turn loose upon the South another era similar to that through which we have passed I can not understand.

[...]

Mr. JONES[27] of New Mexico. Mr. President...

The PRESIDENT pro tempore. Does the Senator from South Carolina yield to the Senator from New Mexico? Mr. SMITH of South Carolina. I yield.

Mr. JONES of New Mexico. I have been listening to the very positive statement made by the Senator from South Carolina, and I have felt like not making any interruption, even for the purpose of asking a question. However, I have finally concluded that unless something be said at this juncture it will go to the people of the State of South Carolina and other Southern States that the remarks just made by the Senator from South Carolina have been universally accepted her in the Senate.

I do not want to provoke any discussion of the subject, but I do want at this time to protest most earnestly against the construction which the Senator from South Carolina has placed upon this proposed constitutional amendment. If I am able to read the English language, the amendment does absolutely nothing more than to prevent discrimination in the franchise on account of sex. I think it requires an extreme imagination for one to draw any inference or to fabricate any argument to the effect that the passage of the amendment is a reaffirmation or readopting of the fifteenth amendment.

Mr. SMITH of South Carolina. Does it not extend suffrage to female Negroes?

Mr. JONES of New Mexico. That is true; but the Senator knows that the fifteenth amendment was directed to a class of people only, and this amendment is intended to liberate the women of the entire country, the millions of white women of the country. It is to operate upon them and is not confined to the black women of the South.

Mr. SMITH of South Carolina. But it includes them.

Mr. JONES of New Mexico. Yes; it includes them.

Mr. SMITH of South Carolina. Certainly. I said it did not differ from the other. He went specifically after the Negro men in the fifteenth amendment. Now you go specifically after the Negro and white women in this amendment. By thus adding the word "sex" to the fifteenth amendment you have just amended it to liberate them all, when it was perfectly competent for the legislatures of the several States to so frame their laws as to preserve our civilization without entangling legislation involving the women of the black race. You simply have amended the fifteenth amendment by adding the Negro women. When we could have had all the white women vote by State action, you want to add the Negro women by Federal action. That is what you have done, and that is what I am protesting against.

Mr. JONES of New Mexico. That, I take it, is the Senator's construction, and, of course, I do not expect to convince him, but I want the statement to go into the Record that in my judgment this amendment is entitled to no such interpretation.

[...]

Mr. BRANDEGEE. Mr. President, I shall be very brief in the statement that I want to make to the Senate upon this question. I heard quite a large portion of the speech made by the Senator from Idaho [Mr. BORAH] yesterday. I was then called from the floor on business, and I did not hear the latter part. I see that it is withheld from publication in the Record, so that I am unable to read it, but, so far as I heard it, I entirely agree with his views upon this matter.

The Senator from Idaho comes from a State that has for years had woman suffrage. I come from a State which has never had it. The legislature of my State has just declined to submit to the people of the State a constitutional amendment providing for it in that State. There is no way of ascertaining, so far as I have been informed, what the sentiment of the voters of my State is upon that question other than the individual opinions that people may entertain upon the question. From information that I have received – and I think I have been in pretty close touch with the sentiment of the State – I believe that a vast majority of the present voters of the State who are men are opposed to woman suffrage in the State of Connecticut. I believe that a vast majority of the women of the State are opposed to woman suffrage in the State of Connecticut. I am absolute certain that a vast majority of both the women and the men of Connecticut are opposed to Congress and three-quarters of the other States of the Union telling them what the qualifications of the electors of the State of Connecticut shall be.

However that may be – and that, of course, I admit is a question of opinion about which I have stated mine, and others are welcome to theirs – I am opposed to putting in the Constitution of the United States a provision which will force the ideas of Congress and three-quarters of the States, if three-quarters of the States concur with the ideas of Congress, upon that State and their ideas of what the qualifications of the electors of the other quarter of the States shall be. I believe that this country has become prosperous and great and strong by the exercise of home rule and the people of the different localities in this country minding their own business and, by minding it, developing a capacity to manage it. I may be wrong about that. It may be that the various localities of this country should transfer all the powers which the States which formed this Union reserved to themselves to the Federal Government here in Washington, but it is contrary to the biological and physiological laws of the world that we will get stronger by abandoning the exercise of these functions than we would be by exercising them. It contradicts the laws of history and experience.

Mr. President, in my judgment the framers of the Constitution designed that instrument to be the broad charter of our liberties and the definition of our form of government. They never expected the use of the process of amending the Constitution to be prostituted to putting a lot of police regulations, ordinances, and laws into the Constitution of the United States. They left the police power and the rules which govern the inhabitants of this country in their respective subdivisions in the hands of the people who were to be affected by these rules. They wisely thought that the people in a country differing in climate, population, habits, and historical traditions could better administer their own affairs in the far-removed sections of the country in accordance with their local traditions and ideas than they could be administered by the fiat of a body sitting in the city of Washington. They wisely thought that the Senator from South Carolina and his colleague were better adapted to say what was for the best interests of the people who elected them, and to whom they are responsible, then the Senator from Connecticut or the Senator from New York, and vice versa. I think the Senator from South Carolina will agree that the Senator from New York and myself from my State are better qualified to state to this body what sort of laws are best adapted for our section of the country than the Senator from South Carolina would be. If that were not so, it would be no sense in having Senators of the United States required to be residents of the States which they pretend to represent here.

[...]

Mr. President, if this process is to be continued, if the people of this country want to be governed in local customs, to be told what they are to eat and what they are to drink and how much, and when they are told to go to bed, and what language they are to use, and to be regulated in every move they make in their daily lives and in their personal habits by a constitutional amendment in the United States Constitution that can never be got out except by a two-thirds vote of each branch of Congress and then a vote of three-fourths of all the State legislatures in addition, you have made a set of police regulations of the Constitution of the United States, as the Senator from New York has wisely warned you, it is a process that is calculated beyond all others to drag the Constitution of the United States into the mire and to destroy all respect for it, because you can not enforce a law or even a constitutional amendment against people who do not believe in it.

[...]

Mr. THOMAS.[28] Mr. President, until the Senator from Idaho [Mr. BORAH] made his very interesting speech yesterday, it had not been my purpose to take any part in this discussion; for I am as anxious as any one to reach a vote, and thus finally dispose of the subject, as it undoubtedly will be disposed of on this occasion. I think, however, in view of the argument submitted by the senior Senator from Idaho, which unquestionably impressed his audience as it did myself, something should be said in reply to one or two of its features.

During its delivery I asked the Senator how he differentiated between his position at the time and that taken by him on the occasion of his vote upon the prohibition amendment; and his explanation, if I correctly comprehended him, was that inasmuch as a number of the States had adopted prohibition, and inasmuch as it could not be made effective so long as other States not having adopted it were permitted to manufacture and import alcoholic liquors therein, which neutralized prohibition, it being necessary to enable the States to enforce their laws, and, in the interest of local self-government, that the constitutional amendment providing for general prohibition should be submitted to the States for ratification or rejection, the Senator voted for the amendment.

I have no doubt that this reason was conclusive and controlling with the Senator from Idaho; but I am unable to perceive the force of that logic which justifies the enactment of a prohibition amendment to the Constitution but which rejects the proposed suffrage amendment. Each of them deals with a subject which was reserved to the States at the time of the adoption of the Constitution. Were it not so, these amendments would be unnecessary. That it is so is most obvious by reference to the general proposition that powers not expressly or by necessary implication delegated to the Federal Government are reserved to the States, or to the people.

If the argument be a substantial, it could be made as I think it has been made, against every amendment hitherto proposed to the Constitution, whether adopted or rejected. Fundamentally, the people of the United States, when conforming to the machinery and the requirements of the Constitution in their action, may incorporate into the Constitution of the United States anything they please. It is a matter of judgment – a matter, if you please, of necessity – in the opinion of that majority which is required to make the fundamental change. Whether it encroaches upon the rights of the States or interferes with local self-government, or abolishes local self-government, is entirely a practical question, and, in my judgment, has nothing to do with the constitutional right and power of the people to amend their organic act as they may see fit.

Prohibition and the suffrage are both matters of local concern; and they will be matters of local concern, subject, of course, to national legislation within the purview of our powers, until constitutional amendments are not only proposed by the Senate and House of Representatives but actually ratified and enforced by a two-thirds majority of the States voting thereon.

[...]

I can readily understand, Mr. President, how a Senator who had cast his vote against the prohibition amendment could consistently oppose this amendment upon the ground that it interferes with local self-government; but I am unable to understand the logic which justifies a favorable vote for the one and an unfavorable vote for the other.

I am as much concerned for the integrity of local self-government as any lover of his country can be. I concede all that was said in his favor yesterday by the Senator from Idaho. I am glad that he has become so fervent and capable a champion of that great principle; and I freely admit that never in this country did it stand in as much jeopardy as at present and in the recent past. The right of the people to meet in their separate and several communities and legislate in their own interest and for their own welfare may be said to lie at the very foundation of Anglo-Saxon liberty – a right which should be safeguarded at all times and respected everywhere; a right the disregard or lowering or abandonment of which will, in my judgment, be inevitably followed by all the consequences so eloquently pictured by the Senator from Idaho. But, Mr. President, I am unable to perceive how this amendment, should it become effective through ratification, can affect the principle of local self-government, while that regarding prohibition certainly will; for the right of a man to eat or to drink or to conduct his personal affairs as he sees fit, provided only that he pays the same respect for the right of others to do the same thing, is infinitely more of a subject for local self-government than the right of suffrage.

I do not refer to the moral or police aspect of the subject. This is not the time or place for that, but I assert fundamentally that the one affects local self-government much more than the other.

Mr. KING.[29] Mr. President –

Mr. THOMAS. In just a moment. If I had been present when the vote was taken upon the prohibition amendment, I should have voted for it, not because I believe it is the best thing for the people, but because I was instructed by the people of my State to do it, and I would have respected that instruction. I yield to the Senator from Utah.

Mr. KING. I agree with what the Senator has said that the support of the prohibition amendment to the Constitution, if a man acted logically, ought to call for a vote in favor of amending the Constitution with respect to suffrage. And yet, does not the Senator think that this amendment is more an assault upon the States than the other, because one of the inevitable characteristics and indispensable qualities of a sovereign State is the right to determine who shall hold office within the State, determine the qualifications of electors, and this amendment is a restriction upon the right of a sovereign State to exercise their sovereign power.

Mr. THOMAS. No, Mr. President, I do not. It is unquestionably an invasion, an absorption, if you please, of a right within the States may now, subject to another amendment regarding suffrage, exercise without national interference, except in so far as national elections are concerned. We had at one time a law upon the statute books enacted by Congress and enforced for many years under which at all elections where any national officer was chosen the entire machinery of the election was in the hands of the Federal authorities represented by United States marshals and supervisors. It was a deliberate and unwarranted intrusion into the affairs of the States, but it was a law, nevertheless, within the power of Congress, if it saw fit to do so, to enact. Inasmuch as State elections are constantly narrowing or decreasing in number, so that State officials and presidential elector and Members of Congress are chosen at the same time, there is no reason in the world why, if Congress saw fit to do so, it might not independently of this proposed amendment take charge of and control those elections.

But, Mr. President, whether that be so or not, that time for applying that argument has gone, for there can be no question that in spite of the obstructive tactics of the so-called National Woman's Party, which has prevented the successful submission of this amendment heretofore, the overwhelming majority of the people of the United States are in favor of the amendment. There can be no more significant evidence of the fact than that the vote about to be taken will be confined to no particular section of the country.

[...]

Mr. KIRBY.[30] Mr. President, I had not intended to speak on this question, and shall do so but briefly. My remarks are chiefly provoked by the statements of the Senator from New York [Mr. WADSWORTH] and the Senator from Connecticut [Mr. BRANDEGEE] that the action of this Congress and the action of the people of the

45 States in the adoption of the prohibition amendment has a tendency to bring the Congress into disrepute, [and] has a tendency to make the people have less regard and respect for the Constitution.

When I heard this statement of the Senator from New York that they were many men in the United States who already now feel aggrieved because of the prohibition amendment to the Constitution, and that they are proceeding to avoid or evade the effect of this amendment, and that such action would have the effect to bring the Constitution into disrepute with the people of this country...

The Senator from Alabama [Mr. UNDERWOOD] has offered this amendment, and he has offered it not to improve the condition but in the hope of defeating the resolution. He is an enemy to the cause. He is not in favor of the proposition of permitting women to vote. He makes no concealment of that fact. He has not been in favor of it. He is not in favor of it now. He offers this amendment to injure the cause and not to help it. Why should the amendment be adopted? No other amendment of the 17 amendments to the Constitution of the United States has ever been submitted to conventions in the States. It has never been attempted to be done before. It is permitted under the Constitution, yes; but has never been availed of. It has never been done heretofore, and why should be employed now on this question, and why should it proposed by an enemy of the resolution and expected to be indorsed [sic] by those who are its friends? I say it should not be done.

There any reason to fear that in the United States of America in the adoption of this amendment the people will not have a fair expression of their views about it? Women only vote in comparatively a very few States. The man in all the States vote. They vote to elect members of the legislature, they vote to elect Members of Congress, they vote to elect United States Senators, and they will vote yonder upon this proposition of the ratification of this amendment, which is proposed in accordance with the rules laid down for amending the Constitution.

Can you say it is wrong to amend the Constitution according to the rules laid down for the purpose. If all the people of the country can not be trusted to amend the Constitution according to the rules provided in the Constitution, then is it not time that we have no further amendments? Some of these gentlemen, I believe from the arguments they have made, would be willing and think it better for the interest of the country in [the] future that we have no further amendments to the Constitution, that the people can not be trusted to amend their own Constitution in the they laid down when the Constitution was made for amending and changing it. That seems to be the idea some of them have.

The Senator from Connecticut [Mr. BRANDEGEE] inveighed against the degeneracy of the times. He talked about those ancient Senators of great ability and great courage who stood here and took the same oath that these Senators in these degenerate days take. He said they were courageous, that they were patriotic, that they regarded their oath when it was taken. I do not know whether the Senator thinks he is more loyal and were patriotic and more courageous than the Senators who are supporting this amendment or not. He may be more able, but I will not even make any concession on that point.

That is the condition we are confronted with here to-day. No other amendment to the Constitution has ever been proposed in such a way as it is attempted to propose this. It never has been done. All the legislatures in the States are elected by the people. They are sent to their different assemblies representing their people. They will vote on this question, and if you had a convention and elected these representatives for this particular purpose they would be no more representatives of the people than they are now. You are attempting here an innovation, so far as that practice is concerned.

As to what as to what the Senator from South Carolina [Mr. SMITH] has said, the Senator still seems to be in the unreconstructed period. I live in the South. I have lived under the fifteenth amendment since I was born, practically. It is the law of the land, and what is the use in discussing conditions under which it became so? Where is the harm that shall come to us if hereafter as to one-half of our people who have been denied the right to vote we shall utilize their ability and their judgment in the settlement of questions that affect local conditions and affect national interests? There has been, so far as I am concerned, no good reason urged here to-day at all why this amendment should not be adopted. I did not expect to say anything to-day and would not have done so except for those remarks from the Senators from New York [Mr. WADSWORTH] and the Senator from Connecticut [Mr. BRANDEGEE] that provoked it.

Mr. UNDERWOOD. Mr. President, only a few words. I have listened with interest to what the Senator from Arkansas [Mr. KIRBY] has just said. Of coarse, I am opposed to the pending joint resolution, and have been from the beginning, but that does not affect the question of the amendment to it, as to which is the better way to reflect popular sentiment in its adoption or rejection.

The Senator says that this is an innovation; that he desires to have this amendment adopted along the lines of the Constitution. It is no more an innovation if my amendment is adopted than the joint resolution would be as it stands as originally drafted, because the Constitution itself provides two modes of ratification, and it is left entirely optional with the Congress as to which mode shall be adopted. The Congress can determine that it shall go to the legislatures for adoption or the Congress can determine that State conventions called for this sole purpose shall pass upon the ratification or the rejection of the amendment.

The Senator from Arkansas says that this amendment of mine is introduced for the purpose of defeating the joint resolution. That is a very candid confession by one of the proponents of the measure. In itself it could not defeat the measure. There can be no question that every State in the Union would call a convention for the ratification or rejection of the amendment if we adopt this method. More than that, if they did not call it, the Federal Congress could call a convention.

But it narrows itself to this, that if a legislature is elected, this, being one of the issues, may become subordinated in many States to other issues. It may become subordinate to the personal equation of the candidates, and men may be elected to vote on this issue who will not directly reflect the mature judgment of their constituents. But if a convention is called for the sole purpose of ratifying or rejecting this measure, then the delegates to that convention will be merely the instrument of the popular will, as the Electoral College is the instrument of the popular will in the election of a President of the United States. When the Senator advances the argument that the adoption of this amendment would defeat the woman-suffrage amendment he concedes n that moment that the popular sentiment is not for the Susan B. Anthony amendment, and that the proponents of the measure dare not submit it to the popular will of the people of America.

Mr. REED. Mr. President, I simply want to add a word in connection with the statement just made by the Senator from Alabama [Mr. UNDERWOOD]. We are already informed through the press that the purpose has taken shape of immediately convening legislatures in extraordinary session to ratify this amendment. Those legislatures were not elected upon the issue of suffrage or nonsuffrage; they were elected upon totally different issues; and now it is proposed that men who were not selected by the for the purpose of passing upon this issue shall pass upon it before the people even have the opportunity to again elect a legislature.

Mr. KIRBY. Mr. President –

The PRESIDENT pro tempore. Does the Senator from Missouri yield to the Senator from Arkansas? Mr. REED. I yield to the Senator.

Mr. KIRBY. The Senator suggests that there is a purpose to call the legislatures of the different States to get immediate ratification. Where does the Senator get such an idea? Where is there anything upon which to base such a statement as a fact?

Mr. REED. I will answer that Senator. I have already stated it, if the Senator had been listening. I said it had been repeatedly stated in the press that that is the purpose of the leaders of this movement. I have seen what professed to be quotations by those who have been leaders of the movement. I have generally found that the newspapers have been pretty able to prognosticate the movements to a reasonable extent in the future of this suffrage program. I have just been informed by a citizen of the State of Texas that two of the great papers of Texas are already advocated the calling of the legislature in extraordinary session for the purpose of ratifying this amendment, although the State of Texas by popular vote held within the last few days has defeated suffrage, I understand, the majority amounting to nearly 30,000.

So we may as well understand that it the purpose of the proponents of this measure to do everything within their power to keep from submitting it in any way to the popular will and to obtain ratification in any manner possible. I expect to hear all of these proponents within the next few months loudly proclaiming their belief in the doctrine that the great people of the country shall in all respects rule. I wish they could bring to an adherence to that doctrine to-day.

[...]

Mr. PHELAN.[31] Mr. President, the objection which has been made to the amendment I the proponents of woman suffrage is that it may delay the final adoption of the suffrage amendment. I plan to hasten consideration. The reason why a delay might be caused is that the House has passed the amendment in one form, and it would facilitate matters to have concurrence by the Senate; but, of course, the Senate is an independent body, and that is no reason which should be advanced to us. Those of us who are in favor of national suffrage, and also in favor of the determination of all questions affecting the amendment of the Constitution by a vote of the people, desire to see that an opportunity shall be given to the people to vote; and to that end I have prepared an amendment to the amendment, with a view of facilitating the early determination by the people of their will upon this subject, so that there will be no needless delay.

I will read the amendment in order to comment upon it.

The amendment proposed by the Senator from Alabama reads as follows:

Resolved, etc., That the following articles be proposed as an amendment to the Constitution, which shall be valid to all intents and purposes as a part of the Constitution when ratified by conventions in three-fourths of the several States.

[...]

Mr. GAY.[32] Mr. President, in February last, when the vote was taken on the woman suffrage question, I explained my position briefly at that time. My position to-day, Mr. President, is the same as it was then. There is no doubt in my mind that women should be given the right to vote. There is doubt, however, that they will ever receive the privilege they are now asking by the methods which some of their supposed friend is have adopted. It is a well-known fact that they have finally secured the necessary two-thirds vote of the Senate of the United States to pass the Susan B. Anthony amendment and to submit that amendment to the legislatures of the various States of the Union. The advocates of the Susan B. Anthony amendment have won a great victory and are justly entitled to all the praise and honor which comes with the winning of a battle which has been fought for so long a time. It is not my intention to attempt to delay this legislation, but I do desire to present here and now an amendment at the next meeting of their legislatures. I present this as a substitute for the amendment which is now before you. The amendment which I am about to present was drafted by the former first attorney general of Louisiana and by the Democratic national committeemen from that State when this matter was under discussion during the last session of Congress. It meets the objection that many have to the Susan B. Anthony amendment and is more liberal perhaps than the amendment which I have already presented for your consideration.

Section 2 reads that the several States shall have the authority to enforce this article by necessary legislation, but if any State shall enforce or enact any law in conflict therewith, then Congress shall not be excluded from enacting appropriate legislation to enforce it.

This, Mr. President, gives to the various States the right to enact and enforce laws giving women the right to vote. It does not leave all questions to Congress, but puts the matter where those who believe in State rights consider the powers should be vested.

Mr. President, it only requires 13 States to prevent the adoption of the Susan B. Anthony amendment, and I predict there are 13 States that will never ratify the amendment which the Congress of the United States is about to present to the American people. The last vote in the State of Texas shows full well how the wind is blowing.

With the passage of the amendment which I am now presenting to you as a substitute for the other amendments which have been offered, the objection would be removed and number of States would soon pass it and thus give the right of suffrage to those noble, patriotic, and splendid women of our country who have so long fought for this right and who so richly deserve the privilege.

Historical Background Documents

Wendell Phillips (1811-1884) was one of the most important abolitionists during the years before the US Civil War, right alongside William Lloyd Garrison. In this speech, republished in 1910 and excerpted below, Phillips asks the question: 'shall women have the right to vote?'

This speech was made at a Convention held at Worcester, on the 15th and 16th of October, 1851, upon the following resolutions, which were offered by Mr. Phillips: –

"1. Resolved, That, while we would not undervalue other methods, the right of suffrage for women is, in our opinion, the corner-stone of this enterprise, since we do not seek to protect woman, but rather to place her in a position to protect herself.

"2. Resolved, That it will be woman's fault if, the ballot once in her hand, all the barbarous, demoralizing, and unequal laws relating to marriage and property do not speedily vanish from the statute-book; and while we acknowledge that the hope of a share in the higher professions and profitable employment of society is one of the strongest motives to intellectual culture, we know, also, that an interest in political questions is an equally powerful stimulus; and we see, beside, that we do our best to insure education to an individual, when we put the ballot into his hands; it being so clearly the interest of the community that one upon whose decisions depend its welfare and safety should both have free access to the best means of education, and be urged to make use of them.

"3. Resolved, That we do not feel called upon to assert or establish the equality of the sexes, in an intellectual or any other point of view. It is enough for our argument that natural and political justice, and the axioms of English and American liberty, alike determine that rights and burdens, taxation and representation, should be coextensive;

hence women, as individual citizens, liable to punishment for acts which the laws call criminal, or to be taxed in their labor and property for the support of government, have a self-evident and indisputable right, identically the same right that men have, to a direct voice in the enactment of those laws and the formation of that government.

"4. Resolved, That the democrat, or reformer, who denies suffrage to women, is a democrat only because he was not born a noble, and one of those levelers who are willing to level only down to themselves.

"5. Resolved, That while political and natural justice accord civil equality to woman; while great thinkers of every age, from Plato to Condorcet and Mill, have supported their claim; while voluntary associations, religious and secular, have been organized on this basis, – there is yet a favorite argument against it, that no political community or nation ever existed in which women have not been in a state of political inferiority. But, in reply, we remind our opponents that the same fact has been alleged, with equal truth, in favor of slavery; has been urged against freedom of industry, freedom of conscience, and the freedom of the press; none of these liberties having been thought compatible with a well-ordered state, until they had proved their possibility by springing into existence as facts. Besides, there is no difficulty in understanding why the subjection of woman has been a uniform custom, when we recollect that we are just emerging from the ages in which might has been always right.

"6. Resolved, That, so far from denying the overwhelming social and civil influence of women, we are fully aware of its vast extent; aware, with Demosthenes, that 'measures which the statesman has meditated a whole ear may be overturned in a day by a woman'; and for this very reason we proclaim it the very highest expediency to endow her with full civil rights, since only then will she exercise this mighty influence under a just sense of her duty and responsibility; the history of all ages bearing witness that the only safe course for nations is to add open responsibility wherever there already exists unobserved power.

"7. Resolved, That we deny the right of any portion of the species to decide for another portion, or of any individual to decide for another individual, what is and what is not its 'proper sphere'; that the proper sphere for all human beings is the largest and highest to which they are able to attain; what this is cannot be ascertained without complete liberty of choice; woman, therefore, ought to choose for herself what sphere she will fill, what education she will seek, and what employment she will follow; and not be held bound to accept, in submission, the rights, the education, and the sphere which man thinks proper to allow her.

"8. Resolved, That we hold these truths to be self-evident: 'That all men are created equal; that they are endowed by their Creator with certain inalienable rights; that among these are life, liberty, and the pursuit of happiness; that, to secure these rights, governments are instituted among men, deriving their just powers from the consent of the governed'; and we charge that man with gross dishonesty or ignorance who shall contend that 'men,' in the memorable document from which we quote, does not stand for the human race; that 'life, liberty, and the pursuit of happiness' are the 'inalienable rights' of half only of the human species; and that, by 'the governed,' whose consent is affirmed to be the only source of just power, is meant that half of mankind only who, in relation to the other, have hitherto assumed the character of governors.

"9. Resolved, That we see no weight in the argument, that it is necessary to exclude women from civil life because domestic cares and political engagements are incompatible; since we do not see the fact to be so in the case of man; and because, if the incompatibility be real, it will take care of itself, neither men nor women needing any law to exclude them from an occupation when they have undertaken another incompatible with it. Second, we see nothing in the assertion that women themselves do not desire a change, since we assert that superstitious fears, and dread of losing men's regard, smother all frank expression on this point; and further, if it be their real wish to avoid civil life, laws to keep them out of it are absurd, no legislator having ever yet thought it necessary to compel people by law to follow their own inclination.

"10. Resolved, That it is as absurd to deny all women their civil rights because the cares of household and family take up all the time of some, as it would be to exclude the whole male sex from Congress, because some men are sailors, or soldiers, in active service, or merchants, whose business requires all their attention and energies."

In drawing up some of these resolutions, I have used, very freely, the language of a thoughtful and profound article in the *Westminster Review*. It is a review of the proceedings of our recent Convention in this city, and states with singular clearness and force the leading arguments for our reform, and the grounds of our claim in behalf of woman.

I rejoice to see so large an audience gathered to consider this momentous subject. It was well described by Mrs. Rose as the most magnificent reform that has yet been launched upon the world. It is the first organized protest against the injustice which has brooded over the character and the destiny of one-half of the human race. Nowhere else, under any circumstances, has a demand ever yet been made for the liberties of one whole half of our race. It is fitting that we should pause and consider so remarkable and significant a circumstance; that we should discuss the question involved with the seriousness and deliberation suitable to such an enterprise. It strikes, indeed, a great and vital blow at the whole social fabric of every nation; but this, to my mind, is no argument against it. The time has been when it was the duty of the reformer to show cause why he appeared to disturb the quiet of the world. But during the discussion of the many reforms that have been advocated, and which have more or less succeeded, one after another, – freedom of the lower classes, freedom of food, freedom of the press, freedom of thought, reform in penal legislation, and a thousand other matters, – it seems to me to have been proved conclusively, that government commenced in usurpation and oppression; that liberty and civilization, at present, are nothing else than the fragments of rights which the scaffold and the stake have wrung from the strong hands of the usurpers. Every step of progress the world has made has been from scaffold to scaffold, and from stake to stake. It would hardly be exaggeration to say, that all the great truths relating to society and government have been first heard in the solemn protests of martyred patriotism, or the loud cries of crushed and starving labor. The law has been always wrong. Government began in tyranny and force, began in the feudalism of the soldier and bigotry of the priest; and the ideas of justice and humanity have been fighting their way, like a thunderstorm, against the organized selfishness of human nature. And this is the last great protest against the wrong of ages. It is no argument to my mind, therefore, that the old social fabric of the past is against us.

Neither do I feel called upon to show what woman's proper sphere is. In every great reform, the majority have always said to the claimant, no matter what he claimed, "You are not fit for such a privilege." Luther asked of the Pope liberty for the masses to read the Bible. The reply was, that it would not be safe to trust the common people with the word of God. "Let them try!" said the great reformer; and the history of three centuries of development and purity proclaims the result. They have tried; and look around you for the consequences. The lower classes in France claimed their civil rights, – the right to vote, and to direct representation in the government; but the rich and lettered classes, the men of cultivated intellects, cried out, "You cannot be made fit." The answer was, "Let us try." That France is not, as Spain, utterly crushed beneath the weight of a thousand years of misgovernment, is the answer to those who doubt the ultimate success of this experiment.

Woman stands now at the same door. She says, "You tell me I have no intellect: give me a chance. You tell me I shall only embarrass politics: let me try." The only reply is the same stale argument that said to the Jews of Europe, "You are fit only to make money; you are not fit for the ranks of the army or the halls of Parliament." How cogent the eloquent appeal of Macaulay, – "What right have we to take this question for granted? Throw open the doors of this House of Commons, throw open the ranks of the imperial army, before you deny eloquence to the countrymen of Isaiah or valor to the descendants of the Maccabees." It is the same now with us. Throw open the doors of Congress, throw open those court-houses, throw wide open the doors of your colleges, and give to the sisters of the Motts and the Somervilles the same opportunities for culture that men have, and let the result prove what their capacity and intellect really are. When, I say, woman has enjoyed, for as many centuries as we have, the aid of books, the discipline of life, and the stimulus of fame, it will be time to begin the discussion of these questions, – "What is the intellect of woman?" "Is it equal to that of man?" Till then, all such discussion is mere beating of the air.

While it is doubtless true that great minds, in many cases, make a way for themselves, spite of all obstacles, yet who knows how many Miltons have died "mute and inglorious?" However splendid the natural endowment, the discipline of life, after all, completes the miracle. The ability of Napoleon, – what was it? It grew out of the hope to be Caesar or Marlborough, – out of Austerlitz and Jena, – out of his battle-fields, his throne, and all the great scenes of that eventful life. Open to woman the same scenes, immerse her in the same great interests and pursuits, and if twenty centuries shall not produce a woman Charlemagne or Napoleon, fair reasoning will then allow us to conclude that there is some distinctive peculiarity in the intellects of the sexes. Centuries alone can lay any fair basis for argument. I believe that, on this point, there is a shrinking consciousness of not being ready for the battle, on the part of some of the stronger sex, as they call themselves; a tacit confession of risk to this imagined superiority, if they consent to meet their sisters in the lecture-hall or the laboratory of science. My proof of it is this: that the mightiest intellects of the race, from Plato down to the present time, some of the rarest minds of Germany, France, and England, have successively yielded their assent to the fact that woman is, not perhaps identically, but equally, endowed with man in all intellectual capabilities. It is generally the second-rate men who doubt, – doubt, perhaps, because they fear a fair field:

"He either fears his fate too much,
Or his deserts are small,
Who fears to put it to the touch,
To gain or lose it all."

In 1869, a group of suffragists banded to form the National Woman Suffrage Association. Among this group were Susan B. Anthony, Elizabeth Cady Stanton, and others who would come to dominate the suffragist movement of the nineteenth century. In December 1871, this petition was sent to both houses of the US Congress, asking that the proposed amendment granting women the right to vote be debated and voted on the floor of both houses.

To the Honorable the Senate and House of Representatives of the United States in Congress assembled.

The undersigned, Citizens of the United States, believing that under the present Federal Constitution all women who are citizens of the United States have the right to vote, pray your Honorable Body to enact a law during the present Session that shall assist and protect them in the exercise of that right.

And they pray further that they may be permitted in person, and in behalf of the thousands of other women who are petitioning Congress to the same effect, to be heard upon this Memorial before the Senate and House at an early day in the present Session.

We ask your Honorable Body to bear in mind that while men are represented on the floor of Congress and so may be said to be heard there, women who are allowed no vote and therefore no representation cannot truly be heard except as Congress shall open its doors to us in person.

Elizabeth Cady Stanton
Isabella Beecher Hooker
Elizabeth L. Bladen
Olympia Brown
Susan B. Anthony
Josephine S. Griffing

Hartford Conn.
Dec. 1871.

This editorial from Harper's Weekly, *XXXVII, 19 May 1894, examines female suffrage in the United States as the nation nears the end of the nineteenth century.*

FEMALE SUFFRAGE.

The tendency of all the governments in the civilized world is to become constitutional, and the tendency of all constitutional governments is to give votes to all people, not being dependents upon the public, who really desire votes. In this country the suffrage is avowedly universal. In Great Britain, since the last reform bill, it has become practically universal. Although in the English manner the last reform bill pretends to hedge the suffrage with qualifications and particulars, the fact is that one of every seven in the population has a vote for a member of the House of Commons. While under our own system the proportion is that of one in five. It is not likely that the admission of the voters now excluded would make any noteworthy difference in the course of British legislation or British politics, or that the enactment of manhood suffrage will be very long delayed if the excluded classes take the trouble to agitate. The abolition of plural voting is sure to come soon, whether the pending measure for that purpose is successful or not.

Is there any good reason why the line should be drawn at the female sex, or why womanhood suffrage should not be added to manhood suffrage? There has for a generation and more been a band of female agitators who have answered this question to their own satisfaction. The logic of the situation has seemed to be all on their side, but they have not impressed the male sex with the belief that women in general really desired votes. If they really do, then probably no one doubts that they will secure them.

A vigorous effort is even now making to admit women to the suffrage in the State of New York by the action of the coming Constitutional Convention. The peculiarity of the movement is that it has not been undertaken by those who have been scoffingly called the "woman women," but that its promoters are ladies of whom many have won distinction in arts about the propriety of women's practising which there is no longer any question. But no sooner has the movement been fairly started than a counter-movement appears, and a number of ladies equally accomplished and distinguished protest that for their part they do not desire votes, and dread the new responsibilities that the possession of votes would entail.

It would be easy but unprofitable to discuss what advantages or disadvantages would accrue to women from the possession of votes. On the one hand, it is argued that women would raise the tone of public life, and that the opening of public careers to them would be of benefit to the State; for pretty obviously the right to hold public office would be a sequel to the right to vote, and it would be impracticable to exclude any class of voting citizens from all the rights of citizenship. On the other, it may be argued that women have already all the protection which reasonable women are disposed to demand, and that their rights of property in particular are very jealously guarded by the laws of the State of New York. But practically the whole question is whether women really desire votes. A plébiscite of the women of New York upon this question, if it could be had, would go far to settle the question. At present it is very far from being settled. Petitions will be sent to Albany from women who desire the suffrage for themselves, and think that the majority of their sex is with them; and counterpetions from other women who deprecate the conferring of votes upon them, and who hold this to be the general view of their sex. With such a schism among the women themselves, it is extremely improbable that the Constitutional Convention will venture upon any action, without much fuller information as to the wishes of women than it now possesses.

Legal expert Henry St. George Tucker collected a series of essays on constitutional matters, including the potentiality of a Suffrage Amendment to the US Constitution. This selection comes from his 1916 work.

The right of woman to vote – if there be such a thing as the right of suffrage in any one – and the arguments with which such right or privilege is presented, constitute a most interesting phase of modern political discussion. My object in these pages is not to intrude upon that question, however interesting it may be, and however important it may be to the future of our country; but without touching the subject of the claim of woman to suffrage, and without expressing any opinion on the subject, to show that the attempt to bring about the right of suffrage for women by an amendment to the Constitution of the United States is opposed to the genius of the instrument itself, and subversive of one of the most important principles incorporated in it. The right of woman to vote and her appeal to the public conscience in the assertion of her claim, however it may be deprecated by some, even when not militant, has at least the virtue of an appeal to the reason and conscience of the country, and should receive the calm consideration of those to whom the appeal is made.

That Idaho, California, Montana, and other States may have yielded to the claim of woman to this right, may be of little concern to the people of Maine, Massachusetts, and New York, for they have the like right to determine the question for themselves; but if Maine, Massachusetts, and New York, refusing to follow the lead of those States which have found it expedient and best to adopt this measure, decline to adopt it for themselves, believing that it may be inexpedient for them, they should be accorded the same respect and the same right to decline to adopt a system which they deem inexpedient as is accorded their sister States in their acceptance of the principle. Maine, under our system of government, has no interest whatsoever in the right of suffrage which may be prescribed by the State of California for her people. Her State government is distinct and separate from that of California. Her social, political, and ethnic conditions may be as different from those of California as the climatic differences which prevail in these two States. And when Maine by authority of our Constitution is debarred the right of interfering with California in this respect, it should be recognized that such prohibition is reciprocal, and that California, exercising her inherent right to determine this question for herself, has no right to impose her conclusions upon her unwilling sister. California has a right to claim exemption from the interference of Maine or any of her sister States in granting the exercise of suffrage to those whom she may see fit to admit to that right, and any attempt to interfere with that right on the part of any other State is an intrusion which can be neither defended nor approved. In short, each State in the federal Union has been granted by the United States Constitution the single and exclusive right of determining this question for itself, and if no one of the States may interfere with any other in the determination of this question, it is seriously to be doubted whether three-fourths of the States, by a violation of this basic principle, would be acting wisely to force upon any unwilling State the acceptance of a doctrine which that State may believe to be subversive of good government. For three-fourths of the States to attempt to compel the other one fourth of the States of the Union, by constitutional amendment, to adopt a principle of suffrage believed to be inimical to their institutions, because they may believe it to be of advantage to themselves and righteous as a general doctrine, would be to accomplish their end by subverting a principle which has been recognized from the adoption of the Constitution of the United States to this day, viz., that the right of suffrage – more properly the privilege of suffrage – is a State privilege, emanating from the State, granted by the State, and that can be curtailed alone by the State.

And so, under the original Constitution, the right of suffrage abides in the State as one of the corner-stones of this imposing structure; and while under Article V when two-thirds of both Houses of Congress shall have proposed amendments to the Constitution and those amendments shall have been ratified by three-fourths of the States, the Constitution may be changed thereby, yet an amendment taking the right of determining suffrage and placing it under the control of the Federal Government would be a radical change of the instrument and contrary to the views of those who originally framed the Constitution. This provision has been accepted during the life of the Government for one hundred and twenty-six years without any serious denial of its wisdom, or any attempt to change its wise and beneficent provisions.

Should the proposed amendment to the Constitution denying the right of the States to deny suffrage to women because of sex be adopted, the following provisions of the Constitution of the United States would be affected directly:

ARTICLE I, Section 2, C[onstitution] U. S.:

"The House of Representatives shall be composed of members chosen every second year by the people of the several States, and the electors of each State shall have the qualifications requisite for electors of the most numerous branch of the State Legislature."

Hearings into continuing the push for a Suffrage Amendment to the US Constitution were held before the US House Committee on Woman Suffrage in January 1918. Dr. Anna Howard Shaw, the President of the National American Woman Suffrage Association (NAWSA), testified before the committee, excerpted below.

"To fail to ask for the suffrage amendment at this time would be treason to the fundamental cause for which we, as a nation, have entered the war. President Wilson has declared that 'we are at war because of that which is dearest to our hearts – democracy; that those who submit to authority shall have a voice in the Government.' If this is the basic reason for entering the war, then for those of us who have striven for this amendment and for our freedom and for democracy to yield today, to withdraw from the battle, would be to desert the men in the trenches and leave them to fight alone across the sea not only for democracy for the world but also for our own country...

"The time of reconstruction will come and when it comes many women will have to be both father and mother to fatherless children, and these mothers and their children will have no representatives in this Government unless it is through the mothers who have given everything that it might be saved and democracy might be secured...

"No men better than those of the South know what it owes to southern women and shall those men stand in the way of freedom for the women who gave everything to retain for our country the very best of southern traditions – shall they plead in vain for the freedom of their daughters? What is true of the women of the South is true of the women of the North...

"We are today a united people with one flag and one country because the women are worthy of their men, and we plead because we are a part of the people, a part of the Government which claims to be a democracy, and in order that this country may stand clean-handed before the nations of the world."

The debate in the US House of Representatives in 1918 that sent proposed language for a Suffrage Amendment to the states is covered here by a selection from suffragist Carrie Chapman Catt's memoirs on the machinations leading up to the debate, as well as the debate itself.

"The time for submitting the federal amendment with a real chance of success had arrived. A previous triumph of the Congressional Committee, under the leadership of the intelligent, effective Maud Wood Park of Boston, had seen the establishment in September 1917 of a Woman Suffrage Committee in the House. Hitherto the woman suffrage bill had been referred to the Judicial [sic] Committee, headed by a strong and immovable opponent of the federal amendment, Edwin Y. Webb of North Carolina. Judge [Rep. John Edward] Raker of California was appointed chair of the Woman Suffrage Committee. He introduced a new amendment resolution, and it went automatically to his committee, which promptly reported it favorably. The House vote was scheduled for January 10, 1918.

"'The wonderful day came at last and with it the vote which put us through,' wrote Catt. It began with Jeannette Rankin, the first congresswoman, who opened the long debate that followed. Suspense vied with tedium as fifty-three more speeches were made during the interminable afternoon. The suffragists barely had their required number of votes and won only because at least five friends came from their sickbeds to vote. Tennessee Representative Thetus W. Sims came with a broken shoulder that would not have set until after the vote because he was afraid the anesthetic would keep him down. In spite of excrutiating pain he stayed on to encourage political friends who were less convinced than he. Henry A. Barnhart of Indiana has himself carried on a stretcher to a place near the Speaker's desk; Robert Crosser of Ohio left a sickbed and the Republican leader James R. Mann of Illinois left a hospital and came in spite of his doctor's warning he was risking his life. Most poignant of all was Frederick C. Hicks, Jr. of New York, who had left his wife's deathbed on her insistence to cast his vote for the resolution. He then went home to her funeral.

"The amendment passed by a single extra vote, 274 ayes to 136 nays, one more than the required two-thirds. On their way out of the Capitol, Catt and the women started singing, as they had so long ago at the victory in Colorado, 'Praise God, from whom all blessings flow.'"

In their 1926 work on the history of the suffragist movement, Carrie Chapman Catt and Nettie Rogers Shuler touched on the last moves to get Congress to enact the language that would become the Nineteenth Amendment to the US Constitution.

So far the story of suffrage, victory and defeat, has been the story of State referenda. We have been covering the time when for years that state-by-state effort spun the main thread of suffrage activity. "Win more States to full woman suffrage," had been the fell word that the suffragists of earlier days had encountered from friend and foe alike. "Go, get another State," Theodore Roosevelt counseled as late as 1908.

I don't know the exact number of States we shall have to have, said Miss Anthony once in a musing hour, but I do know that there will come a day when that number will automatically and resistlessly act on the Congress of the United States to compel the submission of a federal suffrage amendment. And we shall recognize that day when it comes.

As has been seen, that dream of woman suffrage by federal amendment antedated all the efforts to win woman suffrage by the State route. And it is not to be forgotten that from the earliest days the will and the work to make the dream come true went along concurrently with the work for and in State referenda.

Before the Civil War it seems to have occurred to no one that suffrage for women might be gained through federal action. Public opinion in all parts of the country was strongly resentful of any unusual assumption of authority by the federal government and no precedent existed upon which to base a theory for such action. The Civil War welded the loosely federated States into an "indissoluble Union," the word "nation" for the first time found its way into the list of words frequently used as descriptive of the United States of America, and the Acts of Reconstruction represented a degree of centralized authority which before the war would not have been tolerated. Although apologists for the departure from previous custom explained the Acts of Reconstruction as military necessities and although the conflict concerning the distribution of power between federal and State authorities continues today, the fact remains that hostility to federal legislative supremacy was greatly modified after that period.

After suffragists had made their energetic and heroic struggle to prevent the enfranchisement of the Negro without the inclusion of women in the plan, and when, despite their protests, Negro suffrage was achieved with woman suffrage left out, the Fourteenth and Fifteenth Amendments at least furnished precedents for a federal woman suffrage amendment, and this at once became the ultimate aim of the women's campaign. Observing the frequency with which laws, both State and Federal, were set aside by court decisions, and observing, too, that the Fifteenth Amendment had been declared constitutional, the women of that day took pains to frame a woman's amendment in the same precise phraseology. A group, led by Miss Anthony and Mrs. Stanton, wrote the amendment, designated by the suffragists for many years as the Sixteenth, and it was introduced in the Senate by A. A. Sargent of

California on January 10, 1878. Owing to the death of the friendly chairman of the Committee on Privileges and Elections, Senator Oliver P. Morton of Indiana, an adverse report was made, but a minority report, accompanied by a lengthy address, was presented by Senator George F. Hoar of Massachusetts in which he said:

"No single argument of its advocates seems to us to carry so great a persuasive force as the difficulty which its ablest opponents encounter in making a plausible statement of their objections. We trust we do not fail in deference to our esteemed associates on the committee when we avow our opinion that their report is no exception to this rule."

At that same date President Hayes received a deputation of suffragists, and a petition to the Congress was presented, with speeches on behalf of the amendment.

With so promising a beginning, suffrage hopes centered again on federal action. But between that date and June 4, 1919, when the amendment was finally passed by the Congress, lie forty years and six months, During that period the amendment was continuously pending, having been introduced in the same form in every succeeding Congress. In the Senate it was reported with a favorable majority in 1884, 1886, 1889 and 1893, and without recommendation in 1890 and 1896, and with a favorable majority again in 1913, 1914 and 1916. The House Committee gave favorable reports in 1883 and 1890, and adverse reports in 1884, 1886 and 1894, reported without recommendation in 1914, 1916 and 1917, and favorably in 1918, the Senate Committees making six reports only and the House Committees five in the thirty-five years between 1878 and 1913.

While other influences contributed to this record of inaction, the most outstanding cause was that Southern Democrats, although a minority, held the whip and controlled the suffrage situation. In 1878, when the woman suffrage amendment was introduced, the nation consisted of thirty-eight States and was accordingly represented by 76 United States Senators. The constitutional requirement of a two-thirds vote in the Congress for the submission of an amendment and action by three-fourths of the Legislatures for ratification made the support of fifty-one of these Senators and twenty-eight Legislatures necessary to its adoption. To secure this result the vote of five Senators and the ratification of five Legislatures of secession, or border, States had to be obtained, in addition to the united support of all Northern and Western States.

During the earlier portion of this time, Senators from the seceding States would rather have committed hari kari than vote for any federal suffrage amendment, and the border States were little less pronounced in their vindictive denunciation of suffrage by the federal method. Three prospects only for success appeared: (1) An increase in the number of States, so that the total could outvote the South; (2) A change of attitude on the part of Southern Senators; and (3) A more insistent demand for action by Congress than the nation was then in a mood to give. None offered immediate hope, but in the end all three aids were secured.

The suffragists of 1878 could not believe that the nation would long allow its record of enfranchisement of illiterate men, fresh from slavery, and its denial of the same privilege to intelligent white women to stand unchallenged. They turned to the States, firm in the faith that they would soon furnish a mandate to which popular opinion would yield, and through which the congressional impasse would be broken.

Had Republicans recognized the indefensible discrimination against women created by reconstruction history and given party aid to State amendments, which obvious consistency demanded (without whip or bayonet), woman suffrage would have swept from West to East long before corporate interests had gained sway over party councils. The East and South would have yielded then to the momentum of the triumphant movement, as they did forty years later, and there would probably have been no need of a federal woman suffrage amendment. However, the Republicans, in full control of most Northern and Western States, blocked action in these States as effectually as the Southern Democrats did in the Congress and in Southern States.

So it came about that the dismayed suffragists had to gird on their armor in grim preparation for war with the nation's prejudice, should it take till the end of time. They determined to hold fast the demand established in Congress, to bring to its support such gains among the States as they could wrest from the well-nigh impossible conditions imposed, and then, when politics should indicate the hour, to concentrate their efforts again on a federal amendment with the aim of finishing the task by that method. Formulated at that early day, this remained the policy of the National American Woman Suffrage Association to the end.

When it became plain that no action could be secured in Congress from the committees to which national suffrage amendments were referred, the suffragists attempted to induce Senate and House to establish standing woman suffrage committees with more time and sympathy to give their cause. As a result of much labor for three years, a so-called select committee was obtained in both Houses, the Senate renewing this committee in 1883 and the House declining to do so. The Senate Committee in time became a standing committee and so remained until the end. In the House the amendment was usually referred to the Judiciary Committee. A further attempt to renew the suffrage committee in the House was made in 1884, at which time Miss Anthony said: "This is the sixteenth year that we have come before Congress in person, and the nineteenth by petition."

The early Senate Committee did not prove to be an asset to the women's campaign. In the long list of committees, it was held to be of low rank and during the thirty-five years of Republican control the chairmanship was assigned to a Southern Democrat. Senators from the States of Missouri, North Carolina, Florida, Arkansas, Virginia, and Georgia, to whose people the idea of suffrage by federal act was infuriating, held the post during this period. Said one of these chairmen to a fellow Senator:

"There is no man living who can answer the argument of those women, but I'd rather see my wife dead in her coffin than voting, and I'd die myself before I'd vote to submit that amendment."

Upon another occasion, Miss Anthony, bearing her threescore years and ten, closed the hearing with a review of the forty years of effort to secure justice for women and made so pathetic an appeal for action that the great room full of women, with faces drawn and tears running down many cheeks, involuntarily turned their eyes upon the chairman from Virginia. He was clearly perturbed and under the control of emotion. What would he say? What would he do? How could he refuse so unanswerable, so appealing a request? Presently they discovered the source of his emotion—he was in need of the spittoon! And no indication of more sympathetic interest did any of these Southern Democratic chairmen ever show.

During a portion of Grover Cleveland's administration, the Senate became Democratic. Then, the tables being turned, a Republican was given the chairmanship, and that fearless friend of woman suffrage, George F. Hoar of Massachusetts, being appointed, no time was lost in presenting a favorable report.

Based on this favorable report of the Committee in 1886, a vote on the amendment was secured in the Senate in 1887. The vote stood ayes 16, nays 34, absent 26. The debate is a distinct landmark, as Southern Senators laid out with care the argument upon which the Northern opposition was based through the coming years. Already the reaction had set in against the "wholesale and indiscriminate extension of the electorate" and the plea of all opponents for the next generation was "there are too many incompetent voters now, why double them? Let the extension of suffrage stop now."

Said Senator Beck of Kentucky:

"We have been compelled in the last ten years to allow all the colored men of the South to become voters. There is a mass of ignorance there to be absorbed that will take years and years of care in order to bring that class up to the standard of intelligent voters. The several States are addressing themselves to that task as earnestly as possible. Now it is proposed that all the women of the country shall vote; that all the colored women of the South, who are as much more ignorant than the colored men as it is possible to imagine, shall vote. Not one perhaps in a hundred of them can read or write. The colored men have had the advantages of communication with other men in a variety of forms. Many of them have considerable intelligence; but the colored women have not had equal chances. Take them from their washtubs and their household work and they are absolutely ignorant of the new duties of voting citizens.... Why, sir, a rich corporation or a body of men of wealth could buy them up for fifty cents apiece, and they would vote, without knowing what they were doing, for the side that paid most."

Said Senator Morgan of Alabama:

"We have now masses of voters so enormous in numbers as that it seems to be almost beyond the power of the law to execute the purposes of the elective franchise with justice, with propriety, and without crime. How much would these difficulties and these intrinsic troubles be increased if we should raise the number of voters from 10,000,000 to 20,000,000 in the United States? That would be the direct and immediate effect of conferring the franchise upon the women.... The effect would be to drive the ladies of the land, as they are termed, the well-bred and welleducated women, the women of nice sensibilities, within their home circles, there to remain, while the ruder of that sex would thrust themselves out on the hustings and at the ballot-box, and fight their way to the polls through Negroes and others who are not the best of company even at the polls, to say nothing of the disgrace of association with them. You would paralyze one-third at least of the women of this land by the very vulgarity of the overture made to them that they should go struggling to the polls in order to vote in common with the herd of men."

No other vote was obtained in the Senate until 1914 and none at all during this period in the House. The years passed with hearings before the Committees of both Houses of every Congress and the circulation of the printed procedure of these hearings, interviews with members, occasional petitions, deputations to the presidents and, every year, a resolution from the national suffrage convention calling upon Congress to submit the suffrage amendment.

Until 1895 all the annual suffrage conventions were held in Washington, in order that suffrage delegates might plead with their representatives in Congress to submit the amendment, but after 1895 the conventions were held alternate years in other cities, meeting in Washington during the first session of each Congress only. There followed the period between 1896 and 1910 when the business of securing from the country a mandate on woman suffrage made such slow headway. The Congress was accepting the inaction of the country as a cue for inaction in Senate and House, and the inaction in Congress, composed as that body was of the leaders of political parties, was taken as the cue for inaction in the States.

In order to focus the attention of Congress once more upon woman suffrage and that of the country upon congressional obligation to the women of the land, it was voted at the annual suffrage convention held in Buffalo in October, 1908, to roll up another petition calling for the submission of the federal suffrage amendment. This method of agitation had been abandoned many years before, not only because petitions seemed to produce no direct result, but as it was no longer the custom to present such petitions publicly and with speeches, they were robbed of their publicity effect upon the country. It was now proposed to resume the plan, chiefly for its agitational value.

As Submitted to the States

Section 1.
The right of citizens of the United States to vote shall not be denied or abridged by the United States or by any State on account of sex.

Section 2.
Congress shall have power to enforce this article by appropriate legislation.

State Ratifications of the Nineteenth Amendment

The dates below indicates when the state ratified the amendment; an asterisk (*) indicates when the governor signed the ratification, not necessarily when the state legislature approved it.

State	Date
Wisconsin	10 June 1919
Illinois	10 June 1919
Michigan	10 June 1919
Kansas	16 June 1919
New York	16 June 1919
Ohio	16 June 1919
Pennsylvania	24 June 1919
Massachusetts	25 June 1919
Texas	28 June 1919
Iowa	2 July 1919*
Missouri	3 July 1919
Arkansas	28 July 1919
Montana	2 August 1919*
Nebraska	2 August 1919
Minnesota	8 September 1919
New Hampshire	10 September 1919*
Utah	2 October 1919
California	1 November 1919
Maine	5 November 1919
North Dakota	1 December 1919
South Dakota	4 December 1919
Colorado	15 December 1919*
Kentucky	6 January 1920
Rhode Island	6 January 1920
Oregon	13 January 1920
Indiana	16 January 1920
Wyoming	27 January 1920
Nevada	7 February 1920
New Jersey	9 February 1920
Idaho	11 February 1920
Arizona	12 February 1920
New Mexico	21 February 1920
Oklahoma	28 February 1920
West Virginia	10 March 1920*
Washington	22 March 1920
Tennessee	18 August 1920
Connecticut	14 September 1920
Vermont	8 February 1921
Delaware	6 March 1923
Maryland	29 March 1941
Virginia	21 February 1952
Alabama	8 September 1953
Florida	13 May 1969
South Carolina	1 July 1969
Georgia	20 February 1970
Louisiana	11 June 1970
North Carolina	6 May 1971
Mississippi	22 March 1984

Explanation of the amendment

The language behind the Nineteenth Amendment is simple and straightforward: it banned any discrimination in voting based on one's sex. This ended any state laws that banned women from voting in local, state, and/or federal elections.

ORIGINAL PRIMARY DOCUMENTS

In 1870 when there were only 15 amendments to the US Constitution, Rep. George Washington Julian, Republican of Indiana, introduced a potential sixteenth, one to give women suffrage. The effort went nowhere at the time, but here the Daily State Gazette, *6 April 1870, demonstrates one of the earliest congressional moves to gain constitutional protections for women.*

The Sixteenth Amendment

Mr. Julian presented a joint resolution in the House of Representatives on Monday, to amend the Constitution of the United States, by adding article 16, as follows:

Section 1.
The rights of citizens of the United States to vote shall not be denied or abridged by the United States or by any state on account of sex.

Section 2.
Congress shall have power to enforce this article by appropriate legislation.

In this report from The Fort Worth Register *of Texas, 2 June 1901 supporters of a female suffrage amendment meet to plot strategy. The article is headlined "The Sixteenth Amendment" because at that time the last amendment which had been enacted was the Fifteenth in 1870, the subsequent Sixteenth (1913), Seventeenth (1913), and Eighteenth (1919) amendments had yet to be enacted and ratified.*

THE SIXTEENTH AMENDMENT

The Advocates of Woman Suffrage Listen to Report of Susan B. Anthony.

Special to The Register.

Minneapolis, Minn., June 1. – The National American Woman Suffrage association this morning began the third day of its convention with prayer services led by Rev. Celia Parker Woolley of Illinois. Clara B. Colby presented a report dealing with industrial problems affecting women and children, which was followed by the report of the committee on legislation. The convention then received and adopted the report of the committee on resolutions. The report was presented by Susan B. Anthony and was as follows:

"It has been my duty to ask national bodies of all kinds in convention to allow our association to present one question to them, and later to ask the passage of a resolution in favor of woman suffrage. The American Federation of Labor in session at Detroit was addressed by me and the president and secretary authorized to sign a petition asking for a sixteenth amendment. Among the national associations to which petitions have been sent are the National Indian Woman's association, American-Jewish Historical association, Catholic Woman's Benevolent association, American Economic association, National Federation of Educational associations, National Building Trades

Council, Brotherhood of Steam Dredge Engineers of America, National Clothiers' association, National AntiSaloon League, United States Brewers' association and numerous others.

It has also been my duty to notify state presidents of meetings and state associations, and to urge them to present petitions and ask for an audience at such state meetings. I have had hearty co-operation on this direction. It is my belief that although we must continue all our branches of work and be ready to ably present our subject to those who are our willing listeners, yet at the same time we must go to those who will not come to us."

Women try to get a state constitutional amendment added to Connecticut's constitution – as reported in The Hartford Courant, *3 February 1913.*

A SUFFRAGE PETITION.

_____

Appeal for a Constitutional Amendment.

_____

The following circular has been sent out from the woman's suffrage headquarters in Bridgeport in this state to members of the Legislature: –

We, the undersigned, desire our representatives, assembled in the Connecticut Legislature, to pass an amendment to the constitution admitting women to the franchise on the same terms as men. This we desire in order that the question may be submitted directly to the voters in the state. This wording is designed to be as clear and simple as possible for those adult persons who may desire to sign it. That there may be as little confusion as possible to would-be signers, the following explanation on a separate sheet usually accompanies the petition sheet, The franchise for women in Connecticut. To obtain the suffrage for women in Connecticut, a bill must first be submitted to the House of Representatives in the Connecticut Legislature. If this bill to amend the Connecticut constitution passes the House, it then waits two years for another Legislature to convene. It is again submitted to this new house and if it passes, must also pass through the Senate at the same time. After that the amendment goes to the voters to be voted upon in direct referendum.

As the act of amending the constitution is a long and difficult proceeding, it is most important that all men and women who favor a vote of the people on the subject should lend their names to the movement. The question of granting the suffrage to women must be submitted to the regular male voting population before it becomes a law.

This petition asks that it should be so submitted as soon as possible. Many people sign this petition who are not in the ranks of the organized suffragists, because they would like to know the outcome of such a vote taken in Connecticut. To have women vote upon the question of their own enfranchisement does not appear to be constitutional. It is not desired by suffragists nor by non-suffragists.

(Signed) Maud M. Hicks Hincks,
President Conn. Woman Suffrage Association.

This article, from 9 March 1913, was written exclusively for the New-York Tribune *by Dr. Anna Howard Shaw, the President of the National American Woman Suffrage Association (NAWSA), at that time one of the leading woman's suffrage associations agitating for the congressional passage of a Suffrage Amendment to the US Constitution.*

WOMEN ANSWER QUESTION: "WHY FORCE WOMEN TO VOTE?"

Dr. Shaw States Grounds for Her Faith in the Cause, in the Van of Whose Advocates She Has Long Fought.

The object of the National American Woman Suffrage Association, as defined in its constitution, is to secure protection in their right to vote to the women citizens of the United States by appropriate national and state legislation. This has been the well-defined object from the very beginning of the association, forty-four years ago. Prior to that time there were small groups of women banded together to secure certain rights and privileges which were denied to women in all the then civilized nations of the world. Among the other demands made by women at their first national convention suffrage was declared to be the right protective of all other rights, and while the primary object of the association was to secure the vote for women they did not devote all their attention to this one purpose, for in their demands they included the right to personal freedom, to acquiring an education, to earn a living, to claim their own wages, to own property, to make contracts, to bring suits, to testify in court, to possess their children, to claim a fair share of the accumulations during marriage, none of which rights were possessed by the women of this nation when the first woman suffrage convention was held at Seneca Falls, N.Y., in 1848.

Recognizing that these reasonable and just demands of women could be secured only through law, the suffragists realized that unless they could secure the means by which those who enacted and enforced laws were elected to office, the claims of women would not be generally recognized, and while they have been struggling to secure the most valuable of all rights, the right of self-government in a republic, they have also been working to secure changes in the laws affecting women's property and education and children and changes in the industrial world which control all their relations in life.

INFLUENCE OF AN IDEA.

It is claimed by the opponents to woman suffrage that all the changes wrought during the last sixty years would have come naturally through the process of evolution, but it is a remarkable fact, pointed out by Judge Sewell, of Massachusetts, that more good laws have been enacted for the benefit of women and children during the last fifty years, since the woman suffrage agitation began, than had been enacted in five thousand years preceding that time. The various changes which are pointed out as of vast benefit by the anti-suffragists, and of which they take equal advantage with the suffragists, have been secured largely by the suffragists as a by-product of the effort to secure the ballot. But it is the undoubted opinion of every woman who has struggled for these changes that they could have been effected in a much easier, simpler and much shorter period if women had had political power, and that there has been a great waste of the energies of the omen of the United States and vast suffering has accrued to innumerable people because of the delayed legislation, which could have been secured had women had the ballot in the beginning.

The women who began this movement were the foremost thinkers and philanthropists of their day, and there have come to the ranks of suffragists from that time a large majority of the women who have been doing the educational and philanthropic work of the country. There is not a woman president of a leading woman college in the United States today who is not a strong advocate of woman suffrage. All the well known and leading philanthropic workers – Jane Addams, Mrs. Raymond Robbins, Julia Lathrop, Florence Kelley, Mrs. Maud Nathan, Miss Dreit and many others – declare that their work could be better done and more effectively and easily done if the women of these United States were voting citizens.

FLORENCE KELLEY.

Florence Kelley stated in a mass meeting that she felt the last twenty years of her life had been largely wasted in her effort to secure protective legislation for women and children, and that it would have been better if she had devoted the time to securing the ballot for women.

There can be no better evidence of the success of woman suffrage, both in its value to the state as a whole and its influence upon women, than the fact that the continual extension of suffrage is made by those states lying in juxtaposition to those already possessing it.

Among the books recommended by the president of the National Anti-Suffrage Association is one entitled "The Ladies' Battle," by Miss Mollie Elliot Seawell. If all the other books of reference recommended by the AntiSuffrage Association are as inaccurate and as absolutely false in their statements as is this ladies' battle, the information secured will not be very helpful. As a sample of the inaccuracy of the statements made by Miss Seawell in "The Ladies' Battle," she asserts that a certain meeting presided over by the Rev. Anna Shaw, there was such an uproar and confusion and disorder that the police were called in and that Miss Shaw pounded the table with her mallet with tears running down her cheeks, and declaring that the movement had been set back twenty years by the conduct of the ladies present. As a matter of fact, Miss Shaw was not present at the meeting referred to, she did not preside, she knew nothing of the holding of the meeting or what took place in it until she saw the report in a distorted newspaper statement. The entire story, as quoted by Miss Seawell, was entirely made up, utterly false, without one word of truth as far as Miss Shaw's connection with the meeting or in regard to any statement which Miss Shaw made respecting it. In fact, it was a faked affair, and yet Miss Seawell, without making any inquiry, without knowing anything about the truth or falsity of it, inserts it in her book. From the absolute unreliability of this story we can judge of the reliability of the rest of her book.

The claim that there is any attempt on the part of women suffragists to force women to vote is entirely unfounded, as there is no desire on the part of women suffragists to compel any women to vote who does not wish to do so, any more than there is on the part of men to compel men to vote who have no desire to cast their ballots.

The claim, however, on the part of anti-suffragists that granting the suffrage to the women who desire it will compel the women who do not wish to vote to do so because they are conscientious in the performance of their duty, if true, would entirely disprove other statements made by the anti-suffragists and would destroy their entire arguments against woman suffrage.

While making the boast that 90 per cent of the women of every state are opposed to woman suffrage, and also making the claim that if the suffrage is granted the anti-suffragists are so conscientious that they will vote, they try to show that very few women use the suffrage where it is granted. One of the strong points of the anti-suffragists at the present time is that only 37 per cent of the women of San Francisco voted at the last election, though they overlook the point that more than 80 per cent of the women of Los Angeles voted. But taking their own plea that all anti-suffragists vote who have the opportunity, and that only a small number of women would vote when they do have the opportunity, the only conclusion which can be traced is that there are but a few anti-suffragists, or else the vote of women would be very heavy. To try to prove that the large majority of women are anti-suffragists, and that granting the suffrage will compel them to vote, and then immediately try to prove that where women have the suffrage but a few women vote, naturally nullifies the value of any statement based upon these conflicting arguments.

All of the contention of anti-suffragists that granting suffrage to women who desire it would compel the women who do not desire it to vote is completely nullified by facts, for it is very easy to show that where women possess the ballot the women who are opposed to suffrage do not feel any obligation to use it what ever, if they did so the vast majority of women would be voting wherever the suffrage is extended even partially to women.

ANNA HOWARD SHAW.

President, National American Woman Suffrage Association.

Woman continued to protest in both chambers of the US Congress on the so-called "Susan B. Anthony Amendment." Here is a report from the New-York Tribune, *13 January 1915 of one such protest in 1913.*

WOMEN, 500 STRONG, BACKED BY POLICE, BOMBARD CAPITOL

———

Urge Congress to Support Proposed Constitution Amendment Granting Suffrage.

———

AMPLE PROTECTION GIVEN

———

Major Sylvester Personally in Charge, and There is No Sign of Disorder During March.

———

[From The Tribune Bureau]

Washington, April 7. – More than five hundred suffragists stormed the Capitol, the citadel of the law makers, to-day to urge Congress to support the proposed continual amendment giving nation wide enfranchisement to women. The parade to the Capitol followed a mass meeting at the Columbia Theatre, at which the foremost suffragist orators spoke for more than an hour. The speakers were Miss Alice Paul, Mrs. James Lees Laidlaw, Mrs. Beatrice Forbes Robertson and Miss Janet Richards.

Police protection was more than ample to-day. Major Sylvester, superintendent of police, having learned by experience of the disorders possible as a result of such a demonstration, furnished almost one policeman for every woman in the parade. There were policemen on foot, on horses, on bicycles and in automobiles, and, as a consequence, there was not a suggestion of disorder. Major Sylvester personally conducted the police activities.

The policemen were lined up along the route practically a dozen feet apart, and as the marchers passed the policemen turned and marched along with them. A squad of mounted police headed the procession and another brought up the rear. Thus the suffragists marched surrounded by officers.

Representative Bryan,[33] of Washington, greeted the marchers, led by Miss Paul, at the east door of the Capitol, and inside was a delegation of Representatives and Senators from woman suffrage states to complete the welcome. Among them were Senators Brady,[34] La Follette,[35] Jones[36] Shafroth[37] Poindexter,[38] Townsend,[39] Sutherland[40] and Thomas.[41] As each of the women passed the Senators shook hands and assured each that they were in favor of their fight and would support the measure that is to be introduced in Congress.

The women bore petitions from every state and every Congress district. This is a sample of the petitions:

"We ask you, in behalf of the women of your district, to work for the national suffrage amendment in the coming special session of Congress for the following reasons:

"Some state constitutions are practically impossible to amend owing to the necessity for a majority vote of all the qualified voters.

"A national amendment acts as a moral stimulus to backward legislatures.

"It is no greater interference with the theory of states' rights than is the national amendment for the election of Senators or income tax.

"It is easier for the American woman seeking emancipation than is the work of convincing every voter.

"It does not prevent state action.

"It is a natural evolutionary step in American constitutional history.

"Trusting that the righteousness of our appeal and the wisdom of immediate action in the matter will be understood to you, I am ____."

Formal resolutions proposing constitutional amendments giving women the right to vote were introduced in both houses of Congress, together with scores of petitions and memorials from various societies and individuals. Senator Chamberlain,[42] of Oregon, and Representative Mondell,[43] of Wyoming, introduced resolutions in their respective houses for the constitutional amendments.

Source: "Women, 500 Strong, Backed by Police, Bombard Capitol," *New-York Tribune*, 8 April 1913, 16.

A vote to advance the proposed Suffrage Amendment to the US Constitution takes place in the US House of Representatives – and is defeated overwhelmingly. Here, the New-York Tribune, *13 January 1915, covers this historic vote.*

SUFFRAGE MEETS DEFEAT IN HOUSE

———

Resolution to Give Women Vote Beaten by 174 to 204

———

MEMBERS POINT TO STATES

———

Declare Questions of Franchise Should Be Settled There.

———

FAIR ADVOCATES UNSHAKEN

———

Result Anticipated by Crowds of Women Who Fill Galleries During Long Hours 0f Debate – Vice Chairman of Suffragists' Committee Says Strength of Minority Vote Exceeded by 4 "Most Sanguine Count" – "What We Expected," Declares Mrs. Arthur M. Dodge, Leader of the "Anti" Forces.

———

THE PARTY VOTE

———

FOR SUFFRAGE:
Democrats
86
Republicans
72
Progressives
12
Progressive   Republicans
3
Independent
1
Total
174

AGAINST SUFFRAGE:

Democrats
171
Republicans
33
Total
204

At the end of a full day of spectacular debate, in which nearly every member present took part, the House last night turned back upon the States the demand of women for equal suffrage with men. The Mondell-Bristow resolution for an amendment to the Federal Constitution went to defeat by a vote of 174 to 204, a majority of 30 voting against the measure.

Long before the House clerks had finished the roll call, the result as anticipated by the suffragists, who had occupied the galleries throughout the long hours of discussion, which probably did not change a single vote, and many of them had filed out into the Capitol corridors. They announced that they were not discouraged, and that the fight was only slightly interrupted. Mrs. Antoinette Funk, who is vice chairman of the congressional committee of the suffragists, issued a statement in which she declared the vote for the resolution exceeded by four "the most sanguine count of the congressional committee."

Second in History of Congress.

The vote, the second in the history of Congress on the women suffrage issue, came at the close of a day of long prepared for oratory, during which the many speakers were listened to with frequent evidences of approval or disapproval by packed galleries. The question was before the House on the Mondell resolution to submit a constitutional amendment providing that the right of suffrage should not be abridged "because of sex."

A two-thirds affirmative vote was necessary to pass the resolution. It was defeated by a majority of 30.

Party lines were not strictly drawn in the fight, though Democratic Leader Underwood,[44] voicing the attitude of his party that suffrage is a state issue, strongly opposed the resolution, while Republican Leader Mann[45] was one of the chief speakers of the suffragists.

Line-Up of Parties.

The line-up of the political parties on the suffrage resolution follows:

For suffrage – Democrats, 86; Republicans, 72; Progressives, 12; Progressive-Republicans, 3; Independent, 1. Total, 174.

Against suffrage – Democrats, 171; Republicans, 33. Total, 204.

Enthusiasm mingled with dejection when Speaker Clark announced the result, and into the corridors from opposite galleries filed the hundreds of suffragists with their purple and yellow sashes and the red rose bedecked anti suffragists.

Defeated Last March.

This was the second defeat for the suffrage cause in the national legislature within a year. March 19 last an equal suffrage constitutional amendment proposed by Senator Chamberlain,[46] of Oregon, received a vote of 35 to 34 in the Senate, securing a bare majority, but failing of the necessary two-thirds. However, suffragist leaders last night were not dismayed. As they left the galleries led by Dr. Anna Howard Shaw, Mrs. Carrie Chapman Catt, and other champions of the cause they declared that the fight was by no means over, and that the suffrage propaganda would be pressed forward and onward until every woman in America should have the right to cast a ballot.

"What We Expected" – Mrs. Dodge.

"The result was what we expected," said Mrs. Arthur M. Dodge, president of the National Association Opposed to Woman Suffrage. "It means that the suffrage movement, fostered by hysterical women, is on the wane."

Often during the earnest and at times bitter debate preceding the vote, Speaker Clark was forced to interrupt the speakers on the floor, fill the chamber with the deafening battering of his gavel, and warn both members and spectators that order must be preserved. Several times he threatened to have the galleries cleared unless the disturbance subsided. But the murmurs of approval and disapproval persisted as each speaker voiced his support for or opposition to the cause of "votes for women."

Hisses Greet Bowdie.

The turmoil culminated in a storm of hissing that greeted a speech made by Representative Bowdie,[47] of Ohio, opposing the amendment. He had treated the subject humorously and remarked that the "women of Washington are beautiful, but they have no interest in affairs of state."

Opponents of the resolution based their opposition largely upon the argument that for the Federal government to prescribe qualification for suffrage would be an unwarranted invasion of the right of the individual States to control their elections, and further upon the contention that there was no adequate "public demand" for this amendment.

Point to Suffrage States.

Advocates of the amendment contended that the widespread demand for woman suffrage, its success in the States where it has been tried, and the principle of "allowing the people to rule" justified the submission of the proposal to the States for ratification.

Preceding the general debate there was debate of and hour and a half on a special rule providing for consideration of the resolution.

After an hour and a half of debate the House adopted, 209 to 31, a special rule for considering the proposed constitutional amendment for women suffrage and then settled down to six hours actual debate before voting. To the applause and cheers of supporters of both sides of the question, packed in opposite galleries, the House plunged into a debate fully as spectacular as that which attended the vote on the prohibition amendment some weeks ago. Representative Mann, of Illinois, leader of the Republicans, lined up alongside the suffrage advocates, and Representative Underwood, leader of the Democrats, speaking against the amendment, urged the rights of the States to control the franchise.

Webb Leads Opposition.

Representative Webb,[48] chairman of the judiciary committee, led off the debate in opposition to the amendment. He believed that if the question were voted on by women more than 80 per cent would vote against suffrage. He charged that woman suffrage was more or less a fad.

"These agitating women suffragists want something to agitate about and if they should find nothing to agitate about they would be disappointed," said he. "If they can get it they don't want it; if they can't get it, they'll carry on agitation for it. I for one shall vote against this amendment in order to protect womankind against itself."

Representative Taylor,[49] of Colorado, supported the amendment, saying the opposition spoke from prejudice and misinformation.

Representative Mondell,[50] of Wyoming, co-author of the resolution, urged its adoption in a speech which traced the history of the movement.

"The stupid and threadbare argument that the exercise of the elective franchise will have an unfavorable effect upon the character of the women, expose them to undesirable contact, destroy the finer fibre of the sex, and put in jeopardy their natural charm has been utterly refuted by the experience of every State and nation which has enfranchised its women," said Mr. Mondell.

Representative Campbell,[51] Republican, spoke for the resolution.

Progressive party support was voiced by Representative Kelly,[52] of Pennsylvania.

"There is no reason," he said, "why the woman suffrage problem should be met piecemeal and fractionally. There is no reason why it should be decided in 48 different places."

Representative Hobson[53] argued that the resolution did not take any power from the States.

Support for the special rule but opposition to the submission of the amendment was expressed by Representative Lenroot,[54] Republican, of Wisconsin. He declared he was not satisfied there was a sufficient public demand for woman suffrage to indicate that the proposed amendment would be speedily ratified.

Representative Murdock,[55] Progressive, of Kansas, supported the resolution.

In Line for Resolution.

Representative Eulings,[56] of Pennsylvania, and Lindbergh,[57] of Minnesota, made brief speeches favoring the resolution and Representatives Summers,[58] of Texas, and Clark,[59] of Florida, opposed it.

Representative Dies,[60] Democrat, of Texas, opposed the resolution.

"I have no doubt," said he, "that if woman wielded the cleaver at the meat stall we would have cleaner beefsteak. But who wants to court the butcher? Undoubtedly women would make good peace officers. But who wants to marry a policeman?"

Representative Stafford,[61] Republican, of Wisconsin, opposed the resolution.

Representative Bryan,[62] of Washington, and Stephens[63] and Bell,[64] of California, declared woman suffrage a success. Representative Moore,[65] Republican, of Pennsylvania, opposed the amendment.

Representative MacDonald,[66] of Michigan; Brown,[67] of New York, and Stevens,[68] of New Hampshire, spoke for the resolution, and Representatives Abercrombie,[69] of Alabama, and Hardy,[70] of Texas, made brief but vigorous speeches against it. Mr. Abercrombie said he would vote against the amendment, but he had no doubt that the women of the country ultimately would be given the ballot either by State or through a Federal constitutional amendment. He favored woman suffrage granted by the States.

Express Vigorous Opposition.

Representative Bartlett,[71] of Georgia, and Representative Sisson,[72] of Mississippi, vigorously opposed the resolution.

Representative Madden,[73] of Illinois; Towner,[74] of Iowa; Barnhart,[75] of Indiana; and Raker,[76] of California, supported the resolution in brief speeches.

Representative Henry,[77] of Texas, declared that the trend of the times was too strongly in the direction of stripping the States of their power.

Representative Seldomridge,[78] of Colorado, supported the resolution and praised the voting women of his State.

In opposing the resolution, Representative Hughes,[79] of Georgia, declared, that should the proposed amendment be ratified by the States, it would precipitate a serious situation in the Southern States, on account of the race problem.

Arguments for suffrage also were made by Representatives Cramton,[80] Farr,[81] Hayes,[82] Sinnott,[83] and Gorman,[84] while among the opponents, were Representatives Sloan,[85] Carter,[86] and Mulkey.[87]

Representative Decker,[88] of Missouri, supporting the amendment, replied to Representative Bowdie. He declared that the "governmental cooperation of women was a great blessing," and derided the idea that woman's lack of ability for military service disqualified her as a voter.

Representatives Hayden,[89] of Arizona; Keating,[90] of Colorado; Volstead,[91] of Minnesota; Reilly,[92] of Connecticut; Cline,[93] of Indiana; Fess,[94] of Ohio; and Baker,[95] of New York, also supported the amendment.

Representative Miller,[96] of Minnesota, asserted that the amendment was "in contravention of all the principles of free local self-government."

Representatives Sabath,[97] and Evans[98] spoke in favor of the amendment, and Representative Heflin,[99] of Alabama, made a vigorous speech against it.

Representative Stafford closed the debate in opposition to the bill, declaring that no argument advanced in the discussion had shown the necessity for Federal action on the question of woman suffrage.

At 7:45 the reading of the bill for amendment was begun. Representative Cullop,[100] of Indiana, offered an amendment to submit the suffrage proposal to constitutional conventions in the various States instead of to the State legislatures. This was voted down, 108 to 142.

Further reading for amendment was stopped when Representative Garrett,[101] of Tennessee, moved to strike out the enacting clause of the Mondell resolution. This had the effect of bringing a direct vote on the question of submitting the constitutional amendment to the States, because, under the rules of the House, the striking out of the enacting clause is equivalent to defeating a measure.

Debate Is Cut Off.

Efforts were made to have Representative Garrett withdraw his motion, and to allow a straight vote on the resolution, but he declared his determination of cutting off all further amendments. It was asserted that certain amendments had been prepared involving the question of the colored race's suffrage, which will embarrass Southern members.

Representative Garrett moved the previous question to cut off debate on his motion, which was adopted by a vote of 206 to 170.

A unanimous consent agreement then was reached that the vote should be taken directly upon the resolution itself.

The 7 October 1915 publication of The New York Times *covers President Wilson's endorsement of the Nineteenth Amendment.*

WILSON INDORSES WOMAN SUFFRAGE

———

Will Vote for New Jersey Amendment Oct. 19, President Announces in Statement.

———

OPPOSES NATIONAL ACTION

———

Quest for Each State to Settle-Speaks as Private Citizen-Suffragists Delighted.

———

Special to *The New York Times*.

WASHINGTON. – Oct. 6. President Wilson announced today that he would vote for the woman suffrage amendment in New Jersey. He issues this statement:

I intend to vote for woman suffrage in New Jersey because I believe that the time has come to extend that privilege and responsibility to the women of the State, but I shall vote, not as the leader of my party in the nation, but only upon my private conviction as a citizen of New Jersey, called upon by the Legislature of the State to express his conviction at the polls. I think that New Jersey will be greatly benefited by the change.

My position with regard to the way in which this great question should be handled is well known. I believe that it should be settled by the States and not by the National Government and that in no circumstances should it be made a party question, and my view has grown stronger at every turn of the agitation.

The President's statement makes it plain that he will not encourage the so-called Susan B. Anthony amendment to the Federal Constitution. While he may not actively oppose it, the President, it is known, disapproves of any attempt to fasten woman suffrage on States not ready to vote for it themselves. By making a distinction between State and Federal action on suffrage the President avoids offending the Democratic South, where, except in a few states, the movement for woman suffrage is unimportant.

Four members of the President's Cabinet already have declared in favor of woman suffrage-Mr. Garrison, Mr. McAdoo, Mr. Redfield, and Mr. Wilson.

This story in The Washington Post, *11 January 1918, captures the calm that followed the passage in the House of the proposed Suffrage Amendment and the doubt that remained at how the Senate would vote.*

WOMAN SUFFRAGE WINS IN HOUSE BY ONE VOTE

———

274 For to 136 Against Submitting Amendment.

———

DOUBT NOW IN SENATE

———

Polls Indicate Two-Thirds Cannot Be Obtained.

———

WOMEN PUSH THE FIGHT.

———

Encouraged by Wilson's Support Suffragists Hope to Have Enough Members in Line for Success by Time Vote Takes Place – Close Result in the House Surprise to Both Sides – Scenes of Jubilation in the House Galleries, When the Final Result Is Announced.

———

Woman suffrage by Federal constitutional amendment won in the House last night with exactly the required number of affirmative votes.

While members in their seats and throngs in the galleries waited with eager interest, the House adopted, by a vote of 274 to 136, a resolution providing for submission to the States of the so-called Susan B. Anthony amendment for national enfranchisement of women.

Votes That Saved the Day.

But for the promise of Speaker Clark to cast his vote from the chair for the resolution if it were needed, the change of a single vote to the opposition would have meant defeat.

Republican Leader Mann, who came from a Baltimore hospital, where he has been under treatment ever since Congress convened, and Representative Sims, of Tennessee, just out of a sick bed, and hardly able to walk to his seat, brought the votes which settled the issue.

The House hardly had adjourned before the suffrage champions began their fight for favorable action on the Senate side of the Capitol.

Doubt in the Senate.

Recent polls there have indicated that the necessary two-thirds vote could not be mustered, but encouraged by the House victory and counting upon the influence of President Wilson who came to their support last night, the suffragists hope to bring the Senate into line so as to have the amendment before State legislators during the coming year.

They feel sure at least of forcing a vote in the Senate before the present session ends.

Advocates Are Confident.

Advocates of the amendment has been supremely confident of the result in the House after President Wilson advised the members who called upon him last night to support it. They were so confident that the close vote was received with amazement, and some of the opponents were almost as much surprised.

When the first roll call was finished unofficial counts put the result in doubt and before the Speaker could make an announcement there was a demand for a recapitulation. Then the name of each member and the way he recorded was read.

Announcement of the vote was greeted with wild applause and cheering. Women in the galleries literally fell upon each other's necks, kissing and embracing and shouting Glory, glory, hallelujah."

Text of the Resolution.

The resolution as adopted, follows:

Joint resolution proposing an amendment to the Constitution of the United States extending the right of suffrage to women. Resolved by the Senate and House, &c., two-thirds of each house concurring therein, that the following article be proposed to the legislatures of the several States as an amendment to the Constitution of the United States, which, when ratified by three-fourths of said legislatures, shall be valid as part of said Constitution, namely:

"Article ____, section 1. The right of citizens the United States to vote shall not be denied or abridged by the United States or by any State on account of sex.

Section 2. Congress shall have power, by appropriate legislation, to enforce the provisions of this article."

Defeat of Amendments.

Every attempt made to amend this language was beaten. Representative Gard[102] of Ohio, tried unsuccessfully to Put on it the same limitation carried by the resolution for the prohibition constitutional amendment, that it must be ratified by the States within seven years from the date of its submission. Representative Moores ,[103] of Indiana, sought to have a referendum or special convention in each State required. The Gard amendment was rejected, 159 to 246, and the Moores amendment, 131 to 272.

When the final vote came on the resolution Representative Austin,[104] of Tennessee, challenged the vote of Representative Dominick,[105] of South Carolina, who appeared late in the roll call and said he had not heard his name called. Mr. Dominick told the Speaker he was in the hall and listening and did not hear his name called. His vote as then recorded.

Clark Chuckles Over Victory.

The Speaker watched the vote, prepared to cast his own into the breach if necessary. "One more negative vote," he explained afterward, as he chuckled over the victory, "would have changed the situation and the amendment resolution would have been lost, in which event I would have directed the clerk to call my name and that would have been just sufficient to carry it." Of the total membership of 435, there were 410 members who voted. Their line-up follows:

For the resolution: Democrats, 104; Republicans, 165; miscellaneous, 5; total, 274. Against the resolution, Democrats, 102; Republicans, 33; Progressive, 1; total, 136.

Applause for Mann.

Urgent orders had been given by the leaders to bring in everybody possible. When Representative Mann walked slowly to his accustomed place as leader of the Republicans, applause rang over the House, members from all sides rushed over to him and Speaker Clark broke a precedent by announcing from the rostrum that he was sure everybody in the House welcomes him back.

There were two women on the floor during the contest. Miss Jeanette Rankin, of Montana, who as representative of a suffragist State, was accorded the courtesy of not only controlling one-fourth of the time of debate, but of making the opening speech, and Miss May Offterdinger, of this city, who, as clerk of the woman suffrage committee, sat beside the chairman, Representative Raker,[106] of California.

Wilson Helps the Result.

The House met at 11 o'clock yesterday morning, an hour earlier than usual, and began consideration of the resolution under an agreement to close general debate and begin voting on amendments at 5 o'clock in the afternoon. It was 6:25 o'clock when the final roll call began, and just 45 minutes later when Speaker Clark announced the result.

President Wilson's support is credited with changing many Democratic votes. The party divided almost evenly, with a margin of two ayes. Until Wednesday it had been assumed that a large majority of the Democrats would oppose the resolution.

Mrs. Catt's Statement.

Mrs. Carrie Chapman Catt, president of the National American Woman Suffrage Association, said last night:

"It is an incomparable victory which tremendously gratifies, though it does not surprise us. We have felt all along that the House could be relied on to vindicate itself as the forward-looking exponent of democratic progress which America has the right to expect its great law-making body to be.

"Not for a minute did we concede that the American Congress would lag behind the parliaments of Europe in the making of democratic history.

"We now turn to the Senate with complete confidence that our measure will be passed by that body within a very short time. From the Senate we shall start upon our campaign of ratifications, hoping that every State in the Union will ratify and knowing that 36 will – New York among them. We expect that most of the 1918 legislatures – there are only a few in session this year – will dispose of the measure favorably at an early date. The legislatures of 41 States convene next year."

Likens Wilson to Lincoln.

Dr. Anna Howard Shaw, honorary president of the association, said:

"When the name of Lincoln is mentioned today the first thought that enters the mind of the world is that he was the emancipator of the slaves.

"In future generations when the name of Wilson is mentioned, the thought of the world will be that the women of the United States were enfranchised during his administration and largely through his assistance. People forget wars and the incidents of wars, but they never forget a great forward step in human freedom."

Expects Senate Victory.

Miss Alice Paul, the leader of the woman's party, made this statement:

"We rejoice, and for the moment that is all we do. With tomorrow we will begin to press for the immediate passage of the amendment through the Senate. Four years ago we lacked only eleven votes in the Senate.

"Our strength meanwhile has grown enormously and victory should be easy. It is not now a question of victory or defeat, but of how quickly we can secure the submission of the amendment to the States and begin our campaign for ratification. With the official support of every political party we believe that ratification will not require more than two years."

Mrs. Wadworth's View.

Mrs. James W. Wadsworth, Jr., president of the National Association Opposed to Woman Suffrage, issued this statement:

"We thank the men who stood by the principle of local self-government against the policy of surrender to suffrage threats and we are proud that there are still some American men who vote according to their convictions and not according to command.

"We consider the result very close in view of the pressure brought to bear on the members.

"Our hope now is that the Senate will stand firm in defense of our American traditions of true democracy."

This excerpted article from The Chicago Tribune, *11 February 1919 examines what happened in the US Senate for the Suffrage Amendment to fall one vote shy of the three-fourths vote needed to send the proposal to the states.*

SUFFRAGE LOSES BY ONE VOTE; NOW UP TO G.O.P.

————

Amendment, Again Rejected, Likely to Pass Next Congress.

————

(By a Staff Correspondent.)

Washington, D.C., Feb. 10. – [Special] – By the margin of one vote nation wide women's suffrage went down to defeat on the senate again today. Its rejection dooms the suffrage amendment so far as the present session is concerned, but it is confidently expected it will be put through promptly when the Republicans take control of the next congress.

The vote on the resolution to submit the suffrage constitutional amendment to the states for ratification was 55 yeas. If one "anti" had but switched to vote the measure would have had the two-thirds necessary to its adoption.

Bryan's Warning Unheeded.

In the face of William Jennings Bryan' warning to the southern Democrats that their opposition to the suffrage was spelling ruin to the party in the north the dems nevertheless contributed the major share of the voice against the resolution. Democrats favoring the [eso] numbered twenty-four, as against the thirty-one Republicans for it. Eighteen Democrats, especially from the south, and eleven Republicans voted against the resolution.

There was a change of only one vote upon the lineup of Sept. 30 last, when the amendment was rejected by a margin of two votes. Senator Pollock,[107] Democrat, of South Carolina, who succeeded Senator Benet,[108] an "anti" cast his vote for suffrage.

[...]

On Trial in Police Court, Too.

Today's action was taken after a brief [denaye] before galleries crowded with women, both "pros" and "antis." While the amendment was being voted on in the senate thirty-nine members of the Woman's party were being tried in the police court for demanding its passage at a protest demonstration in front of the White House Sunday afternoon, in which President Wilson was burned in effigy as responsible for the threatened defeat of the measure.

Twenty-five women were sentenced to five days, one to two days, and the others dismissed. The charges against them were building fires on government property, standing on the coping around the White House, or attempting to make speeches.

The women announced from the district jail tonight that they would conduct a "hunger strike."

Leaders Undismayed.

Suffrage leaders were undismayed by the defeat and at once declared they would continue the fight. Mrs. Carrie Chapman Catt, president of the American National Woman Suffrage association, said:

"It is not the women, it is the nation that is dishonored. The whole country stand shamed before the world, victimized by a small reactionary minority that holds American back from her rightful place among the standard bearers of democracy."

The Rev. Dr. Anna Howard Shaw, temporary president of the National association, said: "Soon we shall be in the humiliating position of admitting that ours is the only one of the great nations of the earth denying justice to its women."

Still Has Hope.

Mrs. Alice Paul, chairman of the National Woman's party, said: "The time is short, but if dynasties and leaders can be overthrown in the brief span of a few days it should be possible to enfranchise the women of America before this congress ends."

Mrs. George Bass of Chicago, chairman of the women's Democratic committee, wired from California: "Reactionary Republicans, seconded by a little group of 'me too' senators whose democracy is merely a thread-bare tradition, have been able to again postpone the day of victory."

Mrs. Medill McCormick of Chicago, chairman of the Republican women's national executive committee said she was neither surprised nor disappointed at the result.

"We knew exactly how the senate stood on the measure," she said. "As soon as there is a Republican congress the amendment will be adopted."

Mrs. Grace Wilbur Trout, president of the Illinois Suffrage association, said: "The Democrats failed to grasp their opportunity today, but the Republicans will seize it in the next congress."

This story in The Washington Post*, 11 January 1918 reports on the breakthrough that suffragettes have been looking for, when the US Senate passes, by a three-fourths vote, the Suffrage Amendment to the US Constitution.*

SUFFRAGE AMENDMENT IS ADOPTED BY SENATE

_____

Fifty-six Senators Cast Their Ballots in Support of the House Resolution and 25 Against it; Roll Call Shows Two Votes More Than Necessary; Measure Now Goes to the Legislatures of the States for Ratification; Three-fourths of the States Must Vote in Favor of the Incorporation of the Amendment into the Constitution of the Nation Before it Can Before Effective.

_____

Washington, June 4. – Action by congress on equal suffrage – subject of a fight of forty years duration – ended late today in adoption by he senate by a vote of 56 to 25 of the historic Susan B. Anthony constitutional amendment resolution.

The amendment now goes to the state legislatures, ratification of three-fourths of which is required for its incorporation in the federal constitution.

The roll call today showed two votes more than the necessary two-thirds for the resolution, which was drafted by Susan B. Anthony in 1875 and introduced by Senator Sargent[109] of California in 1878.

Loud applause, unchecked by the presiding officer, swept the senate chamber when the final vote was announced following two days debate and many jubilation meetings were in progress tonight at headquarters of various women's organizations.

Although few state legislatures are now in session, woman suffrage champions tonight claimed that certification soon would be secured, probably by next spring. In today's debate, however, Senator Gay[110] predicted that with the southern states opposing the measure because of implied enfranchisement of negro women, the required number of states would refuse to ratify and cause its rejection.

The Philadelphia Evening Ledger, *5 June 1919, reports reactions to the congressional passage of the Suffrage Amendment.*

SUFFRAGISTS HERE FLAUNT THEIR FLAGS

City Advocates Jubilant Over Senate Victory – Start Work for State Ratification

WANT PENNA. TO BE FIRST

Suffragists in this city are jubilant over the victory of the Susan B. Anthony amendment which passed the Senate late yesterday afternoon with a vote of 56 to 25.

Senator Penrose[111] was paired with Senator Calder,[112] of New York, and Senator Townsend,[113] of Michigan, and Senator Knox[114] voted against the amendment.

As soon as the news reached Philadelphia, the house of Miss Marry Burnham, 3401 Powelton Avenue, displayed a suffrage flag for victory. Mrs. Archibald Harmon, 5247 Baltimore Avenue, who returned to this city late yesterday, after watching the amendment go through in Washington, also decorated her house with the suffrage colors.

The last minutes before the roll call was taken were tense and breath-taking, according to Mrs. Harmon. Miss Alice Brock and she were the only Philadelphia representatives present in the gallery of the Senate yesterday.

"Nobody said a word for several seconds after the announcement was made," says Mrs. Harmon. "They just held their breaths and then a shout went up from the galleries."

"The women grabbed each other and hugged one another on the steps and in the halls. Then we went out on the Capitol steps and a 'movie' was taken of us. I felt like a frazzle when I got through."

Mrs. Harmon said that all Washington seemed alive with the news which spread like wildfire.

The National Women's party held an executive committee meeting this morning to discuss future moves. The subject of a local celebration will be brought before the meeting.

Immediately following the passing of the amendment the National Women's party in Washington was ready with printed copies of the amendment for the signatures of the Department of State and the presiding speaker. These copies were signed and sent out last night to all the legislatures.

Illinois opened up the competition of the states for ratification by advising the party to send a certified copy of the amendment with all speed in that state.

The big job is only beginning, according to members of the executive committee. They contend they must concentrate on state ratifications just now and this evening will send out two thousand letters to legislators and members of the party in this state in the hope that Pennsylvania will be the first state to ratify the amendment.

Supreme Court Cases

Bradwell v. Illinois *(83 U.S. 130 {1873}). Decided 15 April 1873 by a vote of 8-1, with Chief Justice Salon P. Chase in dissent. Samuel Freeman Miller wrote the majority opinion.*

The Case: Myra Bradwell, a resident of Illinois, applied to the state bar to be admitted to practice as an attorney. She applied under a state statute which allowed "any adult" who had received proper training in the law and who had a "good character" to be so admitted. However, the state bar refused to grant her a law license solely because she was a woman. Bradwell sued to the Illinois state Supreme Court, which held that if the state bar were to grant such a license, it would cause "strife." Bradwell sued to the US Supreme Court, which agreed to hear the case. Arguments were heard on 18 January 1873.

On 15 April 1873, the Court held 8-1 that the Illinois state bar's refusal to grant a law license to Bradwell was not unconstitutional because the right to practice the law was not one of the listed privileges in the Fourteenth Amendment to the US Constitution. Justice Samuel Freeman Miller was joined in the majority opinion by Justices Nathan Clifford, David Davis (who had once served as a US Senator from Illinois), Ward Hunt, and William Strong, and in concurrence by Justices Joseph P. Bradley, Stephen J. Field, and Noah Haynes Swayne. Chief Justice Salmon P. Chase was all alone in his dissent.

During arguments before the court, Bradwell's attorney, Matthew Hale Carpenter, said to the justices: "The question does not involve the right of a female to vote. It presents a narrow matter:

"Can a female citizen, duly qualified in respect of age, character, and learning, claim, under the fourteenth amendment, the privilege of earning a livelihood by practicing at the bar of a judicial court?"

Justice Miller wrote, "Does admission to the bar belong to that class of privileges which a State may not abridge, or that class of political rights as to which a State may discriminate between its citizens?...It is evident that there are certain 'privileges and immunities' which belong to a citizen of the United States as such; otherwise it would be nonsense for the fourteenth amendment to prohibit a State from abridging them. I concede that the right to vote is not one of those privileges. And the question recurs whether admission to the bar, the proper qualification being possessed, is one of the privileges which a State may not deny."

He added, "The opinion just delivered in the Slaughter-House Cases [83 US 36 {1873}] renders elaborate argument in the present case unnecessary; for, unless we are wholly and radically mistaken in the principles on which those cases are decided, the right to control and regulate the granting of license to practice law in the courts of a State is one of those powers which are not transferred for its protection to the Federal government, and its exercise is in no manner governed or controlled by citizenship of the United States in the party seeking such license."

Chief Justice Chase did not write a dissent; the official decision merely noted that he did dissent, "and [dissented] from all the opinions."

Minor v. Happersett *(88 U.S. 162 {1875}). Decided 29 March 1875 by a vote of 9-0. Chief Justice Morrison Remick Waite wrote the majority opinion.*

The Case: Mrs. Virginia Minor, a citizen of Missouri, wanted to vote in the general election in 1872. Reese Happersett, the state registrar of voters, refused to register her, claiming that under Missouri law "every male citizen of United States shall be entitled to vote." Minor sued him in a district court, as she was deprived of her right to vote. Happersett answered, stating that since she was not a "male citizen," he could not, under state law, register her. The lower court held that Happersett was correct and, without ruling on the merits of the law itself, the Missouri state Supreme Court upheld the verdict. Minor sued to the US Supreme Court, which heard arguments on 9 February 1875.

On 29 March 1875, Chief Justice Morrison Remick Waite held that while Minor was considered a "citizen" under the laws of the United States, nevertheless the right to vote was not a part of being a citizen as prescribed by the Fourteenth Amendment to the US Constitution. He explained, "The right of suffrage was not necessarily one of the privileges or immunities of citizenship before the adoption of the fourteenth amendment, and that amendment does not add to these privileges and immunities. It simply furnishes additional guaranty for the protection of such as the citizen already had." After stating that "[n]either the Constitution nor the fourteenth amendment made all citizens voters," he wrote, "A provision in a State constitution which confines the right of voting to 'male citizens of the United States,' is no violation of the Federal Constitution. In such a State women have no right to vote." Note: There is more on this landmark decision in the introduction to this section.

Leser v. Garnett *(258 U.S. 130 {1922}). Decided 27 February 1922 by a vote of 9-0. Justice Louis D. Brandeis wrote the majority opinion.*

The Case: This case was the first and only constitutional challenge to the constitutionality of the Nineteenth Amendment to the US Constitution. Ironically, however, the case involved two men who sued to have the amendment nullified so that womens' vote could not be counted. From the decision: "On October 12, 1920, Cecilia Streett Waters and Mary D. Randolph, citizens of Maryland, applied for and were granted registration as qualified voters in Baltimore City. To have their names stricken from the list Oscar Leser and others brought this suit in the court of common pleas. The only ground of disqualification alleged was that the applicants for registration were women, whereas the Constitution of Maryland limits the suffrage to men." Leser wanted Garnet, the voting registrar, to strike women from the voting rolls. The trial court dismissed the pleas of Leser and his compatriots; the state Court of Appeals upheld the verdict. Leser sued to the US Supreme Court, which granted certiorari, or, the right to hear the case. Arguments were heard on 24 and 25 January 1922.

A month later, on 27 January 1922, the Court unanimously held that under the Nineteenth Amendment, Waters and Randolph had the right to vote, and, further, that the amendment was wholly constitutional. Justice Louis D. Brandeis broke the decision down into two parts: the constitutionality of the amendment, and hether Maryland could keep women from voting. As to the first, he explained, "The first contention is that the power of amendment conferred by the federal Constitution and sought to be exercise does not extend to this amendment because of its character. The argument is that so great an addition to the electorate, if made without the state's consent, destroys its autonomy as a political body. This amendment is in character and phraseology precisely similar to the Fifteenth. For each the same method of adoption was pursued. One cannot be valid and the other invalid. That the

Fifteenth is valid, although rejected by six states, including Maryland, has been recognized and acted on for half a century."

He then moved on to the second: "The second contention is that in the Constitutions of several of the 36 states named in the proclamation of the Secretary of State there are provisions which render inoperative the alleged ratification by their Legislatures. The argument is thst by reason of these specific provisions the Legislatures were without power to ratify. But the function of a state Legislature in ratifying a proposed amendment to the federal Constitution, like the function of Congress in proposing the amendment, is a federal function derived from the federal Constitution; and it transcends any limitations sought to be imposed by the people of a state."

Finally, he addressed another argument of the plaintiffs: that the states which pushed the amendment over the requisite number of states had voted in an illegal manner. Brandeis wrote, "The remaining contention is that the ratifying resolutions of Tennessee and of West Virginia are inoperative, because adopted in violation of the rules of legislative procedure prevailing in the respective states. The question raised may have been rendered immaterial by the fact that since the proclamation the Legislatures of two other states-Connecticut and Vermont-have adopted resolutions of ratification. But a broader answer should be given to the contention. The proclamation by the Secretary certified that from official documents on file in the Department of State it appeared that the proposed amendment was ratified by the Legislatures of 36 states, and that it 'has become valid to all intents and purposes as a part of the Constitution of the United States.' As the Legislatures of Tennessee and of West Virginia had power to adopt the resolutions of ratification, official notice to the Secretary, duly authenticated, that they had done so, was conclusive upon him, and, being certified to by his proclamation, is conclusive upon the courts."

ৡৢৡৢৡৢৡৢৡৢ

Breedlove v. Suttles *(302 U.S. 277 {1937}). Decided 6 December 1937 by a vote of 9-0. Justice Pierce Butler wrote the majority opinion.*

The Case: Breedlove is not a "woman's suffrage" case per se; however, it does deal with how a woman who wanted to vote – or not vote – could be treated by state officials. The state of Georgia had a law which provided that a poll tax of $1 per year was to be levied against every citizen of Georgia, except for women or blind people who did not vote; further, if a woman didn't pay the poll tax she could not vote. Appellant Breedlove, a white man, sued to have this entire law struck down as unconstitutional, naming Suttles, the Tax Collector, as the defendant. The Superior Court of Fulton County dismissed Breedlove's lawsuit, and, on appeal the Georgia state Supreme Court affirmed. Breedlove then sued to the US Supreme Court, which accepted the case and heard arguments on 16 and 17 November 1937.

Less than a month later, on 6 December 1937, the Court held that the poll tax was legal, and women could be exempt as long as they did not vote. Justice Pierce Butler wrote that "[t]he tax being upon persons, women may be exempted on the basis of special considerations to which they are naturally entitled. In view of burdens necessarily borne by them for the preservation of the race, the state reasonably may exempt them from poll taxes." He added that the "[p]rivilege of voting is not derived from the United States, but is conferred by the state and, save as restrained by the Fifteenth and Nineteenth Amendments and other provisions of the Federal Constitution, the state may condition suffrage as it deems appropriate."

Butler concluded,

"The Nineteenth Amendment, adopted in 1920, declares: 'The right of citizens of he United States to vote shall not be denied or abridged by the United States or by any State on account of sex.' It applies to men and women alike and by its own force supersedes inconsistent measures, whether federal or state...Its purpose is not to regulate the levy or collection of taxes. The construction for which appellant contends would make the amendment a limitation upon the power to tax. The payment of poll taxes as a prerequisite to voting is a familiar and reasonable regulation long enforced in many states and for fore than a century in Georgia. That measure reasonably may be deemed essential to that form of levy. Imposition without enforcement would be futile. Power to levy and power to collect are equally necessary. And, by the exaction of payment before registration, the right to vote is neither denied nor abridged on account of sex. It is fanciful to suggest that the Georgia law is a mere disguise under which to deny or abridge the right of men to vote on account of their sex. The challenged enactment is not repugnant to the Nineteenth Amendment."

Reed v. Reed *(404 U.S. 71 {1971}). Decided 22 November 1971 by a vote of 9-0. Chief Justice Warren Burger wrote the majority opinion.*

The Case: This is the landmark equal protection case involving the rights of women. Upon his death in March 1967, Richard Lynn Reed, a minor, left an estate but no will, and it was fought over by his adopted parents, Cecil R. Reed and Sally M. Reed, both of whom were separated at the time. The court of probate in Ada County, Idaho, held that "[o]f several persons claiming and equally entitled to administer [an estate], males must be preferred to females, and relatives of the whole to those of the half blood." Sally Reed sued her husband in the District Court of the Fourth Judicial District of Idaho, which held the state law violative of the Equal Protection Clause of the Fourteenth Amendment to the US Constitution, and sent the case back for another hearing. Before this could happen, however, Cecil Reed appealed to the Idaho state Supreme Court, which overturned the lower court and ordered that Cecil Reed be named as his adopted son's executor. Sally Reed then appealed this decision to the US Supreme Court, which granted certiorari, or, the right to hear the case. Arguments were held on 29 October 1971.

A month later, on 22 November 1971, the Court held unanimously that the state law treating men and women differently was unconstitutional. Chief Justice Warren Burger spoke for the unanimous Court when he wrote, "Clearly the objective of reducing the workload on probate courts by eliminating one class of contests is not without some legitimacy. The crucial question, however, is whether [the state statute] advances that objective in a manner consistent with the command of the Equal Protection Clause. We hold that it does not. To give a mandatory preference to members of either sex over members of the other, merely to accomplish the elimination of hearings on the merits, is to make the very kind of arbitrary legislative choice forbidden by the Equal Protection Clause of the Fourteenth Amendment; and whatever may be said as to the positive values of avoiding intrafamily controversy, the choice in this context may not lawfully be mandated solely on the basis of sex." He concluded, "The objective of [the state statute] clearly is to establish degrees of entitlement of various classes of persons in accordance with their varying degrees and kinds of relationship to the intestate. Regardless of their sex, persons within any one of the enumerated classes of that section are similarly situated with respect to that objective. By providing dissimilar treatment for men and women who are thus similarly situated, the challenged section violates the Equal Protection Clause."

Frontiero v. Richardson *(411 U.S. 677 {1973}). Decided 14 May 1973 by an 8-1 vote. The majority opinion was written by Justice William Brennan.*

The Case: The petitioner in this case was Sharron Frontiero, an officer in the US Air Force. She tried to obtain a dependent's allowance for her husband. According to federal law, however, while a wife was automatically regarded as a dependent of a husband serving in the armed forces, a husband had to be dependent on his wife serving in the armed forces for more than half of his support in order to receive dependent benefits.

The Court ruled in Frontiero's favor, holding that the statute violated the Due Process Clause of the Fifth Amendment. The Court held that any statute that draws lines between the sexes on the basis of gender alone is unconstitutional.

Justice William Brennan wrote,

"There can be no doubt that our Nation has had a long and unfortunate history of sex discrimination. Traditionally, such discrimination was rationalized by an attitude of 'romantic paternalism' which, in practical effect, put women not on a pedestal, but in a cage....

"As a result of notions such as these, our statute books gradually became laden with gross, stereotyped distinctions between the sexes, and, indeed, throughout much of the 19th century, the position of women in our society was, in many respects, comparable to that of blacks under the pre-Civil War slave codes. Neither slaves nor women could hold office, serve on juries, or bring suit in their own names, and married women traditionally were denied the legal capacity to hold or convey property or to serve as legal guardians of their own children. And although blacks were guaranteed the right to vote in 1870, women were denied even that right – which is itself 'preservative of other basic civil and political rights' until adoption of the Nineteenth Amendment half a century later.

"It is true, of course, that the position of women in America has improved markedly in recent decades. Nevertheless, it can hardly be doubted that, in part because of the high visibility of the sex characteristic, women still face pervasive, although at times more subtle, discrimination in our educational institutions, in the job market and, perhaps most conspicuously, in the political arena....

"With these considerations in mind, we can only conclude that classifications based upon sex, like classifications based upon race, alienage, or national origin, are inherently suspect, and must therefore be subjected to strict judicial scrutiny. Applying the analysis mandated by that stricter standard of review, it is clear that the statutory scheme now before us is constitutionally invalid....

"We therefore conclude that, by according differential treatment to male and female members of the uniformed services for the sole purpose of achieving administrative convenience, the challenged statutes violate the Due Process Clause of the Fifth Amendment insofar as they require a female member to prove the dependency of her husband."

＊＊＊＊＊＊＊＊＊＊＊＊

Cleveland Board of Education v. LaFleur *(414 U.S. 632 {1974}). Decided 21 January 1974, by a vote of 7-2. Justice Potter Stewart delivered the majority opinion.*

The Case: Petitioners in this case consisted of public school teachers in Cleveland, Ohio, who were pregnant. They contested a number of provisions in the school system's regulations bearing on maternity leave, notice to the school system of the intent to take such leave, schedules for returning to the classroom, and the need for certificates from physicians. The petitioners argued that these onerous requirements were unconstitutional.

The Court agreed, holding that the requirement were arbitrary and irrational, based on presumptions about the ability of pregnant women to perform in their jobs. Thus, they violated the Due Process Clause of the Fifth Amendment and the Fourteenth Amendment.

Justice Stewart wrote,

"This Court has long recognized that freedom of personal choice in matters of marriage and family life is one of the liberties protected by the Due Process Clause of the Fourteenth Amendment. As we noted in *Eisenstadt v.*

Baird, there is a right 'to be free from unwarranted governmental intrusion into matters so fundamentally affecting a person as the decision whether to bear or beget a child.'

"By acting to penalize the pregnant teacher for deciding to bear a child, overly restrictive maternity leave regulations can constitute a heavy burden on the exercise of these protected freedoms. Because public school maternity leave rules directly affect 'one of the basic civil rights of man,' *Skinner v. Oklahoma*, supra, at 541, the Due Process Clause of the Fourteenth Amendment requires that such rules must not needlessly, arbitrarily, or capriciously impinge upon this vital area of a teacher's constitutional liberty. The question before us in these cases is whether the interests advanced in support of the rules of the Cleveland and Chesterfield County School Boards can justify the particular procedures they have adopted...."

"We conclude, therefore, that neither the necessity for continuity of instruction nor the state interest in keeping physically unfit teachers out of the classroom can justify the sweeping mandatory leave regulations that the Cleveland and Chesterfield County School Boards have adopted. While the regulations no doubt represent a good-faith attempt to achieve a laudable goal, they cannot pass muster under the Due Process Clause of the Fourteenth Amendment, because they employ irrebuttable presumptions that unduly penalize a female teacher for deciding to bear a child."

Stanton v. Stanton *(421 U.S. 7 {1975}). Decided 15 April 1975 by a vote of 8-1. Justice Harry Blackmun wrote the opinion for the majority.*

The Case: According to a Utah statue, the age of adulthood for males was twenty-one and that for females was eighteen. This discrepancy had implications for the continuance of child support payments by a divorced parent after a daughter turns eighteen. The petitioner in this case was an ex-wife who sought continued child support payments from the daughter's father after the daughter turned eighteen.

The Court struck down the Utah statute as a violation of equal protection under the law.

Justice Blackmun wrote:

"The test here, then, is whether the difference in sex between children warrants the distinction in the appellee's obligation to support that is drawn by the Utah statute. We conclude that it does not. It may be true, as the Utah court observed, and as is argued here, that it is the man's primary responsibility to provide a home, and that it is salutary for him to have education and training before he assumes that responsibility; that girls tend to mature earlier than boys; and that females tend to marry earlier than males. The last mentioned factor, however, under the Utah statute, loses whatever weight it otherwise might have, for the statute states that 'all minors obtain their majority by marriage'; thus, minority, and all that goes with it, is abruptly lost by marriage of a person of either sex at whatever tender age the marriage occurs.

"Notwithstanding the 'old notions' to which the Utah court referred, we perceive nothing rational in the distinction drawn by [the Utah statute] which, when related to the divorce decree, results in the appellee's liability for support for Sherri only to age 18, but for Rick to age 21. This imposes 'criteria wholly unrelated to the objective of that statute.' A child, male or female, is still a child. No longer is the female destined solely for the home and the rearing of the family, and only the male for the marketplace and the world of ideas. Women's activities and responsibilities are increasing and expanding. Coeducation is a fact, not a rarity. The presence of women in business, in the professions, in government and, indeed, in all walks of life where education is a desirable, if not always a necessary, antecedent is apparent, and a proper subject of judicial notice. If a specified age of minority is required for the boy in order to assure him parental support while he attains his education and training, so too is it for the girl. To distinguish between the two on educational grounds is to be self-serving: if the female is not to be supported so long as the male, she hardly can be expected to attend school as long as he does, and bringing her education to an end earlier coincides with the role-typing society has long imposed. And if any weight remains in this day to the claim of earlier maturity of the female, with a concomitant inference of absence of need for support beyond 18, we fail to perceive its unquestioned truth or its significance, particularly when marriage, as the statute provides, terminates minority for a person of either sex."

೭ঌৎঌৎঌৎঌৎঌ

Craig v. Boren *(429 U.S. 190 {1976}). Decided 20 December 1976 by a vote of 7-2. Justice William Brennan wrote the majority opinion; Chief Justice Warren Burger and Justice William H. Rehnquist dissented.*

The Case: Officially titled *Craig v. Boren, Governor of Oklahoma*, this case dealt with whether the Equal Protection Clause of the Fourteenth Amendment gave females a differing standard of treatment that could be considered better than males. Oklahoma enacted a state law that barred males over the age of 18, but over the age of 21, from purchasing or consuming intoxicating beers, labeled as 3.2% alcohol, but did not bar females over 18 from purchasing the product. Curtis Craig, a male who was over 18 but under 21, sued under the Equal Protection Clause in the District Court for the Western District of Oklahoma in 1972. A three-judge court stated that the law was constitutional, and dismissed the suit. Craig bypassed his state Supreme Court and federal appeals courts and appealed directly to the US Supreme Court, which granted certiorari, or the right to hear the case. Arguments were heard before the High Court on 5 October 1976.

Two months later, on 20 December 1976, Justice William Brennan spoke for a 7-2 court which held that under the Equal Protection Clause, males could not be treated differently than females, and struck down the state law. Citing the case (mentioned in this section) of *Reed v. Reed* (404 U.S. 71 {1971}), Brennan wrote,

"*Reed v. Reed* has also provided the underpinning for decisions that have invalidated statutes employing gender as an inaccurate proxy for other, more germane bases of classification. Hence, 'archaic and overbroad' generalizations...concerning the financial position of servicewomen...and working women...could not justify use of a gender line in determining eligibility for certain governmental entitlements. Similarly, increasingly outdated misconceptions concerning the role of females in the home rather than in the "marketplace and world of ideas" were rejected as loose-fitting characterizations incapable of supporting state statutory schemes that were premised upon their accuracy...In light of the weak congruence between gender and the characteristic or trait that gender purported to represent, it was necessary that the legislatures choose either to realign their substantive laws in a gender-neutral fashion, or to adopt procedures for identifying those instances where the sex-centered generalization actually comported with fact."

He added,

"Following this approach, both federal and state courts uniformly have declared the unconstitutionality of gender lines that restrain the activities of customers of state-regulated liquor establishments irrespective of the operation of the Twenty-first Amendment...Even when state officials have posited sociological or empirical justifications for these gender-based differentiation, the courts have struck down discriminations aimed at an entire class under the guise of alcohol regulation. In fact, social science studies that have uncovered quantifiable difference in drinking tendencies dividing along both racial and ethnic lines strongly suggest the need for application of the Equal Protection Clause in preventing discriminatory treatment that almost certainly would be perceived as invidious. In sum, the principles embodied in the Equal Protection Clause are not to be rendered inapplicable by statistically measured but loose-fitting generalities concerning the drinking tendencies of aggregate groups. We thus hold that the operation of the Twenty-first Amendment does not alter the application of equal protection standards that otherwise govern this case." He concluded, "We conclude that the gender-based differential contained in [the state statute] constitutes a denial of the equal protection of the laws to males aged 18-20 and reverse the judgment of the District Court."

In dissent, Justice William H. Rehnquist explained, "The Court's disposition of this case is objectionable on two grounds. First is its conclusion that men challenging a gender-based statute which treats them less favorably than women may invoke a more stringent standard of judicial review than pertains to most other types of classifications. Second is the Court's enunciation of this standard, without citation to any source, as being that 'classifications by gender must serve important governmental objectives and must be substantially related to achievement of those objectives.'...The only redeeming feature of the Court's opinion, to my mind, is that it apparently signals a retreat by those who joined the plurality opinion in *Frontiero v. Richardson*, 411 U. S. 677 (1973), from their view that sex is a 'suspect' classification for purposes of equal protection analysis. I think the Oklahoma statute challenged here need pass only the 'rational basis' equal protection analysis."

WHO'S WHO

This section includes biographies of four individuals who played a significant part in drafting and passing the Nineteenth Amendment. All are mentioned in earlier sections of this chapter.

Carrie Chapman Catt (1859-1947)

Carrie Chapman Catt not only pushed the Suffrage Amendment through Congress, but also helped get it ratified by the states. She signifies all of the women who were there to see the amendment through to its ultimate conclusion.

Carrie Chapman Catt was born Carrie Clinton Lane in Ripon, Wisconsin, on 9 February 1859, the daughter of farmers Lucius Lane and his wife Maria (née Clinton) Lane. She came from a long line of settlers who first settled in the colony of Massachusetts in the early 17th century. Both Lucius Lane and Maria Clinton Lane grew up on a farm near Potsdam, New York, and after marrying they moved west, settling in Ripon. Eventually, they would have two other children, both sons. In 1866, when Carrie was seven, the family moved to a farm near Charles City, Iowa, where the Lane children would attend local schools. When he finished high school, Carrie Lane taught school for one year to pay for college courses. She studied at the Iowa State Agricultural College (now Iowa State University), and, in 1880, graduated with a Bachelor's degree in Science after she studied evolution and the law. She then went to work for a law office in Charles City; afterward, she served as the principal of the Mason City (Iowa) High School, moving up to superintendent in 1883.

From an early age, Carrie Lane became an agitator to improve women's lives, especially when she found out in 1872 that her mother was prohibited from voting in that year's presidential election. At that time, single women, while able to work, were shut out of most opportunities that exist today for women, so in 1885, Lane married Leo Chapman, the editor of the weekly newspaper the *Mason City Republican*, and he made her the co-editor of the paper. She used its pages to rail against the societal norms that pigeonholed women, writing in a column she called "Woman's World." During a local election in Mason City, Chapman alleged in his paper that Henry Shepard, the County Auditor, who was up for re-election, had committed fraud in his office. Shepard sued Chapman for libel, and when Chapman asked a court to dismiss the suit, the court refused and set a date for trial. Afraid of losing everything, Chapman and his wife quickly sold the newspaper and fled Mason City. Carrie Chapman stayed with her parents in Charles City while Leo Chapman went west, to San Francisco, to find work. While there, he came down with typhoid. His wife got on a train to get to his side, but he died in August 1886 before she could reach him. Carrie Chapman was widowed at 26 years old.

She remained in San Francisco to work as a reporter to earn a living, and also lectured on women's issues. After a year, she returned to Iowa, and continued her activities by writing for local newspapers and lecturing there, and became the state organizer and recording secretary for the Iowa Woman Suffrage Association. One issue which also drew her attention was prohibition, which many women embraced because of the toll alcohol took on men and their families. Carrie Chapman joined the Women's Christian Temperance Union (WCTU), one of the nation's leading prohibition organizations, which also stood for woman's suffrage.

The year 1890 was a key moment in the life of this woman. In October 1889, she had attended the Iowa Woman Suffrage Association convention. The following year, she attended and addressed the National American Woman Suffrage Association. This group was the encompassing organization of two leading women's rights groups: the National Woman Suffrage Association, led by Susan B. Anthony and Elizabeth Cady Stanton, and the American Woman Suffrage Association, chaired by Julia Ward Howe and Lucy Stone. At the same time, Carrie Chapman married George Catt, an engineer she had known while attending college in Iowa and had met while in San Francisco. George Catt wholeheartedly supported his wife's life work, to bring suffrage to women.

For the next several years, Carrie Chapman Catt toured the Midwestern states to bring the issue of suffrage to the people, mostly in Colorado and South Dakota. In 1895, after years of such grinding work, she moved to New York City, where she was named the chairman of the National Woman Suffrage Organization Committee (NWSOC) and directed a national campaign of sending lecturers throughout the nation. In 1900, she reached the pinnacle of power when she succeeded Susan B. Anthony as the third president of the National American Woman Suffrage Association (Elizabeth Cady Stanton had been the first president); during her nine years and two tenures in this position – 1900 to 1904, and 1915 to 1920 – she oversaw increased pressure on Congress to finally pass a Suffrage Amendment to the US Constitution. In 1904, George Catt became ill, forcing his wife to resign as president to take care of him, but he died the following year, leaving Carrie Chapman Catt a widow for the second time. She was further struck by tragedy in 1907 when both her mother and her brother William Lane passed away.

In addition to serving as the President of the National American Woman Suffrage Association, Catt also served for nineteen years, from 1904 to 1923, as the President of the International Woman Suffrage Alliance. In this role, she traveled the world to bring the issue of woman's suffrage to every continent of the world except for Australia. She was forced to halt her travels during the First World War.

By 1918, it was clear that the tide had turned and that Congress would, sooner rather than later, pass the Suffrage Amendment to the states. All that was needed were enough votes to gain the three-fourths necessary to pass both houses of the Congress. To this end, Catt and her fellow suffragists sent letters and telegrams, and met in person with numerous legislators. In 1919, in anticipation that the amendment would not only pass Congress but also be ratified by the states, the National American Woman Suffrage Association was dissolved, and she helped to form from its ashes the League of Women Voters (LWV), whose main goal is to "speed the suffrage campaign in our own and other countries." Still in existence today, LWV assists in increasing voting numbers across the nation. In 1915, Catt once more was named as the President of the National American Woman Suffrage Association, and she held the organization's presidency during the last fight for woman's suffrage. In June 1919 the suffrage amendment passed both houses of Congress, and, a year later, in August 1920, Tennessee voted for its ratification, giving the amendment the requisite 38 states and making it an official part of the US Constitution. Carrie Chapman Catt's life work, the life work of so many women and men who had spent either their entire lives or good portions of them had reached its ultimate culmination. Catt wrote upon this momentous moment, "Winning the vote is only the opening wedge. To learn to use it is a bigger task."

When the United States entered the First World War in April 1917, Catt and most of the members of the National American Woman Suffrage Association agreed to support their country and its war aims. Catt, a lifelong pacifist, was criticized by other pacifists for her stand. In the 1920s, she stood once again for pacifism, organizing in 1925 the first annual Conference on the Cause and Cure of War and served as its chairman. Catt believed that since women could now vote, and (as she believed) all women were opposed to war, male politicians who wanted to go to war risked their political careers if they voted for any movement towards war. Such was a naïve belief, which served to pigeonhole all women as having one particular belief. Nevertheless, Catt and the delegates met with President Calvin Coolidge, and they lobbied for world acceptance of the Kellogg-Briand Pact (1928), which called for the outlawing of war.

In her final years, Catt came to believe that her cause for pacifism was a losing one, especially when the Second World War broke out. She served as the chairman of the Committee on the Cause and Cure of War in 1932, although she supported its goals until the group disbanded in 1941. Honored until her final days for her lifelong work, which changed woman's lives across America, Catt died at her home near New Rochelle, New York, of a heart attack on 9 March 1947; she was 88 years old. In her honor, the League of Women Voters established the Carrie Chapman Catt Memorial Foundation to help women earn the right to vote in countries around the world, and to advance that cause.

In an editorial, *The Washington Post* stated, "Mrs. Carrie Chapman Catt was the most distinguished American exemplar of a social genus which might be called 'the old New Woman.' She represented the class which, about the beginning of the century, had become very numerous and insistent and, despite all the derision heaped upon it, very influential. It was comprised for the most part, of intelligent and ambitious women who had fought their way over barriers of prejudice into the professions and into important positions in business and journalism. What the women were clamoring for was a removal of the legal barriers which prevented their sex from direct participation in political life...it is unlikely that Mrs. Catt ever doubted in the least that the net effect of the great victory with which her name is associated was beneficent both to her sex and to her country." Historian Kevin Amidon wrote in 2007, "As one of the main figures in the American woman suffrage movement, Catt has captured the interest of scholars, commentators, and critics for her tireless advocacy, organizational skills, and powerful rhetoric. Catt's primary political interest before 1920 was the expansion of the participation of women in representative political processes. After 1920 she retained her interest in women's political activity, but broadened her sphere of activity into support for international peace through world government. Throughout the several phases of her career, she navigated between the two branches of evolutionary thought, focusing in certain contexts on broad claims about progressive change, and in others more closely on issues of human diversity."

James Robert Mann (1856-1922)

James Robert Mann was one of the earliest advocates for a Suffrage Amendment to the US Constitution, and one of its strongest proponents leading up to its congressional passage in 1919. He is also remembered for his authorship of the Mann Act (1910), which imposed harsh sanctions to end so-called "white slavery" in the first years of the 20th century.

James Robert Mann was born in Gilman, near Bloomington, Illinois, on 20 October 1856, one of three sons of William Henry Mann, a horticulturist, and his wife Elizabeth Dabney (née Abraham) Mann. One of Mann's brothers, William A. Mann, rose to the rank of Brigadier General and headed the Militia Bureau from October 1916 to November 1917 during the First World War, while the other, Frank Irving Mann, was a farmer who served as director of the Illinois State Farmers' Institute. Of William Henry Mann, historian Herbert Margulies wrote, "Born in Kentucky in 1827, William was among a group of men who successfully pioneered as horticulturalists and nurserymen in central Illinois. He enjoyed and became expert in experimental grafting. William served as a private in the Mexican War and as a Union captain in the Civil War. He was civic-minded, he nurtured the Illinois State Normal University at the village of Normal, and he beautified that young community with trees to line the roads." As to Elizabeth Mann, he explained, "His mother, Elizabeth Dabney Abraham Mann, was the product of an unusual marriage between a member of the old and aristocratic Dabney family of Virginia and a Jew-turned-Christian, Mordecai Abraham. She was a person of wide knowledge and devotion to principle. Raised a Baptist, she later joined the Wesleyan Methodist church and then her husband's Christian denomination, and she was a superintendent of a Sunday school shortly before her death."

James Mann attended local schools, and then graduated, first from the University of Illinois at Urbana in 1876 (where he was the valedictorian), and then from the Union College of Law in Chicago five years later. That same year, 1881, he was admitted to the Illinois bar. He joined a law practice in Chicago which that year became Mann, Hayes & Miller. The following year Mann married Emma Columbia. In 1887, he served as a member of the Oakland Board of Education.

Mann rose quickly in Chicago legal circles, serving as a master in chancery of the superior court of Cook County (Chicago) and defending city commissioners in the Hyde Park and South Park sections of the city. He also invested heavily in real estate, so that within a few years, from both his legal practice and his investments, he was a wealthy man. In 1892, he helped to bring the World's Columbian Exposition to Chicago the following year, and for his work he was elected that year as a member of the city council of Chicago, where he served until 1896. In 1894, he served as the chairman of the Illinois state Republican Convention, and as the chairman of the Republican county Conventions for Cook County, Illinois in both 1895 and 1902.

In 1896, Mann was recruited to run for a seat in the US House of Representatives, representing Illinois' First Congressional district. The incumbent, J(ames) Frank Aldrich, a Republican, had been elected to the seat in 1892, but after two terms decided not to seek re-election. (Rumors persist that Aldrich was "pushed out" by party bosses, but Aldrich had in fact written to Mann in 1894 that the next session of Congress would be his last.) Instead, Mann ran for the seat, and he was elected in a district where Republicans won quite easily. Mann took his seat in the Fifty-fifth Congress, which opened in Washington on 15 March 1897. He was a part of a revolutionary wave of Republicans who had been elected by sweeping Democrats out of control of the entire government: the GOP controlled the US House, the US Senate, and, with the election of William McKinley as President, the White House as well. Mann would hold this seat for the next thirteen congresses, until his death in 1922. He was named in his first term to the House Committee on Interstate and Foreign Commerce, where he became an expert in businessrelated matters. A conservative Republican, Mann rode the wave of conservative control of the House through Speaker Joseph "Uncle Joe" Cannon, who ruled the House with an iron hand. By 1908, however, a number of so-called "Progressive Republicans" had had enough of Cannon and plotted his overthrow. Cannon's power was ultimately curtailed, and in the 1910 congressional elections, the Democrats won control of the US House of Representatives. Just as he was rising to the top of his party's leadership in the House, Mann was stuck in the role of Minority Leader, where he remained for the rest of his time as leader. Historian Robert Harrison wrote about Mann, "whose thorough knowledge of parliamentary procedure and sharp attention to detail enabled him to take on many of the day-to-day tasks of floor leadership."

It was during this period, 1905-1920, that Mann was involved in the enactment of numerous pieces of important legislation, some of which bear his name. He co-authored the Mann-Elkins Act of 1910, which gave the Interstate Commerce Commission (ICC) new powers to regulate telephone and telegraph services where they had not been able to before, and he was a key leader in the passage and implementation of the Pure Food and Drugs Act (1906), which sought to make food and drugs safer for people. But he is most remembered for two leading pieces of legislation: the White Slave Traffic Act and the Nineteenth Amendment.

He authored the White Slave Traffic Act in 1910. Athan Theoharis explained, "A moral panic, sometimes referred to as the 'white slave scare,' erupted in the early 1900s, reflecting public fears that girls and women from farms and small towns were being transported to the larger cities, and to other states, for purposes of prostitution. Support mounted for federal intervention, and in 1910, Congress passed the White Slave Traffic Act, more commonly known as the Mann Act. The act, which outlawed the interstate transport of women for immoral purposes, had as its chief aim the control of organized or commercialized prostitution." The act's main purpose was to go after prostitution and armed gangs using women for immoral purposes, but some critics contended that it was used in a racist way by those who prosecuted black men for being with white women. It is obvious that Mann's act had no such intent.

Regarding women's suffrage, during the time he was in the minority, Mann came to believe that women should get the right to vote as men did. He saw President Woodrow Wilson as one of the main obstacles to getting Democrats in the two houses of Congress from agreeing with him. In one debate he said, "The time is right, the people are ready and the beneficiaries of this amendment are eager and willing and able to perform the duties of citizenship."

Marches, picketing, and mass arrests of suffragists did not change Wilson's mind, even as he ran for re-election in 1916. Because he was in the minority, Mann could not bring such a resolution to the floor for a vote. In 1918, however, the Democrats lost control of the House for the first time in eight years; Mann, as the leader of the new majority Republicans, was slated to become Speaker. However, ill health mixed with more support for another candidate lost him the honor to Rep. Frederick Gillett of Massachusetts. He did remain as the chairman of the House Committee on Woman Suffrage, from which he brought forth the resolution that would become the proposed language for a constitutional amendment granting women the vote. He participated in not just the debates on the floor of the House during several important votes, which gradually built support for the resolution, but also in the numerous hearings in the Committee on Woman Suffrage, which Mann served first as ranking member and then chairman, until, in May 1919, the resolution received 42 votes more than the three-fourths vote necessary to send it to the states. Mann deserves credit for not only authoring the language that ultimately became the Nineteenth Amendment to the US Constitution, but for the hours of work that led to its passage.

In 1922, ill from years of overwork, Mann suffered a serious nervous breakdown from which he would never recover. He had been in ill health for some time; in fact, during the floor debate and vote for the Nineteenth Amendment in May 1919, he left his hospital bed in Baltimore against doctor's orders to rush back to Washington to debate and cast his vote. It's not clear why Mann, when realizing that he did not have long to live, destroyed all of his personal papers, leaving only volumes of newspaper clippings on his career behind, all of which comprise his manuscript collect in the Library of Congress. In late November 1922, he contracted pneumonia; during this time, he attempted to travel to the House to argue on the floor over a shipping bill, but was dissuaded by friends. Shortly thereafter, he announced that he would not be a candidate for election for Speaker, even though he said he would run for his House seat again. However, on 30 November 1922 at his home in the Highlands section of Washington, D.C. he died at the age of 66. Remembered for his hard work and parliamentary skill, Mann was lauded by his colleagues. His body was taken back to Illinois, and he was buried in the Oakwood Cemetery in Chicago.

A parliamentary expert, James R. Mann was held in high regard even by his political opponents. Texas Democrat John Nance Garner once wrote that Mann was "the most useful legislator I ever knew." Historian L. Ethal Ellis wrote, "Only by turning dusty pages...can be captured the drive, the pugnacity, the stubbornness, and withal the sheer ability which James R. Mann enlivened and forwarded the legislative process. A terror to his opponents, not always a pure delight to those on his own side, his was always a force to be reckoned with in arriving at the sum total of positive accomplishment."

Frank Wheeler Mondell (1860-1939)

Known primarily for his work on behalf of the conservation movement, particularly in the American West he represented in Congress, Frank Mondell is strongly connected to the enactment of a Suffrage Amendment to the US Constitution as the legislator who sponsored the amendment in the US House of Representatives.

Frank Wheeler Mondell was born in St. Louis, Missouri, on 6 November 1860, the son of St. Louis hotel owner Ephraim Mondell and his wife Nancy (née Brown) Mondell. According to his biographer, Donald Wernimont, "his mother, Nancy, died while he was quite young. Ephraim became a captain in the Union Army and died at the end of the Civil War from wounds received. So young Mondell, an orphan at the age of six years, drifted into Iowa with some distant relatives." Shuffled around, he was eventually given to a family named Upton, religiously Congregationalist, who raised the child on their farm in Dickinson County, Iowa. Due to his adoptive family's economic situation, Mondell had only a limited rural education. When he reached legal age, he studied engineering and the law before he left the Midwest and moved, first to Chicago, Illinois, where he worked for the Chicago, Burlington & Quincy Railroad, and then onto Denver, Colorado, entering into a series of what his official congressional biography calls "mercantile pursuits, [including] mining and railway construction in various western

states and territories." In 1887, when he was 26, Mondell settled in Wyoming and used what money he had to invest in coal and oil properties in and around the towns of Cambria and Newcastle, in Weston County, and, according to his official congressional biography, "took an active part in the establishment and building of the town of Newcastle."

Working for the Chicago, Burlington & Quincy Railroad, Mondell explored coal fields and deposits in Weston County, Wyoming, places where the railroad planned to build a rail line. Mondell helped to found Newcastle, which was named after the British city, Newcastle-upon-Tyne, a coal center of England and the United Kingdom. Mondell was elected as the town' first mayor, and through his machinations the town's streets and sewer system were planned out. He served in this capacity until 1895.

In 1890, Mondell was elected to a seat in the Wyoming State Senate, meeting for its first session under statehood, and, two years later, he served as the president of that body. In 1892, he began the first of numerous trips as a delegate to the Republican National Convention, held in various cities until his last in 1912.

The Republican Party suffered a national defeat at the polls in 1892; Mondell was re-elected to his state Senate seat. Two years later, he announced his intention to run for Governor; however, in a deal with other Republicans, he instead was nominated for the seat of at-large representative (meaning the one person who represents an entire state in one congressional district). The nation was in the midst of the so-called "Panic of 1893," which was blamed on President Grover Cleveland and his fellow Democrats. Republicans made a comeback from their losses in 1892 and took control of the US House of Representatives. In a series of newspaper articles in 1935 and 1936, near the end of his life, Mondell penned his "memoirs" which appeared in a Wyoming state newspaper under the heading of "My Story." As to the 1894 campaign, he explained:

"As we drove into the little village of Afton in the rich mountain-rimmed Star Valley, we were met by a pleasant capable appearing man who bade us welcome as Mayor and Republican committeeman. After these salutations he said smilingly that he thought we ought to know [that] he was a polygamist, in case that might affect our attitude. (Polygamy had been outlawed by Congress in 1887.) We assured our friend we were not disposed to question the propriety of his family affairs and would be glad to accept his hospitality. Thereupon our party partook of a fine supper in the modest home of very pleasant and comely wife No. Three, and thereafter, leaving Miss Reel [one of the group] with her, the remainder of our party was comfortably housed in the large homes of Wives One and Two.

This peculiar situation perhaps requires some explanation. When the federal authorities began action against the polygamists in Utah, the fathers of such households naturally sought means to escape prosecution without abandoning their families, and there came a transplanting of families into the adjacent states...Wisely the Wyoming authorities ignored these family relations and welcomed these capable, orderly, and industrious settlers..."

Mondell won his race against token opposition, and he took his seat in the Fifty-fourth Congress (1895-97). As a westerner with a vast knowledge of issues important to western states, he was named as a member of the House Committees on Mines and Mining as well as the similar committee on the Irrigation of Arid Lands. During his single term, he spoke out strongly against both Republican and Democrat administrations, which had used conservation measures to set aside public lands for preservation. When the Big Horn reservation in Wyoming was set aside, on his final day in office, he took to the House floor to denounce the Cleveland administration:

"Within my state, in the Big Horn Mountains, there is one reservation of 1,129,000 acres. I have traversed the reservation from end to end, time and time again, and there is not over 100,000 acres of that land that has timber of any sort, or character upon it."

Popular in his state when first elected, during his tenure in Congress Mondell took a stand that was to have consequences to his career. All of the major and minor national political parties (with the exception of the Socialist and Socialist Labor parties) were, in 1896, breaking up into pro-gold or pro-silver camps – one side wanted to match the US dollar with the gold standard, while the other wanted to have the dollar tied to the minting of silver, which was less expensive and made dollars easier to earn for the lower classes. Even though most of the western United States desired to stand with the silver crowd, Mondell opposed them and joined the gold camp. In 1896, even as Republican William McKinley was retaking the White House for his party after four years of rule by Democrat Grover Cleveland, and the GOP was increasing its majorities in both the US House and the US Senate, Mondell was being defeated almost entirely because of his stand on the gold-silver controversy, losing his seat to Democrat John Eugene Osborne, a former Governor (1893-95) of Wyoming. In the usual reward for defeated members of both political parties, Mondell was named by President McKinley as the Assistant Commissioner of the General Land Office, at that time the main governmental authority for the management of the nation's public lands. (Established in 1812, it was made a part of the Department of the Interior when that cabinet department was established in 1849, and in 1946 was merged with the United States Grazing Service to become the Bureau of Land Management.)

In 1898, the issue over gold and silver had diminished to such an extent that Mondell returned home to run against Osborne for his former House seat. Osbourne, perhaps realizing that even as former Governor of the state he would have a hard time defeating Mondell a second time without the gold-silver issue to aid him, refused renomination in 1896. Instead, the Democrats nominated Constantine P. Arnold, and the People's Party, also known as the Populist Party, named William Brown for the seat. The Republicans swept all state and federal offices in Wyoming in 1896, among them Frank Mondell, who was returned to Congress. He would remain in that seat until 1923. Because Wyoming had just one representative, Mondell represented the entire state during that period. During his tenure, he served as the chairman of the Committee on Irrigation of Arid Lands in the Fifty-eighth Congress (1903-1905) and the Fifty-ninth Congress (1905-1907), as chairman of the Committee on Public Lands in the Sixtieth Congress (1907-09) and Sixty-first Congress (1909-11), and Majority Leader of the House in the Sixty-sixth Congress (1919-21) and the Sixty-seventh Congress (1921-23).

Mondell used the experience he had gained while working at the General Land Office to become an expert, as well as advocate, for a national policy of the reclamation and irrigation, particularly in the western states of the country. One of the earliest pieces of legislation that he had an impact on was the Newlands Act of 1902, which put the imprimatur of the federal government on this policy. *Forestry and Irrigation* magazine, the leading periodical for that movement, said in its July 1902 issue, "Mr. Mondell has always been an earliest advocate of irrigation, and from his experience in the Land Office, as well as in the arid west, has become convinced of the necessity of carrying out important reforms of the land laws. His energetic championship of the Irrigation Bill and the striking success of this measure when brought before the House testify to his deep interest in the subject."

Although remembered for his work on such issues of concern to his section of the United States, his support for a woman's suffrage amendment to the US Constitution, as well as sponsoring the language of the proposed amendment for the first time in 1905, is as noteworthy. The *New-York Tribune* noted on 8 April 1913 that "Senator [George Earle] Chamberlain, of Oregon, and Representative Mondell, of Wyoming, introduced resolutions in their respective houses for the constitutional amendments." Although Chamberlain's name rarely appears any further in the histories of the push to get that suffrage amendment through both houses of Congress, Mondell's does, as he worked behind-the-scenes to gain passage for it. By 1919, as western states were allowing women to vote in state and local elections (and, in 1918, Montana elected a woman as the first female to sit in the US House of Representatives, Jeannette Rankin), the tide of congressional opinion had turned. When the Sixty-sixth Congress (1919-21) opened in Washington in May 1919, the GOP was in control of both houses for the first time in eight years. The party had a 39-seat majority in the House, and Rep. Frederick H. Gillett of Massachusetts was elected as Speaker of the House. Mondell, who had served in the party leadership since his tenure had begun, was elected Majority Leader, taking the place of Minority Leader Robert Mann, Republican of Illinois, who would have been elected Majority Leader but, due to ill health (he would die in 1922), chose to avoid a leadership position in the new Congress. *The American Review of Reviews* noted two years later, in July 1921, of Mondell that "[h]is method of leadership is that of consultation, rather than of arbitrary dictatorship." However, through the machinations of Mondell, Mann, and others, the suffrage resolution passed the House with more than the required three-fourths vote. Within a year, the requisite number of states would ratify it and make it the Nineteenth Amendment to the US Constitution.

In one of his last acts as a member of Congress, in 1921 Mondell sponsored legislation that authorized the seven states of the so-called Colorado River basin to enter into an agreement that formed what is known as the Colorado River Compact, in which all seven would share portions of the waters of the Colorado River. The compact was signed at Santa Fe, New Mexico, in 1922.

In 1922, Mondell gave up his seat in the House for a run at a US Senate seat, but he faced Democrat and former Governor John Benjamin Hendrick, running for his second term in the upper body of the US Congress. Even though Mondell was a popular figure in his state, he could not overcome Kendrick's popularity and Mondell was defeated. Out of office for the first time since 1897, he was offered a series of government positions, including as US Ambassador to Japan and Governor of Puerto Rico (a post which at that time was named by the president, but which is now elected by the people of that island), but he turned them down. Instead, in 1923, he was named as the Director of the War Finance Corporation, a government entity described by the National Archives as "an independent agency...[which] [p]rovided support to war industries and banks that aided them, and assisted in the transition to peace[;] [it] [f]inanced government-controlled railroads and made loans to U.S. exporters[;] [it] [m]ade agricultural loans to financial institutions and cooperative marketing associations[;] [and] [e]stablished agricultural loan agencies and cooperated with livestock loan companies." Mondell served as the WFC head until his resignation in July 1925. During his tenure at the WFC, he studied the law, and in 1924 was admitted to the bar. He practiced the law in Washington, D.C. until the end of his life. In 1924, he served as the permanent chairman of the Republican National Convention.

In the last years of his life, Mondell suffered from leukemia and died at his home in Washington on 6 August 1939 at the age of 78. Although a son of the American West, he was laid to rest in the Cedar Hill Cemetery in Suitland, in Prince George's County, Maryland. The Mondell Field Airport, which services Mondell's residential town of Newcastle, Wyoming, was named in his honor.

Thetus Willrette Sims (1852-1939)

The changed vote of Tennessee's Thetus Willrette Sims – from nay to aye – on the passage of the Nineteenth Amendment in the US House of Representatives was a turning point in the debate and helped get the amendment enacted and sent to the states for ratification.

Sims was born near (some sources say in) Waynesboro, in Wayne County, Tennessee, on 25 April 1852. He attended a private school located at Martins Mills, Tennessee; however, in 1862, Sims moved with his parents to Savannah, in Hardin County, Tennessee. There, he attended the Savannah College, and eventually graduated from the law department of Cumberland University in Lebanon, Tennessee, in June 1876. He was admitted to the Tennessee state bar, and began a private practice that year in Linden, in Perry County, Tennessee. He had married Nancy Kittrell in December 1867; they remained married until his death in 1939, and together they had five daughters and two sons.

Sims was elected as the superintendent of public instruction for Berry County, Tennessee, from 1882 to 1884. A Democrat, he served as a presidential elector in the 1892 campaign for former President Grover Cleveland, who was elected to a second, non-consecutive term as President that year. In 1896, despite a horrendous national economic downturn blamed on Cleveland that would cost the Democrats dearly that election year, Sims ran for and was elected to a seat in the US House of Representatives, which swung from Democratic control to Republican in that contest. In addition, he had defeated the incumbent, Republican John McCall. Sims took his seat in the Fifty-fifth Congress on 4 March 1897, and he held the seat through eleven additional congresses until the end of the Sixty-sixth Congress in March 1921. He would serve during his tenure as the chairman of the Committee on War Claims in the Sixty-second Congress (1911-13) and the chairman of the Committee on Interstate and Foreign Commerce in the Sixty-fifth Congress (1917-19).

Sims became an unlikely hero to the woman's suffrage movement, coming through for them at a time when previously he had strenuously resisted supporting the franchise for them. In fact, in a heated 1915 House floor debate, he castigated the suffragist movement and condemned it. Yet, four years later, as the House poised to vote on potential language that would be sent to the states for ratification as a constitutional amendment, Sims made a 360° turn and backed the measure. No one knows why, although rumors allege that his daughters implored him to change his mind. In a history of woman's suffrage, penned in multiple volumes in 1922, it was stated:

"A number of men who voted favorably came to the Capitol at considerable inconvenience to cast their votes. Republican Leader Mann of Illinois at much persons risk came from a hospital in Baltimore. He had not been present in Congress for months and his arrival shortly before five o'clock caused great excitement in the chamber. Representative Sims of Tennessee, who had broken his shoulder two days before, refused to have it set until after the suffrage vote and against the advice of his physician was on the floor for the discussion and the vote."

One witness later wrote that "in spite of agonizing pain that he suffered, [Sims] strove...to bring over one or two of his Southern friends to our side or prevail upon them not to vote at all."

In 2010, Rep. Marsha Blackburn (R-TN), who currently occupies the same congressional office in the US Capitol as Sims did nearly a century ago, went to the US House floor to thank Sims for his role in granting women the right to vote. She said,

"I want to tell you about another swing vote that helped to set the stage in the suffrage story. And it is one that is important to our State of Tennessee, and it is one that transpired right here in this Chamber 91 years ago... Ninety-one years ago, before the Nineteenth Amendment could go to the States for ratification, it had to be discharged from this Chamber. The first attempt to do that was in 1915, and it failed. Thetus Sims voted against the Nineteenth Amendment at that point in time.

"Well, he had the opportunity to vote again on the Nineteenth Amendment in 1918. And it was a very dramatic day right here in this Chamber. It was perhaps one of the most important days that had transpired in this Chamber. Supporters of the amendment were unsure they had the votes to discharge the amendment. The galleries around us were packed with suffragettes. They were packed with journalists. Everyone was watching. On that day, Thetus Sims surprised the nation.

"Between 1915 and 1918, the suffrage movement had heated up not only here in D.C., but all across the Nation. Riots had broken out here in D.C., and women were jailed for wanting the right to vote. The D.C. commissioner who put them behind bars was a gentleman named Louis Brownlow. Louis Brownlow was Thetus Sims' son-inlaw. With such influences, it is hard to see how Thetus Sims could see his way to vote "yes" on this amendment.

"But Louis Brownlow wasn't the only person talking to Thetus Sims at the family dinner table. Congressman Sims also had daughters. And in Washington, the Sims daughters were known as consummate hostesses. Back in Tennessee, everyone knew them for being crack shots with their rifles. Well, here in D.C. Elizabeth Sims was a suffragist leader. And her arguments evidently beat out those of her husband, Louis Brownlow.

"So the day finally came in 1918. And on his way to the vote, Thetus Sims took a very bad fall, and he broke his collarbone. He refused to have it set or to take pain killers for fear he would miss the vote. So, he came to the floor and he flipped his vote. He voted "aye," and he became the hero of the day."

In 1920, Sims may have paid for his vote when he lost in the Democratic primary for re-election to his House seat to Captain. Gordon Browning, a First World War veteran, although in an interview Sims says that he attributed the defeat to "the almost universal sentiment of appreciation and gratitude on the part of people toward our ex-servicemen." After eight years of Democratic rule, the country tired of President Woodrow Wilson and threw Democrat out acronyms the country, handing huge majorities to the Republicans in the US House and Senate, and giving the party the White House for the first time in eight years. Sims' seat ultimately went to Republican Lon Allen Scott.

Returning home to Tennessee, Sims went back to the practice of law, this time in the city of Lexington, in Henderson County. In 1930 he retired from all business and legal pursuit and returned to Washington, D.C., where he lived with his wife for the remainder of his life. Sims died in Washington on 17 December 1939, and was buried in Washington, D.C.'s Rock Creek Cemetery.

FOOTNOTES, SOURCES, FURTHER READING

Footnotes

[1] McMillen, Sally G., "Seneca Falls and the Origins of the Women's Rights Movement" (Oxford, United Kingdom: Oxford University Press, 2008), chapter 3: Seneca Falls, unpaginated.

[2] "Woman's Right Convention," *The North Star* [Rochester, New York], 14 July 1848, 2.

[3] Anthony, Susan B., "Woman's Half-Century of Evolution," The North American Review, CLXXV (December 1902), 800-10.

[4] "Selections. Woman's Rights Convention," *The North Star* [Rochester, New York], 11 August 1848, 1.

[5] "Female Suffrage" in Edward McPherson, "A Political Manual for 1869, Including a Classified Summary of the Important Executive, Legislative, Judicial, Politico-Military and General Facts of the Period. From July 15, 1868, to July 15, 1869" (Washington City: Philp & Solomons, 1869), 506.

[6] Feeney, Kathleen, "Woodhull, Victoria Claflin" in John A. Garraty and Mark C. Carnes, gen. eds., "American National Biography" (New York: Oxford University Press; 24 volumes, 1999), 23:800-01.

[7] ["Editorial"], *Boston Daily Advertiser* [Massachusetts], 4 April 1870, 2.

[8] Aynes, Richard L., "*Bradwell v. Illinois*: Chief Justice Chase's Dissent and the 'Sphere of Women's Work,'" *Louisiana Law Review*, LIX:—(Winter 1999), 521-41.

[9] [Historical source for Minor].

[10] Basch, Norma, "Minor v. Happersett" in Donald G. Nieman, ed., "The Constitution, Law, and American Life: Critical Aspects of the Nineteenth-Century Experience" (Athens: The University of Georgia Press, 1992), 56.

[11] Kobach, Kris (May 1994). "Rethinking Article V: term limits and the Seventeenth and Nineteenth Amendments". Yale Law Journal (Yale Law School) 103 (7): 1971-2007.

[12] Mead, Rebecca J., "How the Vote Was Won: Woman Suffrage in the Western United States, 1868-1914" (New York: New York University Press, 2004), 38-39.

[13] Catt, Carrie Chapman; and Nettie R. Schuler, "Woman Suffrage and Politics" (New York: Charles Scribner's Sons, 1926), 133-59.

[14] Initially ratified on 10 June 1919; it was reaffirmed on 17 June 1919.

[15] Date that the state ratification was signed into law by Governor William L. Harding, not the date that the legislature voted for it.

[16] Date that the state ratification was signed into law by Governor Sam V. Stewart, not the date that the legislature voted for it.

[17] Date that the state ratification was signed into law by Governor John H. Bartlett, not the date that the legislature voted for it.

[18] Date that the state ratification was signed into law by Governor Oliver Henry Shoup, not the date that the legislature voted for it.

[19] Although passed on 10 March 1920, for some reason it was not legally confirmed until 21 September 1920.

[20] With Tennessee's passage, the amendment gained the approval of the requisite 36 states (of the 48 then in the Union), confirming its ratification as a part of the US Constitution.

[21] Passed on 14 September 1920, but reaffirmed on 21 September 1920.

[22] This was a second vote; the amendment had initially been rejected by the same body on 2 June 1920.

[23] Ratified on 29 March 1941; the amendment had initially been rejected by the same body on 24 February 1920. The 1941 certification itself was not officially certified until 25 February 1958.

[24] Ratified on 21 February 1952; the amendment had initially been rejected by the same body on 12 February 1920.

[25] The amendment had initially been rejected by the same body on 22 September 1919.

[26] The amendment had initially been rejected by the same body on 28 January 1920; its 1969 ratification was not officially certified until 22 August 1973.

[27] The amendment had initially been rejected by the same body on 24 July 1919.

[28] The amendment had initially been rejected by the same body on 1 July 1920.

[29] The amendment had initially been rejected by the same body on 29 March 1920.

[30] Joseph Hamilton Moore (1864-1950), Republican of Pennsylvania, US Representative (1906-20), Mayor of Philadelphia (1920-23, 1932-35).

[31] John Nance Garner (1868-1967), Democrat of Texas, US Representative (1903-33), Speaker of the US House of Representatives (1931-33), Vice President of the United States (1933-41).

[32] Edward Campbell Little (1858-1924), Republican of Kansas, US Representative (1917-24).

[33] Claude Kitchin (1869-1923), Democrat of North Carolina, US Representative (1901-23).

[34] Rufus Hardy (1855-1943), Democrat of Texas, US Representative (1907-23).

[35] Frank Clark (1860-1936), Democrat of Florida, US Representative (1905-25).

[36] John Edward Raker (1863-1926), Democrat of California, US Representative (1911-26).

[37] John MacCrate (1885-1976), Republican of New York, US Representative (1919-20), Judge, New York state Supreme Court (1920-55).

[38] Oscar Wilderness Underwood (1862-1929), Democrat of Alabama, US Representative (1895-1915), US Senator (1915-27).

[39] James Wolcott Wadsworth, Jr. (1877-1952), Republican of New York, US Senator (1915-27), US Representative (1933-51).

[40] Frank Bosworth Brandegee (1864-1924), Republican of Connecticut, US Representative (1901-05), US Senator (1905-24).

[41] William Edgar Borah (1865-1940), Republican of Idaho, US Senator (1907-40).

[42] Andreius Aristeius Jones (1862-1927), Democrat of New Mexico, US Senator (1917-27).

[43] Ellion DuRant Smith (1864-1944), Democrat of South Carolina, US Senator (1909-44).

[44] Charles Spalding Thomas (1849-1934), Democrat of Colorado, Governor of Colorado (1899-1901), US Senator (1913-21).

[45] William Henry King (1863-1949), Democrat of Utah, Associate Justice, Utah state Supreme Court (1894-97), US Representative (1897-99, 1900-01), US Senator (1917-41).

[46] William Fosgate Kirby (1867-1934), Democrat of Arkansas, Attorney General of Atka (1907-09), Associate Justice, Arkansas state Supreme Court (1910-16), US Senator (1916-21).

[47] James Duval Phelan (1861-1930), Democrat of California, US Senator (1915-21).

[48] Edward James Gay (1878-1952), Democrat of Louisiana, US Senator (1918-21).

[49] James Wesley Bryan (1874-1956), Progressive of Washington State, US Representative (1913-15).

[50] James Henry Brady (1862-1918), Republican of Idaho, US Senator (1911-19).

[51] Robert Marion La Follette (1855-1925), Republican of Wisconsin, US Senator (1905-25).

[52] Wesley Livsey Jones (1863-1932), Republican of Washington State, US Representative (1899-1909), US Senator (1909-32).

[53] John Franklin Shafroth (1854-1922), Democrat of Colorado, US Senator (1913-19).

[54] Miles Poindexter (1868-1946), Republican of Washington State, US Senator (1911-23).

[55] Charles Elroy Townsend (1856-1924), Republican of Michigan, US Representative (1903-11), US Senator (1911-23).

[56] George Sutherland (1862-1942), Republican of Utah, US Representative (1901-03), US Senator (1905-17), Associate Justice, US Supreme Court (1922-38).

[57] Charles Spalding Thomas (1849-1934), Democrat of Colorado, Governor of Colorado (1899-1901), US Senator (1913-21).

[58] George Earle Chamberlain (1854-1928), Democrat of Oregon, US Senator (1909-21).

[59] Frank Wheeler Mondell (1860-1939), Republican of Wyoming, US Representative (1895-97, 1899-1923).

[60] Oscar Wilderness Underwood (1862-1929), Democrat of Alabama, US Representative (1895-1915), US Senator (1915-27).

[61] James Robert Mann (1856-1922), Republican of Illinois, US Representative (1897-1922).

[62] George Earle Chamberlain (1854-1928), Democrat of Oregon, US Senator (1909-21).

[63] Referring not to a "Bowdie" but to Stanley Eyre Bowdie (1868-1919), Democrat of Ohio, US Representative (1913-15).

[64] Edwin Yates Webb (1872-1955), Democrat of North Carolina, US Representative (1903-19). See Section 10, on the Eighteenth Amendment, for a full biography of Webb.

[65] Edward Thomas Taylor (1858-1941), Democrat of Colorado, US Representative (1909-41).

[66] Frank Wheeler Mondell (1860-1939), Republican of Wyoming, US Representative (1895-97, 1899-1923). See this section, under "Influential Biographies," for a full examination of the life of Mondell.

[67] Philip Pitt Campbell (1862-1941), Republican of Kansas, US Representative (1903-23).

[68] Melville Clyde Kelly (1883-1935), Progressive of Pennsylvania, US Representative (1913-15).

[69] Richmond Pearson Hobson (1870-1937), Democrat of Alabama, US Representative (1909-15).

[70] Irving Luther Lenroot (1869-1949), Republican of Wisconsin, US Representative (1909-18), US Senator (1918-27).

[71] Victor Murdock (1871-1945), Progressive of Kansas, US Representative (1903-15).

[72] Referring not to a "Eulings" but to Willis James Hulings (1850-1924), Progressive of Pennsylvania, US Representative (1913-15).

[73] Charles August Lindbergh (1859-1924), Republican of Minnesota, US Representative (1907-17). He was the father of Charles Augustus Lindbergh, who flew the first non-stop solo voyage across the Atlantic Ocean in 1927.

[74] Referring to Hatton William Sumners (1875-1962), Democrat of Texas, US Representative (1913-47).

[75] Frank Clark (1860-1936), Democrat of Florida, US Representative (1905-25).

[76] Martin Dies (1870-1922), Democrat of Texas, US Representative (1909-19).

[77] William Henry Stafford (1869-1957), Republican of Wisconsin, US Representative (1913-19, 1921-23).

[78] James Wesley Bryan (1874-1956), Progressive of Washington State, US Representative (1913-15).

[79] William Dennison Stephens (1859-1944), Progressive of California, US Representative (1911-16), Lt. Governor of California (1917), Governor of California (1917-23).

[80] Thomas Montgomery Bell (1861-1941), Democrat of California, US Representative (1905-31).

[81] Joseph Hampton Moore (1864-1950), Republican of Pennsylvania, US Representative (1906-20), Mayor of Philadelphia, Pennsylvania (1920-23).

[82] William Josiah MacDonald (1873-1946), Progressive of Michigan, US Representative (1913-15).

[83] Lathrop Brown (1883-1959), Democrat of New York, US Representative (1913-15).

[84] Raymond Bartlett Stevens (1874-1942), Democrat of New Hampshire, US Representative (1913-15).

[85] John William Abercrombie (1866-1940), Democrat – of Alabama, US Representative (1913-17).

[86] Rufus Hardy (1855-1943), Democrat of Texas, US Representative (1907-23).

[87] Charles Lafayette Bartlett (1853-1938), Democrat of Georgia, US Representative (1895-1915).

[88] Thomas Upton Sisson (1869-1923), Democrat of Mississippi, US Representative (1909-23).

[89] Martin Barnaby Madden (1855-1928), Republican of Illinois, US Representative (1905-29).

[90] Horace Mann Towner (1855-1937), Republican of Iowa, US Representative (1911-25).

[91] Henry A. Barnhart (1858-1934), Democrat of Indiana, US Representative (1907-19).

[92] John Edward Raker (1863-1926), Democrat of California, US Representative (1911-26).

[93] Robert Lee Henry (1864-1931), Democrat of Texas, US Representative (1897-1917).

[94] This should be Harry Hunter Seldomridge (1864-1927), Democrat of Colorado, US Representative (1913-15).

[95] Dudley Mays Hughes (1848-1927), Democrat of Georgia, US Representative (1909-17).

[96] Louis Convers Cramton (1875-1966), Republican of Michigan, US Representative (1913-31).

[97] John Richard Farr (1857-1933), Republican of Pennsylvania, US Representative (1911-21).

[98] Everis Anson Hayes (1855-1942), Republican of California, US Representative (1905-19).

[99] Nicholas John Sinnott (1870-1929), Republican of Oregon, US Representative (1913-29).

[100] George Edmund Gorman (1873-1935), Democrat of Illinois, US Representative (1913-15).

[101] Charles Henry Sloan (1863-1946), Republican of Nebraska, US Representative (1911-19).

[102] Charles David Carter (1868-1929), Democrat of Oklahoma, US Representative (1907-27).

[103] William Oscar Mulkey (1871-1943), Democrat of Alabama, US Representative (1914-15).

[104] Perl D. Decker (1875-1934), Democrat of Missouri, US Representative (1913-19).

[105] Carl Trumbull Hayden (1877-1972), Democrat of Arizona, US Representative (1912-27), US Senator (1927-69).

[106] Edward Keating (1875-1965), Democrat of Colorado, US Representative (1913-19).

[107] Andrew John Volstead (1860-1947), Republican of Minnesota, US Representative (1903-23).

[108] Thomas Lawrence Reilly (1858-1924), Democrat of Connecticut, US Representative (1911-15).

[109] Cyrus Cline (1856-1923), Democrat of Indiana, US Representative (1909-17).

[110] Simeon Davison Fess (1861-1936), Republican of Ohio, US Representative (1913-23), US Senator (1923-35).

[111] Referring to Jacob Thompson Baker (1847-1919), Democrat of New Jersey (not New York), US Representative (1913-15).

[112] Clarence Benjamin Miller (1872-1922), Republican of Minnesota, US Representative (1909-19).

[113] Adolph Joachim Sabath (1866-1952), Democrat of Illinois, US Representative (1907-52).

[114] John Morgan Evans (1863-1946), Democrat of Montana, US Representative (1913-21, 1923-33).

[115] James Thomas Heflin (1869-1951), Democrat of Alabama, US Representative (1904-20, 1920-31).

[116] William Allen Cullop (1853-1927), Democrat of Indiana, US Representative (1909-17).

[117] Finis James Garrett (1875-1956), Democrat of Tennessee, US Representative (1905-29).

[118] Warren Gard (1873-1929), Democrat of Ohio, US Representative (1913-21).

[119] Merrill Moores (1856-1929), Republican of Indiana, US Representative (1915-25).

[120] Richard Wilson Austin (1857-1919), Republican of Tennessee, US Representative (1909-19).

[121] Frederick Haskell Dominick (1877-1960), Democrat of South Carolina, US Representative (1917-33).

[122] John Edward Raker (1863-1926), Democrat of California, US Representative (1911-26).

[123] William Pegues Pollock (1870-1922), Democrat of South Carolina, US Senator (1918-19).

[124] Christie Benet (1879-1951), Democrat of South Carolina, US Senator (1918). Benet was named to fill the vacancy caused by the death of Senator Ben "Pitchfork Ben" Tillman, yet he only served from 6 July 1918 to 5 November 1918.

[125] Aaron Augustus Sargent (1827-1887), Republican of California, US Representative (1861-73), US Senator (1873-79).

[126] Edward James Gay (1878-1952), Democrat of Louisiana, US Senator (1918-21).

[127] Boies Penrose (1860-1921), Republican of Pennsylvania, US Senator (1897-1921).

[128] William Musgrave Calder (1869-1945), Republican of New York, US Senator (1917-23).

[129] Charles Elroy Townsend (1856-1924), Republican of Michigan, US Senator (1911-23).

[130] Philander Chase Knox (1853-1921), Republican of New York, US Senator (1904-09, 1917-21), US Secretary of State (1909-13).

Sources Arranged by Chapter Sections

Debate in Congress
"The Congressional Record: Proceedings and Debates of the First Session of the Sixty-Sixth Congress of the United States of America" (Washington, D.C.: Government Printing Office, 1919), 78-84.

"The Congressional Record: Proceedings and Debates of the First Session of the Sixty-Sixth Congress of the United States of America" (Washington, D.C.: Government Printing Office, 1919), 615-33.

Historical Background Documents
"Shall Women Have the Right to Vote? Addres by Wendell Phillips at Worcester, Mass. 1851" (Philadelphia: The Equal Franchise Societu of Pennsylvania, 1910), 8-12.

"Petition to Congress, December 1871," in RG [Record Group] 46, The Records of the US Senate, Committee Records Compiled 1816-1982, SEN 42A-H11, Committee on the Judiciary, Suffragist Petition to the US House of Representatives and US Senate, December 1871, 42A-H11.4 woman suffrage, Chronological, 42A-H11.5 various subjects, Chronological, the National Archives and Records Administration, Washington, D.C.

"The Supreme Court Upon the Voting of Women," *Harper's Weekly*, XIX:985 (13 November 1875), 915. "Female Suffrage," Harper's Weekly, XXXVIII:1952 (19 May 1894), 459.

"Woman's Right to Vote," *Harper's Weekly*, LIV:2782 (16 April 1910), 33.

Tucker, Henry St. George, "Woman's Suffrage by Constitutional Amendment" (New Haven: Yale University Press, 1916), 1-6.

Van Voris, Jacqueline, "Carrie Chapman Catt: A Public Life" (New York: The Feminist Press at the City University of New York, 1987), 148.

Governor Albert H. Roberts to Secretary of State Bainbridge Colby, 24 August 1920, in National Archives and Records Administration, "Ratified Amendments, XI-XXVII" (Washington, D.C.: National Archives and Records Administration, 1993), Roll 8: Nineteenth Amendment, State Ratifications, Tennessee.

Currey, Margery, "The Victory Convention," *Life and Labor*, X:3 (March 1920), 67-70.

Catt, Carrie Chapman; and Nettie Rogers Shuler, "Woman Suffrage and Politics: The Inner Story of the Suffrage Movement" (New York: Charles Scribner's Sons, 1926), 227-34.

Original Primary Documents
"The Sixteenth Amendment," *Daily State Gazette* [Trenton, New Jersey], 6 April 1870, 2.

"A Suffrage Petition," *The Hartford Courant* [Connecticut], 3 February 1913, 9.

"Women, 500 Strong, Backed by Police, Bombard Capitol," *New-York Tribune*, 8 April 1913, 16.

"Suffrage Meets Defeat in House," *The Washington Post*, 13 January 1915, 1, 2.

"Wilson Indorses Woman Suffrage," *The New York Times*, 7 October 1915, 1.

"Woman Suffrage Wins in House by One Vote," *The Washington Post*, 11 January 1918, 1, 5.

"Suffrage Loses By But One Vote; Now Up to G.O.P.," *The Chicago Tribune*, 11 February 1919, 3.

"Suffrage Amendment Is Adopted by Senate," *The Miami Herald*, 5 June 1919, 1.

"Suffragists Here Flaunt Their Flags," *The Philadelphia Evening Ledger*, 5 June 1919, 2.

Supreme Court Cases

Bradwell v. Illinois (83 U.S. 130 {1873}).
Sullivan, Kathleen S., "Constitutional Context: Women and Rights Discourse in Nineteenth-Century America" (Baltimore: The Johns Hopkins University Press, 2007); O'Neill, Timothy J., "Bradwell v. Illinois" in David Schultz, ed., "Encyclopedia of the Supreme Court" (New York: Facts on File, 2005), 49.

Minor v. Happersett (88 U.S. 162 {1875}).
Cushman, Claire, "Supreme Court Decisions and Women's Rights: Milestones to Equality" (Washington, D.C.: Supreme Court Historical Society, 2001), 7-12; Ray, Angela G.; and Cindy Koenig Richards. "Inventing Citizens, Imagining Gender Justice: The Suffrage Rhetoric of Virginia and Francis Minor," *Quarterly Journal of Speech*, XCIII:4 (November 2007), 375-402.

Leser v. Garnett (258 U.S. 130 {1922}).
Currie, David P., "The Constitution in the Supreme Court: The Second Century, 1888-1986" (Chicago: The University of Chicago Press; two volumes, 1990), II:177-78; "Judicial Review and Constitutional Amendments" in Donald P. Kommers, John E. Finn, and Gary J. Jacobsohn, "American Constitutional Law: Essays, Cases, and Comparative Notes" (Lanham, Maryland: Rowman & Littlefield Publishers, Inc.; two volumes, 2010), II:70.

Breedlove v. Suttles (302 U.S. 277 {1937}).
Abernathy, Mabra Glenn; and Barbara Ann Perry, "Civil Liberties Under the Constitution" (Columbia: University of South Carolina Press, 1993), 412.

Reed v. Reed (404 U.S. 71 {1971}).
"Suspect Classifications: Sally Reed Fights Back (1971)" in Huang Hoon Chng, "Separate and Unequal: Judicial Rhetoric and Women's Rights" (Amsterdam, the Netherlands: John Benjamin Publishing Co., 2002), 80; Goldstein, Leslie Friedman, "The Constitutional Rights of Women: Cases in Law and Social Change" (Madison: The University of Wisconsin Press, 1989), 112.

Frontiero v. Richardson (411 U.S. 677 {1973}).
Basic, Christine, "Strict Scrutiny and the Sexual Revolution: Frontiero v. Richardson," Journal of Contemporary Legal Issues, XIV (Summer 2004), 117; McKenny, Betsy B., "Frontiero v. Richardson: Characterization of Sex-Based Classifications," Columbia Human Rights Law Review, VI (1974), 239.

Cleveland Board of Education v. LaFleur (414 U.S. 632 {1974}).
"The Case of the Pregnant School Teachers: An Equal Protection Analysis," *Maryland Law Review*, XXXIV (1974), 287-326.

Stanton v. Stanton (421 U.S. 7 {1975}).
Fowler, William G., Stanton (Thelma) v. Stanton (Lawrence) U.S. Supreme Court Transcript of Record with Supporting Pleadings (Farmington Hills, MI: Gale, 2011).

Craig v. Boren (429 U.S. 190 {1976}).
"Craig v. Boren (1976)" in Jeffrey D. Schultz and Laura Van Assendelft, "Encyclopedia of Women in American Politics" (Phoenix, Arizona: The Oryx Press, 1999), 47; Goldstein, Leslie Friedman, "The Constitutional Rights of Women: Cases in Law and Social Change" (Madison: The University of Wisconsin Press, 1989), 165-66.

Who's Who

Carrie Chapman Catt (1859-1947)
Peck, Mary Gray, "Carrie Chapman Catt, a Biography" (New York: The H.W. Wilson Company, 1944), 17-20; Clevenger, Ima Fuchs, "Invention and Arrangement in the Public Addresses of Carrie Chapman Catt" (Ph.D. dissertation, The University of Oklahoma, 1955); Walker, Lola C., "The Speeches and Speaking of Carrie Chapman Catt" (Ph.D. dissertation, Northwestern University, 1951); Croy, Terry Desch, "*The Crisis*: A Complete Critical Edition of Carrie Chapman Catt's 1916 Presidential Address to the National American Woman Suffrage Association," *Rhetoric Society Quarterly*, XXVIII:3 (Summer 1998), 49-73; Katz, David Howard, "Carrie Chapman Catt and the Struggle for Peace" (Ph.D. dissertation, Syracuse University, 1973); "Carrie Chapman Catt" in Deborah G. Felder, "The 100 Most Influential Women of All Time: A Ranking Past and Present" (New York: Citadel Press, 2001), 55-57; "Carrie Chapman Catt Dies; Pioneer Woman Suffragist," *The Washington Post*, 10 March 1947, 1, 2; "[Editorial:] Carrie Chapman Catt," *The Washington Post*, 16 March 1947, B4; Amidon, Kevin S., "Carrie Chapman Catt and the Evolutionary Politics of Sex and Race, 1885-1940," *Journal of the History of Ideas*, LXVIII:2 (April 2007), 305-28.

James Robert Mann (1856-1922)
Wernimont, Donald H., "Frank W. Mondell as a Congressman" (Master's thesis, the University of Wyoming at Laramie, 1956), 2; "Mondell, Frank Wheeler" official congressional biography, online at http://bioguide.congress.gov/scripts/biodisplay.pl?index=M000852; Larson, T.A., "History of Wyoming" (Lincoln: University of Nebraska Press, 1990); Mondell remarks in *The Congressional Record*, 54th Congress, 2nd Session (3 March 1897), 2678; "Hon. Frank W. Mondell," *Forestry and Irrigation*, VIII:7 (July 1902), 275; "Women, 500 Strong, Backed by Police, Bombard Capitol," *New-York Tribune*, 8 April 1913, 16; "Republicans Now Responsible," *The American Review of Reviews*, LIX:4 (April 1919), 350; "Hon. Frank W. Mondell, of Wyoming," *The American Review of Reviews*, LXIV:1 (July 1921), 11; "The Sixty-sixth Congress," *The Independent*, XCVIII:3677 (31 May 1919), 314-15; "Frank W. Modell, GOP Leader, Is Dead at 79," *The Washington Post*, 7 August 1939, 1, 4.

Thetus Willrette Sims (1852-1939)
"Sims, Thetus Wilrette" official congressional biography, online at http://bioguide.congress.gov/scripts/biodisplay.pl?index=S000441; "Sims Is Hurt in Fall; Representative Slips on the Ice After Leaving Capitol," *The Washington Post*, 8 January 1918, 3; Stanton, Elizabeth Cady; and Susan B. Anthony, Matilda J. Cage, and Ida Husted Harper, eds. et. al, "The History of Woman Suffrage" (New York: J.J. Little & Ives Company for The National American Woman Suffrage Association; six volumes, 1922), V:637; Remarks of Rep. Marsha Blackburn, 15 September 2010, in "Recognizing [the] 90th Anniversary of [the] 19th Amendment," courtesy of Capitolwords.org, online at http://capitolwords.org/date/2010/09/15/H6726_recognizing-90th-anniversary-of-19th-amendment/; "Sims Says Gratitud to Soldiers Defeated Him," *The Washington Post*, 7 August 1920, 2; "Thetus Sims To Be Buried Here Today; Former Representative From Tennessee was 87 Years Old," *The Washington Post*, 19 December 1939, 23.

Further Reading

Anzalone, Christopher A., *Supreme Court Cases on Gender and Sexual Equality*, 1787-2001 (Armonk, NY: M. E. Sharpe, 2002).

Baker, Jean H., ed., *Votes for Women: The Struggle for Suffrage Revisited* (New York: Oxford University Press, 2002).

Banaszak, Lee Ann, *Why Movements Succeed or Fail: Opportunity, Culture, and the Struggle for Woman Suffrage* (Princeton, NJ: Princeton University Press, 1996).

Kobach, Kris, "Rethinking Article V: Term Limits and the Seventeenth and Nineteenth Amendments," *Yale Law Journal*, CIII:7 (May 1994), 1971-2007.

McDonagh, Eileen L., "Issues and Constituencies in the Progressive Era: House Roll Call Voting on the Nineteenth Amendment, 1913-1919," *The Journal of Politics*, LI:1 (February 1989), 119-36.

Siegel, Reva B., "She the People: The Nineteenth Amendment, Sex Equality, Federalism, and the Family," *Harvard Law Review*, CXV:4 (February 2002), 947-1046.

Sullivan, Kathleen M., "Constitutionalizing Women's Equality," *California Law Review*, XC:3 (May 2002), 735-94.

AMERICA AT THAT TIME . . .

Although the material in this section may not be directly related to the adoption of the Nineteenth Amendment, it offers valuable insight into what was happening in America at the time the Amendment was adopted. Modeled after Grey House Publishing's Working American *series, whose author, Scott Derks, is responsible for its content, it includes a Historical Snapshot, Selected Prices, significant quotations, newspaper and magazine clips to give a sense of what was on the minds of Americans, and how it may have impacted the amendment process.*

HISTORICAL SNAPSHOT

1919-1920

- Boston police struck against pay scales of $0.21 to $0.23 per hour for 83- to 98-hour weeks

- The cost of living in New York City was up 79 percent from 1914

- The dial telephone was introduced in Norfolk, Virginia

- Wheat prices soared to $3.50 per bushel as famine swept Europe

- Kellogg's All-Bran was introduced by the Battle Creek Toasted Corn Flakes Company

- U.S. ice cream sales reached 150 million gallons, up from 30 million in 1909

- *The New York Daily News* became the first tabloid newspaper, or small-sized picture oriented newspaper

- Boston Red Sox pitcher and outfielder Babe Ruth hit 29 home runs for the year; the New York Yankees purchased his contract for $125,000

- More than four million American workers struck for the right to belong to unions during 1919, including 365,000 steelworkers who struck against the United Steel Workers, which still maintained a 12-hour day. The Federation of Churches backed the strikers, declaring that their average work week of 68.7 hours was inhuman. Big Steel used its $2 billion in war profits and military force to break the strike.

- The Bureau of Labor Statistics reported that 1.4 million women had joined the American work force since 1911

- Following the 1918 strike by the Union Streetcar Conductors protesting the employment of female conductors, the War Labor Board ruled in favor of the continued employment of women

- The southern leaders of the National Association of Colored Women protested the conditions of domestic service workers, including the expectation of White male employers of the right to take sexual liberties with their servants

"Works As Auto Mechanic," *Bismarck Daily Tribune*, March 27, 1915

Celebrated Suffragist Hiker Inspired by Ambition to Become Self-supporting Citizen!

Gen. Rosalie G. Jones, suffragist hiker, began on Monday to earn her bread as a mechanic in the Chevrolet Automobile company's repair shop here, though not without fear that her mother, Mrs. Mary E. Jones, an ardent anti-suffragist, would stop the liberal allowance she has been giving her daughter.

Mrs. Jones inherited $1,147,000 from her husband, Oliver Livingston Jones, who died on August 8, 1913, and is said to have several other millions.

Although, Miss Jones is at present learning the mysteries of the carburetor, magneto and other automobile essentials, her ultimate ambition is to be a chauffeur. In this she is inspired by a desire to become self-supporting but she has some doubts of getting maternal approval.

The Chevrolet company furnished her the famous yellow suffrage car from which she spoke throughout New York last summer. She is still living at the Hotel Brotzell, 3 East Twenty-seventh Street, but does not know how long she can stay there if Mrs. Jones tightens the purse strings. Mrs. Jones lives at the Jones country home in Cold Spring Harbor, L. 1.

"I don't know what mother will say," said Miss Jones last night. "She may stop my allowance; people do strange things sometimes. I couldn't prevent her, it's her money. I telephoned her I was going into the automobile business, but I didn't explain.

"One has to get down and get under, you know, I don't wear overalls. I wear a big apron, which is better than any masculine attire. I hope to get a chauffeur's license and drive a taxicab in the suffrage parade when the amendment passes this fall."

"Haiti's Progress as a Ward of Uncle Sam,"
The Literary Digest, January 10, 1920:

The United States is doing in Haiti today "just what it did in Cuba," say recent observers of conditions in the two Haitian republics of Santo Domingo and Haiti. Great improvements of various kinds are said to have been made in both these miniature republics since Uncle Sam has been keeping an eye on them. Lawlessness has been checked, it appears, and the whole island has been made safe for travelers, with some of the remote mountain locations still the stronghold of bandits. In Port-au-Prince, the capital of Haiti, much progress has been made in cleaning up the city and improving the sanitary conditions. No longer do the "distinct and original" smells, remarked upon by visitors in times gone by, assail the nostrils of the tourist who goes to Port-au-Prince. . . .The conditions are further described in a letter from Seth H. Seelye, also a resident of Port-au-Prince, from which we quote as follows:

"Disembarking from a ship docked at the well-constructed concrete pier at Port-au-Prince, the traveler walks on clean concrete pavements to the custom-house. He then may pass out into the city, and his first impression must be that of cleanliness. A concrete paved street over a hundred feet in width borders the waterfront. Here one may hire a carriage and drive around the city for an hour without leaving similar pavements. . . . The main market is in two large, interconnected steel structures each covering a whole block. Here on the concrete floor, the native venders sit with their produce arranged in neat piles before them. . . . Yet, in these markets one finds surprisingly few flies, and this absence of flies must surely be indicative of cleanliness and sanitation."

"Immigration," Letter to the Editor,
The American Legion Weekly, August 20, 1920:

To the Editor:

What action is to be taken on the dangerous horde of immigration that is coming in every day? We were assured during the war that certain restrictions would be thrown around immigration. Nothing has been done. The economic danger is very grave from these people, and they are being rushed here without even medical inspection. Visit Ellis Island and see the thousands of people from Poland and Russia who are coming in. These nations are urging, and even almost forcing some other people to come here. Meanwhile typhus, bubonic plague and other diseases are at our door. Washington will take no action. The people themselves must save America, for which our dear men died.

Mrs. Emma J. Arnold
New York City

One of the World's Great Women by John Temple Graves, *Cosmopolitan* Magazine, February 1916:

One day, during the memorable suffrage campaign in New York, I asked my fellow speaker, Mrs. Philip Snowden, wife of a member of the British Parliament and regarded by many as the most brilliant woman speaker in the world, if she would mind telling me after ten years' campaigning in the United States, who, in her opinion was the greatest of American women. Without a moments hesitation she replied, "Carrie Chapman Catt."

"I will go further," said the beautiful and distinguished English woman. "Measured by the grasp and power of her mind, by her wisdom, her self-control, and her consecration to a great cause, by the constructive genius of her services, by her power to plan, her capacity to execute, and her genius for leadership, by her unsurpassed eloquence in speech and her absolutely unselfish devotion to the cause of women, I hold Carrie Chapman Catt the first and greatest woman of the English-speaking race."

This intelligent and disinterested judgment from the Old World upon an American woman impressed me deeply and inspired me to consider its foundation.

If men, throughout the world, had neither participation nor representation in government, and if the men of 21 countries organized and we eager to secure these rights, the man whom these 21 nations elected their president and leader might fairly be called the most representative man in all the world.

On the same basis, Carrie Chapman Catt, of New York, president and leader of the International Woman Suffrage Alliance, chosen by 21 organized nations, may just as fairly be regarded as the woman who best represents the women of the civilized world at the present time.

Nobody, man or woman, could be chosen to such a position without deserving it. Mrs. Catt has spoken and fought for woman suffrage in every state of the Union except South Carolina and Florida. She has lectured for the cause in England, Norway, Sweden, Denmark, Holland, Saxony, Bohemia, Prussia, and Hungary.

A Farmer's Daughter

Carrie Chapman Catt is a farmer's daughter, and has shown that the framer's daughter, as well as the farmer's son, may lay a compelling hand upon her day and generation. Her father was Lucius Lane, who lived near Charles City, in Iowa. They were plain people, winning enough by work to have not luxuries but some comforts—with books, always. The daughter earned half the money that sent her, with high honors, through Iowa College, at Grinnell. One day, as censor of the debating society which she organized, she was forced to point out the defects of a new boy who had made his maiden speech. He bore no ill-will but profited by the criticism, and years after, as George W. Catt, became the husband of Carrie Lane. Their married life was exceptionally happy, helpful, and wholesome in united work. George Catt died of typhoid fever in San Francisco before his devoted wife, summoned by telegraph, could reach his side. He fought side by side with his wife effectively for suffrage while he lived.

Continued

One of the World's Great . . . *(Continued)*

Carrie Chapman Catt was always a beautiful woman—perhaps the most beautiful woman who figured in that day of suffrage work. To-day, at fifty years of age, after years of nerve-racking toil, she is still a very pretty woman. Those who remember her twenty-five years ago remember a skin of cream and roses, a mass of soft chestnut hair, a pair of large, dark-blue eyes, a small, delicate face, a willowy figure, making up a type of beauty peculiarly appealing. Naturally, she was the observed of observers, picking her way through the down-town San Francisco markets. Not one of the marketmen was ever rude to her; but men of a different class—men to whom she went to solicit advertising or collect bills, frequently were.

The Ballot for Protection

One day, just at closing-time, her employer asked her to stop at a certain office on her way and present a bill. It was raining furiously, and she was clad in one of the great shapeless rain-coats of a quarter of a century past. The sole idea pervading her mind was to get through her work and get home. She entered the office with her dripping umbrella, asked for the money, and, at the man's request, sat down at the desk to receipt the bill. The man came up behind her, drew back her head, and kissed her repeatedly. When he released her, she burst into tears, and he stood and laughed at her. She stumbled down the stairs and walked a mile and a half to her boardinghouse. She could not endure a street-car; she had to walk off her helpless rage. The gentle breezes of San Francisco in a storm turned her umbrella inside out. No one noticed her. It was only a woman, walking, crying, through the rain.

That incident was a turning-point in her life. She had always been a suffragist. For the first time she determined to devote her life to securing the suffrage. She decided, then and there that woman needed more power, that whatever weapons education, business training, the ballot could place in their hands for their own protection and advancement ought to be so placed. She devoted her life from that time on so to place those weapons.

Mrs. Catt has never, primarily, asked for the ballot for women because of any good which they may presumably do with it. In her own mind, she demands it because they need any possible power that many result from it for their own protection.

This is a people's war. . . .We have made partners of women in this war; shall we admit them only to a partnership of suffering and sacrifice and toil and not to a partnership of privilege and right?

— Writer Helen Gardner

I have sold two dozen eggs, 10 pounds of butter, one peck of crab apples, and engaged two pecks more. This goes to the suffrage fund.

—Letter by Mrs. C. W. (Lizzie) Smith,
—Stockton, Kansas, 1911

THE MIAMI HERALD

EVERYBODY BUYING OR SELLING SHOULD USE THE HERALD WANT ADS.

ONLY ASSOCIATED PRESS LEASED WIRE SERVICE ON LOWER EAST COAST.

VOL. 9; NO. 183.

MIAMI, FLORIDA, THURSDAY MORNING, JUNE 5, 1919.

PRICE FIVE CENTS

INDICATIONS POINT TO IMMENSE BLDG. ACTIVITY DURING JUNE WHICH SOME ESTIMATE WILL REACH ASTONISHING TOTAL OF MORE THAN $2,000,000

With Two Holidays Included in the Four June Days Already Passed Permits Aggregating $50,000 Have Already Been Issued This Month

RESOLUTION 1 FAILS TO PASS

Vote Falls Short of Required Number and Proposed Constitution Revision Fails.

There is a Serious Shortage of Architectural Draftsmen to Take Care of the City's Building Program But Plenty of Other Skilled Labor is Here.

JUDGE F. B. STONEMAN THANKS HIS FRIENDS

SUBWAY EMPLOYES OF PARIS DECIDE TO STRIKE

SEMENOFF SELF-ELECTED DUKE OF MONGOLIA

CIRCULATING THE FULL TEXT OF PEACE TREATY

NO INFORMATION AS TO COSTA RICAN RUMOR

BUENOS AIRES WITHOUT NEWS

City of a Million and a Half Has Had No Papers For Six Days and No Bulletins.

SUFFRAGE AMENDMENT IS ADOPTED BY SENATE

EXECUTIVE BOARD CANVASSES VOTES

Figures Published by The Herald in an Extra Edition Yesterday Morning Are Unchanged by the Final Count of Primary Election Returns.

TERMS TOO SEVERE FOR AUSTRIANS

They, Like the Germans, Ask For a Peace of Right and Justice and Declare Treaty is Based on Might Rather Than Right.

Fifty-six Senators Cast Their Ballots in Support of the House Resolution and 25 Against it; Roll Call Shows Two Votes More Than Necessary; Measure Now Goes to the Legislatures of the States For Ratification; Three-fourths of the States Must Vote in Favor of the Incorporation of the Amerment Into the Constitution of the Nation Before it Can Become Effective.

NOMINEE FOR MAYOR SAYS HE WILL STOP BOOTLEGGING AT ALL COSTS

At Organization Meeting of Miami Baptist Brotherhood Held Last Night W. P. Smith Said He Will Stand by Platform.

(Continued on Page 2)

OCEAN CABLE TO CONNECT MIAMI WITH BRAZIL BY WAY OF BARBADOES PLANNED

Western Union Telegraph Co. and British Co. Have Decided on Mutual Operation of the Cable Which Will Connect the Two Continents.

BOLSHEVIKI DENY THAT PETROGRAD HAS FALLEN

CHANEY KNOCKED OUT

(Continued on Page 2)

ATTENTION BOTANIANS.

The regular weekly luncheon of the Miami Rotary Club will be held today at 12:15 noon at Douglas Tea Room.
JNO. W. CLAUSSEN, Secy.

NOTICE.

"Foundation of Good Health,"
Leslie's Weekly, January 10, 1920:

"American women are horrified at the mention of Chinese foot-binding through which thousands of Chinese children have been crippled for life. Yet how many of these women calmly accept a fashion which makes a crutch of what should be a foot covering? How many of them force their feet to fit their shoes, rather than fit their shoes to their feet? How many of them prefer style to sense? Children, obeying their instinct, toe straight ahead, and are promptly taught to turn their toes outward. Yet the Indians, doubtless the world's champion walkers, set their feet one before the other, as though following an invisible chalk line . . . 95 percent of our women have foot troubles. We could not build the Woolworth Building standing at an angle of 45 degrees. How can we expect the human body to properly do its work if maintained at such an angle?

Because of incorrect shoes few of our women walk gracefully; they either waddle, hobble, or teeter. The pointed-toed, high-heeled shoe causes not only minor torments such as corns and bunions, but it gives the body only two points of contact with the ground, one at the heel and the other at the bunched-up toes. The health troubles due to improper footwear decrease economic efficiency probably on an average of 25 percent. If horses were not properly shoed they would have foot troubles, and consequently become inefficient. Why should we countenance similar inefficiency in human workers?

The American Museum of Safety claims that 95 percent of the people suffer in one form or another from foot troubles which result in an inefficiency from 10 to 50 percent. The Museum strongly advised manufacturers who have their interests at heart as well as those of their employees to compel employees to wear correct shoes. This has been carried out in the case of nurses and war workers. A well-known obstetrician in the country claims that 40 percent of the instrument childbirth are traceable to injurious footwear.

Very few of our stores or firms employ men who are familiar with the anatomy of the foot to fit or design their shoes. Present-day shoes are made to fit the conventionally trained eye, not the foot. If we had indigestion we should not ask the grocer to prescribe our diet; therefore, why should we ask the shoe clerk, knowing nothing of the anatomy of the foot, to prescribe a shoe to cure our foot ills?"

The first time I saw the Statue of Liberty, all the people were rushing to the side of the boat. "Look at her, look at her," in all kinds of tongues. "There she is," like someone was greeting them.

—Elizabeth Phelps, 1920

Selected Prices

Dress Pattern...$0.10

Farmland, per Acre...$20.00

Gin, Fifth..$2.15

Hair Color...$0.25

Hair Curlers...$0.25

Hair Pins...$0.05

Phonograph Record..$0.65

Radium Water, 50 24-Ounce Bottles.................................$25.00

Shampoo..$0.33

Travelers' Checks...$0.50

Year	Value of One Dollar in 2016 US Dollars
1917	$18.16
1918	$15.99
1919	$13.96
1920	$12.07
1921	$13.49
1922	$14.37

The Twentieth Amendment

Chapter 11

S. J. Res. 14

Seventy-second Congress of the United States of America;
At the First Session,

Begun and held at the City of Washington on Monday, the seventh
day of December, one thousand nine hundred and thirty-one.

JOINT RESOLUTION

Proposing an amendment to the Constitution of the United States
fixing the commencement of the terms of President and Vice
President and Members of Congress and fixing the time of the
assembling of Congress.

*Resolved by the Senate and House of Representatives of the United
States of America in Congress assembled (two-thirds of each House
concurring therein),* That the following amendment to the Constitution be, and hereby is, proposed to the States, to become valid as
a part of said Constitution when ratified by the legislatures of the
several States as provided in the Constitution:

"ARTICLE —

" SECTION 1. The terms of the President and Vice President shall
end at noon on the 20th day of January, and the terms of Senators
and Representatives at noon on the 3d day of January, of the years
in which such terms would have ended if this article had not been
ratified; and the terms of their successors shall then begin.

" SEC. 2. The Congress shall assemble at least once in every year,
and such meeting shall begin at noon on the 3d day of January,
unless they shall by law appoint a different day.

" SEC. 3. If, at the time fixed for the beginning of the term of
the President, the President elect shall have died, the Vice President
elect shall become President. If a President shall not have been
chosen before the time fixed for the beginning of his term, or if the
President elect shall have failed to qualify, then the Vice President
elect shall act as President until a President shall have qualified;
and the Congress may by law provide for the case wherein neither
a President elect nor a Vice President elect shall have qualified,
declaring who shall then act as President, or the manner in which
one who is to act shall be selected, and such person shall act accordingly until a President or Vice President shall have qualified.

" SEC. 4. The Congress may by law provide for the case of the
death of any of the persons from whom the House of Representatives
may choose a President whenever the right of choice shall have
devolved upon them, and for the case of the death of any of the
persons from whom the Senate may choose a Vice President whenever the right of choice shall have devolved upon them.

S. J. Res. 14—2

"SEC. 5. Sections 1 and 2 shall take effect on the 15th day of October following the ratification of this article.

"SEC. 6. This article shall be inoperative unless it shall have been ratified as an amendment to the Constitution by the legislatures of three-fourths of the several States within seven years from the date of its submission."

Speaker of the House of Representatives.

Vice President of the United States and
President of the Senate.

Proposed in Congress:	2 March 1932
Sent to States:	2 March 1932
Ratified:	23 January 1933

Chapter 11

THE TWENTIETH AMENDMENT

Section 1.
The terms of the President and the Vice President shall end at noon on the 20th day of January, and the terms of Senators and Representatives at noon on the 3d day of January, of the years in which such terms would have ended if this article had not been ratified; and the terms of their successors shall then begin.

Section 2.
The Congress shall assemble at least once in every year, and such meeting shall begin at noon on the 3d day of January, unless they shall by law appoint a different day.

Section 3.
If, at the time fixed for the beginning of the term of the President, the President elect shall have died, the Vice President elect shall become President. If a President shall not have been chosen before the time fixed for the beginning of his term, or if the President elect shall have failed to qualify, then the Vice President elect shall act as President until a President shall have qualified; and the Congress may by law provide for the case wherein neither a President elect nor a Vice President shall have qualified, declaring who shall then act as President, or the manner in which one who is to act shall be selected, and such person shall act accordingly until a President or Vice President shall have qualified.

Section 4.
The Congress may by law provide for the case of the death of any of the persons from whom the House of Representatives may choose a President whenever the right of choice shall have devolved upon them, and for the case of the death of any of the persons from whom the Senate may choose a Vice President whenever the right of choice shall have devolved upon them.

Section 5.
Sections 1 and 2 shall take effect on the 15th day of October following the ratification of this article.

Section 6.
This article shall be inoperative unless it shall have been ratified as an amendment to the Constitution by the legislatures of three-fourths of the several States within seven years from the date of its submission.

Note: Article I, section 4, of the Constitution was modified by section 2 of this amendment. In addition, a portion of the 12th amendment was superseded by section 3.

Brief Summary

The Twentieth Amendment, often referred to as the Lame Duck Amendment, moved the date of the end of the previous administration and the beginning of the new one to 20 January. The original Constitution, ratified at a time when travel and communication were slow and uncertain, provided that the incoming president and vice president take office on 4 March, creating a lengthy period between the November election and the installation of the new administration. In addition to the change to presidential administration start dates, the Twentieth Amendment moved the beginning and ending terms of members of Congress from 4 March to 3 January.

Timeline

1930	Representative Charles Laceille Gifford proposes an amendment to the Constitution very similar to what would become the Twentieth Amendment.
1 March 1932	The Twentieth Amendment passes in the US House of Representatives.
2 March 1932	The Twentieth Amendment is proposed to the US Senate and passes.
23 January 1933	The Twentieth Amendment is ratified when Missouri becomes the thirty-sixth state to ratify it.
3 January 1935	The Seventy-fourth Congress is the first to convene under the requirements of the Twentieth Amendment.

Introduction

Sir Robert Birley wrote in 1944, "One of the last acts of the Congress of the Confederation had been to declare that the new Constitution would come into force on 4 March 1789, and it followed that from that time all future Presidents, Vice-Presidents, Senators, and Representatives would begin their terms of office on that day in the year. By Acts passed in 1871 and 1872 Congress laid it down that the elections for the House of Representatives should be held in all States, except Maine, on the Tuesday following the first Monday in November. The old Congress, therefore, remained in power for four months after the election of the new, and as a session always began in December, members who had already been defeated would still be legislating for the country. These members were known as 'lame ducks.' The Twentieth Amendment, sometimes known as the 'Norris Amendment,' after its chief sponsor in the Senate, or the 'Lame Duck Amendment,' was passed through Congress in 1932 and ratified on 6 February 1933. The terms of office of the President and Vice-President were to begin on 20 January, and of Senators and Representatives on 3 January, on which day Congress would assemble."[1]

When the Framers established the Constitution in 1787, they lodged in Article I the powers of Congress, one of the three branches – alongside the Executive and the Judiciary – of the federal government. For purposes of our discussion here, the relevant portion of that article is at Section 4, which reads:

"The times, places and manner of holding elections for Senators and Representatives, shall be prescribed in each state by the legislature thereof; but the Congress may at any time by law make or alter such regulations, except as to the places of choosing Senators.

"The Congress shall assemble at least once in every year, and such meeting shall be on the first Monday in December, unless they shall by law appoint a different day."

Thus, the Constitution sets for Congress the right to fix the dates of election, but for Congress only. As well, as we can see from the text of the article, Congress was firmly set to meet on the first Monday of each December, but the right was bestowed on Congress to change this date. In the earliest days of the Republic, it was not a hardship for Congress to meet nearly a year after it was first elected, as members coming from differing sections of the ever-growing nation needed much time to get to the Capitol, whether it was in Philadelphia, New York City, or, as it is now, Washington, D.C.

As a congressional report noted in 1932, "'[W]hen our Constitution was adopted there was some reason for such a long intervention of time between the election and the actual commencement of work by the new Congress... [u]nder present conditions [of communication and transportation] the result of elections is known all over the country within a few hours after the polls close, and the Capital City is within a few days' travel of the remotest portions of the country...'[2]

But this presented a huge problem. Since one Congress was elected in November, and a new one did not meet until the following December, thirteen months later, members of the old Congress who had retired or had been defeated for re-election were able to sit for that thirteen months and continue to vote on legislation. The situation was odd at best, and desperately needed reform. But none came, despite several laws enacted by Congress in the late nineteenth century that changed the dates of election, but nothing else.

The situation continued well into the 20th century – in fact, by the late 1920s a new Congress was still meeting thirteen months after it was first elected, even though transportation, even from the farthest reaches of the nation, had improved drastically. That's not to say that there were some random tries at amending the entire process of electing federal officers. In 1912, Rep. Robert Lee Henry, Democrat of Texas, and a member of the US House

Committee on the Judiciary, proposed an amendment to the Constitution. In his report proposing the amendment, Henry stated:

"The Committee on the Judiciary, to whom was referred House joint resolution No. 204, proposing an amendment to the Constitution of the United States, have given the same due consideration and favorably report the same, embodying the exact language in which the author introduced it. Should the joint resolution be ratified by the requisite number of States, it will become a substitute for Article XII (amendment 12) of the Constitution, as the same now exists...The resolution here reported embraces five proposed changes in our system of constitutional government. First. Beginning with the Sixty-third Congress, the term of office of the President and Vice President chosen at the election (of November, 1912) immediately preceding shall continue until the last Thursday of April, 1917, at noon; and the last Thursday of April, at noon, shall thereafter be the commencement and termination of the official term of the President and Vice President. Second. Upon the ratification of the proposed amendment, the second Tuesday of January, at noon, shall constitute the commencement and termination of the official term of the Senators and Members of the House of Representatives. The Congress in existence when the Members of the first House of Representatives are elected (which is always the short session immediately following the general election for Representatives in Congress) after the ratification of this amendment shall hold no annual session after such election, and such short session of Congress, as now provided for, shall terminate on the second Tuesday of the January immediately following. The Senators whose existing term would otherwise expire on the 4th of day March next succeeding the day on which the term of the first Congress shall commence after the ratification of this amendment shall continue in office until their successors are appointed or elected..."[3]

Henry's proposal went nowhere, and according to the history we could find, that appears to be the last time that Henry proposed it. The idea sat fallow, untouched, for another decade. In 1924, Rep. Hays Baxter White, Republican of Kansas, a member of the House Committee on Election of President, Vice President, and Representatives in Congress, introduced his own amendment. According to his proposal,

"The constitutional amendment which this resolution proposes will accomplish the following:

(1) The newly elected Congress will count the electoral votes, and in case a majority has not been received, the newly elected House of Representatives will choose the President, and the Senate (including the newly elected Senators) will choose the Vice President.

(2) The newly elected President, Vice President, and Members of Congress will take office approximately two months after their election.

The new Congress may assemble approximately two months after the election; and

(3) A necessary amendment will be made to the twelfth amendment and two ambiguities will be removed." Although White's proposed amendment looks completely different from what eventually became the Twentieth Amendment, he did insert into the proposal the following language: "In order that these duties may devolve upon the new Congress, the first section of the proposed amendment provides that presidential terms begin [on] January 24 and the terms of Members of Congress on January 4. This permits the new Congress to assemble and affords it 20 days, before the terms of the President and Vice President begin, in which to count the electoral votes and to make that choice if a majority has not been received. In order to provide ample notice and opportunity to attend, and to prevent any possible retroactive interpretation, the last sentence provides that this section shall take effect on the 15th day of December following the ratification of the amendment."[4]

Again, the proposal went nowhere. Two months after White first introduced his proposal, he tried again. On 15 April 1924, he introduced virtually the same proposed amendment, but again it received no support, and died an early death.[5] In fact, White kept at it, introducing the same proposed amendment in 1926[6] and 1928[7]. In the latter year, debate was actually held on a proposed amendment, although it was not the White amendment;

instead, this one came from Rep. Edward McMath Beers, Republican of Pennsylvania. This appears to be the first major congressional debate, at least in the House of Representatives, on an amendment to try to fix the problem of a lame duck Congress.[8]

In 1930, Rep. Charles Laceille Gifford, Republican of Massachusetts, proposed an amendment that looks very much like what would become the Twentieth Amendment only three years later. In his proposal, modeled along the lines of what White introduced, but adding new language, Gifford's proposal stated:

"Article ____

"Section 1. The terms of the President and Vice President shall end at noon on the 24th day of January, and the terms of Senators and Representatives at noon on the 4th day of January, of the years in which such terms would have ended if this article had not been ratified; and the terms of their successors shall then begin.

"Sec. 2. The Congress shall assemble at least once in every year, and such meeting shall be on the 4th day of January unless they shall by law appoint a different day.

"Sec. 3. If the President-elect dies, then Vice President-elect shall become President. If a President is not chosen before the time fixed for the beginning of his term, if the President-elect fails to qualify, then the Vice Presidentelect shall act as President until a President has qualified; and the Congress may by law provide for the case where neither President-elect nor a Vice President-elect has qualified, declaring who shall then act as President, or the manner in which a qualified person shall be selected, and such person shall act accordingly until a President or Vice President has qualified.

"Sec. 4. The Congress may by law provide for the case of the death of any of the persons from whom the House of Representatives may choose a President whenever the right of choice devolves upon them, and for the case of the death of any of the persons from whom the Senate may choose a Vice President whenever the right of choice devolves upon them.

"Sec. 5. Sections 1 and 2 shall take effect on the 30th day of November of the year following the year in which this article is ratified.

"Sec. 6. This article shall be inoperative unless it shall have been ratified as an amendment to the Constitution by the legislatures of three fourths of the States within seven years from the date of the submission hereof to the States by the Congress, and the act of ratification shall be by legislatures the entire membership of at least one branch of which shall have been elected subsequent to such date of submission."[9]

By 1932, it was apparent that some type of change had to be made to the way that the Congress assembled, ending the threat of what a "lame duck" Congress could do with legislation that may or may not be popular with the American people. In stepped Senator George Norris, Republican of Nebraska. Norris had pushed for such an amendment since 1924. Final approval for his proposal finally passed both houses of Congress, the last step being in the US Senate on 2 March 1932, after which it was sent to the states for ratification[10], and, in a little more than a year, it was ratified by the requisite number of states to become the Twentieth Amendment to the US Constitution. Historians Jeffery Jenkins and Timothy Nokken wrote, "The passage of the Twentieth Amendment – or Lame Duck Amendment, as it has also become known – was accomplished due to the Herculean efforts of Sen. George W. Norris (R-NE). Norris began his crusade against the short session of Congress in 1922, working tirelessly for its own limitation until finally achieving the required two-thirds votes in each chamber a decade later. Norris' arguments for the amendment were many, but all involved the representational dangers inherent in a Congress populated in part by lame ducks. Norris held that democratic accountability and responsiveness were hampered in lame-duck sessions, as departing members were allowed to participate and, more importantly, *vote* after the public had acted to replace them. With the electoral connection severed, Norris argued, lame-duck members were no longer formally beholden to their constituencies and thus were susceptible to influence from congressional party

Footnotes, Sources and Further Reading for this chapter appears on page 711

leaders and (especially) the president, who possessed the ability to bestow valuable rewards in the form of executive appointments. Thus, in Norris' mind, lame-duck sessions were perverse legislative setting, as they produced policy outcomes that were often contrary to the public will and were routinely determined by a small group of political elites."[11]

So, after years of trying, Congress finally got the votes to make this change to the way government works – and, as we see, government sometimes takes a very long time to change itself to work better. In a Congressional Research Service report from 2001, it was noted,

"The primary purpose of this change was to eliminate the historical anomaly of lame duck congressional sessions, while also shortening the period between election and inauguration of the President and Vice President by six weeks. A subsidiary purpose, as revealed by the amendment's legislative history, was to remove the responsibility for contingent election from a lame duck Congress. Section 3 restates the 12th Amendment provision that the Vice President acts as President in the event the House is unable to elect a President in the contingent election process. It also empowers Congress to provide by law for situations in which neither a President nor a Vice President "qualifies," (i.e., neither has been elected)."[12]

The Twentieth Amendment was the first of three amendments – including the Twenty-second and Twenty-fifth amendments – that reformed this system of electing the President and delineating the time in terms he could serve, as well as laying out a plan if a president became incapacitated during his (or, in the future, her) time in office. The Twenty-second came about because Franklin D. Roosevelt refused to adhere to the time-honored tradition of having presidents serve only two consecutive or non-consecutive terms (Grover Cleveland is the only president to have served two non-consecutive terms, 1885-89 and 1893-97), while the Twenty-fifth was added because, during his administration, President Dwight D. Eisenhower suffered a severe heart attack and for a time, no one know what could be done to replace him if he had died. But the Twentieth Amendment is quite important, too. When this amendment kicked in for the first time, impacting the presidential term that had begun in 1933 and ended in 1937, the president, Franklin Delano Roosevelt, served during that term from 4 March 1933 until 20 January 1937, the shortest four-year term for any president in American history. However, because Roosevelt continued to serve, his term wasn't really "short" by any means. Nevertheless, it was an anomaly built in because of the passage of this amendment.

Debate in Congress

On 16 February 1932, the US House of Representatives accepted the proposed elections amendment nearly word-for-word as the US Senate passed it, except for one change that dictated the states had seven years to ratify it. The Senate resisted this change, but Senator George Norris, the amendment's author, realized that it would not pass the House without this provision, so he pushed his fellow Senators, successfully, to accept it. The portion of the debate from the US House that follows indicates little argument over the actual amendment's language other than the insertion of the date-sensitive provision.

COMMENCEMENT OF TERMS OF PRESIDENT, VICE PRESIDENT, MEMBERS OF CONGRESS, ETC.

The SPEAKER. Under the previous order of the House, the question is on agreeing to the amendment to Senate Joint Resolution No. 14.

The amendment was agreed to.

The joint resolution was ordered to be read a third time, and was read the third time.

Mr. RAMSEYER.[13] Mr. Speaker, I offer a motion to recommit.

The SPEAKER. Is the gentleman from Iowa opposed to the bill?

Mr. RAMSEYER. The gentleman from Iowa is not opposed to the bill.

The SPEAKER. Is there any Member of the House opposed to the resolution seeking recognition? If not, the Clerk will report the motion to recommit.

The Clerk read as follows:

Mr. Ramseyer moves to recommit Senate Joint Resolution 14 to the Committee on Election of President, Vice President, and Representatives in Congress, with instructions to report the same back forthwith with an amendment by inserting, after section 5 thereof, the following new section:

"Sec. 6. This article shall be inoperative unless it shall have been ratified as an amendment to the Constitution by the legislatures of three-fourths of the States within seven years from the date of the submission hereof to the States by the Congress; and the act of ratification shall be by legislatures, the entire membership of at least one branch of which shall have been elected subsequent to such date of submission."

The SPEAKER. The question is on the motion of the gentlemen from Iowa to recommit the joint resolution. The question was taken; and on a division (demanded by Mr. Ramseyer) there were – ayes 71, noes 65.

Mr. TAYLOR of Colorado.[14] Mr. Speaker, I make the point of no quorum.

The SPEAKER. Evidently there is not a quorum present. The call is automatic.

The Doorkeeper will close the doors, the Sergeant at Arms will notify absent Members, and the Clerk will call the roll.

The question was taken: and there were – yeas 204, nays 184, not voting 43...

[...]

So the motion to recommit was adopted.

[...]

Mr. JEFFERS.[15] Mr. Speaker, the Committee on Election of President, Vice President, and Representatives in

Congress report back Senate Joint Resolution 14 with the following amendment.

The Clerk read as follows:

Sec. 6. This article shall be inoperative unless it shall have been ratified as an amendment to the Constitution by the legislatures of three quarters of the States within seven years from the date of the submission hereof to the States by the Congress; and the act of ratification shall be by legislatures, the entire membership of at least one branch of which shall have been elected subsequent to such date of submission.

The SPEAKER. The question is on agreeing to the amendment.

The question was taken, and the amendment was agreed to.

The SPEAKER. The question is on the third reading of the amended resolution.

The resolution as amended was ordered to be read a third time, and was read the third time.

The SPEAKER. The question is on the passage of the resolution.

Mr. SNELL.[16] Mr. Speaker, I demand the yeas and nays. The yeas and nays were ordered.

The question was taken; and there were – yeas 336, nays 56, answered "present" 1, not voting 38...

The extended debate in the US Senate is excerpted here, from its initial introduction of the conference report of the two houses of Congress to the final vote, 2 March 1932.

FIXING TERMS OF PRESIDENT, VICE PRESIDENT, AND CONGRESS

Mr. NORRIS. Mr. President, I ask the Chair to lay before the Senate the conference report on Senate Joint Resolution 14, fixing the terms of President and Vice President.

The PRESIDENT pro tempore laid before the Senate the following conference report submitted by Mr. Norris on Monday last:

The committee of conference on the disagreeing votes of the two Houses on the amendment of the House to the joint resolution (S.J. Res. 14) proposing an amendment to the Constitution of the United States fixing the commencement of the terms of President and Vice President and Members of Congress and fixing the time of the assembling of Congress, having met, after full and free conference have agreed to recommend and do recommend to their respective Houses as follows:

That the Senate recedes from its disagreement to the amendment of the House and agree to the same with an amendment as follows: In lieu of the matter proposed to be inserted by the House amendment insert the following:

"That the following amendment to the Constitution be, and hereby is, proposed to the States, to become valid as a part of said Constitution when ratified by of the several States as provided in the Constitution:

"'Article _____

"Section 1. The terms of the President and Vice President shall end at noon on the 20th day of January, and the terms of Senators and Representatives at noon on the 3d day of January of the years in which such terms would have ended if this article had not been ratified; and the terms of their successors shall then begin.

"Sec. 2. The Congress shall assemble at least once in every year, and such meeting shall begin at noon on the 3d day of January, unless they shall by law appoint a different day.

"Sec. 3. If, at the time fixed for the beginning of the term of the President, the President elect shall have died, the Vice President elect shall become President. If a President shall not have been chosen before the time fixed for the beginning of his term, or if the President elect shall have failed to qualify, then the Vice President elect shall act as President until a President shall have qualified; and the Congress may by law provide for the case wherein neither a President elect nor a Vice President elect shall have qualified, declaring who shall then act as President, or the manner in which one who is to act be selected, and such person shall act accordingly until a President or Vice President shall have qualified.

"Sec. 4. The Congress may by law provide for the case of the death of any of the persons from whom the House of Representatives may choose a President whenever the right of choice shall have devolved upon them, and for the case of the death of any of the persons from whom the Senate may choose a Vice President whenever the right of choice shall have devolved upon them.

"Sec. 5. Sections 1 and 2 shall take effect on the 15th day of October following the ratification of this article.

"Sec. 6. This article shall be inoperative unless it shall have been ratified as an amendment to the Constitution by the legislatures of three fourths of the several States within seven years from the date of its submission.'"

And the House agrees to the same.

G.W. Norris,
Wm. E. Borah,
Thos. J. Walsh,
Managers on the part of the Senate.

Lamar Jeffers,
Ralph F. Lozier,
Chas. L. Gifford,
Managers on the part of the House.

Mr. NORRIS. I move that the Senate proceed to the consideration of the conference report.

The motion was agreed to; and the Senate proceeded to consider the conference report.

Mr. NORRIS. Mr. President, I have no desire to take up that time of the Senate unnecessarily. I have an idea that most Senators understand what changes the conferees have made in joint resolution as it passed the Senate.

I will state briefly that section 1 of the proposed amendment to the Constitution as it now appears in the conference report is identical with section 1 as the joint resolution originally passed the Senate, except as to a change in date. The conference report changes the date from the 2d of January to the 3d of January and changes the other date from the 15th day of January to the 20th day of January. With those exceptions, there is no change whatever in section 1.

Senators all realize that section 1 is really the crux of the entire amendment. It is this section that changes the date for the beginning and ending of the terms of President, Vice President, Members of the House, and Members of the Senate, and obviates and does away with what is now known as the short session of Congress. As we have agreed upon it, it provides for the meeting of Congress on the 3d day of January after the November election instead of the 2d day of January as joint resolution passed the Senate.

Section 2 of the conference report is identical with section 2 of the joint resolution as it passed the Senate with the exception of changing the date from the 2d day of January to the 3d day of January. That is the date for the convening of Congress. As it passed the Senate it provided for the convening of Congress on the 2d day of January, but as agreed to in conference the date is changed to the 3d day of January.

Section 3 in substance is the same as it passed the Senate, though several changes have been made by the conferees in the language.

Section 4 of the joint resolution as it passed the Senate is now section 5 and is exactly the same as the passed the Senate except that it applies only now to sections 1 and 2 of the amendment. As it passed the Senate it read:

Sec. 4. The amendment shall take effect on the 15th day of October after its ratification.

As agreed to in conference it now reads:

Sec. 5. Sections 1 and 2 shall take effect on the 15th day of October following the ratification of this article.

That leaves the balance of the section to go into effect as soon as it is ratified.

Mr. SMITH.[17] Mr. President...

The PRESIDENT pro tempore. Does the Senator from Nebraska yield to the Senator from South Carolina?

Mr. NORRIS. Certainly.

Mr. SMITH. May I ask the Senator what date is provided for the convening of Congress?

Mr. NORRIS. The 3d day of January.

Mr. SMITH. Does not the present law provide for the convening of Congress on the first Monday in December?

Mr. NORRIS. Yes; that is true.

Mr. SMITH. To obviate the question of convening on Sunday, might it not be well to provide a certain day instead of a certain date?

Mr. NORRIS. The conference committee and members of the Judiciary Committee in the consideration of other resolutions which we have passed before relating to the subject, have given considerable attention to that question. The law provides that the terms of Senators shall be for six years and that the terms of Members of the House shall be for two years. There might possibly come a conflict if we undertake to make the term commence and end on a certain day of the week instead of a certain date. It might make the term a little more than two years, in the case of Members of the House, or a little less than two years. There might be as much as six days' difference.

When we come to think about it, it might happen and will happen occasionally that we will meet on Sunday, but that would be about the same as the arrangement we have now when we close a session on Sunday. If 4th of March comes on Sunday, nobody thinks of having a session of Congress on Sunday up until noon on that day. That will not occur hereafter. It may happen that beginning instead of the end of the session will fall on Sunday, but there will be no more Sunday work than there ever has been.

Mr. SMITH. The time of convening has been made contemporaneous with the beginning of one term?

Mr. NORRIS. Yes.

Mr. BARKLEY.[18] Mr. President...

The PRESIDENT pro tempore. Does the Senator from Nebraska yield to the Senator from Kentucky?

Mr. NORRIS. Certainly.

Mr. BARKLEY. There is nothing that can be done about it now because the conference report is here, but what was the real objection to having the Congress assembled and beginning of the terms occur on the first Monday in January?

Mr. NORRIS. I do not know whether the Senator was here a moment ago when I explained that. I have just stated that if we had it begin on the first Monday in January we would have at least a technical conflict with other provisions of the Constitution which provide that the term of a Member of the Senate shall be six years and a Member of the House two years. If we had those terms commence on Monday and end on Monday, it might be that they would be six days more than two years or six days less than two years, or at least there might be several days' difference. As I said, the 4th of March is liable to come on a Sunday, but we do not think anything about that. That may be the last day of the session. In this case sometimes the first day of the session may be Sunday, so we will not be any more irreligious under the new plan than we were under the old plan.

Mr. BARKLEY. I was reared in an old-fashioned school of thought which took the position that it is better to work on Sunday when the ox is in the ditch than deliberately to put him in the ditch in order that we might work on Sunday.

Mr. NORRIS. The Senator thinks the ox is more liable to be in the ditch on last day of the session than on the first day?

Mr. BARKLEY. Yes; that is probably so.

Mr. NORRIS. That may be true.

Mr. WALSH of Massachusetts.[19] Mr. President, may I ask the Senator from Nebraska if any change has been made in the period of time for ratification by the legislatures of the several States?

Mr. NORRIS. Yes; I am just coming to that.

Section 4 of the conference report was not in the joint resolution as it passed the Senate. The Senate conferees, however, have no objection to it, but think it is a good provision. It is not necessarily in the amendment changing the terms of office of President, Vice President, and Members of Congress, but it meets a contingency that is liable to occur and reads as follows:

Sec. 4. The Congress may by law provide for the case of the death of any of the persons from whom the House of Representatives may choose a President whenever the right of choice shall have devolved upon them, and for the case of the death of any of the persons from whom the Senate may choose a Vice President whenever the right of choice shall have devolved upon them.

Section 6 was also inserted by the House, but was not in the joint resolution as it passed the Senate. As it passed the House section 6 provided that the amendment would be inoperative unless ratified within seven years after its submission and that it must appear that at least one of the branches of the legislatures passing upon it to ratify it had been elected after the submission of the amendment. The conferees compromised on that, left out the latter clause and put in the first clause, so that section 6 now reads:

Sec. 6. This article shall be inoperative unless it shall have been ratified as an amendment to the Constitution by the legislatures of three-fourths of the several States within seven years from the date of its submission.

In effect, it is the same provision that was in the prohibition amendment to the Constitution.[20]

Mr. BINGHAM.[21] Mr. President, may I ask the Senator a question?

The PRESIDENT pro tempore. Does the Senator from Nebraska yield to the Senator from Connecticut?

Mr. NORRIS. Certainly.

Mr. BINGHAM. If this amendment is ratified by the States, it does away with the December session of Congress?

Mr. NORRIS. Yes.

Mr. BINGHAM. That probably gives us two more months in every alternate year of the session of Congress than we get at the present time.

Mr. NORRIS. Yes; I should think so.

Mr. BARKLEY. Mr. President, under the practice, if the conference report is adopted this morning, when will it be submitted to the several States?

Mr. NORRIS. Immediately, I presume, by the Secretary of State.

Mr. BARKLEY. The legislature in my State is now in session and will adjourn on the 17th of March. I should be very happy to see my State ratify it, because when I came to the House of Representatives in 1913 the first measure I introduced was similar to the one which we are now about to adopt. Personally I should be very much ratified if it could be submitted to the Kentucky Legislature in order that they might vote on it before they adjourn.

Mr. NORRIS. Mr. President, if no Senator wishes to discuss the matter, I will ask for the yeas and nays. The yeas and nays were ordered, and the Chief Clerk proceeded to call the roll

Mr. JONES[22] (when his name was called). I have a general pair with the senior Senator from Virginia (Mr. SWANSON[23]), who is necessarily absent. I understand, however, that if present he would vote as I intend to vote on this question. So I shall vote. I vote "yea."

Mr. McNARY[24] (when his name was called). Announcing my pair with the junior Senator from Arkansas (Mrs. CARAWAY[25]). I am advised that if present she would vote as I am about to vote. I will therefore vote. I vote "yea."

Mr. TOWNSEND[26] (when his name was called). Announcing my pair with the senior Senator from Tennessee (Mr. McKELLAR[27]). I am advised that if present he would vote as I am about to vote. I therefore feel at liberty to vote and vote "yea."

The roll call was concluded.

Mr. HATFIELD[28] (after having voted in the affirmative). I have a general pair with the senior Senator from North Carolina (Mr. MORRISON[29]). I am informed that if present he would vote as I have voted. I therefore feel at liberty to vote and will let my vote stand.

Mr. BINGHAM (after having voted in the negative). In the absence of the junior Senator from Virginia (Mr. GLASS[30]), who is my general pair, I am obliged to withdraw my vote.

Mr. HEBERT.[31] After announcing my pair with this Senator from Louisiana (Mr. LONG[32]), I withhold my vote.

Mr. FESS.[33] I desire to announce the following general pairs:

The Senator from California (Mr. SHORTRIDGE[34]) with the Senator from Georgia (Mr. HARRIS[35]); and The Senator from Delaware (Mr. HASTINGS[36]) with the Senator from Tennessee (Mr. HULL[37]).

I am not advised as to how any of those Senators would vote if present.

Mr. SHEPPARD.[38] I wish to announce that the Senator from Texas (Mr. CONNALLY[39]), the Senator from Georgia (Mr. HARRIS), the Senator from Tennessee (Mr. McKELLAR), the Senator from North Carolina (Mr. BAILEY[40]), the Senator from Missouri (Mr. HAWES[41]), and the Senator from Tennessee (Mr. HULL) are necessarily absent from the Senate. If present, they would vote "yea" on the adoption of the conference report.

Mr. WAGNER.[42] I transfer my general pair with the Senator from Missouri (Mr. PATTERSON[43]) to the Senator from Texas (Mr. CONNALLY) and vote "yea." The result was announced – yeas 74, nays 3, as follows:

YEAS – 74

Ashurst	Cutting	Kendrick	Sheppard
Austin	Davis	Keyes	Shipstead
Bankhead	Dickinson	King	Smith
Barbou	Dill	LaFollette	Smoot
Barkley	Fess	Lewis	Steiwer
Black	Fletcher	Logan	Thomas, Idaho
Blaine	Frazier	McGill	Thomas, Okla.
Borah	George	McNary	Townsend
Bratton	Glenn	Moses	Trammell
Brookhart	Goldsborough	Neely	Tydings
Broussard	Gore	Norbeck	Vandenberg
Bulkley	Hale	Norris	Wagner
Bulow	Harrison	Nye	Walsh, Mass.
Byrnes	Hatfield	Oddie	Walsh, Mont.
Capper	Hayden	Pittman	Watson
Carey	Howell	Reed	Wheeler
Copeland	Johnson	Robinson, Ark.	White
Costigan	Jones	Robinson, Ind.	
Couzens	Kean	Schall	

NAYS – 3

Dale	Metcalf	Waterman

NOT VOTING – 19

Bailey	Glass	Hull	Shortridge
Bingham	Harris	Long	Stephens
Caraway	Hastings	McKellar	Swanson
Connally	Hawes	Morrison	Walcott
Coolidge	Hebert	Patterson	

The PRESIDENT pro tempore. Two-thirds of all Senators present and voting having voted in the affirmative, the conference report is agreed to.

Mr. COOLIDGE[44] subsequently said: Mr. President, I was necessarily absent from the Chamber when the vote was taken on the Senate Joint Resolution 14 – conference report. If I had been present, I would have voted "yea."

Footnotes, Sources and Further Reading for this chapter appears on page 711

Historical Background Documents

This selection from Senator George Norris' autobiography, Fighting Liberal: The Autobiography of George W. Norris *(New York: The Macmillan Company, 1945), illustrates the situation leading up to the passage of the Twentieth Amendment.*

One of the main objectives of the Lame Duck Amendment had been to abolish the fourth day of March as the date of final adjournment of Congress. This was destroyed by the House amendment. The second session of Congress – the shorter, lame-duck session – would have been unlimited, like the first session.

In that first meeting of the conferees it was revealed that a majority of the House conferees would not agree upon any report. Senator Borah, Senator Walsh, and I met by ourselves later and decided it was impossible to get a report before adjournment. The House had held the resolution without action for nearly a year, plainly determined to defeat it by delay.

It had succeeded.

The trail was indubitably clear to the three of us as we sat there talking.

The attitude of the Speaker was established.

There were a number of very important appropriation bills awaiting action that required passage to keep the government going. There was little chance of obtaining action on the conference report, so regretfully we agreed to let the resolution fail. It therefore died in conference, and the fifth attempt to amend the Constitution by eliminating the Lame Duck session of Congress had failed.

When the next Congress convened, I introduced my resolution for the sixth time on December 9, 1931. It was referred to the Judiciary Committee, was reported back promptly to the Senate, and on January 6, 1932, the Senate passed it for the sixth time. It went to the House, was amended, and passed on February 16, 1932. The next day the Senate disagreed to the House amendment, requested a conference to which the House promptly agreed, appointing conferees.

The sun had broken through the clouds after ten years of frustration.

It is important to note that the House had changed its political character in the preceding election.

It was now under control by the Democrats; Speaker Longworth had been succeeded by John Garner of Texas, and the control which had successfully defeated every attempt to pass the resolution had been terminated. Again I had the assistance of Senator Walsh and Senator Borah as conferees, and this time a majority of the House contraries were friendly. There was no difficulty in reaching an agreement. The conferees' report was accepted by the House on March 1, 1932; by the Senate on March 2; and thus the resolution after passing the Senate in six different Congresses became a reality and for approval.

As Submitted to the States

Section 1. The terms of the President and Vice President shall end at noon on the 20th day of January, and the terms of Senators and Representatives at noon on the 3d day of January, of the years in which such terms would have ended if this article had not been ratified; and the terms of their successors shall then begin.

Section 2. The Congress shall assemble at least once in every year, and such meeting shall begin at noon on the 3d day of January, unless they shall by law appoint a different day.

Section 3. If, at the time fixed for the beginning of the term of the President, the President elect shall have died, the Vice President elect shall become President. If a President shall not have been chosen before the time fixed for the beginning of his term, or if the President elect shall have failed to qualify, then the Vice President elect shall act as President until a President shall have qualified; and the Congress may by law provide for the case wherein neither a President elect nor a Vice President elect shall have qualified, declaring who shall then act as President, or the manner in which one who is to act shall be selected, and such person shall act accordingly until a President or Vice President shall have qualified.

Section 4. The Congress may by law provide for the case of the death of any of the persons from whom the House of Representatives may choose a President whenever the right of choice shall have devolved upon them, and for the case of the death of any of the persons from whom the Senate may choose a Vice President whenever the right of choice shall have devolved upon them.

Section 5. Sections 1 and 2 shall take effect on the 15th day of October following the ratification of this article.

Section 6. This article shall be inoperative unless it shall have been ratified as an amendment to the Constitution by the legislatures of three-fourths of the several states within seven years from the date of its submission.

State Ratifications of the Twentieth Amendment

State	Date
Virginia	4 March 1932
New York	11 March 1932
Mississippi	16 March 1932
Arkansas	17 March 1932
Kentucky	17 March 1932
New Jersey	21 March 1932
South Carolina	25 March 1932
Michigan	31 March 1932
Maine	1 April 1932
Rhode Island	14 April 1932
Illinois	21 April 1932
Louisiana	22 June 1932
West Virginia	30 July 1932
Pennsylvania	11 August 1932
Indiana	15 August 1932
Texas	7 September 1932
Alabama	13 September 1932
California	4 January 1933
North Carolina	5 January 1933
North Dakota	9 January 1933
Minnesota	12 January 1933
Arizona	13 January 1933
Montana	13 January 1933
Nebraska	13 January 1933
Oklahoma	13 January 1933
Kansas	16 January 1933
Oregon	16 January 1933
Delaware	19 January 1933

Washington State	19 January 1933
Wyoming	19 January 1933
Iowa	20 January 1933
South Dakota	20 January 1933
Tennessee	20 January 1933
Idaho	21 January 1933
New Mexico	21 January 1933
Georgia	23 January 1933
Missouri	23 January 1933
Ohio	23 January 1933
Utah	23 January 1933
Massachusetts	24 January 1933
Wisconsin	24 January 1933
Colorado	24 January 1933
Nevada	26 January 1933
Connecticut	27 January 1933
New Hampshire	31 January 1933
Vermont	2 February 1933
Maryland	24 March 1933
Florida	26 April 1933

Explanation of the amendment

The so-called "election reform amendment" in fact didn't change elections; what it did do was change the dates that Congress met following election, as well as moving the date of a presidential inauguration from the customary 4 March up to 20 January.

Changes to the amendment

There have been no changes made to the specific language of this amendment. However, through the eventual passage of the Twenty-second amendment (1951) and the Twenty-fifth Amendment (1967), the outlines of the presidential term and presidential disability were made clearer.

ORIGINAL PRIMARY DOCUMENTS

The proposed "lame duck" amendment to the US Constitution passes the US House of Representatives, as announced in The Washington Post, *16 February 1932.*

'LAME DUCK' RESOLUTION CARRIES IN HOUSE, 335-56

Washington, Feb. 16. (AP) – A resolution proposing to the States a constitutional amendment to abolish the "lame duck" session of Congress was adopted today by the House. The vote was 335 to 56.

It was approved by a two-thirds vote as required for a proposed constitutional amendment. Having already been approved by the Senate, it will be sent to conference where minor differences will be composed.

By not fixing a limit on the second annual session the Democratic House terminated a ten-year-old controversy between the two branches.

The resolution must be ratified by three-fourths of the States within seven years.

It provides that a new Congress shall meet two months after the November elections, instead of thirteen months later as at present. Terms of Congressmen would begin on January 4 and of the President and Vice-President on January 24.

As the measure was adopted by the Senate, Congress would convene January 2 and the President and VicePresident would take office on January 15.

Those who voted against the resolution were:

Democrats – Bland, Blanton, Bulwinkle, Larsen, Montague, Tucker, Woodrum – 7.

Republicans – Aldrich, Allen, Andrew of Massachusetts, Bachmann, Bacon, Beckwith, Beers, Brumm, Burdick, Chipperfield, Cole of Iowa, Coyle, Darrow, De Priest, Doutrich, Eaton of Colorado, Erk, Evans of California, Finley, Foss, French, Golder, Hawley, Hess, Hollister, Houston, Kahn, Kinzer, Loofbourow, Murphy, Parker of New York, Ransley, Rich, Rogers of Massachusetts, Sanders of New York, Seiberling, Shott, Shreve, Stokes, Taber, Temple, Tilson, Tinkham, Treadway, Underhill, Watson, Welsh of Pennsylvania, Wigglesworth, and Wolfenden, 49: grand total, 56.

Senator Norris,[45] Republican, Nebraska, author of the constitutional amendment, expressed gratification over the House action, but expressed opposition to the seven-year limitation inserted by the House on ratification. Nevertheless the Nebraskan was confident that the new differences between the Senate and House could be ironed out in conference.

While the Senate seven times has adopted the amendment the House has approved it only once before.

Another perspective on the House approval, as announced in The Chicago Tribune, *3 March 1932.*

LAME DUCK BILL IS APPROVED; UP TO STATES NOW

Washington, D.C., March 2. – [Special.] – The Norris amendment, proposing to change the date of the President's inauguration, the date on which members of congress take office, and the date for the convening of congress, received its final approval at the hands of congress today and now becomes a matter for ratification by the legislatures of the states.

The resolution, embodying amendments to provisions which were written into the constitution in the days of travel by horseback and carriage, received its final congressional sanction when the senate approved the conference report which reconciled differences between the two houses.

The house of representatives agreed to the conference report yesterday.

Only three senators, all Republicans, voted against approval: Dale [Vt.],[46] Metcalf [R.I.],[47] and Waterman [Col.].[48] Senator Bingham [Rep., Conn.][49] cast an adverse vote, but was forced to withdraw it when his pair failed to vote.

If ratified by three-quarters of the states within the seven year period provided in the resolution the amendment will make the following constitutional changes: The terms of the President and Vice President will begin on Jan.

20 instead of March 4; the terms of senators and representatives will begin on Jan. 3 instead of March 4, and congress will meet once each year beginning on Jan. 3 instead of on the first Monday in December.

There was but a brief discussion in the senate as the conference report was agreed to. A point brought up by Senator Alben W. Barkley [Dem., Ky.] was the possibility that Jan. 3 and Jan. 20 might fall on Sunday.

"But the fourth of March may fall on a Sunday – and sometimes does," answered Senator Norris. "Congress, therefore, reaches end of its short session on a Sunday at times. We shall be no more irreligious than we now are."

The proposed amendment passes the US Senate, reported in the Los Angeles Times, *3 March 1932.*

LAME DUCK BAN WINS

Approval Given by Senate

Norris Amendment Carries by Vote of 73-to-3 and Now Goes to States

---

Ratification by Thirty-six of Them in Seven-Year Period Required

---

WASHINGTON, March 2. (AP) – A new constitutional amendment was put before the States today for ratification for the first time since 1924, when the Norris proposal to abolish the "lame duck" session of Congress received the Senate's final approval by 73 votes to 3, and was dispatched to the State Department for submission to the States.

It must be ratified by the required thirty-six States within seven years.

The House approved it yesterday.

Action today on the amendment marked fulfillment of a nine-year struggle, during which it passed the Senate six times previously. It was blocked regularly, however, by the rigid insistence of the House, then under Republican control, on a definite adjournment date for Congress.

LITTLE EXCITEMENT

Although this was the first constitutional amendment adopted since the child-labor proposal of eight years ago, there was little excitement in the Senate. Its approval had been a foregone conclusion since last Saturday, when conferees of the two branches reached agreement.

The record vote was take at the request of Senator Norris after he had explained briefly the changes made by the conferees.

Outstanding among the measure's provisions is elimination of the "short session" of Congress, extending from the first Monday in December until March 4, and the establishment of sessions of indeterminate length to begin each January 3.

At present "lame-ducks" – members of Congress defeated for re-election in November – may continue to legislate throughout the short session.

CHANGES PROVIDED

Under amendment members would take up their duties on January 3 – two months after their election – instead of waiting thirteen months until the following December.

The present system has in referred to in past decades on the amendment as a survival from stage-coach days, when it took months to find out the result of an election and get the legislators to the Capitol.

Terms of the President and Vice-President would begin on January 20, instead of March 4.

The National League of Women Voters announced tonight that State Leagues can be counted on to begin plans to support State ratification of the amendment.

Mrs. Siegel W. Judd of Grand Rapids, Mich. chairman of the league's department of efficiency in government, said in a statement through headquarters here that such preparations already have been started in the eight States where legislatures now are in session.

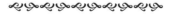

A "Virginia Democrat" denounces the congressional passage of the elections amendment in a letter to the editor, The Washington Post, *14 March 1932.*

Virginia Democrat Praises "Guard the Constitution" Editorial – Opposed to Norris Amendment.

_____

To the Editor of The Post – Sir: All good Americans will thoroughly and enthusiastically agree with your timely editorial, "Guard the Constitution." The manner and speed in which the "lame duck" amendment was railroaded through both houses of the Legislature in Virginia is reminiscent of the days when the eighteenth amendment was being "considered" by the Legislatures of the several States.

Regardless of the merits of any proposed change in an amendment to the Constitution, adequate time for serious thought and the most careful consideration and debate are of prime importance. Moreover, time should be given for the expression of public opinion. This was not done in Richmond. The amendment was railroaded through both houses in the spirit of the public-be-damned attitude.

I do not know how the citizens of Virginia feel about the amendment or how they would vote on it if given the opportunity to do so. Neither did the representatives in the Legislature. For that reason the citizens of Virginia are chagrined rather than elated over the manner in which their representatives railroaded this amendment through both houses.

Personally, if given an opportunity to express my views, I would have voted against it. I am in favor of having the Congress meet soon after election so that the newly elected members will begin their terms as soon as possible. This feature of the amendment is admirable. But to set the date of the inauguration of our President up to January is a step backward instead of an improvement. The inauguration of our President is a national affair in which all the people have an interest. It is an affair which is looked forward to and attended by people from every States in the Union. Because of the national character of this event it was recognized a few years ago that March 4 was too uncertain as to weather and too early a date on which to have the inauguration. Consequently, following the blizzard of March 4, 1909, a great deal of agitation was started both in and out of Congress to have the inauguration date changed to a date later in the spring. The day provided for in the amendment is almost certain to be a disagreeable, wintry one, which will be suitable for no one to attend, and those few who do venture out will do so at the peril of their lives.

This amendment was a great scheme, and I'm certain no other than the fertile (?) mind of Senator Norris would have conceived it.

VIRGINIA DEMOCRAT

Despite having this important constitutional amendment officially ratified, the news barely got any notice in The Sun of Baltimore, *7 February 1933.*

Lame-Duck Amendment Formally Proclaimed

———

Senator Norris And Other Sponsors Unable to Leave Capitol For Ceremony.

———

Washington, Feb. 6. (AP) The "lame duck" amendment was formally proclaimed today by Secretary Stimson[50] as a part of the Constitution, although in actually became effective with ratification by the thirty-sixth State – Missouri – January 23.

Secretary Stimson had hoped to have sponsors of the Twentieth Amendment in Congress, including Senator Norris (Rep., Neb.), attend the ceremony, but pressure of business prevented the legislators from leaving the Capitol.

The amendment provides that hereafter the regular sessions of Congress with begin on January 3 and that beginning with 1937 Presidents will be inaugurated on January 20 instead of March 4.

WHO'S WHO

This section includes a biography of one individual who played a significant part in the passage of the Twentieth Amendment. There is much mention of him earlier in the chapter.

George William Norris (1861-1944)

George Norris is one of the longest-serving members of Congress from Nebraska. He is well known for his participation in the so-called "Progress Revolt" against Speaker of the US House of Representatives "Uncle Joe" Cannon in 1910, which ultimately caused Cannon's fall from power and the takeover the House by the Democrats in 1910. Norris eventually was elected to the US Senate, where he spent the remainder of his life. It was while in the US Congress' upper body that Norris pushed for the passage, and ratification by the states, of an amendment to change the dates that Congress assembled, as discussed here, as well as the date of the presidential inauguration. Although called "The Norris Amendment" in contemporary news articles and works, the closer to the present day discussion of the Twelfth Amendment is, the less mention there is of Norris or his work on the amendment.

Known as "Willie" as a child, Norris was born not in Nebraska, the state with which he was identified for his entire life, but on his family's farm near the village of Clyde, in Sandusky County, Ohio, on 11 July 1861, the son of farmers Chauncey Norris and his wife Marry Magdalene (née Mook) Norris. Walter Locke, writing in *The Antioch Review Anthology* in 1945, explained, "He had been born in Northern Ohio in the atmosphere of the Civil War. He had lost a brother in that war. He grew up among devoted Republicans, firm in the faith that the Republican Party was wholly good and that in political and government that party was the only good there was." Chauncey Norris died suddenly when his son was but three years old, leaving the young child to become the "man of the house." From an early age, he became the lead worker on the family farm, becoming skilled at his craft. Although this would leave little time for school, Norris did attend what were called "district schools" – usually small schools for rural children who could not attend school on a regular basis. Norris also went to Baldwin University in Berea, Ohio, and he completed his education at the Northern Indiana Normal School (now Valparaiso University), from which he graduated in 1880. After studying the law, he was admitted to the Ohio bar in 1883. Believing that opportunity was ahead for him only if he moved, he picked up and began a move west. To pay the bills, he taught schools in several western states before finally settling in Nebraska in 1885. He opened a law practice in Beaver City and then in the city of McCook, in the southernmost portion of the state, near to the Kansas border. (In fact, one of the tourist attractions in McCook is the George Norris House, located at 706 George Norris Avenue.) Norris gradually grew his law practice, at the same time making a good living in the mortgage and loan business. In 1889, he married Pluma Lashley, the daughter of a Beaver City businessman; the couple would have three daughters. Pluma Norris died in 1901, after which Norris married Ella Leonard, a schoolteacher from McCook; the couple had no children.

George Norris became a leading legal expert in both Beaver City, in Red Willow County, and McCook, in Furnas County. Norris served as county attorney for Furnas County for three terms, then as a district judge for the Fourteenth Judicial District from 1895 to 1902. In 1899, two years before his first wife's death, Norris moved his family permanently from Beaver City to McCook.

In 1902, running as a Republican, Norris was elected to a seat in the US House of Representatives, eventually serving five terms, from the Fifty-eighth Congress (1903-1905) until the Sixty-second Congress (1911-13). Although elected as a conservative Republican, Norris gradually moved left while in Congress, and although he remained in the Republican Party, he became a part of that party's so-called "Progressive" wing. When Norris entered the House in 1903, the body was in the firm control of Rep. Joseph Cannon, known as "Uncle Joe," who ran the House with a strong hand and an artful use of the rules to railroad his legislation through the committees, which he stocked with his supporters and backers. Someone who resisted Cannon paid a heavy price, with assignments to negligible committees or a refusal to have their legislation considered for passage. One of those who resisted Cannon was Norris, who joined with the Progressives of the party to fight against Cannon's power. Finally, on 17 March 1910, after two failed attempts to end Cannon's iron grip, Norris and more than 40 Progressive Republicans, joined by all of the 149 Democrats in the House, scheduled a vote on Cannon's ability to hold power just when the House was in a period of little business, and most of Cannon's allies were absent from the House. Norris demanded, through a resolution, that Cannon be stripped of his seat on the all-powerful Rules Committee, and that he be disallowed from naming members to plum committee assignments. Norris told the House, "[T]here will be no change in the rules that will be satisfactory or produce satisfactory results either to the House or the country that does not take away from the Speaker the right to serve on the Committee on Rules and the right to appoint all the standing committees of this House. Any other proposition that may come in here will only blind the real situation. It is to be regretted, Mr. Speaker, that we were not left to settle this question without any outside influences. During the vacation Members of this House have been worked upon by the various departments of this government, especially what are known as the 'Insurgent' part of the House; Senators, cabinet members, and, I regret to say, the President have all been working in behalf of the Speaker and his machine; so that we have had a combination of the Senate, the Cabinet, the Executive, and the 'Knights of the Iron Duke,' all combined in an assault upon that little band of insurgents." A filibuster, led by Cannon to try to stall for time to find his allies, eventually failed, and Cannon was forced to rule the entire exercise out of order on 19 March. Norris appealed to the full House, which, still missing key Cannon allies, voted to overrule Cannon and adopt the Norris resolution. Cannon's power was broken, although a vote engineered by the Speaker asking to be removed from his post failed. Nevertheless, his ability to control the legislation and committee assignments in the House was finished. In the elections held later that year, Democrats won control of the House, and Cannon was relegated to the back benches. Two years later, Cannon lost his seat in the 1912 elections that swept the GOP from power in the White House, which it had held since 1897. The overthrow of Speaker Cannon was one of the two major occurrences in Norris' congressional service; the other was his service as one of the managers for the impeachment proceedings against Judge Robert Wodrow Archbald, a Judge on the United States Commerce Court (since done away with by Congress), impeached in 1912 on charges of having an improper business relationship with litigants before his court, and, in January 1913, convicted by the US Senate and removed from office.

Growing more radical and increasingly out of step with the majority of his party, in 1912 Norris decided to give up a safe seat in the US House of Representatives for one in the US Senate. Senator Norris Brown, who had been elected to the US Senate in 1906 and had, during his term, introduced the resolution that later became the Sixteenth Amendment to the US Constitution, which mandated a federal income tax, was not re-elected by the Nebraska legislature (prior to the ratification of the Seventeenth Amendment in 1913, state legislatures elected US Senators; with the amendment, Senators were elected directly by the people). With the seat now open, Norris declared for it, and he was named as the Republican candidate. Democrats named Ashton C. Shallenberger, a former Governor of Nebraska (1909-11). With the legislature controlled by the GOP, Norris' election was assured, and he won what would become five terms in the US Senate.

An expert in farm matters – especially coming from an agricultural state – Norris made few speeches on foreign affairs, but his opposition to the foreign policy of the administration of President Woodrow Wilson made him an opponent of the President. When the First World War began in 1914, Norris called for American neutrality; in

April 1917, when Wilson asked Congress for a war resolution against Germany, Norris was one of only six US Senators to vote against American entry into the war. Taking to the Senate floor, Norris stated:

"There are a great many American citizens who feel that we owe it as a duty to humanity to take part in this war. Many instances of cruelty and inhumanity can be found on both sides. Men are often biased in their judgment on account of their sympathy and their interests. To my mind, what we ought to have maintained from the beginning was the strictest neutrality. If we had done this, I do not believe we would have been on the verge of war at the present time. We had a right as a nation, if we desired, to cease at any time to be neutral. We had a technical right to respect the English war zone and to disregard the German war zone, but we could not do that and be neutral.

"I have no quarrel to find with the man who does not desire our country to remain neutral. While many such people are moved by selfish motives and hopes of gain, I have no doubt but that in a great many instances, through what I believe to be a misunderstanding of the real condition, there are many honest, patriotic citizens who think we ought to engage in this war and who are behind the President in his demand that we should declare war against Germany. I think such people err in judgment and to a great extent have been misled as to the real history and the true facts by the almost unanimous demand of the great combination of wealth that has a direct financial interest in our participation in the war... I say again that when two nations are at war any neutral nation, in order to preserve its character as a neutral nation, must exact the same conduct from both warring nations; both must equally obey the principles of international law. If a neutral nation falls in that, then its rights upon the high seas-to adopt the President's phrase-are relative and not absolute. There can be no greater violation of our neutrality than the requirement that one of two belligerents shall adhere to the settled principles of law and that the other shall have the advantage of not doing so. The respect that German naval authorities were required to pay to the rights of our people upon the high seas would depend upon the question whether we had exacted the same rights from Germany's enemies. If we had not done so, we lost our character as a neutral nation and our people unfortunately had lost the protection that belongs to neutrals. Our responsibility was joint in the sense that we must exact the same conduct from both belligerents."

From his first days in the US Senate, Norris began to agitate for the inclusion in the US Constitution of an amendment to end the so-called "lame duck" session of Congress. Although he was a "disinterested supporter" of amendments that banned the sale of alcoholic drinks and gave women the right to vote, Norris was more interested in changing the lame-duck session. Historian Shirley Ann Komoruski Lindeen wrote in 1971, "Norris' demands for elimination of the Lame Duck Congress and reform of the electoral college were not so easily disposed. The chief architect of the Lame Duck Amendment, Norris argued that it took more than a year before a new Congress could function while those repudiated by the voters continued to make laws. Almost more controversial than this change was a provision in the original text of the amendment calls for reform of the electoral college. It incorporated retention of the electoral vote of the states, but no longer would candidates be required to offer slates of electors. The electoral vote would be given independently to the winning presidential and vice-presidential candidates – an improvement, said Norris, because a voter could express an absolute freedom of choice for the latter office which he was denied under the present system. His attack on the electoral college revealed his disdain for the twoparty system and his arguments posed the need for change in that system...although Norris was imbued with the immediate need for electoral college reform, advice that the Lame Duck Amendment could secure passage only if this provision were removed resulted in its abolition in the final draft of the amendment presented to the Senate." Norris introduced his so-called "lame-duck" amendment for the first time in 1924; frustration followed over the next several years, and it was not until 1932 that he was able to garner enough support in both houses to send the amendment to the states. In less than a year, enough states ratified it that it became the Twentieth Amendment to the US Constitution.

In the 1920s and 1930s, Norris found himself increasingly out of step with his party as he continuously moved to the left. His only consistency appeared to be his firm support for federal agricultural programs. He also felt that the government should control certain public power centers; to this end, he called for the conversion of the Muscle Shoals power facility in Alabama into a public entity. He also backed organized labor over industry, becoming the co-author with Representative Fiorello La Guardia, Republican of New York, of the Norris-LaGuardia AntiInjunction Act of 1932.

In 1932, Democrat Franklin Delano Roosevelt, the governor of New York, was elected President. Up until this time, Norris had had a love-hate relationship with the presidents he had served with. That all changed with Roosevelt. Though the men belonged to two different parties, Norris voted with liberal Democrats. As such, Roosevelt saw Norris as a handy tool to use to beat over the heads of Republicans who refused to vote for Roosevelt's economic program. Because he backed Roosevelt, Norris had the president's ear – and he was able to effect his plan to convert the Muscle Shoals facility into a public entity; it was converted to the Tennessee Valley Authority (TVA), which supplies cheap energy to Tennessee Valley area. Historian William Leuchtenberg wrote in 1952, "In his message to Congress in the spring of 1933 urging passage of the Tennessee Valley Authority legislation, President Roosevelt observed: 'If we are successful here we can march on, step by step, in a like development of other great natural territorial units within our borders.' In the next few years, glowing reports of the success of the TVA moved regional leaders to urge the President to 'march on, step by step' to extend the TVA idea to the other great river valleys of the nation. On February 5, 1937, Senator George W. Norris of Nebraska capped the agitation by proposing 'enough TVAs to cover the entire country,' and on March 31, on leaving the White House after a conference with Roosevelt, Senator Norris told reporters that he had discussed a national power and flood control plan with the President and that he would draft legislation for regional authorities modeled on [the] TVA." Norris expanded his program, with Roosevelt's help, into the federal program known as the Rural Electrification Administration (REA), one of a so-called "alphabet soup" of government agencies.

By the late 1930s, as the Nazi and Japanese threats to the free world grew in intensity, Norris, a lifelong isolationist, was gradually won over by Roosevelt and his advisors to supporting a stronger role for the United States in the world. Whereas in 1917, Norris had lambasted the prospect of going to war in Europe, by 1940 he was convinced that the United States needed to be strong militarily to fight external threats. His inconsistency was noted by his political opponents, but few others, and Norris would serve in the US Senate nearly until his death. In 1942, at 81 years old, having served for forty years in both the House and Senate, and in failing health, Norris decided not to seek another term. However, as most politicians do, Norris changed his mind and announced that he would run for a sixth term – not as a Republican, but as an Independent Progressive. Norris believed that the same people who had sent him to Washington over four decades would do so again, but he was wrong. Frail, Norris did no campaigning on his own, and as such he had no idea how unpopular his support for President Roosevelt's policies were in Nebraska. Republican Kenneth S. Wherry, a former member of the Nebraska state Senate, squared off against Norris and Democrat Foster May. On election day, Wherry won with 49% of the vote to Norris' 28.6% and May's 22%. The defeat was catastrophic for Norris, who angrily denounced his constituents for not honoring his years of service. With his wife, Norris retired to his home in Washington, DC, where he lived out his last years. Roosevelt offered him various cabinet positions and government jobs, but he turned each one down. He was in McCook, Nebraska, on 2 September 1944 when he suddenly died at the age of 83. Secretary of State Cordell Hull sent a message to Norris' widow, calling his passing "a great loss." Hull wrote, "His outstanding leadership as a great statesman and as a champion of liberalism has contributed immeasurably to the well being of the Nation and will not he forgotten." Norris was laid to rest in the Memorial Park Cemetery in McCook. His grave, in front of a huge obelisk which says "NORRIS" in large letters, is situated next to that of his first wife, Pluma, and is a small affair that simply reads: "George William. 1861-1944."

FOOTNOTES, SOURCES, FURTHER READING

Footnotes

[1] Birley, Sir Robert, ed., "Speeches and Documents in American History" (London: Oxford University Press; four volumes, 1942-44), IV:93-94.

[2] Senate Committee on the Judiciary, Report to Accompany S.J. Res. 14, Senate Report 26, 72nd Congress, 1st Session (1932), 2-4.

[3] "Terms of President, Vice President, Senators, and Representatives. January 18, 1912. – Referred to the House Calendar in order to be printed," House Report No. 239, 62nd Congress, 2nd Session (1912), 1-2.

[4] "Proposing an Amendment to the Constitution of the United States. February 19, 1924. – Referred to the House Calendar in order to be printed," House Report No. 211, 68th Congress, 1st Session (1924), 1-2.

[5] See "Proposing an Amendment to the Constitution of the United States. April 15, 1924. – Referred to the House Calendar in order to be printed," House Report No. 513, 68th Congress, 1st Session (1924), 1-2.

[6] See "Proposing an Amendment to the Constitution of the United States. February 17, 1926. – Referred to the House Calendar in order to be printed," House Report No. 311, 68th Congress, 1st Session (1924), 1-2.

[7] See "Proposing an Amendment to the Constitution of the United States. January 18, 1928. – Referred to the House Calendar in order to be printed," House Report No. 309, 68th Congress, 1st Session (1924), 1-2.

[8] "Fixing the Presidential and Congressional Term: Proceedings and Debate in the House of Representatives on S.J. Res. 47, Proposing an Amendment to the Constitution of the United States[,] Fixing the Commencement of the Terms of President and Vice President and Members of Congress and Fixing the Time of the Assembling of Congress" (House Document No. 331, 70th Congress, 1st Session {1928}).

[9] "Proposing an Amendment to the Constitution of the United States. April 8, 1930. – Referred to the House Calendar in order to be printed," House Report No. 1105, 71st Congress, 2nd Session (1930), 1-2.

[10] "Lame Duck Constitutional Amendment Goes to States," The Sun [Baltimore, Maryland], 3 March 1932, 4.

[11] Jenkins, Jeffery A., and Timothy Nokken, "Legislative Shirking in the Pre-Twentieth Amendment Era: Presidential Influence, Party Power, and Lame-Duck Sessions of Congress, 1877-1933," Studies in American Political Development, XXII:1 (2008), 112.

[12] Neale, Thomas H., "Election of the President and Vice President by Congress: Contingent Election," CRS Report for Congress, 17 January 2001, CRS-5.

[13] The time period, from the time the amendment was passed by Congress and sent on to the states, and when it was officially ratified, was 327 days.

[14] Utah, on 23 January 1933, became the state that gave the proposed amendment the requisite number of states to be considered ratified.

[15] Christian William Ramseyer (1875-1943), Republican of Iowa, Prosecuting Attorney, Davis County, Iowa (1911-15), US Representative (1915-33), Commissioner, US Court of Claims (1933-43).

[16] Edward Thomas Taylor (1858-1941), Democrat of Colorado, state Senate (1896-1908), US Representative (1909-41).

[17] Lamar Jeffers (1888-1983), Democrat of Alabama, US Representative (1921-35).

[18] Bertrand Hollis Snell (1870-1958), Republican of New York, US Representative (1915-39).

[19] Ellison DuRant Smith (1864-1944), Democrat of South Carolina, US Senator (1909-44).

[20] Alben William Barkley (1877-1956), Democrat of Kentucky, US Representative (1913-27), US Senator (1927-49, 1955-56), Vice President of the United States (1949-53).

[21] David Ignatius Walsh (1872-1947), Democrat of Massachusetts, Lt. Governor of Massachusetts (1913), Governor (1914-15), US Senator (1919-25, 1926-47).

[22] Referring to the Eighteenth Amendment to the US Constitution.

[23] Hiram Bingham (1875-1956), Republican of Connecticut, Lt. Governor of Connecticut (1922-24), Governor of Connecticut (1924), US Senator (1924-33).

[24] Wesley LivseyJones (1863-1932), Republican of Washington State, US Representative (1899-1909), US Senator (1909-32).

[25] Claude Augustus Swanson (1862-1939), Democrat of Virginia, US Representative (1893-1906). Governor of Virginia (1906-10), US Senator (1910-11, 1911-33), Secretary of the Navy (1933-39).

[26] Charles Linza McNary (1874-1944), Republican of Oregon, Associate Judge, Oregon Supreme Court (1913-15), US Senator (1917-18, 1918-44).

[27] Mrs. Hattie Wyatt Caraway (1878-1950), Democrat of Arkansas, US Senator (1931-45).

[28] John Gillis Townsend, Jr. (1871-1964), Republican of Delaware, State house of Representatives (1901-03), Governor of Delaware (1917-21), US Senator, 1929-41).

[29] Kenneth Douglas McKellar (1869-1957), Democrat of Tennessee, US Representatives (1911-17), US Senator (1917-53).

[30] Dr. Henry Drury Hatfield (1875-1962), Republican of West Virginia, State Senator (1908-12), Governor of West Virginia (1913-17), US Senator (1929-35).

[31] Cameron A. Morrison (1869-1953), Democrat of North Carolina, Mayor, Rockingham, North Carolina (1893), Governor of North Carolina (1921-25), US Senator (1930-32), US Representative (1943-45).

[32] Carter Glass (1858-1946), Democrat of Virginia, US Representative (1902-18), Secretary of the Treasury (1918-20), US Senator (1920-46).

[33] Felix Hébert (1874-1969), Republican of Rhode Island, US Senator (1929-35).

[34] Huey Pierce Long (1893-1935), Democrat of Louisiana, Governor of Louisiana (1928-32), US Senator (1932-35).

[35] Simeon Davison Fess (1861-1936), Republican of Ohio, US Representative (1913-23), US Senator (1923-35).

[36] Samuel Morgan Shortridge (1861-1952), Republican of California, US Senator (192133), Special Attorney, US Department of Justice, Washington, DC (1939-43).

[37] William Julius Harris (1868-1932), Democrat of Georgia, State Senate (1911-12), Director, United States Census Bureau (1913-15), Acting Secretary, Department of Commerce (1913-15), Member, Federal Trade Commission (1915-18), US Senator (191932).

[38] Daniel Oren Hastings (1874-1966), Republican of Delaware, Deputy Attorney General of Delaware (1904-09), Secretary of State of Delaware (1909), Associate Justice, Delaware state Supreme Court (1909-11), US Senator (1928-37).

[39] Cordell Hull (1871-1955), Democrat of Tennessee, State House of Representatives (1893-97), Judge, Fifth Judicial Circuit of Tennessee (1903-06), US Representative (1907-21, 1923-31), US Senator (1931-33), US Secretary of State (1933-44), Winner, Nobel Prize for Peace, 1945.

[40] Morris Sheppard (1875-1941), Democrat of Texas, US Representative (1902-13), US Senator (1913-41).

[41] Thomas Terry Connally (1877-1963), Democrat of Texas, State House of Representatives (1901-04), US Representative (1917-29), US Senator (1929-53).

[42] Josiah William Bailey (1873-1946), Democrat of North Carolina, US Senator (1931-46).

[43] Harry Bartow Hawes (1869-1947), Democrat of Missouri, US Representative (1921-26), US Senator (1926-33).

[44] Robert Ferdinand Wagner (1877-1953), Democrat of New York, state Assembly (1905-08), state Senate (1909-18), Justice, New York state Supreme Court (1919-26), US Senator (1927-49).

[45] Roscoe Conkling Patterson (1876-1954), Republican of Missouri, US Representative (1921-23), United States District Attorney for the Western District of Missouri (1925-29), US Senator (1929-35).

[46] Marcus Allen Coolidge (1865-1947), Democrat of Massachusetts, mayor of Fitchburg, Massachusetts (1916), US Senator (1931-37).

[47] The newspaper spelled Norris' name as "Morris."

[48] Porter Hinman Dale (1867-1933), Republican of Vermont, Vermont state Senator (1910-14), US Representative (1915-23), US Senator (1923-33).

[49] Jesse Houghton Metcalf (1860-1942), Republican of Rhode Island, US Senator (1924-37), member, Republican National Committee (1935-40).

[50] Charles Winfield Waterman (1861-1932), Republican of Colorado, US Senator (1927-32).

[51] Hiram Bingham (1875-1956), Republican of Connecticut, Lt. Governor of Connecticut (1922-24), Governor of Connecticut (1924), US Senator (1924-33).

[52] Henry Lewis Stimson (1867-1950), US Secretary of War (1911-13), Governor-General of the Philippines (1927-29), US Secretary of State (1929-33), US Secretary of War (1940-45).

Sources Arranged by Chapter Sections

Debate in Congress

"Congressional Record: Proceedings and Debates of the First Session of the Seventy-Second Congress of the United States of America" (Washington, D.C.: Government Printing Office, 1932), 4059-60.

"Congressional Record: Proceedings and Debates of the First Session of the Seventy-Second Congress of the United States of America" (Washington, D.C.: Government Printing Office, 1932), 5084-87.

Historical Background Documents

Norris, George W., "Fighting Liberal: The Autobiography of George W. Norris" (New York: The Macmillan Company, 1945), 341-42.

Original Primary Documents

"'Lame Duck' Resolution Carries in House 335-56," *The Washington Post*, 17 February 1932, 1.

"Lame Duck Bill is Approved; Up to States Now," *The Chicago Tribune*, 3 March 1932, 13.

"Lame Duck Ban Wins; Approval Given by Senate," *Los Angeles Times*, 3 March 1932, 1.

"Letters to the Editor. Virginia Democrat Praises 'Guard the Constitution' Editorial," *The Washington Post*, 14 March 1932, 6.

"Lame-Duck Amendment Formally Proclaimed," *The Sun* [Baltimore], 7 February 1933, 2.

Who's Who
George William Norris (1861-1944)

"Norris, George W.," official congressional biography, online at http://bioguide.congress.gov/scripts/biodisplay.pl?index=n000139; Locke, Walter, "George W. Norris, Independent" in Paul Howard Bixler, ed., "The Antioch Review Anthology: Essays, Fiction, Poetry, and Reviews from the Antioch Review" (Cleveland: World Publishing Company, 1953), 2; Lowitt, Richard, "George W. Norris" (Syracuse, New York: Syracuse University Press, 1963), 15; for more on the fight to challenge Cannon, see George Galloway, "History of the House of Representatives" (New York: Crowell, 1968), 253; see "Articles of Impeachment Presented Against Robert W. Archbald, Additional Circuit Judge of the United States from the Third Judicial District" (Washington: Government Printing Office, 1912); Norris speech against the war declaration, on 4 April 1917, in "*The Congressional Record*: Containing the Proceedings and Debates of the First Session of the Sixty-Fifth Congress. Also Special Session of the Senate of the United States of America" (Washington: Government Printing Office, 1917), 212-14, 223-36; Lindeen, Shirley Ann Komoruski, "The Political Party Philosophies of William Jennings Bryan and George W. Norris" (Ph.D. dissertation, The University of Nebraska at Lincoln, 1971), 276-79; Leuchtenburg, William E., "Roosevelt, Norris and the 'Seven Little TVAs'," *Journal of Politics*, XIV:3 (August 1952), 418; "George W. Norris Succumbs at Home," *The Washington Post*, 2 September 1944, 1; "Hull Wires Note of Sympathy to Sen. Norris' Wife," *The Washington Post*, 4 September 1944, 3.

Further Reading

Beth, Richard S., and Jessica Tollestrup, *Lame Duck Sessions of Congress, 1935-2012* (74th-112th Congresses), CreateSpace, 2014.

Larson, Edward J., "The Constitutionality of Lame-Duck Lawmaking: The Text, History, Intent, and Original Meaning of the Twentieth Amendment," *Utah Law Review*, 2 (2012), 707-58.

Nagle, John Copeland, "A Twentieth Amendment Parable," *New York University Law Review*, LXXII:2 (May 1997), 470-94.

_____, "Lame Duck Logic," *UC Davis Law Review*, XLV:4 (April 2012), 1177-1219.

US Congress, Continuity of Government Commission, The Continuity of the Presidency: The Second Report of the Continuity of Government Commission, June 2009, https://www.brookings.edu/wp-content/uploads/2016/06/06_continuity_of_government.pdf.

AMERICA AT THAT TIME . . .

Although the material in this section may not be directly related to the adoption of the Twentieth Amendment, it offers valuable insight into what was happening in America at the time the Amendment was adopted. Modeled after Grey House Publishing's Working American *series, whose author, Scott Derks, is responsible for its content, it includes a Historical Snapshot, Selected Prices, significant quotations, newspaper and magazine clips to give a sense of what was on the minds of Americans, and how it may have impacted the amendment process.*

HISTORICAL SNAPSHOT

1933

- The first episode of *The Lone Ranger* radio program was broadcast
- The first singing telegram was introduced by the Postal Telegram Company in New York
- President-elect Franklin Roosevelt escaped an assassination attempt in Miami that
- claimed the life of Chicago Mayor Anton J. Cermak
- *Newsweek* and *Esquire* magazines were first published
- Ground was broken for the Golden Gate Bridge in San Francisco
- The U.S. Congress passed the Twentieth and Twenty-first Amendments, the first to eliminate "Lame Duck" sessions and the second to repeal the Eighteenth Amendment, which outlawed the sale of alcohol
- The movie *King Kong* premiered, featuring Fay Wray
- Franklin D. Roosevelt was inaugurated to his first term as president; in pledging to lead the country out of the Great Depression, he said, "We have nothing to fear but fear itself"
- At the start of his administration, Roosevelt ordered a four-day bank holiday in order to stop large amounts of money from being withdrawn from the banks
- In German parliamentary elections, the Nazi Party won 44 percent of the vote, enabling it to join with Nationalists to gain a slender majority in the Reichstag
- The board game Monopoly was introduced
- Adolph Hitler seized power in Germany; the Nazis ordered a ban on all Jews in businesses, professions, and schools
- Congress authorized the Civilian Conservation Corps to relieve rampant unemployment, which exceeded 25 percent
- The United States went off the gold standard
- Gandhi began a hunger strike to protest British oppression in India

The New York Times, February 12, 1933:

What the people who live in the midst of these alarums and excursions . . . see is not Red revolution, not an organized movement to defraud creditors, but a desperate effort to preserve the existing property status from wreckage. In spite of cow-testing wars, farm strikes, highway picketing, and interference with tax and mortgage foreclosure sales, the general level of respect for law and its orderly process remains high.

Before the depression, I wore the pants in this family, and rightly so. During the Depression I lost something. Maybe you call it self-respect, but in losing it I also lost the respect of my children, and I am losing my wife.

—Jobless father to interviewer, 1933

I am a farmer. . . . Last Spring I thought you really intended to do something for this country. Now I have given it all up. Henceforward I am swearing eternal vengeance on the financial barons and will do every single thing I can to bring about communism.

—Indiana farmer to newly elected president Franklin D. Roosevelt, October 16, 1933

The plains are beautiful, but, oh, the terrible, crushing drabness of life here. And the suffering, for both people and animals. . . . Most of the farm buildings haven't been painted in God only knows how long! If I had to live here, I think I'd just quietly call it a day and commit suicide. . . . The people up here . . . are in a daze. A sort of nameless dread hangs over the place.

—Letter from Lorena Hickok to Eleanor Roosevelt, October 1933, while inspecting economic conditions in North Dakota

Selected Prices

Ad in *Ladies' Home Journal,* Full-page $12,500

Babies' Rubber Pants, Three Pairs $0.22

Boys' Knickers $0.77

Cedar Chest $12.95

Cod Liver Oil, Gallon, for Livestock $1.79

Model Airplane $6.50

Movie Ticket, Adult $0.25

Phonograph Records, Five $0.29

Sanitary Napkins, Kotex, Dozen $0.85

Silk Hosiery $0.89

Year	Value of One Dollar in 2016 US Dollars
1930	$14.46
1931	$15.88
1932	$17.62
1933	$18.57
1934	$18.02
1935	$17.62

"Garden Planning Dramatic Policy Change; To End Regular Boxing, Wrestling Dates," by James P. Dawson,

The New York Times, February 13, 1933:

The days of professional boxing and wrestling, on the comprehensive scale on which these two sports events were promoted heretofore, are numbered at Madison Square Garden.

Unless all signs fail, boxing, which, as an entertainment in the old Garden under the late Tex Rickard, was primarily responsible for the present arena, will be relegated to the status of minor importance in the future activities in the Garden.

As far as can be determined, it is proposed, commencing next fall, to eliminate the regular weekly boxing day Friday on the Garden's calendar, and the custom of semi-monthly wrestling attractions. There will be substituted only important boxing and wrestling events when, and if, they develop. Amateur boxing, it is understood, will be encouraged. . . .

Hockey, circus, rodeo, bike races, track meets and various tradeshows all give a good account of themselves, according to reliable information, but boxing and wrestling are not so profitable. Therefore, the conclusion is reached that before long many of the regular Friday night boxing and Monday night wrestling dates will be eliminated, and will be replaced by other attractions which these new improvements are making available.

THE 20TH AMENDMENT, *The Kingsport Times,* January 27, 1933

At last, after ten years of bitter struggle and waiting, the 20th Amendment to the Constitution of the United States has become a reality. The new amendment provides that the newly elected president and members of congress shall take office in January following the November election, thus eliminating the ridiculous abuse of the so-called "lame duck" congress.

The distinction of being the 36th state to ratify the 20th Amendment fell to Missouri, which took favorable action on the amendment Monday.

For many years the lame duck congress has been the skeleton in the closet of our form of government. Heretofore it has been 13 months from the time of the election to the time when the newly elected congressmen actually assumed their seats. In other words it has required more than a year to place in effect the will of the voters as expressed at the polls! It seems to us that nothing could be more utterly absurd than to have congressmen who have been repudiated at the polls sitting at Washington, drawing federal salaries and making laws, while the congressmen-elect have been sitting impotently at home, waiting 13 months for an opportunity to put into effect policies which their constituents have endorsed.

Naturally nothing in the way of really constructive legislation has ever been effected by the lame duck session of congress. We could hardly expect that there would be, with many of the members disgruntled defeated candidates and the other members marking time in uncertainty.

During the latter years there has been no excuse whatever for this long delay between the election and the inauguration of the president and congressmen elected. Perhaps, at the time the Constitution was adopted, the inadequate means of transportation, to some extent justified this system. But whereas a trip across the continent was once a matter of months it is now only a matter of days—even of hours—and this excuse, if it ever were a valid one, is no longer extant.

With the 20th Amendment in effect congress will meet every year on January 3, and the newly-elected president will take office on January 20 instead of March 4. The 17-day difference between the convening of congress and the presidential inauguration will be for the purpose of giving congress time to canvass and certify the election returns.

Also at last we have adopted an amendment to the federal Constitution which will meet with hearty approval on all sides, without one voice of dissent from any quarter. Many of the amendments to the constitution have been unpopular. Particularly after the disappointments of the last two amendments—the pitiful ineffectiveness of the 18th and the disillusionment of the 19th—it will be particularly refreshing to know that we have ratified an amendment which is without sham or humbug and which is based on solid common sense.

"13 Are Sentenced in Scottsboro Row, Each Gets $100 Fine or 60 Days in Jail for March on Capitol in Protest to High Court," *The New York Times,* **November 11, 1932:**

WASHINGTON—Judge Isaac R. Hitt in police court today sentenced 13 participants in the Capitol Monday prior to the Supreme Court's decision in the Scottsboro case to a $100 fine or 60 days in jail.

The charge against all 13 was illegal parading and in six cases assaulting policemen.

The ideal farm worker is "a class of people who have not the ability to rise, who have not the initiative, who are children, who do not want to own land, who can be directed by men in the upper stratum of society."

—Texas Congressman John C. Cox during a House Immigration Committee meeting on Mexican immigration

Visit the barrios of Los Angeles and you will see endless streets crowded with the shacks of the illiterate, diseased, pauperized Mexicans, taking no interest whatever in the community, living constantly on the ragged edge of starvation, bringing countless numbers of American citizens into the world with the reckless prodigality of rabbits.

—Kenneth L. Roberts The Saturday Evening Post

TODO and TOMORROW by Frank Parker Stockbridge,
The State Center Enterprise, March 2, 1933

PRESIDENTS . . . and double-O

Franklin Roosevelt is the third successive President to have a double "o" in his name. He is also the third President whose surname is the same as that of one of his predecessors. We have had two Presidents Adams, two Presidents Harrison and now two Presidents Roosevelt.

Mr. Roosevelt is the third President of Dutch descent. Martini Van Buren and Theodore Roosevelt being the other two. He is likewise the third President elected in his fifty-first first year.

If there is luck in odd numbers President Roosevelt ought to have plenty of it.

X X X

MASONS . . . as Presidents

President Franklin Roosevelt is the thirteenth member of the Masonic Order to be President of the United States. I have often heard some of my Masonic brethren say that every President has been a Mason, but that is not true.

Washington was Master of his Lodge, Monroe, Jackson, Polk, Buchanan, Johnson, Garfield, McKinley, Theodore Roosevelt, Taft and Harding were Masons. There is no Masonic record to prove that Jefferson was a member of the Order, but there is collateral evidence which is taken and accepted Masonically as indicating that he was.

Mr. Taft was not a Mason before he was elected, but the Grand Lodge of Ohio made him a "Mason at sight" between his election and his inauguration.

President Roosevelt was recently initiated into one of the Masonic societies, the Tall Cedars of Lebanon.

"Kidnapping: Epidemic of Seizures for Ransom, with More Adults than Children Abducted, Raises New National Problem, *News-Week,* July 22, 1933:

The sinister word, "Kidnapped," screamed from the front page of the country's newspapers last week. From New York State to the Pacific Coast, aroused communities read of adults snatched from their homes and held for high ransom. In many places guards were thrown around the homes of men of wealth. Defenseless friends and relatives of the victims of what seemed to be organized bands, worked through intermediaries with underworld connections, fearful lest the intervention of police might lead to the killing of the kidnapped.

Definitely a national kidnap fear developed. From city after city came rumors that such and such a prominent resident had received threats. So alarmed by kidnap threats was the Hollywood colony, that many film stars hired special guards. In Chicago, homes of 50 wealthy citizens were being guarded. Baltimore had a bad kidnap scare. Extra guards were assigned to watch the president's grandchildren . . .

PENALTIES: At the present time, the emergence of "Whiskers," as gangsters call Uncle Sam's agents, throws fear into every kidnapper, contemptuous, as a rule, of local police. The Patterson-Cochran bills, passed by Congress in 1932 after the Lindbergh case, impose a maximum penalty of 20 years in prison and a fine of $5,000 "for the use of the mails to convey threats to injure, to kidnap, to accuse of crime, or to demand ransom or reward for the return of an abducted person." Where a kidnapped person is taken across a state line, the judge upon the conviction of the kidnappers may impose any sentence up to life imprisonment. This is the only federal statute with such broad provisions.

"Communications," *The Commonwealth,* November 16, 1932:

To the Editor: May I suggest an argument in favor of the bonus payment which I have not seen advanced so far. Indeed, the argument is good for the payment of pensions to all veterans, widows of veterans, husbands of remarried widows of veterans, their children and grandchildren. The argument is this: The more we pay for the last war, the more likely we are to think twice before starting or being drawn into another war. Let's make war so burdensome for ourselves and the generations to come that it will become financially impossible.

And as for the immediate payment of the bonus, I think that a little inflation will be just the thing. The vast body of American debtors, cracking under the strain of debts incurred under inflated valuation, have a right to relief by being allowed to pay with inflated currency.

—A.R. Bandini, Crockett, California

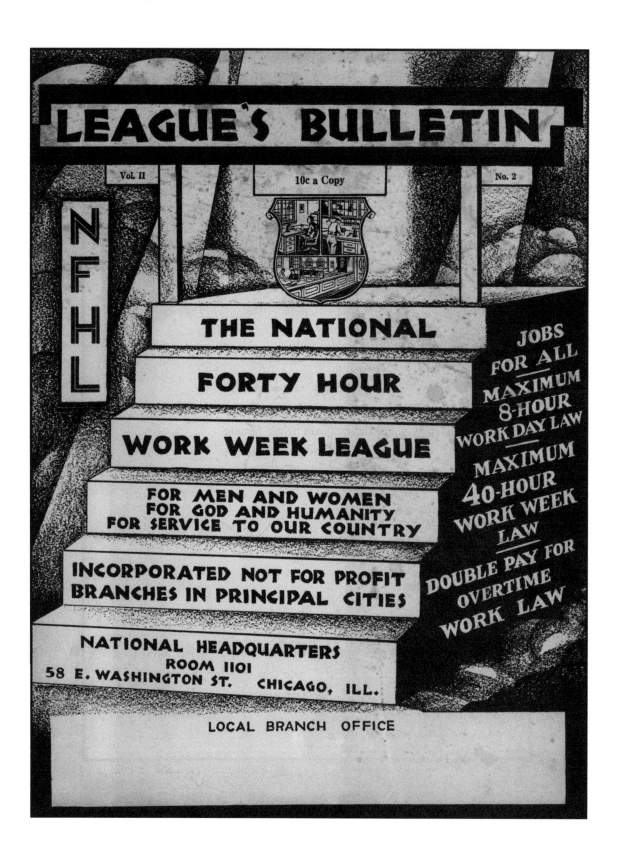

The Twenty-first Amendment

Chapter 12

S. J. Res. 211

Seventy-second Congress of the United States of America;

At the Second Session,

Begun and held at the City of Washington on Monday, the fifth
day of December, one thousand nine hundred and thirty-two.

JOINT RESOLUTION

Proposing an amendment to the Constitution of the United States.

*Resolved by the Senate and House of Representatives of the United
States of America in Congress assembled (two-thirds of each House
concurring therein), That the following article is hereby proposed
as an amendment to the Constitution of the United States, which
shall be valid to all intents and purposes as part of the Constitution
when ratified by conventions in three-fourths of the several States:*

"ARTICLE —

"SECTION 1. The eighteenth article of amendment to the Constitution of the United States is hereby repealed.

"SEC. 2. The transportation or importation into any State, Territory, or possession of the United States for delivery or use therein
of intoxicating liquors, in violation of the laws thereof, is hereby
prohibited.

"SEC. 3. This article shall be inoperative unless it shall have been
ratified as an amendment to the Constitution by conventions in the
several States, as provided in the Constitution, within seven years
from the date of the submission hereof to the States by the Congress."

Speaker of the House of Representatives.

*Vice President of the United States and
President of the Senate.*

724

Proposed in Congress:	**20 February 1933**
Sent to States:	**20 February 1933**
Ratified:	**5 December 1933**

Chapter 12

THE TWENTY-FIRST AMENDMENT

Section 1.
The eighteenth article of amendment to the Constitution of the United States is hereby repealed.

Section 2.
The transportation or importation into any State, Territory, or Possession of the United States for delivery or use therein of intoxicating liquors, in violation of the laws thereof, is hereby prohibited.

Section 3.
This article shall be inoperative unless it shall have been ratified as an amendment to the Constitution by conventions in the several States, as provided in the Constitution, within seven years from the date of the submission hereof to the States by the Congress.

Brief Summary

The Twenty-first Amendment is unique in that it is the only amendment to repeal a previous amendment, the Eighteenth. Section 1 of the Twenty-first Amendment ended the national ban on the manufacture, transportation, and sale of intoxicating liquors – that is, Prohibition. Section 2 turned the regulation of liquor sales, transportation, and distribution over to the states. Section 3 called for the amendment to be ratified in the states by state conventions (rather than by the state legislatures), the only constitutional amendment to carry this provision.

Timeline

16 January 1919   The Eighteenth Amendment is ratified.

16 February 1933   The Twenty-first Amendment passes in the US Senate.

20 February 1933   The Twenty-first Amendment passes in the US House of Representatives.

5 December 1933	The Twenty-first Amendment is ratified when Utah becomes the thirty-sixth state to ratify it; only two additional states out of the forty-eight subsequently ratified the amendment.
1966	Mississippi is the last of the "dry" states to end its ban on alcohol.
28 October 2000	Congress passes the Twenty-first Amendment Enforcement Act, amending the 1913 Webb-Kenyon Act.

Introduction

In 1919, the Eighteenth Amendment, after being ratified by a sufficient number of states, banned the sale of intoxicating liquors, beer, and wine across the nation. Even before the Eighteenth Amendment went into effect, 65% of America banned the sale of intoxicating liquors, so it was not an incredible step for the states to ratify an amendment making such bans part of the US Constitution.

The passage of the Eighteenth Amendment, however, set off a wave of law-breaking and anti-government feeling unseen since Shays' Rebellion in Massachusetts in 1786-87. During Prohibition, there was no army or force of arms that could stop the flow of liquor across the nation. Despite a massive government movement to halt liquor sales, "bootleggers" and "bathtub gin" gradually won the day, and authorities who caught lawbreakers discovered them to be also the leading citizens of these cities, who by day preached against the evils of alcohol but at night sipped the liquid that was supposedly banned. Courts were inundated with liquor prosecutions; in one year in New York City, there were 7,000 arrests, but only 17 convictions. Government agents (originally from the IRS) spread across the nation to hunt down illegal liquor businesses and shipments, also dealing with the residual crime that arose from bootlegging operations, most notably the use of massive firepower (the Thompson submachine gun, better known as the "Tommy" gun, earned its reputation during the Prohibition period). When Prohibition ended, the responsibilities of these government agents were combined into one agency that later became the Bureau of Alcohol, Tobacco, and Firearms (now the Bureau of Alcohol, Tobacco, Firearms and Explosives). Prior to the Eighteenth Amendment, states were slowly banning liquor sales, but after Prohibition they went the other way and, by 1925, six states, including New York, passed laws which forbid the police under state or local jurisdiction to arrest anyone for alcohol-related offenses, effectively overriding federal law, marking the death knell for Prohibition.

In hindsight, we can see that almost from the start, Prohibition's days were numbered. The states were granted extraordinary powers called "concurrent powers" that allowed them to fight the liquor traffic with the same force in law as the federal government, but it also caught them short, unable to fight with the same power as the feds. Bootleggers who traveled across state lines could avoid being chased by one state or the other. Men who smuggled illegal liquor in from Canada, or Mexico, of the Caribbean islands, could avoid certain state law enforcement by bribing the right people. Strapped for cash, especially by the late 1920s as the Depression took hold, the states were unable to fight a national war against a product. Historian Sue Davis wrote in 2004, "Although there had been attempts to repeal Prohibition since the Eighteenth Amendment went into effect in 1920, two major favors made its repeal possible in the early 1930s. First, the Congress that proposed the Eighteenth Amendment had a House of Representatives in which the seats were distributed in accordance with an apportionment based on the census of 1910, when a majority of Americans still lived in rural areas. Although the census of 1920 revealed a major shift of the population to urban areas, Congress did not reapportion those seats in the House after that census, waiting instead until 1929. As a result of reapportionment that year, twenty-one states – primarily in the South and West – lost seats in the House to states in the East. Moreover, the seats that those states gained tended to be located in the more metropolitan areas. In short, the western and southern rural supporters of Prohibition lost considerable power in Congress to eastern urban opponents."[1]

Believing that additional measures were necessary, in May 1929 President Herbert Hoover named former Attorney General George Wickersham to head up a national commission to study the enforcement picture in the United States and to report potential changes. The commission was officially called the US National Commission on Law Observance and Enforcement, but is better remembered as The Wickersham Commission. This group was tasked with "studying exhaustively the entire problem of the enforcement of our laws and the improvement of our judicial system, including the special problem and abuses growing out of the prohibition laws." With Wickersham as the commission chairman, the group included numerous national experts on the liquor problem but also law enforcement leaders, including former Secretary of War Newton D. Baker; Roscoe Pound, dean of the Harvard Law School; and Ada Comstock, the President of Radcliffe College. After two years of meetings and commission hearings, in 1931, the commission released its report.[2] The so-called Wickersham Report was a landmark of its time, breathlessly encapsulating the gist of the national problem in fourteen volumes. While Hoover had established the commission to report on new potential federal laws to make Prohibition stronger, the commission concluded that there should be additional resources sent into the fight against those wishing to break the laws against liquor. However, a minority of the commission's members held that Prohibition was an abject failure, and they split the commission's members into two beliefs: either the law should remain the same, no matter what it was doing to the nation, or the entire exercise should be undone – and the original law should be overturned.[3]

The World of New York, a Democratic newspaper, editorialized, "The commissioners are unanimous in sweeping away the pretension that the experiment of constitution; prohibition is within sight of success. There is apparently not one commissioner who believes that the 11 years trial thus far has given positive evidence that the revolutionary experiment can succeed."[4]

The Wickersham Commission, while not the catalyst that led to the repeal of the Eighteenth Amendment, was the proverbial "stepping stone" that allowed the majority of the American people, quietly demanding an end to Prohibition, to finally look at the issue and see that repeal was the only way forward. Although historians like to state that in the 1932 election, the Democrats rode the Prohibition issue to victory, they wholly ignore the fact that the 1932 GOP platform called for repeal as well. Both parties were playing for an audience already converted to the cause. Newspaper columnist Franklin Pierce Adams, known to the nation's newspaper readers as "F.P.A.," wrote in his column in *The World* on the Wickersham Commission:

"Prohibition is an awful flop.
We like it.
It can't stop what it's meant to stop.
We like it.
It's left a trail of graft and slime,
It don't prohibit worth a dime,
It's filled our land with vice and crime.
Nevertheless, we're for it."[5]

But Adams was not the only journalist or editorial writer to rail against Prohibition – H.L. Mencken wrote, "In brief, Prohibition is a failure, and it grows a worse failure every day. There was a time, shortly after the Eighteenth Amendment went into effect, when it showed some promise of being a success, especially in the farming regions, and on the strength of that promise very optimistic report were sent broadcast by the extremely diligent pressagents of the Anti-Saloon League, and a number of confiding foreigners – for example, Sir Arthur Newholme, the Englishman – were made to believe that the New Jerusalem was actually at hand. But that was simply because the great majority of Americans had not be taking the thing seriously – because they had been caught unawares by the extraordinarily drastic provisions of the Volstead Enforcement Act. The instant [that] they realized what was upon them they applied the national ingenuity and the national talent for corruption to the problem, and in six months it was solved."[6]

Democrat Franklin D. Roosevelt, the governor of New York State, rode to victory in the presidential election of 1932 based on an economy in the deep mire of depression, not the lure of ending prohibition. Nevertheless, the President-elect's promise of ending Prohibition through the amendment process was taken up quickly by Congress soon after the election results came in. According to historian Everett Somerville Brown, "In accordance with this latter pledge Senate Joint Representative 211 was introduced by Senator [John James] Blaine of Wisconsin on December 6, 1932. It proposed submitting the question of repeal of the Eighteenth Amendment to conventions in the states. The report of the Committee on the Judiciary, to which the resolution was referred, was printed in *The Congressional Record* on January 12. The resolution had been amended by the committee to provide for the submission of the proposal of repeal to legislatures of the states, instead of to conventions. This proposed change in procedure immediately aroused the criticism of officers of associations which had fought for years to persuade members of Congress to submit a repeal amendment to conventions in the states. Charles S. Rackemann, president of the Constitutional Liberty League, in a letter of January 9, 1933, to Senator [David Ignatius] Walsh of Massachusetts, wrote: "'The proposal that the amendment should be referred to State legislatures comes as a complete surprise. We had supposed that the plan of referring this question, so important in its relations to the fundamental principles of the Constitution, to conventions of the people meeting in the several States had received practically unanimous support.' Jouett Shouse, president of the Association against the Prohibition Amendment, protested in similar vein. After referring to the platform pledges of the two major parties, he continued: 'It would seem, therefore, wholly improbable that Con in submitting the resolution would flaunt these specific promises and would refer it for action to legislatures instead of to conventions...Moreover, it is obvious that the only method whereby popular expression on this proposition, which deals so intimately with the life and habits of the people, could be had is through the convention method of ratification.'"[7]

The final end of Prohibition came about because of the rise of the "wet" politicians, who favored repealing the Eighteenth Amendment, and the slow demise of the "dry" politicians who had pushed to get the amendment passed and ratified in the years after the First World War. *The Boston Globe* noted in 1932, "It was not until last Spring that any vigorous movement developed within Congress for [the] resubmission of the 18th Amendment, or modification of the Volstead act to legalize beer. On May 18 [1932] the Bingham 4 percent beer amendment failed of passage in the Senate, the vote being 28 for and 60 against. On the same day the Senate defeated the Tydings amendment legalizing 2.75 percent beer. The vote was 24 for and 61 against. An attempt to bring about a direct vote on the Hull-O'Connor beer bill was defeated in the House on May 23, the vote being 169 for and 228 against. On May 25 the Senate defeated the Bingham amendment to legalize and tax 2.75 percent beer."[8] By the early 1930s, the "wets" were outnumbering the "drys" in every office, from local to state to federal – the 1932 election, which brought a wave of liberal, "wet" Democrats into the US Senate and US House of Representatives, set the issue in concrete. Just how would the Congress undo a ratified amendment to the US Constitution? For a time, many in Congress desired a convention system: states would hold conventions and send notices to Washington showing their desire for a specific constitutional amendment to end Prohibition. Never before in our nation's history has such a convention system been utilized to secure an amendment, and the potential that some states would have differing standards for the sale of liquor gave pause to the suggestion. When Senator Blaine introduced his proposed amendment in the US Senate, the potential for a convention system rapidly ended. Instead, as with all of the other amendments, wide debate on what exactly should be done began in earnest. Once all legislation to either "deauthorize" the Volstead Act or to legalize the sale of beer had failed, supporters of ending prohibition realized that only a full-scale amendment, which would fully repeal the original amendment, would suffice. The ultimate proposal to repeal prohibition was introduced in the US Senate through Joint Resolution 211. It passed the US Senate on 16 February 1933 by a vote of 63-23, and passed the US House of Representatives four days later by a vote of 289-121. Signed by the Speaker of the House and the Vice President, Charles Curtis (in his last days in the office), was then sent to the states for ratification. From Graph 1, we can see how quickly the states moved on ratifying the amendment, culminating in its ratification on 5 December 1933, when Utah became the 36th state to ratify it.

For the first time, an amendment, a change to the original Constitution, had been undone, via another amendment. The official ratification of the Twenty-first Amendment set off massive celebrations across the nation, as people came out from the shadows and drank legal liquor for the first time in over 13 years.

As we near 80 years after the end of Prohibition, we ask what came of this "noble experiment." While it did set off an unprecedented wave of crime in America, it did have some positive effects: overall, drinking dramatically decreased (30%-50%), and deaths from alcohol consumption dropped to their lowest levels. Rates of deaths of men from cirrhosis of the liver, the prime disease from alcoholism, dropped from 29.5 per 100,000 men in 1911 to 10.7 per 100,000 men in 1929. Today, with continued abuse of alcohol, tens of thousands of Americans die in DUI-related car crashes, and domestic violence is on the rise, as are alcohol-abuse related illnesses. Three years after the Twenty-first Amendment ended Prohibition, two reformed drinkers, Bill Wilson and Dr. Robert Smith, formed an association to help their fellow alcoholics – known today as Alcoholics Anonymous. Mothers Against Drunk Driving (MADD), founded in 1980 by the mother of a child killed by a drunk driver, is one of the leading organizations aimed at fighting drunk driving and advocating for stronger driving laws relating to drink. Historian Ken-

Footnotes, Sources and Further Reading for this chapter appears on page 785

neth Rose wrote, "Some 15.3 million Americans met the criteria for alcohol abuse, dependence, or both in 1988, and in 1990 alcohol was a factor in half of all fatal traffic accidents and alcohol-related mortality accounted for about 5 percent of all deaths in the United States. In its 1993 report on alcohol and health the Department of Health and Human Services observed that one of the consequences of alcohol use is that ''everyone, even those who abstain, may be adversely affected by someone else's drinking.'''[9] Today, the Temperance movement is seen as a quaint 19th century movement. In fact, the Prohibition Party, the leading political arm of the movement, still runs presidential candidates, although its influence is far below what it once was.

The Twenty-first Amendment, particularly Section 2, has played a prominent role in the nation's judicial history. Shortly after the amendment was ratified, the Court affirmed the principle that the states are authorized to make distinctions in regulating imported liquors (i.e., from another state) and those of domestic (i.e., within the state) origin. Thus, in *State Board of Equalization v. Young's Market Co.* (299 U.S. 59 {1936}), the Court upheld a California statute mandating a $500 annual license fee for beer importers to the state and a $750 fee for the right to manufacture beer. In *Mahoney v. Joseph Triner Corp.* (304 U.S. 401 {1938}), the Court upheld a Minnesota statute that barred a manufacturer or wholesaler from importing intoxicating liquors that contained more than 25 percent alcohol and that are ready for sale without further processing. In *Indianapolis Brewing Co. v. Liquor Commission, et al.* (305 U.S. 391 {1939}) the Court upheld a Michigan statute that barred the importation of beer from a state that discriminated against Michigan beer. These and other cases relinquished to the states broad powers to regulate the liquor and brewing industries.

Later Court decisions had a bearing on the intersection between Section 2 of the amendment and other provisions of the Constitution. In general, these decisions eroded the authority of the states over liquor by holding that the Commerce Clause takes precedence, along with other constitutional guarantees, such as those provided by the Fourteenth Amendment. In 1939 the Court, in *Ziffrin, Inc. v. Reeves* (308 U.S. 132 {1939}), upheld a Kentucky statute requiring transporters of Kentucky liquor to be licensed common carriers. The basis of the ruling, however, was not the state's power to regulate the transportation of liquor under the Twenty-first Amendment but the conclusion that the statute did not burden the Commerce Clause. In *Carter v. Virginia* (321 U.S. 131{1944}), the Court essentially ignored the amendment in upholding statutes that regulated the transport of liquor cargoes that originated and ended outside the regulating states-again basing the decision on Commerce Clause considerations. In *Hostetter v. Idlewild Bon Voyage Liquor Corp.* (377 U.S. 324 {1964}), the Court held that although the Twenty-first Amendment gives a state the power to regulate the transportation of liquor through the state, the Commerce Clause bars the state from preventing transactions supervised by the Board of Customs regarding liquor for delivery to customers in foreign countries. In *Craig v. Boren* (429 U.S. 190 {1976}), the Court rejected Twenty-first Amendment arguments to invalidate a state law that specified different minimum drinking ages for men and women, holding that the law violated the Equal Protection Clause of the Fourteenth Amendment. In *California Retail Liquor Dealers Association v. Midcal Aluminum, Inc.* (445 U.S. 97 {1980}), the Court asserted that there is no "bright line" between the enforcement powers of the state and those of the federal government, which retains power to regulate liquor when the Commerce Clause applies. In *Bacchus Imports, Ltd. v. Dias* (468 U.S. 263, 276 {1984}), the Court rejected Twenty-first Amendment arguments used to justify economic protectionism in the application of discriminatory liquor taxes when those taxes impeded interstate commerce. Finally, in *Granholm v. Heald*, (544 U.S. 460 {2005}), the Court struck down state laws that permitted in-state wineries to ship wine directly to consumers but that prohibited out-of-state wineries from doing the same, holding that the Twenty-first Amendment does not annul the Commerce Clause.

Debate in Congress

During the debate in the US Senate, 16 February 1933, the day that the proposed prohibition repeal amendment passed that body, arguments ranged from a discussion over the attempted assassination of President-elect Franklin D. Roosevelt to whether or not the Eighteenth Amendment, under threat of repeal, should in fact be strengthened.

WITHDRAWAL OF CLOTURE PETITION

Mr. BINGHAM.[10] Mr. President, on behalf of those who signed the cloture petition regarding the motion of the Senator from Wisconsin [Mr. BLAINE] to take up the proposed amendment to the Constitution, in view of the fact that the vote was had on yesterday, I ask to withdraw the petition.

The VICE PRESIDENT. Is there objection? The Chair hears none, and so is ordered.

AMENDMENT TO THE CONSTITUTION – REPEAL OF PROHIBITION

Mr. REED.[11] Mr. President, I wish to enter a motion to reconsider the vote by which the amendment of the Senator from Arkansas [Mr. ROBINSON],[12] striking out section 3 of the committee amendment, was agreed to last night.

The VICE PRESIDENT. The motion will be entered.

Mr. GLASS.[13] Mr. President, I desire formally to offer Senate Joint Resolution 202 as a substitute for Senate Joint Resolution 211.

The substitute is as follows:

Resolved, etc., That the following is proposed as an amendment to the Constitution of the United States, which shall be valid to all intents and purposes as part of the Constitution when ratified by conventions in three-fourths of the several States:

"Article _____

"SECTION 1. Article XVIII of the amendments to this Constitution is hereby repealed. The sale of intoxicating liquors within the United States or any territory subject to the jurisdiction thereof for consumption at the place of sale (commonly known as a saloon), and the transportation of intoxicating liquors into any State, Territory, District, or possession of the United States in which the manufacture, sale, and transportation of intoxicating liquors are prohibited by law, are hereby prohibited. The Congress and the several States, Territories, and possessions shall have concurrent power to enforce this article by appropriate legislation.

"Sec. 2. This article shall be inoperative unless it shall have been ratified as an amendment to the Constitution by conventions in the several States, as provided in the Constitution, within seven years from the date of the submission hereof to the States by the Congress."

[...]

The Senate resumed the consideration of Mr. Blaine's motion that the Senate proceed to consider the joint resolution (S.J. Res. 211) proposing an amendment to the Constitution of the United States.

Mr. ROBINSON of Indiana.[14] Mr. President, in all that has been said by the eminent Senator from Arkansas [Mr. ROBINSON] and my good friend the distinguished Senator from West Virginia [Mr. HATFIELD][15] I am in hearty accord. The incident at Miami was deplorable;[16] the entire country is shocked and grieved.

Mr. FESS.[17] Mr. President, will the Senator yield for a moment? Mr. ROBINSON of Indiana. I yield.

Mr. FESS. I wanted to ask the Senator, who is a good lawyer, whether, in his judgment, there could not be some additional protection accorded to the man who occupies the Presidency of the country by the imposition of a more drastic penalty upon those who undertake to do a dastardly deed and yet fail, and by the fact of failure are relieved of the penalty that otherwise would be administered?

Mr. ROBINSON of Indiana. The Senator means the death penalty?

Mr. FESS. Yes; whether it is not feasible to undertake some additional protection to the high office of the Presidency.

Mr. ROBINSON of Indiana. I do not know what the result would be, Mr. President, but, so far as I am personally concerned, I believe that anybody who attempts to assassinate the President of the United States or the President elect of the United States ought to suffer the death penalty.

I desired now, Mr. President, to discuss the joint resolution which is pending before the Senate. The PRESIDENT pro tempore. The unfinished business is before the Senate.

Mr. ROBINSON of Indiana. Mr. President, for the past three days we have been discussing the question of whether or not intoxicating alcoholic beverages should be permitted to return legally. Three valuable days, three days during every one of the 24 hours of each of which untold thousands of people in America have been crying for bread, have been wasted in an academic discussion of the resolution that can have no effect possibly for the next 2, 3, 4, or 5 years. While measures are before this body that, if enacted into law, would provide relief for suffering humanity in America and alleviate agricultural conditions that are well-nigh intolerable, we continue to discuss the question of booze and the American saloon and whether or not they shall be tolerated in the future. We fiddle while the Nation burns, discussing a resolution which, if adopted, can only bring more misery to the country, and fail to consider measures that would unquestionably bring relief to millions of people the American flag.

Mr. President, let nobody be deceived. This resolution is not for submission. Any one voting for the adoption of this resolution votes for the return of the American saloon with all its evils.

I have heard that some legislators occasionally believe that when they vote to submit an amendment of this kind somehow or other they are relieved of any responsibility either way. They take a neutral position. As a matter of fact, Mr. President, whoever votes for the joint resolution now before the Senate votes directly and deliberately for the return of the saloon. No other interpretation can be placed upon any vote in the affirmative. Not only that, but whoever votes for the adoption of this joint resolution requests the people in the State from which he comes to support that vote when the question comes up for decision by the various Commonwealths.

Mr. President, I understand perfectly well that anything I may say on this subject will doubtless have little effect. I assume it will influence no votes in his body; but I should feel myself derelict in duty did I not present to the Senate and to the country some observations that suggest my own line of reasoning with reference to this problem.

[...]

Mr. GLASS. Mr. President, on last July 16 the Senate voted on Senate Joint Resolution 202 offered by me and by a recorded vote of 37 yeas to 21 nays decided to make it the order of business. Subsequently it was displaced by an appropriation bill. I have now offered it as a substitute for the pending Senate Joint Resolution 211.

I had hoped, Mr. President, to discuss the question in a practical way. I have never in either House of Congress in a service of 30 years felt it desirable to speak only for home consumption. If the Senate has no desire to hear these grave matters discussed I am not going to exhaust my reserve strength or that of the Senate either by undertaking a discussion of the question. Therefore, with a meager attendance of Senators, I shall accordingly abbreviate as much as possible my intended exposition of Senate Joint Resolution 202.

Mr. President, I have never voted anything but the prohibition ticket in my life when the issue was live and practical. I am not a zealot on the subject, but whenever opportunity has afforded I have invariably voted to banish intoxicating drinks. However, I must realize, as other observant persons must realize, that the experiment of national prohibition seems to have proven an utter failure. What the causes may be, no man may accurately say. There are a multiplicity of them and they are of a varied nature. One of them in my considered judgment is the fact that moral lepers and statutory criminals have had the effrontery to assume leadership of the moral forces in the country. I think that fact had made a tremendous contribution to the reaction throughout the United States against prohibition as a national problem. There are some few things worse than liquor. But in any event, whatever the causes are, whatever their nature, every observant person must know that there had been this reaction.

There has been a tremendous demand for a resubmission of the question to the States for further determination. It has always been my view that there is just as much reason and equity in the general demand for resubmission of the prohibition problem as there was in the demand in the first instance for the submission of the eighteenth amendment to the States for ratification or rejection. Therefore, reluctantly I have joined the forces which are demanding a resubmission of the question.

I was on the platform committee of the national Democratic convention at Chicago, and there was no difference of judgment as to the desirability of submitting the question to the States for further consideration. The Democratic convention of my own State, to which I owe primary allegiance and of which I am their representative here in the Senate and not of any national convention, declared for a resubmission of the question. But concurrently with that declaration the Virginia Democratic State platform denounced the return of the saloon and by implication advocated a submission in the form of a proclamation against the return of the saloon.

The Democratic National Convention at Chicago denounced the return of the saloon. It may be said that by implication at least it advocated action by the States against the return of this alone and that is granted. But that declaration, I contend, did not necessarily preclude a constitutional reservation against the return of the saloon. On the other hand, the Republican National Convention at Chicago textually and in terms demanded a constitutional reservation against the return of the saloon.

[...]

Mr. BULKLEY.[18] Mr. President, will the Senator from Virginia yield to me?

The VICE PRESIDENT. Does the Senator from Virginia yield to the Senator from Ohio?

Mr. GLASS. I yield.

Mr. BULKLEY. The Republican platform expressly declares that as to this particular subject no one may be bound by the platform announcement.

Mr. GLASS. The Republican platform expressly declares that while in dealing "with the evils inherent in the liquor traffic," the States shall be allowed "to deal with the problem as their citizens may determine," such dealing shall always be subject "to the power of the Federal Government to protect those States where prohibition may exist and safeguard our citizens everywhere from the return of the saloon and attendant abuses."

Mr. BULKLEY. But the platform goes on to declare...

Mr. GLASS. Oh, I know.

Mr. BULKLEY. The platform goes on to declare that no Republican need be bound by its declaration on this subject, and that it shall not come in conflict with anybody's conscience.

Mr. GLASS. I do not intend that my party platform shall ever come in conflict with either my judgment or my conscience, if the Senator from Ohio wants my view on the subject.

[...]

Mr. FLETCHER.[19] Mr. President, will the Senator yield?

The VICE PRESIDENT. Does the Senator from Virginia yield to the Senator from Florida?

Mr. GLASS. I yield.

Mr. FLECTCHER. I am wondering if the Senator would be willing to change his amendment, in the nature of a substitute, beginning in line 7, page 2, where it reads:

The Congress and the several States, Territories, and possessions shall have concurrent power to enforce this article by appropriate legislation.

In other words, I do not like the "concurrent power" provision.

Mr. GLASS. I will say to the Senator when the proper time arrives I will be glad to make any reasonable concession that will assure us the prospect of submitting this question to the States.

Mr. FLETCHER. Very well. I should like, however, to have the Senator devote a little thought to this phase of the question. I recognize, of course, that the Congress has power to regulate interstate commerce and to prohibit the movement of wet goods into dry States and that sort of thing. That is in the law now; we do not need to express that in a new amendment to the Constitution.

Mr. GLASS. Oh, I understand that, Mr. President.

Mr. FLETCHER. But as to the control of the saloon and the provision of the proposal the Senator offers with reference to the sale on the premises, it seems to me that that might well be left entirely to the States and not have the power concurrently vested in the Federal Government and the States.

Mr. WALSH of Montana.[20] Mr. President...

The VICE PRESIDENT. Does the Senator from Virginia yield to the Senator from Montana?

Mr. GLASS. Yes; I yield to the Senator from Montana.

Mr. WALSH of Montana. I wish to say a word, in view of what has just been stated by the Senator from Florida in relation to the second paragraph of the joint resolution as tendered by the committee.

It is true that the original Constitution authorizes Congress to prohibit the transfer of intoxicating liquors in interstate commerce. It is held, however, that that authority simply indicates the intention to have commerce free except as Congress otherwise direct. It has been held that under the existing Constitution the right obtains on the part of any citizen to pass his goods into another State, and they remain under the protection of the Federal Constitution until they actually reach the hands of the cosignee; so that they can not be stopped at the State line nor there fall under the jurisdiction of the State authorities, but the goods will not fall under the jurisdiction of the State authorities until they actually get into the possession of the cosignee who may live in the center of the State. Meanwhile all manner of opportunity is afforded for the diversion of the intoxicating liquors from the cosignee to whom they are addressed. Likewise, even then, the intoxicating liquor is protected by the commerce clause; if it remains on the siding in the car of the transportation company, it still remains under that protection, and if it goes into a warehouse belonging to the transportation company it remains under the protection of the Federal statute, and is immune from any control by State statutes until it actually reaches the possession of the cosignee. The purpose of the provision in the resolution reported by the committee was to make the intoxicating liquor subject to the laws of the State once it passed the State line and before it gets into the hands of the cosignee as well as thereafter. It was so decided in a case reported in One hundred and seventieth United States Reports, with which, I think, the profession generally is not particularly familiar.

Mr. GLASS. Mr. President, in my own interpretation of the resolution as I have presented it, there can be no cosignee of intoxicating liquors in a dry State. Liquors may be shipped across a State in interstate commerce from one wet State to another wet State, but the resolution as I have drafted it prohibits the shipment of intoxicating liquors into a State whose laws prohibit the manufacture, sale, or transportation of liquors. So I have met the objection that we are undertaking to interfere with interstate commerce as between States which authorize the manufacture, transportation, and sale of liquors; but there can be no cosignee in dry territory under the terms of my proposed amendment to the Constitution.

Mr. President, at every point in the presidential campaign when submission of this question was discussed, and whenever the objection was raised as to the return of the saloon, assurances were given that both parties, with unexampled unanimity, were opposed to the return of the saloon. The Democratic national platform, in spirit and by suggestion – indeed, by denunciation – objected to the return of the saloon. The Republican platform in text insisted upon a constitutional guaranty against the return of the saloon. So my joint resolution complies with both the Democratic and the Republican platforms; and that is the only way you are ever going to get the question submitted at all, as it requires a two-thirds vote. Moreover, not only is it the only way you are ever going to get it submitted but it is the only way you are ever going to get it ratified by 36 States of the Union.

[...]

Mr. REED. Mr. President, will the Senator yield for a question?

The VICE PRESIDENT. Does the Senator from Virginia yield to the Senator from Pennsylvania?

Mr. GLASS. I do.

Mr. REED. May I preface the question by saying that I am in sympathy with every word the Senator has thus far uttered on this subject.

A good many Senators are obviously bothered by the continuance of Federal control in this matter; and while they are anxious to see the saloon outlawed, they would like to see it done by prohibition on State action rather than continuing this unsuccessful Federal effort to carry its police power into the States. I am wondering whether the Senator feels that the last sentence in section 1 of his amendment is essential. That is the one which gives concurrent power to Congress.

Mr. GLASS. No; I do not think it is essential. If I could be brought to believe that the joint resolution stands a better chance of passage by the elimination of that sentence, I should be glad to eliminate it, because the balance of the joint resolution gives us a constitutional prohibition against any return of the saloon.

Mr. REED. That is just what I want to see; and the question of the Senator from Florida [Mr. FLETCHER] a little while ago seemed to be animated by the same thought I had – that there are many votes that would be secured for the joint resolution if that grant of concurrent power to Congress were eliminated.

Mr. GLASS. That being so, I should be perfectly willing to eliminate that one sentence from the measure. All I want is a constitutional guaranty against the return of this abominable saloon system of dispensing intoxicating liquors – that is all – and if we write it into the Constitution I assume that no State would ever even undertake to violate the text of the Constitution by licensing a saloon.

Mr. REED. Obviously, if it did, its licensing law would be invalid. Mr. GLASS. Why, absolutely so.

[...]

Mr. GORE.[21] Mr. President, the purpose of the substitute offered by the Senator from Virginia is to prevent the return of the saloon. I share his views upon that subject. I do not wish to see the saloon resurrected. I have often said that the saloon was as dead as human slavery. I have often said that it had no more chance to rise from the dead than human slavery. I can not vote to falsify my own words. I can not help to roll the stone from its grave. I shall, therefore, vote for the Senator's substitute. But I feel obliged to say that, whether his substitute is adopted or rejected, owing to an obligation imposed upon me by the organized Democracy of Oklahoma, I can not vote for either of the resolutions.

[...]

Mr. President, when, some 14 years ago, 46 States voted through their legislatures to place the eighteenth amendment in the Constitution it was not due to any sudden, overnight change of heart. Adoption of the eighteenth amendment was the culmination of many years of observation and experience; the result of testing many and various means for the control of liquor. It was the culmination of a long series of "noble experiments."

The States had tried, with high license, with local option, with State dispensaries, with other means, to make a law-abiding person of John Barleycorn. All these efforts had failed. The fact is John Barleycorn is not cut out for a law-abiding citizen. So that States and the people were looking for something better. They believed that with State and Federal regulation combined John could be looked after and guarded and held in restraint a little more closely in the public interest than he ever had been before.

A good start was made with prohibition. Then New York State, with a great liquor stronghold within its borders and a city government that never had obeyed any liquor law, went back on its agreement. New York early became a backslider. It repealed its State enforcement act and has insisted ever since that prohibition is a failure. A few other States in which the liquor interests and liquor parties have always been strongly – intrenched [sic] followed New York's example in nullifying the Constitution.

Of course, this did not help the experiment in national prohibition, nor has it been helped by the constant stream of propaganda against the law that has come from that part of the country.

Frankly, I am for continuing the experiment nationally. We went through similar experiences in Kansas for 30 years before we had really effective prohibition enforcement. It must be admitted that national prohibition has not been entirely successful up to date; but I am satisfied, and the most authentic statistics we have all indicate, that prohibition is doing more good than harm – if it is doing harm. The records of the Treasury and of the Department of Justice, studied calmly and dispassionately, prove the increasing efficiency of the law's enforcement.

I do not believe we should expect to wipe out an age-old curse like the liquor evil by statutory law in a dozen years nor in a score of years. If we are really making progress, as in many respects we undoubtedly are, we should be encouraged by this progress, not discouraged, and should proceed to make more progress.

It is said that in spite of prohibition a man can get a drink almost anywhere in the United States. Doubtless that is more or less true. Also a man may still commit murder anywhere in United States, and many men do, although laws against murder has been on the statute books for ages.

Mr. President, if there is any ideal way of handling the liquor traffic I do not believe the world has yet discovered it. In Canada the wets told the people if they would repeal prohibition, lawlessness would decline. Statistics from the office of the Dominion's attorney general show that during the eight years, from 1923 to 1930, lawlessness in the Dominion increased from 18 to 153 per cent. Canada's jails have never been so full as they are now, nor her courts so crowded with business.

All over the world a colossal struggle is going on between right and wrong. Crime has increased everywhere. As the population of the world is larger than ever before, I doubt if it ever has witnessed so gigantic a contest between good and evil as is now taking place.

[...]

MR. BORAH.[22] Mr. President, after listening to the debate to-day, particularly on the subject of the saloon, I have become convinced that there will be no way to prevent the return of the saloon if the eighteenth amendment shall be repealed. I agree with everything the able Senator from Virginia [Mr. GLASS] has said with reference to the saloon, and I am just as much opposed to its return as anyone could possibly be. No power on earth could keep that institution clean, or make it respectable, and I do not want to see it returned. For that reason I am going to vote against the repeal of the eighteenth amendment.

Mr. President, what is the situation now? We have in the Constitution the eighteenth amendment, which prohibits the sale of intoxicating liquors, and prohibits their being sold and drunk upon the premises where sold. Gentleman come to us now and say that we must repeal that amendment because we can not enforce it. Yet they say to us in the next breath, "If you legalize the sale of intoxicating liquors, the National Government can effectively prevent their being drunk on the premises where sold." In other words, we are asked to turn back to the States the power to do everything except control the places where liquor may be consumed. In my opinion, under any possible amendment which can be drawn, that would be a practical impossibility. If we cannot prevent liquor being drunk on the premises of 5,000 saloons in New York to-night, when it is illegal to sell it, could we prevent it being drunk upon those premises after it was made legal to sell it?

The only way to fight the American saloon is to fight it as it was fought when we adopted the eighteenth amendment, that is, to outlaw the liquor traffic and make it an outlaw under the laws of the United States. If we have not the courage to enforce the law against sale, shall we have the courage to enforce the infinitely more difficult task of preventing the place of drinking legally sold liquor?

[...]

Can we expect the States of the Union which have now repealed all enforcement laws, which have repealed all laws by which to enforce the Constitution, to give us aid in controlling the places where liquor shall be drunk, after we have given authority to sell it and dispose of it? Certainly not. It would be practically an impossible proposition.

Mr. President, I venture to say here upon the floor of the Senate to-day that, just so surely as the eighteenth amendment shall be repealed and the liquor traffic turned back to the States, the saloon as it was known in the old days will return, and that brutal institution, where criminals consort and crime is bred will be running in full blast in less than 60 days after the eighteenth amendment shall have been repealed. Yea, more than that, it would be running within 30 days after the beer bill, which is now upon the calendar for action, shall have been passed.

Governments have tried to deal with the liquor question for a hundred years – yes; for 200 years – yet they have never been able to devise any scheme by which they could control the lawlessness of the liquor traffic. The liquor traffic itself is lawless, and to say that we can control it by permitting liquor to be sold, but providing that it shall not be drunk that at this or that particular place, is imposing an impossibility which no governmental agency could execute. Make the sale legal and give the States power and right to set up a system for sale and distribution; make the drinking where sold illegal but give the Government which makes it illegal no power to execute its will or enforce its laws; that is the most consummate legal riddle yet devised by the genius of man.

[...]

Mr. TYDINGS.[23] Mr. President, I would like to offer an amendment to the substitute of the Senator from Virginia. On page 2, line 10, and a new sentence, as follows:

No national taxes shall be laid for collection against any intoxicating liquor for beverage purposes which shall be prohibited as a commodity in interstate commerce by the laws of the United States.

I ask unanimous consent to have one minute to explain my amendment.

Mr. BORAH. I object.

The VICE PRESIDENT. Objection is made. The question is on the amendment of the Senator from Maryland to the substitute of the Senator from Virginia.

The amendment was rejected.

The VICE PRESIDENT. The question is on a substitute of the Senator from Virginia [Mr. GLASS] for the amendment of the Senator from Wisconsin [Mr. BLAINE].[24]

Mr. WATSON.[25] Let us have the yeas and nays.

The yeas and nays were ordered.

Several SENATORS. Let the substitute be read.

The VICE PRESIDENT. It will be read.

The CHIEF CLERK. Is proposed to substitute for Senate Joint Resolution 211 the following:

Senate Joint Resolution 202

Joint resolution proposing an amendment to the Constitution of the United States relative to the eighteenth amendment

Resolved by the Senate and House of Representatives of the United States of America in Congress assembled (two-thirds of each House concurring therein), That the following is proposed as an amendment to the Constitution of the United States, which shall be valid to all intents and purposes as part of the Constitution when ratified by conventions in three-fourths of the several States:

"ARTICLE ____

"SECTION 1. Article XVIII of the amendments to this Constitution is hereby repealed. The sale of intoxicating liquors within the United States or any territory subject to the jurisdiction thereof for consumption at the place of sale (commonly known as a saloon), and the transportation of intoxicating liquors into any State, Territory, District, or possession of the United States in which the manufacture, sale, and transportation of intoxicating liquors are prohibited by law, are hereby prohibited. The Congress and the several States, Territories, and possessions shall have concurrent power to enforce this article by appropriate legislation.

"Sec. 2. This article shall be inoperative unless it shall have been ratified as an amendment to the Constitution by conventions in the several States, as provided in the Constitution, within seven years from the date of the submission hereof to the States by the Congress."

The VICE PRESIDENT. The yeas and nays have been ordered, and the Secretary will call the roll.

The Chief Clerk proceeded to call the roll.

Mr. BRATTON[26] (when his name was called). Repeating the announcement of my pair and its transfer, I vote "nay."

Mr. WAGNER[27] (when Mr. COPELAND's[28] name was called). I wish to announce that my colleague the senior Senator from New York [Mr. COPELAND] is absent because of the death of his father. If he were present and not paired, he would vote "nay."

Mr. FESS (when his name was called). I'm announcing my pair as before with the Senator from New York [Mr. COPELAND], I wish to state that were I at liberty to vote I would vote "yea."

Mr. FRAZIER[29] (when his name was called). On this question I have a pair with the junior Senator from Louisiana [Mr. LONG].[30] Not knowing how he would vote, I withhold my vote.

Mr. NORRIS[31] (when Mr. HOWELL's[32] name was called). The junior Senator from Nebraska [Mr. HOWELL] is absent on official business of the Senate. He is paired with the Senator from New Mexico [Mr. BRATTON]. If my colleague [Mr. HOWELL] were present and voting, on this question he would vote "yea."

Mr. THOMAS of Idaho[33] (when his name was called). Making the same announcement as before, I withhold my vote. If permitted to vote, I would vote "nay."

The roll call was concluded.

Mr. FESS. I wish to announce that the Senator from Virginia [Mr. SWANSON][34] has a general pair with the Senator from Illinois [Mr. GLENN].[35]

The result was announced – yeas 38, nays 46

[...]

Editorial note: Other amendments, including one from Senator Reed, were also voted on, but were all defeated. Debate then turned to the original amendment introduced, that of Senator Blaine of Wisconsin.

Mr. REED. Mr. President, the sentiment of the Senate has been sufficiently shown, I think, to make it clear that there would be nothing gained by taking the time to vote on the motion to reconsider the action of the Senate in striking out section 3. Therefore I will not make the motion.

The VICE PRESIDENT. The motion entered by the Senator from Pennsylvania is withdrawn.

Mr. WATSON. Mr. President, may I renew the motion?

Mr. ROBINSON of Arkansas. Mr. President, I rise to a point of order.

The VICE PRESIDENT. The Senator will state it.

Mr. ROBINSON of Arkansas. Under the unanimous consent agreement under which the Senate is proceeding, a vote on a motion to reconsider is not in order.

The VICE PRESIDENT. The unanimous consent agreement limits the voting to amendments.

If there be no further amendments, the question is, Shall the joint resolution, as amended, be ordered to be engrossed for a third reading and read the third time?

The joint resolution, as amended, was ordered to be engrossed for a third reading, and read the third time. The question is, Shall the joint resolution pass?

Mr. BARKLEY[36] and other Senators demanded the yeas and nays, and they were ordered.

[...]

The roll call resulted – yeas 63, nays 23, as follows:

YEAS – 63

Ashurst	Bulow	Glenn	Keyes
Austin	Byrnes	Grammer	King
Bailey	Clark	Hale	LaFollette
Bankhead	Connally	Harrison	Lewis
Barbour	Coolidge	Hastings	McKellar
Barkley	Couzens	Hayden	McNary
Bingham	Cutting	Hébert	Metcalf
Black	Davis	Hull	Moses
Blaine	Dill	Johnson	Neely
Bratton	Fletcher	Kean	Nye
Bulkley	Frazier	Kendrick	Oddie

Note: the vote's results were split on a single page, owing for the "un-alphabetical" listing which follows:

Patterson	Russell	Trammell	Walsh, Mass.
Pittman	Shipstead	Tydings	Walsh, Mont.
Reed	Shortridge	Vandenberg	Watson
Reynolds	Smith	Wagner	White
Robinson, Ark.	Swanson	Walcott	

NAYS – 23

Borah	Dickinson	McGill	Smoot
Brookhart	Glass	Norbeck	Steiwer
Capper	Goldsborough	Norris	Stephens
Caraway	Gore	Robinson, Ind.	Thomas, Okla.
Costigan	Hatfield	Schuyler	Townsend
Dale	Logan	Sheppard	

NOT VOTING – 10

Broussard	Fess	Long	Wheeler
Carey	George	Schall	
Copeland	Howell	Thomas, Idaho	

The VICE PRESIDENT. On this question the yeas are 63, the nays are 23. More than two-thirds having voted in the affirmative, the joint resolution is passed.

کویوکویوکویوکویوکو

The debate in the US House occurred 20 February 1933, four days after the debate in the Senate. It was apparent from the beginning that those who wanted the Eighteenth Amendment repealed knew they had enough votes, and those opposed to repeal knew that they could not stop the movement towards passage of the Twenty-first Amendment.

REPEAL OF THE EIGHTEENTH AMENDMENT

Mr. RAINEY.[37] Mr. Speaker, I move to suspend the rules and take from the Speaker's table the Senate joint resolution [sic] (S.J. Res. 211) proposing an amendment to the Continue of the United States and agree to the same.

The Clerk read the Senate joint resolution, as follows:

Resolved by the Senate and House of Representatives of the United States of America in Congress assembled (two-thirds of each House concurring therein), That the following is proposed as an amendment to the Constitution of the United States, which shall be valid to all intents and purposes as part of the Constitution when ratified by conventions in three-fourths of the several States:

"ARTICLE _____

"Section 1. The eighteenth article of amendment to the Constitution of the United States is hereby repealed.

"Sec. 2. The transportation or importation into any State, Territory, or possession of the United States for delivery or use therein of intoxicating liquors, in violation of the laws thereof, is hereby prohibited.

"Sec. 3. This article shall be inoperative unless it shall have been ratified as an amendment to the Constitution by conventions in the several States, as provided in the Constitution, within seven years from the date of the submission hereof to the States by the Congress."

The SPEAKER. Is a second demanded? Mr. DYER.[38] I demand a second.

Mr. BLANTON.[39] A point of order, Mr. Speaker.

The SPEAKER. The gentleman will state it.

Mr. BLANTON. It is impossible for Democrats over on this side to get any time to oppose this repeal resolution from the majority leader, who has moved to pass it under suspension of the rules, and it is necessary to have some one demand a second who is against it, and who will yield his time to the opposition, and we will have only 20 minutes' debate to the side.

The SPEAKER. The general will have some one against it when the Member qualifies.

Mr. DYER. I demand a second.

The SPEAKER. Is the gentleman from Missouri opposed to the resolution?

Mr. DYER. I am not.

The SPEAKER. The gentleman does not qualify.

Footnotes, Sources and Further Reading for this chapter appears on page 785

Mr. MOORE of Ohio.[40] Mr. Speaker, I demand a second.

The SPEAKER. Is the gentleman opposed to the resolution?

Mr. MOORE of Ohio. I am opposed to the resolution.

Mr. RAINEY. Mr. Speaker, I ask unanimous consent that a second be considered as ordered.

Mr. SNELL.[41] Mr. Speaker, I would like to ask the gentleman from Illinois if it is his purpose to divide the time between those in favor and those opposed, or will he yield to those only who are in favor of the resolution?

Mr. RAINEY. I am going to yield only to those who are for the resolution, but I intend to yield to gentlemen on that side.

Mr. SNELL. And the gentleman from Ohio, Mr. Moore, will yield time to those opposed to the resolution?

Mr. RAINEY. Yes.

Mr. DYER. Reserving the right to object...

Mr. BLANTON. There is no question of objection. I make a point of order. I ask for the regular order.

The SPEAKER. The regular order is, a second has been demanded, and it takes unanimous consent to agree that the second shall be considered as ordered. Is there objection to the request of the gentleman from Illinois?

There was no objection.

The SPEAKER. The gentleman from Illinois is recognized for 20 minutes, and the gentleman from Ohio [Mr. MOORE] for 20 minutes.

Mr. RAINEY. Mr. Speaker, I am not going to discuss this resolution except to quote from a speech made by the proponent of prohibition, Senator Sheppard, of Texas, in the Senate, July 30, 1917, Congressional Record, pages 5553 and 5554, in which he states among other statements...

Mr. RANKIN.[42] Mr. Speaker, I make the point of order that the gentleman from Illinois has no right to attack a Senator on the floor of the House.

Mr. RAINEY. I am not attacking any Senator, I am approving of what he said.

Mr. RANKIN. It is an indirect attack, and he can not read from the Senate proceedings.

The SPEAKER. The point of order made by the gentleman from Mississippi is well taken. Speaker Longworth held in an elaborate ruling that a Member of the House could not refer to a Senator and quote what he said. The gentleman from Illinois is recognized.

Mr. SABATH.[43] A parliamentary inquiry.

The SPEAKER. The gentleman will state it.

Mr. SABATH. Has not a Member a right to quote anything that a Senator said?

The SPEAKER. The Chair has just ruled on that.

Mr. RAINEY. Then, Mr. Speaker, I say this on my own responsibility. I would vote to submit any amendment to the States in order to preserve the right of petition, and for that reason I am voting for this. I voted for the submission of the five amendments which have been added to the Constitution since I have been a Member of this House.

During my period of service here I have voted to submit to the States every amendment which seemed to have the support of any considerable bloc of people. I have already voted to submit five amendments, the income-tax amendment, the amendments providing for the direct election of Senators, the prohibition amendment – the eighteenth – the woman's suffrage amendment, and the lame-duck amendment, and I expect to vote now to submit this amendment.

I refuse to stand in the gateway in an attempt to prevent the people of the United States from amending their own Constitution in the way provided by the Constitution itself. I am not arrogant enough to do that.

A Member of this House is not voting wet or dry when he votes to submit this amendment. He is simply conceding to the States the right of petition and enormous petitions have been filed here for the resubmission of this amendment. There seem to be a great many people in the United States who would like to see the Federal Government obtain as revenue the profits now made by bootleggers, and I must confess that personally I sympathize with them in the position they take, and this Government certainly needs revenue. At the present time we are borrowing just half the amount it costs to run this Government. This can not go on forever. We are going to reach the end of our borrowing power sooner than some people think. Every time we borrow five hundred million or a billion dollars we are in effect mortgaging all the homes and all the farms in every State in this Union for that amount of money, and we are placing a mortgage on them which must be paid in advance of the mortgages these owners have been compelled to place on their property, and unwillingly compelled to place there. Every dollar of profit in this country is pledged to the payment of the immense sums we are adding now to the national debt.

[...]

In conclusion, I desire to say that I hope this amendment will pass. It will take three-fourths of the States to ratify it. Opposition to its passage now by prohibition leaders shows a decided weakness on their part. Framers of the Constitution have provided that it is not easily changed and can only be changed by three-fourths of the States, and if three-fourths of the States want to amend the Constitution they have the right to do so. If this amendment is adopted the question will be remitted to the States in compliance with the provisions of the Constitution, and the States will have the right to amend, to reject, or to adopt it in the manner provided by the Constitution itself.

[...]

Mr. MOORE of Ohio. Mr. Speaker, I yield two minutes to the gentleman from Maine [Mr. NELSON].

Mr. NELSON of Maine.[44] Mr. Speaker and Members of the House, the success or failure of national prohibition is of peculiar interest to the people of my State. It was in Maine some 87 years ago that the first prohibitory law ever enacted was placed upon our statute books. In 1884 it was written into our State constitution. Since I came to manhood and cast my first vote I have seen going on in Maine the same struggle as regards prohibition, resubmission, and repeal that is to-day being enacted on a larger scale in the Nation. For 27 years before coming to this Congress I voted dry, voted against the money and efforts of out-of-state liquor organizations to nullify our State laws, voted for what I believed and still believe to be for the best interests of the homes of Maine and the women and children of my State. For 11 years as a Member of this House I have voted to support and enforce the eighteenth amendment. My convictions remain unchanged.

I realize, of course, that I am one of a very definite minority, and that the result of the coming vote is a foregone conclusion. The Republican leaders of this House are supporting this resolution, which to my mind does violence to a solemn promise made to the people of this country in our party platform, while the Democratic leaders have had recourse to arbitrary caucus methods seeking to override the very consciences of their members. Nevertheless, I make this prediction: That the experience of Maine will be the experience of the Nation, and that unless some definite assurance against the return of the saloon is given to the American people no Member of this House will live to see national prohibition wiped from the pages of the Federal Constitution.

The great danger, however, as all must realize, lies in the breakdown of enforcement and the nullification of law that is already foreshadowed and bound to exist during the years of the interregnum between the passage of this resolution and its final disposition. The recent election was an economic revolution, a demand on the part of the people, not for rum, but for better economic and social conditions. The demand has not yet been met, nor will this resolution meet it. It is a poor time to encourage lawlessness or to let loose a flood of intoxicating liquor on a mechanized world seething with social unrest.

[...]

Mr. MOORE of Ohio. Mr. Speaker, I yield two minutes to the gentleman from Georgia [Mr. TARVER].

Mr. TARVER.[45] Mr. Speaker, there are only two sides to this war. A man ought to be on one side or the other. He ought to be dry or he ought to be wet. I respect the views of any man who thinks the eighteenth amendment ought to be repealed and stands by his convictions. For the man who deep down in his heart does not think it ought to be repealed, and believes that its repeal would endanger every fireside in America, but nevertheless votes for repeal and assigns as his reason the declarations of some delegates to some convention or the action of some party caucus, I have only profound sympathy. No job in the world is worth a sacrifice like that. I pity the man who says that he is going to vote for repeal here and then go home and vote against repeal. He is neither a soldier nor a sailor. He might he a marine, fighting first on water and then on land, except for the fact that the marines are good fighters and are always loyal to the flag. The Bible speaks about him when it says:

Thou art neither hot nor cold; I will spew thee out of my mouth.

But my profoundest commiseration goes out to men who have voted on both sides of this question, and especially to those who, as lately as last December, voted against repeal and now vote for repeal. The same platform declarations existed then that exist now. A party caucus may have intervened, but whoever heard of a party caucus being more powerful than a party platform? Will gentlemen who voted "no" in December, despite their party platform, vote "aye" now and attempt to excuse themselves by pointing to a party caucus? The suggestion is absurd.

[...]

Mr. RAINEY. Mr. Speaker, I yield one minute to the gentleman from Pennsylvania [Mr. LICHTENWALNER].

Mr. LICHTENWALNER.[46] Mr. Speaker, ladies and gentlemen of the House. I am very proud to have the opportunity of doing my part here to-day to bring about the repeal of the eighteenth amendment and prohibition. I have no doubt this result will follow within a year if we pass this resolution to-day.

In season and out of season I have fought against the principle involved in the eighteenth amendment, when Congress and the State legislatures amended the Constitution to try to regulate the personal habits of the people and when it invaded their private rights and liberties it wrote into the Constitution what might better have been passed as town ordinances in those communities which desired to be bone dry.

I did not believe at the time that prohibition was passed that it represented the majority will of the people at all, and I think that the results of 13 years of attempted enforcement justify that belief, because no law can be enforced that is against the will of the people.

The Government has been most liberal in appropriating money for enforcement and those of us who are willing to face the facts know the results. Prohibition has not brought about temperance. We know now that it has had the opposite effect. We know that for every saloon that has been eliminated that there have been three speakeasies to replace it. Where local authorities were formally able to enforce the laws preventing liquor being sold to minors and to intoxicated persons and on Sundays, it is now an undercover business and therefore passed out of control. So that prohibition must now be pronounced a national failure.

But more important and most serious of all is the fact that billions of dollars which would have slowed into the United States Treasury in revenue, and which might have gone to the reduction of taxes and of the public debt have reverted instead to racketeers and gangsters in most of our cities and created lawlessness much more serious than the breaking of liquor laws.

So that while I was and am against prohibition in principle, my opinion has been further confirmed by its results: but irrespective of my views, now that the Government under the present economic conditions needs the revenue so badly, this alone would be sufficient for me to form my opinion regarding it. I therefore hope that this resolution will pass.

[...]

Mr. MOORE of Ohio. Mr. Speaker, I yield one minute to the gentleman from Washington [Mr. SUMMERS].

Mr. SUMMERS.[47] Mr. Speaker, the resolution now before us would decide the policy of a Nation. Within the hour and without opportunity for debate or amendment we must vote for or against the return of the saloon. I am against it. The resolution does not comport with the Republican nor the Democratic platforms. It gives no guarantee against the old-time saloon. This resolution opens wide the door. It will pass to-day because a great political party has bound and gagged its members and prevented the exercise of their individual rights and judgment. Feeding the hungry and solving economic problems are pushed aside.

[...]

You talk of revenues. Taxes come directly or indirectly from the pockets of the people. I know and you know this is not the sound, unselfish judgment of the American people but the hue and cry of paid propagandists. This is the culmination of a deep-laid plan of heartless millionaires to shift the tax burden from their pockets to the cravings of the helpless.

This is an economic crime you would perpetrate to-day. The free flow of liquor never did and never can solve the problems of this or any other country. Wet Britain and Germany are suffering worse to-day than us.

[...]

Mr. MOORE of Ohio. Mr. Speaker, I yield one minute to the gentleman from Kansas [Mr. GUYER].

Mr. GUYER.[48] Mr. Speaker, if the House passes this resolution to-day, every Republican and every Democrat who votes for it votes not only to repudiate the most solemn and binding pledge of his party platform but also for the return of the saloon, the most sinister influence that ever cursed American life and politics. The final ratification of this proposed amendment insures the return of the saloon. It will be here the moment the thirty-sixth State gives it final approval to this proposed amendment to the Constitution.

Never in the political history of the United States was there such a betrayal of a party-platform pledge. Both the Republican and Democratic platforms contained the most solemn and unequivocal pledge that there should be no return of the saloon. The Republican platform pledged "to safeguard our citizens everywhere from the return of the saloon." The Democratic platform likewise promised "such measures by the several States as will actually promote temperance, effectively prevent the saloon."

Never did parties state in more unequivocal language a more positive position, and never in the political history of this country did congressional party leadership more brazenly violate the pledge of their parties. Does a platform declaration mean nothing to the party leadership in this House? If such a party pledge is thus so violently repudiated, what confidence do we justify in the judgment of the people? Can we complain if they lose confidence in the parliamentary machinery of our country?

[...]

Mr. RAINEY. Mr. Speaker, I yield one minute to the gentleman from Illinois [Mr. SABATH].

Mr. SABATH. Mr. Speaker, I am, indeed, gratified to have the chance of voting for this resolution. The resolution carries out the pledges and the promises not only of the Democratic convention but of the Republican convention, and has been approved by over 22,000,000 people in 42 States, notwithstanding that the Anti-Saloon League in Washington has been endeavoring to thwart the mandate of the 22,000,000 people by injecting sectionalism into the matter and to mislead willfully the membership of this House, as was done when the eighteenth amendment was first submitted.

All this resolution does is to submit the question to the people for approval or disapproval, and it protects the rights of every State. The charges by gentlemen that this will bring back the saloon is unjustifiable and unwarranted, and I hope will not mislead anyone. The threats by the forces of Bishop Cannon[49] will be of no avail, as the membership of this House must recognize that this law-destroying, crime-breeding prohibition law should and must repealed if law and order are to be restored. The sooner favorable action is taken the sooner law and order will be reestablished and the will of the people carried out.

Historical Background Documents

Senator John James Blaine of Wisconsin introduces a proposed amendment to the US Constitution to repeal prohibition, 6 December 1932.

PROHIBITION AMENDMENT OF THE CONSTITUTION

Mr. BLAINE. Mr. President, I ask unanimous consent to make a very brief statement in connection with the presentation of a joint resolution for an amendment to the eighteenth amendment.

The VICE PRESIDENT. Is there objection to the request of the Senator from Wisconsin? The Chair hears none.

Mr. BLAINE. Mr. President, the joint resolution which I am about to propose amends the eighteenth amendment. The effect of the joint resolution is to effectuate a complete repeal of the eighteenth amendment and to take out of the Federal Constitution the power of Congress relating to prohibition, except in so far as the Congress may assist the several States which desire prohibition in the protection of those States.

Moreover, the joint resolution proposes to amend the interstate commerce law so as to make intoxicating liquor for beverage or other purposes, for use in States which prohibit intoxicating liquors, subject to the laws of such States, leaving all other States which choose to adopt any of liquor control free to legislate without any constitutional inhibition or control by the Congress.

I ask that the joint resolution be printed in full in the RECORD, and that it be referred to the Committee on the Judiciary.

Resolved by the Senate and House of Representatives of the United States of America in Congress assembled (two-thirds of each House concurring therein), That the following is proposed as an amendment to the Constitution of the United States, which shall be valid to all intents and purposes as part of the Constitution when ratified by conventions in three-fourths of the several States:

"ARTICLE ____

"SECTION 1. The eighteenth article of amendment of the Constitution of the United States is hereby amended to read as follows:

"'ARTICLE XVIII

"'SECTION 1. The provisions of clause 3 of section 8 of Article I of the Constitution, vesting in the Congress the power to regulate commerce with foreign nations and among the several States and with the Indian tribes, shall not be construed to confer upon the Congress the power to authorize the transportation or importation into any State or Territory of the United States for use therein of intoxicating liquors for beverage or other purposes within the State or Territory if the laws in force therein prohibit such transportation or importation; and any such transportation or importation of intoxicating liquors into any State or Territory for use therein in violation of its laws is hereby prohibited. If any such transportation or importation of intoxicating liquors in violation of law is made, the liquors so transported or imported shall become subject to the laws of the State or Territory on arrival therein.

"'SEC. 2. The Congress shall have the power to enact laws in aid of the enforcement of, and not inconsistent with, the laws enacted by any State or Territory of the United States which has prohibited the transportation or importation of intoxicating liquors for beverage or other purposes into such State or Territory for use therein.'"

AMENDMENT OF THE NATIONAL PROHIBITION ACT

Mr. BINGHAM submitted an amendment in the nature of a substitute intended to be proposed by him to the bill (S. 436) to amend the national prohibition act, as amended and supplemented, in respect to the definition of intoxicating liquor, which was ordered to lie on the table and to be printed.

Source: "The Congressional Record: Proceedings and Debates of the Second Session of the Seventy-Second Congress of the United States of America. Volume 76 – Part 1: December 5, 1932, to December 30, 1932" (Washington: Government Printing Office, 1933), 64-65.

As with all of the amendments to the US Constitution, the Secretary of State must certify the ratification of the amendment. Here, Acting Secretary of State William Phillips certifies the amendment after it is ratified by the requisite number of states, 5 December 1933.

William Phillips

Acting Secretary of State of the United States of America.

TO ALL TO WHOM THESE PRESENTS SHALL COME, GREETING:

KNOW YE, That the Congress of the United States, at the second session, seventy-second Congress begun and held at the city of Washington on Monday, the fifth day of December, in the year one thousand nine hundred and thirty-to, passed a Joint Resolution in the words and figures as follows: to wit –

JOINT RESOLUTION

Proposing an amendment to the Constitution of the United States.

———

Resolved by the Senate and House of Representatives of the United States of America in Congress assembled (two-thirds of each House concurring therein), That the following article is hereby proposed as an amendment to the Constitution of the United States, which shall be valid to all intents and purposes as part of the Constitution when ratified by conventions in three-fourths of the several States:

"ARTICLE ____

"Section 1. The eighteenth article of amendment to the Constitution of the United States is hereby repealed.

"Sec. 2. The transportation or importation into any State, Territory, or possession of the United States for delivery or use therein of intoxicating liquors, in violation of the laws thereof, is hereby prohibited.

"Sec. 3. This article shall be inoperative unless it shall have been ratified as an amendment to the Constitution by conventions in the several States, as provided in the Constitution, within seven years from the date of the submission hereof to the States by the Congress."

And, further, it appears from official notices received at the Department of State that the Amendment to the Constitution of the United States proposed as aforesaid has been ratified by conventions in the States of Alabama, Arizona, Arkansas, California, Colorado, Connecticut, Delaware, Florida, Idaho, Illinois, Indiana, Iowa, Kentucky, Maryland, Massachusetts, Michigan, Minnesota, Missouri, Nevada, New Hampshire, New Jersey, New Mexico, New York, Ohio, Oregon, Pennsylvania, Rhode Island, Tennessee, Texas, Utah, Vermont, Virginia, Washington, West Virginia, Wisconsin, Wyoming.

And, further, that the States wherein conventions have so ratified the said proposed Amendment, constitute the requisite three-fourths of the whole number of States in the United States.

NOW, therefore, let it be know that I, William Phillips, Acting Secretary of State of the United States, by virtue and in pursuance of Section 160, Title 5, of the United States Code, do hereby certify that the Amendment aforesaid has become valid to all intents and purposes as a part of the Constitution of the United States.

IN TESTIMONY WHEREOF, I have hereunto set my hand and caused the seal of the Department of State to be affixed.

DONE at the City of Washington this fifth day of December, in the year of our Lord one thousand nine hundred and thirty-three.

[SEAL]

WILLIAM PHILLIPS
Acting Secretary of State.

Following the certification of the ratification of the Twenty-first Amendment by Acting Secretary of State William Phillips, President Franklin D. Roosevelt released the following official proclamation to the American people on the occasion of the first-ever repeal of a constitutional amendment, 5 December 1933.

Date of Repeal of the Eighteenth Amendment

By the President of the United States of America

A PROCLAMATION

WHEREAS the Congress of the United States in second session of the Seventy-second Congress, begun at Washington on the fifth day of December in the year one thousand nine hundred and thirty-two, adopted a resolution in the words and figures following, to wit:

"JOINT RESOLUTION

Proposing an amendment to the Constitution of the United States

"Resolved by the Senate and House of Representatives of the United States of America in Congress assembled (two-thirds of each House concurring therein), That the following article is hereby proposed as an amendment to the Constitution of the United States, which shall be valid to all intents and purposes as part of the Constitution when ratified by conventions in three-fourths of the several States:

"ARTICLE ____

"'Section 1. The eighteenth article of amendment to the Constitution of the United States is hereby repealed.

"'Sec. 2. The transportation or importation into any State, Territory, or possession of the United States for delivery or use therein of intoxicating liquors, in violation of the laws thereof, is hereby prohibited.

"'Sec. 3. This article shall be inoperative unless it shall have been ratified as an amendment to the Constitution by conventions in the several States, as provided in the Constitution, within seven years from the date of the submission hereof to the States by the Congress.'"

WHEREAS section 217 (a) of the act of Congress entitled "AN ACT To encourage national industrial recovery, to foster competition, an to provide for the construction of certain useful public works, and for other purposes," approved June 16, 1933, provides as follows:

"Sec. 217. (a) The President shall proclaim the date of the close of the first fiscal year ending June 30 of any year after the year 1933, during which the total receipts of the United States (excluding public-debt receipts) exceed its total expenditures (excluding public-debt expenditures other than those chargeable against such receipts), or (b) the repeal of the eighteenth amendment to the Constitution, whichever is the earlier."

WHEREAS it appears from a certificate issued December 5, 1933, by the Acting Secretary of State that official notices have been received in the Department of State that on the fifth day of December 1933 conventions in 36 States of the United States, constituting three fourths of the whole number of the States had ratified the said repeal amendment;

Footnotes, Sources and Further Reading for this chapter appears on page 785

NOW, THEREFORE, I, FRANKLIN D. ROOSEVELT, President of the United States of America, pursuant to the provisions of section 217 (a) of the said act of June 16, 1933, do hereby proclaim that the eighteenth amendment to the Constitution of the United States was repealed on the fifth day of December 1933.

FURTHERMORE, I enjoin upon all citizens of the United States and upon others resident within the jurisdiction thereof to cooperate with the Government in its endeavor to restore greater respect for law and order, by confining such purchases of alcohol beverages as they may make solely to those dealers or agencies which have been duly licensed by State or Federal license.

Observance of this request, which I make personally to every individual and every family in our Nation, will result in the consumption of alcoholic beverages which have passed Federal inspection, in the break-up and eventual destruction of the notoriously evil illicit liquor traffic, and in the payment of reasonable taxes for the support of Government and thereby in the superseding of other forms of taxation.

I call specific attention to the authority given by the twenty-first amendment to the Government to prohibit transportation or importation of intoxicating liquors into any State in violation of the laws of such State.

I ask the whole-hearted cooperation of all our citizens to be end that this return of individual freedom shall not be accompanied by the repugnant conditions that obtained prior to the adoption of the eighteenth amendment and those that have existed since its adoption. Failure to do this honestly and courageously will be a living reproach to us all.

I ask especially that no State shall by law or otherwise authorize the return of the saloon either in its old form or in some modern guise.

The policy of Government will be to see to it that the social and political evils that have existed in the preprohibition era shall not be revived nor permitted again to exist. We must remove forever from our midst the menace of the bootlegger and such others as would profit at the expense of good government, law, and order.

I trust in the good sense of the American people that they will not bring upon themselves the curse of excessive use of intoxicating liquors, to the detriment of health, morals, and social integrity.

The objective we seek through a national policy is the education of every citizen towards a greater temperance throughout the Nation.

IN WITNESS WHEREOF, I have hereunto set my hand and caused the seal of the United States to be affixed.

DONE at the City of Washington this fifth day of December, in the year of our Lord nineteen hundred and thirtythree, and of the Independence of the United States of America the one hundred and fifty-eighth.

[SEAL]

FRANKLIN D. ROOSEVELT.

By the President:
WILLIAM PHILLIPS
Acting Secretary of State

Upon ratification of the prohibition repeal amendment, The Atlanta Constitution, *6 December 1933, published "Pertinent Facts About Prohibition" with statistics of certain events during the years that John Barleycorn was illegal in America.*

Ratification of the eighteenth prohibition amendment was proposed by congress on December 19, 1917. It was accomplished two years later.

The joint congressional repeal resolution was submitted to the states on February 20, 1933.

Michigan, voting on April 3, 1933, was the first state to ratify repeal. Utah, voting today, was the 36th.

A total of 3,765 persons now are serving sentence in federal prisons for violation of prohibition law.

Enforcement of the dry law cost the lives of 79 investigators and police officers and 175 civilians.

The census bureau reported that 45,549 persons died of alcoholism during the prohibition years from 1920 to 1932.

The twenty-first amendment, ratified today, is the first ever adopted which absolutely repeals another section of the constitution.

Liquor may be served at once in 20 states after ratification.

The Volstead act will apply after repeal in Alaska, Hawaii, Panama Canal Zone, Puerto Rico, Virgin Islands and the District of Columbia.

As Submitted to the States

Section 1. The eighteenth article of amendment to the Constitution of the United States is hereby repealed.

Section 2. The transportation or importation into any State, Territory, or possession of the United States for delivery or use therein of intoxicating liquors, in violation of the laws thereof, is hereby prohibited.

Section 3. This article shall be inoperative unless it shall have been ratified as an amendment to the Constitution by conventions in the several States, as provided in the Constitution, within seven years from the date of the submission hereof to the States by the Congress.

State Ratifications of the Twenty-first Amendment

The dates below indicate when the state ratified the amendment; an asterisk (*) indicates when the governer signed the ratification, not necessarily when the state legislature approved it.

State	Date
Michigan	10 April 1933
Wisconsin	25 April 1933
Rhode Island	8 May 1933
Wyoming	25 May 1933
New Jersey	1 June 1933
Delaware	24 June 1933

Indiana	26 June 1933
Massachusetts	26 June 1933
New York	27 June 1933
Illinois	10 July 1933
Iowa	10 July 1933
Connecticut	11 July 1933
New Hampshire	11 July 1933
California	24 July 1933
West Virginia	25 July 1933
Arkansas	1 August 1933
Oregon	7 August 1933
Alabama	8 August 1933
Tennessee	11 August 1933
Missouri	29 August 1933
Arizona	5 September 1933
Nevada	5 September 1933
Vermont	23 September 1933
Colorado	26 September 1933
Washington State	3 October 1933
Minnesota	10 October 1933
Idaho	17 October 1933
Maryland	18 October 1933
Virginia	25 October 1933
New Mexico	2 November 1933
Florida	14 November 1933
Texas	24 November 1933
Kentucky	27 November 1933
Ohio	5 December 1933
Pennsylvania	5 December 1933
Utah	5 December 1933*
Maine	6 December 1933
Montana	6 August 1934

ORIGINAL PRIMARY DOCUMENTS

Presidential Proclamation 2065, 5 December 1933 – the repeal of Prohibition.

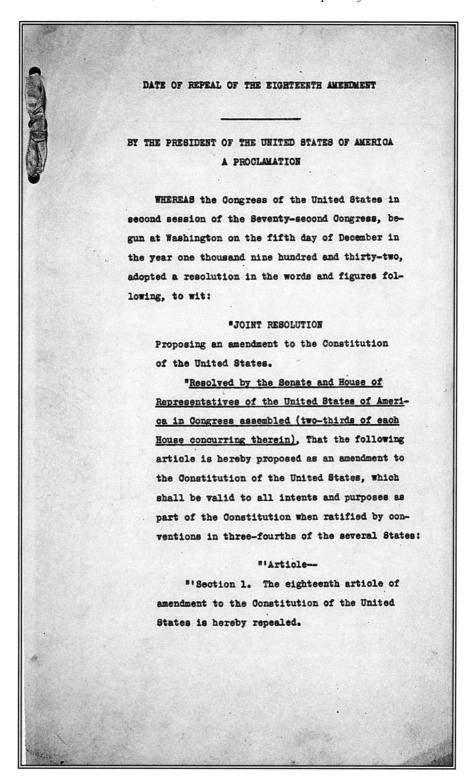

- 2 -

"'Sec. 2. The transportation or importation into any State, Territory, or possession of the United States for delivery or use therein of intoxicating liquors, in violation of the laws thereof, is hereby prohibited.

"'Sec. 3. This article shall be inoperative unless it shall have been ratified as an amendment to the Constitution by conventions in the several States, as provided in the Constitution, within seven years from the date of the submission hereof to the States by the Congress.'"

WHEREAS section 217 (a) of the act of Congress entitled "AN ACT To encourage national industrial recovery, to foster competition, and to provide for the construction of certain useful public works, and for other purposes", approved June 16, 1933, provides as follows:

"Sec. 217. (a) The President shall proclaim the date of --

(1) the close of the first fiscal year ending June 30 of any year after the year 1933, during which the total receipts of the United States (excluding public-debt receipts) exceed its total expenditures (excluding public-debt expenditures other than those chargeable against such receipts), or

(2) the repeal of the eighteenth amendment to the Constitution, whichever is the earlier."

- 3 -

WHEREAS it appears from a certificate issued
December 5, 1933, by the Acting Secretary of State
that official notices have been received in the Department of State that on the fifth day of December
1933 conventions in 36 States of the United States,
constituting three fourths of the whole number of
the States had ratified the said repeal amendment;

NOW, THEREFORE, I, FRANKLIN D. ROOSEVELT,
President of the United States of America, pursuant
to the provisions of section 217 (a) of the said
act of June 16, 1933, do hereby proclaim that the
eighteenth amendment to the Constitution of the
United States was repealed on the fifth day of
December 1933.

FURTHERMORE, I enjoin upon all citizens of
the United States and upon others resident within
the jurisdiction thereof to cooperate with the
Government in its endeavor to restore greater respect for law and order, by confining such purchases
of alcoholic beverages as they may make solely to
those dealers or agencies which have been duly
licensed by State or Federal license.

Observance of this request, which I make personally to every individual and every family in
our Nation, will result in the consumption of alcoholic beverages which have passed Federal inspection, in the break-up and eventual destruction of
the notoriously evil illicit liquor traffic, and
in the payment of reasonable taxes for the support
of Government and thereby in the superseding of
other forms of taxation.

- 4 -

I call specific attention to the authority given by the twenty-first amendment to the Government to prohibit transportation or importation of intoxicating liquors into any State in violation of the laws of such State.

I ask the whole-hearted cooperation of all our citizens to the end that this return of individual freedom shall not be accompanied by the repugnant conditions that obtained prior to the adoption of the eighteenth amendment and those that have existed since its adoption. Failure to do this honestly and courageously will be a living reproach to us all.

I ask especially that no State shall by law or otherwise authorize the return of the saloon either in its old form or in some modern guise.

The policy of the Government will be to see to it that the social and political evils that have existed in the pre-prohibition era shall not be revived nor permitted again to exist. We must remove forever from our midst the menace of the bootlegger and such others as would profit at the expense of good government, law, and order.

I trust in the good sense of the American people that they will not bring upon themselves the curse of excessive use of intoxicating liquors, to the detriment of health, morals, and social integrity.

The objective we seek through a national policy is the education of every citizen towards a greater temperance throughout the Nation.

- 5 -

IN WITNESS WHEREOF, I have hereunto set my
hand and caused the seal of the United States to
be affixed.

DONE at the City of Washington this fifth day
of December, in the
year of our Lord
nineteen hundred
and thirty-three,
and of the In-
dependence of
the United
States of America
the one hundred and
fifty-eighth.

Franklin D. Roosevelt

By the President:

William Phillips
Acting Secretary of State.

2065

❧❧❧❧❧❧❧❧❧

The Wickersham Commission findings gave support to those who wanted to end Prohibition. Here, the report's release is covered in The Hartford Courant *of Connecticut, 21 January 1931.*

HOOVER FIRM AGAINST CHANGE IN DRY LAW AS WICKERSHAM BOARD IS SPLIT ON REVISION

————

Admit Enforcement Has Not Succeeded

————

Report Goes on Record Against Repeal and Urges Large Expansion of Facilities to Make Law Effective – Six of Eleven Members Favor Modification – Baker and Lemann Declare for Outright Repeal, the Latter Refusing to Sign – Finding Referred to Committees – Amendment Proposed by Senator Blaine.

————

Washington, Jan. 20 (AP.) – The report of the Wickersham Commission, broadly upholding constitutional prohibition but leaving the door ajar for basic revision, was put on the crowded calendar of a divided Congress today by President Hoover.

The President agreed with the commission that the dry amendment should not be repealed. He disagreed with a suggestion that revision might be the better part of wisdom. He pointed out to the lawmakers that all the commissioners favored large expansion of enforcement facilities, and said he hoped Congress would consider that at some appropriate time.

The arrival of the report on Capitol Hill set off explosions there that promised to be heard in the next election.

Borah For Appeal to People.

Senator Borah of Idaho, an advocate of prohibition, said repeal or no repeal of the Eighteenth Amendment was the issue and demanded that it be taken to the people.

"I should like to see those opposed to the Eighteenth Amendment present their alternative and let the people choose between them in an orderly and proper fashion," he said.

Blaine Offers Resolution.

Senator Blaine, Republican, Wisconsin, an opponent of the dry law, introduced a resolution for a substitute prohibition amendment similar to that the commission outlined. His proposal would give Congress the power to regulate liquor traffic but not to prohibit.

No Action This Session.

After the first storm of words subsided, Congress turned back to its burdensome legislative task. The report was sent to the judiciary committees of the House and Senate with indications that it would remain there until next session at least.

Chairman Norris[50] of the Senate Judiciary Committee said he expected no action by it at this session, although he would name a sub-committee to study the Blaine proposal if the Wisconsin senator desired.

With the report went the letter of President Hoover. The President briefly reviewed the personnel of the commission and the scope of its 16 months study.

Mr. Hoover made no direct reference to the fact that six of the 11 commissioners asked for repeal or modification, nor did he mention the statement by the whole commission that a revision to give concurrent power to the state and nation would be wise.

Hoover Against Repeal.

He reviewed the general recommendations for improvement of the reinforcement machinery and said:

"The commission by a large majority does not favor repeal of the Eighteenth Amendment as a method or cure for the inherent abuses of the liquor traffic. I am in accord with this view.

"I do, however, see serious objections to, and, therefore, must not be understood as recommending the commission's proposed revision of the Eighteenth Amendment which is suggested by them for possible consideration at some future time if the continued effort at enforcement should not prove successful. My own duty and that of all executive officers is clear – to enforce the law with all the means at our disposal without equivocation or reservation.

President's Letter.

The text of Mr. Hoover's letter follows:

"To the Congress:

"The first deficiency appropriation act of March 4, 1929, carried an appropriation for a thorough investigation as to the enforcement of the prohibition laws, together with the enforcement of other laws.

"In pursuance of this provision I appointed a commission consisting of former Attorney General George W. Wickersham, chairman, former Secretary of War Newton D. Baker, Federal Judges William S. Kenyon, Paul J. McCormick and William L. Grubb, former Chief Justice Kenneth Mackintosh of the Supreme Court of Washington, Dean Roscoe Pound of the Harvard Law School, President Ada L. Comstock of Radcliff College, Henry W. Anderson of Virginia, Monte M Lemann of New Orleans and Frank J. Loesch of Chicago.

"The commission thus comprises an able group of distinguished citizens of character and independence of thought, representative of different sections of the country. For 13 months they have exhaustively and painstakingly gathered and examined the facts as to enforcement, the benefits and the abuses under the prohibition laws, both before and since the passage of the Eighteenth Amendment.

"I am transmitting their report immediately.

"Reports upon the enforcement of other criminal laws will follow.

Says Improvement Is Shown.

"The commission considers that the conditions of enforcement of the prohibition laws in the country as a whole are unsatisfactory but it reports that the Federal participation in enforcement has shown continued improvement since and as a consequence of the act of Congress of 1927 placing prohibition under civil service, and the act of

1930 transferring prohibition enforcement from the Treasury to the Department of Justice, and it outlines further improvement.

"It calls attention to the urgency of obedience to law by our citizens and to the inoperative necessity for greater assumption and performance by state and local governments of their share of responsibilities under the 'concurrent enforcement' provision of the Constitution if enforcement is to be successful.

"It recommends that further and more effective efforts be made to enforce the laws.

"It makes recommendations as to Federal administrative methods and certain secondary legislation for further increase of personnel, new classification of offenses, relief of the courts, and amendments to the national prohibition act clarifying the law and eliminating irritations which arise under it.

"Some of these recommendations have been enacted by the Congress or are already in course of legislation. "I commend these suggestions to the attention of the Congress at an appropriate time.

"The commission, by a large majority, does not favor the repeal of the Eighteenth Amendment as a method of cure for the inherent abuses of the liquor traffic.

"I am in accord with this view.

"I am in unity with the spirit of the report in seeking constructive steps to advance the national ideal of eradication of the social and economic and political evils of this traffic to preserve the gains which have been made and to eliminate the abuse which exist[s], at the same time facing with an open mind the difficulties which have arisen under this experiment.

Against Revision.

"I do, however, see serious objections to, and therefore must not be understood as recommending the commission's proposed revision of the Eighteenth Amendment which is suggested by them for possible consideration at some future time if the continued effort at enforcement should not prove successful. My own duty and that of all executive officials is clear – to enforce the law with all the means at our disposal without equivocation or reservation.

"The report is the result of a thorough and comprehensive study of the situation by a representative and authoritative group.

"It clearly recognizes the gains which have been made and is resolute that those gains shall be preserved. "There are necessarily differences in views among its members. It is a temperate and judicial presentation. "It should stimulate the clarification of public mind and the advancement of public thought.

"Herbert Hoover."
Two For Outright Repeal.

Of the commissioners, two advocated outright repeal of the Eighteenth Amendment, four urged revision of the constitutional clause and the remaining five favored further trial and strict enforcement. All of the commission except one, however, joined in proposing strengthening of enforcement agencies.

The commission opposed the return of the saloon, or Federal or state liquor sale.

One of its members, Henry W. Anderson, presented a plan for Federal controlled privately operated mercantile liquor establishments. Three members indorsed the idea, and two others gave it a qualified recommendation that it be considered.

The commission opposed modification to permit light wines and beer.

Diversity of Views.

Widespread diversity of views as to the best solution of the problem were spread over 100 pages of the full document, comprising the 11 reports of the individual members.

Standing flatly for outright repeal were Newton D. Baker of Cleveland, former Secretary of War, and Monte Lemann, New Orleans lawyer. The former declared in favor of having the "whole question of policy and enforcement with regard to prohibition remitted to the states."

Four for Early Revision.

The four members united for early revision of the prohibition laws were Anderson, Miss Ada Comstock, president of Radcliffe College; Dean Roscoe Pound of Harvard and Frank J. Loesch, Chicago attorney.

Prior to presenting his liquor control plan, Anderson concluded that prohibition "will not be observed and cannot be enforced."

Miss Comstock declared herself convinced that adequate enforcement "is impossible without the support of a much lager proportion of our population than it now commands," but that in the hope Federal regulation would be more effective than that of the states she favored "revision rather than repeal."

Dean Pound said he believed it "futile to seek a nationally enforced general total abstinence." To preserve the gains of prohibition and eliminate its abuses he said he favored a "redrawing of the amendment," to eliminate the saloon but to allow control adapted to local condition.

Loesch set forth that experience had convinced him that "effective national enforcement of the Eighteenth Amendment in its present form is unattainable; therefore steps should be taken immediately to revise the amendment."

In contending for a further trial of the present prohibition system, with a national referendum to determine "the feeling of the people," Federal Judge William S. Kenyon of Fort Dodge, Ia., said he would favor change if these tests demonstrated further unenforceability.

Joining in this stand, Federal Judge Paul J. McCormick, of Los Angeles, said prohibition's "gain should not be jeopardized until it has been demonstrated that the experiment is completed and has proven to be a failure."

The remaining three members, Chairman Wickersham, Federal Judge William Grubb of Birmingham, and former Judge Kenneth Mackintosh of Tacoma, Wash., declared for further trial and stricter enforcement.

The commission chairman said: "I cannot believe that an experiment of such far reaching and momentous consequence as this of national prohibition should be abandoned after seven years of such imperfect enforcement and only three years of reorganization and effort to repair the mistakes of the earlier period."

Mackintosh placed himself in accord with the view that if "further effort is not productive of reasonable enforcement and observance and private and state cooperation," revision of the Eighteenth Amendment would be desirable.

Grubb stood flatly for further trial on the grounds the prohibition experiment is not yet completed and that "no satisfactory substitute for it has been presented or shown to exist."

The report left the White House at noon by messenger and ten minutes later his presence was announced in the Senate. That branch laid aside its work to hear the President's message of transmittal.

It was received a few minutes later on the House side, where already a prohibition dispute was raging in debate over the proposal to increase the personnel of the enforcement bureau.

Immediate repercussions came from the Capitol and downtown Washington. Senators and representatives, prohibitionists and anti-prohibitionists joined in praising and condemning it, according to the view by which they measured the recommendations.

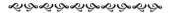

Utah ratifies the Twenty-first Amendment, making the change an official part of the US Constitution. This report is from the Salt Lake City newspaper, The Deseret News, *5 December 1933.*

US PROHIBITION ENDS

Uncertainty Faces Nation as Liquor Ban Falls

UTAH CASTS 36TH VOTE FOR REPEAL

Action Comes After, Pennsylvania, Ohio Ratify

Twenty-one affirmative votes by members of the Utah State Constitutional convention at the capitol today, put an end to prohibition, both within the state and within the nation.

Shortly after the recess for lunch, members reconvened at 2:45 and started the form of procedure leading up to the ratification of the Twenty-first amendment.

Earlier in the day, two other states, Pennsylvania and Ohio, had completed the same formalities, leaving the way open for Utah's final action on repeal.

A plan to postpone the presentation of the ratification resolution and the final vote until 7 p.m., so that the proceedings could be broadcast over the nation, was abandoned.

By its action Utah became the thirty-sixth state to ratify the Twenty-first amendment and thereby put repeal immediately into effect throughout the entire country.

The resolution for ratification of repeal was presented to the convention by Franklin Writer, chairman of the delegates' committee on arrangements.

Both delegates at the state capitol voted today to make prohibition a matter of history, and place the problem of liquor control on a totally new plan of development.

Promptly at noon the 21 delegates elected at the general election Nov. 7, were called to order by Gov. Henry H. Blood and proceedings started which would place Utah as the 36th state in the union to ratify the twenty-first amendment to the state constitution.

So determined were delegates to the convention that Utah would be the deciding state in the battle for repeal that they voted in a caucus previous to the call to order, to postpone actual ratification proceedings until 6:45 p.m., by which time it was thought certain, Ohio would have ratified the amendment leaving the way open for Utah to cast the vote putting repeal into immediate effect.

Prayer Offered

In his prayer, which opened the session, Rev. Elmer I. Goshen, of the First Congressional church, voiced the thought that the delegates "had come with the determination to perform their duty loyally, and win the nation to a return from lawlessness, and away from debauchery outside the law.

"May our state become better by our action here today," he said. "May our law come into higher respect, and our children and their children look back to this day as one when the nation returned to integrity.["]

The business of ratifying the Twenty-first amendment, in obedience to the mandate of the people on Nov. 7, went ahead without delay.

Olson Made President

Ray L. Olson, Ogden Democratic leader, was unanimously elected president of the convention. Clarence E. Bamburger, Salt Lake Republican, vice president; and Mrs. Paul F. Keyser, who was elected by the delegates to take the place of Mrs. S. Grover Rich, now living in Washington, DC, was named recording secretary.

E.M. Garnet, was made official reporter.

Governor Blood, in his speech to the delegates, called attention to the fact "that the eyes of the nation are at this moment turned toward Utah. This commonwealth, situated high in the mountains, far removed from the populace centers of the east, and distant also from the golden western coast of our country, is suddenly placed in a position which will make history.

Two Precedents Set

"Utah, the 36th state to complete its vote for ratification of the 21st amendment of the federal constitution, today is accorded the privilege and the solemn responsibility of taking final action officially to remove from the constitution the 18th amendment.

"The proceedings to this end are being taken in a legally, and orderly and dignified manner, wholly benefiting the signal importance and unusual character of the event. Never before has an amendment to the federal constitution been repealed, and never before has a constitution been amended through the medium of state conventions."

Gov. Blood stressed the fact that the last year has been marked by a pronounced shift of popular sentiment on the liquor question.

"The change of thought has swept the nation from the Atlantic to the Pacific, and whenever the people have been given the opportunity of expressing themselves, the thought has been almost universally against the constitutional restrictions. Once before I have taken occasion to say, that there has appeared an almost irresistible mass movement of such potency and force that everything in opposition to it has been swept aside.

"After the recording of the vote of this convention today, this state and the country at large, will be facing the serious and highly important problem, of what shall be the new method of control.

For Temperance

"I am convinced that there is a widespread and perhaps almost unanimous desire to promote temperance. Such differences as have arisen have to do in a large part with the bringing about of this accomplishment. Surely there is wisdom enough available to meet the issue here presented."

Governor Blood expressed the hope that calm, clear minded study would be given to the subject, before any drastic action was taken. He reminded the gathering that he had already acted in line with this desire and appointed a committee to study the liquor control problem.

"This is a democracy," he said, "and the will of the majority, as expressed through duly constituted representatives has binding force and effect, which must be respected. It therefore becomes a duty of prime importance, that the change effected today, shall be the final step in a purposeful plan to promote respect for and observance of the provisions of the constitution, and the laws based thereon, it shall be my pleasure, as it is my duty to support and sustain and defend the constitution as amended by the will of the majority."

Interest in the proceedings seemed to be rather of a perfunctory measure. Provisions had been made to take care of a large crowd, and all of the desks but 21 in the house of representatives were removed, and the floor space filled with chairs.

This space was occupied by state officials, members of the supreme court, and representatives of various organizations throughout the state. The galleries, rather sparsely filled at first, were not crowded to capacity.

The proceedings, while carried on in a dignified manner, never reached any point of enthusiasm, calling for demonstration and the attitude of the audience seemed to be one more of curiosity in seeing the legal steps of repeal carried out.

Pres. Anthony W. Ivins, in his speech stated that he felt something like Mark Anthony [sic] at Julius Ceaser's [sic] funeral, inasmuch as he came to talk not about this convention and its problem, but about the constitutional convention of 1895, when Utah's constitution was written preliminary to the emergence of the state from the condition of a territory to that of one of the 48 states.

President Ivins sounded a note of optimism, stating that "in this translation coming upon the country, although conditions are constantly changing and new methods of living are developing all the time nevertheless I am convinced that we are going forward and never backward to cons of 20 years ago."

For his experience as one of the legislators in his constitutional convention of 1895, President Ivins said he would never cease to be grateful "though nearly 40 years have passed, and this constitution has proved to be a good piece of work. I remember when I came to the convention I drove a fine team of horses and a buggy, and it took me 10 days to reach Salt Lake City.

"This, I relate, as an illustration of how our methods of living have changed in a [span] of time less than 50 years. In reminiscing about members of that legislation, President Ivins recalled that it was at the convention that he first came to know and admire the late Thomas Kearns, "[w]hom I always found to be a friend to the people of Utah and Salt Lake City."

"Of men active at that convention, we had such men as William J. Kerr, representing the educational side of life; S.R. Thurman, and Franklin S. Richards, representing the law; Anthony C. Lund, new leader of the Tabernacle

Choir, representing music; Noble Warrum, Heber M. Wells, representing literature; Judge C.C. Goodwin was another man and George M. Cannon, Able John Evans, and Judge E.E. Corfman, now chairman of the state utilities commission."

President Ivins said that at this convention he learned that the more you come into close contact with these representatives, the better he liked them, for they were fair minded, patriotic and loyal citizens.

Here, The Atlanta Constitution, *6 December 1933, covers the end of Prohibition in America.*

ROOSEVELT PROCLAIMS REPEAL OF DRY AMENDMENT; LIQUOR SHOPS OPEN DOORS IN EIGHTEEN STATES

HEAVY IMPORTS FROM CANADA ARE AUTHORIZED

Way Cleared To Permit Medicinal Liquor Stocks Go Into Beverage Channels; Drive Opens on Bootleg Industry.

GAY CELEBRATIONS IN MANY SECTIONS

Supplies Restricted in Some Areas; Court Rejects Application To Block Repeal Order.

WASHINGTON, Dec. 5. (AP) – President Roosevelt late today signed a proclamation declaring the prohibition amendment had been repealed.

In the proclamation, the president called upon all citizens to co-operate with the government in efforts to restore "greater respect for law and order" by confining purchases of alcoholic beverages to dealers or agencies licensed by the state or federal governments.

He asked the whole-hearted co-operation of all citizens to the end that the return "of individual freedom" should not be accompanied "by the repugnant conditions that occurred prior to the adoption of the eighteenth amendment and those that have existed since its adoption." He said failure to do this honestly and courageously would be "a living reproach to us all."

By CECIL B. DICKSON.

WASHINGTON, Dec. 5. (AP) – With a dash of ceremony, Utah late today wrote an end to national prohibition in a decree that opened the doors of liquor shops in 18 states.

Almost half a dozen other states were completing plans for legalizing sale under their own laws. The remainder of the nation remained dry.

Word that Utah – the 36th state – had ratified repeal was flashed to the capital a few hours after Pennsylvania and Ohio. But a little later, the final formalities were completed with the issuance of proclamations by the state department and President Roosevelt declaring prohibition at an end.

There was little ceremony at the signing of the presidential or the state department proclamations, but in wet states and some dry ones there were celebrations.

Nearly 14 years of alcoholic draught, enforced by the eighteenth Amendment of World War dry inception, was ended by the Utah vote.

It found the federal government prepared to control the flow of liquor in wet states, through a virtual dictatorship over the industry, and to protect the arid ones. Several of the 18 states where liquor could be sold immediately, however, were without regulations.

Repeal celebrations, however, found liquor supplies for immediate consumption restricted in some sections.

Importation Authorized.

In a hurried effort to meet the demand and thereby thwart the bootlegger, the government today decided to allow large importation of American type Bourbon and rye whiskies from Canada. It also planned to release for beverage purposes medicinal liquors held in bonded warehouses and customs houses.

A move of the International Reform Federation to block the issuance of the repeal proclamation was rejected in District of Columbia supreme court, when Justice F. Dickinson Letts rejected a petition filed by Canon William Sheafe Chase, of Brooklyn, N.Y., on the ground there was no basis for the action. He ruled repeal was effective upon ratification by the 36th state and not through the proclamation.

Repeal was brought about through the convention system, authorized under the constitution, but used for the first time in this case. The eighteenth amendment is the first to be ejected from the constitution in the history of the republic.

Thirty-nine states, beginning Michigan, had ratified the twenty-first amendment previously. Pennsylvania's delegates were the first to ratify today. Ohio soon followed. Utah had determined to have the 36th position.

Meantime, in the capital government officials hurried their preparations for liquor control. The federal alcohol control administration was the dominating group. Under the directorship of Joseph H. Choate, Jr., of New York, it was passing on import quotas of foreign liquors and bringing other branches of the liquor industry under its authority.

Attorney-General Cummings[51] issued an order transferring the prohibition unit of the justice department into the alcoholic beverage unit. The 1,200 agents will assist the internal revenue bureau in enforcing liquor tax laws in wet states and will have a duty of protecting dry ones.

Acting Secretary Henry Morgenthau Jr., of the treasury, issued an order placing the internal revenue bureau directly under him. The bureau of industrial alcohol, which supervised alcohol production and medicinal liquor in prohibition days was transferred to the internal revenue bureau.

Doran Relinquishes Post.

Dr. James M. Doran, who for many years was industrial alcohol commissioner, relinquished his duties today to become director of the national distillers code authority, which is to work with the control administration.

The customs bureau had prepared regulations to prevent American citizens from carting into this country from Canadian and Mexican border points duty-free whisky in allotments of $100 and less, now permitted under the tariff laws.

Determined to keep bootleg whisky from entering legitimate channels, government officials said that though smugglers were seeking to pay the import duties and taxes for that purpose, it would not be permitted. They said the spirits would be subject to seizure.

The decision to let in a large quantity of Canadian whisky was made by the temporary liquor import committee headed by Administrator Choate. In making the announcement, it said:

It was estimated in official circles that Canada has nearly 20,000,000 gallons for export and that the dominion would receive the largest quota of all foreign countries in the initial allotments.

It was not announced how much would be permitted.

Choate Works on Foreign Quotas.

Choate worked throughout the day on foreign quotas, while state department officials continued negotiations with representatives of exporting countries for trade pacts, whereby their spirits and wines might be exchanged for surplus products of American farms.

"Equitable quotas are being set up for countries," said Choate, adding that licenses up to the maximum quota based on four month imports in 1910 to 1914 would be allowed importers.

Because the visible supply of domestic potable liquors is only about 15,000,000 gallons and the established Consumption for the first year of repeal is 105,000,000, it was leaned that larger imports, especially from Canada were contemplated.

Approximately 500,000 gallons of imported and domestic medicinal liquors are expected to be made available. Taxes and import duties will have to be paid before those stocks may be withdrawn, it was explained.

The domestic distillers, importers and brewers already were under government proposed codes for their control by the federal alcohol administration and today hearings were held on a pact to put rectifiers and blenders under the authority granted in the farm and recovery acts.

At a hearing on the rectifiers' and blenders' code, Dr. William V. Linder, head of the technical division of the industrial alcohol bureau, said:

"Unless the government takes over control, 5,000 to 10,000 people could qualify as rectifiers using bootleg spirits to evade taxes."

He urged limitation of the number of rectifiers.

During the day, Pennsylvania officials arrived from Harrisburg by airplane and motorcycle with the official certificate that Pennsylvania was the thirty-fourth state to ratify repeal.

The Pennsylvania convention was held despite an effort of drys to prevent action through the courts. Ratification came at 12:50 p.m.

Ohio's action came at 2:43 p.m., making it the thirty-fifth state. All the 52 delegates voted wet. But Ohio's state constitutional amendment remains on the document until Thursday.

Footnotes, Sources and Further Reading for this chapter appears on page 785

New Jersey is having trouble with its liquor control bill, Governor A. Harry Moore threatening to veto it unless the legislature makes certain amendments.

Maine, which voted repeal in September, holds its ratifying convention tomorrow. North and South Carolina, the other states that have voted on repeal, went against ratification.

States that have had no popular vote on repeal are Georgia, Kansas, Louisiana, Mississippi, Montana, Nebraska, North Dakota, Oklahoma and South Dakota.

Latest figures show 20,813,208 votes have been cast, of which 15,279,216 favored repeal against 5,533,992 for retention.

Here, The Boston Globe, *6 December 1933, covers the repeal of the Eighteenth Amendment.*

BOSTON REMAINS STAID AS IT SIPS LIQUOR IN 115 PLACES LICENSED TO SELL BY DRINK

———

City Gay But Orderly in Celebrating Prohibition Repeal, Following Plea of President in His Proclamation, Although Most Persons Had Not Read It

———

REPEAL ACTUAL IN 18 STATES

———

Proclamation by President Asks Citizens to Exercise Wisely New "Individual Freedom"

———

With an admonition from President Roosevelt to use wisely their newly-restored "individual freedom," citizens in 18 States last night drank legal liquor, The Associated Press reports.

Drinking places opened wide their doors in the early evening immediately after the word had flashed through the land that Utah, following closely behind Pennsylvania and Ohio, had become the 36th State to ratify repeal of National prohibition.

Five other States were getting regulatory laws into shape for the sale of liquor. More than score, however, remained dry under their own statutes.

Supreme Court Cases

State Board of Equalization v. Young's Market Co. *(299 U.S. 59 {1936}). Decided 9 December 1936 by a vote of 8-0. Justice Louis Brandeis wrote the Court's opinion.*

The Case: Young's Market Co. of California brought suit in the District Court of the United States for the Southern District of California, challenging the validity, under the Twenty-first Amendment, of a state statute, and the regulations arising from that statute, which imposed a license fee of $500 for the right to import beer from any point outside the state to inside the state; however, the license does not give the importer the right to sell the imported beer. According to the decision, "the plaintiffs are domestic corporations and individual citizens of California who sue on behalf of themselves and of others similarly situated. Each is engaged in selling at wholesale at one or more places of business within the State beer imported from Missouri or Wisconsin; and has a wholesaler's license which entitles the holder to sell there to licensed dealers beer lawfully possessed, whether it be imported or is of domestic make." The company sued the State Board of Equalization, which carried out the regulations of the statute. Officials of the board argued that the regulations were constitutional under the Twenty-first Amendment, which reads, in part, "The transportation or importation into any State, Territory, or possession of the United States for delivery or use therein of intoxicating liquors, in violation of the laws thereof, is hereby prohibited." The district court found for the plaintiffs, and the State of California appealed directly to the US Supreme Court; arguments were heard on 19 October 1936.

On 9 November 1936, Justice Louis Brandeis, speaking for a 8-0 Court (Justice Harlan Fiske Stone did not participate) in reversing the district court's decision. Writing for the Court – Justice Pierce Butler concurred, the only other opinion published – Justice Brandeis explained, "The Amendment which 'prohibited' the 'transportation or importation' of intoxicating liquors into any state 'in violation of the laws thereof,' abrogated the right to import free, so far as concerns intoxicating liquors. The words used are apt to confer upon the State the power to forbid all importation which do not comply with the conditions which it prescribes. The plaintiffs ask us to limit this broad command. They request us to construe the Amendment as saying, in effect: The State may prohibit the importation of intoxicating liquors provided it prohibits the manufacture and sale within its borders; but if it permits such manufacture and sale, it must let imported liquors compete with the domestic on equal terms. To say that, would involve not a construction of the Amendment, but a rewriting of it." He further argued, "The plaintiffs argue that limitation of the broad language of the Twenty-first Amendment is sanctioned by its history; and by the decisions of this Court on the Wilson Act, the Webb-Kenyon Act and the Reed Amendment. As we think the language of the Amendment is clear, we do not discuss these matters. The plaintiffs insist that to sustain the exaction of the importer's license-fee would involve a declaration that the Amendment has, in respect to liquor, freed the States from all restrictions upon the police power to be found in other provisions of the Constitution. The question for decision requires no such generalization." He concluded, "The claim that the statutory provisions and the regulations are void under the equal protection clause may be briefly disposed of. A classification recognized by the Twenty-first Amendment cannot be deemed forbidden by the Fourteenth. Moreover, the classification in taxation made by California rests on conditions requiring difference in treatment. Beer sold within the State comes from two sources. The brewer of the domestic article may be required to pay a license-fee for the privilege of manufacturing it; and under the California statute is obliged to pay $750 a year...The brewer of the foreign article cannot be so taxed; only the importer can be reached. He is subjected to a license-fee of $500."

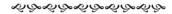

Mahoney v. Joseph Triner Corp. *(304 U.S. 401 {1938}). Decided 23 May 1938 by a vote of 8-0. Justice Louis Brandeis wrote the Court's opinion.*

The Case: The Twenty-first Amendment was declared as ratified on 5 December 1933. In February 1934, the Joseph Triner Corporation, an Illinois company engaged in the manufacture of alcoholic drinks, went to the state of Minnesota and secured from that state's Liquor Control Commission a license to sell their liquors in the state of Minnesota. However, on 29 April 1935, the legislature of Minnesota enacted a law which stated, "No licensed manufacturer or wholesaler shall import any brand or brands of intoxicating liquors containing more than 25 per cent of alcohol by volume ready for sale without further processing unless such brand or brands shall be duly registered in the patent office of the United States." The Joseph Triner Corporation sold many alcoholic drinks with more than 25 per cent alcoholic content. The company went to court to enjoin the Liquor Control Commissioner of Minnesota from interfering with the sale of any intoxicating liquor with more than 25 per cent alcoholic content. The court, the District Court of the United States for the District of Minnesota, granted a preliminary injunction against state officials from carry out the new state statute, including the unnamed Mr. Mahoney, the state Liquor Control Commissioner. Mahoney and the state of Minnesota appealed to the US Supreme Court. Arguments were heard on 25 April 1938; a decision came down one month later, on 23 May 1938.

Holding for an 8-0 Court (Justice Stanley Reed concurred in the court's decision, and Justice Benjamin Cardozo did not take part in the decision), Justice Louis Brandeis reversed the lower court's decision. Brandeis wrote, "The statute clearly discriminates in favor of liquor processed within the State as against liquor completely processed elsewhere. For only that locally processed may be sold regardless of whether the brand has been registered. That, under the amendment, discrimination against imported liquor is permissible although it is not an incident of reasonable regulation of the liquor traffic, was settled by *State Board of Equalization v. Young's Market Co.*" He added, "Joseph Triner Corporation insists that the statute is unconstitutional because it permits unreasonable discrimination between imported brands. That is, the registered brands of other foreign manufacturers may be imported while its unregistered brands may not be, although 'identical in kind, ingredient and quality.' We are asked to limit the power conferred by the amendment so that only those importations may be forbidden which, in the opinion of the Court, violate a reasonable regulation of the liquor traffic. To do so would, as stated in the *Young's Market Case*, 'involve not a construction of the amendment, but a rewriting of it.'" Brandeis concluded, "The fact that Joseph Triner Corporation had, when the statute was passed, a valid license and a stock of liquors in Minnesota imported under it, is immaterial. Independently of the Twenty-first Amendment, the State had power to terminate the license. Reversed."

Indianapolis Brewing Co. v. Liquor Commission, et al. *(305 U.S. 391 {1939}). Decided 3 January 1939 by a vote of 9-0. Justice Louis Brandeis wrote the Court's opinion.*

The Case: The Indianapolis Brewing Company, Inc., an Indiana corporation, was a manufacturer of beer. In the years after the ratification of the Twenty-first Amendment, the company sold beer and shipped the product to dealers in this state of Michigan. In July 1937, however, the Michigan legislature enacted an amendment to the Michigan Liquor Control Act, prohibiting Michigan alcohol dealers and sellers who sold beer from selling any beer from a state whose laws discriminated against beer manufactured in Michigan. Under the Indiana Liquor Control Act of 1936, and amended in 1937, wholesalers and sellers of alcoholic beverages in Indiana could not purchase and import any beer that they did not intend to use for themselves; further, a "port of entry" permit would have to be purchased by the Indiana dealers for a license fee of $1,500, and pay a bond of $10,000. Because of this law in Indiana, Michigan halted all imports of beer from Indiana. The Indianapolis Brewing Company then initiated a lawsuit in the District Court of the United States for the Eastern District of Michigan, asking for an injunction against the new Michigan law. The court held that the law was valid, noting that the Twenty-first Amendment stated, "The transportation or importation into any State, Territory or possession of the United States for delivery or use therein of intoxicating liquors, in violation of the laws thereof, is hereby prohibited." The Indianapolis Brewing Company appealed directly to the US Supreme Court, which granted certiorari. Arguments were heard on 7 December 1938, and a decision came down one month later, on 3 January 1939.

Speaking for a unanimous Court, Justice Louis Brandeis affirmed the district court's holding. In a short decision, Brandeis explained, "Whether the Michigan law should not more properly be described as a protective measure, we have no occasion to consider. For whatever its character, the law is valid. Since the Twenty-first Amendment, as held in the Young case, the right of a state to prohibit or regulate the importation of intoxicating liquor is not limited by the commerce clause; and, as held by that case and *Mahoney v. Joseph Triner Corp.*, discrimination between domestic and imported intoxicating liquors, or between imported intoxicating liquors, is not prohibited by the equal protection clause. The further claim that the law violates the due process clause is also unfounded. The substantive power of the State to prevent the sale of intoxicating liquor is undoubted."

࣯࣯࣯࣯࣯࣯ࣷࣷࣷࣷࣷࣷࣷ

Ziffrin, Inc. v. Reeves (308 U.S. 132 {1939}). Decided 13 November 1939 by a vote of 8-0, with one justice abstaining. The Court's opinion was delivered by Justice James McReynolds.

The Case: The petitioner challenged the lengthy and detailed Kentucky Alcohol Beverage Control Act, arguing that various requirements having to do with transportation of liquor were invalid under the Commerce Clause of the Constitution.

The Kentucky statute forbidding the transportation of liquor by carriers other than licensed common carriers and forbidding distillers to deliver their goods to an unauthorized carrier are not invalid under the Commerce Clause, or under the Due Process and Equal Protection Clauses of the Fourteenth Amendment.

Justice McReynolds wrote,

"The Twenty-first Amendment sanctions the right of a state to legislate concerning intoxicating liquors brought from without, unfettered by the Commerce Clause. Without doubt, a state may absolutely prohibit the manufacture of intoxicants, their transportation, sale, or possession, irrespective of when or where produced or obtained or the use to which they are to be put. Further, she may adopt measures reasonably appropriate to effectuate these inhibitions and exercise full police authority in respect of them.

"Having power absolutely to prohibit manufacture, sale, transportation, or possession of intoxicants, was it permissible for Kentucky to permit these things only under definitely prescribed conditions. Former opinions here make an affirmative answer imperative. The greater power includes the less. The state may protect her people against evil incident to intoxicants, and may exercise large discretion as to means employed.

"Kentucky has seen fit to permit manufacture of whiskey only upon condition that it be sold to an indicated class of customers and transported in definitely specified ways. These conditions are not unreasonable, and are clearly appropriate for effectuating the policy of limiting traffic in order to minimize well known evils, and secure payment of revenue. The statute declares whiskey removed from permitted channels contraband subject to immediate seizure. This is within the police power of the state; and property so circumstanced cannot be regarded as a proper article of commerce."

࣯࣯࣯࣯࣯࣯ࣷࣷࣷࣷࣷࣷࣷ

Carter v. Virginia (321 U.S. 131 {1944}). Decided 31 January 1944 by a vote of 9-0. Justice Stanley Reed delivered the opinion of the Court.

The Case: The petitioners challenged various provisions of Virginia law regulating the transportation of alcoholic beverages from one state to another through Virginia. Their contention was that the relevant provisions of the Virginia law impeded interstate commerce and thus violated the Commerce Clause of the Constitution.

The Court held that the Virginia law, independent of Section 2 of the Twenty-first Amendment, was not an unconstitutional violation of the Commerce Clause.

Justice Reed wrote,

"The appellants argue, first, that the Twenty-first Amendment gives Virginia no power to prohibit absolutely the shipment of liquor from Maryland to North Carolina through Virginia; second, that its power to regulate such shipments is limited by the Commerce Clause to regulations reasonably necessary to enforce its local liquor laws and not unduly burdensome on interstate commerce; third, that Virginia has no authority to penalize prospective violations of the criminal laws of North Carolina or the United States. It will be observed that the intoxicating liquors in question are intended for continuous shipment through Virginia, so that here...a different question arises from those considered under the Twenty-first Amendment, where transportation or importation into a state for delivery or use therein was prohibited. But we may put aside the first and third contentions, for we are satisfied that Virginia may, notwithstanding the Commerce Clause and independently of the Twenty-first Amendment, in order to protect herself from illicit liquor traffic within her borders, subject the shipment of liquor through Virginia to the regulations here in question....

"Whatever may be the effect of the Twenty-first Amendment, this record presents no problem that may not be resolved under the Commerce Clause alone. That Clause remains in the Constitution as a grant of power to Congress to control commerce and as a diminution pro tanto of absolute state sovereignty over the same subject matter."

৵৵৵৵৵৵৵৵৵৵

Hostetter v. Idlewild Bon Voyage Liquor Corp. *(377 U.S. 324 {1964}). Decided 1 June 1964 by a vote of 7-2. Justice Potter Stewart wrote the majority opinion.*

The Case: The Idlewild Bon Voyage Liquor Corporation sold bottled wines and liquors at the departing international lounge at Idlewild International Airport, renamed John F. Kennedy International Airport after President Kennedy was assassinated in 1963. Its place of business was leased from the Port Authority of New York for use solely as "an office in connection with the sale... of in-bond wines and liquors." The company opened its business at the airport in Spring 1960. Only a few weeks later, the New York State Liquor Authority informed the company that its business was illegal under the provisions of the New York Alcoholic Beverage Control Law, better known as the ABC Law, because the business was unlicensed and could not be licensed under that law. Idlewild then sued Hostetter, the Chairman of the State Liquor Authority in the United States District Court for the Southern District of New York, claiming that the law was unconstitutional under the Twenty-first Amendment. The courts found for Idlewild, and the State Liquor Authority appealed to the US Supreme Court, which granted certiorari. Arguments were heard before the high Court on 23 March 1964.

More than nine weeks later, Justice Potter Stewart spoke for a 7-2 Court (Justice William Brennan did not participate, and Justices Hugo Black and Arthur Goldberg dissented), in affirming the lower court ruling. Stewart wrote, "[T]he basic issue we face is whether the Twenty-first Amendment so far obliterates the Commerce Clause as to empower New York to prohibit absolutely the passage of liquor through its territory, under the supervision of the United States Bureau of Customs acting under federal law, for delivery to consumers in foreign countries. For it is not disputed that, if the commodity involved here were not liquor, but grain or lumber, the Commerce Clause would clearly deprive New York of any such power." He continued, "This Court made clear in the early years following adoption of the Twenty-first Amendment that by virtue of its provisions a State is totally unconfined by traditional Commerce Clause limitations when it restricts the importation of intoxicants destined for use, distribution, or consumption within its borders. Thus, in upholding a State's power to impose a license fee upon importers of beer, the Court pointed out that '[p]rior to the Twenty-first Amendment it would obviously have been unconstitutional to have imposed any fee for that privilege. The imposition would have been void,...because the fee would be a direct burden on interstate commerce; and the commerce clause confers the right to import merchandise free into any state, except as Congress may otherwise provide'...In the same vein, the Court upheld a Michigan statute prohibiting Michigan dealers from selling beer manufactured in a State which discriminated against Michigan beer."

Stewart then added, "To draw a conclusion from this line of decisions that the Twenty-first Amendment has somehow operated to 'repeal' the Commerce Clause wherever regulation of intoxicating liquors is concerned would, however, be an absurd oversimplification. If the Commerce Clause had been pro tanto 'repealed,' then Congress would be left with no regulatory power over interstate or foreign commerce in intoxicating liquor. Such a conclusion would be patently bizarre and is demonstrably incorrect. In *Jameson & Co. v. Morgenthau...* 'the Federal Alcohol Administration Act was attacked upon the ground that the Twenty-first Amendment to the Federal Constitution gives to the States complete and exclusive control over commerce in intoxicating liquors, unlimited by the commerce clause, and hence that Congress has no longer authority to control the importation of these commodities into the United States.' The Court's response to this theory was a blunt one: 'We see no substance in this contention.'"

Stewart then concluded,

"Both the Twenty-first Amendment and the Commerce Clause are parts of the same Constitution. Like other provisions of the Constitution, each must be considered in the light of the other, and in the context of the issues and interests at stake in any concrete case... A like accommodation of the Twenty-first Amendment with the Commerce Clause leads to a like conclusion in the present case. Here, ultimate delivery and use is not in New York, but in a foreign country. The State has not sought to regulate or control the passage of intoxicants through her territory in the interest of preventing their unlawful diversion into the internal commerce of the State. As the District Court emphasized, this case does not involve 'measures aimed at preventing unlawful diversion or use of alcoholic beverages within New York.' Rather, the State has sought totally to prevent transactions carried on under the aegis of a law passed by Congress in the exercise of its explicit power under the Constitution to regulate commerce with foreign nations. This New York cannot constitutionally do."

Joseph E. Seagram & Sons, et al. v. Hostetter, Chairman, New York State Liquor Authority, et al. *(384 U.S. 35 {1966}). Decided 19 April 1966 by a vote of 9-0. Justice Potter Stewart wrote the majority opinion.*

The Case: Did a state have the right to monitor the prices of alcoholic beverages? This was the main issue in this case. In 1943, the legislature of New York enacted an amendment to its Alcoholic Beverage Control Law, better known as the ABC Law. Under the original act, companies which manufactured alcoholic beverages for sale in the state of New York had to publish monthly schedules listing the bottle and case price of their product. The amendment forced these companies to list the minimum retail price of their alcoholic beverages. In 1963, however, the governor of New York, —, appointed a commission to study the sale and distribution of alcohol beverages in the state, as well as the effectiveness of the ABC law. The commission found that the reporting of prices had had "no significant effect upon the consumption of alcoholic beverages, upon temperance or upon the incidence of social problems related to alcohol." The commission recommended that the mandatory reporting of prices be eliminated from the law, which was done. In its place, however, was a more stringent law that mandated that monthly price schedules be filed with the State Liquor Authority, and accompanied by an affirmation that "the bottle and case price of liquor...is no higher than the lowest price" of sales made anywhere in the United States. Joseph E. Seagram and Sons, the lead among the appellants, was a distiller, wholesaler, and importer of distilled spirits. They sued in a New York court for an injunction, and, ultimately, declaratory judgment against state law. Over a period of years, that case reached the Court of Appeals of New York State, which held for Hostetter, the Chairman of the New York State Liquor Authority. The Seagram Company and their fellow litigants appealed to the United States Supreme Court, which accepted the case. Arguments were heard on 23 February 1966.

On 19 April 1966, Justice Potter Stewart held for a unanimous Court in affirming the lower court's decision. Stewart explained, "Consideration of any state law regulating intoxicating beverages must begin with the Twentyfirst Amendment, the second section of which provides that: 'The transportation or importation into any State, Territory, or possession of the United States for delivery or use therein of intoxicating liquors, in violation of the laws thereof, is hereby prohibited.' As this Court has consistently held, 'That Amendment bestowed upon the states broad regulatory power over the liquor traffic within their territories.'" He added, "As the *Idlewild* case made clear, however, the second section of the Twenty-first Amendment has not operated totally to repeal the Commerce Clause in the area of the regulation of traffic in liquor. In *Idlewild* the ultimate delivery and use of the liquor was in a foreign country, and the Court held that under those circumstances New York could not forbid sales made under the explicit supervision of the United States Customs Bureau, pursuant to laws enacted by Congress under the Commerce Clause for the regulation of commerce with foreign nations...Unlike Idlewild, the present case concerns liquor destined for use, distribution, or consumption in the State of New York. In that situation, the Twenty-first Amendment demands wide latitude for regulation by the State. We need not now decide whether the mode of liquor regulation chosen by a State in such circumstances could ever constitute so grave an interference with a company's operations elsewhere as to make the regulation invalid under the Commerce Clause...No such situation is presented in this case. The mere fact that § 9 [of the New York law] is geared to appellants' pricing policies in other States is not sufficient to invalidate the statute. As part of its regulatory scheme for the sale of liquor, New York may constitutionally insist that liquor prices to domestic wholesalers and retailers be as low as prices offered elsewhere in the country. The serious discriminatory effects of § 9 alleged by appellants on their business outside New York are largely matters of conjecture. It is by no means clear, for instance, that § 9 must inevitably produce higher prices in other States, as claimed by appellants, rather than the lower prices sought for New York. It will be time enough to assess the alleged extraterritorial effects of § 9 when a case arises that clearly presents them. 'The mere fact that state action may have repercussions beyond state lines is of no judicial significance so long as the action is not within that domain which the Constitution forbids.'"

Stewart concluded,

"Moreover, as the Court of Appeals observed, the regulatory procedure followed by New York is comparable to that practiced by those States, 17 in number, in which liquor is sold by the State itself and not by private enterprise. Each of these monopoly States, we are told, requires distillers to warrant that the price charged the State is no higher than the price charged in other States. In at least one of these States, the distillers are required to adjust the sales price to include all rebates and other allowances made to purchasers elsewhere, and the State has taken positive precautions to insure that the contractual commitments are fulfilled. In some respects, the burden of gathering information for the warranties made to the monopoly States may be more onerous than that required for the affirmations under § 9, since the warranties generally cover prices in other States at the very time of sale to the monopoly State, whereas the affirmations filed under § 9 cover prices charged elsewhere during the preceding month."

Craig v. Boren *(429 U.S. 190 {1976}). Decided 20 December 1976 by a vote of 7-2. The majority opinion was written by Justice William Brennan Jr.*

The Case: An Oklahoma statute banned the sale of 3.2 percent beer to males under the age of twenty-one and to females under the age of eighteen. The petitioner challenged the law as an unconstitutional violation of the Fourteenth Amendment's Equal Protection Clause by establishing different drinking ages for men and women.

The Court held that the law made an unconstitutional gender distinction and that the power granted to the state by Section 2 of the Twenty-first Amendment did not override the Equal Protection Clause of the Fourteenth Amendment.

Justice Brennan wrote,

"Appellees argue...that §§ 241 and 245 enforce state policies concerning the sale and distribution of alcohol and by force of the Twenty-first Amendment should therefore be held to withstand the equal protection challenge. The District Court's response to this contention is unclear. The court assumed that the Twenty-first Amendment 'strengthened' the State's police powers with respect to alcohol regulation, but then said that 'the standards of review that [the Equal Protection Clause] mandates are not relaxed.' Our view is, and we hold, that the Twenty-first

Amendment does not save the invidious gender-based discrimination from invalidation as a denial of equal protection of the laws in violation of the Fourteenth Amendment.

"This Court's decisions since have confirmed that the Amendment primarily created an exception to the normal operation of the Commerce Clause. See, e.g., *Hostetter v. Idlewild Bon Voyage Liquor Corp.*; *Carter v. Virginia*; *Finch & Co. v. McKittrick*. Even here, however, the Twenty-first Amendment does not pro tanto repeal the Commerce Clause, but merely requires that each provision 'be considered in the light of the other, and in the context of the issues and interests at stake in any concrete case.' *Hostetter v. Idlewild Bon Voyage Liquor Corp.*; cf. *Department of Revenue v. James Beam Distilling Co....*

"Once passing beyond consideration of the Commerce Clause, the relevance of the Twenty-first Amendment to other constitutional provisions becomes increasingly doubtful. As one commentator has remarked:

'Neither the text nor the history of the Twenty-first Amendment suggests that it qualifies individual rights protected by the Bill of Rights and the Fourteenth Amendment where the sale or use of liquor is concerned.'

"P. Brest Processes of Constitutional Decisionmaking, Cases and Materials, 258 (1975). Any departures from this historical view have been limited and sporadic. Two States successfully relied upon the Twenty-first Amendment to respond to challenges of major liquor importers to state authority to regulate the importation and manufacture of alcoholic beverages on Commerce Clause and Fourteenth Amendment grounds. See *Mahoney v. Joseph Triner Corp.*; *State Board v. Young's Market Co.* In fact, however, the arguments in both cases centered upon importation of intoxicants, a regulatory area where the State's authority under the Twenty-first Amendment is transparently clear, *Hostetter v. Idlewild Bon Voyage Liquor Corp.*, and touched upon purely economic matters that traditionally merit only the mildest review under the Fourteenth Amendment. Cases involving individual rights protected by the Due Process Clause have been treated in sharp contrast....

"Following this approach, both federal and state courts uniformly have declared the unconstitutionality of gender lines that restrain the activities of customers of state-regulated liquor establishments irrespective of the operation of the Twenty-first Amendment."

৵৽৵৽৵৽৵৽৵৽

California Retail Liquor Dealers Association v. Midcal Aluminum, Inc. *(445 U.S. 97{1980}). Decided 3 March 1980 by a vote of 9-0. The Court's opinion was delivered by Justice Lewis Powell Jr.*

The Case: A California law provided penalties for wine wholesalers who sold below the prices established by producers in fair trade contracts and price schedules filed with the state. A wholesaler challenged the law asking for an injunction against the state's pricing policies as a restraint of trade under the Sherman Antitrust Act.

The Court held that California's pricing policies for wine violated the Sherman Antitrust Act and that the Twenty-first Amendment does not bar the application of the act to the state's wine-pricing system.

Justice Powell wrote,

"Petitioner contends that even if California's system of wine pricing is not protected state action, the Twenty-first Amendment bars application of the Sherman Act in this case. Section 1 of that Amendment repealed the Eighteenth Amendment's prohibition on the manufacture, sale, or transportation of liquor. The second section reserved to the States certain power to regulate traffic in liquor: 'The transportation or importation into any State, Territory, or possession of the United States for delivery or use therein of intoxicating liquors, in violation of the laws thereof, is hereby prohibited.' The remaining question before us is whether § 2 permits California to countermand the congressional policy-adopted under the commerce power-in favor of competition.

"In determining state powers under the Twenty-first Amendment, the Court has focused primarily on the language of the provision rather than the history behind it. *State Board v. Young's Market Co.* In terms, the Amendment gives the States control over the 'transportation or importation' of liquor into their territories. Of course, such control logically entails considerable regulatory power not strictly limited to importing and transporting alcohol. *Ziffrin, Inc. v. Reeves.* We should not, however, lose sight of the explicit grant of authority.

"This Court's early decisions on the Twenty-first Amendment recognized that each State holds great powers over the importation of liquor from other jurisdictions. Young's Market concerned a license fee for interstate imports of alcohol; another case focused on a law restricting the types of liquor that could be imported from other States, *Mahoney v. Joseph Triner Corp.*; two others involved 'retaliation' statutes barring imports from States that proscribed shipments of liquor from other States, *Joseph S. Finch & Co. v. McKittrick*; *Indianapolis Brewing Co. v. Liquor Control Comm'n.* The Court upheld the challenged state authority in each case, largely on the basis of the States' special power over the 'importation and transportation' of intoxicating liquors. Yet even when the States had acted under the explicit terms of the Amendment, the Court resisted the contention that § 2 'freed the States from all restrictions upon the police power to be found in other provisions of the Constitution.' *Young's Market.*

"Subsequent decisions have given 'wide latitude' to state liquor regulation, *Joseph E. Seagram & Sons, Inc. v. Hostetter*, but they also have stressed that important federal interests in liquor matters survived the ratification of the Twenty-first Amendment. The States cannot tax imported liquor in violation of the Export-Import Clause. Nor can they insulate the liquor industry from the Fourteenth Amendment's requirements of equal protection, *Craig v. Boren*, and due process....

"More difficult to define, however, is the extent to which Congress can regulate liquor under its interstate commerce power. Although that power is directly qualified by § 2, the Court has held that the Federal Government retains some Commerce Clause authority over liquor.... [I]n *Ziffrin, Inc. v. Reeves*, the Court did not uphold Kentucky's system of licensing liquor haulers until it was satisfied that the state program was reasonable.

"The contours of Congress' commerce power over liquor were sharpened in *Hostetter v. Idlewild Liquor Corp.*

'To draw a conclusion...that the Twenty-first Amendment has somehow operated to 'repeal' the Commerce Clause wherever regulation of intoxicating liquors is concerned would, however, be an absurd oversimplification. If the Commerce Clause had been pro tanto 'repealed,' then Congress would be left with no regulatory power over interstate or foreign commerce in intoxicating liquor. Such a conclusion would be patently bizarre and is demonstrably incorrect'....

"These decisions demonstrate that there is no bright line between federal and state powers over liquor. The Twenty-first Amendment grants the States virtually complete control over whether to permit importation or sale of liquor and how to structure the liquor distribution system. Although States retain substantial discretion to establish other liquor regulations, those controls may be subject to the federal commerce power in appropriate situations. The competing state and federal interests can be reconciled only after careful scrutiny of those concerns in a 'concrete case.' *Hostetter v. Idlewild Liquor Corp.*"

Bacchus Imports, Ltd. v. Dias *(468 U.S. 263, 276 {1984}). Decided 29 June 1984 by a vote of 5-3 with one abstention. Justice Byron White delivered the opinion on the majority.*

The Case: Hawaii imposed a 20 percent excise tax on wholesale liquors, although certain locally produced alcohol products, including okolehao and fruit wines, were exempt from the tax. An importer challenged the law as a violation of the Import-Export Clause and the Commerce Clause of the Constitution.

The Court held that the discriminatory tax policy of Hawaii was a violation of the Constitution's Commerce Clause and was not protected by the Twenty-first Amendment.

Justice White wrote,

"The State argues in this Court that even if the tax exemption violates ordinary Commerce Clause principles, it is saved by the Twenty-first Amendment to the Constitution. Section 2 of that Amendment provides:

'The transportation or importation into any State, Territory, or possession of the United States for delivery or use therein of intoxicating liquors, in violation of the laws thereof, is hereby prohibited.'

"Despite broad language in some of the opinions of this Court written shortly after ratification of the Amendment, more recently we have recognized the obscurity of the legislative history of § 2....

"It is by now clear that the Amendment did not entirely remove state regulation of alcoholic beverages from the ambit of the Commerce Clause. For example, in *Hostetter v. Idlewild Bon Voyage Liquor Corp.*, the Court stated:

'To draw a conclusion...that the Twenty-first Amendment has somehow operated to 'repeal' the Commerce Clause wherever regulation of intoxicating liquors is concerned would, however, be an absurd oversimplification.'

"We also there observed that '[b]oth the Twenty-first Amendment and the Commerce Clause are parts of the same Constitution, [and] each must be considered in light of the other and in the context of the issues and interests at stake in any concrete case.'

"Similarly, in *Midcal Aluminum*, the Court, noting that recent Twenty-first Amendment cases have emphasized federal interests to a greater degree than had earlier cases, described the mode of analysis to be employed as a 'pragmatic effort to harmonize state and federal powers.' The question in this case is thus whether the principles underlying the Twenty-first Amendment are sufficiently implicated by the exemption for okolehao and pineapple wine to outweigh the Commerce Clause principles that would otherwise be offended. Or, as we recently asked in a slightly different way, 'whether the interests implicated by a state regulation are so closely related to the powers reserved by the Twenty-first Amendment that the regulation may prevail, notwithstanding that its requirements directly conflict with express federal policies.' *Capital Cities Cable, Inc. v. Crisp.*

"Approaching the case in this light, we are convinced that Hawaii's discriminatory tax cannot stand. Doubts about the scope of the Amendment's authorization notwithstanding, one thing is certain: the central purpose of the provision was not to empower States to favor local liquor industries by erecting barriers to competition. It is also beyond doubt that the Commerce Clause itself furthers strong federal interests in preventing economic Balkanization. State laws that constitute mere economic protectionism are therefore not entitled to the same deference as laws enacted to combat the perceived evils of an unrestricted traffic in liquor. Here, the State does not seek to justify its tax on the ground that it was designed to promote temperance or to carry out any other purpose of the Twenty-first Amendment, but instead acknowledges that the purpose was 'to promote a local industry.' Consequently, because the tax violates a central tenet of the Commerce Clause but is not supported by any clear concern of the Twenty-first Amendment, we reject the State's belated claim based on the Amendment."

Granholm v. Heald *(544 U.S. 460 {2005}). Decided 16 May 2005 by a vote of 5-4. Justice Anthony Kennedy wrote the opinion for the majority.*

The Case: Petitioners challenged New York and Michigan statutes that allowed in-state wineries to ship their products directly to consumers but prohibited out-of-state wineries from doing the same.

The Court held that the Twenty-first Amendment does not annul the Commerce Clause; thus, any law that prohibits the direct sale of wine and other alcoholic beverages by out-of-state wineries but permits such sales by in-state producers is unconstitutional.

Justice Kennedy wrote,

"The ratification of the Eighteenth Amendment in 1919 provided a brief respite from the legal battles over the validity of state liquor regulations. With the ratification of the Twenty-first Amendment 14 years later, however, nationwide Prohibition came to an end. Section 1 of the Twenty-first Amendment repealed the Eighteenth Amendment. Section 2 of the Twenty-first Amendment is at issue here.

"Michigan and New York say the provision grants to the States the authority to discriminate against out-of-state goods. The history we have recited does not support this position. To the contrary, it provides strong support for the view that §2 restored to the States the powers they had under the Wilson and Webb-Kenyon Acts. 'The wording of §2 of the Twenty-first Amendment closely follows the Webb-Kenyon and Wilson Acts, expressing the framers' clear intention of constitutionalizing the Commerce Clause framework established under those statutes.' *Craig v. Boren.*

"The aim of the Twenty-first Amendment was to allow States to maintain an effective and uniform system for controlling liquor by regulating its transportation, importation, and use. The Amendment did not give States the authority to pass nonuniform laws in order to discriminate against out-of-state goods, a privilege they had not enjoyed at any earlier time....

"Our more recent cases, furthermore, confirm that the Twenty-first Amendment does not supersede other provisions of the Constitution and, in particular, does not displace the rule that States may not give a discriminatory preference to their own producers....

"States have broad power to regulate liquor under §2 of the Twenty-first Amendment. This power, however, does not allow States to ban, or severely limit, the direct shipment of out-of-state wine while simultaneously authorizing direct shipment by in-state producers. If a State chooses to allow direct shipment of wine, it must do so on evenhanded terms. Without demonstrating the need for discrimination, New York and Michigan have enacted regulations that disadvantage out-of-state wine producers. Under our Commerce Clause jurisprudence, these regulations cannot stand."

WHO'S WHO

This section includes biographies of two individuals who played a significant part in drafting and passing the Twenty-first Amendment. Both men are mentioned in earlier sections of this chapter.

John James Blaine (1875-1934)

Not to be confused with US Senator James Gillespie Blaine of Maine who served 50 years earlier, Senator John James Blaine of Wisconsin was responsible for introducing the language that became the Twenty-first Amendment to the US Constitution. Historian Patrick O'Brien wrote in 1976, "Historians have been somewhat inconsistent in their judgment of the small circle of insurgent progressives who inhabited the US Senate during 'normalcy.' William E. Borah of Idaho, George W. Norris of Nebraska, and Robert M. La Follette, Jr., of Wisconsin have been assigned prominent historical status for their progressivism. Other authentic reformers, including South Dakotan William H. McMaster, Nebraskan Robert B. Howell, and Wisconsinite John James Blaine, have received only casual attention. It may be that Blaine has been neglected because he was in La Follette's shadow, served only one term in the US Senate, and had an unimpressive public image." Despite O'Brien's pronouncements, Blaine in fact did have an impressive career as the Governor of his state and a term in the US Senate.

Blaine was born on his family's farm near the village of Wingville, in Grant County, Wisconsin, in the southwest corner of the state, west of the capital, Madison, on 4 May 1875, the son of James Ferguson Blaine and his wife Elizabeth (née Johnson-Brunstad) Blaine, both farmers. Some sources claim that the Blaines lived not in Wingville but in Boscobel, Wisconsin, and there is no village named Wingville, but there is a village of Preston, in Wingville township. It is possible that John James Blaine was born at a relative's home near Preston, and the address has come to be thought at "owned" by his parents. Elizabeth Blaine was an immigrant from Norway, while James Blaine was born in Scotland, and was a staunch abolitionist. While a child, John James Blaine severely injured his left arm, leaving him unable to perform farm duties, and knew from that early age that he would have to get an education to advance in life. He attended local schools, including the Dixon school a mile east of Preston, teaching during the day to earn money for his family. He then went to Valparaiso University, a Lutheran school in Valparaiso, Indiana. In 1896, Blaine graduated from the Valparaiso law school and returned to Wisconsin, where he opened a law practice in Montfort, in Grant County, earning experience by serving with a noted Boscobel attorney.

It was during this period that Blaine became interested in politics, joining the Republican Party. The GOP was then in a fight between the more conservative elements of the party, known as the "standpatters" or "stalwarts," and the more liberal, or progressive, members, and Blaine, coming from a poor background, slid earnestly into the latter group. In 1901, Blaine was elected for the first of three terms as the Mayor of Boscobel (1901-04, 1906-07). At the same time, he served four terms on the Grant County Board of Supervisors (1901-04). In 1902, Blaine moved to become a state, rather than a local, politician, when he was elected as a delegate to the Republican State Convention. Deeply under the influence of fellow progressive and fellow Wisconsinite Robert La Follette, Blaine would remain in the progressive camp for the remainder of his life. In 1904, he married Anna McSpaden; together the couple would have one child, a daughter.

In 1908, Blaine was elected to a seat in the Wisconsin state Senate for the first of two two-year terms. One of the issues closest to his heart was that of political corruption. Allegations arose that Senator Isaac Stephenson, Republican of Wisconsin, had won his election in 1909 through bribery and other forms of corruption; the Wisconsin legislature was tasked with investigating the potential criminality, and Blaine took a leading role. On 30 June 1911, the legislature informed the US Senate that Stephenson's claim to the seat was invalid because he had committed crimes to get it. As a result of Blaine's actions, the Wisconsin legislature enacted a tough corrupt practices act. Blaine also helped to write and get past a workmen's compensation act. Although he did not seek re-election in 1912, Blaine decided to run for governor in 1914 when then-Governor Francis McGovern ran for the US Senate. Announcing his candidacy as a so-called "Independent Progressive," Blaine faced off against a crowded field of Republican Emanel Lorenz Phillip, Democrat John C. Karel, and Social Democrat Oscar T. Ameringer. Philipp ultimately won with 43% of the vote, with Karel in second with 36.7%, Blaine in the third with 10%, and Ameringer last with 8%. Blaine saw the poor showing as a blow to his burgeoning political career, but he decided to continue. In 1918, he was elected as state Attorney General, and two years later he defeated Governor Philipp, who was running for a fourth term, by a 52%-35% margin. In what turned out to be three two-year terms as governor (1921-27), Blaine delivered on a range of promises, including granting equal rights to women, fighting the Ku Klux Klan, and establishing a large number of state parks. In 1929, "The Wisconsin Blue Book" stated: "The ten years since the war had seen recovery and steady progress in Wisconsin under the administration of Governors Blaine (1921-27) and [Fred R.] Zimmerman. Wisconsin of yesterday becomes Wisconsin of today and tomorrow."

In 1925, Blaine suffered a blow when his political mentor, Robert La Follette, died. It became important that Blaine fill the shoes of the Wisconsin political giant. The following year, Blaine challenged Senator Irvine L. Lenroot in the Republican primary as Lenroot ran for a second term in the US Senate. Blaine defeated Lenroot in the primary, then went on to win the general election. In s single six-year tem in the Senate, Blaine railed against national prohibition, and consistently argued for repeal of the Eighteenth Amendment, which legalized the ban on intoxicating liquors. Although he was a Republican, Blaine was a consistent opponent of the administrations of Presidents Calvin Coolidge and Herbert Hoover; in January 1929, when the US Senate was ratifying the Kellogg-Briand Treaty to Outlaw War by a vote of 85-1, Blaine was the sole dissenting vote. In 1932, Blaine virtually abandoned his party when he supported Democrat Governor Franklin D. Roosevelt for President. This was the final straw for Republicans back in Wisconsin, and party regulars put up the name of John Bowman Chapple, a newspaper editor, against Blaine. The Republican primary was held on 20 September 1932. Chapple won the party nomination, although in the general election that November, he went down to defeat to Democrat F. Ryan Duffy, 57%-36%. Blaine, in the final months of his term, introduced on 6 December 1932 what was called Senate Joint Resolution 211, specific language that called for a constitutional amendment to repeal the Eighteenth Amendment to the US Constitution, and end the period known as Prohibition. Although it took some time, on 16 February 1933, just two weeks before he left the Senate, Blaine voted for passage of the final language that would be submitted to the states. Four days later, the US House of Representatives also passed the amendment, and it was sent to the states. Blaine prepared to return to Wisconsin after his term ended on 3 March 1933. Soon after, President Roosevelt appointed Blaine as a commissioner of the Reconstruction Finance Corporation, a position he held until his death. He worked in Washington, despite the fact that for the remaining year of his life he was in apparent failing health.

On 6 April 1934, Blaine returned to Wisconsin with a severe case of pneumonia. Within days he was in a coma, and on 16 April, Blaine succumbed to his illness; he was three weeks shy of his 59th birthday. He was buried in the Hillside Cemetery in Boscobel. In an editorial, *The Milwaukee Journal* stated, "The career of John J. Blaine demonstrated the value to a public man of boldness. Blaine would go ahead and act. Not always sure of his facts, not always seeing the way ahead, he would take a strong position. In this he went much farther than his leader and associate, the elder La Follette. It was this which kept him in the La Follette circle when other followers who showed leadership were dropped. They were afraid of Blaine...Blaine was always doing the unexpected. When the Republican party was split between Taft and Roosevelt in 1912, Blaine went the whole way. The elder La Follette had attacked Taft as reactionary, but he did not come out against him. Blaine came out for [Woodrow] Wilson and went to Chicago headquarters to work for him...We have spoken of boldness because that is outstanding. Other qualities went to the making of John J. Blaine's career. Ruthless in politics, he was known as a man loyal to his friends. He had a keen sense of the human values..."

Carter Glass (1858-1946)

Best known for his involvement in financial and economic matters, Senator Carter Glass of Virginia helped to shepherd through the proposed language that eventually became the amendment that repealed Prohibition.

Glass was born in Lynchburg, Campbell County, Virginia, on 4 January 1858, one of five children of Robert Henry Glass, the editor of the *Lynchburg Daily Republican* and local postmaster, and Elizabeth (née Christian) Glass. Historians Rixey Smith and Norman Beasley wrote in 1939, "Born in Lynchburg...Carter Glass came into a heritage of freedom. Thomas Glass, the immigrant, came to Virginia in 1648, patented land in New Kent County in 1650...near the present village of Studley. The Glasses were among the first of the pioneers who pushed on into the interior. About one hundred years after Thomas Glass landed, his grandson, Robert Glass, was among the residents of Goochland County. Forty years late, Thomas W. Glass, the grandfather of Carter Glass, was born in Goochland County, where he lived until he was about fifteen years old. Later he went to the adjoining county of Fluvanna where, apparently, he worked in the tavern of Robert Cawthorne, whose daughter, Lucinda, he married about 1818. Carter Glass' mother was Elizabeth Christian, great-granddaughter of Henry Christian, a captain in the Revolutionary War; also, the forebears of his father, Robert Henry Glass, had fought in Washington's armies." Elizabeth Glass died suddenly when her son was just two years old, and his older sister, Nannie, became his surrogate mother.

Despite the political title of Robert Glass' newspaper, it was a staunchly Democratic Party organ in Virginia, hewing the line of that party's pro-slavery political bent. Glass felt sure that slavery would be protected by the US Constitution – and if not, then Virginia, along with the other slaveholding southern states, would depart the Union and start anew. To that end, he served as a delegate to the Democratic National Convention held in Charleston, South Carolina. The Democratic Party split down the middle over the slavery issue: those who wanted to keep slavery protected as long as possible, arguing that the mere threat of secession was enough to send the Northern states into a frenzy, versus the so-called "fire eaters" who wished for a full-on confrontation with abolitionists, which would cause a crisis and force the southern states to secede. The party's leading presidential candidate, Senator Stephen A. Douglas of Illinois, was a moderate who wished to compromise and avoid war. The delegates, however, wanted a fight – Douglas battled several other candidates, including US Senator James Guthrie of Kentucky, who was serving as Secretary of the Treasury. Douglas could not win an outright majority, and more than 100 pro-secession delegates walked out. After 57 ballots, the convention was adjourned with no nomination. Six weeks later, the party reassembled in Baltimore for another convention, and after two ballots, Douglas was declared the victor. This set off more walkouts, with those who bolted forming their own political entity – The Southern Democratic Party – and nominated Vice President John C. Breckinridge of Kentucky, a "fire-eater," for the presidential nomination. Robert Glass was probably one of these latter delegates. In the election, the party split caused the Democrats to lose to Republican Abraham Lincoln. Southern states, starting with South Carolina, seceded. Robert Glass, wholly backed Virginia's walkout from the Union.

Robert Glass became Major Robert Glass, and served, and was wounded, in the Confederate Army. The following year, he married Meta Sandford of North Carolina. During the war and after it concluded, Carter Glass attended private and then public schools. At 13, however, he was forced to quit school to go to work to help out his struggling father. Glass learned the printers' trade, moving up to reporter, then editor in place of his father and, finally, publisher of one of his father's papers, the *Petersburg Post*. Tiring of this work, however, he decided to further his education; in 1886, he married Aurelia McDearmon Caldwell, and together until her death in 1937 they had four children. Soon after that, he went back to work, starting in 1877 as a clerk for the Atlantic, Mississippi, and Ohio Railroad. He joined the *Lynchburg Daily News*, became editor in 1887 and, a year later, purchased the paper. In 1896, he purchased the *Lynchburg Virginian* and merged it with the *Daily News*.

In the last years of the 19th century, Carter Glass became an influential voice in the politics of post-Civil War Virginia. A devout states' rights advocate, he similarly called for labor reforms in the state. But, mostly, Glass was what we call today a segregationist, believing freed slaves inferior and deserving of no rights in the state, particularly voting rights. To this end, in 1894 Glass entered the political arena running for mayor of Lynchburg, but had little support and withdrew his candidacy prior to the vote. He remained in politics, and a speech he delivered at the 1897 state Democratic convention in support of Democrat J. Hoge Tyler for governor earned him increased respect. Two years later, he was elected as state Senator, and again to a second term in 1901. He also served as a delegate to the Virginia constitutional convention, held in 1901 and 1902, where he supported a poll tax to keep blacks from voting.

Following the death of Representative Peter J. Otey, Democrat of Virginia, a special election to fill his seat was held, and Glass was elected for his first of eight two-year terms in the House. Named to the influential Hour Committee on Banking and Currency, Glass rose to become chairman in 1912. In 1913, he authored the law that established the Federal Reserve System and rose to be one of the nation's experts in banking, finance, and currency. In December 1918, when Secretary of the Treasury William Gibbs McAdoo resigned, President Woodrow Wilson reached out to Glass as McAdoo's successor. Nominated on 15 December 1918, Glass was confirmed by the US Senate the following day, and he resigned his House seat. During his tenure, which ended on 1 February 1920, Glass' sole accomplishment was pushing a Victory Loan of war bonds to raise funds to pay for the First World War, which had just concluded, a drive totaling some $5 billion.

During his nearly three decades in the US Senate, Glass became known as "The Father of the Federal Reserve," working to pass additional acts in 1933 and 1935 that updated the system and eventually moved it from the sphere of the Department of the Treasury. In 1941, Glass was elected president pro tempore of the Senate. He earned additional respect as a leader in foreign affairs, especially after he helped to draft the pro-League of Nations plank to the Democratic Party platform at the 1920 Democratic National Convention. Although he remained a segregationist his entire life, in 1928, he supported Governor Al Smith of New York, a Roman Catholic, for President, bucking many in his party from southern states for their refusal to support any Roman Catholic. It was at this time that Glass made his deepest impression on congressional legislation, when he co-authored, with Representative Henry Steagall, Democrat of Alabama, the Glass-Steagall Act of 1932, Historians Randall S. Kroszner and Raghuram G. Rajam wrote in 1994, "The Glass-Steagall Act of 1933 prohibits commercial banks from underwriting, holding, or dealing in corporate securities, either directly or through securities affiliates. The driving force behind the Act was Senator Carter Glass, who strongly believed that direct commercial-bank involvement with corporate securities was detrimental to the stability of the financial system. The co-mingling of investment and commercial banking functions, Glass and others argued, creates significant conflicts of interest." [Glass and Steagall may have been right. In 1999, Congress enacted the Gramm-Leach-Bliley Act, which expanded the functions that banks could be involved in, and some economists blame this act for the collapse of the housing market that led to the recession of 2007.]

Glass backed New York Governor Franklin D. Roosevelt for President in 1932, and after Roosevelt's election, he offered Glass the Secretary of Treasury portfolio, but Glass declined the honor, preferring to remain in the US Senate. Just before Roosevelt took office, Glass took a leading role in helping to pass through the Senate the language which became the Twenty-first Amendment to the US Constitution, which repealed the Eighteenth, or Prohibition, Amendment, enacted in 1918 and ratified in 1919.

When Roosevelt devalued the dollar so that it was no longer backed by gold, Glass broke with the President, and stayed in opposition to his policies from then on. Working with Steagall again, in 1933 Glass co-authored the Banking Act of 1933, which modernized the Federal Reserve System.

As the 1930s progressed, Glass became more opposed to Roosevelt's policies, specifically the administration's massive deficit spending to end the Depression, as well as the President's program of governmental programs called "The New Deal." In 1936, when Glass ran for re-election, he opposed Roosevelt openly and denounced the President's entire economic program. In 1940, he actively opposed Roosevelt's attempt to gain a third presidential term, and, although he accepted the verdict of his party to nominate Roosevelt for that third term, he did not campaign for the President, who won in a landslide. When the United States entered the Second World War, Glass backed the President unconditionally; as a member of the Senate Committee on Foreign Relations, he called for increased appropriations for war measures.

In 1942, Glass suffered health conditions that left him nearly invalid and, although he refused to resign from his US Senate seat, he never again appeared in on the floor of the US Senate. On 28 May 1946, Glass died at his home in Washington at the age of 88. His remains were taken back to his native Virginia, and he was laid to rest in Lynchburg's Spring Hill Cemetery. Senator Harry Byrd, Glass' fellow Virginian in the US Senate, went to the floor of that body to announce Glass' death. "It is with profound sorrow that I announce to the Senate the passing of the senior Senator from Virginia my beloved colleague, Senator Carter Glass. He was one of the outstanding Americans of this generation. This is not the occasion to recall in detail the great services that Senator Glass had rendered Virginia and his country during a public life of nearly 50 years... For myself, I feel the deepest personal sorrow. Senator Glass and I have been intimately associated for many years. I have been his close and devoted friend and he has been mine. I shall never cease to be eternally grateful for the privilege of being his colleague in the representation of Virginia in the Senate of the United States." He concluded, "My admiration for him was only exceeded by my love and devotion for him. Today I voice the sorrow of all Virginians and express in their behalf their gratitude for his great public service."

FOOTNOTES, SOURCES, FURTHER READING

Footnotes

[1] Davis, Sue, "Corwin and Peltason's Understanding the Constitution" (Belmont, California: Thomson Higher Education, 2004), 503.

[2] Wickersham, George W., commission chairman, "Enforcement of the Prohibition Laws. Official Records of the National Commission on Law Observance and Enforcement Pertaining to its Investigation of the Facts as to the Enforcement, the Benefits and the Abuses under the Prohibition Laws, both Before and Since the Adoption of the Eighteenth Amendment to the Constitution" (Washington, DC: Government Printing Office, 1931).

[3] See Kim, Deok-Ho, "'A House Divided': The Wickersham Commission and National Prohibition" (Ph.D. dissertation, State University of New York at Stony Brook, 1992) and Blowers, Malcolm E., "The Wickersham Commission, 1929-1931" (Master's thesis, Ohio State University, 1964).

[4] Editorial in The World [New York], undated, appearing in part in *The Hartford Courant*, 21 January 1931, 1.

[5] Stuntz, William J., "The Collapse of American Criminal Justice" (Cambridge, Massachusetts: The Harvard University Press, 2011), 158.

[6] Mencken, H.L., "A Mencken Chrestomathy" (New York: Vintage Books, 1982), chapter XXIII.

[7] Brown, Everett Somerville, comp., "Ratification of the Twenty-First Amendment to the Constitution of the United States: State Convention Records and Laws" (Ann Arbor: University of Michigan Press, 1938), 4.

[8] "Prohibition Has Never Been a Partisan Issue in Congress," The Boston Globe, 6 December 1922, 14.

[9] Rose, Kenneth D., "American Women and the Repeal of Prohibition" (New York: New York University Press, 1996) 145.

[10] South Carolina rejected the amendment when it voted on it, 4 December 1933.

[11] From the time it was submitted to the states, until it was officially ratified, 288 days had passed.

[12] Hiram Bingham (1875-1956), Republican of Connecticut, Lt. Governor of Connecticut (1922-24), Governor of Connecticut (1924), US Senator (1924-33).

[13] David Aiken Reed (1880-1953), Republican of Pennsylvania, US Senator (1922-35).

[14] Joseph Taylor Robinson (1872-1937), Democrat of Arkansas, US Representative (1903-13), Governor of Arkansas (1913), US Senator (1913-37), unsuccessful Vice Presidential candidate, Democrat Party, 1928.

[15] Carter Glass (1858-1946), Democrat of Virginia, US Representative (1902-18), Secretary of the Treasury (1918-20), US Senator (1920-46). See the "Influential Biographies" section for his full biography.

[16] Arthur Raymond Robinson (1881-1961), Republican of Indiana, US Senator (1925-35).

[17] Dr. Henry Drury Hatfield (1875-1962), Republican of West Virginia, State Senator (1908-12), Governor of West Virginia (1913-17), US Senator (1929-35).

[18] On 15 February 1933, anarchist Giuseppe Zangara fired a gun at President-elect Franklin D. Roosevelt while he toured Miami with Chicago Mayor Anton Cermak. Cermack, shielding the president-elect, was struck several times and eventually died of his wounds. Zangara was later executed in the election chair.

[19] Simeon Davison Fess (1861-1936), Republican of Ohio, US Representative (1913-23), US Senator (1923-35).

[20] Robert Johns Bulkley (1880-1965), Democrat of Ohio, US Representative (1911-15), US Senator (1930-39).

[21] Duncan Upshaw Fletcher (1859-1936), Democrat of Florida, State Representative (1893), Mayor, Jacksonville, Florida (1893-95), President, Gulf Coast Inland Waterwats Association (1908), US Senator (1909-36).

[22] Thomas James Walsh (1859-1933), Democrats of Montana, US Senator (1913-33), named as Attorney General by President-elect Franklin D. Roosevelt, but died en route to Washington from Montana before he could take office.

[23] Thomas Pryor Gore (1870-1949), Democrat of Oklahoma, Member, Oklahoma Territorial Council (1903-05), US Senator (1907-21, 1931-37), member, Democratic National Committee (1912-16).

[24] William Edgar Borah (1865-1940), Republican of Idaho, US Senator (1907-40).

[25] Millard Evelyn Tydings (1890-1961), Democrat of Maryland, Member, State House of Delegates (1916-21), State Senate (1922-23), US Representative (1923-27), US Senator (1923-51).

[26] John James Blaine (1875-1934), Republican of Wisconsin, Mayor, Boscobel, Wisconsin (1901-04), State Senate (1909-13), Attorney General of Wisconsin (1919-21), Governor of Wisconsin (1921-27), US Senator (1927-33). See the "Influential Biographies" section for his full biography.

[27] James Eli Watson (1864-1948), Republican of Indiana, US Representative (1899-1909), US Senator (1916-33).

[28] Sam Gilbert Bratton (1888-1963), Democrat of New Mexico, Judge, Fifth Judicial District of New Mexico (1919-21), Judge, Ninth Judicial District of New Mexico (1921-23), Associate Justice, New Mexico Supreme Court (1923-24), US Senator (1925-33), Judge, US Court of Appeals for the Tenth Circuit (1933-61).

[29] Robert Ferdinand Wagner (1877-1953), Democrat of New York, state Assembly (1905-08), state Senate (1909-18), Justice, New York state Supreme Court (1919-26), US Senator (1927-49).

[30] Royal Samuel Copeland (1868-1938), Democrat of New York, Commissioner of Public Health and President of the New York Board of Health (1918-23), US Senator (1923-38).

[31] Lynn Joseph Frazier (1874-1947), Republican of North Dakota, Governor of North Dakota (1917-21), US Senator (1923-41).

[32] Huey Pierce Long (1893-1935), Democrat of Louisiana, Governor of Louisiana (1928-32), US Senator (1932-35).

[33] George W. Norris (1861-1944), Republican of Nebraska, US Representative (1903-13), US Senator (1913-43).

[34] Robert Beecher Howell (1864-1933), Republican of Nebraska, State Senate (1902-04), Member, Republican National Committee (1912-20), US Senator (1923-33).

[35] John Thomas (1874-1945), Republican of Idaho, Mayor, Gooding, Idaho (1917-19), Member, Republican National Committee (1925-33), US Senator (1928-33, 1940-45).

[36] Claude Augustus Swanson (1862-1939), Democrat of Virginia, US Representative (1893-1906). Governor of Virginia (1906-10), US Senator (1910-11, 1911-33), Secretary of the Navy (1933-39).

[37] Otis Ferguson Glenn (1879-1959), Republican of Illinois, State's Attorney, Jackson County, Illinois (1906-08, 1916-20), State Senate (1920-24), US Senator (1928-33).

[38] Alben William Barkley (1877-1956), Democrat of Kentucky, US Representative (1913-27), US Senator (1927-49, 1955-56), Vice President of the United States (1949-53).

[39] Henry Thomas Rainey (1860-1934), Democrat of Illinois, US Representative (1913-21, 1923-34), Speaker of the House (1933-34).

[40] Leonidas Carstarphen Dyer (1871-1957), Republican of Missouri, US Representative (1913-14, 1915-33).

[41] Thomas Lindsay Blanton (1872-1957), Democrat of Texas, Judge, Forty-second Judicial District of Texas (1912-17), US Representative (1917-29, 1930-37).

[42] Charles Ellis Moore (1884-1941), Republican of Ohio, Prosecuting Attorney, Guernsey County, Ohio (1914-18), US Representative (1919-33).

[43] Bertrand Hollis Snell (1870-1958), Republican of New York, US Representative (1915-39), Publisher, the Potsdam Courier-Freeman newspaper, Potsdam, New York (1934-49).

[44] John Elliott Rankin (1882-1960), Democratic Mississippi, US Representative (1921-53).

[45] Adolph Joachim Sabath (1866-1952), Democrat of Illinois, US Representative (1907-52).

[46] John Edward Nelson (1874-1955), Republican of Maine, US Representative (1922-33).

[47] Malcolm Connor Tarver (1885-1960), Democrat of Georgia, State House of Representatives (1909-12), State Senate (1913-14), Judge, Superior Courts of the Cherokee Circuit, Georgia (1917-27), US Representative (1927-47).

[48] Norton Lewis Lichtenwalner (1889-1960), Democrat of Pennsylvania, US Representative (1931-33).

[49] Dr. John William Summers (1870-1937), Republican of Washington State, State House of Representatives (1917), US Representative (1919-33).

[50] Ulysses Samuel Guyer (1868-1943), Republican of Kansas, Judge, First Division City Court, Kansas City (1907-09), Mayor of Kansas City, Kansas (1909-10), US Representative (1924-25, 1927-43).

[51] Bishop James Cannon, Jr. (1864-1944) was a strong proponent and supporter of the prohibition movement in the 1930s.

[52] George W. Norris (1861-1944), Republican of Nebraska, US Representative (1903-13), US Senator (1913-43), had authored the Twentieth, or "lame duck," Amendment to the US Constitution in 1932.

[53] Homer Stillé Cummings (1870-1956), served as major of Stamford, Connecticut (1900-05) and chairman of the Democratic National Committee (1919-21) before he served as Attorney General from 1933 to 1939.

Sources Arranged by Chapter Sections

Debate in Congress
"The Congressional Record: Proceedings and Debates of the Second Session of the Seventy-Second Congress of the United States of America. Volume 76 – Part 4: February 6, 1933, to February 20, 1933" (Washington: Government Printing Office, 1933), 4211-31.

"The Congressional Record: Proceedings and Debates of the Second Session of the Seventy-Second Congress of the United States of America. Volume 76 – Part 4: February 6, 1933, to February 20, 1933" (Washington: Government Printing Office, 1933), 4508-12.

Historical Background Documents
"*The Congressional Record*: Proceedings and Debates of the Second Session of the Seventy-Second Congress of the United States of America. Volume 76 – Part 1: December 5, 1932, to December 30, 1932" (Washington: Government Printing Office, 1933), 64-65.

Certification of the Ratified Amendment in The Department of State, "Ratification of the Twenty-First Amendment to the Constitution of the United States" (Washington: Government Printing Office, 1934), 9-10.

Official Proclamation by President Roosevelt on the Occasion of the Certification of the Ratification of the Twentyfirst Amendment, 5 December 1933, in The Department of State, "Ratification of the Twenty-First Amendment to the Constitution of the United States" (Washington: Government Printing Office, 1934), 11-13.

"Pertinent Facts About Prohibition," *The Atlanta Constitution*, 6 December 1933, 3.

Original Primary Documents

"Hoover Firm Against Change in Dry Law As Wickersham Board is Split On Revision," *The Hartford Courant*, 1 January 1931, 1, 2.

"US Prohibition Ends," *The Deseret News* [Salt Lake City, Utah], 5 December 1933, 1, —.

"Roosevelt Proclaims Repeal of Dry Amendment; Liquor Shops Open Doors in Eighteen States," *The Atlanta Constitution*, 6 December 1933, 1, 3.

"Boston Remains Staid as it Sips Liquor in 115 Places Licensed to Sell by Drink," *The Boston Daily Globe*, 6 December 1933, 1.

Supreme Court Cases

State Board of Equalization v. Young's Market Co. (299 U.S. 59 {1936}).
Mendelson, Richard, "From Demon to Darling: A Legal History of Wine in America" (Berkeley: The University of California Press, 2009), 122.

Mahoney v. Joseph Triner Corp. (304 U.S. 401 {1938}).
R.F.S.H., "Power of State to Restrict One's Right to Engage in Lawful Occupation," Virginia Law Review, XXV;2 (December 1938), 219-25; I.S.B., "Retaliation and "Equal Protection" in State Liquor Regulations," *Virginia Law Review*, XXV:2 (December 1938), 225-31.

Indianapolis Brewing Co. v. Liquor Commission, et al. (305 U.S. 391 {1939}).
Martin, Susan Lorde, "Wine Wars – Direct Shipment of Wine: The Twenty-first Amendment, the Commerce Clause, and Consumers' Rights," *American Business Law Journal*, XXXVIII:1 (September 2000), 1-40; Cote, Pamela R., "Constitutional Law – The 'Grape' March on Washington: The Twenty-first Amendment, The Dormant Commerce Clause, and Direct Alcohol Shipments," *Western New England Law Review*, XXVI:2 (2004), 343-86.

Ziffrin, Inc. v. Reeves (308 U.S. 132 {1939}).
"Liquor," *Indiana Law Journal*, XVI: 2 (1940), 266-69.

Carter v. Virginia (321 U.S. 131 {1944}).
U.S. Supreme Court Transcript of Record Carter v. Commonwealth of Virginia (Farmington Hills, MI: Gale, 2011).

Hostetter v. Idlewild Bon Voyage Liquor Corp. (377 U.S. 324 {1964}).
Greenberg, Ward A., "Liquor Price Affirmation Statutes and the Dormant Commerce Clause," *Michigan Law Review*, LXXXVI:1 (October 1987), 186-211; Roberts, Dennis J., II, "Interstate and Foreign Commerce–Power of the States to Regulate Traffic in Intoxicating Liquor.–Department of Revenue v. James B. Beam Distillery; Hostetter v. ldlewild Bon Voyage," *Boston College Law Review*, VI:2 (January 1965), 336-44.

Joseph E. Seagram & Sons, et al. v. Hostetter, Chairman, New York State Liquor Authority, et al. (384 U.S. 35 {1966}).
Westerner, Ray O., "Marketing and the United States Supreme Court, 1965-1968," *Journal of Marketing*, XXXIII:1 (January 1969), 16-23; Schubert, Glendon A., "Judicial Policy Making: The Political Role of the Courts" (Chicago: Scott, Foresman, 1974), 179.

Craig v. Boren (429 U.S. 190 {1976}).
Pedrioli, Carlo A., "The Heightened Standard of Judicial Review in Cases of Governmental Gender-Based Discrimination: Ruth Bader Ginsburg's Influence on the U.S. Supreme Court in Craig v. Boren," *Critical Problems in Argumentation: Selected Papers from the Thirteenth NCS/AFA Conference on Argumentation*, edited by Charles Arthur Willard (Washington, DC: National Communication Association, 2005).

California Retail Liquor Dealers Association v. Midcal Aluminum, Inc. (445 U.S. 97 {1980}).
Wannamaker, Caroline, "Midcal Aluminum, Inc. v. California Retail Liquor Dealers Association: Federal Power under the Twenty-First Amendment," *Washington and Lee Law Review*, XXXVIII:1 (January 1981), 302-14.

Bacchus Imports, Ltd., v. Dias (468 U.S. 263, 276 {1984}).
Steele, K. David, "Prospective Overruling and the Judicial Role After James B. Beam Distilling Co. v. Georgia," *Vanderbilt Law Review*, XLV (October 1992), 1345.

Granholm v. Heald (544 U.S. 460 {2005}).
Stanzione, Noah J., "Granholm v. Heald: Wine in, Wit Out," *Widener Law Review*, XVII (2011), 95-126.

Who's Who

John James Blaine (1875-1934)
"Blaine, John James" official congressional biography, online at http://bioguide.congress.gov/scripts/biodisplay.pl?index=B000520; O'Brien, Patrick G., "Senator John J. Blaine: An Independent Progressive during 'Normalcy'," *The Wisconsin Magazine of History*, LX:1 (Autumn 1976), 2, 25-41; Daffer, James Hatfield, "Progressive Profile: John James Blaine From 1873 to 1918" (Master's thesis, University of

Wisconsin, 1951); Mallach, Stanley, "Red Kate O'Hare Comes to Madison: The Politics of Free Speech," *The Wisconsin Magazine of History*, LIII:3 (Spring 1970), 204-22; Anderson, William A. (ed.), "The Wisconsin Blue Book, 1929" (Madison: Democrat Printing Company, State Printer, 1929), 28-29; "John James Blaine, Former US Senator and Governor, Dies," *Fennimore Times* [Boscobel, Wisconsin], 18 April 1934, 38; "John James Blaine Dies; Ill a Week, Collapses and Slips Into Coma, Succumbs 2 Hours Later," *The Wisconsin State Journal* [Madison, Wisconsin], 17 April 1934, 1; "John James Blaine," *The Milwaukee Journal*, 17 April 1934, 8.

Carter Glass (1858-1946)
Smith, Rixey; and Norman Beasley, "Carter Glass: A Biography" (New York: Longmans, Green and Co., 1939), 3-4; "Glass, Carter," official congressional biography, online at http://bioguide.congress.gov/scripts/biodisplay.pl?index=G000232; Poindexter, Harry Edward, "From Copy Desk to Congress: The Pre-Congressional Career of Carter Glass" (Ph.D. dissertation, University of Virginia, 1966); Grantham, Dewey W., Jr., "Virginia Congressional Leaders and the New Freedom, 1913-1917," *The Virginia Magazine of History and Biography*, LVI:3 (July 1948), 304-13; Koeniger, Alfred Cash, "'Unreconstructed Rebel': The Political Thought and Senate Career of Carter Glass, 1929-1936" (Ph.D. dissertation, Vanderbilt University, 1980); Lyle, John Douglas, "The United States Senate Career of Carter Glass, 1920-1933" (Ph.D. dissertation, University of South Carolina, 1974); Kroszner, Randall S.; and Raghuram G. Rajam, "Is the Glass-Steagall Act Justified? A Study of the U.S. Experience with Universal Banking Before 1933," *The American Economic Review*, LXXXIV:4 (September 1994), 810; Koeniger, A. Cash, "The Politics of Independence: Carter Glass and the Elections of 1936," *South Atlantic Quarterly*, LXXX (Winter 1981), 95-106; Syrett, John, "Jim Farley and Carter Glass: Allies Against a Third Term," *Prologue*, XV (Summer 1983), 89-102; Hall, Alvin L., "Politics and Patronage: Virginia's Senators and the Roosevelt Purges of 1938," *The Virginia Magazine of History and Biography*, LXXXII:3 (July 1974), 331-50; "U.S. Leaders Pay Tribute to Sen. Glass," *The Washington Post*, 29 May 1946, 1; "Remarks In Senate on Death of Carter Glass," *The Washington Post*, 29 May 1946, 10.

Further Reading

Chen, Charles, "Supremacy Clause vs. Twenty-First Amendment: Low Cost Military Liquor over State Antidiversion Regulations in United States v. North Dakota," *St. John's Law Review*, LXIII:1 (Fall 1988), 83-96.

Engdahl, Sylvia, ed., *Amendments XVIII and XXI: Prohibition and Repeal* (Detroit, MI: Greenhaven Press, 2009).

Epstein, Richard A., *The Classical Liberal Constitution: The Uncertain Quest for Limited Government* (Cambridge, MA: Harvard University Press, 2014).

Foust, John, "State Power to Regulate Alcohol under the Twenty-First Amendment: The Constitutional Implications of the Twenty-First Amendment Enforcement Act," *Boston College Law Review*, XLI:3 (May 2000), 659-97.

Jurkiewicz, Carole L., and Murphy J. Painter, *Social and Economic Control of Alcohol: The 21st Amendment in the 21st Century* (Boca Raton, FL: CRC Press, 2007).

Levin, William, "Constitutional Law-Twenty-First Amendment-Effect of Section Two on State's Regulatory Power over Intoxicating Liquors," *DePaul Law Review*, XIV:2 (Spring-Summer 1965), 445-49.

Spaeth, Sidney J., "The Twenty-First Amendment and State Control over Intoxicating Liquor," *California Law Review*, LXXIX:1 (January 1991), 161-204.

Staples, Christian Hart, "In Vino Veritas: Does the Twenty-First Amendment Really Protect a State's Right to Regulate Alcohol: An Overview of the North Carolina Wine Industry and the Continuing Wine Distribution Litigation," *Campbell Law Review*, XXXI:1 (Fall 2008), 123-55.

Whitman, Glen, *Strange Brew: Alcohol and Government Monopoly* (Oakland, CA: Independent Institute, 2003).

AMERICA AT THAT TIME . . .

Although the material in this section may not be directly related to the adoption of the Twenty-first Amendment, it offers valuable insight into what was happening in America at the time the Amendment was adopted. Modeled after Grey House Publishing's Working American *series, whose author, Scott Derks, is responsible for its content, it includes a Historical Snapshot, Selected Prices, significant quotations, newspaper and magazine clips to give a sense of what was on the minds of Americans, and how it may have impacted the amendment process.*

HISTORICAL SNAPSHOT

1933

- The Tennessee Valley Authority Act was created

- The first drive-in movie theater opened in Camden, New Jersey

- Aviator Wiley Post completed the first solo flight around the world in seven days, 18 and three-quarter hours

- Albert Einstein fled Hitler's Germany and emigrated to the United States

- Pennsylvania voted to legalize Sunday sports

- The first of the great dust storms of the 1930s hit North Dakota

- Workers staged the first sit-down strike against Hormel meat packers in Austin, Minnesota

- Jack Kirkland's *Tobacco Road* premiered in New York City

- The ban on James Joyce's book *Ulysses* was lifted

- The Pope condemned the massive Nazi sterilization of Jews

- The Twentieth Amendment to the Constitution was declared in effect, changing the inauguration date of members of Congress from March 4 to January 3

- President-elect Franklin Roosevelt escaped an assassination attempt in Miami by Giuseppe Zangara, an unemployed New Jersey bricklayer from Italy

- *Newsweek* magazine was first published under the title *News-Week*

- President Franklin D. Roosevelt ordered a four-day bank holiday in order to stop large amounts of money from being withdrawn

- The first All-star baseball game was played

- American aviator Wiley Post completed the first solo flight around the world in seven days, 18 hours and 45 minutes

- Francis Perkins was appointed Secretary of Labor, the first woman in the Cabinet

---

**"Hoover Favors Change in Prohibition
and an Attack on Depression,"**

The Washington Post, **August 11, 1932:**

President Hoover declared tonight, in accepting renomination to the presidency, that he believed a change in national prohibition is necessary "to remedy present evils" that have grown up under it.

As to the economic situation, he spoke of new plans looking into a movement "from defense to a powerful attack upon the depression," an assertion that was said in high quarters to embrace the carrying out of his recently enunciated nine-point program as well as other propositions not ready for announcement.

FINAL ACTION AT CAPITAL

President Proclaims the Nation's New Policy as Utah Ratifies.

PHILLIPS SIGNS DECREE

Orders 21st Amendment in Effect on Receiving Votes of Three Final States.

RECOVERY TAXES TO END

$227,000,000 A Year Automatically Dropped—Canadian Whisky Quota Is Raised.

Special to The *New York Times.*

WASHINGTON, Dec. 5. – Legal liquor today was returned to the United States, with President Roosevelt calling on the people to see that "this return of individual freedom shall not be accompanied by the repugnant conditions that obtained prior to the adoption of the Eighteenth Amendment and those that have existed since its adoption."

Prohibition of alcoholic beverages as a national jolicy ended at 5:32½ P.M., Eastern Standard Time, when Utah, the last of the thirty-six states, furnished by vote of its convention the constitutional majority for ratification of the Twenty-first Amendment. The new amendment repealed the Eighteenth, and with the demise of the latter went the Volstead Act which for more than a decade held legal drinks in America to less than one-half of 1 per cent of alcohol and the enforcement of which cost more than 150 lives and billions in money.

Earlier in the day Pennsylvania had ratified as the thirty-fourth State and Ohio as the thirty-fifth.

Proclamation by President.

President Roosevelt at 6:55 P.M. signed an official proclamation in keeping with terms of the National Industrial Recovery Act, under which prohibition ended and four taxes levied to raise $227,000,000 annually for amortization of the $3,300,000,000 public works fund were repealed.

But the President went further. Accepting certification from Acting Secretary of State Phillips that thirty-six States had ratified the repealing amendment, he improved the occasion to address a plea to the American people to employ their regained liberty first of all for national manliness.

Mr. Roosevelt asked personally for what he and his party had declined to make the subject of Federal mandate—that saloons be barred from the country.

"I ask especially," he said, "that no State shall by law or otherwise, authorize the return of the saloon, either in its old form or in some modern guise."

Makes Personal Plea.

He enjoined all citizens to cooperate with the government in its endeavor to restore a greater respect for law and order, especially by confining their purchases of liquor to duly licensed agencies. This practice, which he personally requested every individual and every family in the nation to follow, would result, he said, in a better product for consumption, in addition to the "break-up and eventual destruction of the notoriously evil *illicit* liquor traffic" and in tax benefits to the government. . . .

Celebrating the repeal of the 18th Amendment, workers celebrated the reopening of their brewery and Americans took to the bars.

Economic Problems of the Family, by Hazel Kyrk, 1933:

"In her book, *Successful Family Life on a Moderate Income*, Mrs. Abel lays down as her first principle for success—the money income of the family tolerably certain and earned wholly or chiefly by the man. Is the latter one of the requirements that should be set up? There is no doubt that the ideal home as many would picture it is one in which the whole of the money income is furnished by the husband and father. The reasons presented for taking this position would, it is believed, be of very diverse character.

There are those who view with complacence the gainful employment of working class wives and mothers but object to it in the case of women in their own family or class. No concern may be felt over the widespread practice of employment outside the home by Negro women but a similar condition among White women, especially the native-born, may be considered most alarming. This dual standard suggests the basis for certain of the objections to the wife as a contributor to the money income."

American Automobile Workers, 1900–1933, Stan Coulthard, a Chrysler worker talks about getting a job:

"I didn't know what a milling machine was; in fact I'd never worked in a machine shop before. I was taken on in the morning and told to report for the night shift the same day. As soon as I got in I was asked where were my tools? I lied by saying that I'd had no time to go home to get them. I got to the milling machine and didn't even know how to switch it on. I mucked about for a while pretending to be busy until the foreman had gone. Then I told the feller next to me that I'd just got in from Boston, that I didn't know one end of the machine from the other, that I needed a job and could he help me? He said he came from Boston, too, and showed me what to do. After a while he said that the stock I was making was scrap, that there was some good stuff in a pan behind me and to let on that I'd produced it. When the foreman came round to check and he passed it all right! I went on like that for two or three days until I'd got the hang of things. They got it out of my hide before I'd finished so I had no qualms whatever about cheating them."

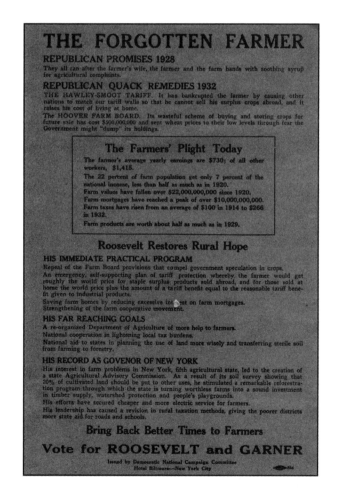

CONSTITUTION SEEN AS SURVIVING STORM

Roanoke College Head Speaks at Annual Dinner Here
of Southern Society.

The New York Times, October 28, 1933

The Constitution of the United States was the only charter of the first rate powers of the world which remained intact after the troublous times of the last decade, said Dr. Charles Jacob Smith, president of Roanoke College, at the annual dinner of the Southern Society at the Waldorf-Astoria last night.

"And even this great doctrine has had a narrow escape, as is demonstrated by the unanimous votes of the several States to take out of it an amendment which is utterly contrary to its original genius," he added.

The rest of the world, which never completely has accepted the republican experiment, he said, watches the United States critically, and although annoyed at American political virility, has had small confidence in the political ideas espoused in this country. . . .

Selected Prices

Brace and Bit Set	$2.80
Chifforobe	$18.95
Electric Iron	$1.00
Lathe	$340.00
Radio	$39.85
Sanitary Pads, Five Boxes	$1.00
Sewing Machine	$19.95
Shave Cream	$0.25
Shortwave Receiver	$14.70
Soda	$0.39

Year	Value of One Dollar in 2016 US Dollars
1932	$17.62
1933	$18.57
1934	$18.02
1935	$17.62
1936	$17.37
1937	$17.12

"Former Local Man Is Cup Contender," *The New Castle News* (Pennsylvania), September 29, 1933:

Newcastle people are looking to the President's Cup Race in the Pontiac River Friday and Saturday with more than ordinary interest this year. A former New Castle man, George C. Reis, is entered in the race and is considered the leading contender for the cup.

The race is for motor boats of 625 cubic inches displacement. When Calvin Coolidge was in the president's chair he donated a gold cup to be sought for each year. Mr. Reis won the cup two years ago, and tradition says no one wins it twice. That's a tradition he hopes to break.

Mr. Reis has already won two major racing events of the year, the National Sweepstakes at Montauk, Long Island, and the Gold Cup Race in Detroit, which he won the same day Gar Wood kept America supreme in the motor boat racing.

1933

FM radio, which Edwin H. Armstrong invented, was patented; FM used frequency modulation of the radio wave to minimize static and interference from electrical equipment and the atmosphere in the audio program.

****

Wheaties advertisement featuring baseball great Lou Gehrig:

I believe any man who wants to go places in any sport has to keep in good physical shape. I always watch my eating pretty closely and make it a point to put away a good breakfast in the morning. But I want my food to taste good, too. And there's nothing better than a big bowl of Wheaties with plenty of milk or cream and sugar. That's a Breakfast of Champions" you want to try. You'll be glad you did. Because Wheaties sure taste great!

The Twenty-second Amendment

Chapter 13

H. J. Res. 27

Eightieth Congress of the United States of America
At the First Session

Begun and held at the City of Washington on Friday, the third
day of January, one thousand nine hundred and forty-seven

JOINT RESOLUTION

Proposing an amendment to the Constitution of the United States
relating to the terms of office of the President.

*Resolved by the Senate and House of Representatives of the United
States of America in Congress assembled (two-thirds of each House
concurring therein)*, That the following article is hereby proposed as
an amendment to the Constitution of the United States, which shall
be valid to all intents and purposes as part of the Constitution when
ratified by the legislatures of three-fourths of the several States:

"ARTICLE —

"SECTION 1. No person shall be elected to the office of the President
more than twice, and no person who has held the office of President,
or acted as President, for more than two years of a term to which
some other person was elected President shall be elected to the office
of the President more than once. But this Article shall not apply
to any person holding the office of President when this Article was
proposed by the Congress, and shall not prevent any person who may
be holding the office of President, or acting as President, during the
term within which this Article becomes operative from holding the
office of President or acting as President during the remainder of
such term.

"SEC. 2. This article shall be inoperative unless it shall have been
ratified as an amendment to the Constitution by the legislatures of
three-fourths of the several States within seven years from the date
of its submission to the States by the Congress."

Speaker of the House of Representatives.

Acting President of the Senate pro tempore.

Proposed in Congress:	**21 March 1947**
Sent to States:	**21 March 1947**
Ratified:	**27 February 1951**

Chapter 13

THE TWENTY-SECOND AMENDMENT

Section 1.
No person shall be elected to the office of the President more than twice, and no person who has held the office of President, or acted as President, for more than two years of a term to which some other person was elected President shall be elected to the office of President more than once. But this Article shall not apply to any person holding the office of President when this Article was proposed by Congress, and shall not prevent any person who may be holding the office of President, or acting as President, during the term within which this Article becomes operative from holding the office of President or acting as President during the remainder of such term.

Section 2.
This article shall be inoperative unless it shall have been ratified as an amendment to the Constitution by the legislatures of three-fourths of the several States within seven years from the date of its submission to the States by the Congress.

Brief Summary

The Twenty-second Amendment sets a term limit for the US president, stating that a person can be elected to the presidency no more than twice. It further specifies that a person who assumes the office of president without being elected to it (because of, for example, the death or resignation of a sitting president) and holds the office for more than two years cannot be elected to the presidency more than once.

Timeline

1947-49	The Commission on Organization of the Executive Branch of the Government, known as the Hoover Commission, recommends, among other proposals, what would become the Twenty-second Amendment.
3 January 1947	Representative Earl C. Michener introduces House Joint Resolution 27, proposing the Twenty-second Amendment.

12 March 1947	The US Senate passes the Twenty-second Amendment.
21 March 1947	The US House of Representatives passes the Twenty-second Amendment.
24 March 1947	The US Congress formally proposes the Twenty-second Amendment.
27 February 1951	The Twenty-second Amendment is ratified when Minnesota becomes the thirty-sixth state to ratify it. Two states rejected the amendment and five took no action.

Introduction

By reason of the lack of a positive expression upon the subject of the tenure of the office of President, and by reason of a well-defined custom which has risen in the past that no President should have more than two terms in that office, much discussion has resulted upon this subject. Hence it is the purpose of this...[proposal]...to submit this question to the people so they, by and through the recognized processes, may express their views upon this question, and if they shall so elect, they may...thereby set at rest this problem."[1]

So noted a report by the US House of Representatives in 1947 on an amendment to the US Constitution to establish only two four-year terms for all Presidents of the United States. Enacted by both houses of Congress that year, there was much ambivalence to changing the US Constitution on this matter, and it took four years before the amendment was ratified in 1951.

Historians Paul and George Willis wrote in 1952, "On February 27, 1951, the thirty-sixth state ratified the Twentysecond Amendment. Thus ended efforts made since 1789 to fill in the omission left in the Constitution by the framers concerning presidential re-eligibility."[2] However, just what is "presidential re-eligibility"? And why was a constitutional amendment needed to fix this potential problem in the American system of government?

The desire to limit the terms of the "chief executive" of what would become the United States existed even before the American nation did. Article 31 of the Declaration of Rights of the Maryland Constitution of 1776 stated "[t]hat a long continuance, in the first executive departments of power or trust, is dangerous to liberty; a rotation, therefore, in those departments, is one of the best securities of permanent freedom."[3] Another example of this same feeling can be found in Section 5 of the Bill of Rights of the Virginia constitution of 1776, which declared "[t]hat the [elected officials in the state and nation] may be restrained from oppression, by feeling and participating the burdens of the people, they should, as fixed periods, be reduced to a private station, return into that body from which they were originally taken, and the vacancies be supplied by frequent, certain, and regular elections, in which all, or any part of the former members, to be again eligible, or ineligible, as the laws shall direct."[4]

At the Constitution Convention in 1787, the issue over the length of the term, and the number of terms itself, for the President under the Constitution, was discussed widely; George Mason said, "a temptation on the side of the Executive to intrigue with the Legislature for a re-appointment."[5] Gouverneur Morris and James Wilson argued for the direct election of the president, with either a two-year or three-year term, with no limits on re-election.[6] In the end, nothing came of any of the potential ideas for a presidential term limitation that would end up in the Constitution as it was first drafted. If changes were to be made, especially in this area, they would have to come through the amendment process. During the convention, delegate Mason spoke out forcefully that the issue should be addressed in the original document, that being the Constitution:

"Mr. Chairman, there is not a more important article in the Constitution than this. The great fundamental principle in republicanism is here sapped. The President is elected without rotation. It may be said that a new election may remove him, and place another in his stead. If we judge from the experience of all other countries, and even our own, we may conclude that, as the President of the United States may be re-elected, so he will. How is it in every government where rotation is not required? Is there a single instance of a great man not being re-elected? Our governor is obliged to return, after a given period, to a private station. It is so in most of the states. This President will be elected time after time; he will be continued in office for life. If we wish to change him, the great powers in Europe will not show us." He continued, "Will not the great powers of Europe, as France and Great Britain, be interested in having a friend in the President of the United States? And will they not be more interested in his election than in that of the king of Poland? The people of Poland has a right to displace their king. But do they ever do it? No. Prussia and Russia, and other European powers, would not suffer it. This clause will open a door to the dangers and misfortunes which the people of Poland undergo. The powers of Europe will interpose, and we shall have a civil war in the bowels of our country, and the subject to all the horrors and calamities of an elective monarchy."[7]

Footnotes, Sources and Further Reading for this chapter appears on page 843

In "The Federalist Papers," No. 72, Alexander Hamilton defended the convention's inability to add a presidential eligibility clause to the Constitution:

"With a positive duration of considerable extent, I connect the circumstance of re-eligibility. The first is necessary to give to the officer himself the inclination and the resolution to act his part well, and to the community time and leisure to observe the tendency of his measures, and thence to form an experimental estimate of their merits. The last is necessary to enable the people, when they see reason to approve of his conduct, to continue him in his station, in order to prolong the utility of his talents and virtues, and to secure to the government the advantage of permanency in a wise system of administration...Nothing appears more plausible at first sight, nor more ill-founded upon close inspection, than a scheme which in relation to the present point has had some respectable advocates, I mean that of continuing the chief magistrate in office for a certain time, and then excluding him from it, either for a limited period or forever after. This exclusion, whether temporary or perpetual, would have nearly the same effects, and these effects would be for the most part rather pernicious than salutary."[8]

Chancellor James Kent wrote in an undated letter, "The mode of his [the President] appointment presented one of the most difficult and momentous questions that occupied the deliberations of the assembly which framed the Constitution; and if ever the tranquility of this Nation is to be disturbed and its liberties endangered by a struggle for power, it will be upon this very subject of the choice of a President. This is the question that is the eventually to test the goodness and try the strength of the Constitution; and if we shall be able for half a century hereafter to continue to elect the chief magistrate of the Union with discretion, moderation, and integrity, we shall undoubtedly stamp the highest value on our national character, and recommend our republican institutions, if not to the imitation yet certainly to the esteem and admiration of the more enlightened part of mankind."[9]

From the first administration of President George Washington, starting in 1789, until 1940, no President dared to go to the voters to get elected to a third term in office. In 1796, after serving two presidential terms, George Washington refused a third, believing that any such re-election would make him, or any future President, a potential dictator. Washington believed that the nation needed new blood in the presidency every eight years, after two four-year terms were completed – that two terms was enough for any leader to accomplish what he needed to accomplish. Even Andrew Jackson refused a third term, although many historians believed that he pushed his Vice President and close associate Martin Van Buren as his successor to have, in effect, a third term. But Van Buren, once elected, became his own man, and Jackson was frustrated. However, it appears that, according to historian Herman V. James, Jackson called for a constitutional amendment that would limit the president to a single term of either four or six years.[10] By the middle of the 19th century, two-thirds of the states in the Union had clauses in their state constitutions limiting the chief executive of the state to certain limited terms. In 1844, the Whig Party placed in their national party platform a call for a constitutional amendment limiting the president to a single term of an undetermined number of years.[11]

Even before and after the Civil War, attempts were made to change this part of the Constitution; in fact, by 1866, there had been ten total attempts. Senator John J. Ingalls, Republican of Kansas, said on 1 February 1866, "No less than ten methods of choosing a President were seriously proposed and debated. How to call forth one of the people to be their executive chief for a limited period of years, and how to clothe him with just sufficient powers, long baffled the convention. Federal governments, in Greece, in Switzerland, and in Holland, like the confederation of the United States, had been without a separate executive branch; and the elective monarchies of Poland, of the Papal states, and of Germany offered no available precedents. The report of the committee of detail of the sixth of August introduced no improvement in the manner of selecting a president; and the transferred to the senate the power to make treaties and to appoint ambassadors and judges of the Supreme Court. Questions relating to his duties long remained in doubt; the mode of his election was reached only just before the close of the convention."[12]

A potential turning point came just prior to the 1876 presidential election. President Ulysses S Grant, serving near the end of his second term in the White House, was called upon by some Republicans to run for an unprecedented third term. Many Republicans and most Democrats denounced even the thought of such a campaign. Representative William McKendreee Springer, Democrat of Illinois, introduced a resolution calling the idea of a third Grant term as "unwise, unpatriotic and fraught with peril to our free institutions." On 15 December 1875, the US House of Representatives, in a nonbinding vote, overwhelmingly supported the Springer resolution, 234-18. Despite this, Grant's name was put in nomination at the 1876 Republican National Convention, where he led all other candidates during the 33 rounds of balloting, rising to 314 votes, 64 shy of the total needed for the nomination. That nomination, after Grant pulled his name out, went to Ohio Governor Rutherford B. Hayes, who was elected president next year.

In 1892, Grover Cleveland, who had been defeated for a second term in 1888, ran again, and was elected – the only President to serve two non-consecutive terms as the Chief Executive. (This is why Cleveland is listed as both the 22nd and 24th Presidents.) From the time that Cleveland left the White House in 1897 until 1940, any talk of a third term was quickly dashed by the nation's political leaders and media sources, most notably newspapers and magazines. In 1912, when former President Theodore Roosevelt ran as an independent for what would have been his second elected but third presidential term, an assassin, John Schrank, tried to murder the former President, claiming that he was stopping Roosevelt from gaining an unprecedented third term. Roosevelt survived the attack (he was shot in the chest, but the papers of a thick speech took much of the impact of the bullet) and lost the election, but the message hung loudly in the air: no President should seek a third elected term, even though there was no actual law against such a campaign run. In 1913, shortly before President-elect Woodrow Wilson was inaugurated, the Senate passed, by a vote of 47-23, a nonbinding resolution that would limit all future presidents to a single six-year term. In 1928, the Senate voted, by a vote of 56-26, the so-called La Follette resolution, which was an exact rehash of the Springer resolution from 1875. Once again, Congress was unable to get the sufficient number of votes to pass a proposed constitutional amendment.

In 1936, the staunch opposition against changing the time a President serves in office, or even limiting the time or terms of service, seemed to remain strong: *The Washington Star* newspaper in Washington, D.C. conducted a poll, asking, "Do you favor a single six-year term for the President instead of the present tenure" of two fouryear terms? The results were 26.7% in favor, 66.4% against, and 6.9% with no opinion. Perhaps anticipating that the controversy could arise, on 5 January 1937 Rep. Donald McLean, Republican of New Jersey, introduced a proposed constitutional amendment that, as of 20 January 1941, would change the presidential term to one single term of six years and no more, and that the President and Vice President could not run for re-election. Senator Edward Burke, Democrat of Nebraska, introduced on 6 January 1937 his own resolution in the US Senate, which also called for a single six-year term, and would allow no present or past President to run for a second term, addressing what Grover Cleveland had done. At the same time, Burke's proposed amendment did away with the Electoral College, allowing for the direct election of both the President and Vice President by the people. Senator Royal Copeland, Democrat of New York and a member of the Senate Committee on Judiciary, introduced his own proposed amendment, calling for a specific law limiting the President to election to no more than two terms of four years each; men who advanced to the presidency, for whatever reason, could only serve the remainder of that term and be elected to one more four-year term. At the end of the day, however, there did not appear to be any danger to the structure of electing the President or his service of two four-year terms, and the proposed amendments never got out of the respective committees that they were referred to.

As the 1940 presidential election moved forward, that statement appeared to hold, as President Roosevelt signaled to his aides and to the nation that he would soon support a candidate to succeed him as the Democratic presidential nominee. Paul Appleby, an advisor to Roosevelt, later wrote, "To no one other then Harry Hopkins has the role of convention manager ever been attributed. Yet Hopkins himself told me, as we mapped our common program for the day following the nomination, that he had had no word of Roosevelt's desires or intentions and no word of instruction-indeed, that he had had no direct communication with the President at all during the convention until the morning after the nomination had been overwhelmingly voted. Even then Roosevelt had not said that he would accept. The conversation had been a mulling over of the convention situation and a discussion of the vice-presidential nomination still to come."[13] But at the Democratic National Convention in Chicago, Roosevelt sprung a secret campaign on the party, asking the delegates and party leaders for another nomination. The Democrats were ill-disposed to deny this man, who had won two landslide elections, his wishes, so they did as they were told and Roosevelt was nominated for an unprecedented third term. Vice President John Nance Garner, angry that Roosevelt had lied to him and had denied him the nomination he felt he deserved for eight years of loyal service as the President's number two, refused to be nominated for another term as Vice President, and his name was substituted by that of Henry A. Wallace, who had served as Secretary of Agriculture (1933-40), and would later serve as Secretary of Commerce (1945-46). Garner and Postmaster General James Farley, both close Roosevelt confidants for many years, decided to challenge Roosevelt for the nomination anyway; they were ultimately crushed by a convention that seemed unwilling and unable to find any candidate other than Franklin D. Roosevelt. But even though Roosevelt seemed to have pushed his candidacy at the last moment, a study of the record shows that he was making overtures to supporters as early as 1939. Historian Michael Korzi explained, "What is fascinating about the increasing calls for Roosevelt's service in late 1939 and 1940 is how many still appealed to preserving the New Deal and the Roosevelt legacy, in addition to the foreign crisis, to justify the third term. While Democratic Senator Byron (Pat) Harrison would abandon his opposition to the third term in January 1940 because of the 'world crisis,' and Paul McNutt – federal security administrator and Democratic presidential aspirant in 1940 – would pledge his support to a Roosevelt third term due to 'the threat of total war,' others would persist in appealing to the preservation of the New Deal and the Roosevelt domestic legacy."[14]

Not all of Roosevelt's supporters were happy with his breaking of tradition in running for a third term. Lewis W. Douglas wrote in *The Saturday Evening Post* in November 1940, before the American people went to the polls, "[B]ecause I have a strongly sympathetic feeling toward much of what the New Deal stands for, and because, finally, my full sympathy is extended to the President during these days of heavy responsibility and grave decisions, I have reluctantly but unqualifiedly [come to] believe that to continue the present Administration in office beyond what is almost a constitutional limitation on tenure is to add to the dangers that are pressing in on American democracy."[15] But Douglas' pleas fell on deaf ears, and Roosevelt was elected not just to a third term, but, in 1944, a fourth term.

At the same time that Roosevelt was winning an unprecedented third and fourth term, there was talk, especially among Republicans, of limiting the number of terms a President could be elected to. What held the Republicans back was the fact that from 1931 until 1947, they controlled neither house of the US Congress, and from 1933 until 1953, they did not control the White House, either. In April 1945, Roosevelt died suddenly from a brain hemorrhage, and he was succeeded by his third Vice President, former US Senator Harry S. Truman of Missouri. Within a year of his taking office, Truman became exceedingly unpopular in the nation. This led, in November 1946, to the Republicans winning control of the US House of Representatives for the first time in fifteen years. Once the Republicans took control of the House in January 1947, they made immediate moves to open debate on a proposed constitutional amendment to limit the number of terms a president could be elected to.

What eventually became the proposed constitutional amendment began as House Joint Resolution 27, introduced in the House on 3 January 1947 by Rep. Earl C. Michener, Republican of Michigan, and the chairman of the House Committee on the Judiciary, after which it was referred to the House Committee on the Judiciary. After hearings were held, it was voted out of committee favorably on 5 February 1947. The next day, 6 February 1947, Rep. Leo Ellwood Allen, Republican of Illinois, went to the floor of the House and called for the passage of just such an amendment. Opposing him was Rep. Adolph Joachim Sabath, Democrat of Illinois, who mocked the Republican argument, claiming that the American people did not support such an amendment, and that the only reason it was being pushed was because the Republicans were jealous for not having a presidential candidate to win a third or fourth or even a fifth, if possible, term in office. Sabath called the proposed resolution the "antiRoosevelt amendment."[16] Next to speak was Rep. John McCormack, Democrat of Massachusetts. He argued that Americans in the future would be denied by this amendment to elect a president who they wanted to serve more than two terms, which he felt was something the Framers had tried to fix with the US Constitution. He called this action the placing of a "dead hand of the past" on future generations. McCormack concluded his argument by stating that any limitations that the US Constitution placed on any segment of American government or society were placed there as protective measures. He stated, "[T]hose limitations were imposed to protect the rights of the individuals to assure that the legislative body would not take away the fundamental rights that the American people believe in and for which the framers of the Constitution fought."[17] Rep. Raymond Springer, Republican of Indiana, then stated, "[T]his resolution has but one purpose: that purpose is to submit to the people of the country by and through their state legislatures the important problem of Presidential tenure, and permit the people through their state legislatures to decide whether or not they desire that limitation fixed or to leave the question of Presidential tenure just as it is now set forth in the Constitution of the United States of America."[18]

Finally, after two hours of debate in the US House, the resolution passed by a vote of 285-121, with 26 members not voting. The proposal then moved to the US Senate, where it was referred to the Senate Committee on the Judiciary. Reported out of committee favorably on 21 February by Senator Alexander Wiley, Republican of Wisconsin, and Chairman of the Assented Committee on the Judiciary, debate began on 3 March 1947, and continue on 7 March, 10 March, and 12 March, with the resolution coming up for a final vote on the final date. In the Senate, debate was just as passionate for and against the proposed amendment. Senator Millard Tydings, Democrat of Maryland, said, "[T]he people ought to have right to elect a man to two full terms...and we ought not to deny them the right to elect a President for two full terms, but we ought to provide that a man cannot be elected President for more than two terms."[19] Senator Herbert Romulus O'Conor, Democrat of Maryland, disagreed, stating, "Certainly nothing could act more definitely too halt or impede development of potential leadership in the city, State, or Nation than to permit any one man or any one party to persuade the people that he or they alone are competent and therefore must be perpetuated in office."[20] Senator Warren Magnuson, Democrat of Washington State, introduced a substitute amendment: "A person who has held [the] office of President, or acted as President, on 365 calendar days or more in each of two terms shall not eat eligible to hold the office of President, or to act as President, for any part of another term; but this article shall not prevent any person who may be holding the office of President or acting as President during the term within which this article becomes operative from holding the office of President or acting as President during the remainder of such term." Other Senators argued that under the House resolution, a vice president could become president near the end of his second term and then be elected to two full terms as president. Although Magnuson did receive some support from across the aisle, notably from Senator Robert Taft, Republican of Ohio, Taft felt that a US president should serve no more than eight years as the Chief Executive.. It was because of this stalemate that Senate debate lasted for several days. It was not until 12 March 1947 that Senate started voting on the resolution itself, as well as potential amendments and substitutes for the House proposal. The Senate voted first on Senator Magnuson's substitute, which received 34 yeas and 50 nays, with 11 members not voting. Senator Wilbert Lee O'Daniel, Democrat of Texas, introduced a substitute for House Joint Resolution 27, establishing a federal government-wide schedule of maximum tenure for all elected federal officials that gave them a single term of six years and no chance of re-election; the measure was defeated, 82-1, with 12 members not voting. A joint substitute, pitched by Republican William Lander of North Dakota and Democrat Glen Taylor of Idaho, read, "no person shall be elected to the office of President more than twice, and no person who had held the office of President, or acted as President, for more than two years of a term to which some other person was elected President, shall be elected to the office of President more than once." The Lander-Taylor proposal, while addressing the chief concern over electing a person more than two times as president, also disallowed this person from ever running for president again. For some reason, combining the first matter, the subject of the original debate, with the second, which had never been brought up, doomed the proposal: the Senate vote was 14 yeas, 66 nays, and 15 members not voting. The Senate then adjourned until later that evening. When they returned, Senator Claude Pepper, Democrat of Florida, began an attack on Senator Taft and the entire Republican Party. He accused the Republicans of using the amendment to harm" the legacy of the deceased Franklin Delano Roosevelt. He called the proposal an illegal move against "the right and present power of the people of the country to elect one to be the highest magistrate in the land."[21] After Pepper had finished, Senator Scott Lucas, Democrat of Illinois, stated that he felt that the Senate should vote on the resolution already. Cries of "Vote! Vote!" were chanted by Senators who wanted the proposed amendment to pass. Realizing that the debate was over, Senator Taft ordered a roll call vote. The vote was 59 yeas, 23 nays, and 13 members not voting. Amendments added to the Senate version had to be sent to a conference committee so that both houses could vote on the same exact language. Following the conference, the resolution was returned to the Senate on 13 March, then to the House, where it also passed with the requisite two-thirds on 21 March 1947, 81 to 29. The following day, it was submitted to the states for ratification.

There was not the urgency attached to the ratification of this amendment as seen, for example, in the ratification of the Twenty-first Amendment, which repealed the Eighteenth Amendment and ended Prohibition. When Minnesota ratified the amendment on 27 February 1951, it had taken 1,439 days from the time the US Congress submitted it to the states, while the Twenty-first amendment took 288 days.

Although it can be argued that the Twenty-second Amendment is less important than other amendments, in today's political climate, its significance has risen. The amendment might have been invoked after the assassination of President John F. Kennedy in 1963, but Kennedy had served more than half of his four-year term, so his successor, Lyndon Johnson, was eligible to run for the office twice (although he elected not to seek reelection in 1968). Gerald R. Ford, the thirty-eighth president, assumed the office on the resignation of Richard Nixon. In his subsequent election bid in 1976, he lost (to Jimmy Carter), but had he won, the Twenty-second Amendment would have precluded him from running again in 1980 because he served out more than two years of Nixon's term. In 1984, as Ronald Reagan was running for his second term, some of his adherents wished that there were no amendment that could stop him from running for a third term, and in fact numerous proposals for the repeal of the amendment have been introduced in Congress.

Commenting on the effect of the Twenty-second Amendment on the American political system, historian Joseph Kallenbach explained in 1952, "The ultimate effect on the Presidency of the now-formalized rule of compulsory retirement after two terms is difficult to assess. A backward projection gives some indication of its future impact. If the Twenty-second Amendment had been in effect since 1789, it appears that the outcome of two presidential elections in addition to those of 1940 and 1944 would have been affected. If General Grant had not been a strong contender for a third-term nomination in 1880, the 'dark horse' Garfield might well have never emerged as the candidate of the Republicans, and the election of that year would probably have placed sore one else in the White House. Again in 1912 Theodore Roosevelt would not have been eligible for the Presidency, and the split in the Republican party which resulted from his candidacy and made possible the election of Woodrow Wilson conceivably would not have occurred. Of the 32 persons who have occupied the office of President, ten would have been rendered ineligible for further service. Those who would have been forever disqualified include six of the seven Presidents who are generally recognized as having been our most outstanding and able ones."[22]

Debate in Congress

On 6 February 1947, debate opened on the proposed presidential term amendment. The debate quickly became heated, as Republicans desired to stop the chance of a future President serving more than two terms, and Democrats saw the amendment as an attack on the now-deceased President Franklin D. Roosevelt.

AMENDMENT TO THE CONSTITUTION RELATING TO THE TERMS OF OFFICE OF THE PRESIDENT

Mr. ALLEN of Illinois.[25] Mr. Speaker, I call up House Resolution 91 and ask for its immediate consideration.

[...]

Mr. Speaker, immediately upon the adoption of this resolution it shall be in order to move that the House resolve itself into the Committee of the Whole House on the State of the Union for the consideration the joint resolution (H.J. Res. 27) proposing an amendment to the Constitution of the United States relating to the terms of the office of the President. That after general debate, which shall be confined to the joint resolution and shall continue not to exceed 2 hours, to be equally divided and controlled by the chairman and ranking minority member of the Committee on the Judiciary, the joint resolution shall be read for amendment under the 5-minute rule.

[...]

This resolution has but one purpose. That purpose is to submit to the people, by and through their State legislatures, this very important problem of the Presidential tenure of office, and to let the people decide whether or not this limitation should be written into the Constitution.

Heretofore many resolutions have been introduced upon this very question, but for some reason or another they have fallen by the wayside, and no legislation has been passed upon this question, and our Constitution remains without amendment to this date respecting the tenure of the office of President.

Section 1, article II, of the Constitution provides:

The executive power shall be vested in a President of the United States of America. He shall hold his office during the term of 4 years.

Again, under amendment 20, section 1, of our Constitution, we find, in that amendment, the following language:

The terms of the President and Vice President shall end at noon on the 20th day of January, and the terms of Senators and Representatives at noon on the 3d day of January, of the years in which such terms would have ended if this article had not been ratified; and the terms of their successors shall then begin.

By reason of the lack of a positive expression upon the subject of tenure of the office of President, and by reason of a well-defined custom which has arisen in the past that no President should have more than two terms in that office, much public discussion has resulted upon this subject. Hence it is the purpose of this legislation, if passed, to submit this question to the people as they, by and through the recognized processes, may express their views upon this question, and, if they shall so elect, they may amend our Constitution and thereby set at rest this problem.

This is not a political question. The importance of the problem to the people transcends all political implications and considerations. This proposed amendment to our Constitution, if adopted, will continue throughout the future years, unless and until a further amendment may be adopted upon this subject. Therefore, in the face of general public discussions, in the face of the custom which has developed throughout the years, we are here presenting a resolution to submit this basic problem to the people.

[...]

Mr. SABATH.[26] Mr. Speaker, I yield myself such time as I may desire.

Mr. Speaker, the rule has been correctly stated by my colleague, the new chairman of the Committee on Rules, with whom I have had the pleasure of serving for many years. I have always found him to be fair, and consequently I was rather surprised that he should have yielded to the demands for depriving the House of a reasonable time for general debate on this important legislation.

If I am not mistaken, this is the first time that any resolution amending the Constitution that has served us so well for 170 years has been brought before the House under a rule which permits only two short hours for general debate...

[...]

For 170 years this country has prospered and grown strong under the Constitution, without any amendment deviating from our true course toward more and more democracy, nor from the true principles of representative government laid down by the founding fathers. Today we are enjoying greater prosperity and greater liberty and greater equality than ever before in our history. I hope the Republicans will not be able to do anything to destroy that prosperity, which was brought about by the Democratic Party under the inspired leadership of our greatest

President, Franklin Delano Roosevelt, during the third and even the first part of the fourth term, until his untimely death, and despite the incalculable burdens of carrying a world-wide war to final victory.

What hurts most, and what I strongly resent, are statements made by several Republican Members that they "must vote for this anti-Roosevelt resolution." Perhaps, had I not overheard these remarks, I should not have said anything at all here today.

Can we not be fair enough to let rest in peace a man who has done so much for our country and for humanity? I think it is manifestly unfair for anyone to make such remarks. It was a Godsend to the world that we had Franklin D. Roosevelt, whom the people freely chose four times to direct our Government and our destinies, and who served the Nation and all mankind as no other man has ever done before.

Though Franklin Roosevelt now rests in eternal sleep, I trust and I hope that his views and his policies, for which he fought and for which he gave his life, will continue for years to come to shape our national destiny, and that this country will continue in the great material prosperity which he brought about. Most of all, Mr. Speaker, I hope that the people of the world can reach his greatest objective – a just and lasting peace – not only for America, but for all people everywhere. That is his dream, and my dream, and the dream of the common people Roosevelt so loved.

[...]

But, Mr. Speaker, there are other reasons why the people will rise up in anger against this constitutional amendment once the facts are known.

[...]

Mr. Speaker, I yield 15 minutes to the gentleman from Massachusetts [Mr. McCORMACK].

Mr. McCORMACK.[27] Mr. Speaker, this is one of the most important questions that any Member of this body will have to pass upon and I hope each Member will determine the question in accordance with his conscience. It is not my purpose to discuss politics in connection with the proposed amendment to the Constitution, an amendment which will not have any effect upon you and me of this generation but which might have a very important effect upon generations to come after you and I are dead and gone. If this amendment is incorporated in the Constitution, it will make the Constitution rigid. It ties the hands of future generations of Americans and deprives them of the opportunity to meet any problem that might confront them.

[...]

Mr. ALLEN of Illinois. Mr. Speaker, I yield 10 minutes to the gentleman from Indiana [Mr. HALLECK].

Mr. HALLECK.[28] Mr. Speaker, while I do not agree with the burden of the argument just made by the gentleman from Massachusetts, I have listened with interest to what he had to say. I commend him for his approach, which is clearly one devoid of partisanship. I join with him in the statement that the matter we are discussing today is not one of partisanship but rather of what best to do, be we Democrats or Republicans, looking to the future of this great land of ours. He has pointed out certain things which he says might be dangerous in their effects. Without undertaking to say that there is no force at all to his argument, speaking for myself I think that the dangers that the gentleman envisages, if they may be said to be dangers, are certainly outweighed by the danger that obtains from the absence of the constitutional amendment as now proposed.

We are discussing here a proposal to protect our American system of constitutional government. In such a discussion there can be no divisions on mere lines of partisanship, for in this House, Democrats, no less than Republicans, are devoted to our Constitution. We all want to see our system work for the benefit of the entire Nation, and for posterity.

Throughout our entire national history, we have amended the Constitution from time to time as experience appeared to dictate.

The Constitution has served us well. It was once described by the great Gladstone as the most wonderful work ever struck off at a given time by the brain and purpose of man.

Yet the Constitution itself clearly provides the methods of amendment, demonstrating that it was never the intention of the founding fathers to regard their work as finished for all time.

These are the reasons why I am happy today to all to call as our witness for this proposal one of the founders of the Democratic Party, a man who was himself one of the principal architects of the Bill of Rights, so vital a part of our Constitution today – Thomas Jefferson.

Toward the end of Jefferson's second administration, in 1808, there arose an insistent demand among many of his supporters that he stand for re-election.

When the legislatures of 7 of the then 17 States had adopted petitions urging a third term, Jefferson responded: That I should lay down my charge at the proper period is as much a duty as to have borne it faithfully.

If some termination to the services of the Chief Magistrate be not fixed by the Constitution, or supplied by practice, his office, nominally for 4 years, will, in fact, become for life; and history shows how easily that degenerates into an inheritance.

Believing that a representative government, responsible at short periods by election, is that which produces the greatest sum of happiness to mankind, I feel it a duty to do no act which shall essentially impair that principle; and I should unwillingly be the person who, disregarding sound precedent set by an illustrious predecessor, should furnish the first example of prolongation beyond the second term of office.

Now, we do not need a Philadelphia lawyer to interpret what Thomas Jefferson thought about the principle embodied in the proposal before us today.

[...]

By way of illustrating how deeply the two-term tradition had become imbedded in our legal and political assumptions, let me read to you a plank from the Democratic national platform for 1896. The plank is headed, "Third term." It reads:

We declare it to be the unwritten law of this Republic established by custom and usage of 100 years, and sanctioned by the examples of the greatest and wisest of those who founded and have maintained our Government, that no man should be eligible for a third term of the Presidential office.

With Thomas Jefferson as his mentor, and with the Democratic national platform as his guide, no Democrat in this Congress need experience the slightest qualms of partisan conscience in giving unequivocal patriotic support to the amendment before us.

[...]

Mr. McCORMACK. Mr. Chairman, will the gentleman yield?

Mr. SPRINGER.[29] I yield to my colleague from Massachusetts.

Mr. McCORMACK. Does my friend agree with my contention that if in the future our country should be involved in war and the-then President were in his second term, that no matter what the emergency, no matter what situation might confront the people at that time, that President must retire if this resolution becomes part of the Constitution?

Mr. SPRINGER. I understand the gentleman's question, and thanks for submitting it. May I say that if our country were involved in any grave emergency in the future, such as war, the President does not fight the war. Our chiefs of staff, our generals, our admirals are the ones who fight our wars. Our President takes advice, of course, and acts in conjunction with them. But where is the President, of whatever political party he may be a member, who would not take that same counsel, that same advice, for the safety and for the protection of our Nation and the people in it?

Mr. McCORMACK. Mr. Chairman, will the gentleman yield further?

Mr. SPRINGER. May I proceed further? I have but a short time. I appreciate the gentleman's interest.

Mr. Chairman, during the past many resolutions of this kind have been submitted but none have ever been enacted by both Houses of the Congress, and this question has not been submitted to the people. Throughout the years the Constitution has stood as originally written, and may I read just for our own consideration, as we deal with this vitally important problem, section 1 of article II of the Constitution which contains this provision. I know all of you are familiar with it, but let us review it once more:

The executive power shall be vested in a President of the United States of America, who shall hold his office during the term of 4 years.

The CHAIRMAN. The time of the gentlemen from Indiana has expired.

Mr. MICHENER.[30] Mr. Chairman, I yield the gentleman three additional minutes.

Mr. SPRINGER. May I say, Mr. Chairman, that until the lame-duck amendment to this article, amendment No. 20, there had been no amendment adopted on this question. That amendment provided -

That the terms of President and Vice President shall end at noon on the 20th day of January and the terms of Senators and Representatives at noon on the 3d day of January of the year in which such terms should have ended if this article had not been ratified and the terms of their successors shall then begin.

Mr. RANKIN.[31] Mr. Chairman, will the gentleman yield? Mr. SPRINGER. I yield to the gentleman from Mississippi.

Mr. RANKIN. Let me call attention to the fact that in 1861 when everyone knew we were on the verge of a war, the Confederate constitutional convention met, at a time when we had one of the greatest soldiers of all time as President of the Confederacy, and they adopted a constitutional provision limiting the Presidency of the Confederacy to 6 years and providing that he could not succeed himself.

Mr. SPRINGER. In other words, they wanted to protect to some extent against any man perpetuating himself in public office.

Mr. Chairman, I want to recur to the words of Woodrow Wilson. Let us think for a minute what he said on this question. I obtained this interesting statement from his own remarks, now on file in the Congressional Library.[32] This is what Woodrow Wilson said on this subject:

To change the term to 6 years would be to increase the likelihood of its being too long, without any assurance that it would, in happy cases, be long enough. A fixed constitutional limitation to a single term of office is highly arbitrary and unsatisfactory from every point of view.

He was thinking about the one-term proposal.

Put the present customary limitation of two terms into the Constitution, if you do not trust the people to take care of themselves, but make it two terms (not one, because 4 years is often too long), and give the President a chance to win the full service by proving himself fit for it.

Before closing I want to quote the words of Abraham Lincoln when he left Springfield, Ill., to come to Washington to assume the Presidency. He came to Indianapolis. He was worried and distressed. He stopped there. A great group of people had assembled. They asked them to speak. He spoke, and in the course of his remarks he said this to the American people:

Remember, it is not with the President nor the officeholder, nor with the politician, but with the people alone rests the power of determining our politics of government.

Mr. Chairman, we are today proposing to submit this highly important question to the people, just as Lincoln proposed.

Mr. CELLER.[33] Mr. Chairman, I yield myself 10 minutes.

Mr. Chairman, a number of the members of the minority of the Committee on the Judiciary realize that the Constitution sets no limitation on the number of terms a President may serve. The Members also realize that a tradition was established by Washington, followed by Jefferson, Madison, Jackson, Cleveland, McKinley, and Wilson. Now attempts are being made to change the Constitution as to [the] number of terms a President may serve.

These Members feel a change is unnecessary, but if there is to be any change these Members feel it would be preferable to change the Constitution so that a President could serve only 6 years and not be eligible for re-election.

It has always been natural for the incumbent President to have his eyes fixed on re-election, and all the acts of the first term, directly or indirectly, in some measure, are affected by the ambition for a second term. It is only natural for the incumbent President to make appointments even to his Cabinet with due consideration for political repercussions. Even appointments to important judicial positions have been at times tinctured with politics. I make no specific charge against any specific President. I speak generally. The President is one to ask himself and his intimates, "Will the appointment enhance or diminish my prospects for re-election?" You know and I know that even Ambassadors and Ministers have been appointed because of political campaign aid and assistance and in the hope of renewal of that aid at re-election time. If there is no possibility, we feel, for re-election, there is no need for the President and his Cabinet and those associated with him to canvass for delegates at the national convention; no need for the President to placate certain sections of the country that may be hostile; no need to suggest legislation that might mean the garnering of additional votes that might be useful at the national convention.

During the first term the ambition for re-election to a second term and to serve four additional years casts an ominous shadow, in my humble estimation, over all the acts and all the work of the incoming President. I could, but shall not, quote you at length the arguments advanced by numerous Presidents, notably Jackson and Hayes and Taft, in favor of a 6-year-them, with no re-eligibility, but I will give you the statement made by Grover Cleveland when he accepted the nomination for President. He argued for a 6-year term, with no right to re-election. He said:

Then an election to office shall be the selection by the voters of one of their number to assume for a time a public trust, instead of his dedication to the profession of politics; when the holders of the ballot, quickened by a sense of duty, shall avenge truth betrayed and pledges broken, and when the suffrage shall be altogether free and uncorrupted the full realization of a government by the people will be at hand. And of the means to this end not one would, in my judgment, be more effective than an amendment to the Constitution disqualifying the President from re-election. When we consider the patronage of this great office the allurements of power, the temptations to retain public place once gained, and more than all, the availability a party finds in an incumbent when a horde of office-holders, with a zeal born of benefits received and fostered by the hope of favors yet to come, stand ready to aid money and trained political service, we recognize in the eligibility of the President for re-election a most serious danger to that calm, deliberate, and intelligent political action which must characterize a government by the people.

[...]

Mr. CELLER. Mr. Chairman, I yield 5 minutes to the gentleman from South Carolina [Mr. BRYSON].

Mr. BRYSON.[34] Mr. Chairman, the age-old question of the third term for President is before us again. The question arose in the early days of the Republic. In 1787 when our Constitution was first adopted our founding fathers debated the question of tenure of office for the President. First, it was proposed that the President should have one 7-year term. That proposal was adopted and later thrown out. Then a 6-year term was proposed, but rejected. Finally, in its great wisdom, the Convention settled on a 4-year term, with no limit to the number of terms. During the 170 years since the establishment of tenure of office for all our elective Federal officials many proposals have been made to change or limit the length of their service, but no change has ever been made. For many years, some Americans, particularly Republicans, believed that the precedents set by Washington and Jefferson, when they refused to serve three terms, had established an unwritten law that no President should ever serve his country more than 8 years.

In 1940 opponents of Franklin D. Roosevelt called on that unwritten l to help them prevent his election for a third term. But this so-called precedent or tradition proved a poor substitute for the will of the people, who swept the President back into office for a third and a fourth term. To have had a continual limitation on the presidential tenure of office in 1940 and again in 1944 would have been disastrous. Mr. Speaker, I submit that the gross fallacy of such a proposal as we have before us today was proved beyond the shadow of a doubt when in the face of a grave national crisis in 1940 the people of the United States believed it inadvisable to change their Chief Executive; and the utter stupidity of such a proposal was proved in 1944 when the people believed that such a change would have thrown our Nation into chaos and jeopardized our security in the face of the gravest military crisis in our Nation's history.

The proposal before us utterly ignores the possibility of future crises and exigencies which could well make it mandatory that we continue a Chief Magistrate in office beyond an 8-year period.

Before 1940 the precedent for the President's tenure of office had been established by the Presidents themselves, notably Washington and Jefferson. But in 1940 the precedent was established by the people, and that is as it should be. The President is the servant of the people, and each 4 years the people themselves should have the privilege of deciding whether their chief servant is to continue in office or be replaced. President Wilson said, "We singularly belie our own principles by seeking to determine by fixed constitutional provision what the people shall determine for themselves."

[...]

Mr. SPRINGER. Mr. Chairman, I yield such time as he may desire to the gentleman from Ohio [Mr. JENKINS]. Mr. JENKINS.[35] Mr. Chairman, I shall favor this resolution. The two-term rule for the position of Pre is an American tradition which was established by Washington, ratified by Jefferson in forceful and unambiguous language and likewise ratified expressly or implied by every President until the day of Franklin D. Roosevelt. The tenure of Franklin D. Roosevelt proved that Washington and Jefferson were wise.

I introduced a [response] to the same import as the resolution that we are now considering. I would have voted for my resolution and I shall vote for he one before us today.

[...]

Mr. SPRINGER. Mr. Chairman, I yield 5 minutes to the distinguished gentleman from Kentucky [Mr. ROBSION]. Mr. ROBSION.[36] Mr. Chairman, I am in support of House Joint Resolution 27. The gentleman from Michigan [Mr. MICHENER], one or two others, and myself introduced identical resolutions, proposing an amendment to the Constitution of the United States to limit the tenure of office of the President to the whole or any part of each of two separate terms; in other words, making ineligible any person who has served a President for a whole or part of two separate terms, and thereby placing a maximum limit of 8 years. No man could serve more than 8 years if this proposed amendment is submitted to the States and ratified NY 36 of the 48 States.

I am expressing the view that I have entertained over a long period of years. My experience and observations have strengthened my position on this matter. There has been so much discussion of this subject that I feel that we should at least give the American people, through the respective legislatures, the right to determine whether or not they desire such a limitation.

President George Washington, the Father of Our Country, in his wide experience and great wisdom, declined to be considered for a third term even though there was a universal demand that he do so and at a time when out country was having serious problems with France and other nations. Thomas Jefferson, another one of our very great Americans, the author of the Declaration of Independence, and who had served our country in the highest offices in this country and in foreign countries, certainly believed in representative democracy and in protecting the liberties and freedom of the American people. He had seen at first hand in Europe how free people had lost their freedom, not through parliaments and congresses, but through ambitious heads of the executive branch of the government. Therefore, 2 years before his second term expired, he made the following statement:

The general solicitations I have received to continue another term give me great consolation, but considerations for public as well as personal determine me inflexibly on that measure. That I should lay down my charge at a proper season is as much a duty as to have borne it faithfully...These changes are necessary, too, for the security of republican government. If some period be not fixed, either by the Constitution or by practice, to the service of the First Magistrate, his office, though nominally elective, will in fact be for life; and that will soon degenerate into an inheritance. I have therefore requested my fellow citizens to think of a successor for me, to whom I shall deliver the public concern with greater joy than I received them.

The Senate debate over the proposed presidential term amendment lasted for three days; the following are excerpts of the debate from 7, 10, and 12 March 1947.

THE PRESIDENTIAL TERM

The PRESIDENT pro tempore. The question is on the first committee amendment, which will be stated.

The Chief Clerk. On page 1, line 6, after the word "by," it is proposed to strike out "the legislatures of threefourths of the several States" and insert "conventions in the several States, as provided in the Constitution."

Mr. HILL.[37] Mr. President, the pending amendment to the Constitution would place the wisdom of the people in a strait-jacket. It would be a limitation on their right of free election. No matter what the emergency or what the danger, no matter how strongly the people might wish to continue a man in the Presidency, at the end of his second term they would be prohibited from doing so. The proposed amendment to the Constitution would place in the

Constitution a rigid prohibition against the right of the people to re-elect a man at the end of his second term. There is a vast difference between a rigid prohibition in the Constitution, absolutely denying such a right to the people, and a custom under which the people ordinarily do not exercise the right. I have no disagreement with the custom of ordinarily electing our Presidents for not more than two terms. The custom is well and good in customary times to meet ordinary conditions, but the difficulty about the proposed amendment is that once this rigid prohibition is imposed on the people, they are absolutely bound by it until and unless, at some future date, the Constitution is again amended and the rigid prohibition removed.

We all know the difficulties attendant upon amending the Constitution. We realize what a long, slow, and tedious process it is. No man can possibly know what the future holds; no man can know what tomorrow may bring forth, what dangers there may be for our country, what emergencies the Nation may face. Who, standing on this floor 10 years ago, could have foreseen the momentous and revolutionary events which have occurred in the history of the United States and of the world during the past 10 years? When we contemplate the world today and recall what it was like 10 years ago we can readily realize how violent and revolutionary have been the changes. We are accustomed to think we live in the air age. Yet the world is moving forward so rapidly that before we have passed out of the adolescence of the air age we find ourselves in the atomic age.

Within the past week many of us have been shocked by the revelations of conditions in Greece and Turkey, by the challenge should of certain obligations and duties resting upon our country in those far-away lands which perhaps most of us had not even considered. Only a few days ago even so wise and level-headed and able a Member of this body as the distinguished junior Senator from Georgia [Mr. RUSSELL][38] suggested that constituent members of the United Kingdom, England, Wales, Scotland, and Ireland be admitted into the American Union as States. This shows, Mr. President, how uncertain conditions are in the world today, and it suggests that many of the old moorings and the old landmarks seem to have disappeared. No one, I repeat, can know what may lie ahead of us or what danger or emergency may confront our Nation in the days ahead. Why then, should we suggest writing into the Constitution of the United States a rigid prohibition which might prevent the American people from meeting a danger or an emergency as they in their wisdom may think best?

Mr. President, during the history of our country approximately 170 joint resolutions have been introduced, either in this body or in the House of Representatives proposing to limit the term of office of the President. No one of those resolutions has ever been able to command sufficient support on the part of the people of the United States to be passed by the necessary votes in both Houses of Congress. Why should we now, at this late date after more than 150 years of our history under the Constitution, submit such a rigid prohibition for incorporation into the Constitution?

When we speak of a third term we think of George Washington, our first President, because it is said that he set the custom, that he established the precedent of a President's serving only two terms in office. Washington spoke very directly on the question of the wisdom of placing such a limitation on the people and the free election of their President. On April 28, 1788, he wrote a letter to the Marquis de Lafayette in which he spoke of the Constitutional Convention having given most careful consideration to this question, and of having finally come to the conclusion that there should be no limit on the people's right in the matter of the election of their President. Washington closed his letter to the Marquis de Lafayette with these words:

Under an extended view of this part of the subject I can see no propriety in precluding ourselves from the service of any man who, in some great emergency, shall be deemed universally most capable of serving the public.

That was George Washington speaking 170 years ago. It illustrates the wisdom of Washington. He did not foresee the air age or the atomic age. He did not even foresee the railroads, the telegraph, the telephone, or any of the other inventions which have made the world one common neighborhood; but in his wisdom he foresaw that a great emergency might arise in which the people might wish to continue a man in office. So he said he saw no propriety in limiting the people in their right to meet an emergency as they deemed wisest and best.

Mr. LUCAS.[39] Mr. President, will the Senator yield for a question? Mr. HILL. I yield.

Mr. LUCAS. The fact that George Washington refused a third term has been referred to as evidence that Washington was opposed to anyone serving a third term. I think the able Senator will agree with me that that is an inaccurate conclusion.

Mr. HILL. It is a wholly inaccurate conclusion. Not one word, not one expression, is to be found in George Washington's statements or his writings against a President serving more than two terms. On the contrary, there is the express opinion which I have just read to the Senate. Anyone who has studied the history of George Washington should know that the principal reason stated in his Farewell Address for his not even considering a third term was a personal reason. He had been in command of the Continental Army for 7 or 8 years; he had been away from his beloved Mount Vernon; he had served 8 years as President; and the desire closest to his heart was to retire from public service, to be relieved of the burdens and labors of public office, and return to his beautiful acres at Mount Vernon.

[...]

Mr. WILEY.[40] Mr. President, in regard to the pending amendment which proposes to strike out "the legislatures of three-fourths of the several States," and insert the words "conventions in the several States, as provided in the Constitution," I desire to state that in committee, as I recall the change was brought about largely due to the insistence of some of the Democratic Members, and I believe I am stating their argument correctly when I say they felt that conventions to consider and act on proposed constitutional amendments were nearer to the people. I could not agree with that, but their contention was that if under the Constitution conventions were held, representatives to the conventions would be elected on the specific issue. That was their position.

[...]

Mr. REVERCOMB.[41] Mr. President, will the Senator yield?

Mr. WILEY. I yield to the Senator from West Virginia.

Mr. REVERCOMB. I join the able chairman of the Judiciary Committee in the statement that there was some disagreement in the committee. As a matter of fact, I was one of those who thought that perhaps the best method of passing on the proposed amendment was through action by the State legislatures. However, after some discussion it was generally agreed to submit the amendment in the form in which it now appears.

The question was addressed to me, which I now want to address to the chairman of the Committee on the Judiciary, whether or not it is incumbent upon the Senate to set up the machinery for holding conventions, or whether that must be left to the separate States; that is, in allocating the number of delegates to a convention, and prescribing how the convention shall be held. I would like an answer on that question while the pending amendment is before us.

Mr. WILEY. Mr. President, in seeking an answer to that question, I turned to the Constitution itself to see if there were any annotations in relation to it. I could find none. It seems to me that the machinery of the several States would go into operation without further direction from the Congress. In other words, power is conferred on the States to organize conventions.

After continued debate that focused exclusively on the right of states to hold constitutional conventions regarding this amendment, the Senate adjourned to debate pending action on the Wagner Act. The Senate returned to the discussion over the proposed presidential term amendment on 10 March 1947.

THE PRESIDENTIAL TERM

The Senate resumed the consideration of the joint resolution (H.J. Res. 27) proposing an amendment to the Constitution of the United States relating to the terms of office of the President.

[...]

Mr. MAGNUSON.[42] Mr. President, a parliamentary inquiry.

The PRESIDING OFFICER.[43] The Senator will state it.

Mr. MAGNUSON. Does the Senator from Wisconsin intend to ask for the adoption of the second committee amendment that this time?

Mr. WILEY. Yes.

Mr. MAGNUSON. I have an amendment at the desk which I wish to offer as a substitute.

The PRESIDING OFFICER. The clerk will state the second amendment of the committee.

The CHIEF CLERK. On page 1, after line 9, it is proposed to strike out "Any person who has served as President of the United States during all, or portions, of any two terms, shall thereafter be ineligible to hold the office of President; but this article shall not prevent any person who may hold the office of President during the term within which this article is ratified from holding such office for the remainder of such term" and to insert "A person who has held the office of President, or acted as President, on 365 calendar days or more in each of two terms shall not be eligible to hold the office of President, or to act as President, for any part of another term; but this article shall not prevent any person who may be holding the office of President or acting as President during the term within which this article becomes operative from holding the office of President or acting as President during the remainder of such term."

The PRESIDING OFFICER. Does the Senator from Washington offer his amendment as a substitute for the committee amendment?

Mr. MAGNUSON. I offer my amendment as a substitute, and ask that it be stated.

The PRESIDING OFFICER. The clerk will state the amendment offered by the Senator from Washington.

Mr. GEORGE.[44] Mr. President, before the amendment is offered formally, and read at the desk, I assume there will be no objection to taking the same action with reference to the amendment in section 2 as the Senate has just taken as to section 1, that is, to restore the provision calling for ratification by the legislatures rather than by the convention method. I make that suggestion to the Senator from Wisconsin, in charge of the joint resolution.

Mr. WILEY. If there is no objection, Mr. President, I ask that, in accordance with the vote just had in relation to the amendment in section 1, similar action be taken with regard to the amendment in section 2.

The PRESIDING OFF. Without objection, it is so ordered, and the committee amendment on page 2, lines 15 and 16, is rejected.

Mr. MAGNUSON. I now offer my amendment as a substitute.

The PRESIDING OFFICER. The clerk will state the amendment.

The CHIEF CLERK. In lieu of the language proposed to be inserted on page 2, beginning in line 4, and extending down to and including line 12, is proposed to insert the following:

No person shall be elected to the office of the President more than twice.

Mr. MAGNUSON. Mr. President, to my mind, the suggested amendment is in the nature of a perfecting amendment. There was much discussion in committee, legal and otherwise, regarding not only the House bill but the committee amendment which is now before the Senate. Many questions were raised: for example, as to whether a man who was acting as President was actually a President; and as to the period during which a man could hold office as acting President, and if he were elevated to the office of President through circumstances beyond his control, to what period should he be limited.

The committee amendment is in very complicated legal language. I doubt if many State legislators could really understand its wording, but in effect it was an honest attempt to provide a restriction, so that if, through an unfortunate circumstance, such as the death of the President, or otherwise, the Vice President should assume the office of President, or act as President for any one year, meaning one calendar year of 365 days, thereafter he would be eligible to run for the Presidency only once.

[...]

Mr. TYDINGS.[45] Mr. President, I stated that I am not a member of the committee; that there may be good reasons why the committee amendment is preferable to the amendment offered by the Senator from Washington, but that, so far as I have been able to think my way through, I am convinced that the amendment of the Senator from Washington is preferable to the committee amendment. What we are trying to do is to stop any man from being elected President more than twice. I am for that. I think it is a fine thing to put in the Constitution. But under the committee amendment a man could be prohibited from being elected President more than once, provided that he had served more than 1 year prior to the time he was elected President. Therefore it is conceivable that a man would be limited, under the committee amendment, to serving in the Presidency only 5 years. I think that provision is a little stringent. I think if we limit the Presidency to two elected terms in that office we will do what I believe a great many Americans want done. If we were to strain it still further I am afraid we would bring about opposition in some of the legislatures to the adoption of the proposed constitutional amendment. Whereas if the constitutional amendment provided for two elected terms, and that is all that was put before the legislature, in my judgment it would secure more votes and have a better chance of adoption. I should like to see the Presidency limited to two terms.

[...]

Mr. TAFT.[46] Mr. President, will the Senator yield?

Mr. MAGNUSON. I yield to the Senator from Ohio.

Mr. TAFT. If I correctly understand the difference between the two amendments, under the committee amendment a man might be held to a service of 5 years. The longest he could serve would be 8 years. Under the amendment proposed by the Senator from Washington, he might serve 8 years, or he might serve as long as 11 1/2 years. My objection to the Senator's argument is that 11 1/2 years is too long. I think the general precedent has been the other way.

Mr. MAGNUSON. Does not the Senator feel that 5 years is too short?

Mr. TAFT. Strange to say, Presidents have died in the first year of their terms. Garfield died in the first year of his term. Arthur served 3 years. William Henry Harrison died in the first year, Tyler served 3 years. McKinley died in the first year of his second term, and Theodore Roosevelt served for 3 years and was elected for a full term, serving a total of 7 years. At that time that was considered to be in conformity with the two-term rule, as then applied. He did not run for re-election.

In the case of Coolidge, Harding died almost within his first year.[47] Coolidge served for 3 years, and for an elective term of 4 years in addition, and did not run again, apparently feeling that the total of 7 years was in conformity with the two-term rule.

It is not only a question of power. It seems to me that it is a question of whether a man should serve that long as President of the United States. By reason of the Vice Presidential situation, we cannot say "8 years or nothing." I should be perfectly willing to vote for one term of 6 years and say that no one should be President more than 6 years. The provision of the committee amendment that no man shall be President for more than 5 years is perfectly reasonable to me. If the Senator wishes to make it 6 years, I am willing to compromise with him. But I think it is a great mistake to say that a man may serve for 11 years. I think that is too long. I think it would break down his health. I do not believe that any man ought to serve that long, from the standpoint of his welfare or that of the Nation.

Mr. TYDINGS. Mr. President, will the Senator yield? Mr. MAGNUSON. I yield.

Mr. TYDINGS. I will say to the Senator from Ohio that I think there is a great deal in what he says, that 11 1/2 years in the Presidency is too long. My point is that 5 years in the Presidency may be too short. If this amendment were changed so that a man could serve 7 years in the Presidency, then I think we might prevent him from running for a second elective term. But this amendment takes the other extreme, so to speak. The two extremes are 11 years and 5 years, instead of 8. If we are to allow some Presidents to serve 8 years, then in good faith we ought to permit Vice Presidents who are elected President after they serve a part of the term of their predecessor, due to his death, a longer time than 5 years in which to be President. If it is right to have a limitation of 8 years for a twice-elected President, then why in heaven's name is it not right to give a Vice President the 3 years which he may serve in the term of his predecessor plus one full term, rather than limit him to 5 years?

Mr. TAFT. Mr. President, will the Senator yield? Mr. MAGNUSON. I yield.

Mr. TAFT. Under the amendment of the Senator from Washington he could serve for 11 years, and be elected twice.

Mr. MAGNUSON. We are talking about extremes.

Mr. TAFT. The people can end his service at 4 years, if they so desire. It is the extreme in which we are interested, and not the short term.

Mr. MAGNUSON. In any event, the people of the United States should have the right once to vote for a man and say, "We want him as our President." They should also have the right to say, "He has been a good President, and we want to elect him again." Under the committee amendment that would not be possible.

Mr. TAFT. I am willing to vote for one term of 6 years, instead of two terms totaling 8 years. I should like to read a resolution adopted by the Senate...

Mr. MAGNUSON. Am I to understand that the Senator from Ohio favors one term of 6 years? Mr. TAFT. I do not care whether it is one term of 6 years or two terms of 4 years.

I should like to read the resolution adopted by the Senate near the end of Coolidge's term, after he had served 3 years of the term of his predecessor and 4 years of an elective term. Apparently the question worrying the Senate was whether Coolidge intended to run for another term, and thereby serve 11 years. The Senate adopted the following resolution:

Resolved, That it is the sense of the Senate that the precedent established by Washington and other Presidents of the United States in retiring from the Presidential office after their second term has become, by universal concurrence, a part of our republican system of government, and that any departure from this time-honored custom would be unwise, unpatriotic, and fraught with peril to our free institutions.

Mr. MAGNUSON. Was that after Coolidge declined to run?

Mr. TAFT. No. That was near the end of Coolidge's term, before he had declined to run. It was in the nature of a warning. The Senate did not think he ought to run. I may say that the distinguished Senator from Kentucky [Mr. BARKLEY][48] voted for that resolution, as did the distinguished Senator from Maryland [Mr. TYDINGS].

Mr. TYDINGS. I am still for it.

Mr. TAFT. The Senator from Tennessee [Mr. McKELLAR][49] and several other Senators now Members of this body voted for it.

I think the generally accepted belief has been that if a man has served 3 years of the term of his predecessor and 4 years of an elected term, that conforms to the two-term rule, and he should not be re-elected. Whether the 1 year of service mentioned in the committee amendment is perhaps too short, I am not prepared to say. But I think it would be a great mistake to say that after a man had been President for 3 years, he should then be eligible for two more terms, serving a total of 11 years. If that is all that is to be accomplished by the joint resolution I do not believe it is worth while to pass it. Personally I would prefer one 6-year term. But certainly the length of service should not be more than 9 years, in accordance with the committee amendment. I think that is as long as anyone should be permitted to serve.

[...]

Mr. MYERS.[50] Mr. President, will the Senator yield to me?

Mr. HATCH.[51] It occurred to me that the limitation might be better placed upon political parties, rather than upon individuals, because I have seen it happen that there have been three different Presidents during 12 years' time, and yet the result has been merely to change the person in the Executive office, rather than to change the policy or the philosophy, since the same fundamental political philosophy has continued.

So, Mr. President, if the proponents of this resolution desire to cure what they believe to be an evil, the limitation might be better placed upon parties, rather than upon individual candidates for the Presidency.

[...]

Mr. WILEY. Mr. President, I am about to propound a unanimous consent request. However, before doing so, I wish to say a few words.

The debate which has taken place during the last hour – for this subject has been discussed today for only 1 hour – is similar to the debate which occurred at the time of the formation of the Republic, with one exception; namely, that in those days, there was no insinuation that the debate was for political purposes. In those days the founding fathers saw the challenge which certainly those of us today who have eyes to see with, see now. The House saw it, and so indicated by voting by such a vast majority in favor of the joint resolution. Five or six or seven Senators saw it, and so indicated by submitting resolutions. In the subcommittee Democratic and Republican Senators saw it, and indicated as much by reporting this resolution. What they saw was simply that power vested too long in the hands of anyone is dangerous to the community and to the Nation.

Even President Roosevelt saw that, and even that great Democrat, Thomas Jefferson, saw it when he endorsed the two-term tradition, which has become the unwritten law of the land. He said:

No pretext should ever be permitted to dispense with it...

He was referring to the principle of rotation in the Executive Office:

Because there will never be a time when real difficulties will not exist to furnish a plausible pretext for dispensation. When I quoted that language at the time when I opened the debate on this subject some days ago, I showed once the pretext was in the case of President Roosevelt.

No, Mr. President; we are not afraid of shadows. We are not even fearful of realities. But we feel it is our obligation to face them.

Under the joint resolution as passed by the House, and as it has been discussed here, provision is made that anyone who has occupied the Office of President of the United States during all, or portions, of any two terms, shall thereafter be ineligible to serve in that office in a succeeding term.

Under the Senate committee's version of the resolution, the Chief Executive might in one case serve for as long as 9 years.

Those who have read the debates which occurred in the early days of this Republic know fact up to the very last the founding fathers debated the question whether the President should be eligible for only one term and whether such a term should be for 7 years. Mr. President, I have been glad to hear Senators on the other side of the aisle expressing their admiration for the founding fathers. Finally, in order to compromise and get things accomplished, the founding fathers left the question undecided. But the first President of the United States, George Washington, recognized the validity of the arguments and of the ideas which had been presented at that great period in our history, when our Nation was being formed; and he established the principle of not more than two terms for any President. The other founding fathers indicated their concurrence in that view.

Now we have arrived at a period in the history of the world in which we have seen demonstrated on a world scale how dangerous it is for power to gravitate into the hands of one man or one group. I do not think there should be any insinuation that partisanship or mere politics is responsible for the bringing of this resolution before the Senate. In the debate in the Committee on the Judiciary, I do not think partisan politics was ever mentioned. There was unanimity on this subject, with the exception of one member of the committee; and now, as I understand, even that Senator has indicated a desire to have the Congress legislate explicitly that those who serve in the office of Chief Executive of the Nation shall not serve more than two terms.

So, Mr. President, I ask unanimous consent that the Senate vote on the amendments and on joint resolution on Wednesday at not later than 3 o'clock, and, if that is agreed to, I shall ask [that] a recess be taken.

[...]

After a recess, the debate was returned to on 12 March 1947 – here is the exact moment of the "re-opening" of the floor arguments.

THE PRESIDENTIAL TERM

Mr. REVERCOMB. Mr. President, there is now pending before the Senate as the unfinished business House Joint Resolution 27 which proposes an amendment to the Constitution of the United States relating to the terms of office of the President. The purpose of joint resolution is to submit to the several States a proposed amendment to the Constitution which would limit the tenure of the office of the President. We have debated this subject of several days. Amendments have been made to the measure reported from the Committee on the Judiciary, and the next vote will be upon an amendment offered by the able Senator from Washington.

[...]

Certain Senators have indicated that they prefer the amendment which may be offered if the amendment of the Senator from Washington does not prevail, providing a minimum limitation of 6 years and a maximum of 10. I shall support that amendment. But I cannot support the amendment of the Senator from Washington.

The appeal has been made upon the ground that we would unduly limit individuals from holding office. That is not the real purpose of the amendment. The real heart of the amendment is to prevent any individual from holding too long the office of Chief Executive. As is well known, it became a custom firmly implanted in the tradition of this country for many years that one individual should not serve more than two terms as President of the United States. This custom began with the end of the second term of office of the first President, George Washington, when he declined to accept nomination after he had completed two terms. That custom lasted for more than 150 years, and was the subject of positive statement, sustained by a number of eminent men who had held the office of President.

Among them I cite the name of Thomas Jefferson, who time and again endorsed the rule that no man should serve for more than two terms. He gave his reasons. He feared that a despotism might grow in this country if any individual were permitted to occupy for too long the office of Chief Executive. Jefferson was a great believer in preserving the democracy of this country and setting up every possible barrier against autocratic rule.

Likewise, during his term of office, Andrew Jackson expressly subscribed to the limitation of the tenure of office in the Presidency, and he went so far in those early days as to say that there should be a constitutional amendment limiting the term of occupancy of the Presidency to 6 years.

Grover Cleveland, who held office for two terms which were not consecutive, ably expressed his opposition to any one man continuing in office for too long. He took a more extreme position than any taken on the floor of the Senate. This position was that no man should hold the office of President beyond one term.

The reason for the rule is apparent and sound. Our fundamental concept is that government shall be in the will of the people. That at once makes us guarded against vesting power for too long a time in any man in any office. To grant extended power to any one man would be a definite step in the direction of autocracy, regardless of the name given the office, whether it be president, king, dictator, emperor, or whatever title the office may carry. It would be a definite step toward the destruction of real freedom of the people.

[...]

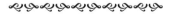

Senator Theodore Green of Rhode Island moved to have the debate on the proposed resolution continued until 26 March 1947, in effect tabling the measure and potentially sending it to its "legislative death." Republicans in the Senate moved to defeat the motion.

The PRESIDENT pro tempore. The question is on agreeing to the motion of the Senator from Rhode Island.

Mr. TAFT. Mr. President, is the motion debatable?

The PRESIDENT pro tempore. The motion is debatable.

Mr. TAFT. I only wish to point out that we have considered this measure for 3 or 4 days. Senators have made up their minds, and I see no reason why we should not vote on the joint resolution tonight.

The PRESIDENT pro tempore. The question is on agreeing to the motion of the Senator from Rhode Island [Mr. GREEN][52] that further consideration of the pending joint resolution be postponed until Wednesday, March 26. [Putting the question.]

The motion was not agreed to.

The PRESIDENT pro tempore. The question is on the engrossment of the amendment and the third reading of the joint resolution.

The amendment ordered to be engrossed and the joint resolution to be read a third time.

The joint resolution was read the third time.

The PRESIDENT pro tempore. The joint resolution having been read the third time, the question is, Shall it pass?

Mr. PEPPER.[53] Mr. President, as I have notified the majority leader, I wish to address myself for a few moments to the joint resolution. I suggested to the majority leader that inasmuch as we are to return for a night session anyway, I would naturally much prefer to make my remarks when we reconvene at 7 o'clock. I wish that might be possible.

Mr. WHITE.[54] Mr. President, the understanding has been that we would take a recess at approximately half past five and reassemble at 7 o'clock. If the Senator's remarks are to be brief, and would consume only 10 or 15 minutes, that would be one thing. But if the Senator warms to his subject, as he sometimes does, I am apprehensive that he may run beyond the suggested limitation of time. Is the Senator in a position to indicate how long he wishes to speak?

Mr. PEPPER. A Senator can never tell when he begins a speech in the Senate just how long it will last or how many interruptions there will be. I would not wish to violate my obligation to my friend, so I had better not make an estimate.

[...]

Debate began again when the Senate reconvened later in the evening, 26 March 1947.

Mr. PEPPER. Mr. President, the pending question is whether or not the Senate by a two-thirds vote shall agree to submit to the people of the United States for ratification, through their legislatures, the following proposed amendment to the Constitution of the United States:

No person shall be elected to the office of the President more than twice, and no person who has held the office of the President, or acted as President, for more than 2 years of age term to which some other person was elected President shall be elected to the office of the President more than once. But this article shall not apply to any person holding the office of President when this article was proposed by the Congress, and shall not prevent any person may be holding the office of President, or acting as President, during the term within which this article becomes operative from holding the office of President or acting as President during the remainder of such term.

Mr. President, that it is the language proposed by the distinguished senior Senator from Ohio [Mr. TAFT] and adopted by the Senate this afternoon. In express language it excerpts from the operation of the proposal the present occupant of the White House, and it would also except the President of the United States at the time the amendment should become operative, should it be properly ratified by the legislatures of three-fourths of the States.

Mr. President, I shall not, directly or indirectly, question or attack the motives of those who are either the sponsors or the supporters of the proposed amendment. But I cannot refrain from saying that in my opinion the effect of it, the way it will be construed by the people of our country and of the world, is that it is aimed directly at the Presidency and the record of Franklin D. Roosevelt.

Why do I say that, Mr. President? The intended amendment to the Federal Constitution is of course a constitutional limitation upon the right and present power of the people of this country, in free elections, to elect one to be the highest magistrate in the land. I say that not only because the proposal emanates from a party other than the party of President Franklin D. Roosevelt. I dare say its principal supporters are in that party, as has been manifest on the floor. I say that, Mr. President, because in the 158 years of the duration of this Government under the Constitution of the United States with the present unlimited power of the people to elect a qualified man to the office of President as many times as they see fit to elect him, no Congress has ever proposed to the country an amendment to the Constitution to deprive the people of that power, and no man has ever thrice, much less four times, been elected to the highest office within the gift of a sovereign people, save Franklin Delano Roosevelt. And, as Patrick Henry said, Mr. President:

We have no light to guide our footsteps in the future except the lamp of the past.

Therefore those who are the sponsors and the supporters of the proposed amendment to the Constitution must find in the record of Franklin D. Roosevelt something which in their opinion justifies this radical deprivation of free franchise from the people of the United States to elect their own President.

Therefore I say, Mr. President, it seems to me it was intended to and it does submit to the Congress and to the country a referendum on the question of whether the people of the United States, under the circumstances then prevailing, were right in the election of Franklin D. Roosevelt to a third and to a fourth term as President of the United States.

Mr. President, what is proposed to be done by this resolution is in a time of relative calm and quietue to deprive the people of the power to choose their President in a moment of crisis. Let is be remembered that this Senate, this country, this world, are not the same Senate, the same county, the same world as they were in November 1940, nor the same as in November 1944. All we have to do, Mr. President, is to imagine the rivers of blood that have flowed since November 1940 and 1944 to give this country its present calm and quietue, to give democracy on earth the stability and the assurance which it enjoys today.

Mr. President, it is not easy for us as we sit here now in the calm which has been won by the blood and maimed bodies of so many who have given themselves for their country, to remember the crisis which faced the world in 1940, in November, when the people of the United States elected Franklin D. Roosevelt for the first time in their history to a third term. It is not always remembered how decisive was the judgment of the people in November 1940, and November 1944.

[...]

❧❧❧❧❧❧❧❧❧

The Senate returned to the proposed amendment, and finally, the vote, in the evening of the third day of debate.

Mr. TAFT. Mr. President, the program contemplated a vote early in the day on House Joint Resolution 27. It was not expected that it would be debated at length all afternoon and all evening. Everything that was to be said on it had been said. Nevertheless the debate continued. It disrupted all the plans, which involved taking up the portalto-portal pay measure this afternoon and seeing how far we could get with it before turning to the Lilienthal nomination.[55] It was repeatedly stated that the Lilienthal nomination was to be taken up this evening.

Unfortunately the plans were disrupted. I regret very much that that was the fact. But I do not see how Senators can foresee the length of debate. Perhaps we were mistaken in assuming that the debate would be shorter than it proved to be.

Now the question is on the passage of the joint resolution, which I think is in such form that anyone who is in favor of the principle of limiting the number of terms a President may serve can properly support it.

The PRESIDENT pro tempore. The joint resolution having been read three times, the question is, Shall it pass? On this question the yeas and nays have been ordered, and the clerk will call the roll.

[...]

The result was announced – yeas 59, nays 23, as follows:

YEAS – 59

Aiken	Eastland	Langer	Saltonstall
Baldin	Ecton	Lodge	Smith
Ball	Ferguson	Martin	Taft
Brewster	Flanders	Maybank	Thomas, Okla.
Bricker	George	McCarthy	Thye
Bridges	Gordon	McClellan	Tydings
Brooks	Gurney	McKellar	Vandenberg
Buck	Hawkes	Millikin	Watkins
Bushfield	Hickenlooper	Moore	Wherry
Byrd	Hoey	Morse	White
Capehart	Ives	O'Conor	Wiley
Capper	Jenner	O'Daniel	Williams
Cooper	Johnson, Colo.	Reed	Wilson
Donnell	Kern	Reverscomb	Young
Dworshak	Knowland	Robertson, Va.	

NAYS – 23

Connally	Hill	McFarland	Sparkman
Downey	Holland	McGrath	Stewart
Ellender	Johnson, S.C.	McMahon	Taylor
Fulbright	Kilgore	Murray	Thomas, Utah
Green	Lucas	Myers	Umstead
Hayden	Magnuson	Pepper	

NOT VOTING – 13

Barkle	Hatch	Overton	Wagner
Butler	Malone	Robertson, Wyo.	
Cain	McCarran	Russell	
Chavez	O'Mahoney	Tobey	

Historical Background Documents

This report, submitted 5 February 1947 by Rep. Raymond Springer, Republican of Indiana and a member of the House Committee on the Judiciary, goes into great depth as to the issues behind the historical move to limit how many terms a president may serve.

This resolution has but one purpose. That purpose is to submit to the people, by and through their State legislatures, this very important problem of the Presidential tenure of office, and to let the people decide whether or not this limitation should be written into the Constitution.

Heretofore many resolutions have been introduced upon this very question, but for some reason or another they have fallen by the wayside, and no legislation has been passed upon this question, and our Constitution remains without amendment to the state respecting the tenure of the office of President.

Section 1, article II, of the Constitution provides:

The executive Power shall be vested in a President of the United States of America. He shall hold his Office during the Term of four years...

Again, under amendment 20, section 1 of our Constitution, we find, in that amendment, the following language:

The terms of the President and Vice President shall end at noon on the 20th day of January, and the terms of Senators and Representatives at noon on the 3d day of January, of the years in which such terms would have ended if this article had not been ratified, and the terms of their successors shall then begin.

By reason of the lack of a positive expression upon the subject of tenure of the office of President, and by reason of a well-defined custom which has arisen in the past that no President she would have more than two terms in that office, much public discussion has resulted upon this subject. Hence it is the purpose of this legislation, if passed, to submit this question to the people so they, by and through the recognized processes, may express their views upon this question, and, if they shall so elect, they may amend our Constitution and thereby set at rest this problem.

This is not a political question. The importance of the problem to the people transcends all political implications and considerations. This proposed amendment to our Constitution, if adopted, will continue throughout the future years, unless and until a further amendment may be adopted upon this subject. Therefore, in the face of general public discussions, in the face of the custom which has developed throughout the years, we are here presenting a resolution to submit this basic problem to the people.

ACTION TAKEN IN CONSTITUTIONAL CONVENTION

The tenure of the Presidential office proposed under the new Constitution was one of the most difficult and perplexing problems to come before the Convention of 1787. How long should the term of the President be? Should he be eligible for re-election? It was not until the closing days of the Convention that a decision was reached, and then only in the final report of the Committee on Revision, submitted on September 12, 1787. In that report provision was made for the term of 4 years and election by the electoral college.

In the plan submitted by Mr. Randolph[56] on May 29, 1787, however, the term of years was left blank, as was also the case in the resolutions introduced by Mr. Patterson [sic].[57] A proposal for a tenure of 7 years, accompanied by a provision of ineligibility for a second time, appeared in a series of resolutions referred to the Committee of Detail on July 23, but throughout the debates the matter recurred constantly without decision. A draft of the Constitution, reported from the Committee of Five on August 6, provided for a term of 7 years without reeligibility. The report of the Committee of Eleven file on September 4, 1787, provided for a 4-year term without reference to reeligibility, and that provision appeared in the revised and final test of September 12, 1787.

[...]

MINORITY VIEWS OF MR. CELLER[58]

A number of the members of the House Judiciary Committee oppose House Joint Resolution 27, which limits, in general, the Presidential tenure of office to two terms of 4 years each.

We believe if there is to be any change in Presidential tenure, it should be in the nature of a 6-year term, with no right of re-election, and that no one shall be eligible for the Presidency who has served in that office any part of two previous times.

It has always been natural for the incumbent President to have his eyes fixed on re-election, and all the acts of the first term, directly or indirectly, in some measure, are affected by the ambition for a second term. It is only natural for the incumbent President to make appointments to his Cabinet with due consideration for political repercussions. Even appointments to important judicial posts are tinctured with politics. He is wont to ask himself and his intimates, "Will the appointment enhance or diminish my prospects for re-election?"

[...]

It is interesting to take the views of some of our Presidents [into consideration]. I quote from the sixth annual message of Andrew Jackson to Congress, December 1, 1834:

I trust that I may be also pardoned for renewing the recommendation I have so often submitted to your attention in regard to the mode of electing the President and Vice President of the United States. All the reflection I have been able to bestow upon the subject increases my conviction that the best interests of the county will be prompted by the adoption of some plan which will secure in all contingencies the important right of sovereignty to the direct control of the people. Could this be attained, and the terms of those offices be limited to a single per of either 4 or 6 years, I think our liberties would possess an additional safeguard.

In his inaugural address, Rutherford B. Hayes stated:

In furtherance of the reform we seek, and in other important respects a change of great importance, I recommend an amendment to the Constitution prescribing a term of 6 years for the Presidential office and forbidding a re-election.

Grover Cleveland, in accepting the nomination for President, wrote:

Then an election to office shall be the selection by the voters of one of their number to assume for a time a public trust, instead of his dedication to the profession of politics; when the holders of the ballot, quickened by a sense of duty, shall avenge truth betrayed and pledges broken, and when the suffrage shall be altogether free and uncorrupted, the full realization of a government by the people will be at hand. And of the means to this end not one would, in my judgment, be more effective than an amendment to the Constitution disqualifying the President from re-election. When we consider the patronage of this great office, the allurements of power, the temptations to retain public place once gained, and, more than all, the availability a party finds in an incumbent when a horde of officeholders, with a zeal born of benefits received and fostered by the hope of favors yet to come, stand ready to aid with money and trained political service, we recognize in the eligibility of the President for re-election a most serious danger to that calm, deliberate, and intelligent political action which must characterize a government by the people.

William Howard Taft, in 1915, wrote:

I am strongly inclined to the view that it would have been a wiser provision, as it was at one time voted in the Constitution, to make the term of the President 6 or 7 years, and render him ineligible thereafter. Such a change would give to the Executive greater courage and independence in the discharge of his duties. The absorbing and diverting interest in the re-election of the incumbent, taken by those Federal civil servants who regard their own tenure as dependent on his, would disappear and the efficiency of administration in the last 18 months of a term would be maintained.

One of the best minds that ever sat in the Senate was Senator Root[59] of New York. He stated:

I think the possibility of renomination and re-election of a President who is in office seriously interferes with the working of our governmental machinery during the last 2 years of his term; and, just about the time he gets to the highest efficiency, people in the Senate and in the House began to figure to try to beat him. You cannot separate the attempt to beat an individual from the attempt to make ineffective the operations of government which that individual is carrying on in accordance with his duty. Legislation in this Congress has been largely dominated for 2 years past by considerations of that sort; and I should like to see those considerations exiled from these Halls.

The possibility of re-election tends to build up a dangerous political machine. It interferes with the highest efficiency of the President as the Nation's Executive. A single 6-year term of office will remedy these evils and will remove the menace of rigidity. It will relieve the President of the tremendous political strain of trying to be all things to all men. Likewise, the present burdensome cost of re-election borne by the people would be reduced. There would be fewer disturbances in trade and markets, less changes in our financial system.

In all, I say the President will be able to do a better job. He would not have to curry too selfish groups, and thus would be better able to enforce the policies he thought best.

Frankly, under the present system, the fourth year of the first term is mainly devoted to campaigning for re-election. The tenure of the first term is only 3 years in relation to concentration on affairs of office.

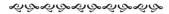

In this letter to Thomas Swope, the sports editor for the Cincinnati Post, *Senator Robert A. Taft discusses Senate business, including the debate over the Twenty-second Amendment, which he alludes to in the final paragraph of this letter as stated in* The Kent State University Press, *3 July 1947.*

July 3, 1947
[Washington, DC]

Dear Mr. Swope:

I have your letter of June twenty-first, and I am glad to hear that you approve the passage of the labor bill over the President's veto.

We considered the different methods of providing for the succession to the Presidency, but finally adopted the one which makes the Speaker of the House the President's successor if there is no Vice President. We adopted this course partly because it seemed to have more support than any other proposal, and partly because it was recommended by the President and therefore could not be vetoed by him. If we are going to choose one of the officers of the government, the Speaker seems to be the closest to the people.

We had your proposal also before us, and it is certainly an interesting possibility. People generally, however, don't like the idea of one Vice President, because he really has nothing to do and no one has ever been able to work out a plan by which he has anything to do. Feeling this way about the Vice President, a good many members of the Senate didn't like the idea of having two of them.

With best wishes,

Sincerely yours,

As Submitted to the States

No person shall be elected to the office of the President more than twice, and no person who has held the office of President, or acted as President, for more than two years of a term to which some other person was elected President shall be elected to the office of President more than once. But this Article shall not apply to any person holding the office of President when this Article was proposed by Congress, and shall not prevent any person who may be holding the office of President, or acting as President, during the term within which this Article becomes operative from holding the office of President or acting as President during the remainder of such term.

Section 2.
This article shall be inoperative unless it shall have been ratified as an amendment to the Constitution by the legislatures of three-fourths of the several States within seven years from the date of its submission to the States by the Congress.

State Ratifications of the Twenty-second Amendment

State	Date[23]
Maine	31 March 1947
Michigan	31 March 1947
Iowa	1 April 1947
Kansas	1 April 1947
New Hampshire	1 April 1947
Delaware	2 April 1947
Illinois	3 April 1947
Oregon	3 April 1947
Colorado	12 April 1947
California	15 April 1947
New Jersey	15 April 1947
Vermont	15 April 1947
Ohio	16 April 1947
Wisconsin	16 April 1947
Pennsylvania	29 April 1947

Connecticut	21 May 1947
Missouri	22 May 1947
Nebraska	23 May 1947
Virginia	28 January 1948
Mississippi	12 February 1948
New York	9 March 1948
South Dakota	21 January 1949
North Dakota	25 February 1949
Louisiana	17 May 1950
Montana	25 January 1951
Indiana	29 January 1951
Idaho	30 January 1951
New Mexico	12 February 1951
Wyoming	12 February 1951
Arkansas	15 February 1951
Georgia	17 February 1951
Tennessee	20 February 1951
Texas	22 February 1951
Nevada	26 February 1951
Utah	26 February 1951
Minnesota	27 February 1951[24]
North Carolina	28 February 1951
South Carolina	13 March 1951
Maryland	14 March 1951
Florida	16 April 1951
Alabama	4 May 1951

Note: From the time it was submitted to the states by Congress until it was ratified was a period of 1,439 days.

Explanation of the amendment

From the birth of the nation until 1940, no sitting President dared to run for a third elected presidential term. That year, President Franklin D. Roosevelt decided to "break the tradition" of not running for that third term; Roosevelt won in 1940, and, four years later, he ran for an unprecedented fourth term and was elected, although he died only three months into his fourth term. With Roosevelt gone, in 1946 the Republican Party won control of the US House of Representatives, and instantly pushed for a constitutional amendment limiting all future presidents to two four-year terms only. Although many critics condemned the advocacy of changing the Constitution for this solitary reason, four years after the Congress sent the amendment to the states, it was ratified. To this day, more than sixty years after its ratification, the amendment stands like a sentinel against all presidents, of both major parties and, perhaps, in the future, presidents of other parties, from serving more than eight years as President of the United States.

ORIGINAL PRIMARY DOCUMENTS

A hearing is ordered in a House Judiciary subcommittee on the multitude of proposals for a potential presidential election term, The Chicago Tribune, *2 February 1947.*

Order Hearing on Bills to Limit Presidential Term

Washington, Feb. 2 (AP) – A house judiciary subcommittee today ordered public hearings Monday to speed action on measures limiting the time one man may hold the presidency. Nine proposals are before the committee, all constitutional amendments which would require approval of the house and senate by two-thirds majorities and ratifications by three-fourths of the states. Seven, differing in detail, would limit a president to two terms of four years each. The other two would make the presidential term six years and limit an executive to one term.

A House of Representatives subcommittee recommends a proposed amendment regarding presidential terms, as reported in The New York Times, *4 February 1947.*

PRESIDENCY LIMIT OF 8 YEARS ASKED

———

Committee in House Approves Amendment – Expects Floor Action This Week

———

WASHINGTON, Feb. 3 (AP) – A House Judiciary Subcommittee to-day approved a constitutional amendment that would prevent any President from serving more than eight years.

Chairman Earl C. Michener, Republican of Michigan, said the full Judiciary Committee may approve it tomorrow. He hopes to have the House vote on it late this week.

Before the amendment could become effective it must be approved by two-thirds of the House and Senate and ratified by at least thirty-six of the forty-eight States.

The measure would limit Presidential tenure to two terms of four years each, whether consecutive or not, and construe a term to mean all or part of one. A Vice President succeeding to the Presidency because of a vacancy could be elected only for one additional four-year term.

The proposal as hailed by Republicans during the subcommittee hearing today as a bar to dictatorship and condemned by Democrats as an attempt to let the "dead past" govern the future.

Representative John W. McCormack, Democrat, of Massachusetts, declared that any such restrictions would impose "the dead hand of the past" on future generations and prevent "a free choice in their own best interest and the national interest."

Representative Ellsworth B. Buck, Republican, of New York, recalling that Franklin D. Roosevelt was elected to four consecutive terms, said "dictatorships are spawned by the repeated election of one man."

Representative Everett M. Dirksen, Republican, of Illinois, advocating a single term of six years, told the committee six years is "long enough for any President, wise or weak, to carry out his program."

Representative William Lemke, Republican, of North Dakota, supported a six-year term and nomination of the President by direct vote instead of a convention.

This editorial in The Washington Post, *13 February 1947, discusses the political impact of the proposed presidential term amendment, and comments on its partisan nature.*

Two-Term Amendment

An unfortunate thing about the anti-third-term resolution is the partisan vote by which the House approved it. Every Republican voted for it, and a large majority of the Democrats voted against it. Former Speaker Rayburn decried partisan division by advising the Republicans to "wait a little while and cool off a bit." But history does not sustain his inference that only the Republicans were actuated by political motives. As a matter of fact, the most memorable anti-third-term moves in the past have found their support in the Democratic Party.

Only one strong objection was raised against the resolution: that in time of emergency it might operate to prevent the people from choosing the leader they prefer. It is a plausible argument. Nor has the last been heard of it, for the resolution has a long way to go before it can become part of the Constitution. The answer is that an unscrupulous Executive might perpetuate himself in office by manipulation of the tremendous power that now centers in the White House. It would be foolish in these days of necessarily strong Presidents to minimize this danger. In this complicated age we must entrust them with great power during the period they remain in the White House. Now that the two-term tradition has been broken, every President of this sort will be under strong temptation to make a third and possibly a fourth try. A safeguard against evolution toward the dictatorship is thus felt to be necessary by many Americans with no partisanship in their systems.

"Presidency Limit Put Before Senate" as reported in The New York Times, *6 March 1947. Senator Alexander Wiley argues in the US Senate for the proposed amendment.*

PRESIDENCY LIMIT PUT BEFORE SENATE

———

Wiley Offers a Constitution Amendment
Making Nine Years Most in the Office

———

By C.P. TRUSSELL
Special to *The New York Times*

———

WASHINGTON, March 5 – A proposed Constitutional amendment to limit the tenure of a President of the United States to a maximum of nine years went before the Senate today with the principal sponsor, Senator Alexander Wiley, Judiciary Committee chairman, sounding this keynote:

"This resolution should be considered apart from the discussion of the personality of the late President Roosevelt. It is not intended as a criticism of him; prejudices for or against him should not be considered. We should be taking this step in terms of what the American people used for the future.

"This resolution merely puts into writing in the Constitution a custom which the American people have observed throughout their history prior to President Roosevelt's tenure."

Both Sides Predict Adoption

Senate adoption of the measure by the required two-thirds majority, perhaps on Friday, was predicted from both Republican and Democratic sides. The resolution in somewhat different form, was adopted by the House on Feb. 6 by a vote of 285 to 121, with forty-seven Democrats joining 238 Republicans in giving approval.

The House version would limit the tenure to two terms, one of them not necessarily complete, and would submit the amendment for ratification by three-fourths of the State Legislatures. The Senate version would limit tenure to two full terms of four years, by would not disqualify a president from seeking a second full term if he had entered the White House to serve no more than a year of an unfinished term. The Senate ratification plan would put the decision up to the state constitutional conventions.

In putting the resolution under consideration, Senator Wiley advanced five other reasons, besides the one of custom, for submitting the proposed amendment to the states.

"Too long occupancy of the presidential office and too long continuance of the same administration," he said, "always make for danger of dictatorship. Power corrupts even when it is in the hands of angels."

Statement in 1932 Quoted

He quoted President Roosevelt's agreement with President Coolidge in 1932 in opposition to a third term.

"If we do not enact this resolution," Mr. Wiley continued, "there will be a constant temptation to Presidential incumbents to attempt to achieve a third and a fourth term.

"When a man occupies the Presidential office, there is always a reluctance in his party not to nominate him for another term. It is the President, of course, who is the head of his party and who, through disposition of a large number of jobs, can win the allegiance of many members of his party. Thus, he has 'an inside track' on nomination for a third and fourth term.

"A President can create an emergency and thus create reasons for his continuance in office."

He quoted President Jefferson's refusal of a third term.

Senator Wiley's sixth point was that the proposed amendment would provide a guarantee that no individual would occupy the Presidency more than two full terms and thus "serve to encourage political leadership in other individuals."

The Senate Rules Committee decided today to start hearings Friday on several proposals for setting up a line of succession in the event of the death of a President and a Vice President.

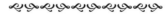

The proposed amendment passes both houses of Congress and is sent to the states, as reported here in The Chicago Tribune, *13 March 1947.*

VOTES TO PLACE TWO TERM ISSUE BEFORE STATES

Senate Would Allow 10 Years' Service

[*Chicago Tribune* Press Service]

Washington, March 12. By a vote of 59 to 23, the necessary two-thirds majority, the senate tonight passed a resolution providing for submission to the states of a constitutional amendment to prohibit future Presidents from being elected to more than two terms.

The resolution would permit vice Presidents who succeeded to the Presidency thru death of the chief Executive to serve a maximum of 10 years.

The measure goes back to the house, which has passed a similar resolution by a vote of 285 to 121. It probably will be sent to a conference between the two houses for adjustment of differences. The house resolution provides that no person who has served all or part of any two terms shall be eligible to hold the Presidency.

Democrats Fight Curb

A small but vociferous Democratic opposition protested to the last in the senate that the action was an affront to the memory of the late President Roosevelt, the only chief executive in history to violate the two term tradition established by George Washington.

But when the test came, 33 Democrats joined 46 Republicans to put the resolution over. All opposing votes came from Democrats.

Legislatures of 36 of the 48 states must ratify the amendment within seven years if it is to become part of the constitution.

The senate resolution carries an amendment, proposed by Sen. Taft, [R., O.], which provides that President Truman may be reelected for two terms altho he is serving three years and four months of his predecessor's unexpired term. If reelected twice, Mr. Truman could serve a total of 11 years and four months.

Taft Applauds Compromise

But all future Vice Presidents who succeeded to the White House seat would be barred from serving two elective terms if they had served two years or more of their predecessor's unexpired term, if they served less than two years, they could be elected for two four year terms.

"This seems a fair and sensible compromise," Taft told the senate. "A president may serve eight to 10 Years under this provision – except in that case of Mr. Truman who ran for vice president when there was no limitation in the law. We do not want to make it retroactive."

The senate defeated 50 to 34 an amendment by Sen. Magnuson [D., Wash.] to restrict a President to two successive terms. By a vote of 66 to 14 it rejected an amendment By Sen. Langer [R., N.D.] providing for direct primary elections of the President and vice president. Beaten by a vote of 82 to 1 was an amendment by Sen. O'Daniel [D., Tex.] which would have permitted only one six year term for the President and senators and three two year terms for representatives.

The US house votes to send the proposed presidential term limit amendment to the states, as reported in The Sun, *22 March 1947.*

HOUSE VOTE O.K.'S PRESIDENCY LIMIT

Congress Action On Proposed Amendment Completed

By Robert W. Ruth

[Washington Bureau of The Sun]

Washington, March 21 – The House today completed congressional action, by a standing vote of 81 to 29, on a proposed constitutional amendment limiting the tenure of future Presidents to a maximum of ten years.

Thus Congress has taken the most far-reaching step ever accomplished in this country on the question of presidential tenure, which provided the constitutional convention in 1787 with its hardest-fought issue and which again brought up a bitter controversy when the late Franklin D. Roosevelt shattered the two-term precedent.

Copies To Go To States

The House action now sends the joint resolution to the State Department, where certified copies will be forwarded to the states. If 36 state legislatures ratify the proposed amendment within seven years, it will become effective, probably as the Twenty-second Amendment.

However, it is likely that approval by the states, if it comes at all, will await future election changes since well over twelve of the states at the present have either one or both houses of the Legislature controlled by the Democrats. And most Democrats have looked with disfavor on what many consider an attempt by the Republicans to gain revenge for their long term out of power. Not since March, 1933, has the GOP controlled the executive branch of the Federal Government.

Elections Fixed At Two

The proposed constitutional amendment, one of 50 resolutions for constitutional changes already introduced in the present Congress provides that no person shall be elected to the presidency more than twice.

The House concurred in the Senate amendment, proposed by Senator Taft[60] (R., Ohio) to the effect that any person who serves two years or longer as President, could be elected to serve only one more four-year term. However, any person serving less than two years as part of a term will be eligible for two additional four-year terms, or a maximum of ten years, less one day.

President Truman is specifically exempted from the proposal.

McCormack Objects

Representative McCormack[61] (D., Mass.), minority whip, today renewed his earlier argument that the constitutional amendment "will tie the hands of future generations of Americans."

In addition, most Democrats, although their own 1912 platform favored a single-term amendment, are mindful of the 1940 GOP pledge recommending a two-term limit.

But from the Republican side the joint resolution, introduced by Representative Michener[62] (R., Mich.), has brought assurances that it is a nonpartisan measure, since it would affect all future executive regardless of party.

Not all Democrats are against the present proposal. In early February the House Republicans voted solidly for a two-term limit, but were joined by 47 Democrats. And Senate passage last week, by a vote of 59 to 23, found some members of the minority party, including both Maryland legislators, supporting the constitutional limitation.

Author's note: There have been no US Supreme Court decisions regarding the application or constitutionality of this amendment. In a work on the analysis and interpretation of the US Constitution, it was noted, "The Twentysecond Amendment has yet to be tested or applied. Commentary suggests, however, that a number of issues could be raised as to the Amendment's meaning and application, especially in relation to the Twelfth Amendment. By its terms, the Twenty-second Amendment bars only the election of two-term Presidents, and this prohibition would not prevent someone who had twice been elected President from succeeding to the office after having been elected or appointed Vice-President. Broader language providing that no such person 'shall be chosen or serve as President...or be eligible to hold the office' was rejected in favor of the Amendment's ban merely on election. Whether a two-term President could be elected or appointed Vice President depends upon the meaning of the Twelfth Amendment, which provides that 'no person constitutionally ineligible to the office of President shall be eligible to that of Vice-President.' Is someone prohibited by the Twenty-second Amendment from being 'elected' to the office of President thereby 'constitutionally ineligible to the office'? Note also that neither Amendment addresses the eligibility of a former two-term President to serve as Speaker of the House or as one of the other officers who could serve as President through operation of the Succession Act."[63]

WHO'S WHO

This section includes biographies of two individuals who played a significant part in drafting and passing the Twenty-second Amendment. They are also mentioned in earlier sections of this chapter.

Earl Cory Michener (1876-1957)

Earl Michener served seven terms in the US House of Representatives, and introduced the proposed language in the US House that ultimately became the Twenty-second Amendment to the US Constitution.

Michener was born near Attica, in Seneca County, Ohio on 30 November 1876. In 1889, when he was 12 or 13 years old, his parents moved to the town of Adrian, Michigan. Michener attended schools in Adrian. In 1898, when he was 21, the Spanish-American War broke out between the United States and Spain, mostly over the latter's treatment of the people in the Spanish possessions of Cuba and the Philippines. Michener volunteered for service, and he was given the rank of private, seeing service in Company B, of the Thirty-first Regiment of the Michigan Volunteer Infantry. He served from 26 April 1898 until 17 May 1899. When he returned to Michigan, Michener began the study of the law at the University of Michigan at Ann Arbor. In 1902 he transferred to Columbian University (now George Washington University) in Washington, DC, from which he graduated the following year with a law degree.

In 1903 he was admitted to the state bar, he proceeded to open a law practice in his new hometown of Adrian. He quickly became an important local attorney; in 1907, he rose to serve as the Assistant Prosecuting Attorney for Lenawee County, where he served until 1910. The following year he advanced to become the Prosecuting Attorney for the county, serving until 1914.

In 1918, Michener ran for a seat in the US House of Representatives as a Republican. The 1918 election was a pivotal one – it was held just as the war in Europe was grinding to a close, a conflict which had cost the United States 100,000 dead in less than a year and a half of fighting. At the same time, the American economy was starting to slow down, giving the Republicans, out of power in both chambers of the US Congress as well as the White House, a sturdy political weapon. Michener used the sharp edge of this weapon in his race, against incumbent Rep. Samuel Willard Beakes, a Democrat who had held the seat for two terms and was looking for a third. But in this year when the war and the economy were two important issues, and President Wilson was highly unpopular, Michener easily defeated Beakes, and he took his seat in the Sixty-sixth Congress (1919-21). Michener ultimately served from 4 March 1919 until 3 March 1933, to the close of the Seventy-second Congress. During this first tenure in the US House of Representatives, Michener was involved as one of the managers in the impeachment proceedings against Judge George W. English, a judge of the United States District Court for the Eastern District of Illinois, who was impeached in 1926 on charges that he abused his power. (English resigned from the bench on 4 November 1926, and the impeachment proceedings against him were dismissed for lack of jurisdiction).

Footnotes, Sources and Further Reading for this chapter appears on page 843

In 1932, the US economy was suffering in its third year of the depression which had hit the nation in October 1929. Running for re-election that year, Michener was accused of the same charges he used to such great effect in 1918 – that his party, controlling the entire US government, had been unresponsive to the economic downturn. Michener ultimately lost his seat to Democrat John Camillus Lehr, a former city attorney. On 3 March 1933, Michener departed from Congress, and returned to Michigan to practice law. He was not out of politics long, however. In 1934, just two years after his defeat, Michener challenged Lehr in a rematch of the 1932 race. This time, Michener won during a period when Democrats controlled most of the US government in overwhelming numbers. Michener would ultimately serve during this tenure from 3 January 1935 (the Twenty-first Amendment had changed the dates of the congressional term from 4 March to the first Monday in January) until 3 January 1951, from the Seventy-fourth through the Eighty-first congresses.

During this second tenure, Michener introduced, on 3 January 1947, the first day of the Eightieth Congress, the language which would eventually become the Twenty-second Amendment to the US Constitution. As chairman of the House Committee on the Judiciary, Michener instantly referred the measure to that committee. Hearings were held, and the proposed amendment was voted out of the committee with a favorable vote on 5 February 1947. Michener took part in the floor debate that raged between Republicans and Democrats over the amendment's potential language. Republicans wished to limit the number of terms a President could be elected to; Democrats felt that the amendment was an attack on former President Franklin D. Roosevelt, who had died two years earlier after being elected to his unprecedented fourth term. Ultimately, the amendment garnered enough support to pass both houses of Congress, and was submitted to the states, which ratified it in 1951.

When the amendment was ratified, Michener was no longer in Congress, deciding not to run in 1950. He left the House on 3 January 1951, and returned to Michigan as an attorney in his hometown of Adrian. Michener worked there until his death on 4 July 1957 at the age of 80. He was laid to rest in the Oakwood Cemetery in Adrian, next to his wife, Belle, who died the same year.

Alexander Wiley (1884-1967)

Senator Alexander Wiley introduced the proposed amendment in the US Senate, and pushed for its ultimate passage in that body. Wiley was born in Chippewa Falls, in Chippewa County, Wisconsin, on 26 May 1884. He attended public schools and went to Augsburg College in Minneapolis, Minnesota, and the University of Michigan at Ann Arbor. He graduated from the University of Wisconsin with a law degree in 1907, was admitted to the Wisconsin state bar that same year, and opened a law practice in Chippewa Falls.

In 1908, Wiley was elected as the District Attorney for Chippewa County, serving from 1909 to 1915. In 1934, Progressive Phillip La Follette, the son of famed Wisconsin politician Robert La Follette, was elected governor of Wisconsin; two years later, Wiley was nominated as the Republican candidate to oppose him. The Democrats, a shadow of what their party had once been in the state, nominated Arthur Lueck. La Follette won a narrow victory with 46% of the vote; Wiley came in second with 29%, and Lueck came in third with 22%.

In 1938, Wiley won a seat in the US Senate, just two years after his gubernatorial loss, by defeating the incumbent and so-called "Townsend Republican" Democrat F. Ryan Duffy, and served from 3 January 1939 until 3 January 1963. During the Eightieth Congress (1947-49), Wiley served as the chairman of the Senate Committee on the Judiciary. It was in this role that Wiley introduced, in the Senate, the proposed language for a constitutional amendment to limit the number of terms a President could serve to two elected terms. Historian Michael Korzi wrote, "The arguments offered...ranged from subtle treatments of the balance of power in Washington and the American system to general screeds linking FDR to the dictatorships of Europe. Republican Senator Alexander Wiley (WI) argued that the necessity of the Twenty-second Amendment was supported by the historical record. 'Continuance of power in the hands of an individual or party over a considerable period of time made positive a Hitler, a Mussolini, and all the little Fascists. That, Mr. President, is the reason for the proposed constitutional amendment.' Some members took exception to the proposed amendment as a vilification of FDR. Most other supporters of the amendment, however, were less heavyhanded in their criticisms of long presidential tenure." In the Eighty-third Congress, Wiley served as the chairman of the Senate Committee on Foreign Relations.

Wiley was known as a prankster and joke teller who kept his fellow Senators laughing, regardless of party. In his 1947 memoir *Laughing with Congress*, Wiley wrote that a Russian observer, Boris Marshalov, visited Congress, after which Marshalov explained, "Congress is so strange. A man gets up to speak and says nothing. Nobody listens – and then everybody disagrees." In 1954, *Life* magazine profiled Wiley, alongside an up-and-coming Senator from Massachusetts, John F. Kennedy. The magazine said of the Wisconsinite, "As the Administration's principal foreign policy spokesman in the Senate, Wisconsin's Alexander Wiley works hard, but he is always cracking jokes. He has posed for photographers banging a fellow senator over the head with a gavel, sometimes addresses government officials as 'you handsome men,' and once attended a hearing of John Forster Dulles wearing a comical black string tie."

Although he was a moderate-to-conservative Republican, Wiley served from a state with a history of progressive politics. In 1944, he was challenged in the Republican primary by Joseph R. McCarthy, and Wiley narrowly won. By 1962 , at 76 years old, Wiley faced re-election against Democrat Gaylord Nelson, 32 years Wiley's junior. Nelson defeated Wiley, 53% to 47%. On 3 January 1963, Wiley departed from the Senate for the first time in 24 years. He remained in Washington, however, where he lived until a few days before his death. He was at the High Oaks Christian Science Church Sanitarium in Germantown, Pennsylvania where he died on 26 May 1967, his 83rd birthday. His body was returned to his hometown, and he was laid to rest in the Forest Hill Cemetery in Chippewa Falls.

FOOTNOTES, SOURCES, FURTHER READING

Footnotes

[1] "Proposed Amendment to the Constitution of the United States Relating to Terms of Office of the President," House Report No. 17, 80th Congress, 1st Session (1947), 2.

[2] Willis, Paul G.; and George L. Willis, "The Politics of the Twenty-second Amendment," *The Western Political Quarterly*, V:3 (September 1952), 469-82.

[3] Thorpe, Francis Newton, "The Federal and State Constitutions, Colonial Charters and Other Organic Laws of the States, Territories and Colonies" (Washington: Government Printing Office; seven volumes, 1909), III:1689.

[4] Ibid., VII:3813.

[5] See Charles C. Tansill, ed., "Documents Illustrative of the Formation of the Union of the American States" (Washington: Government Printing Office, 1927), 135.

[6] Ibid., 134, 410-11.

[7] Elliot, Jonathan, "The Debates in the Several State Conventions, of the Adoption of the Federal Constitution, as Recommended by the General Convention at Philadelphia, in 1787, Together with the Journal of the Federal Convention, Luther Martin's Letter, Yates's Minutes, Congressional Opinions, Virginia and Kentucky Resolutions of '98-'99, and Other Illustrations of the Constitution" (Philadelphia: J.B. Lippincott & Co.; five volumes, 1876), III:483-84.

[8] Hamilton, Alexander; James Madison, and John Jay, "The Federalist: A Commentary on the Constitution of the United States, Being a Collection of Essays Written in Support of the Constitution Agreed Upon September 17, 1787" (New York: G.P. Putnam's Sons, 1892), 451.

[9] Kent, James (William M. Lacy, ed.), Commentaries on America Law by James Kent" (Philadelphia: The Blackstone Publishing Group; four volumes, 1889), I:285.

[10] Ames, Herman V., "The Proposed Amendments to the Constitution of the United States During the First Century of its History" (Washington: Government Printing Office, 1897), 124-25.

[11] Porter, Kirk Harold., comp., "National Party Platforms" (New York: The Macmillan Company, 1924), 15.

[12] Ingalls remarks in Dougherty, J. Hampden, "The Electoral System of the United States. Its History, Together a Study of the Perils That Have Attended its Operations, an Analysis of the Several Efforts by Legislation to Avert These Perils, and a Proposed Remedy by Amendment of the Constitution" (New York: G.P. Putnam's Sons, 1906), 14-15.

[13] Appleby, Paul H., "Roosevelt's Third-Term Decision," *The American Political Science Review*, XLVI:3 (September 1952), 755.

[14] Korzi, Michael J., "Presidential Term Limits in American History: Power, Principles & Politics" (College Station: Texas A&M University Press, 2011), 83-84.

[15] Douglas, Lewis W., "No Third Term," *The Saturday Evening Post*, (2 November 1940), 27.

[16] Sabath remarks in "*The Congressional Record*: Proceedings and Debates of the First Session of the 80th Congress, First Session. Volume 99 – Parts 1-4" (Washington: Government Printing Office, 1947), 842.

[17] McCormack remarks in ibid., 844.

[18] Springer remarks in ibid., 846.

[19] Tydings remarks in ibid., 1864.

[20] O'Conor remarks in ibid., 1780.

[21] Pepper remarks in ibid., 1965.

[22] Kallenbach, Joseph E., "Constitutional Limitations on Reeligibility of National and State Chief Executives," *The American Political Science Review*, XLVI:2 (June 1952), 451.

[23] Two states rejected the amendment: Oklahoma in June 1947, and Massachusetts on 9 June 1949.

[24] Minnesota became the state which gave the amendment the requisite number of state ratifications to be considered a ratified amendment.

[25] Leo Elwood Allen (1898-1973), Republican of Illinois, US Rep. (1933-61).

[26] Adolph Joachim Sabath (1866-1952), Democrat of Illinois, US Rep. (1907-52).

[27] John William McCormack (1891-1980), Democrat of Massachusetts, US Rep. (1928-71), Speaker of the House of Representatives (1953-71).

[28] Charles Abraham Halleck (1900-1986), Republican of Indiana, US Rep. (1935-69).

[29] Raymond Smiley Springer (1882-1947), Republican of Indiana, County Attorney, Fayette County, Indiana (1908-14), Judge, thirtyseventh judicial circuit of Indiana (1916-22), US Rep. (1939-47).

[30] Earl Cory Michener (1876-1957), Republican of Michigan, Assistant Prosecuting Attorney, Lenawee County, Michigan (1907-10), Prosecuting Attorney (1911-14), US Rep. (1919-33, 1935-51).

[31] John Elliott Rankin (1882-1960), Democrat of Mississippi, Prosecuting Attorney, Lee County, Mississippi (1911-15), US Rep. (1921-53).

[32] The speaker is referring here to the Library of Congress.

[33] Emanul Celler (1888-1981), Democrat of New York, US Rep. (1923-73).

[34] Joseph Raleigh Bryson (1893-1953), Democrat of South Carolina, Member, South Carolina state House of Representatives (1921-24), Member, state Senate (1929-32), US Rep. (1939-53).

[35] Thomas Albert Jenkins (1880-1959), Republican of Ohio, Prosecuting Attorney, Lawrence County, Ohio (1916-20), Member, Ohio state Senate (1923-24), US Rep. (1925-59).

[36] John Marshall Robsion (1873-1948), Republican of Kentucky, US Rep. (1919-30, 1935-48), US Senator (1930).

[37] Joseph Lister Hill (1894-1984), Democrat of Alabama, US Rep. (1923-38), US Senator (1938-69).

[38] Richard Brevard Russell, Jr. (1897-1971), Democrat of Georgia, Member, Georgia state House of Representatives (1921-31), Governor of Georgia (1931-33), US Senator (1933-71).

[39] Scott Wike Lucas (1892-1968), Democrat of Illinois, State's Attorney, Mason County, Illinois (1920-25), US Rep. (1935-39), US Senator (1939-51).

[40] Alexander Wiley (1884-1967), Republican of Wisconsin, District Attorney, Chippewa County, Wisconsin (1909-13), US Senator (1939-63).

[41] William Chapman Revercomb (1895-1979), Republican of West Virginia, US Senator (1943-49, 1956-59).

[42] Warren Grant Magnuson (1905-1989), Democrat of Washington State, Special Prosecuting Attorney, King County, Washington State (1931), Member, Washington State House of Representatives (1933-34), US District Attorney (1934), Prosecuting Attorney, King County (1934-36), US Rep. (1937-44), US Senator (1944-81).

[43] On this day, the presiding officer was identified as Senator William Fife Knowland, Republican of California (1908-1974).

[44] Walter Franklin George (1878-1957), Democrat of Georgia, Solicitor General, the Cordele judicial circuit (1907-12), Judge, Georgia Superior Court (1912-17), Judge, Georgia state Court of Appeals (1917), Associate Justice, Georgia state Supreme Court (1917-22), US Senator (1922-57), Special Ambassador to the North Atlantic Treaty Organization (NATO) (1957).

[45] Millard Evelyn Tydings (1890-1961), Democrat of Maryland, Member, Maryland state House of Delegates (1916-21), Member, Maryland state Senate (1922-23), US Rep. (1923-27), US Senator (1927-51).

[46] Robert Alphonso Taft (1889-1953), Republican of Ohio, Member, Ohio state House of Representatives (1021-26), Member, Ohio state Senate (1931-32), US Senator (1939-53).

[47] Harding died on 2 August 1923, 2 years and 4 months into his term.

[48] Alben William Barkley (1877-1956), Democrat of Kentucky, US Rep. (1913-27), US Senator (1927-49, 1955-56), Vice President of the United States (1949-53).

[49] Kenneth Douglas McKellar (1869-1957), Democrat of Tennessee, US Rep. (1911-17), US Senator (1917-53).

[50] Francis John Myers (1901-1956), Democrat of Pennsylvania, Deputy Attorney General of Pennsylvania (1937), US Rep. (1939-45), US Senator (1945-51).

[51] Carl Atwood Hatch (1889-1963), Democrat of New Mexico, Assistant Attorney General of New Mexico (1917-18), District Judge, the Ninth Judicial District of New Mexico (1923-29), US Senator (1933-49), US District Judge for the District of New Mexico (1949-63).

[52] Theodore Francis Green (1867-1966), Democrat of Rhode Island, Governor of Rhode Island (1933-36), US Senator (1937-61).

[53] Claude Denson Pepper (1900-1989), Democrat of Florida, Member, Florida state House of Representatives (1929-30), US Senator (1936-51), US Rep. (1963-89).

[54] Wallace Humphrey White, Jr. (1877-1952), Republican of Maine, US Rep. (1917-31), US Senator (1931-49).

[55] The big fight in the US Senate was not over the proposed constitutional amendment, but over the nomination of David E. Lilienthal to be the chairman of the Atomic Energy Commission.

[56] Edmund Jenings Randolph (1753-1813), of Virginia, Aide-de-camp to General George Washington during the Revolutionary War, Attorney General, state of Virginia (1776), Member, Continental Congress (1779, 1781, 1782), Governor of Virginia (1786-88), Delegate, Constitutional Convention (1787), Attorney General of the United States (1789-94), Secretary of State of the United States (1794-95).

[57] Referring actually to William Paterson (1745-1806), Pro-Administration member from New Jersey, Delegate and secretary, Provincial Congress (1775-76), Member, State Legislative Council (1776-77), Attorney General, state of New Jersey (1776-83), Delegate, Constitutional Convention (1787),US Senator (1789-90), Governor, states of New Jersey (1790-93), Associate Justice, US Supreme Court (1793-1806).

[58] Emanul Celler (1888-1981), Democrat of New York, US Rep. (1923-73).

[59] Elihu Root (1845-1937), Republican of New York, US Attorney for the Southern District of New York (1883-85), Secretary of War (1899-1904), Secretary of State (1905-09), US Senator (1909-15), President, Carnegie Endowment for International Peace (1910-25), winner, Nobel Prize for Peace (1912), President, The Hague Tribunal of Arbitration, the Netherlands (1913), Special US Ambassador Extraordinary to Russia (1917).

[60] Robert Alphonso Taft (1889-1953), Republican of Ohio, Member, Ohio state House of Representatives (1021-26), Member, Ohio state Senate (1931-32), US Senator (1939-53).

[61] John William McCormack (1891-1980), Democrat of Massachusetts, US Rep. (1928-71), Speaker of the House of Representatives (1953-71).

[62] Earl Cory Michener (1876-1957), Republican of Michigan, Assistant Prosecuting Attorney, Lenawee County, Michigan (1907-10), Prosecuting Attorney (1911-14), US Rep. (1919-33, 1935-51).

[63] "The Constitution of the United States of America: Analysis and Interpretation – 2020 Edition" (Washington, D.C.: Government Printing Office, 2002), 2104.

Sources Arranged by Chapter sections

Debate in Congress

"The Congressional Record: Proceedings and Debates of the 80th Congress, First Session. Volume 93 – Part 1. January 3, 1947, to February 24, 1947" (Washington" US Government Printing Office, 1947), 841-49.

"The Congressional Record: Proceedings and Debates of the 80th Congress, First Session. Volume 93 – Part 2. February 26, 1947, to March 28, 1947" (Washington" US Government Printing Office, 1947), 1770-80, 1862-67, 1964-78.

Historical Background Documents

"Proposed Amendment to the Constitution of the United States Relating to Terms of Office of the President," House Report No. 17, 80th Congress, 1st Session (1947), 1-37.

Robert A. Taft to Thomas Swope, 3 July 1947, in Clarence E. Wunderlin, Jr., ed., "The Papers of Robert A. Taft" (Kent, Ohio: The Kent State University Press; four volumes, 1997-2006), III:298-99.

Original Primary Documents

"Order Hearing on Bills to Limit Presidential Term," *The Chicago Tribune*, 2 February 1947, 2.

"Presidency Limit of 8 Years Asked," *The New York Times*, 4 February 1947, 18.

"Two-Term Amendment," *The Washington Post*, 13 February 1947, 6.

"Presidency Limit Put Before Senate," *The New York Times*, 6 March 1947, 2.

"Votes to Place Two Term Issue Before the States," *The Chicago Tribune*, 13 March 1947, 1.

"House Vote O.K.'s Presidency Limit," *The Sun* [Baltimore, Maryland], 22 March 1947, 1, 2.

Who's Who

Earl Cory Michener (1876-1957)
"Michener, Earl Cory," official congressional biography, online at http://bioguide.congress.gov/scripts/biodisplay.pl?index=M000693; Michener election numbers in James Langland, ed., "The Chicago Daily News Almanac and Year-Book for 1922" (Chicago, Illinois: The Chicago Daily News Company, 1922), 251; "Presidency Limit of 8 Years Asked," *The New York Times*, 4 February 1947, 18.

Alexander Wiley (1884-1967)
"Wiley, Alexander," official congressional biography, online at http://bioguide.congress.gov/scripts/biodisplay.pl?index=W000465; "Wiley, Alexander" in Caryn Hannan, "Wisconsin Biographical Dictionary: 2008-2009 Edition" (—:State History Publications, 2009), 460-61; Wiley, Alexander, "Laughing with Congress" (New York: Crown Publishers, 1947), 58; McConaughy, James L., "The World's Most Exclusive Clubmen," Life, XXXVI:16 (19 April 1954), 115; "State Voters Reelect Wiley, Support Dewey," *The Wisconsin State Journal* [Madison], 8 November 1944, 1; Korzi, Michael J., "Presidential Term Limits in American History: Power, Principles, and Politics" (College Station: Texas A&M University Press, 2011), 132.

Further Reading

Beermann, Jack M., "A Skeptical View of a Skeptical View of Presidential Term Limits," Connecticut Law Review, XLIII:4 (May 2011), 1105-23.

Brands, H.W., "Traitor to His Class: The Privileged Like and Radical Presidency of Franklin Delano Roosevelt' (New York: Doubleday, 2008).

Coenen, Dan T., "Two-Time Presidents and the Vice-Presidency," *Boston College Law Review*, LVI:4 (October 2015), 1287-1344.

Davis, Paul B., "The Results and Implications of the Enactment of the Twenty-Second Amendment," *Presidential Studies Quarterly*, IX:3 (Summer 1979), 289-303.

Korzi, Michael J., *Presidential Term Limits in American History: Power, Principles, and Politics* (College Station, TX: Texas A&M University Press, 2011).

Maltz, Gideon, "The Case for Presidential Term Limits," *Journal of Democracy*, XVIII:1 (January 2007), 128-42.

Paul, Jeremy, "If It Quacks Like a Lame Duck, Can It Lead the Free World? The Case for Relaxing Presidential Term Limits," *Connecticut Law Review*, XLIII:4 (May 2011), 1097-1104.

Peabody, Bruce G.; and Scott E. Gant, "The Twice and Future President: Constitutional Interstices and the Twenty-Second Amendment," *Minnesota Law Review*, LXXXIII (1999), 565-635.

Stathis, Stephen W., "The Twenty-Second Amendment: A Practical Remedy or Partisan Maneuver?," *Constitutional Commentary*, VII:1 (Winter 1990), 61-88.

AMERICA AT THAT TIME . . .

Although the material in this section may not be directly related to the adoption of the Twenty-second Amendment, it offers valuable insight into what was happening in America at the time the Amendment was adopted. Modeled after Grey House Publishing's Working American *series, whose author, Scott Derks, is responsible for its content, it includes a Historical Snapshot, Selected Prices, significant quotations, newspaper and magazine clips to give a sense of what was on the minds of Americans, and how it may have impacted the amendment process.*

HISTORICAL SNAPSHOT

1951

- Nationwide 3.8 million people played golf on approximately 5,000 courses, comprising 1.5 million acres of land

- North Korean forces crossed the thirty-eighth parallel, took Seoul, and rejected American truce offers

- Color television was first introduced

- H&R Block, formed in 1946 in Kansas City, began offering tax preparation services when the IRS stopped preparing people's taxes

- Margaret Sanger urged the development of an oral contraceptive

- The Metropolitan Life Insurance Company reported a link between being 15 pounds overweight and dying younger than the average life span

- The Twenty-second Amendment to the U.S. Constitution passed Congress, limiting the service of the president to two terms

- The latest census reported that eight percent of the population was more than 65 years old, up from four percent in 1900

- For the first time in history, women outnumbered men in the United States; Washington, D.C., had the highest percentage of single women (27 percent), while Nevada had the lowest (13 percent)

- Julius and Ethel Rosenberg were sentenced to death for espionage against the United States

- President Truman dispatched an air force plane when Sioux City Memorial Park in Iowa refused to bury John Rice, a Native American who had died in combat; his remains were interred in Arlington National Cemetery

- Entertainer Milton Berle signed a 30-year, million-dollar-plus contract with NBC

- New York and other major cities increased the cost of a phone call from $0.05 to $0.10

"Dr. Earnest Diehter, New York Consulting psychologist, told the Pacific Council of the American Association of Advertising Agencies convention that he has conducted six exhaustive studies to find out why people drink. His findings: 'To get drunk.' "

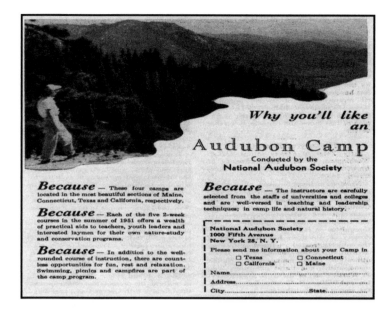

"The West's Most Fabulous Highway," Claire Noall, *Deseret News Magazine,* Salt Lake City, Utah, June 10, 1951:

A million dollars for 30 miles of highway to reach a town of 217 people sounds fantastic, not just in regard to the money spent or the emancipation of the last packhorse-mail-route town in the United States—but in beauty.

Boulder would still be isolated in winter were it not for the amazing highway. In summer the town can be reached from Wayne County (on the north) via a narrow precipitous dirt road over Boulder Mountain. Between Escalante (30 miles southwest) and Boulder lies the romantic Hell's Backbone dirt road. But the Boulder Mountain road reaches an altitude of nearly 11,000 feet. Hell's Backbone strikes out at about 9,000. Both are closed in winter. Calf Creek, the most gloriously beautiful of the three, remains open all winter.

Prior to 1935, the way into Boulder from Escalante was by packhorse or mule back, over the Death Hollow trail if you took the shortcut. If you wanted to play safe, you might take the much longer but easier trail over the backbone. In winter, however, it was mighty cold in Hell and the Death Hollow trail was the best bet, though one's mule might slide off the narrow path down a rocky descent towards the infernal pit.

The Calf Creek turnpike has banished the use of both pack trails as a necessity. Hand-built by the CCC [Civilian Conservation Corps] boys, it has made the drive between Escalante and Boulder one of the most spectacularly beautiful in the whole United States. Yet how few people are aware of this treat in scenic novelties!

Not long ago we had a game where a receiver in the backfield was hit on a pass play. It was an early hit but not a vicious one. The fans were screaming for pass interference, but since the play occurred behind the line of scrimmage, it wasn't pass interference and we didn't call it. That was an example of a good "no all."

—NFL Veteran Referee Jerry Markbreit

Selected Prices

1951 Nash Rambler...$1,732.00

Admiral Dual-Temp Refrigerator..$189.95

Aerowax Floor Wax, Quart $0.55

Chapstick Lip Balm $0.25

Charvin Girdle $6.95

Collette Basketball, Official Size $2.98

Columbia Records' Record..$4.85

Corning Glass Double Boiler..$3.45

Evenflow Baby Nipple...$0.25

Ford Custom Victoria Automobile $1,925.00

Goodyear Glide Garden Hose...$5.95

Imperial Gas Range, Full Size $99.00

Moran Wee-Walker Shoes..$1.19

Noxema Home Facial, Big Jar $0.59

Oscar Mayer Wieners, per Pound $0.49

Parker Brothers Monopoly Game $4.00

Scott Television, 16 Inch...$299.00

Serta Perfect Sleeper Mattress $49.50

Year	Value of One Dollar in 2016 US Dollars
1947	$10.83
1948	$10.02
1949	$10.14
1950	$10.02
1951	$9.29
1952	$9.11

22nd Amendment Now Law;
States OK President Term Limit,
Independent Journal, February 27, 1951

WASHINGTON (/P) — From now on, no president of the United States—except for Harry Truman—may be elected to more than two terms. And under the Twenty-second amendment to the Constitution, which for all practical purposes became law last night, no man or woman may serve more than ten years in the White House.

The amendment, while limiting future presidents to two elective terms, allows a person who has served two years or less of an unexpired term to be elected twice on his own.

As president at the time the amendment was approved by the Republican controlled 80th Congress, Truman was specifically exempted. Thus he would be permitted to run for a second full term in 1952 even though his White House tenure would then fall within the ban set out in the new amendment. He has not said whether he will run. Utah and Nevada legislature acted in quick succession yesterday to approve the amendment. Nevada completed action at 4:30 p.m. (PST), becoming the 38th state to ratify the amendment.

The Constitution requires that amendments to it be ratified by three-fourths of the states—or 36 at present—to become law. A two-thirds majority in Congress is required to submit amendments to the states.

The new amendment could be repealed by the same procedure, of course, just as the 18th—prohibition—amendment was repealed by the 21st, it was ratified on Dec. 5, 1933.

Nevada legislators had stood by to grab for their state the honor of being the 36th state to ratify the new amendment. Minutes after learning that Utah had approved, Nevada senators voted 16 to 1 for ratification. The assembly had a proved earlier, 29 to 12.

At least two other states also were near ratification votes—Minnesota and Maryland. The Minnesota legislature had suspended the rules to schedule a vote this afternoon in the hope of becoming the 36th and deciding state to act.

The amendment has been before the states since March, 1947. After an initial spurt of ratification votes, interest in the proposal apparently lagged and only 24 states had acted favorably by the start of this year. Then came another rush, bringing approval by legislatures of a dozen states within the past few weeks.

When it submitted the amendment to the states, Congress provided that to be effective it had to be ratified by the required number within seven years, or before March 26, 1954.

"I Have Two Mothers and Two Fathers," by Louise Horner, *Good Housekeeping*, February 1951:

"It had always seemed to me that we were an essentially happy family. Divorces happened in other families, not in ours. But the week after I graduated from high school, my two brothers and I were called into our parents' room for one of our infrequent family conferences. We sat in a row on the edge of the big bed and watched the rain beat against the windows. 'Children, please try to understand what we are going to tell you,' Mother said. 'Your father and I—' there was a catch in her voice and she could not go on. Dad looked at a spot on the wall above our heads. Finally his words came in a rush. 'After thinking it over, your mother and I have decided that it would be better for all of us if we lived apart from each other.' He turned his back to us and stared out the window at the rain . . . Eight years have elapsed since then, and because I have gained perspective, I can appreciate the wisdom with which our parents handled the situation. They told us there had been no quarrel. Their life together had to end because they had grown away from each other. They promised that when any problems concerning us arose, they would do their best to solve them together."

"It seems clear to the committee that too many of the men running gambling operations in Nevada are either members of existing out-of-state gambling syndicates or have had histories of close association with the underworld characters who operate these syndicates. The licensing system which is in effect in this state has not resulted in excluding the undesirables from the state but has merely served to give their activities a seeming cloak of respectability."

—Sen. Estes Kefauver, 1951

Inventions: 1950 to 1959

1950

Ralph Schneider invented the credit card.

1951

Super Glue was invented.
Francis W. Davis invented power steering.
Charles Ginsburg invented the first video tape recorder (VTR).

1952

Mr. Potato Head was patented.
The first patent for bar code was issued to inventors Joseph Woodland and Bernard Silver.
The first diet soft drink, a sugar-free ginger ale intended for diabetics, was sold.
Edward Teller and his team built the hydrogen bomb.

1953

Radial tires were invented.
RCA invented the first musical synthesizer.
David Warren invented the black box flight recorder.
Texas Instruments invented the transistor radio.

1954

An oral contraceptive for women (the "pill") was invented.
The first nonstick Teflon pan was produced.
Chaplin, Fuller and Pearson invented the solar cell.

1955

Tetracycline was invented.
Optical fiber was invented.

1956

The first computer hard disk was used.
Christopher Cockerell invented the hovercraft.
Bette Nesmith Graham invented "Mistake Out," later renamed Liquid Paper, to paint over mistakes made with a typewriter.

1957

The Fortran computer language was invented.

1958

The computer modem was invented.
Gordon Gould invented the laser.
Richard Knerr and Arthur "Spud" Melin invented the Hula Hoop.
Jack Kilby and Robert Noyce invented the integrated circuit.

1959

Wilson Greatbatch invented the internal pacemaker.
Ruth Handler (the co-founder of Mattel) invented the Barbie Doll, named after her own daughter Barbara.
Jack Kilby and Robert Noyce both invented the microchip.

Gardner Cowles Says All-Out War Not Inevitable
Corpus Christie Times, February 27, 1951

BEVERLY HILLS. Calif., Feb. 27. (AP)— "If we keep our heads, the United States is not going to get involved in an all-out war with Russia, but will enjoy the greatest era of prosperity in history," says Publisher Gardner Cowles.

Russia is not the terror many people think, the publisher of *Look Magazine* told a Screen Producers Guild banquet last night. We've been oversold on the idea, he declared.

"Russia has been having troubles at home and plenty of troubles in her satellite nations," Cowles said. "Meanwhile this country is getting fantastically stronger—and strength breeds friends."

He added he is all for rearmament and the Atlantic Pact.

The national consumer expenditures
(per capita income) in 1951 were:

Auto Parts	$9.72
Auto Usage	$143.24
Clothing	$113.42
Dentists	$6.48
Food	$393.42
Furniture	$20.74
Gas and Oil	$39.54
Health Insurance	$5.83
Housing	$157.49
Intercity Transport	$6.48
Local Transport	$12.96
New Auto Purchase	$55.74
Personal Business	$46.02
Personal Care	$17.49
Physicians	$17.49
Private Education and Research	$12.31

The Twenty-third Amendment

Chapter 14

S. J. Res. 39

Eighty-sixth Congress of the United States of America

AT THE SECOND SESSION

Begun and held at the City of Washington on Wednesday, the sixth day of January,
one thousand nine hundred and sixty

Joint Resolution

Proposing an amendment to the Constitution of the United States granting representation in the electoral college to the District of Columbia.

Resolved by the Senate and House of Representatives of the United States of America in Congress assembled (two-thirds of each House concurring therein), That the following article is hereby proposed as an amendment to the Constitution of the United States, which shall be valid to all intents and purposes as part of the Constitution only if ratified by the legislatures of three-fourths of the several States within seven years from the date of its submission by the Congress:

"ARTICLE —

"SECTION 1. The District constituting the seat of Government of the United States shall appoint in such manner as the Congress may direct:

"A number of electors of President and Vice President equal to the whole number of Senators and Representatives in Congress to which the District would be entitled if it were a State, but in no event more than the least populous State; they shall be in addition to those appointed by the States, but they shall be considered, for the purposes of the election of President and Vice President, to be electors appointed by a State; and they shall meet in the District and perform such duties as provided by the twelfth article of amendment.

"SEC. 2. The Congress shall have power to enforce this article by appropriate legislation".

Speaker of the House of Representatives.

Vice President of the United States and Acting President of the Senate pro tempore.

Proposed in Congress:	**16 June 1960**
Sent to States:	**16 June 1960**
Ratified:	**29 March 1961**

Chapter 14

THE TWENTY-THIRD AMENDMENT

Section 1.
The District constituting the seat of Government of the United States shall appoint in such manner as Congress may direct:

A number of electors of President and Vice President equal to the whole number of Senators and Representatives in Congress to which the District would be entitled if it were a State, but in no event more than the least populous State; they shall be in addition to those appointed by the States, but they shall be considered, for the purposes of the election of President and Vice President, to be electors appointed by a State; and they shall meet in the District and perform such duties as provided by the twelfth article of amendment.

Section 2.
The Congress shall have power to enforce this article by appropriate legislation.

Brief Summary

The Twenty-third Amendment granted voting rights to the District of Columbia. Historically, residents of the District of Columbia did not have the right to vote in presidential elections, for the district is not a state but rather a federal territory. As such, it did not appoint electors to the Electoral College. The Twenty-third Amendment changed that. In granting voting rights to the district in presidential elections, it specifies that the district is to appoint members to the Electoral College. The number of electors is equal to the number the district would have if it were a state: one for each of two US senators plus one for each representative in the House. The amendment further specifies that the number of electors is not to exceed that of the nation's least populous state. As of 2016, the district has three electors.

Timeline

1888   Theodore Noyes of the Washington Star launches a campaign to promote an amendment to the Constitution giving DC citizens the right to vote in presidential elections.

14 June 1960	The US House of Representatives passes the Twenty-third Amendment.
16 June 1960	The US Senate passes the Twenty-third Amendment.
29 March 1961	The Twenty-third Amendment is ratified when Ohio becomes the thirty-eighth state to ratify it; Arkansas rejected the amendment, and nine states took no action on it.
24 December 1973	Congress passes the District of Columbia Home Rule Act, giving DC features of home rule such as the right to elect a mayor.
25 July 1977	House Joint Resolution 554 is introduced in an effort to amend the Constitution to give the District of Columbia statehood privileges, including representation in Congress.
2 March 1978	The District of Columbia Voting Rights Amendment proposed by HJR 554, which would repeal the Twenty-third Amendment, passes in the US House of Representatives.
22 August 1978	The proposed amendment passes in the US Senate.
22 August 1985	The proposed amendment expires as the requisite number of states fail to ratify it by the deadline for ratification.

Introduction

When the US Constitution was first ratified in 1789, there was no District of Columbia to speak of. The nation's capital city was in New York, where the first President of the United States, George Washington, was inaugurated. The infant Congress met there; the even younger US Supreme Court had just begun its momentous work. W.H. Muller, writing in 1922, explained, "The first meeting of the Supreme Court was held in temporary quarters in the Exchange Building in the city of New York on February the first, 1790."[1]

The men who drafted the Constitution, and who helped to write the first twelve amendments to that document, did not see fit to include the "voting rights" of a capital city. They reasoned that both New York, as the current capital, and Philadelphia, a former capital, each had "voting rights" when they served as capitals, and too, once their status changed to non-capital.

This matter, however, was evident in the fight to get first the Constitution itself, and then its amendments, ratified. In *The Federalist*, No. 42, James Madison explained "to the people of the State of New York, '[C]omplete authority at the seat of government...is a power exercised by every legislature of the Union...Without it, not only the public authority might be insulted and its proceedings interrupted with impunity; but a dependence of the members of the general government on the State comprehending the seat of the government, for protection in the exercise of their duty, might bring on the national councils an imputation of awe or influence...[and] abridge its necessary independence.'"[2] In a counter-argument, Richard Henry Lee, of the famed Lee family of Virginia (which includes "Lighthorse Harry" Lee as well as Civil War military commander Robert E. Lee), wrote in *The Antifederalist*, Nos. 41-43, "What would be the consequence if the seat of the government of the United States, with all the archives of America, was in the power of any one particular state? Would not this be most unsafe and humiliating? Do we not all remember that, in the year 1783, a band of soldiers went and insulted Congress? The sovereignty of the United States was treated with indignity. They applied for protection to the state they resided in, but could obtain none. It is to be hoped such a disgraceful scene will never happen again; but that, for the future, the national government will be able to protect itself."[3]

What changed the argument was the actual formation of a national "capital" in 1800, when the center of the American government moved to the new city of Washington, carved out of a small area that belonged to Virginia and Maryland. The site, originally selected in 1790 and given by both states, was about 10 miles (16 kilometers) square, located along the Potomac River. President Washington named Andrew Ellicott to survey the new federal city site, and, once that survey was completed, the President appointed a French military engineer, Pierre Charles L'Enfant, whom Washington knew during L'Enfant's military service in the Continental Army during the American Revolution, to lay out a plan for buildings for the city. L'Enfant sketched a city with wide boulevards that intersected, and placed a home for the President, styled as the "Executive Mansion" on Pennsylvania Avenue, looking down the broad street to a building that would someday house the two houses of Congress.

Styled initially as the "District" of Columbia, instead of the "State" of Columbia, its creation was actually figured by the Founding Fathers: in Article I, section 8, clause 17 of the US Constitution, the Congress was given the power "[t]o exercise exclusive Legislation in all Cases whatsoever, over such District (not exceeding ten Miles square) as may, by Cession of particular State, and the Acceptance of Congress, become the Seat of the Government of the United States." This specific portion of the founding document gave the Congress the right to "accept" land from any state to be set aside as a federal capital, and to be administered by the federal government. No one knew where this place might be; in addition, there was nothing in the article that stated that the "federal capital" could be a separate state, or a separate entity, with the right to vote for any federal official. As such, from that starting point in 1800 until 1961, the "federal capital" had a confrontational – at best – relationship with the federal government that oversaw its every action. Construction on many government buildings, hotels (to house federal officials, including Senators and Representatives), and other structures, began in earnest, and within a decade of the first plodding steps placed upon its grounds, a city quickly rose. There was a major setback in August 1814, when the British invaded the city and burned both the Executive Mansion and the unfinished buildings of the Capitol, as well as fair number of other pieces of the District. Rebuilding began, and by the 1820s, Congress gave the District the right to vote for a mayor and a city council. The city, however, remained much of a scourge: a huge canal, through which ran an open sewer, was situated through the central part of the city, slaves were sold in massive pens, and there were houses of prostitution and bars operating openly. Famed British writer Charles Dickens visited, and in 1842 he wrote, "It is sometimes called the City of Magnificent Distances, but it might with greater propriety be termed the City of Magnificent Intentions." He explained that the city consisted of "Spacious avenues, that begin in nothing, and lead nowhere; streets, mile-long, that only want houses, roads and inhabitants, public buildings that need but a public to complete; and ornaments of great thoroughfares, which only lack great thoroughfares to ornament – as it leading features...To the admirers of cities it is a Barmecide Feast; a pleasant field for the imagination to rove in; a monument raised to a deceased project, with not even a legible inscription to record its departed greatness."[4] In 1846, the land that Virginia had given to be used for the District was returned, shrinking the District from 10 square miles to 6.8 square miles.

Some Presidents during this period pushed Congress to give the District's citizens (and denizens) voting rights. On 6 December 1831, President Andrew Jackson, in his Third Annual Message (now called the State of the Union), sent Congress a message asking that the District be endowed "with the same privileges that are allowed to other territories of the United States":

"I deem it my duty again to call your attention to the condition of the District of Columbia. It was doubtless wise in the framers of our Constitution to place the people of this District under the jurisdiction of the general government, but to accomplish the objects they had in view it is not necessary that this people should be deprived of all the privileges of self-government. Independently of the difficulty of inducing the representatives of distant states to turn their attention to projects of laws which are not of the highest interest to their constituents, they are not individually, nor in Congress collectively, well qualified to legislate over the local concerns of this District. Consequently its interests are much neglected and the people are almost afraid to present their grievances, lest a body in which they are not represented and which feels little sympathy in their local relations should in its attempt to make laws for them do more harm than good...Is it not just to allow them at least a delegate to Congress, if not a local legislature, to make laws for the District, subject to the approval or rejection of Congress? I earnestly recommend the extension to them of every political right which their interests require and which may be compatible with the Constitution."[5]

The period just before the outbreak of the Civil War brought the scourge of slavery to the city, though it was always practiced in the District, even from the earliest days of the District's existence. In 1803, a bill was introduced in Congress by Rep. John Randolph of Virginia to return the parcels of land which made up the district back to Maryland and Virginia to avoid "political slavery." However, by the late 1850s, as more and more anti-slavery Whigs, and then Republicans, were elected to Congress and the US Senate, calls arose to ban at least open slave pens from being allowed. But any move to abolish these slave pens – not slavery itself, but the public sight of human beings being sold just blocks away from where Congress was meeting and where the President lived – was met with opposition from the Congress, still dominated by southerners and pro-slavery Democrats. By the time of the Civil War, however, the fight against slavery had become a nationwide issue, including in the District of Columbia.

In 1871 the District was established as a territory, giving the people who lived there a territorial form of government, in which all of the District's officials would be appointed by the President of the United States instead of being elected. Instead of a mayor, a "governor" was named – but only two would eventually hold that title: Henry D. Cooke (served 1871-73) and Alexander Robey Shepherd (served 1873-74), before the stench of political corruption, most notably during Shepherd's tenure, ended the practice. In 1874, Shepherd was forcibly removed from his position, and Congress established a Board of Commissioners, which served as the District's leadership from 1874 until 1975, even after the Twenty-third Amendment had been enacted.[6] Whereas under the territorial government scenario, the "governor" had been named by the President, now the entire Board of Commissioners would be named by the President. Still, the people who resided in the District of Columbia had no real voice in how their city was run.

From the end of the Shepherd era until the late 1950s, Congress looked at a myriad of ways to tackle the problem of District representation in Congress once and for all. As historian Judith Best explained, "the movement to provide national representation for the District of Columbia...[has] produced more than 150 congressional resolutions."[7] The first real attempt to address the situation through the method of a constitutional amendment came in 1888, when newspaper reporter Theodore Noyes of *The Washington Star* began a crusade in the pages of his newspaper for just such an amendment. He wrote, "National representation for the capital community is not in the slightest degree inconsistent with control of the capital by the nation through Congress." The call was taken up by Senator Henry William Blair, Republican of New Hampshire, who introduced in the US Senate a proposed constitutional amendment that would give the District congressional representation and electoral votes. The proposal soon died when it lacked any substantial support, and it never left the upper body of the US Congress.[8] Fourteen years later, in 1902, Senator Jacob Gallinger, Republican of New Hampshire, and the chairman of the Senate Committee on the District of Columbia, introduced a proposed constitutional amendment that would make the District an official state. Again, the effort never got out of the Senate. In 1909, President William Howard Taft, at a banquet, explained his opposition to establishing a "State of Columbia" on constitutional grounds:

"This was taken out of the application of the principle of self-government in the very Constitution that was intended to put that in force in every other part of the country, and it was done because it was intended to have the representatives of all the people of the country control this one city, and to prevent it being controlled by the parochial spirit that would necessarily govern men who did not look beyond the city to the grandeur of the nation and this as the representative of that nation."[9]

It was not until 1940 that the first real progress in the movement to gain voting status for the District was made. Congress passed a statute that gave the residents of the District, as well as territories of the United States, the jurisdiction of states in diversity actions in federal courts. Based on the legislation, a legal action was begun that reached the US Supreme Court in 1949: in *National Mutual Insurance Co. v. Tidewater Transfer Co., Inc.* (337 US 582 {1949}), the Court upheld the 1940 act; however, Justice Robert H. Jackson, who penned the plurality decision of the Court, refused to overturn the 1805 *Hepburn* decision, which originally held that the District is not a "state" under the strictures of the US Constitution. Thus, while the residents of the District had equal rights, as other American citizens, under the Constitution, they did not have the rights of statehood.

At this point, it appeared that the only way the District of Columbia would get voting rights would be through an act of Congress – but constitutional scholars argued that since the US Supreme Court stated specifically that the Constitution did not allow the District to be considered a state within the meaning of the document, only an actual constitutional amendment could undo the Court's decision in *National Mutual Insurance Co.* Democrats and Republicans worked for years to put together language that would appease both those who wanted voting rights for the District and those who did not want to bestow representation in the Congress for the district. In the House, Rep. Emanuel Celler, Democrat of New York, and Rep. James G. Beall, Sr. of Maryland, worked for several Congresses to do just this, but they were stymied, specifically by southern Democrats, especially when Celler and his fellow Democrat, Senator Spessard Holland, Democrat of Florida, paired the potential and proposed amendment with language that would end the poll tax in the states.

It bears reminding that Supreme Court decisions and congressional legislation had already given blacks, specifically in the American South, more voting rights, but certain state leaders, usually Democrats, countered with various state laws designed to keep black citizens from voting, for example, the poll tax. By the 1950s, the poll tax had pretty much eliminated the possibility of any black person being able to vote, even in federal elections, in the southern states. Republicans tried for years to outlaw the poll tax, but their efforts were halted by allies of the poll tax in both the US House and the US Senate. Certain members of Congress pushed for a dual amendment (outlawing the poll tax and giving the District voting rights). Rep. Joel T. Broyhill, Republican of Virginia, offered to split the DC voting rights amendment into two parts: one part would take care of the District's representation in the

Congress, and the other would give the District relevant numbers in the Electoral College, but this just complicated matters, and was eventually tabled.

US Senator, and former Governor of Florida, Spessard Holland, working with Beall and Celler, crafted a dualpurpose amendment that would give voting rights to the District of Columbia and, at the same time, end the poll tax in the southern states, in one fell swoop.

While the amendment could pass both houses, it could not gain the two-thirds support needed for a constitutional amendment to be submitted to the states for ratification. By early 1960, those pushing for the poll tax addition to the proposed amendment realized that they needed to break that part of the amendment from the whole proposal to get at least the DC voting rights amendment through the Congress. Also, any language that gave the District voting representatives (one member of the House and two US Senators) would have to be stripped from the amendment.

In a report put together by Celler in early 1960, he explained:

"The purpose of this...constitutional amendment is to provide the citizens of the District of Columbia with appropriate rights of voting in national elections for President and Vice President of the United States. It would permit District citizens to elect Presidential electors who would be in addition to the electors from the States and who would participate in electing the President and Vice President.

"The District of Columbia, with more than 800,000 people, has a greater number of persons than the population of each of 13 of our States. District citizens have all the obligations of citizenship, including the payment of Federal taxes, of local taxes, and service in our Armed Forces. They have fought and died in every U.S. war since the District was founded. Yet, they cannot now vote in national elections because the Constitution has restricted that privilege to citizens who reside in States. The resultant constitutional anomaly of imposing all the obligations of citizenship without the most fundamental of its privileges will be removed by the proposed constitutional amendment..."[10]

Utilizing this language, the proposed amendment passed the Senate, then went to the US House, where that body's Judiciary Committee added and subtracted language that changed it substantially. The House then passed this measure on 14 June 1960, and the US Senate, rather than open the amendment up to new hearings and cause the House to rebel, passed it on 16 June 1960. Both votes were by voice vote, so there is no official record as to who voted for it and who voted against it. But it passed both houses by two-thirds, and was submitted to the states, which ratified it by 29 March 1961 as the Twenty-third Amendment. It took another year before the anti-poll tax amendment received enough support in both houses to be likewise submitted to the states, and it was ratified as the Twenty-fourth Amendment on 23 January 1964.

Since 1962, there have been many attempts to give the District of Columbia either complete statehood rights, or extend the right of representation in Congress, or pieces of both, but as of this writing none appear to have enough support to make it through both houses of Congress. In 1967, just six years after the Twenty-third Amendment was ratified, Congress considered enacting an additional amendment that would give the same representation in Congress – two US Senators and members of the US House of Representatives based on population – as all other states; this effort went nowhere for more than a decade, until 25 July 1977, when Rep. Don Edwards, Democrat of California, introduced House Joint Resolution 554, giving the District such statehood privileges through the constitutional amendment process. The measure passed the US House on 2 March 1978, and the US Senate on 22 August 1978, and was submitted to the states for ratification. The proposed amendment had a deadline for ratification of 1985; by the time that that deadline came, only 16 states had ratified it, well short of the 38 that are presently required, three-fourths of all the states in the Union.

In 2002, Senator Joe Lieberman, Democrat (and, later, Independent) of Connecticut, then the chairman of the Senate Committee on Government Affairs, submitted a report with regards to the No Taxation Without Representation Act of 2002. In the report, he explained, "Congress already treats the District as though it were a state for over 500 statutory purposes – from federal taxation to military conscription to highway funds, education funds, and national motor voter requirements. The Supreme Court has also deemed DC the equivalent of a state for certain constitutional purposes, including the Fourteenth Amendment's Privileges and Immunities Clause and the Full Faith and Credit Clause under Article IV of the Constitution. Even where the Supreme Court has held that DC residents do not have the same rights granted to inhabitants of a state by the Constitution, it has ruled in at least one case that Congress could extend those rights to DC residents. That 1949 case, *National Mutual Insurance Co. v. Tidewater Transfer Co.*, considered the constitutional provision regarding diversity jurisdiction, which allows cases arising under state law to be brought in federal courts where the controversy exists between 'citizens of different states.' An 1805 Supreme Court case had held that DC did not constitute a state for the purposes of that clause, and therefore that DC residents could not sue or be sued in diversity in federal court. Justice [John] Marshall indicated, however, that the matter was one for 'legislative, not judicial consideration.' It took over a hundred years, but Congress eventually took the cue: in 1940, Congress passed a law that extended diversity jurisdiction to cases involving DC residents, thereby essentially treating the District as if it were a state for the purposes of that provision of the Constitution."[11]

Today, the District of Columbia has its own local government, but has no representation in Congress or anywhere else. Thus the Twenty-third Amendment solved one problem but did not address another. However, as Professor David A. Crockett has pointed out, the amendment has caused a different problem altogether: there are now 3 more electoral votes than total members of Congress (435 in Congress, with 438 electoral votes available). He explained, "The current 'problem' in election mechanics began in 1961, with the ratification of the Twenty-third Amendment. The Twenty-third Amendment gave the Federal District what has turned out to be three electoral votes, but no voting representation in Congress. For most of American history the electoral votes mirrored representation in Congress, and an odd number of federal legislators should have given us an odd number of electoral votes. However, because the Federal District has no voting representation in Congress, the Twenty-third Amendment disrupts this elegant constitutional dynamic. Despite the fact that House membership has been a constant 435, the addition of three electors that do not have counter partisan Congress has given us an even number of electoral votes in all 10 presidential elections since 1964. Although the elections of 1968 and 1976 were very close, the 2000 contest was the closest this nation has come to a House contingency election since the last one in 1824."[12]

Crockett adds, "Constitutionally, statehood for the District also has problems. Article One, Section Eight, of the Constitution allowed for the creation of a federal district through the cession of land from particular states, and it would seem that statehood for that federal district would require a constitutional amendment. Some scholars argue that, at the very least, the Twenty-third Amendment would have to be repealed, while others rest their argument on the original intent of the Framers, who desired a federal capital free of state interference. Whatever the relative merits of the constitutional arguments, there is sufficient partisan support for the arguments opposing statehood to make the matter moot. Even the argument that the District is bigger than many states a common argument as recently as the early 1990s is losing strength. The District of Columbia now ranks number 50 of 51 entities in population, beating only Wyoming."[13]

Despite its flaws, the Twenty-third Amendment was the third-to-last such constitutional change that granted the rights of voting to a specific group. Later, the Congress extended these rights (again) to blacks in the Twenty-fourth Amendment, and to those under the age of 21 in the Twenty-sixth Amendment in 1971. Historians Michael Kazin, Rebecca Edwards, and Adam Rothman wrote, "The Twenty-third Amendment (1961), granting the District of Columbia three electoral votes, and the Twenty-fourth (1964), eliminating the poll tax, were small steps toward civic participation for African Americans, symbolic victories for proponents of major civil rights reform, but so modest that even congressional opponents did not strenuously object."[14]

Debate in Congress

The original amendment began in the US Senate. After passage, it went to the House of Representatives where, after much work in the House Committee on the Judiciary, several important changes were made to the proposed language, 15 June 1960.

GRANTING REPRESENTATION IN THE ELECTORAL COLLEGE TO THE DISTRICT OF COLUMBIA

Mr. Smith of Virginia.[15] Mr. Speaker, by direction of the Committee on Rules, I call up House Representative 554 and ask for its present consideration. The Clerk read the resolution, as follows:

Resolved, That upon the adoption of this resolution it shall be in order to move that the house resolve itself into the Committee on the Whole House on the State of the Union for the consideration of the resolution (H.J. Res. 757) proposing an amendment to the constitution of the United States granting representation in the electoral college to the District of Columbia. After general debate, which shall be confined to the resolution, and continue not to exceed two hours, to be equally divided and controlled by the chairman and ranking minority member of the Committee on the Judiciary, the resolution shall be considered as having been read for amendment. No amendment shall be in order to said resolution except amendments offered by direction of the Committee on the Judiciary. Amendments offered by direction of the Committee on the Judiciary may be offered to any section of the resolution at the conclusion of the general debate, but said amendments shall not be subject to amendment. At the conclusion of the consideration of the resolution for amendment, the Committee shall rise and report the resolution to the House with such amendments as may have been adopted, and the previous question shall be considered as ordered on the resolution and amendments thereto to final passage without intervening motion, except one motion to recommit, with or without instructions.

Mr. SMITH of Virginia. Mr. Speaker, I yield 30 minutes to the gentleman from Ohio [Mr. BROWN] and now yield 10 minutes to the gentleman from Pennsylvania [Mr. WALTER].

[...]

Mr. BROWN of Ohio.[16] Mr. Speaker, I yield myself such time as I may consume.

Mr. Speaker, House Resolution 554, by the gentleman from Virginia [Mr. SMITH], makes in order, with 2 hours of general debate, the consideration of House Joint Resolution 757, a resolution which would amend the Constitution of the United States. The resolution provides not only for 2 hours of general debate but also for a closed rule under which no amendments, except those offered by the Committee on the Judiciary, may be considered. That was done because this joint resolution deals with an amendment to the Constitution of the United States.

I think perhaps I also should point out that a two-thirds vote of the House and of the other body is required to approve a joint resolution of this type, submitting to the various States of the Union, for ratification, a constitutional amendment.

The House joint resolution, of course, does not require approval or disapproval by the President, but is first the action of the Congress and then later comes the action of ratification by the States. That ratification requires an affirmative vote of three-fourths of all the States, or 38 States.

This amendment to the Constitution, as proposed in the House joint resolution is a very simple one. It would give to the people of the District of Columbia who are legal residents – not residents of some others State, but legal residents of the District itself – the right and privilege to vote for President and Vice President, or perhaps I should say, rather, for not more than three electors to represent them in the electoral college which actually selects the President and Vice President, following the general election which is held in November each 4 years. This constitutional amendment would restrict to three the numbers of electors the District of Columbia would be permitted to have, which is the equal in number to that allowed the smallest State, but actually would be about the number the District would be entitled to on a population basis, if it were a State. But this resolution in no way creates the District of Columbia as a State. It simply confers upon the electors, the legal electors, the right to vote for President and Vice President.

The amendment does not carry any provision for delegates to sit in the House, or in either branch of the Congress. Neither does it have any connection whatsoever with the various home rule questions we have had before us for a long time.

Mr. MASON.[17] Mr. Speaker, will the gentlemen yield?

Mr. BROWN of Ohio. I yield to the gentleman from Illinois.

Mr. MASON. Let us suppose that I land here in the District of Columbia and make it my home. I have come from Poland or some other place, and am not a citizen of the United States; would I have the right to vote?

Mr. BROWN of Ohio. No. The gentleman would have to be a citizen of the United States; he would have to meet all citizenship requirements, as I understand it.

Mr. Speaker, this resolution has received perhaps more consideration by the House Committee on the Judiciary than almost any piece of legislation which has come before this House in many, many years. There have been a great many constitutional and other legal questions raised in connection with this matter. I feel, as do most of the members of the Committee on Rules, that the Committee on the Judiciary has not only worked long and arduously, but has brought about a very simple and a very effective resolution which will in no way take away from the Congress of the United States the right and authority to control the affairs of the District of Columbia as the seat of the Federal Government, or give to the people of the District any powers except those which I have designated, to vote for electors for President and Vice President.

Mr. MEADER.[18] Mr. Speaker, will the gentleman yield?

Mr. BROWN of Ohio. I yield to the gentleman from Michigan.

Mr. MEADER. I should like to refer to the question directed to the gentleman from Ohio by the gentleman from Illinois [Mr. MASON], namely, whether or not residents of the District of Columbia who were not citizens might participate in the selection of electors. I think section 1 of the proposed amendment is very clear and reads as follows:

The District constituting the seat of Government of the United States shall appoint in such manner as the Congress may direct.

In other words, the answer of the gentleman from Ohio to the question of the gentleman from Illinois should have been that that entire matter was left to the Congress of the United States and was not specifically either provided for or prohibited in the terms of the amendment itself.

Mr. BROWN of Ohio. That is right. But the Congress of the United States has the power to fix those voting rights, just as the legislature of any State may fix them in any particular State.

As I pointed out a moment ago, this does not take away from the Congress the power to control the public activities within the District of Columbia, what ever they may be, whether it deals with transportation or whether with the right of suffrage. As we have it now, the District elects delegates to party national conventions.

Mr. MEADER. The gentleman is absolutely correct on that point. I should like to call attention to the language I have just read in section 1. The proposed amendment is the same phraseology as appears in article II, section 1 of the Constitution of the United States. The only difference is that we put in the word "Congress" instead of "legislature." This is the language of the Constitution:

Each State shall appoint, in such manner as the legislature thereof may direct...

And so forth. We have simply taken the pattern established in the Constitution of the United States and left it completely within the discretion of Congress to set up the qualifications of electors, and how electors for President and Vice President shall be selected.

Mr. BROWN of Ohio. I appreciate the gentleman making his clarifying statement. I had hoped and thought that I had made the situation clear, but certainly the gentleman's explanation leaves no doubt in the mind of anyone that the Congress retains to itself the powers provided under the Constitution to deal with District of Columbia matters.

Mr. Speaker, I yield 5 minutes to the gentleman from Virginia [Mr. BROYHILL].

Mr. BROYHILL.[19] Mr. Speaker, I rise in support of this rule and the joint resolution the rule makes in order. I see no earthly reason why we should not grant the same rights to the citizens of the District of Columbia who are American citizens to vote for President and Vice President as all other citizens of the United States have. In fact I would go so far as to say we should grant them the right to have full national representation, full representation in the House and the Senate, the same as all other American citizens enjoy. I have maintained that position for the past three Congresses. I have introduced similar resolutions in each Congress, one to grant the people of the District of Columbia the right to vote for President and Vice President, and the other to grant Congress the authority to give the people of the District of Columbia full voting representation in the House and the Senate.

The joint resolution which we will have before us is practically identical to the resolution is I have introduced in previous Congresses. It is, however, somewhat of a compromise, in that it limits the number of votes in the electoral college to no more than those of the least populous State. Of course it is a compromise. All major legislation gets through as a result of compromise.

It is unfortunate that while we are at it, going through the long, complicated process of a constitutional amendment, we do not do the job right and give them the full vote, the same vote they would have in the electoral college if they were a State of the same population. Yet, as I stated before, sometimes a compromise is necessary and I agree to this compromise.

I should like to address myself for just a moment to the confusion that has existed between this proposal for a constitutional amendment and the proposal for home rule in the District of Columbia. During that hearings the chairman of the Committee on the Judiciary admonished the witnesses, and properly so, not to confuse this issue with home rule, but it is confused. Not more than one out of a hundred Americans who are familiar with this problem really understand the difference between this constitutional amendment we are proposing today and the problem of home rule. I venture to say a very small percentage of the advocates of home rule really understand the difference between the two measures. The two measures are similar in only one respect, that is, they give the citizens the right to vote. That is what we want to do, to give the citizens of the District of Columbia the right to vote. The right to vote for President and Vice President does not infringe on the rights of the other people of this great Nation. If we granted the people of the District of Columbia representation in the House and Senate, it would not infringe on the rights of the other people of this Nation. However, if we attempt to turn over the government of the Nation's Capital to the people who live within its boundaries to rule and control, then we do impinge on the right of the other people of the Nation, because all the people of the States have a stake and a vested right and interest in the government of the Nation's Capital.

[...]

Mr. BROWN of Ohio. Mr. Speaker, I yield such time as he may consume to the gentleman from Ohio [Mr. McCULLOCH], the ranking member of the Committee on the Judiciary.

Mr. McCULLOCH.[20] Mr. Speaker, with the Civil Rights Act of 1957 and the Civil Rights Act of 1960, the law of the land now, in full force and effect, every qualified citizen of this country, except those legally domiciled in the District of Columbia, has the right to exercise the elective franchise so far as electors for President and Vice President are concerned.

The rule which is under discussion now will make in order a resolution submitting to the States for ratification a constitutional amendment which will give the people legally domiciled in the District of Columbia the right to vote for presidential and vice presidential electors. This, indeed, is a historic occasion. I trust the rule will be adopted and that the resolution submitting the question to the States will have the unanimous approval of the House of Representatives.

Mr. BROWN of Ohio. Mr. Speaker, I have no further requests for time and yield back the balance of my time. Mr. SMITH of Virginia. Mr. Speaker, I yield myself such time as I may require.

Mr. Speaker, this resolution has been thoroughly explained by those who have preceded me. It simply provides that the citizens of the District of Columbia shall be entitled to vote for the President and Vice President of the United States and to elect electors for the purpose of electing the President.

I hope the House will not confuse it with many of the confusing things concerning the District of Columbia, because it deals solely with the one problem of the right of the people who are citizens of the United States to vote for their President. It is an entirely different question, as has been mentioned before, from the present agitation about home rule in the District, because there you run into a constitutional prohibition which has not only constitutional but also historic reasons why the Congress should exercise, as the Constitution requires, exclusive legislation over the District of Columbia. I will not go into that, because it has no relationship whatsoever to the bill before us. I hope this resolution may be adopted and that the constitutional resolution also may be adopted by the House, because I can see no valid reason why any citizen of the United States should be denied the right to vote for President and Vice President.

The joint resolution requires a two-thirds vote. After studious consideration by the Committee on the Judiciary, it has been stripped down to this one, as I regard it, non-controversial question; and in this late day of the session it is my hope that this may be gotten through and go to the States for ratification. It is the one chance, because if it is complicated further with other matters that do not directly relate to the question of the right to vote for President, the whole thing is going to fail in this late day of the session. I hope very much it can be enacted by the Congress.

If it is enacted, then the question of who can vote in these elections in the District of Columbia is a matter to be determined by the Congress; in other words, the qualifications of the voters and all the details with respect to voting will have to be dealt with in an additional act of Congress. I hope the joint resolution may be passed by the House without objection.

[...]

Mr. CELLER.[21] The bill, Senate Joint Resolution 39, which passed the Senate particularly contained the provision for the abolition of the poll tax. The distinguished and dedicated senior Senator from Florida, Senator HOLLAND, was the faithful and courageous sponsor of the poll tax repeal. He has assured me that in the interest of getting at least the vote for the District in national elections he would yield on his amendment. If he does not make this sacrifice there might not be any bill passing the House. The Senator graciously yielded on his amendment. I hope he will press for the poll tax repeal in the next session. I pledge every possible help to him in that repeal. I shall do all and sundry to support such repeal on the House side as he will on the Senate side.

The right, the privilege, the duty to vote – whatever characterization you may ascribe to it – is the foundation upon which rests what is the essence of a democracy, namely, government by discussion. Therefore, unjustifiable segregation from political life is a cruel exercise in isolation.

Under Anglo Saxon concepts, since the year 1215 when the Magna Carta declared that exceptional feudal aids were not to be levied without the common counsel of the realm, the extension of the body of the electorate has been the universal goal. At first, the counsel demanded by the Magna Carta was given by an assembly consisting of great lords, ecclesiastical prelates and tenants in chief, but there were in essence local assemblies or town meetings. They met twice a year to determine questions of law, inflict criminal punishment and to transact other kinds of business. This was the skeleton of the true representative system.

In 1265 the leaders of the barons embattled with the king and hold for a parliament of two knights out of each shire, two burgesses from the towns, and from five sports each, four men. Thirty years later, there was summoned what is known as the "model parliament" by King Edward I which consisted of 2 archbishops, all of the bishops, the more important abbots, 7 earls, 41 barons, and in addition to these, each sheriff "shall cause to be elected 2 knights from each shire, 2 burgesses each from 115 cities and boroughs." At first the clergy, the barons, and the commoners met separately. This, of course, could not work and gradually there evolved the House of Lords which was comprised of lords temporal and lords spiritual and a House of Commons representing all of the classes.

I have gone back to English history because our own institutions derived therefrom. In my review I am again struck with the thought that the extension of the franchise was the most civilizing element in the development of national entities.

The French Revolution and the American Revolution gave radical impetus to this extension of the franchise. Basic to our understanding is the historical statement in the Declaration of Independence [that] "all governments derived their just powers from the consent of the governed."

It has been said another way, "Either no individual member of the human race has any real rights or else all have the same." Widening the electorate has been no easy victory. At the outbreak of the American Revolution there was not a colony which did not require the ownership of property for the privilege of voting. Eight colonies imposed religious or moral tests upon either officers or electors. New Hampshire excluded Roman Catholics; and South Carolina deemed unsafe all citizens who did not believe in God and a future life. Several required that assemblymen should be Protestants, while others demanded that they should believe in God and the divine inspiration of the Scriptures.

By 1830 it may be said that a broad, though not universal, suffrage had been acquired in practically all the Original Thirteen States. There were exceptions like North Carolina, or Rhode Island, where Dorr[22] and his followers acquired the vote only by rebellion. Where a property qualification occurred in the State went of the Alleghenies, it was of little consequence, so long as an abundant supply of cheap land made it easy for all to obtain property. By the end of the Civil War, practically universal, manhood suffrage had been established for all whites.

It took until the second decade of the 20th century to remove the disqualification of sex. The paramount question there before us is – shall the citizens of the District of Columbia be classed with idiots, insane people, and persons convicted of serious crimes which today constitute the major classes of people who are disenfranchised? Great efforts have been made by this Congress to assure the right to vote to all inhabitants under the 15th amendment of the constitution, although this amendment speaks of abridgements of the vote on racial groups. Our Civil Rights Act of 1957 through 1960 are based upon that amendment. There can be, therefore, no logic, no justification, no indifference to the disenfranchisement of the residents of the District of Columbia. Under this bill, the enfranchisement is a limited one.

The people of the District of Columbia want to participate in national elections, even if it were to be as abortive a such participation was back in 1924 when the Alabama Democratic delegation in Madison Square Garden said "24 for Underwood" through 103 ballots. Without any kind of vote, the people of the District of Columbia are mere wards of Congress. They are declassed. That reflects upon their dignity; it wounds their pride; they are disqualified, though qualified. They are written off like excess baggage.

What useful purpose would be served to deny them the right to vote at least in the presidential election? There is no skin off anyone's back in granting that right. None is hurt but many will be helped. It is not fair to have a whole Nation possessed of the ballot, but not the people of the District of Columbia. Why place a hex on them? Denial of any vote in not like cutting out a useless appendix; it goes to the heart and pride of the citizen, and pride is one of our most precious human emotions.

[After a series of amendments to the Senate resolution were voted on, the new House version of the proposed DC electoral amendment was voted on that same day. There was no roll-call vote; instead, the supporters of the proposed amendment had a voice vote, of which few voices expressed opposition. The new proposed amendment now went back to the US Senate for further debate and possible changes.]

After originally passing in the US Senate, the proposed DC electoral amendment was changed substantially by the House Committee on the Judiciary. After passage in the House, the resolution went back to the US Senate for a new debate and a vote, 16 June 1960.

AUTHORIZATION TO FILL TEMPORARY VACANCIES IN HOUSE OF REPRESENTATIVES – ABOLITION OF CERTAIN TAX AND PROPERTY QUALIFICATIONS, AND ENFRANCHISEMENT OF PEOPLE OF DISTRICT OF COLUMBIA

Mr. JOHNSON of Texas.[23] Mr. President, I ask the Chair to lay before the Senate a message from the House of Representatives on Senate Joint Resolution 39.

The PRESIDING OFFICER laid before the Senate the amendments of the House of Representatives to the joint resolution (S.J. Res. 39) proposing amendments to the Constitution of the United States to authorize Governors to fill temporary vacancies in the House of Representatives, to abolish tax, and property qualifications for electors in Federal elections, and to enfranchise the people of the District of Columbia, which were, to strike out all after the enacting clause and insert:

That the following article is hereby proposed as an amendment to the Constitution of the United States, which shall be valid to all intents and purposes as part of the Constitution only if ratified by the legislatures of three fourths of the several States within seven years from the date of its submission by the Congress:

"ARTICLE ____

"SECTION 1. The District constituting the seat of Government of the United States shall appoint in such manner as the Congress may direct:

"A number of electors of President and Vice President equal to the whole number of Senators and Representatives in Congress to which the District would be entitled if it were a State, but in no event more than the least populous State; they shall be in addition to those appointed by the States, but they shall be considered, for the purposes of the election of President and Vice President, to be electors appointed by a State; and they shall meet in the District and perform such duties as provided by the twelfth article of amendment.

"Sec. 2. The Congress shall have power to enforce this article by appropriate legislation."

And to amend the title so as to read: "Joint resolution proposing an amendment to the Constitution of the United States granting representation in the electoral college to the District of Columbia."

Mr. JOHNSON of Texas. Mr. President, I move that the Senate concur in the House amendments.

Mr. JAVITS.[24] Mr. President, will the Senator yield at that point?

Mr. CASE of South Dakota.[25] Mr. President...

Mr. JOHNSON of Texas. I yield to the Senator from South Dakota.

Mr. CASE of South Dakota. As I understand, the amendment to which we are asked to agree is an amendment submitted by the House of Representatives which would adopt one feature of the three-pronged joint resolution, the constitutional amendment which was earlier passed by the Senate, to survive, namely, that dealing with a vote for presidential and vice presidential electors. Is that correct?

Mr. JOHNSON of Texas. That is my understanding.

Mr. CASE of South Dakota. I should like to speak for a few moments upon the joint resolution.

Mr. MANSFIELD.[26] Mr. President, is the resolution before the Senate and, if so, is the Senator from South Dakota about to make a speech on a reservation of objection?

Mr. JOHNSON of Texas. Mr. President, I will yield the floor if there is any question.

Mr. CASE of South Dakota. Mr. President, the joint resolution which comes before us with a House amendment marks a long way down the road toward extending the right of suffrage to the people of the District of Columbia. In December of 1952 the-then President-elect of the United States, Dwight Eisenhower, sent word to me that he would like to have me come to New York in order to discuss some legislative matters affecting the District of Columbia.

The prospect was that I would be chairman of the Committee on the District of Columbia of the Senate. Among subjects discussed was the possibility of getting the right to vote for the people of the District of Columbia. The President spoke very feelingly upon the fact that he believed taxation without representation was contrary to the principle of our country. He said he felt there was something basically wrong if we taxed people and did not give them the right to vote. He thought there was something basically wrong if we drafted their sons for military service and did not give them the right to vote.

During the preceding 2 years I had been a member of the Committee on the District of Columbia and had been accorded the honor by the-then chairman of the committee, the late Senator Neely of West Virginia,[27] and the majority leader of that day, Senator McFarland of Arizona,[28] of piloting the so-called home rule bill through its consideration by the Senate in January of 1952.

So I was very glad to accede to the suggestion of the President that we devote some energy to the possibility of getting [the] suffrage for the District of Columbia.

During 1953-54 we passed a home rule bill. We also passed a bill giving the people of the District of Columbia the right to vote for delegates to national conventions. The matter of voting for President and Vice President called for a constitutional amendment. We get some consideration to it but, of course, that was a proposal which would have to go to the Judiciary Committee.

My interest in this subject has continued throughout the years. The interest of the President has continued throughout the years. On various occasions he has continued to express an interest in this goal.

Early in this Congress the distinguished Senator from Maryland [Mr. BEALL][29] introduced a constitutional amendment proposing that the citizens of the District of Columbia be given the right to vote in presidential elections. The junior Senator from South Dakota introduced a similar constitutional amendment.

In the amendment which I proposed I suggested that the District of Columbia be given three delegates to the House of Representatives with a like number of electoral votes for President and Vice President, in every way preserving the traditional basis upon which a State has votes in the electoral college.

Early this year, when the District of Columbia Committee reported the so-called home rule bill, I offered that constitutional amendment as an amendment to that home rule bill, in fact as a substitute for the home rule bill. Watching the course of these proposals through the years has convinced me that there was little practical possibility of getting home rule, as such, through both Houses of Congress in the same Congress.

Also I knew that every home rule bill which had been presented in the previous 10 years had included a provision to recognize the basic constitutional provision that Congress is given the exclusive legislative jurisdiction for the District of Columbia.

Believing that the people of the District of Columbia should have an effective voice in the Government which governs them, namely, Congress, plus the appointive power of the President, I came to the conclusion that the practical thing to do was to press for a constitutional amendment which would give them a voice in the electoral college for the election of President and Vice President and, if possible, delegates in the House of Representatives.

So I introduced the constitutional amendment on the floor as a substitute for the home rule bill on the floor of the Senate. The most important result was the interest which developed. Many Members of the Senate said to me, "We would like to support that kind of measure as an independent proposal."

The most helpful interest developed was the interest that was taken by the distinguished Senator from New York [Mr. KEATING].[30] Not only did he say he believed that that constitutional amendment should be adopted at that time, but, as a member of the Committee on the Judiciary, he took an earnest and unrelenting interest in the subject. When the distinguished Senator from Tennessee [Mr. KEFAUVER][31] arranged to hold hearings on the subject, it was the Senator from New York [Mr. KEATING] who took up the cudgels for the constitutional amendment in a most effective fashion.

The outgrowth of that effort was the reporting of a proposed constitutional amendment to the Senate, built upon the language that had been proposed by the Senator from Maryland [Mr. BEALL], the Senator from New York [Mr. KEATING], and myself. That proposal was reported to the full Committee on the Judiciary by the Kefauver subcommittee.

Mr. KEATING. It reported it to the full committee. However, it was on the floor that the amendment was added. Mr. CASE of South Dakota. Yes. Then there came before the Senate a proposal to deal with the problem of the election of Members of the House of Representatives in case of an emergency which incapacitated a majority of the Members of the House from acting at any time. The Senator from Tennessee [Mr. KEFAUVER] was in charge of that amendment when it came to the floor.

The Senator from Florida [Mr. HOLLAND][32] proposed an addition to that proposed constitutional amendment. His proposal was an amendment for the abolition of the poll tax in Federal or national elections. That was agreed to.

So, then the distinguished Senator from New York [Mr. KEATING] performed the master stroke of presenting the District of Columbia amendment which had been reported by the Kefauver subcommittee to the full Judiciary Committee. It drew wide support and was agreed to by more than the two-thirds required for a constitutional amendment.

I believe that is an accurate reflection of the record, and the course that this matter has taken. As we adopted the amendment in the Senate, it provided for both representation in the House of Representatives and representation in the electoral college for the voters of the District. The three-pronged resolution then passed by the required two-thirds vote for a constitutional amendment, and it went to the House of Representatives.

The Senator from New York, the Senator from Maryland, and I and others testified before the House Judiciary Committee urging action upon this particular proposition to provide suffrage for the voters of the District of Columbia in the election of President and Vice President. We also urged delegate representation in the House of Representatives.

Of course, under the Constitution, the House of Representatives is the judge of its own membership. In its wisdom the Judiciary Committee of the House of Representatives reported a constitutional amendment to the House of Representatives in a form which left only the provision for the election of presidential electors for President and Vice President by the District of Columbia.

Mr. JAVITS. Mr. President, will the Senator yield?

Mr. CASE of South Dakota. I yield.

Mr. JAVITS. I think it is very sad that even this very minimum point in the constitutional amendment, which it was said when the matter was debated would be approved very promptly in a year or two, has now been completely dropped out of the bill so far as the poll tax is concerned. I think is sad. I shall not contest the matter here. Of course, I shall support what is before us. I intend when we next have an opportunity, in the next Congress, again to put before the Senate the opportunity to support a bill to eliminate the poll tax. It appears that that is the only way to do it, was it only takes a majority vote to do it.

I should like also to join with the Senator from South Dakota in the fine things he is saying about my colleague from New York [Mr. KEATING], which are very richly deserved. I agree with the Senator from South Dakota that the junior Senator from New York acted with the greatest wisdom and celerity in seizing the opportunity which was before us in supporting the excellent measure which the Senator had himself authored and in bringing into being something so deserving for the people of the District of Columbia.

I enthusiastically join the Senator from South Dakota in extending congratulations to my colleague [Mr. KEATING], who I think in is first 2 years in the Senate has, through this particular effort, already performed a very signal service, very easy to identify and fix for the people of the District of Columbia, who will be so proud to have this opportunity to exercise the right of suffrage.

[...]

Mr. HOLLAND. Mr. President, as Senators will remember, the joint resolution, as passed by the Senate, and as it went to the House of Representatives, contained, in addition to a proposed constitutional amendment dealing with the subject now before the Senate, two other provisions. The first was a constitutional amendment proposed by my distinguished colleague the Senator from Tennessee [Mr. KEFAUVER]. It provided for the prompt filling the by the Governors of the several States of any vacancies in the membership of the House of Representatives, in the event an atomic catastrophe were to remove one-half or more of the membership of that body. In the second place, that joint resolution included an amendment which I have been sponsoring for approximately 11 years, and in that sponsorship I have been joined, and am honored that I have been joined, by many outstanding and extremely able Senators, such as the late Senator George, of Georgia;[33] the Senator from Virginia [Mr. BYRD],[34] who more lately has withdrawn from that sponsorship; the late Senator Hoey, of North Carolina;[35] the Senator from Arkansas [Mr. McCLELLAN];[36] the Senators from Louisiana [Mr. ELLENDER][37] and [Mr. LONG];[38] and numerous others who come from the same region of the country from which I come, and whom I have regarded over the years, and still regard, as among the finest Americans ever to serve in the Senate.

That amendment, which they and I have sponsored for some 11 years, proposed once and for all to remove the payment of a poll tax as a prerequisite to voting in an election in which a President, a Vice President, a Senator, or Members of the House of Representatives were being elected – that is to say, in Federal elections.

Mr. President, for 11 years we have tried to get that amendment before this body. We finally got it before this body during consideration of the so-called Kefauver amendment, some months ago.

The RECORD will show that the amendment received an overwhelming vote of approval from the Senate; the amendment was adopted by largely more than a two-thirds vote, and with a very large attendance of Senators, representing the 50 States of the Nation. But notwithstanding that fact, and because of the peculiar situation existing in the House of Representatives – which I do not criticize, and on which I make no comment at this time – it was thought best by the advocates of the District of Columbia amendment to drop the poll tax amendment and to drop the amendment so ably sponsored by Senator from Tennessee [Mr. KEFAUVER], and to confine this amendment to the one subject matter of granting to the citizens of the District of Columbia the right to participate in the election of Presidents and Vice Presidents.

I have talked at some length with the distinguished sponsor of this amendment in the House of Representatives, the Representative from New York, Mr. CELLER[39]; and I am fully satisfied that the course he adopted was one which he felt compelled to adopt because of the situation existing in the House of Representatives...

[...]

Mr. EASTLAND.[40] Mr. President, will the Senator yield? Mr. HOLLAND. I yield to my friend from Mississippi.

Mr. EASTLAND. Does the Senator think this joint resolution should go to the Judiciary Committee for study?

Mr. HOLLAND. I think if there were any prospect of its being passed upon upon with any degree of expedition, that would be a good course. My experience with the poll tax amendment, after it had been subjected to three hearings, after the record had been printed three times, after a subcommittee had reported it three times to the able Committee on the Judiciary, approvingly, after we found we could not get any action at all before the Judiciary Committee leads me to think it would at least be a debatable question as to whether it would be wise to submit the measure to that committee.

Mr. EASTLAND. Has not the House shown we were right? What did it do with the amendment? It kicked it out.

Mr. HOLLAND. The Senator from Mississippi speaks with a little heat on this question. Perhaps he does not have the experience in this field that the Senator from Florida has had. The Senator from Florida, as a member of the State senate of his own State, helped to knock out the poll tax requirement as a prerequisite to voting in all elections – not merely Federal elections, but all elections. He found, from actual experience, how good results came to his State by the immediate participation of more white citizens in greater numbers, and by the gradual participation by Negro citizens, who, up to that time, had been banned from participation not only by the poll tax requirement, but by the requirement of white primaries.[41]

I mention to my friend that we also abolished a little later, but in connection with the same movement, the requirement of white primaries.

The Senator from Florida has stated repeatedly to all his friends in the Senate that he and every other student of government in his State has found that we have had purer politics and sounder government, and a government nearer to the people, than we had before, when, by the device of the poll tax, too frequently, in some counties, a few of the court house officials were able, by paying the poll tax for others, particularly impecunious persons, to dominate elections.

[...]

Mr. GOLDWATER.[42] Mr. President, will the Senator yield?

Mr. HOLLAND. The point I make is simply this: For 14 years we struggled with the tidelands bill before e obtained a decision. When one is right, I think one should not count time too heavily. I am willing to wait another year. I would rather do that than defeat another good effort in its chance to be submitted to 50 States, and to be decided by the collective wisdom of the people representing those 50 States through their legislatures.

Mr. GOLDWATER and Mr. EASTLAND addressed the Chair.

Mr. HOLLAND. I agree to yield first to the Senator from Arizona. Then I shall yield again to the Senator from Mississippi.

Mr. GOLDWATER. Mr. President, I think the Senator from Florida is making his customarily convincing argument as to his views.

I am hard put to place my remarks in the form of a question, so if the Senator will indulge me, perhaps I can support him in part of his thesis. I may have to oppose him in others.

At the outset, I am unalterably opposed to the poll tax idea, but I think it is a matter for the States to decide. I do not think it is something that should be influenced by people outside the States. Elections are matters for the States to determine for themselves.

In respect to my feeling in this matter, which is a States' rights feeling. I should like to read a part of the joint resolution that we are being asked to consider tonight:

A number of electors of President and Vice President equal to the whole number of Senators and Representatives in Congress to which the District would be entitled if it were a State...

Here is an outside controlling factor – but in no event more than the least populous State.

I think this provision is consistent with the Senator's argument that we should not have outside controlling influences upon elections in a State or in the District of Columbia, if the District is given this privilege. I suggest that the outside influence that would be exerted upon the District of Columbia would come from the conglomeration of philosophies and ideas of people who populate the District and who originate from different sections of the country. It would also be controlled in expect to the number of electors that it could have by comparison with the least populous State, even though the population of the least populous State might well be, as it is today, well before the population of the District of Columbia.

I am sure the Senator from Florida will agree with me that we hear very liberal Senators argue in the Senate that there should be no control such as is exercised with respect to interstate traffic in money during elections, and no control by outside groups. I myself have been vociferous in the Senate about organized labor acting in the political arena on behalf of Senators and Congressmen when they have no interest in the State at all.

I believe the Senator has been touching indirectly upon a very important part of our entire election procedures in this country. Up to this time in our history I have been concerned about outside influences coming into my own State of Arizona, and while I realize a Senator is elected to represent not only his own State but to represent the people of the United States, nevertheless he is bound to reflect the feelings of his own people more than he would reflect the feelings of the people of a State rather distant from him.

The whole question of outside influence in American politics is an important and rather insidious one. I am very reluctant to discuss this subject, but we have an important election approaching us in 1960. We shall select a President for the next 4 years. I have been very much disturbed about the apparent efforts of forces outside the United States trying to influence our elections. In my capacity as chairman of the Republican senatorial campaign committee, I abhor these tactics, and I hope that we shall not be influenced by what other governments think of our candidates or of our parties. I think that we as Republicans and Democrats can refrain from insinuating that one candidate might be influenced this way, that way, or the other...

I repeat that I am against the poll tax as I am against segregation, but I do not believe that it is a problem of the States and not the Federal Government I am hopeful that the Senator from Florida will keep up his dedicated fight in the effort that he has launched, with not too much success this year, but possibly success in the future.

Mr. HOLLAND. I thank the Senator from Arizona for his kind remarks...

There are three matters I would like to mention briefly before I close my remarks. The first is this: It seems to me that during the debate some Senator should remark on a situation which is almost ridiculous if it were not rather serious. I refer to the approach which is now being made in this amendment that completely reverses the attitude of the Founding Fathers with reference to the rights and privileges of citizens or residents of the District of Columbia.

Anyone who has read the minutes of the Constitutional Convention, anyone who has read the Federalist Papers, knows that it was understood that local government should continue in the District of Columbia. Everyone knows that history knows that local government did continue here for many years, and people in the District continued to elect their mayor, their councilmen, their commissioners, or whatever they were called, their school district members, and their various local officials, just as people do in any other normal American city.

Everyone who has read this history knows that it was the distinct conviction of the Founding Fathers that he would be unwise to give to the residents of the District of Columbia the right to participate in the election of President and Vice President. Why? For the very reason I recited in the beginning, that they would be too close to Congress, would have too good an opportunity to exert pressure, making life miserable for Senators and Members of the House of Representatives, by continuing and assiduous expressions for local objectives. The minutes show quite well that the pressure that had been inserted upon Congress in some of the other cities where for a time the capital had been maintained was the reason for that decision.

Mr. President, times change. The attitude of the citizens of the United States at the present time, the attitude of Senators and Members of the House at this time, may well be different on this subject from the attitude of the Founding Fathers. However, I want the RECORD to show, because it is an interesting observation, and I think people should ponder it a little, that the Founding Fathers very definitely and devotedly felt that the residents of the seat of Government, the residents of the District of Columbia – not then established, when the Constitution was written, but later established – should not have the right to participate in the selection of the President and Vice President, but should have the right of local self-government. They did have it for many, many years, as every Senator knows. So it is interesting, and I wanted this observation to be a part of the RECORD of this debate, and to observe that in the judgment of those who are suggesting the amendment at this time that there is a purpose completely variant and completely opposite and contradictory to the expressed purpose of the Founding Fathers in this matter, at the same moment that we are withholding local self-government from the District.

Mr. CASE of South Dakota. Mr. President, will the Senator yield?

Mr. HOLLAND. I yield.

Mr. CASE of South Dakota. That is a very interesting observation. I think along with it there should be noted the fact that at the time the Founding Fathers were writing the Constitution, there were very few States. There were Thirteen Original Colonies, and I do not recall what the electoral vote of the respective States was to be. Certainly the electoral vote of the first States was much less than that of the present 50 States, with 435 Representatives and 100 Senators, a total of 535. The provision in the amendment limiting the electoral vote of the District to that of the least populous State would mean that it would not have more than three. Certainly 3 votes out of 535 is a very small proportion, and the impact would be much less, proportionately, than it could possibly have been at the time the Constitution was adopted.

Mr. HOLLAND. I thank the Senator for his comment. Of course it is needless for me to remind the Senator, because he knows it already, that when the electoral representation of the District of Columbia is being recorded, is being credited for having two Senators, which it does not have and will not have.

In addition, the amendment as now submitted does not require the very careful and meticulous separation of citizens that would be required if we had to find out who were really entitled to vote in the District of Columbia in these elections, because we all know that several hundred thousand residents maintain their legal residence and their right to vote back in their own States.

For example, in the office of the Senator from Florida, where there are 12 employees, all of them except 1, as I recall, now maintain their residence in Florida, casting their votes in Florida, and several of them have families – wives or husbands or other members of their families who also cast absentee ballots.

Therefore, no one can pretend for a moment that the area of the District of Columbia is comparable, on the question of citizenship of those who live here with, for example, the citizenship and the residents in the State so ably represented by the Senator from North Dakota [Mr. CASE], where those who live there all are residents and voters by a great preponderance, certainly 98 or 99 percent.

So one of the improvements of the amendment that comes back from the House is in this very matter. The representation of the District of Columbia in the electoral college is placed much more nearly in accord with the merits of the situation than was the case with the one against which the Senator from Florida voted.

Another change which the Senator from Florida thinks is desirable is with reference to the provision which permitted the election of delegates to the House of Representatives and, what made it worse, submitted to Congress itself the question as to what power to give those delegates, whether full power or not. The Senator from Florida was utterly opposed to that proposal, because it would put pressure in the maximum degree against the men and women sitting in the Senate and in the House. The Senator from Florida is glad that that provision was omitted in the draft of the resolution which comes back from the House of Representatives.

Mr. President, the sole purpose of my making these remarks was to say just this: I shall vote for the amendment. I will do so with some misgivings, because I realize it runs counter to the wisdom of the Founding Fathers, who wanted to insulate Congress against the type of pressure and type of influence which may be exercised against Members of Congress, if this amendment is adopted.

We have come a long way in the school of democratic government and democratic living. It is not for me to say that that may not be a proper change in the philosophy of our Government. The people eventually will determine that question through the action of their State legislators. I have some misgivings on that subject. That was the first thing I wanted to say.

The second was that by no means shall I desist from continuing to offer the poll tax amendment. I think it is fundamental in this country that citizens who otherwise are qualified should have the right to vote for their President, their Vice President, and those who represent them in the Senate and in the House of Representatives. I believe that cleaner government and purer government will come with the recognition of that right, in which I very strongly and profoundly believe.

I shall be back in the Senate, offering that amendment early in the next session. I hope the Senate will, without being annoyed by too much other discussion, be given the chance to vote. I am sorry I have had to take this long. I appreciate the colloquys [sic] with distinguished Senators.

It is my own firm conviction that in the case of the poll tax amendment, those who believe in the civil rights program, which in some of its particulars I strongly disagreed with – that is the one which has been voted – will find in five States that most of the enforcement which it is believed will occur under the terms of that act will be defeated by the nonpayment of the poll tax by persons who otherwise would be qualified. I want the RECORD to show that, because that is what I firmly believe. I believe that if Senators and Representatives realized that fact, and if they realized that the right to vote of vastly more persons than the total population of the District of Columbia is affected by the poll tax amendment, there would have been a different attitude long since expressed toward that amendment.

[...]

Mr. DIRKSEN.[43] Mr. President, I suggest the absence of a quorum.

The PRESIDING OFFICER. The clerk will call the roll.

The legislative clerk proceeded to call the roll.

Mr. JOHNSON of Texas. Mr. President, I ask unanimous consent that the order for the quorum be rescinded.

The PRESIDING OFFICER. Without objection, it is so ordered.

Mr. BEALL. Mr. President, I ask for the yeas and nays. The yeas and nays were not ordered.

Mr. JOHNSTON of South Carolina.[44] Mr. President, if there is not to be a yea-and-nay vote, I desire the

RECORD to show that I shall vote against the amendment.

Mr. EASTLAND. Mr. President, I desire the RECORD to show that I am against the joint resolution. I ask for a yea-and-nay vote.

The yeas and nays were not ordered.

The PRESIDING OFFICER. The question is on agreeing to the motion of the Senator from Texas that the Senate concur in the amendments of the House. [Putting the question.]

In the opinion of the Chair, two-thirds of the Senators present and voting having voted in the affirmative, the motion is agreed to.

Mr. CASE of South Dakota. Mr. President, I move that the Senate reconsider the vote by which the amendments were agreed to.

Mr. KEATING. I move to lay that motion on the table.

Mr. EASTLAND. Mr. President, I ask for the yeas and nays on the motion to lay on the table. The yeas and nays were not ordered.

The PRESIDING OFFICER. The question is on agreeing to the motion of Senator from New York to lay on the table the motion of the Senator from South Dakota to reconsider the vote by which the amendments were agreed to.

The motion to lay on the table was agreed to.

Historical Background Documents

During the fight to get the original US Constitution ratified, James Iredell of North Carolina, who later served on the US Supreme Court, gave this argument calling for a federal capital that would have all of the voting rights of any American state, 30 July 1788.

Mr. IREDELL continued: They are to have exclusive power of legislation, – but how? Whenever they may have this district, they must possess it from the authority of the state within which it lies; and that state may stipulate he conditions of the cession. Will not such state take care of the liberties of its own people? What would be the consequence if the seat of the government of the United States, with all the archives of America, was in the power of any one particular state? Would not this be most unsafe and humiliating? Do we not all remember that, in the year 1783, a band of soldiers went and insulted Congress? The sovereignty of the United States was treated with indignity. They applied for protection to the state they resided in, but could obtain none. It is to be hoped such a disgraceful scene will never happen again; but that, for the future, the national government will be able to protect itself. The powers of the government are particularly enumerated and defined; they can claim no other but such as are so enumerated. In my opinion, they are excluded as much from the exercise of any other authority as hey could be by the strongest negative clause that could be framed. A gentleman has asked, What would be the consequence if they had the power of the pure and sword? I ask, In what government under heaven are there not given up to some authority or other? There is a necessity of giving both the pure and the sword to every government, or else it cannot protect the people.

But have we not sufficient security that those powers shall not be abused? The immediate power of the pure is in the immediate representatives of the people, chosen every two years, who can lay no tax on their constituents but what they are subject to at the same time themselves. The power of taxation must be vested somewhere. Do the committee wish it to be as it has been? They must suffer the evils which they have done.

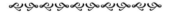

Rep. John Randolph made these remarks in February 1803 on the role of self-government for the infant District of Columbia, one of the earliest such speeches on this subject recorded in American history.

Mr. RANDOLPH said that, whatever reasons might be advanced on the ground of expediency against the adoption of the resolutions, he wished to at a few words on the Constitutional objections which had been offered to them. The gentleman from Delaware (Mr. BAYARD) told us, on a very late occasion, that the power to create involved the power to destroy; and although I may not be willing to adopt this maxim in all the latitude in which it was urged by that gentleman, I have no hesitation in averring my belief that Congress possess the rights, with the assent of these States, respectively, to cede the several portions of this territory to Maryland and Virginia. Nor, in my opinion, does this doctrine militate against that construction of the Constitution, which regards that instrument in the light of a limited grant of power. In this construction I heartily concur with the gentleman from Delaware, or rather, if he will permit me to say so, I am glad to find he agrees with me, as I have retained my opinion, whilst he seems to have changed his. I readily admit that Congress possesses no power but that which is devolved on them by the Constitution, explicitly, or which is evidently included in, or deducible from its plain provisions. The Constitution no where gives Congress the express power of repealing laws; but the repeal of laws is essentially connected with the power of passing them, as in this case, the right to recede is involved in the right to accept the cession. The parties to this compact are the United States, of the one part, and the States of Maryland and Virginia, of the other. We speak the voice of the United States, and, among others, of Maryland and Virginia, in their confederate capacity. The Legislatures of those States answer for them in their individual capacity. If all these parties are agreed to revoke their act, I wish to know who is to dissent to it, or what obstacle can prevent its being rescinded?

Mr. R. said, that he was of the number of those who voted against assuming the jurisdiction of this territory. He did it from a predilection for those principles in which the American Revolution originated. From the firm belief that men ought not to be bound by laws in whose formation they had no influence. It was the violation of that principle, and not the extent to which it was carried, which laid the foundation of our independence. For, let it be remembered that the demand of Great Britain went only to a peppercorn; but that we disdained the admission of so odious a doctrine, and commenced a determined and successful resistance. But it is denied that this territory is in a state of slavery, because, says the gentleman, it implies that we are tyrants. The term slavery, sir, excites in the mind of man an odious idea. There are, however, various species of this wretched condition. Domestic slavery, of all others, the most oppressive; and political slavery, which has been well defined, to be that state in which any community is divested of the power of self-government, and regulated by laws to which its assent is not required, and may not be given. Nor have I ever before understood that slavery, particularly of the last description, necessarily implied tyranny, although it too frequently is productive of it. But, so far from being slaves, the people within this territory are, it seems, our children, who are to experience every indulgence at our hands. Sir, the form of government, such as has been described, however mild and beneficent it may be in its administration, places those subjected to it in a state of political slavery, and they are as completely divested of self-control as the infant who is dandled on the knee of its parents. As to the existence, then, of this species of slavery, it mattered not whether the people within the limits of this District were regarded as the favorite son, and feasted on the fatted calf, or were exposed to the cruel rigor of a stepmother.

An idea had been held out from a very respectable quarter that this District might, in time, become a State. As to Congress, what difference will be found between being under the jurisdiction of the State of Columbia, or the State of Maryland. But, if this objection were removed, it is impossible that this territory can become a State. The other States can never be brought to consent that two Senators and, at least, three electors of President, shall be chosen out of this small spot, and by a handful of men.

ৡৎৼ৽ৡৎৼ৽ৡৎৼ৽ৡৎৼ৽ৡৎৼ৽

In these excerpts from a congressional report on a proposed series of amendments, including DC voting rights, a ban on the poll tax, and setting up elections in the US House should there be an atomic attack on the United States, Rep. Emanuel Celler (D-New York) lays out some of the reasons behind the amendment and its language, 31 May 1960.

Mr. CELLER, from the Committee on the Judiciary, to whom was referred the joint resolution (S.J. Res. 39) proposing amendments to the Constitution of the United States to authorize Governors to fill temporary vacancies in the House of Representatives, to abolish tax and property qualifications for electors in Federal elections, and to enfranchise the people of the District of Columbia, having considered the same, reports favorably thereon with amendments and recommends that the joint resolution do pass.

The amendments are as follows:

Amendment No. 1: Page 1, line 3, strike out all the language after the resolving clause and substitute the following: "That the following article is hereby proposed as an amendment to the Constitution of the United States, which shall be valid to all intents and purposes as part of the Constitution only if ratified by the legislatures of three fourths of the several States within seven years from the date of its submission by the Congress:

"ARTICLE ____

"SECTION 1. The District constituting the seat of Government of the United States shall appoint in such manner as the Congress may direct:

"A number of electors of President and Vice President equal to the whole number of Senators and Representatives in Congress to which the District would be entitled if it were a State, but in no event more than the least populous State; they shall be in addition to those appointed by the States, but they shall be considered, for the purposes of the election of President and Vice President, to be electors appointed by a State; and they shall meet in the District and perform such duties as provided by the twelfth article of amendment.

"Sec. 2. The Congress shall have power to enforce this article by appropriate legislation."

Amendment No. 2: Amend the title to read:

"A joint resolution proposing an amendment to the Constitution of the United States granting representation in the Electoral College to the District of Columbia."

[...]

Purpose

The purpose of this proposed constitutional amendment is to provide the citizens of the District of Columbia with appropriate rights of voting in national elections for President and Vice President of the United States. It would permit District citizens to elect Presidential electors who would be in addition to the electors from the States and who would participate in electing the President and Vice President.

The District of Columbia, with more than 800,000 people, has a greater number of persons than the population of each of 13 of our States. District citizens have all the obligations of citizenship, including the payment of Federal taxes, of local taxes, and service in our Armed Forces. They have fought and died in every US war since the District was founded. Yet, they cannot now vote in national elections because the Constitution has restricted that privilege to citizens who reside in States. The resultant constitutional anomaly of imposing all the obligations of citizenship without the most fundamental of its privileges, will be removed by this proposed constitutional amendment.

[...]

MINIMUM IMPACT; PRESERVATION OF ORIGINAL CONCEPT OF CONSTITUTION

The proposed amendment would change the Constitution only to the minimum extent necessary to give the District appropriate participation in national elections. It would not make the District of Columbia a State. It would not give the District of Columbia any other attributes of a State or change the constitutional powers of the Congress to legislate with respect to the District of Columbia and to prescribe its forms of government. It would not authorize the District to have representation in the Senate or the House of Representatives. It would not alter the total number of presidential electors from the States, the total number of Representatives in the House of Representatives, or the apportionment of electors or Representatives among the States. It would, however, perpetuate recognition of the unique status of the District as the seat of [the] Federal Government under the exclusive legislative control of Congress.

AMENDMENT NOT RELATED TO HOME RULE

This proposed constitutional amendment with respect to voting by citizens of the District in national elections is a matter entirely separate from questions as to possible changes in the form of local government which the Congress might establish for the District. The president constitutional provisions relating to the District already vest plenary power in the Congress to legislate in this respect and the present constitutional powers would not be modified by the a [e[ed. Questions as to the possible changes [the] possible changes in the structure of the District government, are matters which may properly be brought before other committees of the Congress and will not be affected by the constitutional amendment here proposed.

Following the official ratification notification of the Twenty-third amendment, President John F. Kennedy released the following statement, The Washington Post, *30 March 1961.*

"Ratification of the 23d Amendment giving the residents of the District of Columbia the right to vote in Presidential elections by the required 38 states is a major step in the right direction.

"The speed with which this Constitutional Amendment was approved by the required number of States demonstrates the interest of the nation at large in providing to all Americans citizens of the most valuable of human rights – the right to share in the election of those who govern us. Hearings on enabling legislation to implement the amendment will be held shortly by the District of Columbia Commissioners and a legislative proposal will be submitted to the Congress at the earliest possible time.

"It is equally important that resident of the District of Columbia have the right to select the officials who govern the District. I am hopeful that the Congress, spurred by the adoption of the 23d Amendment, will act favorably on legislative proposals to be recommended by the Administration providing the District of Columbia the right of home rule."

As Submitted to the States

Section 1. The District constituting the seat of Government of the United States shall appoint in such manner as the Congress may direct:

A number of electors of President and Vice President equal to the whole number of Senators and Representatives in Congress to which the District would be entitled if it were a State, but in no event more than the least populous State; they shall be in addition to those appointed by the States, but they shall be considered, for the purposes of the election of President and Vice President, to be electors appointed by a State; and they shall meet in the District and perform such duties as provided by the twelfth article of amendment.

Section 2. The Congress shall have power to enforce this article by appropriate legislation.

State Ratifications of the Twenty-third Amendment

State	Date
Hawaii	23 June 1960
Massachusetts	22 August 1960
New Jersey	19 December 1960
New York	17 January 1961
California	19 January 1961
Oregon	27 January 1961
Maryland	30 January 1961
Idaho	31 January 1961
Maine	31 January 1961
Minnesota	31 January 1961
New Mexico	1 February 1961
Nevada	2 February 1961
Montana	6 February 1961
South Dakota	6 February 1961
Colorado	8 February 1961
Washington State	9 February 1961
West Virginia	9 February 1961
Alaska	10 February 1961
Wyoming	13 February 1961
Delaware	20 February 1961
Utah	21 February 1961
Wisconsin	21 February 1961
Pennsylvania	28 February 1961
Indiana	3 March 1961
North Dakota	3 March 1961
Tennessee	6 March 1961
Michigan	8 March 1961
Connecticut	9 March 1961
Arizona	10 March 1961
Illinois	14 March 1961
Nebraska	15 March 1961
Vermont	15 March 1961
Iowa	16 March 1961
Missouri	20 March 1961
Oklahoma	21 March 1961
Rhode Island	22 March 1961
Kansas	29 March 1961
Ohio	29 March 1961
New Hampshire	30 March 1961
Alabama	16 April 2002

Explanation of the amendment

The Twenty-third Amendment's goal was to give the District of Columbia voting rights in presidential elections. Because of this amendment, the District has three electoral votes out of a total of 538 in the Electoral College, even though the District has no voting representation in either body of the Congress.

Organic changes to the amendment

Since its passage in 1960 and its ratification the following year, there have been no changes to the amendment, although in 1978 the Congress submitted to the states a proposed constitutional amendment to give the District statehood which would be embodied in the US Constitution. The proposed amendment had a deadline of seven years, and, in 1985, the deadline ran out without the requisite number of states ratifying the potential amendment.

ORIGINAL PRIMARY DOCUMENTS

Compromise is the key word written all over this story, underlying the difficulty arising in getting this amendment through both Houses. This report shows why the House had to take the original Senate resolution and "blow it up" into a completely new potential amendment, The Washington Post, *9 June 1960.*

Suffrage Bill to Get Clear Path

Sponsors Expect Change to Insure Affirmative Vote

By Morton Mintz, Staff Reporter

The proposal to give District residents the vote for President and Vice President was transferred yesterday to a new parliamentary road which sponsors believe will move it with equal speed and greater safety.

Rep. Emanuel Celler (D-N.Y.), chairman of the House Judiciary Committee, said he expected his resolution for a Constitutional amendment will be before the House next week. It was understood that it will be under a closed rule, which allows no further amendment.

The House Rules Committee gave the resolution its blessing after a half-hour hearing yesterday. Chairman Howard

W. Smith (D-Va.) said it will meet "no trouble if we get it to the floor in clean shape, and that's what we aim to do."

The form of the resolution was rejected by the Committee because it carried the title of a resolution, passed by the

Senate in February, that packaged a District suffrage amendment with two unrelated amendments.

Poll Tax Issue

One of the unrelated amendments would bar the poll tax as a prerequisite of voting in Federal elections. Celler said his fear was that zealous house enemies of the poll tax might sink District suffrage rather than vote or a resolution from which the poll tax ban had been eliminated.

His solution was to introduce the suffrage amendment as a new resolution, unrelated to any other issue. The Judiciary Committee is to meet this morning to approve it. The new resolution then is expected to go at once to the Rules Committee where prompt action appears assured.

Once the resolution wins a two-thirds vote in the House, Celler said, he will ask unanimous consent to give it the Senate resolution's title. This would restore the legislative shortcut under which the resolution would go directly to Senate-House conference committee.

Celler and the ranking Republican on the Judiciary Committee, Rep. William M. McCulloch (Ohio) agreed that the resolution's chances are good only if no attempt is made to broaden the suffrage it provides.

The amendment would limit presidential electors to the number had by the least populous state, or three. Otherwise, the District would have four.

కుపుకుపుకుపుకుపుకుపు

The US House of Representatives passes the proposed DC electoral amendment by voice vote, and the story gets little coverage in the nation's newspapers. This, from The New York Times, *16 June 1960, began as a small story on page 1 and concluded on page 33.*

Suffrage for Capital Approved by House

By C.P. Trussell
Special to *The New York Times.*

WASHINGTON, June 14 – The House of Representatives voted today to give the vote-less citizens of the nation's capital the right to help elect Presidents and Vice Presidents.

Approval was given by voice, rather than a roll-call, but so few voices were raised in opposition that there was no doubt that a two-thirds majority required for presenting a proposed Constitutional amendment had been registered.

The resolution now goes to the Senate.

The Senate has approved a District of Columbia voting amendment but has linked it with two other proposed amendments. One would outlaw poll taxes and the other would permit Governors to appoint temporary members of the House of Representatives should a majority of the House be wiped out by a disaster.

Acceptance Expected

However, the Senate is expected to accept the single amendment as approved by the House and send it to the states for ratification.

Three-fourths, or thirty-eight, of the states must agree before a Constitutional amendment becomes effective, but seven years are allowed to complete the ratification. Affirmative action by the states could make the Twenty-third Amendment to the Constitution effective for elections of 1964.

Today's strategy was worked out largely by the House Judiciary Committee, headed by Representative Emanuel Celler, Democrat of Brooklyn. Mr. Celler saw that if the House considered the Senate-approved resolution, enough trouble might develop to deprive it of many Southern votes because of the poll-tax feature.

Sponsors of this phase of the Senate proposal were reported to have agreed to drop it for this session of Congress. It was also found that there would apparently be no pressure at this time to demand the provision for appointment of House members.

Today's debate found few Southerners opposing the granting of voting rights for Washingtonians. Residents of the capital have been denied national suffrage since the development of the District of Columbia on land donated by Maryland and Virginia.

Another question was settled. It had been feared in some quarters that the district's population could give it stronger representation in the Electoral College than that of at least four states – Delaware, Nevada, Wyoming and Alaska. Each of these has three electoral votes.

Today's action held the District of Columbia's electoral votes to the number held by "the least populous states." This means three, although the district's estimated population is greater than that of Alaska, Nevada and Wyoming combined.

It was emphasized in debate today that no attempt was being made to "displease" the Constitution. The proposed amendment, it was insisted, is designed to "correct an omission" rather than find fault with the Founding Fathers.

The Senate accepts the new language passed by the House, and sends it to the states, as noted here in The Washington Post, *17 June 1960.*

Suffrage Bill Passed By Senate

_____

Measure Goes Directly to States for Ratification

_____

By John J. Lindsay, Staff Reporter

The Senate approved a constitutional amendment last night to give District residents a vote for President and that Vice President. The measure goes directly to the states for ratification.

Approval of the resolution proposing the amendment was by voice vote with a sprinkling of negative votes among the fewer than 30 Senators present.

The constitutional amendment which has cleared both houses must be ratified by three fourths – or 38 – of the 50 states within seven years.

The amendment, a weaker version of one previously passed by the Senate, would give the District only three votes in the Electoral College. There is no provision for a House delegate and the electoral votes would be fixed permanently at the level of the least populous state, a proviso strongly objected to last night by Sens. Kenneth B. Keating (R-N.Y.) and Francis Case (R-S.Dak.).

Case and Keating joined in support of the bill on the floor along with Sen. Jennings Randolph (D-W.Va.); Clifford Case (R-N.J.) and Jacob K. Javits (R-N.Y.).

Sen. Spessard Holland (D-Fla.), who supported the amendment, with reservations, told the Senate he believes the "founding fathers" desired local government for the District, but were leery of the presidential vote.

The requisite number of states ratify the proposed DC electoral amendment, giving the US Constitution its newest addition. Here is the coverage from The Washington Post, *30 March 1961.*

Presidential Vote for District Wins, Kansas Beating Ohio as 38th State

_____

23rd Amendment Adopted 9 Months after 'Hill' Action; Event Is Broadcast to World

_____

By Morton Mintz, Staff Reporter

Washington won the right to vote for President and Vice President at 1:14 p.m. EST yesterday.

At that historic moment the Kansas House of Representatives supplied the 38th and crucial ratification of the 23d Amendment to the United States Constitution.

But only 14 minutes earlier minimum, New Hampshire had provided the 37th ratification that Kansas and Ohio spurned. Then Ohio came through with the one-for-good measure 39th at 1:56 p.m., 42 minutes after Kansas.

Enabling legislation drafted yesterday by District officials would enfranchise Washingtonians 21 years old or older. It would set up a one-year residence requirement.

A public hearing will be held Monday and Congressional approval will be sought. Congressional leaders have promised swift action.

The 23d Amendment achieved final ratification 91/2 months after leaving Congress – more swiftly than any of the 12 Amendments adopted in the last 157 years.

President Kennedy said that the speed shown by the states in granting Washington residents the presidential vote "demonstrates the interest of the Nation at large in providing to all American citizens the most valuable of human rights – the right to share in the election of those who govern us."

Told in 35 Languages

The Voice of America beamed the news worldwide in 35 languages.

The Kansas House had just recessed when a phone call brought the New Hampshire tidings to the office of Speaker William L. Mitchell in Topeka, who quickly summoned the body back into session. The ratification resolution flashed through 88 to 0.

The Kansas Senate had cleared the road on March 3 when it approved 36 to 0.

Kansans thus achieved their goal of being 38th. They regard it as an honor and a unique celebration of the centennial year of Kansas statehood.

And they won a tense countdown with Ohio, which had also sought to be 38th, in a memorable vindication of the official Kansas motto: "To the Stars Through Difficulties."

Ohio Is Outmaneuvered

Ohio Senate Republicans, outmaneuvered by Kansas, caught before their session had begun by New Hampshire, were chided on the floor by the Democratic minority.

The Ohio House had approved an Amendment resolution 125 to 6 on March 7. The Senate approved unanimously 36 to 0.

The New Hampshire, Kansas and Ohio Legislatures became the 11th, 12th and 13th controlled by Republicans to ratify the Amendment. They provided the final proof – if any were needed – that the Amendment could not have succeeded without bipartisan support.

Nor could have it succeeded, at least this year, without the dedicated work of countless members of Congress, governors, state legislators, organizations and individuals.

District residents will vote in the 1964 presidential election under ground rules that Congress will establish.

As citizens of Maryland, residents of Washington voted in the presidential elections of 1792, 1796 and 1800. That was before the City formally became the official seat of the Federal Government.

But Washington's citizens have not voted for any public office – have been taxed without representation of any kind – for 87 years, because of what is generally recognized as an historical accident.

The District population is 53.9 per cent Negro, by Census estimate. It is also strongly Democratic, if the results of the 1960 primary are a guide – but there is serious doubt as to their reliability.

Opposed by Segregationists

The racial makeup of the city evoked segregationist opposition – not always openly expressed – in the South. To date, only one Southern state, Tennessee, has ratified.

In some Northern states, including Wyoming and Illinois, many Republican legislators opposed ratification because of their fear that Washington would become another urban Democratic stronghold. But every non-Southern state except Texas, where a ratification resolution is pending, ratified.

President Kennedy, who began working actively for complete District suffrage in 1947 as a freshman member of the House of Representatives, termed the Amendment "a major step in the right direction."

He said he is hopeful that Congress will be spurred to "act favorably on legislative proposals to be recommended by the Administration providing the District of Columbia with home rule."

Oath Required

The indication at the moment is that District residents wishing to vote for President will have to swear that they claim voting rights nowhere else. They had to take this oath to ballot in the 1956 and 1960 primaries, at which delegates to the Democratic and Republican National Conventions and members of the District party committees were elected.

Assuming that this requirement holds, Ernest Schein, chairman of the District Board of Elections, has estimated that between 200,000 and 250,000 District residents will vote here in 1964.

The Amendment won the approval of the required three-fourths of the states 286 days after it won final, overwhelming approval from Congress last June 16. Its deadline was June 16, 1967.

Only one other Amendment, the 12th, which set up the system for the election of President and Vice President in 1804, made better time – less than 230 days.

But the 23d even beat by two days the speed record of the 21st, which repealed prohibition in 1933.

The 23d was the first in the Nation's history to require the approval of so many states – 36 was the previous minimum. It is the eighth Amendment to be approved in the 20th century and the 13th since the Bill of Rights took effect in 1791.

Hawaii Was First

The 23d was ratified by Hawaii on June 30, 14 days after it left Congress; by Massachusetts on Aug. 22, and by New Jersey on Dec. 19.

The big push came after the first of the year, when most state legislatures convened. Paced by New York, which approved on Jan. 17, a total of 35 legislatures ratified in the first 88 days of 1961, an average of one each 21/2 days.

Before releasing the Amendment to the states, Congress stripped away proposals to give the District as many electoral votes as it would have if it were a state – four – and representation in the House.

This dilution evoked widespread disappointment. But in recent weeks it became clear that an Amendment broader than the presidential voting proposal would have met with possibly fatal opposition, at least this year, in several states legislatures where the 23d had close calls. These included the legislatures of Tennessee, Illinois, Missouri, Wyoming, North Dakota and South Dakota, in some of which approval required two-thirds majorities.

The General Services Administration, which sent the Amendment to the governors of the states by registered, receipt-requested mail (only to find that copies got lost in several states capitols), has received official certification from 36 states.

Administrator John L. Moore said that on receipt of two more he will hold a ceremony in his office.

Citing the US Constitution, the Bush administration told Congress in 2007 that it would oppose any statehood vote for the District of Columbia. This is how the story was reported in The Washington Post, *17 March 2007.*

White House Opposes D.C. Vote

by Mary Beth Sheridan
Washington Post Staff Writer
Saturday, March 17, 2007

The White House declared its opposition yesterday to a bill that would give the District its first full seat in the House of Representatives, saying it is unconstitutional, and a key Senate supporter said such concerns could kill the measure.

"The Constitution specifies that only 'the people of the several states' elect representatives to the House," said White House spokesman Alex Conant. "And D.C. is not a state."

He declined to say whether President Bush would veto the bill, but the White House appeared to be sending a message to Congress just as momentum for the measure was building. It cleared two House committees this week, and the Democratic leadership has vowed to pass it on the House floor next week.

The bill seeks to increase the House permanently to 437 seats, from 435. In a bipartisan compromise, one seat would go to the overwhelmingly Democratic District, which has a nonvoting delegate in the House. The other would go to the next state in line to pick up a seat based on the 2000 Census: Utah, which leans Republican.

Several Republican House members assailed the bill this week, noting that the Constitution reserves representation for residents of states, not districts. Supporters countered with a section of the Constitution known as the "District Clause," which gives Congress sweeping powers over the city. Legal scholars have disagreed over who is right.

The bill's advocates knew that the White House had constitutional concerns. But Conant said the White House hadn't formally opposed the bill until it had cleared the Judiciary Committee on Thursday and was headed for the House floor. "We had not taken a position until after the committee vote," he said.

Bush has not commented directly on whether he thinks the District should have a vote in Congress. In December, he said that he would "look carefully" at whatever Congress proposes.

Asked about the prospects of a veto, Conant said: "We'll have to wait and see what happens to the legislation. But the White House does oppose the bill."

Supporters of the measure have anticipated a difficult fight in the Senate, where few Republicans have embraced it. The bill's sponsors, Del. Eleanor Holmes Norton (D-D.C.) and Rep. Thomas M. Davis III (R-Va.), have pinned their hopes on the Republican senators from Utah, believing they could persuade colleagues to pass it.

But both Utah senators indicated yesterday that the bill could be in trouble. A spokeswoman for Sen. Robert F. Bennett (R) said he continues to support it. However, "based on the constitutional concerns raised by the White House and others in Congress, it may be difficult to get the 60 votes to move this bill," said the spokeswoman, Emily Christensen, referring to the threshold necessary to avoid a filibuster.

A spokesman for the senior Utah senator, Orrin G. Hatch (R), said he was traveling and unavailable to respond to the White House statement. But the spokesman, Peter Carr, said the senator is unhappy with another part of the bill, which would make the extra Utah seat "at large" until the 2012 reapportionment after the next census.

"He does have serious concerns about the constitutionality of an at-large seat," Carr said.

House Democrats had insisted the Utah seat be at large to avoid a redistricting process that could hurt the lone Democratic member of the state's three-member House delegation.

The flurry of statements appeared to indicate a darkening future for the vote bill. But supporters said they were still hopeful that it could pass.

Davis, who crafted the legislation, said Bush had signed bills in the past that had raised constitutional questions, including a ban on what abortion opponents call "partial-birth" abortion, which is being examined by the Supreme Court. With the voting bill, too, Bush could ultimately choose to "err on the side of letting the courts decide," Davis said.

He also pointed out that prominent Republican lawyers, including Kenneth W. Starr, a former federal appellate judge and onetime independent counsel, and Viet D. Dinh, a former assistant attorney general, had analyzed the D.C. vote bill and deemed it constitutional.

"I'm hopeful that when this gets to the president, he will follow the writings of Judge Starr and Viet Dinh, who he relied on to write the Patriot Act," Davis said.

Norton also noted the support of the former top government attorneys. "With District residents among the troops on the ground in Iraq and Afghanistan, and other residents here paying taxes to support our government, it is unthinkable that this or any president would cast one of his few vetoes to deny our citizens representation," she said in a statement.

D.C. Mayor Adrian M. Fenty (D) said in a statement that he still hopes the measure will quickly pass the House and Senate and be signed into law by the president.

"We will continue to do all we can to make sure that happens," he said.

Supreme Court Cases

Hepburn & Dundas v. Ellzey *(2 Cranch {6 US} 445 {1805}). Decided in the February term, 1805, by a vote of 5-0. Chief Justice John Marshall wrote the Court's opinion.*

The Case: Few of the facts of the case are known; the Court's opinion, as short as it is, lays out the story behind the case. According to the opinion, "A citizen of the District of Columbia cannot maintain an action in the circuit court of the United States, not being a citizen of a state within the meaning of the provision in the law of the United States regulating the jurisdiction of the courts of the United States." Hepburn and Dundas were citizens and residents of the District of Columbia who sued Ellzey, a citizen of the Commonwealth of Virginia. The lawsuit was dismissed by the Circuit Court of the United States of the District of Virginia, with the judges on that court holding that Hepburn and Dundas could not sue citizens of another state because they were not citizens of the state. Hepburn and Dundas sued to the US Supreme Court. Because the case was so early in the Court's history, all that appears in the opinion is that the decision was handed down in the February term of 1805.

Chief Justice John Marshall, joined Justices William Cushing, William Paterson, Samuel Chase, and Bushrod Washington (a nephew of former President George Washington), held that since the District of Columbia was not a state under the terms of the US Constitution, Hepburn and Dundas could not sue a citizen of another state. Marshall explained,

"The question in this case is whether the plaintiffs, as residents of the District of Columbia, can maintain an action in the Circuit Court of the United States for the District of Virginia.

"This depends on the act of Congress describing the jurisdiction of that court. That act gives jurisdiction to the circuit courts in cases between a citizen of the state in which the suit is brought and a citizen of another state. To support the jurisdiction in this case, therefore, it must appear that Columbia is a state.

"On the part of the plaintiffs, it has been urged that Columbia is a distinct political society, and is therefore 'a state' according to the definitions of writers on general law.

"This is true. But as the act of Congress obviously uses the word 'state' in reference to the term as used in the Constitution, it becomes necessary to inquire whether Columbia is a state in the sense of that instrument. The result of that examination is a conviction that the members of the American confederacy only are the states contemplated in the Constitution.

"The House of Representatives is to be composed of members chosen by the people of the several states, and each state shall have at least one representative. The Senate of the United States shall be composed of two senators from each state. Each state shall appoint, for the election of the executive, a number of electors equal to its whole number of Senators and Representatives.

"These clauses show that the word 'state' is used in the Constitution as designating a member of the union, and excludes Page 6 U. S. 453 from the term the signification attached to it by writers on the law of nations. When the same term, which has been used plainly in this limited sense in the articles respecting the legislative and executive departments, is also employed in that which respects the judicial department, it must be understood as retaining the sense originally given to it. Other passages from the Constitution have been cited by the plaintiffs to show that the term state is sometimes used in its more enlarged sense. But on examining the passages quoted, they do not prove what was to be shown by them.

"It is true that as citizens of the United States and of that particular district which is subject to the jurisdiction of Congress, it is extraordinary that the courts of the United States, which are open to aliens and to the citizens of every state in the union, should be closed upon them. But this is a subject for legislative, not for judicial consideration. The opinion to be certified to the Circuit Court is, that that court has no jurisdiction in the case."

Loughborough v. Blake *(5 Wheaton {18 US 317 {1820}). Decided in the February term 1820 by a unanimous vote. Chief Justice John Marshall wrote the majority opinion.*

The Case: Like the earlier case of *Hepburn and Dundas v. Ellzey,* this case opened with nearly the same question being asked by Chief Justice Marshall: "This case presents to the consideration of the court a single question. It is this: Has Congress a right to impose a direct tax on the District of Columbia?" And, like Hepburn, few facts of this case are noted in the opinion, making it hard to adequately discuss the case itself. In fact, Marshall wrote in the first sentence of the official opinion, "The facts in this case are unimportant. The sole question is stated that the beginning of the opinion of the court as delivered by the chief justice [sic]." That being said, it appears that Loughborough was a citizen of the District of Columbia, who claimed that since he was a "stateless person," he could not taxed by the Congress under the US Constitution. There is no record which court first heard this case; all we know is that it made its way to the US Supreme Court. Chief Justice Marshall delivered the opinion of the Court; there is no record of any dissenting opinions.

Chief Justice Marshall wrote, "The counsel who maintains the negative has contended, that congress must be considered in two distinct characters. In one character, as legislating for the states; in the other, as a local legislature for the district. In the latter character, it is admitted, the power of levying direct taxes may be exercised; but it is contended, for district purposes only, in like manner as the legislature of a state may tax the people of a state for state purposes."

Marshall then argued that under the Constitution, Congress could "levy taxes" without regard for the place of the residence of the specific citizen being taxed. He explained, "The 8th section of the 1st article gives to congress the 'power to lay and collect taxes, duties, imposts and excises,' for the purposes thereinafter mentioned. This grant is general, without limitation as to place. It, consequently, extends to all *places over which the government extends. If this could be doubted, the doubt is removed by the subsequent words which modify the grant. These words are, 'but all duties, imposts and excises shall be uniform throughout the United States.' It will not be contended, that the modification of the power extends to places to which the power itself does not extend. The power, then, to lay and collect duties, imposts and excises may be exercised, and must be exercised, throughout the United States. Does this term designate the whole, or any particular portion of the American empire? Certainly, this question can admit of but one answer. It is the name given to our great republic, which is composed of states and territories. The district of Columbia, or the territory 147*147 west of the Missouri, is not less within the United States, than Maryland or Pennsylvania; and it is not less necessary, on the principles of our constitution, that uniformity in the imposition of imposts, duties and excises should be observed in the one, than in the other. Since, then, the power to lay and collect taxes, which includes direct taxes, is obviously co-extensive with the power to lay and collect duties, imposts and excises, and since the latter extends throughout the United States, it follows, that the power to impose direct taxes also extends throughout the United States."

Marshall then wrote, "If, then, the language of the constitution be construed to comprehend the territories and district of Columbia, as well as the states, that language confers on congress the power of taxing the district and territories as well as the states. If the general language of the constitution should be confined to the states, still, the 16th paragraph of the 8th section gives to congress the power of exercising 'exclusive legislation in all cases whatsoever within this district.'"

He concluded, "If it were true, that, according to the spirit of our constitution, the power of taxation must be limited by the right of representation, whence is derived the right to lay and collect duties, imposts and excises, within this district? If the principles of liberty, and of our constitution, forbid the raising of revenue from those who are not represented, do not these principles forbid the raising it by duties, imposts and excises, as well as by a direct tax? If the principles of our revolution give a rule applicable to this case, we cannot have forgotten, that neither the [S]tamp [A]ct, nor the duty on tea, were direct taxes. Yet, it is admitted, that the constitution not only allows, but enjoins, the government to extend the ordinary revenue system to this district.

"If it be said, that the principle of uniformity, established in the constitution, secures the district from oppression in the imposition of indirect taxes, it is not less true, that the principle of apportionment, also established in the constitution, secures the district from any oppressive exercise of the power to lay and collect direct taxes.

"After giving this subject its serious attention, the court is unanimously of opinion, that congress possesses, under the constitution, the power to lay and collect direct taxes within the [D]istrict of Columbia, in proportion to the census directed to be taken by the constitution, and that there is no error in the judgment of the circuit court."

Note: In 1902, Secretary of War Elihu Root wrote of this decision, "That the Chief Justice did not intend to declare the Constitution to be enforce in the District of Columbia appears clearly when the facts upon which the action was founded are known. The law assailed by the taxpayers was a special act imposing a direct tax upon the District alone. That is, the act did not impose a tax upon the country at large and simply require[d] the District to pay a share proportionate with that of the several States...the protesting property owners of the District contended that Congress was not authorized to impose a direct tax except in those parts of the country afforded Representatives in Congress and embraced in the language 'the several States which may be included within the Union;' and if this contention was not sustained, and the power of the Congress to impose a direct tax extended beyond the States of the Union, the Constitution required that the amount to be raised by such tax 'be apportioned among the several States' and not confined to one, to with, the District of Columbia."

National Mutual Insurance Co. v. Tidewater Transfer Co., Inc. *(337 US 582 {1949}). Decided 20 June 1949 by a vote of 8-1. Justice Robert Jackson wrote the Court's opinion; Justice Felix Frankfurter was the lone dissenter.*

The Case: This case did not deal specifically with the representation in Congress or the statehood matter of the District of Columbia; instead, it went to the issue of whether the Congress could pass a law that gave jurisdiction regarding diversity to non-state actors, such as, for instance, territories of the United States and the District of Columbia. On 20 April 1940, Congress enacted a law, codified at 54 Stat. 28 (now 28 U.S.C. §1332), that bestowed jurisdiction upon these entities to be able to sue in federal court. The National Mutual Insurance Company, a corporation located in the District of Columbia, sued the Tidewater Transfer Co., Inc., of Virginia, on a claim resulting from an insurance contract; for some reason, the lawsuit was instigated in the US District Court for Maryland instead of the District of Columbia or Virginia, mainly because the plaintiff did business in Maryland. The judge on the District Court held that while the lawsuit was proper under the 1940 act of Congress, under the US Constitution, which does not recognize the District of Columbia as a state, the lawsuit had to be dismissed. The National Mutual Insurance Co. then sued to the US Court of Appeals for the Fourth Circuit, which upheld the lower court's ruling. The National Mutual Insurance Co. then appealed to the US Supreme Court, which granted certiorari, or the right to hear the case, and arguments were heard on 8 November 1948.

Seven-plus months later, on 20 June 1949, the Court unanimously upheld the act of Congress as constitutional, in effect overturning 200 years of constitutional law. Speaking for the Court, Justice Robert Jackson, joined in signed opinions by Justice Hugo Black and Horace H. Burton, explained his reasoning. He penned, "This case calls up for review a holding that it is unconstitutional for Congress to open federal courts in the several states to action by a citizen of the District of Columbia against a citizen of one of the states. The petitioner, as plaintiff, commenced in the United States District Court for Maryland an action for money judgment on a claim arising out of an insurance contract. No cause of action under the laws or Constitution of the United States was pleaded, jurisdiction being predicated only upon an allegation of diverse citizenship. The diversity set forth was that plaintiff is a corporation created by District of Columbia law, while the defendant is a corporation chartered by Virginia, amenable to suit in Maryland by virtue of a license to do business there. The learned District Judge concluded that, while this diversity met jurisdictional requirements under the Act of Congress, it did not comply with diversity requirements of the Constitution as to federal jurisdiction, and so dismissed. The Court of Appeals, by a divided court, affirmed." He continued, "The history of the controversy begins with that of the Republic. In defining the cases and controversies to which the judicial power of the United States could extend, the Constitution included those 'between citizens of different States.' In the Judiciary Act of 1789, Congress created a system of federal courts of first instance and gave them jurisdiction of suits 'between a citizen of the State where the suit is brought and a citizen of another State.' In 1804, the Supreme Court, through Chief Justice Marshall, held that a citizen of the District of Columbia was not a citizen of a State within the meaning and intendment of this Act. This decision closed federal courts in the states to citizens of the District of Columbia in diversity cases, and, for 136 years, they remained closed. In 1940, Congress enacted the statute challenged here. It confers on such courts jurisdiction if the action 'is between citizens of different States, or Page 337 U. S. 585 citizens of the District of Columbia, the Territory of Hawaii, or Alaska, and any State or Territory.' The issue here depends upon the validity of this Act, which, in substance, was reenacted by a later Congress as part of the Judicial Code."

Jackson further delved into the history of the caselaw, most notably in the cases examined here. "Our first inquiry is whether, under the third, or Judiciary, Article of the Constitution, extending the judicial power of the United States to cases or controversies 'between citizens of different States,' a citizen of the District of Columbia has the standing of a citizen of one of the states of the Union. This is the question which the opinion of Chief Justice Marshall answered in the negative, by way of dicta if not of actual decision. *Hepburn and Dundas v. Ellzey*, 2 Cranch 445. To be sure, nothing was before that Court except interpretation of a statute which conferred jurisdiction substantially in the words of the Constitution with nothing in the text or context to show that Congress intended to regard the District as a state. But Marshall resolved the statutory question by invoking the analogy of the constitutional provisions of the same tenor, and reasoned that the District was not a state for purposes of the Constitution, and, hence, was not for purposes of the Act. The opinion summarily disposed of arguments to the contrary, including the one repeated here, that other provisions of the Constitution indicate that 'the term state is sometimes used in its more enlarged sense.' Here, as there, 'on examining the passages quoted, they do not prove what was to be shown by them.'"

Despite ruling that, for the sake of federal lawsuit jurisdiction, District of Columbia residents must be considered as persons of a state, with all of the rights such a finding bestows, Justice Jackson cautioned the victorious plaintiffs, as well as the nation and the Congress: the Court was not overruling the Court's 1805 decision in Hepburn, in which the Court held that the District of Columbia could not be considered a state under the US Constitution. For the District to gain that right, it had to come through the constitutional amendment process.

WHO'S WHO

This section includes biographies of two individuals who played a significant part in drafting and passing the Twenty-third Amendment. Both are mentioned in earlier sections of this chapter.

Francis Higbee Case (1896-1962)

A Progressive Republican in an era when that strain of politics carried little weight in the Republican Party, Francis H. Case became one of the most powerful US Senators during his time in office. In the months leading up to the ultimate passage of the proposed District of Columbia voting rights amendment, Case worked quietly behind the scenes to get the language for the proposed amendment through the upper body of the US Congress. Historian Guy G. deFuria, an attorney from Pennsylvania, wrote in 1956, "Senator Francis Case, of South Dakota, a publisher and former Congressman, was known for his power of analysis and parliamentary expertness."

Case was born not in South Dakota but in Everly, in Clay County, Iowa, on 9 December 1896, the son of the Rev. Herbert Case, a roaming preacher, and his wife Mary (née Grannis) Case. Historian Richard Chenoweth wrote for a dissertation in 1977, "The Cases were of English extraction. Mary's ancestors migrated to New England before the 1650s and including such patriarchal names as Fairbanks, Sumner, Ashley, and Higbee. Her father, Samuel Grannis, moved from New England to Mankato, Minnesota where he became a moderately successful businessman. The history of the Case name is less clear. Family records show a Jonathan Case living in New York by the 1750s. He had a large family; the story goes that he had twelve boys and each one had four sisters. One grandson, Jerome I., established a farm machinery company that bears the family name. Herbert's father left the New York family home for Iowa following the Civil War where he farmed and practiced veterinary surgery." Herbert Case was ordained at a small Methodist college in 1894. With his wife and growing family, he moved across the Midwest; Francis was born in Iowa, where they stayed for 12 years. They moved to Sturgis, South Dakota, in 1909.

Case attended local schools, graduating from the Dakota Wesley University in Mitchell, South Dakota, in 1918. When he graduated, WWII was coming to a close, and Case enlisted in the US Marine Corps and trained for eight months, although he never saw any action. Upon his return in 1920, he earned a Master's degree from Northwestern University in Evanston, Illinois, and worked as a publicist for the Methodist Church before he entered the world of newspapers. He became the editor and eventual publisher of *The Custer Chronicle* of South Dakota, as well as the *Rapid City Daily Journal* and several other South Dakota newspapers.

In 1924, Case entered the political arena, and was elected the Republican chairman of the South Dakota Third Congressional District, overseeing elections of Republicans to local and federal office. Two years later, Case married Myrle Lucille Graves, and the couple would have two children. It appeared that Case would not rise any further in the Republican Party, especially after 1928, when he was defeated in the Republican primary for a seat in the US House of Representatives. Six years later, in 1934, he again tried and won the Republican nomination for a House seat, but he was defeated in the general election. In 1936, although President Franklin D. Roosevelt was easily winning a second term in the White House, Republicans were gradually taking back some of the seats they had lost in the last four midterm elections – and Case defeated incumbent Rep. Theodore B. Werner for one of those seats. During his career in the House, which lasted for seven total terms, from the Seventy-fifth Congress (1937-39) to the Eighty-first Congress (1949-51), Case served as a member of the House Appropriations Committee. After the end of WW II, he sponsored the Case Labor Disputes Act, which was intended to level the playing field and give employers and equal footing to negotiate contracts with unions. Condemned by those same unions, the bill was vetoed by President Harry S Truman, who wrote, "This bill was undoubtedly passed by the members of the Congress in the sincere belief that it would remedy certain existing conditions which cause labor strife and produce domestic turmoil. I cannot agree with the Congress with reference to the results that would be achieved by it. I trust that there will be no confusion in the minds of the members of the Congress or in the minds of the public between this bill and my request on May twenty-fifth for emergency legislation. At that time I requested temporary legislation to be effective only for a period of six months after the termination of hostilities, and applicable only to those few industries which had been taken over by the Government and which the President by proclamation declared that an emergency had arisen which affected the entire economy of the country."

Case was also involved in issues important to his state. He sponsored legislation in 1939 and 1940 that led to the ultimate passage in 1944 of the Missouri River Flood Control Act. As with many other Republicans, Case was a staunch isolationist until the United States was attacked by Japan on 7 December 1941.

After seven terms in the House, Case desired higher office – he decided to challenge fellow Republican, Senator Chan Gurney, in the 1950 Republican primary. Case defeated Gurney easily, and won in the general election. Taking his seat in the US Senate in January 1951, Case remained in that body until his death. While in the Senate, Case became an expert in legislative affairs. *The New York Times* called Case "one of the most quiet and unobtrusive men in Washington politics."

During his first years in the Senate, Case worked behind the scenes on legislation that would grant the District of Columbia voting rights along the lines of other states, without bestowing actual statehood on the district. Coordinating with fellow Democrats Senator Spessard Holland of Florida and Rep. Emanuel Celler of New York, as well as others, Case eventually pushed through language that managed, with some alterations, to get a two-thirds vote in both chambers. Submitted to the states, it was ratified in 1961.

During his final years, Case turned from a more progressive Republican to a more conservative one. Although he sat as a member of a special Senate committee to investigate charges of possible censure against fellow Senator Joseph R. McCarthy of Wisconsin, Case defended McCarthy for going against alleged Communists in the US government, and ultimately voted against one of the two resolutions against McCarthy. During the first year of the administration of President John F. Kennedy, Case opposed much of Kennedy's program, including federal unemployment assistance and federal aid to education. In January 1962, Case joined a group of 11 other senators who opposed the nomination of John A. McCone as Kennedy's nominee for director of the Central Intelligence Agency, calling McCone unqualified, even though McCone was a fellow Republican. Despite the opposition, McCone was ultimately confirmed as director.

As the 1962 election approached, many in Case's party feared that he could lose in the Republican primary to A.C. Miller, the South Dakota state Attorney General and a former Lieutenant Governor. Case ultimately won the party primary, but suffered a heart attack in March 1962. He recovered, but as he campaigned against newcomer George McGovern, Case suffered a second, fatal heart attack, and died on 22 June 1962 in a hospital in Bethesda, Maryland. He was 65 years old. His body was returned to South Dakota, and he was buried in the Mountain View Cemetery in Rapid City. *The Washington Post* said in an editorial, "The death of Francis H. Case takes from the Senate a...conservative friend of the District of Columbia and a legislator who was spunky enough to report on the offer of a bribe...Senator Case deserves to be remembered for more than his connection with a notorious incident. He served as chairman of the Senate District Committee for many years and showed a diligent concern for the welfare of Washington. Always an advocate of economy, he is credited with saving the taxpayers millions when he introduced a bill during World War II requiring renegotiations of war contracts. A former newspaperman, a politician who inclined more to the colorless than the flamboyant, Senator Case was an agrarian conservative whose earnest sincerity was a credit to Midwest Republicanism."

Kenneth Barnard Keating (1900-1975)

Kenneth Keating is known mostly for his 1964 US Senate defeat at the hands of former Attorney General Robert F. Kennedy, and then for his legislative work, including his support and assistance in the framing of the language that later became, in part, the Twenty-third Amendment to the US Constitution.

Keating was born in Lima, in upstate New York, on 18 May 1900, the son and eldest of two children of Thomas Mosgrove Keating, a grocer of Irish heritage, and Louise (née Barnard) Keating, a high school teacher whose family had been in America since before the American Revolution. Keating received much of his earliest education at home from his mother; it was not until the sixth grade that he attended a local village school. In 1911, he entered the Genesee Wesleyan Seminary, and graduated four years later. He then attended the University of Rochester in Rochester, New York, and, after graduating, he taught Latin and Greek for one year at a high school in Rochester. He completed his education at the Harvard Law School, graduating with a law degree in 1923. That same year, he was admitted to the New York bar. Over the next several years, Keating worked for some of the largest law firms in Rochester.

Keating would have remained an attorney in Rochester had not the Second World War intervened. On 15 April 1942, Keating was commissioned as a Major and assigned to duty as a staff officer at the Department of War, later the Department of Defense. That October, he was promoted to the rank of lieutenant colonel and, in 1944, to full colonel. He was sent to the China-India-Burma theater of operations to serve as a liaison to the Lend-Lease program, serving from November 1943 to January 1946 as the assistant to Lt. Gen. Raymond A. Wheeler, the Deputy Supreme Commander of the Southeast Asia Command. For his service during the war, Keating was given the Legion of Merit and the Pacific Theater campaign ribbon with three battle stars. When he returned home in 1946, he was prompted to the rank of Brigadier General. Back in Rochester, Keating discovered that while he was gone, he was nominated by the Republican Party for a seat in US House of Representatives, which he easily won.

Taking his seat in the Eightieth Congress (1947-49), Keating would serve in the House until the end of the Eightyfifth Congress (1957-59). He served on the Committee on the Judiciary, rising to become the chairman and then ranking member of the committee; he also served on the Joint Committee on Immigration and National Policy. In the Eighty-third Congress (1953-55), when the Republicans had control of the House, Keating served as the chairman of the Judiciary committee, during which time he investigated the administration of the Department of Justice in the Truman administration and had it censured for blocking House investigations. While in the House, Keating became interested in the subject of voting rights for the District of Columbia.

In 1958, Keating gave up his House seat to run for the US Senate against Democrat Frank Hogan, the Manhattan District Attorney with ties to Tammany Hall in New York City. Despite Hogan's connection, Keating was able to score a victory, and entered the US Senate in January 1959. Keating was a firm believer in the rights of black Americans; while in the House, he had sponsored a civil rights bill and, in the Senate, backed civil rights legislation. In 1960, Keating worked behind the scenes to help get a proposed constitutional amendment for electoral voting rights for the District of Columbia, an effort that culminated in the eventual ratification of the Twenty-third Amendment. While he supported the civil rights program of President John F. Kennedy, Keating disagreed with the administration on its policy towards Cuba, advocating a tougher position on the Communist government on that island.

By 1964, Keating found himself increasingly at odds with the base of the Republican Party, which was becoming more conservative. The full break came when Keating refused to endorse the Republican presidential candidate that year, fellow Senator Barry Goldwater of Arizona. Also, Keating had little chance of winning his race for the Senate that year – his opponent was former Attorney General Robert F. Kennedy, the brother of President John F. Kennedy, who had been assassinated in November 1963. The Kennedy name alone was more than enough for Keating to take on, but his abandonment of his party was the icing on the cake. He was defeated by an overwhelming wave of support for the murdered President's brother.

In January 1965, Keating was out of politics for the first time in nearly two decades. He did not return to his formal law firm, from which he had resigned in 1963, and he turned down a nomination for Commissioner of Major League Baseball. In April 1965, he joined the New York law firm of Royall, Koegel, and Rogers, and ran for a seat as an Associate Judge on the New York Court of Appeals, one of the state's highest courts. He was elected and served until 1969, when President Richard Nixon nominated Keating to be the United States Ambassador to India, where he served until1972. Nixon then nominated Keating to serve as the US Ambassador to Israel, where he served from August 1973 to 5 May 1975, when he suffered a fatal heart attack, 13 days shy of his 75th birthday. Because of his service during the Second World War, Keating was given the honor of burial in Arlington National Cemetery in Virginia. Vice President Nelson Rockefeller said in a statement, "Our nation has lost a great American. I have lost a dear friend. With courage in war-time, with effectiveness in both the House and Senate, with justice on the bench of the highest court of New York State, with diplomatic acumen in India and Israel, Ambassador Keating served this nation and its people brilliantly and tirelessly. His death at this time is a particular loss because of the key role he had been playing in the search for peace in the Middle East."

FOOTNOTES, SOURCES, FURTHER READING

Footnotes

[1] Muller, W.H., "Early History of the Federal Supreme Court" (Boston: The Chipman Law Publishing Company, 1922), 18.

[2] Publius [James Madison], "Fourth Class of Powers Vested in the Union" in "The Federalist: A Collection of Essays by Alexander Hamilton, John Jay, and James Madison" (New York: The Co-Operative Publication Society, 1901), 236.

[3] Lee remarks in Bernard Bailyn, ed., "The Debate on the Constitution: Debates in the Press and in Private Correspondence, January 14, 1788-August 1788; Debates in the State Ratifying Conventions: South Carolina, Virginia, New York, North Carolina" (New York: The Library of America, 1993), 914.

[4] Dickens' writing on the Capitol in Ovason, David, "The Secret Architecture of Our Nation's Capital: The Masons and the Building of Washington, D.C." (London: Century Books Ltd., 1999), 191.

[5] Jackson's Third Annual Message in "Appendix to the Register of Debates in Congress" in "Register of Debates in Congress, Comprising the Leading Debates and Incidents of the First Session of the Twenty-Second Congress: Together with an Appendix, Containing Important State Papers and Public Documents, and The Laws Enacted During the Session: With a Copious Index to the Whole" (Washington: Printed and Published by Gales and Seaton, 1830), 6.

[6] Maury, William Magruder, "The Territorial Period in Washington, 1871-1874, With Special Emphasis on Alexander Shepherd and the Board of Public Works" (Ph.D. dissertation, The George Washington University, 1975).

[7] Best, Judith, "National Representation for the District of Columbia" (Frederick, Maryland: University Publications of America, 1984), 14.

[8] Franchino, Roy P., "The Constitutionality of Home Rule and National Representation for the District of Columbia," *The Georgetown Law Journal*, XLVI:2 (Winter 1957-58), 207-59.

[9] Hodgkin, George W., "The Constitutional Status of the District of Columbia," *Political Science Quarterly*, XXV:2 (June 1910), 257.

[10] "Granting Representation in the Electoral College to the District of Columbia. May 31, 1960. Referred to the House Calendar and ordered to be printed," House Report 1698, 86th Congress, 2nd Session (1960), 1, 2.

[11] "No Taxation Without Representation Act of 2002" (Senate Report 107-343, 107th Congress, 2d Session {15 November 2002}), 6.

[12] [FN] Crockett, David A., "Dodging the Bullet: Election Mechanics and the Problem of the Twenty-Third Amendment," *PS: Political Science and Politics*, XXXVI:3 (July 2003), 423-26.

[13] Ibid., 424.

[14] "Amendment Process" in Michael Kazin, Rebecca Edwards, and Adam Rothman, eds., "The Concise Princeton Encyclopedia of American Political History" (Princeton, New Jersey: Princeton University Press, 2011), 11.

[15] Howard Worth Smith (1883-1976), Democrat of Virginia, Commonwealth Attorney, city of Alexandria, Virginia (1918-22), Judge, Corporation Court, Alexandria (1922-28), Judge, Sixteenth Judicial Circuit of Virginia (1928-30), US Representative (1931-67).

[16] Clarence J. Brown (1893-1965), Republican of Ohio, Publisher, newspapers of the Brown Publishing Company; Lieutenant Governor of Ohio (1919-23), Secretary of State of Ohio (1927-33), US Representative (1939-65).

[17] Noah Morgan Mason (1882-1965), Republican of Illinois, City Commissioner, Oglesby, Illinois (1918-26), Member, Illinois State Normal School Board (1926-30), Member, Illinois state Senate (1930-36), US Representative (1937-63).

[18] George Meader (1907-1994), Republican of Michigan, Prosecuting Attorney, Washtenaw County, Michigan (1941-43), Assistant Counsel, United States Senate Special Committee Investigating the National Defense Program (1943-45), Chief Counsel of the same United States Senate Committee (1945-47), Chief Counsel, United States Senate Banking and Currency Subcommittee (1950), US Representative (1951-65), Associate Counsel, Joint Committee on the Organization of the Congress (1965-67), Chief Counsel of the same committee (1967-68).

[19] Joel Thomas Broyhill (1919-2006), Republican of Virginia, US Representative (1953-74).

[20] William Moore McCulloch (1901-1980), Republican of Ohio, US Representative (1947-73).

[21] Emanuel Celler (1888-1981), Democrat of New York, US Representative (1923-73). See the comprehensive biography for Celler in the "influential biographies" section of the Twenty-fourth Amendment.

[22] Thomas Wilson Dorr (1805-1854) was an early 19th century American politician and reformer who, although being born into a wealthy family, agitated for universal suffrage for men who did not own property and were unable to gain the vote. He formed a political party in his native Rhode Island, and in the 1842 election elected a competing slates of candidates against Samuel H. King. When both parties tried to take power, Dorr and his forces used violence to try to storm the state capital. This has come to be known as the Dorr Rebellion. Two years after the insurrection, Dorr returned, stood trial, and was found guilty. Although given a life term, he spent only a year in prison before his health collapsed, and he was released just prior to his death.

[23] Lyndon Baines Johnson (1908-1973), Democrat of Texas, US Representative (1937-49), US Senator (1949-61), Vice President of the United States (1961-63), President of the United States (1963-69).

[24] Jacob Koppel Javits (1904-1986), Republican of New York, US Representative (1947-54), Attorney General, New York State (1954-57), US Senator (1957-81).

[25] Francis Higbee Case (1896-1962), Republican of South Dakota, Editor and Publisher of various newspapers in South Dakota (1925-33), US Representative (1937-51), US Senator (1951-62). See the comprehensive biography for Case in the "influential biographies" section of this amendment.

[26] Michael Joseph (Mike) Mansfield (1903-2001), Democrat of Montana, US Representative (1943-53), US Senator (1953-77), US Ambassador Extraordinary and Plenipotentiary to Japan (1977-88).

[27] Matthew Mansfield Neely (1874-1958), Democrat of West Virginia, Mayor, Fairmont, West Virginia (1908-10), Clerk, West Virginia state House of Delegates (1911-13), US Representative (1913-21), US Senator (1923-29, 1931-41, 1949-58), Governor of West Virginia (1941-45).

[28] Ernest William McFarland (1894-1984), Democrat of Arizona, Assistant Attorney General of Arizona (1923-24), County Attorney, Pinal County, Arizona (1925-30), Judge, Superior Court, Pinal County (1934-40), You Senator (1941-53), Governor of Arizona (1955-59), Associate Justice, Arizona state Supreme Court (1964-68), Chief Justice, Arizona state Supreme Court (1968-70).

[29] James Glenn Beall (1894-1971), Republican of Maryland, Member, Maryland state Senate (1930-34), Member and Chairman, Maryland State Road Commission (1938-39), US Representative (1953-65).

[30] Kenneth Barnard Keating (1900-1975), Republican of New York, US Representative (1947-59), US Senator (1959-65), Judge, New York State Court of Appeals (1965-69), US Ambassador to Israel (1973-75). See the comprehensive biography for Keating in the "influential biographies" section of this amendment.

[31] Carey Estes Kefauver (1903-63), Democrat of Tennessee, Tennessee state Commissioner of Finance and Taxation (1939), US Representative (1939-49), US Senator (1949-63).

[32] Spessard Lindsey Holland (1892-1971), Democrat of Florida, Prosecuting Attorney, Polk County, Florida (1919-20), County Judge, Polk County (1921-29), Member, Florida state Senate (1932-40), Governor of Florida (1941-45), US Senator (1946-71). See the comprehensive biography for Holland in the "influential biographies" section of the Twenty-fourth Amendment.

[33] Walter Franklin George (1878-1957), Democrat of Georgia, Solicitor General, Cordele Judicial Circuit (1907-12), Judge, Cordele Superior Court (1912-17), Judge, Georgia state Court of Appeals (1917), Associate Justice, Georgia state Supreme Court (1917-22), US Senator (1922-57).

[34] Harry Flood Byrd (1887-1966), Democrat of Virginia, Member, Virginia state Senate (1915-25), State Fuel Commissioner (1918), Governor of Virginia (1926-30), US Senator (1933-65).

[35] Clyde Roarke Hoey (1877-1954), Democrat of North Carolina, Member, North Carolina state House of Commons (1898-1902), Member, North Carolina state Senate (1902-04), Assistant US Attorney for the Western District of North Carolina (1913-19), US Representative (1919-21), US Senator (1945-54).

[36] John Little McClellan (1896-1977), Democrat of Arkansas, Prosecuting Attorney, Seventh Judicial District of Arkansas (1927-30), US Representative (1935-39), US Senator (1943-77).

[37] Allen Joseph Ellender (1890-1972), Democrat of Louisiana, City Attorney, Houma, Louisiana (1913-15), District Attorney, Terrebonne Parish (1915-16), Member, Louisiana state House of Representatives (1924-36), US Senator (1937-72).

[38] Russell Billiu Long (1918-2003), Democrat of Louisiana, US Senator (1948-87).

[39] Emanuel Celler (1888-1981), Democrat of New York, US Representative (1923-73). See the comprehensive biography for Celler in the "influential biographies" section of the Twenty-fourth Amendment.

[40] James Oliver Eastland (1904-1986), Democrat of Mississippi, US Senator (1941, 1943-78).

[41] A "white primary" is defined strictly as a legislative device utilized by Southern states to keep black Americans from voting. Political parties were given full control over who could vote in their specific party elections, and as such, Democrats, the party that ran much of if not all of the American South, required that only white citizens could vote in party primaries, effectively keeping blacks from voting. A series of US Supreme Court decisions in the early 20th century struck down the white primary as unconstitutional; it was not until 1963, in *Terry v. Adams*, that the entire white primary system was held to be unconstitutional.

[42] Barry Morris Goldwater (1909-1998), Republican of Arizona, US Senator (1953-65, 1969-87).

[43] Everett McKinley Dirksen (1896-1969), Republican of Illinois, US Representative (1933-49), US Senator (1951-69).

[44] Olin DeWitt Talmadge Johnston (1896-1965), Democrat of South Carolina, Member, South Carolina state House of Representatives (1923-24, 1927-30), Governor of South Carolina (1935-39, 1942-45), US Senator (1945-65).

Sources Arranged by Chapter Sections

Debate in Congress

"The Congressional Record: Proceedings and Debates of the 86th Congress, Second Session. Volume 106 – Part 10: June 14, 1960, to June 22, 1960" (Washington: Government Printing Office, 1960), 12551-56, 12558-71.

"The Congressional Record: Proceedings and Debates of the 86th Congress, Second Session. Volume 106 – Part 10: June 14, 1960, to June 22, 1960" (Washington: Government Printing Office, 1960), 12856-59.

Historical Background Documents

Statement of Iredell, 30 July 1788, in Jonathan Elliot, coll., "The Debates in the Several State Conventions, on the Adoption of the Federal Constitution, as Recommended by the General Convention at Philadelphia in 1787, Together with the Journal of the Federal Convention, Luther Martin's Letter, Yates's Minutes, Congressional Opinions, Virginia and Kentucky Resolutions of '98-'99, and Other Illustrations of the Constitution" (Washington: Printed for the Editor; four volumes, 1836), IV:219-20.

Remarks of Rep. John Randolph of Virginia in "The Debates and Proceedings of the Congress of the United States; With an Appendix, Containing Important State Papers and Public Documents, and All the Laws of a Public Nature; With a Copious Index. Seventh Congress – Second Session, Comprising the Period from December 6, 1802, to March 3, 1803, Inclusive. Compiled From Authentic Materials" (Washington: Printed and Published by Gales and Seaton, 1851), 498-99.

"Granting Representation in the Electoral College to the District of Columbia. May 31, 1960. -Referred to the House Calendar and ordered to be printed," House Report 1698, 86th Congress, 2nd Session (1960), 1-4.

"President Kennedy's Statement," *The Washington Post*, 30 March 1961, A1.

Original Primary Documents

"Suffrage Bill to Get Clear Path," *The Washington Post*, 9 June 1960, A1.

"Suffrage for Capital Approved by House," *The New York Times*, 15 June 1960, 1, 33.

"Suffrage Bill Passed by Senate," *The Washington Post*, 17 June 1960, A1.

"Presidential Vote for District Wins, Kansas Beating Ohio as 38th State," *The Washington Post*, 30 March 1961, A1, A20.

Supreme Court Cases

Hepburn & Dundas v. Ellzey (2 Cranch {6 US} 445 {1805}).
"Hepburn and Dundas v. Ellzey" in John M. Dillon, ed., "John Marshall: Complete Constitutional Decisions" (Chicago: Callaghan & Company, 1903), 48-50; "The Constitutionality of the 1940 Extension of Diversity Jurisdiction," *The Yale Law Journal*, LV:3 (April 1946), 600-03.

Loughborough v. Blake (5 Wheaton {18 U,S. 317 {1820}).
"The Writings of John Marshall, Late Chief Justice of the United States, Upon the Federal Constitution" (Washington, DC: William H. Morrison, 1890), 211-17; Magoon, Charles, "Reports on the Law of Civil Government in Territory Subject to Military Occupation by the Military Forces of the United States. Submitted to Hon. Elihu Root, Secretary of War, by Charles E. Magoon, Law Officer, Bureau of Insular Affairs, War Department" (Washington: Government Printing Office, 1902), 91-92.

National Mutual Insurance Co. v. Tidewater Transfer Co., Inc. (337 US 582 {1949}).
Kurland, Philip B., "Mr. Justice Frankfurter, the Supreme Court and the Erie Doctrine in Diversity Cases," *The Yale Law Journal*, LXVII:2 (December 1957), 187-218; "National Mutual Insurance Co. v. Tidewater Transfer Co., Inc." in "Casenote Legal Briefs: Federal Courts" (New York: Aspne Publishers, 2002), 19.

Who's Who

Francis Higbee Case (1896-1962)
deFuria, Guy G., "The McCarthy Censure Case: Some Legal Aspects," *American Bar Association Journal*, XLII:4 (April 1956), 330; "Case, Francis Higbee," official congressional biography, online at http://bioguide.congress.gov/scripts/biodisplay.pl?index=C000221; Chenoweth, Richard Rollin, "Francis Case: A Political Biography" (Ph.D. dissertation, The University of Nebraska at Lincoln, 1977), 4-5; Lamport, Nancy Lee, "Francis Case: His Pioneer Background, Indian Legislation and Missouri River Construction" (Master's thesis, University of South Dakota, 1972); Pressler, Larry, "Francis H. Case" in "US Senators from the Prairie" (Vermillion, South Dakota: Dakota Press, 1982), 140-49; "Sen. Francis H. Case, In Congress 25 Years," *The Washington Post*, 23 June 1962, C4; "[Editorial:] Francis H. Case," *The Washington Post*, 23 June 1962, A10.

Kenneth Barnard Keating (1900-1975)
"Keating, Kenneth Barnard" official congressional biography, online at http://bioguide.congress.gov/scripts/biodisplay. pl?index=K000036; Giannottasio, Gerard, "The Judgeship of Kenneth B. Keating and the Limits of Judicial Reform" (Ph.D. dissertation, Sate University of New York at Stony Brook, 1994); Paterson, Thomas G., "The Historian as Detective: Senator Kenneth Keating, the Missiles in Cuba, and His Mysterious Sources," *Diplomatic History*, XI (Winter 1987), 67-70; Hailey, Jean B., "Kenneth B. Keating Dies at 74," *The Washington Post*, 6 May 1975, C6; Whitman, Alden, "Keating Dies at 74; Envoy, Ex-Senator," *The New York Times*, 6 May 1975, 1, 32.

Further Reading

Franchino, Roy P., "The Constitutionality of Home Rule and National Representation for the District of Columbia," *The Georgetown Law Journal*, XLVI:2 (Winter 1957-58), 207-59.

Frankel, Lawrence M., "National Representation for the District of Columbia: A Legislative Solution," *University of Pennsylvania Law Review*, CXXXIX (1991), 1659-1709.

McMurtry, Virginia A., *A Legislative History of the 23rd Amendment* (Washington, DC: Library of Congress, Congressional Research Service, 1977).

Raskin, Jamin B., "The Constitutional Importance of the District of Columbia," *American University Law Review*, (1999), 591-93.

_____, "Is This America? The District of Columbia and the Right to Vote," *Harvard Civil Rights-Civil Liberties Law Review*, XXXIV:1 (Winter 1999), 39.

Rosenthal, Albert J., "The Constitution, Congress, and Presidential Elections," *Michigan Law Review*, LXVII:1 (November 1968), 1-38.

Schrag, Philip G., "The Future of District of Columbia Home Rule," *Catholic University Law Review*, XXXIX:2 (Winter 1990), 311-71.

Vile, John R., *Encyclopedia of Constitutional Amendments, Proposed Amendments, and Amending Issues, 1789-2015,* 4th ed. (Santa Barbara, CA: ABC-CLIO, 2015).

Vose, Clement, "When District of Columbia Representation Collides with the Constitutional Amendment Institution," *Publius*, IX:1 (Winter 1978), 105-25.

AMERICA AT THAT TIME . . .

Although the material in this section may not be directly related to the adoption of the Twenty-third Amendment, it offers valuable insight into what was happening in America at the time the Amendment was adopted. Modeled after Grey House Publishing's Working American *series, whose author, Scott Derks, is responsible for its content, it includes a Historical Snapshot, Selected Prices, significant quotations, newspaper and magazine clips to give a sense of what was on the minds of Americans, and how it may have impacted the amendment process.*

HISTORICAL SNAPSHOT

1961

- President Kennedy launched an exercise campaign urging all Americans to be more fit

- The Interstate Commerce Commission banned segregation on all interstate facilities

- The Civil War Centennial celebration began

- The minimum wage rose from $1.00 to $1.25

- Civil Defense officials distributed 22 million copies of the pamphlet *Family Fallout Shelter*

- FCC Chairman Newton Minow called television "a vast wasteland" during a speech at the National Association of Broadcasters

- President Kennedy appointed a committee to study the status of women

- The DNA genetic code was broken

- A university poll reported that 72 percent of elementary and high school teachers approved of corporal punishment as a disciplinary measure

- Clark Gable died at the conclusion of filming *The Misfits*

- Robert Zimmerman, known as Bob Dylan, began singing in Greenwich Village nightclubs; his first recording opportunity was as a backup harmonica player

- Ray Kroc borrowed $2.7 million to buy out the McDonald Brothers and began the McDonald's empire

- The IBM Selectric typewriter was introduced

- Four thousand servicemen were sent to Vietnam as advisors

- The words Peace Corps, high rise, New Frontier, soul, zonked, and new wave all entered the language

- A poll of 16- to 21-year-old girls indicated that almost all expected to be married by age 22 and most wanted four children

Consumer Expenditures and Income, Urban Places in the Western Region, 1960–61, *Bureau of Labor Statistics*:

"Urban families in the Western region spent an average of $5,971 for current annual living expenses in 1960–61. In addition, they made gifts and contributions averaging $324, put $334 into various types of life insurance and retirement funds, paid $844 in income and other personal taxes, and showed savings of $157, on the average, through a net increase in assets over liabilities. . . Families enjoyed a substantial rise in incomes, both before and after taxes, between 1950, when the Bureau conducted its previous nationwide survey, and 1960–61. Annual income after taxes rose by about 62 percent to an average of $6,324. Consumer units increased their spending for current consumption by only 52 percent, however. With this widened margin between their incomes and expenditures, families were able to increase their gifts and contributions, as well as personal insurance, and to set aside more for savings than in 1950. The amount classified as going into personal insurance was almost equally divided between various types of life insurance and social security and other public and private retirement funds.

Dollar expenditures were higher in 1960–61 than in 1950 in all major categories of family expenses, but there were significant shifts in the proportion of total current living expenses going for different purposes. The relative importance of expenditures for food and beverages declined from 30.0 percent in 1950 to 25.6 percent in 1960–61. The declines continued trends shown by the Bureau's surveys since the early 1900s. Spending for shelter, fuel, light, etc., by homeowners and renters moved in the opposite direction, increasing from 14.9 percent of total consumption expenditures in 1950 to 17.8 percent in 1960–61. However, the combined share for the three basic categories of family expense—food, clothing, and shelter—decreased over the decade between surveys from 56 to 53 percent. Expenditures for the purchase and operation of automobiles were almost unchanged over the period, although the proportion of families owning cars rose from 70 percent in 1950 to 80 percent in 1960–61."

"There should be no misunderstanding of our position: We shall render the Cuban people and their government all necessary assistance. . . We are sincerely interested in a relaxation of international tension, but, if others aggravate it, we shall reply in full measure."

—Soviet Union Premier Nikita Khrushchev, April 18, 1961

Speech: Newly appointed FCC Chairman Newton Minow, March 9, 1961, at the National Association of Broadcasters:

"I invite you to sit in front of your television set when your station (or network) goes on the air and stay there without a book, magazine, newspaper, profit-and-loss sheet, or ratings book to distract you—and keep your eyes glued to that set until the station signs off. I can assure you that you will observe a vast wasteland. You will see a procession of game shows, violence, audience participation shows, formula comedies about totally unbelievable families, blood and thunder, mayhem, violence, sadism, murder, Western bad men, Western good men, private eyes, gangsters, more violence, cartoons, and—endlessly—commercials, many screaming, cajoling, and offending, and most of all, boredom. True, you will see a few things you enjoy, but they will be very, very, few, and if you think I exaggerate, try it. Is there one person in this room who claims that broadcasting can't do better? Is there one network president in this room who claims he can't do better? Why is so much of television bad? We need imagination in programming, not sterility; creativity, not imitation; experimentation, not conformity; excellence, not mediocrity."

"Working Girls Beat Living Cost," *San Francisco Examiner*, March 2, 1961:

"The working girl kept a skip and a jump ahead of the rise in the cost of living last year. In fact, she received the equivalent of an extra week's pay—enough to buy one good suit.

John Dana of the Department of Labor disclosed yesterday that the average office girl received a 4.3 percent raise in salary while the cost of living was going up 1.6 percent. This gave her a 1.9 percent increase in real earnings after allowing for high prices sand taxes.

Her boyfriend received a somewhat smaller percentage increase, but about the same amount of cash if he worked the year 'round. One analyst remarked that the lower increase for the boyfriend was the more important statistic. The analyst, a woman, explained: 'After all, how is the poor working girl going to get married if her boyfriend can't earn more money?'

Dana, the department's assistant to the Regional Director of Labor Statistics, said local stenographers, with an average weekly salary of $84.00, have received a 47.3 percent boost in wages since January, 1952. In the same period, the cost of living has risen 18.5 percent, giving her a net increase in real spendable earnings of 21.5 percent.

The weekly salaries of women office workers ranged from an average $60.50 for file clerks to $96.50 for secretaries. The report showed that the average woman elevator operator receives $2.05 an hour, $0.22 more than the average male elevator operator, while the average woman janitor or cleaner received $2.08, $0.07 less than the male janitor. In most skilled occupations studied, men averaged more than $3.10 an hour, with tool and dye makers drawing $3.53, carpenters $3.22, and painters $3.15."

"A Word to Wives, by JFK's Doc," *San Francisco Examiner*, June 16, 1961. "Dr. Janet Travell, President Kennedy's physician,' today offered some rules for housewives":

"Scramble your work. Don't spend all of one day cleaning, another day doing laundry, and a third ironing. That way you use some muscles too much, others not enough.

Cultivate a rhythmic pattern. Don't hurry; don't jerk the movements. Just do your housework as if you're doing a modern dance.

Take short rests at frequent intervals.

Don't tolerate uncomfortable chairs or too-low sinks.

Counteract housework with an entirely different kind of muscle movement, a variety of exercises."

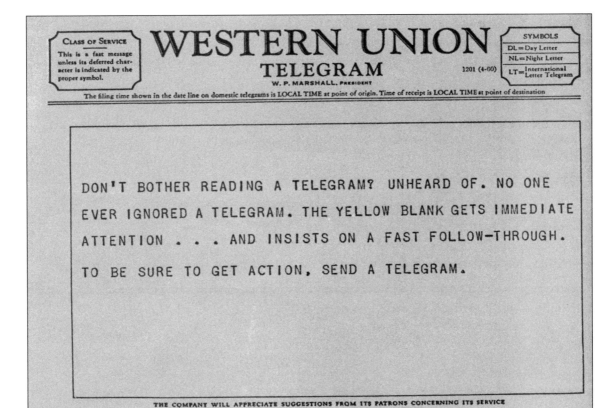

911

"Your Life Easily May Depend on How Well You Are Prepared, If an ATTACK Comes," by John D. Hacket, *The Evening Sun*, Baltimore, Maryland, August 1961:

Baltimore is a "critical target" for an enemy bomb.

It is the sixth-largest United States city, a principal railroad hub with the fourth-largest ocean port. The largest single steel mill, a major missile factory and a modern jet airport are next-door.

The area is a major production center for steel, copper, aluminum, chemicals, ships, missiles, electronics, automobiles, apparel, food and research.

Some 939,000 people live in Baltimore.

You are one of them. If the enemy dropped an H-bomb in this area right now—could you come out alive . . . ?

CONELRAD May Say: EVACUATE

There are 115 air raid sirens in Baltimore today.

They work.

They are checked out once a month by telephone company technicians.

The entire Baltimore area civil defense communications network, which includes police, fire, military, rescue, hospitals, factory and others, is tested every Monday.

These sirens are a part of the nationwide Civil Defense Warning System. They are set off only in an emergency. (However, these sirens do scream once a year in Baltimore, on "Operation Alert" day. They sounded last April. . . .)

Possible Attack

The ALERT signal, the STEADY BLAST for three to five minutes, blares out only when the military and CD people feel planes or missiles are headed for the United States.

It means—PROBABLE ATTACK.

What is the other signal?

Sirens give off a WARBLING sound. It goes up and down, up and down, up and down in tone.

It is the UNDER ATTACK warning.

It screams for three minutes, then stops.

It means the Baltimore area is going to get it, but good—and soon, maybe in minutes.

The first Black employee of the company, Katie Fuller, described the early days of her employment in 1961:

"I didn't know I was the only colored person. I thought they had hired a bunch of them, you know. And when I got out there—nobody but me and the good Lord knows what I went through. But I just pray. I asked God to help me. I said: 'Help me Jesus, I got to work somewhere…'

And they would have to come down this certain aisle going out. See, they would be getting off, while we would still be working. They'd get off at 3:10, and we'd be working almost to 4:20. And they come through there hollering 'Nigger,' and talking all kind of ugly talk. Cursing. And I would look over to the side, to the space next to me. And I thought these people are crazy. And I'd look at 'em and I would laugh. I'd kinda smile. It took a whole lot out of me, you know. And I never worked with anybody like this before. A whole plant of people in here were—I don't know how to describe it. Devil Action."

Year	Value of One Dollar in 2016 US Dollars
1958	$8.35
1959	$8.30
1960	$8.16
1961	$8.07
1962	$7.99
1963	$7.89

Selected Prices

Bluebrook Margarine, per Pound	$0.15
Boy's Life Magazine, Monthly	$0.25
Chap-et Lip Balm	$0.35
Chrysler Newport Automobile	$2,964.00
Daisey BB Gun	$12.98
Ethan Allen Desk, Four-Drawer	$85.60
Flintstones Child's Feeding Set	$1.99
Kelvinator Air Conditioner	$169.00
Kodak Brownie Super 27 Camera	$22.00
Kraft Miracle Whip Salad Dressing, Quart	$0.43
Little Star Dress for Teens	$5.00
Magnavox Broadway Stereo Theater	$495.00
Magna-Lite Shop Light	$6.95
McGregor Meteor Slacks	$10.00
Pakula Necklace	$3.00
Pioneer Ebonetts Kitchen Gloves	$0.98
RCA Victor Tape Recorder, Reel-to-Reel	$99.95
Scott Tissues, Two Packages of 400	$0.39

1961

James Meredith became the first Black student to enroll at the University of Mississippi; President John Kennedy was forced to send 5,000 federal troops to control the rioting.

The National Indian Youth Council was organized to encourage greater self-sufficiency and autonomy.

Investigators in the U.S. Adirondacks confirmed that acid rain was killing some animal species living in and around the lakes.

President John Kennedy appointed a special President's Panel on Mental Retardation.

The Hockey Hall of Fame opened in Toronto.

The Twenty-fourth Amendment

Chapter 15

Eighty-seventh Congress of the United States of America

AT THE SECOND SESSION

*Begun and held at the City of Washington on Wednesday, the tenth day of January,
one thousand nine hundred and sixty-two*

Joint Resolution

Proposing an amendment to the Constitution of the United States relating to the
qualifications of electors.

*Resolved by the Senate and House of Representatives of the
United States of America in Congress assembled,* That the following
article is hereby proposed as an amendment to the Constitution of the
United States, which shall be valid to all intents and purposes as part
of the Constitution only if ratified by the legislatures of three-fourths
of the several States within seven years from the date of its submission by the Congress:

"ARTICLE —

"SECTION 1. The right of citizens of the United States to vote in
any primary or other election for President or Vice President, for
electors for President or Vice President, or for Senator or Representative in Congress, shall not be denied or abridged by the United States
or any State by reason of failure to pay any poll tax or other tax.

"SEC. 2. The Congress shall have power to enforce this article by
appropriate legislation."

Speaker of the House of Representatives.

*Vice President of the United States and
President of the Senate pro tempore*

Proposed in Congress:	**27 August 1962**
Sent to States:	**27 August 1962**
Ratified:	**23 January 1964**

Chapter 15

THE TWENTY-FOURTH AMENDMENT

Section 1.
The right of citizens of the United States to vote in any primary or other election for President or Vice President, for electors for President or Vice President, or for Senator or Representative in Congress, shall not be denied or abridged by the United States or any State by reason of failure to pay poll tax or other tax.

Section 2.
The Congress shall have power to enforce this article by appropriate legislation.

Brief Summary

The Twenty-fourth Amendment abolished the use of poll taxes in federal elections. In the post-Civil War era, some states made it difficult, if not virtually impossible, for African Americans to vote. One obstacle was the poll tax – a fee that the voter had to pay to register to vote. Such taxes not only kept African American voters away from the polls but also acted as a barrier to poor whites, Native Americans, and even some women. The Supreme Court later held that the amendment applied to elections at all levels of government.

Timeline

1937	The Supreme Court, in *Breedlove v. Suttles*, upholds the imposition of poll taxes.
1939	California representative Lee E. Geyer introduces the first of a series of bills to abolish the poll tax.
October 1942	The Geyer bill passes in the House but is filibustered in the US Senate.
27 March 1962	The Twenty-fourth Amendment passes in the US House of Representatives.
27 August 1962	The Twenty-fourth Amendment passes in the US Senate.

Footnotes, Sources and Further Reading for this chapter appears on page 967

23 January 1964   The Twenty-fourth Amendment is ratified when South Dakota becomes the thirty-eighth state to ratify it. Mississippi rejected the amendment, and eight additional states did not ratify it.

6 August 1965   The Voting Rights Act of 1965 becomes effective.

Introduction

A poll tax might sound like a strange law from a far away time. But until the middle of the 20th century, it meant that the equivalent of $1.50-$2.00 per year was levied on every male adult, and was usually used for educational in the states that originally levied the tax. The Founding Fathers felt that a poll tax, also called a "capitation tax," was good, and actually placed language in the US Constitution, Article I, Section 9, giving Congress the right – never used to this day – to levy a poll tax on the American people based on the US Census apportionment figures. Today, historians view the poll tax merely as a small fee to vote. Perhaps today, this might be something people would support – especially if the tax was to be used for education.

But the poll tax was, in fact, one more way that segregationists and racists kept blacks and others from voting. States, all in the South, used the poll tax in conjunction with literacy tests and other methods to keep their black voting population down. On the surface, it was tied to land and/or property ownership. If one did not own land, one had to pay a fee – a poll tax – or take a literacy test. Historian Frank B. Williams, Jr., wrote in 1952, "The poll tax as a prerequisite for voting was effectively adopted by most of the southern states in the last decade of the nineteenth century and the early years of the twentieth."[1] In fact, we know now that the poll tax was first instituted in the years following the end of the American Civil War when whites, who had controlled the government in the southern states during the war, lost some of their power when blacks were freed , and they plotted their return to power by instituting measures that would keep the blacks from voting.

Sidney Robert Crawford, in a 1944 thesis, gives further explanation on how the poll tax originated, "Contrary to current impression among many Americans, the poll, capitation, or head tax did not originate as a tax on voting. Moreover, it has been utilized as a source of revenue and has been levied on person as such from the earliest historical times. One of the very early forms taken by the poll tax was 'the requirement that citizens render personal service to the social organization of which they were members. Poll taxes also appeared in ancient times as metamorphosed from voluntary or gift tribute. The earliest Hellenic historiographers record that Darius, the son of Hystapes, was the first in the vast empire of ancient Persia to transform this voluntary or gift tribute into a poll tax. In this instance, it as to be paid partly money and partly in kind."[2]

In the United States, poll taxes were instituted as a restriction of the suffrage to anyone but men who owned property. Oliver Chitwood, in his 1931 history of colonial America, explained that "the right to vote was not extended to all freemen at any time except in a very few colonies...The suffrage as restricted by property, religious, and other qualifications."[3] So that more people could be brought into the orbit of voting for local, state, and federal candidates for office, certain northern states allowed those who did not fall into these specific categories to vote – *if they paid a poll tax*. In fact, this went so well that in 1784, a year after the American Revolution ended, New Hampshire removed all property qualifications for voting and instead instituted an across-the-board poll tax for all citizens. Other states followed; in 1790, South Carolina amended its state constitution which did away with a property or religious voting qualification and instituted a poll tax. These remained in force for many years; it was not until Andrew Jackson pushed for universal suffrage for all white men, and states, to make the suffrage available to people based not on their property or monetary value, that the cost of a poll tax was brought up. By the time of the Civil War, only seven states had retained a poll tax.

Reconstruction, instituted at the end of the Civil War, brought an end to this movement. The Congress, in a rough mood to punish the Southern states, pushed first for any southern state to agree to the Thirteenth and Fourteenth Amendments before they could re-enter the Union, and, after that, freed blacks and so-called "carpetbaggers" (Northern anti-slavery men who went South after the war to look for fame and fortune, carrying these belongings in bags allegedly made of carpet) took power together and passed laws barring former Confederates from voting. Starting in 1870, the Republicans in the US Congress enacted a series of equally harsh measures, beginning with the Enforcement Acts, which were back-up mechanisms for the Thirteenth and Fourteenth Amendments, and gave the US government the power to intervene in any state that denied the right to vote based on race, color, or previous condition of servitude. When radical white groups formed into the Ku Klux Klan to harass blacks, the Congress enacted the Ku Klux Klan Act of 1871, which allowed the President to suspend the writ of habeas corpus if any election was threatened by such groups. The end of Reconstruction in 1877 allowed whites to once again take power, dislodging the carpetbag governments and ending the rights of blacks to vote. Because these new governments could not fight the power of the US government, they established a wide range of laws to go around the Enforcement Acts and the Ku Klux Klan Act. Such actions, some of which have been listed already, included the white primary, the poll tax, in land ownership the "grandfather clause," and other actions.

Democrats who, by 1880 were in firm control of all of the former Conference states, were not shy about their program of excluding blacks from voting and other facet of life in their areas. The US government in general, and the US Supreme Court in particular, did their utmost to make sure that the rights of blacks to vote were not protected. In *The Civil Rights Cases* (109 US 3), decided 15 October 1883, the court struck down the 1875 Civil Rights Act, which had strengthened the Thirteenth and Fourteenth Amendments through government action to protect blacks in areas of public accommodations, as unconstitutional. Justice Joseph Bradley, writing for the majority, wrote, "On the whole we are of opinion that no countenance of authority for the passage of the law in question can be found in either the Thirteenth or Fourteenth Amendment of the Constitution; and no other ground of authority for its passage being suggested, it must necessarily be declared void, at least so far as its operation in the several States is concerned."[4] Although this decision did not give government protection to blacks in public accommodations – restaurants, hotels, etc. – the southern states used the decision to institute a wide range of policies designed to go around the Thirteenth and Fourteenth Amendments. Within 30 years of the end of the Civil War, blacks had as few rights as they had had prior to the war, except that they were not slaves. They were, however, citizens without rights.

In 1900, Senator John T. Morgan of Alabama, in defending his section, and, by definition, the number of laws established in the southern states to deny blacks the right to vote, said in a speech on the floor of the US Senate,

"In physical, mental, social, inventive, religious, and ruling power the African race holds the lowest place...and it is no idle boast that the white man holds the highest place. To force this lowest stratum into a position of equality with the highest is only to clog the progress of all mankind in its march...toward the highest places of human aspiration...It is a vain effort and is fatal to the spirit and success of free government to attempt to use its true principles as a means of disturbance of the natural conditions of the races of the human family and to reestablish them on the mere theoretical basis, which is not true, that in political power all men must be equal in order to secure the greatest happiness to the greatest number [of people]...No great body of white people in the world could be expected to quietly accept a situation so distressing and demoralizing as is created by negro suffrage in the South. It is a thorn in the flesh, and will irritate and rankle in the body politic until it is removed as a factor in government. It has been one unbroken line of political, social, and industrial obstruction to progress and a constant disturbance of the place in a vast region of the United States...The people of the South are justified, and it would be inexcusable if they failed, by every constitutional measure in their power to preserve in their own hands the power of government in their own states, they being responsible for their welfare, their business interests, and the interests of civilization."[5]

For the white power structure in the Southern states, dominated by the Democratic Party, the poll tax was just one more instrument in a bag of tricks used to make sure that blacks did not vote. If they could not be scared away from the polls, if they could not be kept away through the use of the so-called "white primary," in which only those persons who were "qualified" by the Democratic Party would be allowed to vote in party primaries, then the former Confederate states could use a harsh tax on these same people to finally send them a message: we do not want you to vote, period. Future US Senator Carter Glass, Democrat of Virginia, at one time, before he became a major political figure in his state, told the Virginia Convention of his plan to keep black voters from the polls: "By fraud, no; by discrimination yes. But it will be discrimination within the letter of the law... Discrimination! Why, that is precisely what we propose; that, exactly, is what this convention was elected for-to discriminate to the very extremity of permissible action under the limitation of the Federal Constitution, with a view to the elimination of every Negro voter who can be gotten rid of, legally, without materially impairing the numerical strength of the white electorate...It is a fine discrimination, indeed, that we have practiced in the fabrication of this plan."[6]

By the 1920s and 1930s, as the depression took hold of the nation's economy, many whites were impacted by poll tax requirements and, unable to pay the $1 or $2 tax, were struck off the voting rolls. Democrats viewed with alarm the growing number of their own constituents who could not vote, even as the numbers of black voters likewise continued to go down. Historian William M. Brewer noted in 1944, "Examination of statistics revealed an established disenfranchisement of 64% of the height adult voters in the poll-tax States and in every one of these jurisdictions more whites than colored people were barred by this tax from voting." In 1939, a number of leading Southerners from all walks of life formed the Southern Policies Committee to call for the abolition of the poll tax – again, because it was now impacting whites, where it had not before.[7] The National Committee to Abolish the Poll-Tax supplied the following statistics for the 1942 midterm elections in the Southern states with a poll tax at that time:

States	Whites Disenfranchised	Blacks Disenfranchised	Total
Alabama	815,000	685,000	1,500,000
Arkansas	730,000	320,000	1,030,000
Georgia	980,000	740,000	1,720,000
Mississippi	490,000	755,000	1,245,000
South Carolina	650,000	570,000	1,220,000
Texas	2,220,000	570,000	2,790,000
Virginia	935,000	430,000	1,365,000
Total	6,820,000	4,070,000	10,890,000[8]

However, even while Franklin D. Roosevelt was in the White House (followed by fellow liberal Harry S Truman), and the Democrats had near-veto control of both houses of Congress from 1933 until 1953 (barring two years), neither administration pushed to get the poll tax overturned.

After the end of the Second World War, the "politics" of the poll tax were such that each major political party feared what might happen if the poll tax were done away with. Historians Sarah A. Binde and Steven S. Smith wrote, "A more partisan overlay on the issue was the implication of new African-American voters for the parties. Some Democrats feared of threatened that the new voters would be Republican in the context of southern politics; some Republican feared that the new voters would be New Deal Democrats." They continued, "The poll tax fights illustrate the difficulty of interpreting votes on cloture [in the US Senate]. Bills banning poll taxes died under filibusters in 1942, 1944, and 1946. Only in 1946 did the cloture motion related to the bill garner majority support... But in both 1942 and 1944 at least some contemporary observers believed that the Senate majority would have voted for the bill if a direct vote on the bill had occurred. In 1942, *The New York Times* reported that some Democrats hid behind the filibuster – they would vote for a bill if a vote occurred by preferred not to 'deliver the Democratic South into the hands of the Republican Party' by reducing barriers to voting by African Americans."[9]

What changed to make the situation different? The election of one man: Spessard L. Holland of Florida. During service in the Florida state Senate, then as Governor of the Sunshine state, and then in the US Senate (1946-71), Holland, despite being against the civil rights movement as a whole, felt that the poll tax harmed Florida citizens, black and white. In his state service, he helped to get the poll tax banned in Florida. Once in the US Senate, Holland continually introduced language for a proposed constitutional amendment ending the poll tax in federal elections, because, as Holland continually said, he believed that a mere congressional statue – a law, nothing more – was not "constitutional enough" to overcome original language in the US Constitution that might be found by the courts to allow for such a tax. A constitutional amendment, Holland argued, could not be struck down by the courts.

At the same time that Holland was working in Florida, and then in the US Senate, to gain support for a constitutional amendment, others were working on the issue as well. Holland's fellow Democrat, Rep. Emanuel Celler of New York, was also pushing for language in a proposed constitutional amendment. Celler, however, worked on a different track: during the 1950s, he had combined language giving the District of Columbia voting rights in Congress, as well as electoral votes, with an abolition of the poll tax. Believing that both measures improved voting and electoral strength, Celler demanded an all-incorporated amendment addressing both issues. However, Celler and others, including other Democrats in the House and many Republicans, hit a rather imposing stonewall: Southern Democrats in the US Senate, some of whom had built up years of seniority and power in the Congress' upper body, did their utmost, even employing the filibuster, to fight any attempt to end the poll tax. So, by 1960, it was apparent that those who wanted both issues addressed by a constitutional amendment could not have both of them done at the same time – it was either voting rights for the District of Columbia or nothing. Holland proposed a standalone amendment for the District of Columbia, which eventually became the Twenty-third Amendment, passed by Congress in 1960 and ratified in 1961.

By 1962, enough of the Southern Democrats in the US Senate who had halted progress to end the poll tax had either died or retired, replaced by fellow Democrats who were not as wholly against it as had been their previous seat holders, or by Republicans who wanted to end the poll tax altogether (there were far fewer in the latter group). This was before the GOP took almost complete control of the seats from southern states in the US Senate.

Working with Celler and others, Holland drafted his standalone amendment in 1962. With Holland's support, and the lack of opposition from Southern Democrats, the amendment passed the Senate with barely any debate on 27 March 1962. (In a rather strange motion, Holland's proposed amendment was "attached" to a bill that established Alexander Hamilton's home as a national monument. When Holland attached the amendment, Senator Richard Russell, Democrat of Georgia, objected and made a point of order questioning the constitutionality of the action. Senator Mike Mansfield introduced a motion to table Russell's point of order, which the Senate approved, 58 to 34. The Senate then voted for the Holland language, 77 to 16.)

One criticism from supporters of the movement to end the poll tax was that the amendment language only ended the use of the tax in federal elections, not state or local ones. During the House debate, which was far more involved – and rancorous – than that in the Senate, Rep. John V. Lindsay, Republican of New York, stated, "If we're going to have a constitutional amendment, let's have a meaningful one." He ultimately voted for the amendment, but his remarks were ignored by Celler, who, as the chairman of the House Committee on the Judiciary, was the floor leader for the amendment language. Having passed the US Senate, on 27 August 1962, the anti-poll tax amendment passed the House, 295 to 86, and the amendment was sent on to the states for ratification. On 23 January 1964, when South Dakota ratified it, it received the requisite number of states – 38 – and it was declared as the Twenty-fourth Amendment. Historians Bruce Ackerman and Jennifer Nou wrote in 2009, "Once Congress proposed the Twenty-fourth Amendment in August 1962, its ratification in the states was propelled forward by the rising tide of support for the civil rights movement. With blinding speed, Senator Holland's quixotic struggle over the decades had suddenly become a relatively uncontroversialif painfully inadequate-response to the country's racial and economic problems. Within the short span of sixteen months, the amendment gained the approval of thirty-eight states. When the Secretary of State declared its formal reception into the constitutional canon, his announcement was greeted with a yawn from the general public. Rather than celebrating the moment of formal canonization, Americans were on the threshold of a modern constitutional revolution marked by presidential electoral mandates, landmark statutes, and judicial super precedents."[10]

However, because the amendment only covered federal elections, the five states where the poll tax was still used broke their elections into federal and local. In 1965, the Congress sought to do away with this loophole: it passed an anti-poll tax stipulation in the landmark Voting Rights Act of 1965. However, this only had the backing of courts if it was not struck down as unconstitutional. The US Supreme Court would have to make a final judgment on this matter. It took an additional year, but in 1966, the US Supreme Court held in *Harper v. Virginia Board of Elections* that any poll tax violated the Equal Protection Clause of the US Constitution, and struck them down across the country. The end had come for the poll tax, which was now illegal in every state, every county, and every locality.

In recent years, the Supreme Court has heard a variety of cases that bear on an individual's right to vote. In *Burdick v. Takushi* (504 U.S. 428 {1992}), the Court held that Hawaii's prohibition against write-in votes did not violate the petitioner's rights under the First and Fourteenth Amendments and that the prohibition was consistent with the state's right to conduct elections in an orderly fashion. Further, the Court has ruled on the contentious issue of voter identification in the states. Various states have contended that requiring voters to present identification, including picture IDs, is a reasonable step to prevent voter fraud and ensure orderly elections, and they have passed laws to achieve that end. Opponents of voter ID laws argue that they too often discriminate against minorities, the elderly, and the poor, who often lack the resources to procure the necessary identification, and on this basis opponents see picture IDs as a kind of "poll tax" in violation of the Twenty-fourth Amendment. The Court took up this issue in *Crawford v. Marion City Election Board* (553 U.S. 181 {2008}), holding that the voter ID law in Indiana advanced a legitimate state interest in preventing voter fraud.

By 2016 the issue had not dissipated, and challenges to voter ID laws arose in various state courts and US Circuit Courts of Appeals. In 2014 and again in 2016, the Supreme Court declined to block implementation of a strict voter ID law in Texas. However, in 2016, a deadlocked Court let stand a lower court order blocking enforcement of a restrictive North Carolina voter ID law that opponents argued restricted the voting rights of African Americans. In that case, *North Carolina Conference of the NAACP et al. v. McCrory et al.* (2016), the Fourth Circuit Court of Appeals remarked: "But the totality of the circumstances-North Carolina's history of voting discrimination; the surge in African American voting; the legislature's knowledge that African Americans voting translated into support for one party; and the swift elimination of the tools African Americans had used to vote and imposition of a new barrier at the first opportunity to do so-cumulatively and unmistakably reveal that the General Assembly used [the law] to entrench itself. It did so by targeting voters who, based on race, were unlikely to vote for the majority party. Even if done for partisan ends, that constituted racial discrimination."[11]

Other issues that have arisen in the court system involve the right, or lack thereof, of convicted felons, including tax felons, to vote; the legitimacy of early voting procedures; the inadequacy of employers' time-off provisions allowing people to leave work to vote (the "time tax"); and state residency requirements, any one of which could impose economic hardships on voters and could thus be construed as akin to an unconstitutional "poll tax."

Debate in Congress

The debate over the constitutional amendment in the US Senate in March 1962, was rather short, involving long speeches mostly by the Senate sponsor of the proposed amendment, Senator Spessard Holland of Florida, with other senators only peppering him with queries. The real fireworks came during the House debate, which occurred five months later in August 1962.

Here, Holland attaches his proposed amendment to a resolution honoring the first Secretary of the Treasury, Alexander Hamilton, 27 March 1962.

THE ALEXANDER HAMILTON NATIONAL MONUMENT – AMENDMENT TO THE CONSTITUTION DEALING WITH POLL TAXES

The Senate resumed the consideration of the joint resolution (S.J. Res. 29) providing for the establishing of the former dwelling house of Alexander Hamilton as a national monument.

Mr. MANSFIELD.[12] Mr. President, what is the pending question?

The VICE PRESIDENT. The question is on agreeing to the amendment of the Senator from Florida [Mr. HOLLAND], striking out all after the resolving clause, as amended, of Senate Joint Resolution 29, and inserting in lieu thereof certain other words.

Mr. MANSFIELD. This is a proposed constitutional amendment seeking to abolish the poll tax in the several States, is it?

The VICE PRESIDENT. It is a proposed constitutional amendment.

Mr. HOLLAND rose.

Mr. RUSSELL.[13] Mr. Pre, I suggest the absence of a quorum.

Mr. HOLLAND. Mr. President, I believe I have the floor.

The VICE PRESIDENT. The Senator from Florida has not yet been recognized; he has not yet addressed the Chair.

Mr. HOLLAND. Mr. President, I did not get here...

Mr. RUSSELL. Mr. President...

The VICE PRESIDENT. Does the Senator from Georgia yield?

Mr. RUSSELL. Yes, Mr. President; I yield to the Senator from Florida.

Mr. HOLLAND. Mr. President, I did not get here in time to consult with the majority leader and the Senator from Georgia. Of course I am willing to have whatever procedure they see fit to propose followed in connection with the things we understood will happen today.

Mr. MANSFIELD. Mr. President, will the Senator from Florida seek recognition?

Mr. HOLLAND. I have already been recognized.

The VICE PRESIDENT. No; the Chair did not hear the Senator from Florida address the Chair first. The Senator from Georgia first addressed the Chair and the Senator from Georgia has been recognized.

Mr. RUSSELL. Mr. President, inasmuch as this question has arisen, let me say that I understood the Senator from Montana to state, last evening, just before the recess was taken, that the order of business today would be that the Senator from Florida would offer his amendment and would address himself to it, and that then the Senator from Georgia would have an opportunity to make a point of order.

I came here prepared to follow that procedure, as outlined by the majority leader. I do not always agree with the positions taken on various issues on the floor of the Senate by the majority leader, but in order to retain my standing in the Democratic Party, I support him on matters of procedure. [Laughter.]

Mr. HOLLAND. Mr. President, will the Senator from Georgia yield?

Mr. RUSSELL. Yes, I yield.

Mr. HOLLAND. I am very happy to follow any course of action which will be satisfactory to the majority leader and to the Senator from Georgia. I was simply seeking advice as to whether the two distinguished Senators had agreed on a course of action. I am perfectly willing to follow the course which has been suggested by the Senator from Georgia.

[...]

Mr. HOLLAND. Mr. President, I appreciate the fact that after considerable delay the Senate is about to take up the amendment which I sent to desk and offered yesterday afternoon. I understand that amendment is now the pending question. Am I correct in my understanding?

The PRESIDING OFFICER (Mr. BURDICK[14] in the chair). The Senator is correct.

Mr. HOLLAND. Mr. President, first I wish to give a little history about the amendment. The amendment is in substantially the same form now – only a few words different – that it was in when offered by me first in 1949, 13 years ago, with the concurrence of eight very fine Senators from that part of the country from which I come. They agreed with me that not only was the principle involved in the amendment right, but also that the South, which had already knocked out poll taxes entirely in six States, going much further than the amendment would go, should show its willingness to recognize the conviction of the country that people who are American citizens and citizens of a State and who are otherwise qualified to vote shall not be prevented from voting for their President, Vice President, Senators, and Representatives in Congress – that is, the elective Federal officials – by reason of any failure or unwillingness or inability to pay a poll tax or any other tax which might be substituted therefor.

[...]

Mr. RANDOLPH.[15] Mr. President, will the Senator yield further?

Mr. HOLLAND. I yield.

Mr. RANDOLPH. It is appropriate to add that Senators are deeply conscious of the painstaking and effective manner in which the subject under consideration has been presented on recurring occasions in this body by the distinguished Senator from Florida.

Our franchise of freedom, the American ballot, is an instrument to be used by citizens not only as a right and an opportunity granted by law, but also as an expression of a responsibility which stems from the law. So, to vitiate in any degree the representative use of the American ballot would weaken the system under which we operate as a democracy.

For the record, I commend wholeheartedly the leadership which has been exemplified over and over again in this vital matter, and I applaud the worthy efforts of the diligent senior Senator from Florida.

I do not desire to over paint the picture of a situation inherent in the subject about which we are talking, and which causes me to characterize the measure as "a franchise of freedom," but I urge that we do everything necessary to guard against forfeiture of our freedom. We would even drift, rather than be driven, into a dictatorship. We could lose democracy by default if, in this Nation, we should fail to encourage maximum use of the ballot. The Senator from Florida proposes a method by which the number of persons qualified to vote would be increased. The attainment of this end result would be wholesome.

Mr. HOLLAND. Mr. President, I greatly appreciate the kind remarks of the distinguished Senator from West Virginia. Again I thank him for joining me in presenting the amendment on various occasions since he became a Member of this body.

Mr. President, at this time I should like to place in the RECORD section 1 only of the amendment which I offered yesterday, which states all of the substance of the proposed constitutional amendment. I shall read it:

SECTION 1. The right of citizens of the United States to vote in any primary or other election for President or Vice President, for electors for President or Vice President, or for Senator or Representative in Congress, shall not be denied or abridged by the United States or any State by reason of failure to pay any poll tax or other tax.

Mr. President, in the amendment are minor changes from Senate Joint Resolution 58, which I explained, and was happy to explain, yesterday in a colloquy with the distinguished Senator from Illinois [Mr. DOUGLAS]. If any further explanation is desired, I shall be glad to yield for the purpose of making it.

Mr. LAUSCHE.[16] Mr. President, will the Senator yield?

Mr. HOLLAND. I am happy to yield to the distinguished Senator from Ohio.

Mr. LAUSCHE. A suggestion has been made that the amendment proposed by the Senator from Florida contains provisions which would eliminate the disqualification that now exists in some States with regard to a poll tax, but in place of such a poll tax disqualification, the amendment would allow States to pass laws making the payment of taxes a qualification for the right to vote. I read the amendment, and I found no such language in it. Will the Senator explain whether, under the opposed amendment, States could disqualify a citizen from voting on the basis of failure to pay either a poll tax or any other tax?

Mr. HOLLAND. Mr. President, I am happy to reply. The opposed amendment covers the subject of possible disqualification to vote by nonpayment of any other tax in exactly the same words that it covers the poll tax requirement.

The Senator may have received his information from the fact that, as originally introduced this year, as introduced every year since 1953, and as approved by a yea-and-nay vote 72 to 16 in the Senate, in 1960, the resolution included two provisions which are not now in the proposed amendment. They were as follows:

In addition to mentioning failure to pay a poll tax or other tax, there was mention of failure to meet a property requirement. There was also a section 2 in the measure which, recognizing the fact that 12 States had laws that disqualified such people as paupers from voting, excluded the amendment from application in that kind of case. There was no case in which property ownership was the only qualification for a finding that a person was a pauper. That provision, inserted in the amendment for the past 8 years, was put there at the suggestion of the legal staff of the Library of Congress and the legal staff of the Senate in order to preclude any fear on the part of any Senator representing 1 of the 12 States which had a provision disqualifying paupers from voting, and assure him that his State was not affected. There was never any intention to disqualify anyone by that provision, but instead, to show that the States that had so acted were protected in the continuance of their action.

Incidentally, the Library of Congress informed me specifically that in every instance in which measures affecting paupers had been placed in the laws of the respective 12 States, they were enacted as measures to preserve the purity of the ballot, because it had been found that in the case of the ballots of inhabitants of poorhouses and the like they were likely to be voted by others who had become political iron in the fire. Such was the salutary purpose in each of the 12 States.

However, at the suggestion of the majority leader, and after a conference with the distinguished gentleman from New York [Mr. CELLER], the leader in the House on that question, we all came to the conclusion that there would be no prospect or possibility of any State now imposing a property qualification, because while property qualifications have existed in the distant past, and some time or other have been found in the laws in nearly every State in the distant past, there have been none enacted for many years. Any legislature confronted with such a situation would have to realize that it was disqualifying many of its people, of all colors, and of humble situation in life, from voting.

[...]

Mr. HOLLAND. Mr. President, I recall that some Senators who are not greatly interested in the Alexander Hamilton resolution wept bitter tears over the fact that that resolution was interfered with here. I call attention to the fact that a second resolution of the same sort has been introduced and reported by the committee, and is on the calendar. No harm has been done to anyone. To the contrary, the Senate, through its appropriate committee, has shown very proper concern in consideration to the two distinguished Senators from New York [Mr. JAVITS and Mr. KEATING], who were the cosponsors of the original Alexander Hamilton resolution, and, as I understand, are also the cosponsors of the substituted Alexander Hamilton resolution, which is now on the calendar.

Mr. JAVITS.[17] Mr. President, will the Senator yield?

Mr. HOLLAND. I yield to the Senator from New York.

Mr. JAVITS. I should like to state that what needed to be done has been done with respect to the Alexander Hamilton resolution. As I expressed myself when the first action on the resolution was taken in the Senate, I had no doubt about the fact that that the Senator from Florida, as he states quite properly, would not wish anything untoward to happen to the resolution.

[...]

Mr. HOLLAND. Mr. President, I should like to talk about the full text of the requirement of the resolution very briefly, from two different standpoints: In the first place, I should like to speak from the standpoint of one who is a citizen of a State which until 1937 had the full poll tax requirement. I realized how many good people were deprived of their privilege of voting by reason of the existence and enforcement of the poll tax provision. I saw the repeated cases prior to 1937 – and I am talking about my own observations in my own State of Florida – where fine citizens of undoubted patriotism, through absence from the State at the time it was necessary to pay the poll tax, or through forgetfulness – and the State of Florida required the payment of the tax well ahead of time – had not paid the poll tax, and were, as a result, deprived of their opportunity to vote. I am speaking not only about Federal officials, but also of all officials at the State and local level.

I also saw during these early days [of] machine rule of several counties in my State. That has now ceased. That machine rule was perpetuated by the practice of bloc payment of the poll tax in some counties, in order to retain in office certain critical officials within those counties...

[...]

In 1936, when Florida repealed its poll tax, the total vote cast in the Democratic primary was 328,749. In 1940, the primary vote was 481,437, an increase of 152,688. Comparing that increase with the gain in population in the 5 years from 1935 to 1940, we find that the increase in the participation in our elections was 46-plus percent, whereas the percentage of census gain from 1935 – that being a State census – to 1940, the year of the Federal census, was only 18 percent. So the increase in voting was almost three times as great as the increase in Florida's population. This was an increase in the participation of white citizens in voting, because in 1940, in the Democratic primary, Florida still had the white primary system. As we all know, the white primary was knocked out shortly thereafter by the Supreme Court of the United States. But I am talking now about the phenomenal increase in those 4 years of the number of white citizens alone, as shown by the actual election figures.

We have found since the white primary was abolished, and since Negroes have been participating more and more in our elections, that the number of their participants has risen from 20,000 in the general election of 1936 to 183,197 on the registration books in 1960.

There are persons who think we are interested only in white voters, and there are persons who think we are only interested in Negro voters. So far as I am concerned, I think a citizen is entitled to vote for his President, his Vice President, his Senators, and his Representatives, regardless of what may be the law of the State with reference to local elections. I think the results accomplished in our State, where in 1960 1,540,000-plus voted, indicate rather conclusively the beneficent nature of what Florida has done.

It is not for me to belabor any other States. The States about which I shall speak briefly are States of which I am very fond. I am very fond of their Senators. I do not have to tell Members of the Senate that that is true, because they know it is the case. But when we look at the results in the good States of Mississippi and Alabama, in the 1960 general election, we are bound to see what has happened there in large part, of the imposition of a poll tax.

[...]

Mr. HOLLAND. Mr. President, before I take up the situation Alabama, I shall be glad to yield to the distinguished Senator from Connecticut.

Mr. BUSH.[18] Mr. President, will the Senator from Florida be so kind as to yield for a minute, in order that I may send to the desk for printing an amendment which I have discussed with the Senator? I should like to do this with the understanding that my statement will not interrupt the continuity of the remarks of the Senator from Florida.

Mr. HOLLAND. Mr. President, I am glad to yield for that purpose.

The PRESIDING OFFICER. Without objection, it is so ordered.

Mr. BUSH. I thank the Senator from Florida for his courtesy.

Mr. President, I send to the desk and amendment of the pending measure. The amendment provides that the people of the District of Columbia, which constitutes the seeds of the Government of the United States, shall be entitled to elect two Members to the US Senate and a number of Members to the House of Representatives equal to the number of Members of the House of Representatives to which States having the same population as the District of Columbia would be entitled.

The Members of Congress authorized by this article shall be elected at such time and in such manner, and the electors of such Members shall have such qualifications, as Congress shall provide by law.

Debate in the US House of Representatives on the "Qualification of Electors" Amendment, 27 August 1962, was lengthy, and, in some cases, bitter and divided. The issue did not split along party lines; Democrats and Republicans spoke up in favor of the proposed amendment, while a handful of members from both parties either denounced it or claimed that it was stretching the Constitution to areas it was not supposed to go.

QUALIFICATIONS OF ELECTORS

Mr. Celler.[19] Mr. Speaker, I move to suspend the rules and pass Senate Joint Resolution 29, proposing an amendment to the Constitution of the United States relating to [the] qualifications of electors.

Mr. ABERNETHY.[20] Mr. Speaker, a point of order.

The SPEAKER.[21] The gentleman will state his point of order.

Mr. ABERNETHY. Mr. Speaker, I will make the point of order that this is District Day, that there are District bills on the calendar, and as a member of the Committee on the District of Columbia, I respectfully demand recognition so that these bills might be considered.

[...]

The SPEAKER. The gentleman from New York [Mr. CELLER] is recognized for 20 minutes.

Mr. CELLER. Mr. Speaker, I yield myself such time as I may consume.

Mr. Speaker, our late lamented Speaker, Sam Rayburn, President Kennedy, Vice President Lyndon Johnson, our present Speaker, John McCormack, all have at one time or another inveighed against the poll tax. Both party platforms have repeatedly pledged abolition of the poll tax. For example in the party platforms, the Republicans had the abolition of the poll tax as a platform plank in 1944, 1948, and 1952, as follows:

In 1944:

The payment of any poll tax should not be a condition of voting in Federal elections, and we favor immediate submission of a constitutional amendment for its abolition.

In 1948:

We favor the abolition of the poll tax as a requisite for voting. In 1952:

We will prove our good faith by...Federal action toward the elimination of the poll tax as a prerequisite for voting. In 1960:

(1) To continue the vigorous enforcement of civil rights laws to give the right to vote to all citizens in all areas of the country (from party pledge).

Democrat – no specific reference to the poll tax by name in [the] platforms of 1948 and 1952, but it is obviously referred to in the Democratic platform of 1948 in the following manner:

We call upon the Congress to support our President in guaranteeing the basic and fundamental American principles: (1) the right of full and equal political participation.

In 1952: We find and approval of the removal of the poll tax:

We favor Federal legislation effectively to secure these rights to everyone: ...(3) the right to full and equal participation in the Nation's political life, free from arbitrary restraints.

In 1960:

We will support whatever action is necessary to eliminate literacy tests and the payment of poll taxes as requirements for voting.

I regret that this constitutional amendment is brought up under suspension of the rules [after] only 40 minutes of debate. I applied for a rule. A rule is not forthcoming. A discharge petition was filed but not processed. Such a petition is rarely used and has its attendant difficulties if not embarrassments. Hence this suspension of the rules.

In espousing this amendment I regret that I must differ with my esteemed colleagues of the Judiciary Committee, Representatives WILLIS,[22] ASHMORE,[23] FORRESTER,[24] DOWDY,[25] and TUCK.[26] Their opposition is as strong as it is sincere. In this we are as different as Hamlet is from Hercules, as a pig's tail is from the tail of a comet. But remember, democracy's strength lies in differences of opinion and the right to utter them.

The House has passed an antipoll tax bill five times, the Senate twice, including the resolution before you. Antipoll tax legislation, since 1942, passed by the House in [the] 77th, 78th, 79th, 80th, and 81st Congresses. Debated in the Senate during each of these Congresses but passed by the Senate only during the 86th and 87th.

No bills passed by either House or Senate [in the] 82d through the 85th.

In each instance the bill which passed the House contemplated Federal legislation to prevent a poll tax prerequisite to voting in Federal elections. No such bill was passed by the Senate and at least one – H.R. 7, 78th Congress – was prevented from coming to a vote through [the use of a] filibuster.

[The] only time it passed the Senate was during the 86th Congress, and that took the form of [a] constitutional amendment.

[...]

Only five States maintain poll taxes – Alabama, Arkansas, Mississippi, Texas, and Virginia. Here is how it operates in those States.

Alabama: Poll tax of $1.50 for persons over 21 and under 45. Maximum such requirement, including arrears, is a payment of $3 – or for 2 years. Must be paid February 1, next preceding the election, all poll taxes due from him for the last 2 years.

Arkansas: Poll tax of $1. Tax must be paid on or before October 1 preceding the election.

Mississippi: $2 per year, poll tax. Must be paid on or before February 1 of that election year in which he wishes to vote. Must have proof of payment for 2 preceding years.

Texas: $1.50 poll tax fee – $1 goes to support of schools. Must be paid before February 1 of the year in which [the voter] seeks to vote.

Virginia: $1.50 poll tax fee. Must be paid at least 6 months before [the] election in which [the voter] seeks to vote. Must have paid taxes – State poll taxes – assessed against him during the 3 years next preceding the year of the election.

And it is interesting to note that these five States which still require the payment of a poll tax were among the seven States with the lowest voter participation in the 1960 presidential election. The fear that a constitutional amendment would take too long is illusory. The first 10 amendments, constituting the Bill of Rights, were ratified in approximately 9 months. The 17th, 18th, 19th, and 20th amendments each required only approximately 1 year, while the 21st and 23d amendments took less than a year. And remember, 45 States do not have a poll tax.

Reasonable minds differ as to the method to be adopted to abolish the poll tax. Some would travel the statutory route, others the constitutional route. As the Attorney General stated, "a constitutional amendment is a realistic and commendable" approach.

In testifying before the Senate Constitutional Amendments Subcommittee on June 28, 1961, Assistant Attorney General Nicholas deB. Katzenbach said:

While we think from the recent trend in decisions that the courts would ultimately uphold such a statute, the matter is not free from doubt. In any event, as a practical matter and in view of the widespread support offered by the many sponsors of Senate Joint Resolution 58, the poll tax may possibly be laid forever to rest faster by [a] constitutional amendment than by [an] attempt to enact and litigate the validity of a statute. All of us know that long delays are inherent in litigation generally, and this is particularly true when important constitutional issues are at stake. Accordingly, the Justice Department supports the proposed amendment as a realistic technique which seeks the early demise of the poll tax.

Later, during that hearing, Mr. Katzenbach said:

I am authorized on this to speak for the administration and for the President.

If the statutory method were pursued there would ensue a long period of litigation to test the statute's constitutionality.

Furthermore, a statute would be difficult to enact in both Houses – as difficult as trying to grasp a shadow.

This amendment has passed the Senate, I repeat. I am a pragmatist. I want results, not debate. I want a law, not a filibuster. I crave an end to the poll tax, not unlimited, crippling amendments.

I say to you gentlemen and ladies, "Stretch your feet according to your blanket." It is wiser to recognize the exigencies under which we operate.

I do not wish to try for too much and fail. I do not want to keep rolling a boulder up a high hill like Sisyphus, only to have it fall down constantly upon me. I would have inordinate trouble trying to get a mere statute passed. Hence this constitutional amendment.

I am aware that this resolution only affects voting in Federal elections. States could inflict the tax on ballots in State or local elections. This might mean double or bobtailed ballots. That would be unfortunate.

It is hoped that this constitutional amendment, when ratified, will liberate the minds of the members the State legislatures of the five poll tax States and cause these men to realize that the fungus growth on their own local body politic could very well strangle progress in many directions.

Excuse is offered that the poll tax receipts are used for educational purposes in some States. This is a specious argument. Poll tax proceeds might be used for many good causes – for bird sanctuaries, homes for inebriates, baseball parks, or what have you. But since the poll tax is inherently obnoxious, the good does not justify the evil. It is like the fruit of a poisoned tree or water from a tainted well.

The constitutional amendment is in exactly the form that it passed the Senate. I fought down all amendments before the Judiciary Committee so that we could pass upon the resolution as it had passed the Senate. This will avoid any conference and thus prevent delay. Delay has dangerous ends.

There has been sufficient delay in removing this unfair burden on the right to vote, a burden on the white man's ballots as well as on the colored man's ballot.

[...]

Mr. HALLECK.[27] Mr. Speaker, will the gentleman yield?

Mr. McCULLOCH.[28] I yield to the gentleman from Indiana.

Mr. HALLECK. Mr. Speaker, I believe it might be well for me to say at this point that the proposition before is not new or novel. I have voted for antipoll tax legislation, I would guess, at least half a dozen times. I remember voting for such a bill in 1942. I voted for such a bill in 1943, and I voted for one in 1945. In June of 1947, as may leader of the 80th Congress, we called up under suspension of the rules an anti-poll tax bill. It passed by substantially more than the two-thirds majority.

So, as I said at the outset, this is nothing new or novel; it is something that the House of Representatives has been trying to write into law for a long, long time. This proposal is a constitutional amendment. I think most of the measures we have heretofore dealt undertook to accomplish this by statute law. Is that correct?

Mr. McCULLOCH. I thank the gentleman from Indiana, our minority leader, and I am pleased that he has brought the record up to date.

Mr. Speaker, it is indeed regrettable that a constitutional amendment should be brought to the floor of the House with only 40 minutes of debate thereon. I hope it does not happen again.

Mr. ROGERS of Texas.[29] Mr. Speaker, will the gentleman yield?

Mr. McCULLOCH. I yield to the gentleman from Texas.

Mr. ROGERS of Texas. Can the gentleman tell me whether if this amendment is adopt it will destroy a right that is presently vested in the States?

Mr. McCULLOCH. I am not convinced that that is the case.

Mr. ROGERS of Texas. The States now have the right to make this determination. If you pass this amendment it destroys the right of the States in that regard, does it not?

Mr. McCULLOCH. I am not convinced that it does. Some of the ablest lawyers in the country are of the opinion that the intended result can be accomplished either by congressional action or constitutional amendment.

Mr. CELLER. Mr. Speaker, I yield 5 minutes to the gentleman from Louisiana [Mr. WILLIS].

Mr. WILLIS. Mr. Speaker, Louisiana was one of the first States in the Union to repeal the poll tax. I voted to repeal it. And I would hope that some of these days the three or four remaining States still having the poll tax requirement as a condition to vote will repeal it.

Thus far, therefore, the proponents of the measure before us today and I are together. Beyond that point, however, we part company. Why? I disagree on the basis of two great constitutional concepts. In other words, I part company with my friends who favor this proposal because I believe I have the Constitution on my side.

The first constitutional provision is this. With great humility and out of consideration for all the people, the Founding Fathers put a provision in the Constitution which says that the qualification of people to vote for Members of Congress and national offices shall be the same as those who votes for members of the State legislature and local offices. The resolution before the House today would read reverse this principle. It would make a special provision applicable to Members of Congress and national offices only. It would provide that when a person enters a polling booth to vote for a Member of Congress or national office, he could not be required to pay a poll tax, but when voting for a local officer on the same ballot he could be forced to pay a poll tax. Strangely enough, the proponents of this measure use this very argument to get votes for the pending proposal. On reflection I say to you that this is the greatest argument against a vote for it.

Why make a special provision for Members of Congress and national offices only? Where is our humility? Those of you who vote for this resolution must face the fact that you will not be able to tell the folks back home, "Look what I did for you." You will have to tell the mayor of your hometown, your sheriff, your justice of the peace, and on up to your Governor, "Look what I did for me."

Oh, I know, you might be able to whisper to these local officials that you could not make such a provision for them and so for the time being you made the provision only for your self. But they might well say to you, "Did you try? Did you make a fight for us? Did you offer an amendment to include us?"

And then, too, you might be able to tell your political friends that to match the tactics of those of the opposite party that you had to do something special for a special minority group – a minority group incidentally for whom I have the greatest compassion and a majority of whom I think vote for me. But the truth of the matter is that this great country of ours is made up of conglomerate people of innumerable minority groups. For example, the Catholics as such are not in a majority and in that sense are a minority group. No one sect of the Protestants constitute a majority and in that sense they, too, are minority groups. Suppose some of these days any one of these groups tells you, "Out of political consideration you always seem to justify doing something special for one minority group: when are you going to start doing something for us?" What are you going to say?

Of course you might be able to tell them, "Your turn will come next." But this, in my opinion, would violate another constitutional provision, which, in plain language, states that the time, place, and manner of conducting elections shall be left up to the States. The constitutional amendment before us today, if passed, would be an entering wedge and a foot in the door which through pressure groups, however sincere, would inevitably lead to other amendments concentrating the entire election procedure and machinery in the Federal Government – and then goodbye [to] States['] rights.

The proposal before us today is reminiscent of one made by President Eisenhower. You will remember, I am sure, that he proposed an amendment to the Constitution which would give the right to vote to all people 18 years of age [and over]. The argument was that if a person was old enough to fight for his country, he was old enough to vote, and it had great temporary emotional appeal. But then the people were heard from with a great voice saying, "The proposal has great merit, but on reflection we should heed the admonition of the Founding Fathers to the effect that the qualification of voters and the time, place, and manner of conducting elections should be left up to the States." And the proposal was abandoned.

[...]

Mr. CELLER. Mr. Speaker, I yield such time as he may consume to the gentleman from Virginia [Mr. TUCK]. Mr. TUCK. Mr. Speaker, I said the distinguished gentleman from New York [Mr. CELLER] for allotting me this brief time in which to discuss such an important question.

Mr. Speaker, I rise in opposition to Senate Joint Resolution 29, proposing an amendment to the Constitution of the United States relating to the qualifications of electors, with specific reference to the payment of a poll tax as a prerequisite for voting in Federal elections. I respectfully submit that the House could be utilizing its time more profitably and devoting its attention to far more important matters.

This resolution is a political gesture addressed to powerful minority groups who neither live nor vote in the five poll tax States.

The power of the Congress to pass a resolution of this nature is not questioned; however, to do so will be to subvert hallowed constitutional principles. The principle involved here is the right of the States to control their own election machinery and to set forth [the] qualifications of voters. That right is upheld in the decision of *Butler v. Thompson*, 341 US 937, wherein the Supreme Court held that "the decisions generally hold that a State statute which imposes a reasonable poll tax as a condition of the right to vote does not abridge the privileges or immunities of the citizens of the United States which are protected by the 14th amendment. The privilege of voting is derived from the State, and not from the National Government."

The Supreme Court in *Minor v. Happersett*, 21 Wall. 162, held that "the Constitution of the United States does not confer the right of suffrage on anyone." Suffrage is basically a privilege and becomes a right only if denied under the guarantees of the 15th and 19th amendments. A person may vote only if he meets the qualifications prescribed by his State.

The operation of the poll tax does not create a problem which requires [a] solution by a constitutional amendment. The unbroken precedents of upholding the poll tax against constitutional attack should not be ignored by this House. This body will not be justified in the passage of the proposed resolution

[...]

Mr. LINDSAY.[30] Mr. Speaker, I am very much opposed to poll taxes, and therefore I will vote for this bill, but I do so with a heavy heart.

This is probably the greatest piece of legislative gamesmanship that has come to the floor of the House in the 87th Congress. This is a great day also for the anti civil rights proponents. It may sound strange to some of you, but I am going to agree pretty much with my good friend, the gentleman from Louisiana [Mr. WILLIS]. First of all, this is a fantastic procedure under which to amend the Constitution – an up or down vote, no amendments permitted, no motion to recommit possible, a total of 40 minutes of debate. Secondly, the result sought to be achieved by a simple spot vote.

The leadership on the majority side, who are running this show, Mr. Speaker, ought to be proud of themselves for handing us this dish of tea. Under this kind of gag procedure they usually and cynically tinker with the US Constitution, for political reasons, to get off the hook on civil rights. They would amend the Constitution to abolish the poll tax in Federal elections only. Why only Federal elections? That was the point made by my friend from Louisiana [Mr. WILLIS] – in Federal elections only. The impact is on two States. Only five States still have a poll tax of any kind and only two of these continue to use the poll tax in order to disenfranchise voters. The Civil Rights Commission, in its 1961 report, said as follows:

The absence of complaints to the Commission, actions by the Department of Justice, private litigation, or other indications of discrimination, have led the Commission to conclude that, with the possible exception of a deterrent effect of the poll tax – which does not appear generally to be discriminatory upon the basis of race or color – Negroes now appear to encounter no significant racially motivated impediments to voting in 4 of the 12 Southern States.

Mr. Speaker, it is dangerous to alter the US Constitution when the same result can be reached by statute. Some of the Members on the majority side who think of themselves as great liberals ought to worry about this a little bit. There are any number of proposals, for example, to amend the US Constitution on the school prayer issue, and if you can do it as easily as we do here today, to correct a relatively minor matter that can be corrected by simple statute, just think of what can occur in the future in the event the extreme right should be in the ascendancy. This is using a sledge hammer, a giant cannon, in order to kill a gnat.

Of course, Mr. Speaker, what we really have here is the last act and the last scene of this bad charade that we have been forced to watch for almost 2 years in which the administration and the majority side of the aisle step by step have delivered on the deal not to give the country significant or meaningful civil rights legislation. I think it is a pretty sorry show. This is known as an "off the hook" bill – a show device that will get the administration off the hook for breaking its pledges with the American people on civil rights.

[...]

934

Mr. SMITH of Virginia.[31] Mr. Speaker, 4 minutes; 4 minutes. I have been here a long time. I hope that the walls of this Hall will never ring again with the kind of a farce that has been put out here today, with the Constitution of the United States to be amended, when no one can offer an objection or an amendment to it, when no one can raise his voice in extended debate, but 20 minutes for and 20 minutes supposedly against it. Is unprecedented in the annals of this Government for an amendment to the Constitution, no matter how insignificant it may be, to be considered here under this procedure.

Mr. ROGERS of Colorado.[32] Mr. Speaker, will the gentleman yield?

Mr. SMITH of Virginia. I decline to yield. I have only 4 minutes, and I regret very much, much more than a gentleman does, I am sure, that we do not have additional time.

I heard one of the speakers – and by the way, the best arguments I have heard for the defeat of this resolution have come from the Republican side. This should not be done in this way. It shows the utmost disrespect and disrepute to which a great Constitution of the United States has fallen. Think on the origin of this resolution in the other body. There was a little bill to honor the great Alexander Hamilton, one of the great Republicans of his country, and it was displaced so that they might get onto the floor this disgraceful exhibition of disrespect and disrepute of the great Constitution of the United States.

Gentlemen, how many of you are going to be proud of the vote you are about to cast, about to cast under the pressure of both parties, because the Republican leadership is just as much responsible for this as the Democrats. They do not put bills of this controversy on the "Suspense" Calendar unless they have the consent and approval of the minority leadership. So do not lay it on the Democratic side, and I am not excusing the Democratic leadership because they could have brought this up in the regular way.

Mr. HALLECK. Mr. Speaker, will the gentleman yield?

Mr. SMITH of Virginia. I decline to yield. If you had cooperated with us in fixing this thing so that we would have some time to debate a proposed amendment to the Constitution we would have been glad to discuss it and discuss it fully and on its merits. But this resolution could have been brought up here in the regular way. Some of you will remember that just 18 months ago the leadership of this House packed the Committee on Rules so that they would have a majority vote on it. They could have gotten it out of the Committee on Rules with a majority vote, if they had wanted to do it in the democratic way and permit the House to vote on it. Yet, this House is going to vote for this in this extraordinary situation, and they are going to do it under political pressure to please a minority group. We all know that, everybody knows that, the country knows that. What is this country going to come to when we, supposedly responsible and dignified Members of the Congress, "crook the pregnant hinges of the knee" at every call and at every demand of any minority group in this country in order that some votes may be controlled? Is that the kind of government that we are going to run from now on? Think it over. Vote for it, as you will. Vote for it, as I know you will; and knowing so, vote for it under pressure – under political pressure from a minority group – and then regret it as long as you live.

The SPEAKER. The time of the gentleman has expired.

Mr. RAY. Mr. Speaker, I yield one-half minute to the gentleman from Georgia [Mr. FORRESTER].

Mr. FORRESTER. Mr. Speaker, Georgia levies no poll tax. Only 5 of our 50 States do. Nevertheless, the levying of poll taxes has always been a matter for decision by the respective States, and I hope it will continue to be. The 5 States still collecting a poll tax have as good morals, as much respect for law, and as efficient government as the other 45 States. This statement cannot be challenged. To say that a $1 or $2 poll tax prevents anyone from exercising the privilege to vote is laughable. Maybe a poll tax serves no good purpose but, conversely, it serves no evil purpose. It is a right that the States have exercised from the beginning and a right that can be destroyed only by a constitutional amendment prohibiting such tax.

[...]

Mr. RAY. Mr. Speaker, I yield the balance of the time remaining to the gentleman from New York [Mr. HALPERN].

Mr. HALLECK. Mr. Speaker, will the gentleman yield?

Mr. HALPERN.[33] I yield to the gentleman.

Mr. HALLECK. Mr. Speaker, I do not want to get into any controversy with any of my colleagues, but I just wanted clearly stated for the record and understood that today is the regular day for considering legislation under [the] suspension of the rules under the arrangement made last Monday; and so far as the suspensions are concerned, it was within the province of the Speaker and the majority leadership to schedule them, and that is what has been done.

Mr. HALPERN. Mr. Speaker, I am in favor of any step taken in the direction of outlawing this undemocratic, feudal practice of placing a price tag on the right to vote.

Mr. Speaker, I would much prefer that the poll tax be outlawed by statute rather than by an amendment to the Constitution, as this House has authorized five times previously. There is a big question as to the effectiveness of going the amendment route – obtaining approval of three-fourths of the State legislatures is a long, difficult, and tedious process, to say the least.

We are now, however, faced with no other alternative under the rule and the circumstances here today but to support this constitutional amendment. Despite the question of the effectiveness of this method, I definitely shall support this Senate joint resolution.

It is vital that the Congress go on record before our people that the poll tax be repealed. Mr. Speaker, I urge a massive vote for passage.

Mr. CELLER. Mr. Speaker, I yield the 1 minute remaining on this side to the gentleman from Colorado [Mr. ROGERS].

Mr. ROGERS of Colorado. Mr. Speaker, I regret that the gentleman from Virginia should say that we were placed under a gag rule, that we could not present the matter to the House so that this constitutional proposal could be amended.

[...]

Mr. POFF.[34] Mr. Speaker, in my first campaign for Congress 10 years ago, I registered my opposition to the poll tax as a price tag on the voting privilege.

I prefer to see the States repeal the poll tax.

I am opposed to a Federal statute on the subject.

I am opposed to a constitutional amendment if that amendment reaches into State and local elections.

However, a constitutional amendment which is confined to Federal elections and which is ratified by the States as the Constitution provides is not an unconstitutional invasion of States' rights, and such an amendment I feel obliged to support.

[...]

Mr. JOELSON.[35] Mr. Speaker, I want to express my complete support of this measure designed to eliminate the poll tax. It is my opinion that the poll tax is a denial of the basic elements of democracy.

It is unthinkable that in the United States, there are still areas in which American citizens are required to pay for the right to vote. Such a system tends to discourage our poorer citizens from the exercise of their precious right of choosing their officials.

There is no doubt that in certain sections of our country, our poorer citizens among the Negroes have been prevented from voting by the poll tax as well as by other less subtle forms of persuasion.

Mr. Speaker, the poll tax is undemocratic and un-American. It is a blight that must be eliminated from our Nation.

Historical Background Documents

Statement of Senator Spessard Holland, Democrat of Florida, on a proposed Anti-Poll Tax Amendment to the US Constitution, 17 August 1959, in which Senator Holland spoke out in favor of a constitutional amendment giving the District of Columbia voting rights – a provision that dealt with the poll tax still in use in several Southern states. Although this portion of the proposed amendment – which became the Twenty-third – was eventually dropped to gain southern support, Holland continued to agitate for doing away with the tax. The following is a statement by Holland in hearings on the proposed DC amendment. The chairman of the subcommittee was Sen. Estes Kefauver, Democrat of Tennessee.

Senator HOLLAND. Thank, Mr. Chairman.

I am grateful for the opportunity to appear and testify briefly in support of Senate Joint Resolution 126, proposing an amendment to the Constitution of the United States relating to the qualifications of electors.

[...]

Mr. Chairman, in the 81st Congress and in every succeeding Congress, I have introduced for several other Senators and myself a joint resolution proposing an amendment to the Constitution of the United States relating to the qualifications of electors participating in the election of elective Federal officials, including electors for President or Vice President, and Senators and Representatives in Congress.

The first five Congresses in which I introduced this joint resolution I was joined by outstanding Senators from the South, and I ask to have inserted in the hearing record at this point the names of those cosponsors[.]

[At this point, the list of the Senators spoken about was inserted. It has been excised for reasons of space.]

In fairness to the Senator from South Carolina, Mr. Thurmond, let me state for the record that he withdrew his name as a cosponsor soon after the bill was introduced in the 84th Congress.

Hearings were held by a subcommittee of the Senate Judiciary Committee on this proposal in the 81st, 83d, and 84th Congresses, and in each instance the hearing record was printed and is now available.

It is interesting to note that in the 81st Congress there was no opposition to the joint resolution in the hearings; the same was true in the 83d Congress; and in the 84th Congress, two opposition witnesses appeared, the Honorable Thomas A. Wofford, then a US Senator from South Carolina, and Clarence Mitchell, director, Washington bureau, NAACP, who filed a statement by J. Pohlhaus, counsel, Washington bureau, NAACP.

Mr. Chairman, in past years my testimony has been directed largely on the question of whether a constitutional amendment is necessary or whether a mere Federal statute would legally accomplish the purpose of prohibiting the imposition of a poll tax as a prerequisite to voting in Federal elections.

I think the carefully documented argument I have made down through the years as to the absolute necessity of a constitutional amendment is unanswerable, and the fact that I am joined this year in cosponsoring this proposed constitutional amendment by 65 other Senators leads me to conclude that I need not take the time of this subcommittee to go into that question in detail.

However, Mr. Chairman, in order that Senators may have before them in this record the complete argument on that question, I ask that my remarks beginning at page 2 and concluding on page 55 of the hearings of April 11, 1956, on Senate Joint Resolution 29 of that Congress, be printed at the conclusion of my remarks today.

Senator KEFAUVER. Without objection, that will be done.

Senator HOLLAND. Briefly, Mr. Chairman, the basic argument as to whether a constitutional amendment is necessary centers around the question of whether the required payment of a poll tax (or other tax) or the meeting of any property qualification are "qualifications" within the meaning of article I, section 2 of the US Constitution and the 17th amendment to the Constitution.

The pertinent provisions of each are included in the Constitution in the same words, though article I, section 2 was incorporated by the Constitutional Convention of 1787 and the 17th amendment was ratified by 36 States in 1912 and 1913.

I may say parenthetically, Mr. Chairman, this is the only provision in the Constitution which appears in the same language in two parts of the Constitution, much less into parts adopted at such different times.

I quote first that part of section 2 of article I of the original Constitution which is applicable:

The House of Representatives shall be composed of Members chosen every second year by the people of the several States, and the electors in each State shall have the qualifications requisite for electors of the most numerous branch of the State legislature.

The first paragraph of the 17th amendment reads as follows:

The Senate of the United States shall be composed of two Senators from each State, elected by the people thereof, for 6 years: and each Senator shall have one vote. The electors in each State shall have the qualifications requisite for electors of the most numerous branch of the State legislatures.

The testimony I asked to have printed in the record a few moments ago contains the pertinent constitutional provisions – or colonial charter provisions where a State was operating under such a document – at the time the US Constitution was written. It also includes pertinent excerpts from various State constitutions in effect when the 17th amendment was submitted, showing the use of the words "qualify," "qualification," "qualified," and so forth, in connection with poll tax payment requirements or other tax payment requirements or property ownership requirements.

It is significant that each of the Thirteen Original States had, in the fundamental documents under which they were operating at the time the Federal Constitution was formed, either a poll tax requirement, as in New Hampshire – and that is the only one that had a poll tax requirement at that time – or property-ownership requirements or tax paying requirements, both of which were more severe than a mere poll tax payment requirement, or 2 or even 3 of these conditions, and that in 8 of the 13 documents the word "qualified" or "qualifications" or both were used in referring to those particular requirements and conditions.

Mr. Chairman, there could be no question at all that the framers of the original Constitution, men who probably knew more about the fundamental setup of the Thirteen Original Colonies and the new States that had come in prior to the adoption of the Constitution than any group living, must have known that the word "qualifications" as then used embraced the payment of [a] poll tax, the payment of property taxes, and the requirement of property ownership, as the case might be, in the various States.

It seems to me to be so completely proved beyond any question of doubt that those who participated in the Constitutional Convention of 1787 and used the words "qualifications requisite for electors of the most numerous branch of the State legislature" would be bound to know that these States had prescribed, not as a prerequisite of voting, but as a complete qualification for voting, payment of poll taxes, payment of other kinds of taxes, and ownership of properties of various kinds and descriptions, and that all of these conditions for voting had been styled over and over and over again in these various constitutions as "qualifications" or as being necessary to "qualify" electors or as, when existing, having "qualified" persons to serve as electors.

Mr. Chairman, I do not want to indulge in a lot of semantics in this argument, but it seems so completely clear to me that the framers of the Constitution understood the word "qualification" to comprise and include such things as the payment of a poll tax, the payment of property taxes, and the ownership of property, that the matter is not arguable.

It seems to me – and I am joined in this opinion by many constitutional lawyers throughout the country – that the present Constitution of the United States completely prevent and prohibits the accomplishment of the removal of the poll tax as a requirement for voting in Federal election in any way other than by a constitutional amendment.

We sponsors of this joint resolution strongly believe that the proposed constitutional amendment should be speedily submitted by this Congress to the States for ratification and, if so submitted, we believe it will be quickly ratified by at least the required 38 States.

Because we are so sure that the requisite number of States would speedily ratify the proposed amendment, we are quite agreeable to the allowing of any reasonable period to accomplish its consideration and ratification by the various States. I suggest a limitation of 2 years. The ratification of the 17th amendment, which was in some respects comparable to our proposed amendment, was completed in a little less than 1 year.

The poll tax requirement now limited to five States – namely, Alabama, Arkansas, Mississippi, Texas, and Virginia – has been accorded far greater importance than it deserves. The fact of the matter is that the amount of poll tax required to be paid in the several States is so small as to impose only a slight economic obstacle for any citizen who desires to qualify to cast a ballot. This requirement operates, of course, equally on citizens of all races and colors, and is generally subject to important exemptions which limit its application, such as the exemption of veterans, of women, and of citizens beyond a certain age. Nevertheless the question has remained a vexing one.

May I say, Mr. Chairman, outside of by prepared statement, that in 1937, as a member of the State Senate of Florida, I was one of those who participated in outlawing the poll tax requirement in Florida which was permitted to be levied as requirement for voting by our constitution. We outlawed it as a requirement for all kinds of voting, that is, going much further than this proposed amendment, which of course confines itself to the Federal field.

We have had nothing but good results from that action. It has freed certain countries from control by political machines, which was exercised through the payment of a poll tax, by the so-called "courthouse ring" in most cases, or others who had some selfish interest. It has resulted in a greater participation in voting by people of both races. It has had salutary effects.

I am strongly sold upon the proposition that to impede the casting of ballots, as is done by the imposition of poll tax requirements or these other requirements which would be outlawed under this proposed amendment, is a hurtful process which prevents full realization of the democratic possibilities which are best realized when a large proportion of the people come to the polls and vote. I strongly believe that it is sound democracy to have as full participation as possible in our elections.

I have been asking for [the] submission of a constitutional amendment on this subject by Congress for a long time, and I still feel that it is much more important to accomplish our purpose in this strictly legal way rather than to waste the time of Congress and the courts in some petty passing of legislation and going ahead with litigation, which operates at most as to only a very few individuals here or there.

Mr. Chairman, I would like to call attention briefly to five details in this proposed amendment, as follows:

First, that it is applicable to primaries and other elections in which Federal officials are nominated or elected, namely, presidential electors, Senators, and Representatives to Congress.

Second, that the proposed amendment prohibits the imposition of a poll tax as a prerequisite for such voting for Federal officials only, not relating to the voting for State or local officials or upon State or local matters. Senator KEFAUVER. Let us have a brief recess.

(Short recess.)

Senator KEFAUVER. We will proceed.

Senator HOLLAND. I was just calling attention to the five details.

In this regard, Mr. Chairman, in the 1956 hearings I had printed in the record a document prepared for me by the Library of Congress entitled "Poll Taxes as Levied in New England States," which illustrated so clearly the type of local control which the cosponsors of the resolution feel should be allowed to continue. I will not ask to have that document printed again, but I call attention to the fact that in several of the New England States the payment of a poll tax was a prerequisite for obtaining such things as hunting and fishing licenses, automobile licenses or motor vehicle registrations, and the like.

Up until recent years, several of the New England States had the payment of a poll tax as a condition for participating in their cherished town meetings. One New England State, Vermont, still retains such a requirement.

The varying requirements in New England alone illustrates the wisdom of our staying away from the general effort to intervene in the field of [the] control of elections.

Incidentally, in my own State of Florida, the constitution contains a requirement that participants in county, district, and municipal bond elections must be "freeholders," and such provision is found in other States as well.

Third, that the remedial effects of this amendment would apply not only to the State laws of all of the States, but to the laws of the United States; in other words, would not rest upon the assumption that the present sentiment so dominant in the Congress of the United States will continue to exist, but would protect the right of citizens to vote for Federal officials notwithstanding any possible later change of attitude by the Congress of the United States.

Fourth, that the proposed amendment would prohibit any other tax that is different from the ordinary poll tax, socalled, from being prescribed as a prerequisite for voting.

Diverting from my prepared statement, Mr. Chairman, the last State to have such a tax was the State of Pennsylvania, as is shown in my statements at earlier hearing is, and the year of its repeal was 1933. So you see this is not a fancied problem, but one that could be...

Senator KEFAUVER. What kind of tax was that, Senator Holland, in Pennsylvania?

Senator HOLLAND. Would you wait a moment until I look it up?

Senator KEFAUVER. Yes.

Senator HOLLAND. It was a property tax of some kind. [...]

Senator HOLLAND. Fifth, that the proposed amendment would prevent either the United States or any State from setting up any property qualification as a prerequisite for participation in an election of Federal officers, with the exception of qualifications relating to those citizens who by law are denied the right to vote because they are paupers or persons supported at public expense or by charitable institutions.

I would like to amplify that point, Mr. Chairman.

I would like to explain briefly why that particular exemption has been made. Some years ago when I referred the proposed amendment to the Library of Congress and to the Office of the Legislative Counsel of the Senate, they called to my attention the fact that if we excluded property qualifications in general terms, that we might run into opposition from States which have, either in their constitutions or statutes, provisions which prohibit participation in elections by paupers, or persons who are inhabitants of public institutions and charges upon the general public.

The Library of Congress called my attention to the fact that various States have adopted such procedures because it had been found that corruption in their State elections had resulted from efforts to dominate the voting of inhabitants of poorhouses and institutions of that kind to the degree that they felt that it was important to prohibit the voting of such public charges.

For the record, the following 12 States, which are widely scattered, have varying provisions on this subject: Delaware, Louisiana, Maine, Massachusetts, Missouri, New Hampshire, Oklahoma, Rhode Island, South Carolina, Texas, Virginia, West Virginia.

Mr. Chairman, in my judgment it would be wholly futile to prohibit a denial of the right of suffrage under the imposition of the poll tax while at the same time leaving the way open to any State which might want to limit the number of its electors, to do so by the imposition of another tax or the enacting of any property qualification which it might see fit to impose, thus leaving those two additional possibilities in the picture. This same restriction would apply to the Congress.

I call attention of the distinguished chairman that when the Constitution was first drawn, the matter of limitation of electors under tax payment requirements, meaning taxes other than poll taxes, and under property qualifications, was any greater general deterrent to voting than was the poll tax, which at the time existed as a prerequisite to voting in only one State, the State of New Hampshire.

It seems to me, particularly in view of the fact that the property qualification and the tax payment qualification, other than poll taxes, have been included within the various qualifications for voting by various States as late as 1930 or thereafter, that any method of dealing with this subject should be sufficiently broad to prevent the defeat of the wholesome of objectives of the joint resolution by simply having various States turn to other means is of gaining the same end.

అంక్రాంక్రాంక్రాంక్రాంక్రాం

"Abolition of [the] Poll Tax in Federal Elections": Hearings before the House Committee on the Judiciary, March and May 1962 in which members of the House Judiciary Committee adjusted language of the proposed amendment that came out of the US Senate.

Monday, March 12, 1962

The subcommittee met at 10:30 a.m., pursuant to notice, in room 346 Old House Office Building, Hon. Emanuel Celler (chairman of the committee) presiding.

Present: Representatives Celler, Rogers, Brooks, Toll, and McCulloch.

Also present: William R. Foley, general counsel; William H. Copenhaver, associate counsel. The CHAIRMAN. The committee will come to order.

We are assembled this morning for the purpose of consideration of various resolutions pertaining to the abolition of the poll taxes [sic]. This committee has jurisdiction over constitutional amendments, among those constitutional amendments which would abolish poll taxes.

This committee has no jurisdiction over those bills that will abolish the poll taxes where the bills are in statutory form in contradistinction to constitutional form. Those bills are the separate matter of the Committee on House Administration which has jurisdiction over Federal election [sic]. So, our hearings will be in general on the constitutional amendments.

[The clerk then proceeded to read into the record the numerous numbers of the proposed bills which laid out language which could be included in the proposed constitutional amendment.]

[...]

The CHAIRMAN. I have been informed by the Senator from Florida, Senator Holland, that he favors a constitutional amendment doing away with poll taxes. Up to this juncture, there are five States that still maintain poll taxes. They are Arkansas, Alabama, Mississippi, Texas, and Virginia. All other States have done away with poll taxes.

We hope to finish the hearings on poll taxes today, if possible, although the Attorney General personally wishes to testify. He may not be present until Thursday of this week.

We will also take up during these hearings not only the question of poll taxes but also bills having to do with literacy tests.

Mr. McCULLOCH.[36] Mr. Chairman, I would like to make a brief statement, too, as the ranking minority member of this committee.

I was very pleased, Mr. Chairman, to learn that the committee was scheduling these hearings to consider civil rights legislation as it relates to the abolition of the poll tax and probably in some other fields. It is my opinion that we should have had some hearings in these matters even last year.

Of course, it is well known that my party has long been an advocate of anti-poll tax legislation.

As will be recalled, the House of Representatives in the 80th Congress passed with an overwhelming vote a proposal to nullify poll tax statutes in the various States of the country. That proposal failed in the other body for reasons which are, of course, well known to everyone who is here today.

In the meantime, little or no evidence has been developed linking voting discrimination to the poll tax. And within the last year, the Civil Rights Commission in its report said as much.

The Chairman has already indicated that there are only five States that now have poll taxes in this country. And there is little, if any, evidence on the record that those poll tax statutes have been a material deterrent to voting in those States.

You know, Mr. Chairman, the annual poll tax assessment from these States ranges from $1 to $2 a year. And the funds so collected are used to support public education. Of course, one of the most, if not the most, worthwhile uses of public moneys [sic] is support of education.

In addition, the Civil Rights Commission has reported that of the 12 States of the South, Negroes encounter no significant racially motivated impediments to voting in Arkansas, Oklahoma, Texas, and Virginia. This means that of the five States having poll taxes, only Alabama and Mississippi could be possibly said to use the poll tax as a voter discriminatory device.

If one examines the counties in Alabama and Mississippi which have less than 10 percent Negro registration, it will be seen that this amendment could only benefit that the most, if every person would otherwise exercise his or her voting rights, about 450,000 to 470,000 individuals, assuming that they were all disenfranchised because of the poll tax.

Having said the above, however, I believe that the antipoll tax amendment is a worthwhile proposal.

This is so particularly because many inhabitants and even though leaders of the foreign nations have sought to make anti-American propaganda from the fact that the poll tax is still being levied in a few of our States, not mentioning, of course, that the majority of the States have long since abolished such a practice, including the States of Louisiana, Florida, Georgia, South Carolina, and Tennessee in recent years.

❦❦❦❦❦❦❦❦❦❦

Following the House passage of the proposed anti-poll tax amendment, President John F. Kennedy released the following statement, 28 August 1962.

"Today' action by the House of Representatives in approving the poll tax amendment culminates a legislative effort of many, many years to bring about the end of this artificial bar to the right to vote in some of our states. This is a significant action which I am confident will be approved quickly by the required 38 state legislatures."

❦❦❦❦❦❦❦❦❦❦

Congressional passage of the anti-poll tax amendment was hailed in the black American magazine Jet*, February 1964.*

Poll Taxes For Voting Now Banned By Constitution

The Twenty-fourth Amendment, banning payment of poll taxes as a requirement for voting in federal elections, was finally ratified as a part of the US Constitution as a result of the last-minute race between Georgia and South

Dakota for the honor of becoming the 38th state to approve the amendment. South Dakota won when the state senate suspended its rules and passed the measure unanimously, 34-0. Georgia acted swiftly when its senate approved the amendment unanimously and sent it to the State House for speedy action.

As Submitted to the States

Section 1. The right of citizens of the United States to vote in any primary or other election for President or Vice President, for electors for President or Vice President, or for Senator or Representative in Congress, shall not be denied or abridged by the United States or any State by reason of failure to pay any poll tax or other tax.

Section 2. The Congress shall have power to enforce this article by appropriate legislation.

State Ratifications of the Twenty-fourth Amendment

State	Date
Illinois	14 November 1962
New Jersey	3 December 1962
Oregon	25 January 1963
Montana	28 January 1963
West Virginia	1 February 1963
New York	4 February 1963
Maryland	6 February 1963
California	7 February 1963
Alaska	11 February 1963
Rhode Island	14 February 1963
Indiana	19 February 1963
Utah	20 February 1963
Michigan	20 February 1963
Colorado	21 February 1963
Ohio	27 February 1963
Minnesota	27 February 1963
New Mexico	5 March 1963
Hawaii	6 March 1963
North Dakota	7 March 1963
Idaho	8 March 1963
Washington	14 March 1963
Vermont	15 March 1963
Nevada	19 March 1963
Connecticut	20 March 1963
Tennessee	21 March 1963
Pennsylvania	25 March 1963
Wisconsin	26 March 1963
Kansas	28 March 1963
Massachusetts	28 March 1963
Nebraska	4 April 1963
Florida	18 April 1963
Iowa	24 April 1963
Delaware	1 May 1963
Missouri	13 May 1963

New Hampshire	12 June 1963
Kentucky	27 June 1963
Maine	16 January 1964
South Dakota	23 January 1964*
Virginia	25 February 1977
North Carolina	3 May 1989
Alabama	11 April 2002
Texas	22 May 2009

Explanation of the amendment

As noted in the introduction and the body of the amendment, Southern states utilized poll taxes; this amendment did away with any instance of a state pushing a tax or any other property or qualification to vote in federal elections only, such as those for President and Vice President, US Senator or US Representative. The amendment was ratified in 1964; two years later, the US Supreme Court, in *Harper v. Virginia Board of Elections* (383 US 663 {1966}), struck down all poll taxes, even those impacted on local elections not covered by this amendment, as unconstitutional.

*Note: *South Dakota's ratification gave the amendment the requisite number of states needed to make it a part of the US Constitution.*

ORIGINAL PRIMARY DOCUMENTS

In covering the US Supreme Court decision in Breedlove v. Suttles, *7 December 1937, The At-lanta Constitution reviews the issues behind the case, which is covered here as the second most important story behind a decision on aluminum.*

HIGH COURT RULES U.S. FREE TO RESUME ALUMINUM CASE

Georgia Poll Tax Law Upheld in Opinion by Justice Butler

WASHINGTON, Dec. 6. (AP) – The Supreme Court decided today that the Justice Department is free to resume prosecution in New York of its anti-trust case against the Aluminum Company of America.

[...]

The court, convening after a two weeks' recess, announced decisions in 22 cases and issued 38 orders.

Income Levy Upheld

In a 5-to-4 decision, it held that states have the right to levy gross income taxes by contractors from the federal government for construction work on locks and dams. Justice Hughes read the majority opinion, from which Justice Roberts, Butler, McReynolds and Sutherland dissented.

The tribunal also upheld a Georgia statute forbidding male citizens to vote unless they have paid all accumulated poll taxes. Nolen R. Breedlove, of Atlanta, who challenged the law, contended it was discriminatory because women were required to pat the tax only for the year in which they desired to vote.

Power Is Equal

The opinion, read by Justice Butler, said imposition of a poll tax without enforcement would be "futile," that "power to levy and power to collect are equally necessary," and that it was "fanciful to suggest that the Georgia law was a mere disguise under which to deny or abridge the right of men to vote because of their sex."

Breedlove argued the tax was discriminatory because it was required of women voters only for the years in which they actually registered, because it applied only to persons 21 to 60 years of age, and because it made payment a prerequisite to voting.

Men who have reached 60 years of age, it pointed out, are given various other exemptions, and to levy against minors would place the burden upon their fathers.

One source of information on the movement to ban poll taxes is what used to be called the "black press": newspapers specifically aimed at the black American audience. This story, from the Baltimore Afro-American *of Maryland, 28 August 1962, discusses the movement to get an anti-poll tax amendment through both houses of Congress.*

Poll Tax Goes Seen Planning New Move

A plan has been approved to put a proposed anti-poll tax amendment to the Constitution to a vote in the House of Representatives Aug. 27, it was learned Saturday.

Backers of the Amendment said House Speaker John W. McCormack has approved the tentative plan in order to avoid a contest in the Rules Committee.

By taking the resolution directly to the floor, the requirement of a two-thirds vote in committee would thus be by-passed, but this procedure involves some risk for routine legislation that usually requires a majority vote only.

* * * * * *

HOWEVER, THERE would be little risk on the floor in this instance because the Constitution requires a twothirds vote of all members of Congress on a constitutional amendment.

The resolution has been approved in the Senate and its supporters believe that it would pass easily in the House if put to a roll call vote.

Only five states still require payment of the poll tax, a device that has been used in the South to limit voting by non-whites. The states are Virginia, Alabama, Arkansas, Mississippi, and Texas.

The amendment reads:

"The right of citizens of the United States to vote in any primary or other election for President or Vice President, for electors for President, or for Senator or Representative in Congress, shall not be denied or abridged by the United States or any State by reason of failure to pay any poll tax or any other tax."

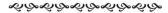

In this editorial from the St. Petersburg Times *[Florida], 28 August 1962, the issue of the poll tax is discussed and the lengthy work of Senator Spessard Holland is noted.*

Poll Tax On Way Out

House passage yesterday of a constitutional amendment outlawing the poll tax, following similar Senate action last March, is a victory for American democracy. It is also a personal triumph for Florida's Sen. Spessard Holland, who has introduced and sponsored the measure in every Congress since 1949.

Since the poll tax as a prerequisite for voting lingers on in only five of the 50 states, it can be taken for granted that the amendment will be ratified by the necessary three-fourths of the states and will become a part of the Constitution.

The Florida Legislature should, and we hope will, be the first to act – specifically as a tribute to Sen. Holland's leadership in the long Battle for this amendment. In fact, we would be glad to see Gov. Bryant[37] call a one-day special session for this purpose right after the November election, in order to get the jump on other legislatures which will meet in January.

IT IS TO BE recalled that Florida abolished its own poll tax two decades ago, during Holland's term as governor. In the five states which still have a poll tax, it is regarded as a serious impediment to voting in only two – Alabama and Mississippi. (The other states are Arkansas, Texas and Virginia.)

The important thing, though, is establishment of the principle that no price tag shall be placed on the right to vote in any national election.

The proposed anti-poll tax amendment passes the US House of Representatives, as reported here in The Sun *of Baltimore, Maryland, 28 August 1962.*

Anti-Poll Tax Amendment For US Elections Passed

HOUSE O.K.'S VOTING PLAN 295 TO 86

Ratification Is Needed Within 7 Years By 38 States

By Peter J. Kumpa
[Washington Bureau of The Sun]

Washington, Aug. 27 – By an overwhelming vote of 295 to 86, the House today completed congressional approval of a constitutional amendment which outlaws the payment of a poll or other tax as a qualification for voting in Federal elections.

If 38 states ratify the resolution within the next seven years, it will become the Twenty-fourth Amendment to the Constitution.

The Administration-backed measure, the only civil rights legislation that had a chance of passage this year, won only after stubborn procedural resistance by a bloc of Southern Democrats and a handful of conservative Republicans.

Supported By Leadership

With the support of both the Democratic and Republican leadership, the votes proved exactly 40 more than the two thirds required under the Constitution amending process and the suspension of rules in effect for the House today.

Voting for the Senate-approved amendment were 163 Democrats and 132 Republicans. Voting against were 71 Democrats and 15 Republicans.

All seven members of the Maryland delegation voted for the amendment.

President Kennedy hailed today's House action for culminating "a long legislative efforts of many, many years to bring about an end of this artificial bar to the right to vote in some of our states."

"Significant Action"

"This is a significant action which I am confident will be approved quickly by the required 38 state legislatures," he said.

The President had singled out the poll tax amendment as one of the five "must" bills at his last press conference when he declared that "Americans should not have to pay to vote."

The amendment, however, will apply to elections for President and Vice President and to Senate and House races.

It will not affect voters' qualifications in the states that still have the poll tax for state and other local elections.

Used In Five States

Five Southern states – Mississippi, Alabama, Virginia, Arkansas and Texas – still have the poll-tax requirement for voter registration on the books. These states were among the seven lowest in voter participation during the 1960 elections.

In only two, Mississippi and Alabama, did the Civil Rights Commission find that the poll tax requirement discriminated against potential Negro voters. In 1960, the two states had 25.6 and 30.9 percent persons of voting age casting ballots.

When other Southern states such as Florida, Tennessee, South Carolina and Georgia abolished the poll tax, there were increases in registration and voting.

It was agreed in the brief House debate today that the poll tax is not a major hindrance to increased Negro voting.

Protest Made

Representative Lindsay[38] (R., N.Y.), a GOP liberal, protested the amendment was like "using a sledge hammer to kill a goat."

He wanted a stronger amendment to outlaw the poll tax in local elections as he protested about the lack of opportunity to propose further amendments.

Though he voted for it, Lindsay griped that it was not a significant piece of civil-rights legislation.

Representative Celler[39] (D., N.Y.), chairman of the House Judiciary Committee, called Lindsay's complaint "a lot of malarkey."

The New York Republican, said Celler reminded him of a "bull that charges into an express train – commendable in courage but deficient in judgment."

Representative Williams[40] (D., Miss.) and Representative Smith[41] (D., Va.), chairman of the powerful Rules Committee, led the emotional Southern opposition.

For 2 hours and 45 minutes they prevented the House from considering the amendment by continuous calls for quorums and five roll-call votes on procedural steps.

They were overruled by Speaker McCormack[42] (D., Mass.) on their final protest on a point of order.

Smith shook his finger at the Republican side, blaming them as well as his own party leadership for forcing the measure that he said showed "disrespect and disrepute" for the Constitution.

Southerners argued that the amendment was invading a sacred prerogative of states rights in setting qualifications for voting.

States Rights Cited

They also pointed out in that in most states, Virginia, for one, the poll taxes collected were used for educational purposes.

Chairman Smith was stung back by his argument that the amendment should have been debated at greater length rather than the twenty minutes provided for each side under the rules suspension.

Representative Rogers[43] (D., Col.) reminded the Rules Committee chairman that his group had been requested to hold hearings and report the bill to the floor with debating time. In fact, Smith never bothered to hold hearings.

Federal legislation to eliminate the poll tax, either by statute or by constitutional amendment, has been introduced in every Congress since 1939.

Previous Actions Cited

On five different occasions, the House has passed anti-poll tax bills.

The stumbling block was the Senate where the threat of Southern filibuster prevented any action until the last Congress when a constitutional amendment was slipped through as part of a larger bill. The House, however, failed to act.

This year the Senate voted the amendment 77 to 16 on the motion of Senator Holland[44] (D., Fla.).

Southern Democrats let it pass without full-scale filibuster on the theory that it would relieve the leadership of pressure to push more reaching civil-rights legislation.

❧❧❧❧❧❧

We get a unique perspective of how the work to enact a constitutional amendment in Washington affects small town America from this article on the ratification of the Twenty-fourth Amendment, Big Spring Daily Herald of Texas, *24 January 1964.*

Poll Tax Receipt Needed To Vote in All Elections

It may well be that the action of South Dakota in ratifying the national poll tax amendment could create a confused situation in Texas in the matter of voting, but one thing remains crystal clear:

If you want to ensure your right to vote in all elections this year, pay the poll tax and get a poll tax receipt.

What may or may not happen after the General Services Agency[45] certifies that the 38th state has now banned payment of poll tax or other fee as a qualification for voting in federal elections in any state, it is assured by special provision of the Texas election laws that the person who has paid his poll tax for the current year can vote in all elections held this year.

FEDERAL VOTES

Later on this spring when the plans have been worked out, a system will be put in operation so that voters who do not want to pay the poll tax required to vote for county, district and state officials, can qualify themselves to vote for president, vice president, US senators and congressmen.

This program will probably require that such voters go to the tax assessor's office and obtain a registration receipt. This paper in Texas will consist of a poll tax receipt on which has been stamped "poll tax not paid." Such receipts will be issued without charge to all qualified voters who demand them. They will entitle the holder, when he presents the receipt at the polls, to vote in federal elections for federal officials.

However, all of these things are for the future.

30-DAY PERIOD

There will be a little interval before the certification of the South Dakota ratification is made. And after that, there will be a 30-day period set up for people to qualify themselves.

If you have paid your poll tax and hold a receipt or if you have a certificate of exemption issued for the current poll tax year, these documents qualify you to vote in all elections held in Texas this year. You do not have to come back to the tax office later for a second receipt or certificate.

If you do not have a poll tax receipt or an exemption certificate and do not want to get one before Jan. 31, but still have a desire to vote in federal elections, wait for an announcement of the proper time to go to the tax assessorcollector's office to register.

◞◟◞◟◞◟◞◟◞◟

Every Southern state that still had a poll tax by the time the Twenty-fourth Amendment was ratified debated the end of the tax and its effects on their particular state. Here is a view from Fayetteville, Arkansas, Northwest Arkansas Times, *25 January 1964, giving a detailed history of the poll tax in that state.*

In Arkansas As Everywhere: Poll Tax Problem Old

By JIMMIE "RED" JONES (AUDITOR OF STATE)

LITTLE ROCK – In Arkansas, as in most Southern states, poll and poll tax are the alpha and omega of city, county, and state government on all levels. In order for our democratic form of government to survive, we must have registered voters. Many ways of polling have been tried. Laws have been written, appealed, repealed, amended, and killed.

For 124 years, ever since Arkansas was admitted to the Union, people have paid a poll tax, but not until 1920 has the poll tax been a requirement for voting. History lists all five constitutions included the poll tax. The years 1836, 1861, 1864, 1868, and 1874.

At present the poll tax originates in the state auditor's office. Forms are drawn up and the blank receipts are distributed to county clerks of the 75 counties. The county clerk then delivers the poll tax receipts to the county tax collector, who in most cases is the sheriff and collector. There are 16 counties in the state where the collector's office is separate from the sheriff's office. To him falls the big job of selling every eligible voter a poll tax, and his ways and means are many. Persons who make application for a certain license or permit, designated under the laws of the state, shall present with such application his or her poll tax receipt, or evidence that the poll tax has been paid.

It hasn't always been so simple and clear-cut. The 1836 Constitution states: "No poll tax shall be assessed for other than county purposes"; the 1861 Constitution added, "for county or cooperation purposes"; the 1864 Constitution brought in the "free and equal" phrase. And by 1868 the poll tax issue had become so acute that the law makers saw fit to write into the Constitution: "The levying of taxes by the poll is grievous and oppressive; therefore, the General Assembly shall never levy a poll tax except for school purposes."

The people will go along with being taxed for school purposes, and that is the way it is today. Ninety-five cents out of each dollar paid for poll tax goes to the general or common fund for schools, which is disbursed by the county school superintendent and county treasurer to the school districts of each county. The disbursement is on a per student basis as to [the] number of pupils in the school district.

Not always have the state and county had close check and balance control systems as reassuring as today. It was in 1868 when the poll tax first appeared as [a] levy connected to property tax, known as the Clayton Law. This law was in direct contradiction to the fourth Arkansas Constitution, better known as the Carpetbag Constitution of 1868. Although this Clayton Carpetbag reign was the first to establish public schools in Arkansas, most of the tax money collected was said to be squandered and misused. The county originating as Clayton County later changed its name to Clay County because of the stigma of the former name. The fifth Arkansas Constitution of 1874 did not mention a poll tax as a prerequisite to vote.

Positive action began to take shape when Act. No. 88 was signed [on] March 23, 1885. This measure meted a levy annually of "one dollar per capita on every male inhabitant over 31 years of age." This was slated for common school purposes, but it too failed to mention anything about voting. However, by then it was a practiced requirement even though the legal status was not by definite law.

Five years later, in 1890, Mississippi and other Southern states made the poll tax requirements for voting a part of their constitutions.

The first constitutional amendment in Arkansas pertaining to [a] poll tax was submitted in 1893 and was known as Amendment No. 2. The vote was 75,940 for – 56,601 against, but since the total number of voters in that election for governor was 156, 192 the vote did not carry a majority. So this left a loophole for more wrangling.

The 1893 action was ruled as adopted and poll taxes were required for voting for twelve years, until in 1905 a federal judge ruled it invalid, and the Arkansas Supreme Court backed him in 1906, the following year.

In 1907 the Legislature resubmitted the question to the people and it was approved as Amendment No. 9, but here too there was not a majority of all the votes cast in that election. The vote was 88,386 for – 46,835 against. Voters numbered 183,000 in that election.

Regardless of the vote, the counties continued to collect the poll tax and made holding a receipt a requirement to vote.

The Arkansas Legislature, in 1919, submitted the woman's suffrage amendment to supersede the poll tax. When voted upon in 1920, it carried strong. The vote was 87,237 to 49,751. This also was declared lost because a majority of voters failed to mark the ballot on this particular issue. So in attack was made from another angle. Some thing was wrong with the voting regulations. The Arkansas Supreme Court ruled that, under the Initiative and Referendum Amendment of 1910, only a majority voting on a question was necessary for passage.

There was a time in 1936 when Arkansas voted on abolishing the poll tax, but the answer from the voters was a big NO. The fight for a true poll was a hard-earned victory and the voters did not forget.

Five Southern states still have a poll tax as requirement for voting.

The State Constitution sets out that a qualified elector must be a citizen of the United States, of the age of 21 years, who has resided in the state twelve months, in the county six months, and in the precinct, town or ward one month, and who has paid his or her poll tax.

Poll taxes are paid to the collector from October 2 through October 1 of the following year. In other words, 1963 poll tax paid any time from October 2, 1962 to October 1, 1963 inclusive, Entitles the tax payer, if otherwise qualified to vote in any election held in the State between October 2, 1963 and October 1, 1964, inclusive. 1964 poll tax receipts are now being issued by the collector in each county.

Supreme Court Cases

Breedlove v. Suttles *(302 U.S. 277 {1937}). Decided 6 December 1937 by a vote of 9-0. Justice Pierce Butler wrote the majority opinion.*

The Case: According to the case opinion, "[a] Georgia statute provides that there shall be levied and collected each year from every inhabitant of the State between the ages of 21 and 60 a poll tax of one dollar, but that the tax shall not be demanded from the blind or from females who do not register for voting. The state constitution declares that to entitle a person to register and vote at any election he shall have paid all poll taxes that he may have had opportunity to pay agreeably to law. The form of oath prescribed to qualify an elector contains a clause declaring compliance with that requirement. Tax collectors may not allow any person to register for voting unless satisfied that his poll taxes have been paid." Breedlove, whose first name is not given, was a Georgia citizen who sued Settles, the Georgia state Tax Collector, claiming that the collection of the tax violated his right to vote under the US Constitution. Ironically, Breedlove is identified as "a white male, 28 years old," who applied to vote in both federal and state elections, but stated quite clearly that he had not paid, and did not intend to pay, any tax so that he could vote; he demanded to vote anyway. The registrar refused him a ballot, and Breedlove did not vote. He filed suit in district court alleging that the poll tax was a violation of his rights. The case wound up to the Georgia state Supreme Court, which held for Suttles, the Tax Collector, in upholding the tax. Breedlove sued to the US Supreme Court, which granted certiorari, or the right to hear the case, and arguments were heard on 16 and 17 November 1937.

Less than a month later, on 6 December 1937, the Court upheld the state poll tax statute as constitutional. Writing for the Court, Justice Pierce Butler explained, "Levy by the poll has long been a familiar form of taxation, much used in some countries and to a considerable extent here, at first in the Colonies and later in the States. To prevent burdens deemed grievous and oppressive, the constitutions of some States prohibit or limit poll taxes. That of Georgia prevents more than a dollar a year. Poll taxes are laid upon persons without regard to their occupations or property to raise money for the support of government or some more specific end. The equal protection clause does not require absolute equality. While possible by statutory declaration to levy a poll tax upon every inhabitant of whatsoever sex, age or condition, collection from all would be impossible for always there are many too poor to pay. Attempt equally to enforce such a measure would justify condemnation of the tax as harsh and unjust."

He added, "Payment as a prerequisite is not required for the purpose of denying or abridging the privilege of voting. It does not limit the tax to electors; aliens are not there permitted to vote, but the tax is laid upon them, if within the defined class. It is not laid upon persons 60 or more years old, whether electors or not. Exaction of payment before registration undoubtedly serves to aid collection from electors desiring to vote, but that use of the State's power is not prevented by the Federal Constitution."

Butler concluded,

"To make payment of poll taxes a prerequisite of voting is not to deny any privilege or immunity protected by the Fourteenth Amendment. Privilege of voting is not derived from the United States, but is conferred by the State and, save as restrained by the Fifteenth and Nineteenth Amendments and other provisions of the Federal Constitution, the State may condition suffrage as it deems appropriate."

Harper v. Virginia State Board of Elections *(363 U.S. 663 {1966}). Decided 24 March 1966 by a vote of 6-3. Justice William O. Douglas wrote the majority opinion; Justices Hugo Black, John Marshall Harlan, and Potter Stewart dissented.*

The Case: The facts of the case were laid out in the US District Court for the Eastern District of Virginia at Alexandria, the decision of which came down in November 1964: "Poll tax payment as a prerequisite to voting in State and local elections, exacted by the Constitution and statutes of Virginia, is attacked in these two consolidated actions as violate of the no-abridgment and equal protection commands of the Federal Fourteenth Amendment. A corollary attack is made upon the provision of the State constitution excluding 'paupers' as persons entitled to vote in any election...The common premise of the assaults is: that the plaintiffs are financially unable to pay the tax – $1.50 for each of the 3 preceding years for which the elector was assessable; and that they and other State citizens similarly impecunious are thereby deprived, solely on account of their poverty, of the privilege to vote, and at the same time they are also denied a privilege accorded other citizens not so poor." Using the original finding of the US Supreme Court in the original "poll tax decision," Breedlove v. Suttles (302 US 277 {1937}), in which poll taxes had originally been held as constitutional, the District Court found for the state of Virginia. The plaintiffs, led by Annie E. Harper and Evelyn Butts, sued for relief to the US Supreme Court, which granted certiorari. Arguments were heard on 25 and 26 January 1966.

Almost exactly two months later, the court held by a 6-3 vote that all poll taxes, including those used in local elections out of the reach of the Twenty-fourth Amendment, were all wholly unconstitutional. Writing for the Court, Justice William O. Douglas stated,

"While the right to vote in federal elections is conferred by Art. I, § 2, of the Constitution...the right to vote in state elections is nowhere expressly mentioned. It is argued that the right to vote in state elections is implicit, particularly by reason of the First Amendment and that it may not constitutionally be conditioned upon the payment of a tax or fee. We do not stop to canvass the relation between voting and political expression. For it is enough to say that once the franchise is granted to the electorate, lines may not be drawn which are inconsistent with the Equal Protection Clause of the Fourteenth Amendment. That is to say, the right of suffrage 'is subject to the imposition of state standards which are not discriminatory and which do not contravene any restriction that Congress, acting pursuant to its constitutional powers, has imposed.' We were speaking there of a state literacy test which we sustained, warning that the result would be different if a literacy test, fair on its face, were used to discriminate against a class."

He concluded, "We conclude that a State violates the Equal Protection Clause of the Fourteenth Amendment whenever it makes the affluence of the voter or payment of any fee an electoral standard. Voter qualifications have no relation to wealth nor to paying or not paying this or any other tax. Our cases demonstrate that the Equal Protection Clause of the Fourteenth Amendment restrains the States from fixing voter qualifications which invidiously discriminate."

The Court's decision directly overruled its 1937 decision in *Breedlove v. Suttles*.

Sources: See the lower court decision in *Harper v. Virginia State Board of Elections* (240 F. Supp. 270 {Dist. Court, ED Va.}, 1964) for some additional underlying facts in the case; Ely, John Hart, "Interclausal Immunity," *Virginia Law Review*, LXXXVII:6 (October 2001), 1185-99.

Harman v. Forssenius *(380 U.S. 528 {1965}). Decided 27 April 1965 by a unanimous vote. Chief Justice Earl Warren wrote the majority opinion.*

The Case: The facts in this case were simple, and were laid out in the first lines of the Supreme Court decision: "We are called upon in this case to construe, for the first time, the Twenty-fourth Amendment to the Constitution of the United States...[t]he precise issue is whether § 24-17.2 of the Virginia Code – which provides that in order to qualify to vote in federal elections one must either pay a poll tax or file a witnessed or notarized certificate of residence – contravenes this command." Before the passage and ratification of the Twenty-fourth amendment to the US Constitution, the Virginia legislature enacted this statute, which laid out the qualification requirements for voting: 1. United States citizenship; 2. a minimum age of 21 years; 3. residence in the State for one year, or in the city or county for six months, and in the voting precinct for thirty days prior to an election; and 4. payment "at least six months prior to the election" a charge of $1.50 for a poll tax. In anticipation of the ratification of the Twenty-fourth amendment, Gov. Albertis S. Harrison, Jr., a Democrat, convened the state legislature in special session and they enacted an amended law, which ended the use of the poll tax for federal elections but retained them for local and state elections. Virginia residents Lars Forssenius and Horace E. Henderson sued A.M. Harman, Jr. (who may have been the Officer in charge of Elections in Virginia), claiming that the new law was violative of the Twenty-fourth Amendment. However, the United States District Court for the Eastern District of Virginia at Richmond held that even though the constitutional amendment only banned poll taxes for *federal* elections and not state or local elections, the Virginia statute was unconstitutional. Harman appealed to the US Supreme Court. Arguments were heard on 1 and 2 March 1965, with the court opinion being handed down less then eight weeks later, on 27 April 1965.

Speaking for a unanimous 9-0 Court, Chief Justice Earl Warren held that even though the constitutional amendment did not address poll taxes for local election, they were still in violation of the amendment and were unconstitutional. Warren wrote,

"Reaching the merits, it is important to emphasize that the question presented is not whether it would be within a State's power to abolish entirely the poll tax and require all voters – state and federal – to file annually a certificate of residence. Rather, the issue here is whether the State of Virginia may constitutionally confront the federal voter with a requirement that he either pay the customary poll taxes as required for state elections or file a certificate of residence. We conclude that this requirement constitutes an abridgment of the right to vote in federal elections in contravention of the Twentyfourth Amendment...Upon adoption of the Amendment, of course, no State could condition the federal franchise upon payment of a poll tax. The State of Virginia accordingly removed the poll tax as an absolute prerequisite to qualification for voting in federal elections, but in its stead substituted a provision whereby the federal voter could qualify either by paying the customary poll tax or by filing a certificate of residence six months before the election."

He continued,

"It has long been established that a State may not impose a penalty upon those who exercise a right guaranteed by the Constitution. Thus in order to demonstrate the invalidity of [statute] §24-17.2 of the Virginia Code, it need only be shown that it imposes a material requirement solely upon those who refuse to surrender their constitutional right to vote in federal elections without paying a poll tax. Section 24-17.2 unquestionably erects a real obstacle to voting in federal elections for those who assert their constitutional exemption from the poll tax. As previously indicated, the requirement for those who wish to participate in federal elections without paying the poll tax is that they file in each election year, within a stated interval ending six months before the election, a notarized or witnessed certificate attesting that they have been continuous residents of the State since the date of registration (which might have been many years before under Virginia's system of permanent registration) and that they do not presently intend to leave the city or county in which they reside prior to the forthcoming election. Unlike the poll tax bill which is sent to the voter's residence, it is not entirely clear how one obtains the necessary certificate. The statutes merely provide for the distribution of the forms to city and county court clerks, and for further distribution to local registrars and election officials."

He continued,

"Construing the statutes in the manner least burdensome to the voter, it would seem that the voter could either obtain the certificate of residence from local election officials or prepare personally 'a certificate in form substantially' as set forth in the statute. The certificate must then be filed 'in person, or otherwise' with the city or county treasurer. This is plainly a cumbersome procedure. In effect, it amounts to annual re-registration which Virginia officials have sharply contrasted with the 'simple' poll tax system.[21] For many, it would probably seem far preferable to mail in the poll tax payment upon receipt of the bill. In addition, the certificate must be filed six months before the election, thus perpetuating one of the disenfranchising characteristics of the poll tax which the Twenty-fourth Amendment was designed to eliminate. We are thus constrained to hold that the requirement imposed upon the voter who refuses to pay the poll tax constitutes an abridgment of his right to vote by reason of failure to pay the poll tax."

Warren concluded,

"The poll tax was later characterized by the Virginia Supreme Court of Appeals as a device limiting 'the right of suffrage to those who took sufficient interest in the affairs of the State to qualify themselves to vote.' Whether, as the State contends, the payment of the poll tax is also a reliable indicium of continuing residence need not be decided, for even if the poll tax has served such an evidentiary function, the confrontation of the federal voter with a requirement that he either continue to pay the customary poll tax or file a certificate of residence could not be sustained. For federal elections the poll tax, regardless of the services it performs, was abolished by the Twentyfourth Amendment. That Amendment was also designed to absolve all requirements impairing the right to vote in federal elections by reason of failure to pay the poll tax. Section 24-17.2 of the Virginia Code falls within this proscription."

ভাগ্যভাগ্যভাগ্যভাগ্য

Burdick v. Takushi *(504 U.S. 428 {1992}). Decided 8 June 1992 by a vote of 5-3. Justice Byron White delivered the opinion of the Court.*

The Case: A Hawaii statute prohibited write-in votes. The petitioner challenged the statute, arguing that it violated his rights to free speech and association under the First and Fourteenth Amendments.

The Court held that the statute did not unduly burden the petitioner and did not violate his rights under the First and Fourteenth Amendments.

Justice White wrote,

"Indeed, the foregoing leads us to conclude that when a State's ballot access laws pass constitutional muster as imposing only reasonable burdens on First and Fourteenth Amendment rights-as do Hawaii's election laws-a prohibition on write-in voting will be presumptively valid, since any burden on the right to vote for the candidate of one's choice will be light and normally will be counterbalanced by the very state interests supporting the ballot access scheme.

"In such situations, the objection to the specific ban on write-in voting amounts to nothing more than the insistence that the State record, count, and publish individual protests against the election system or the choices presented on the ballot through the efforts of those who actively participate in the system. There are other means available, however, to voice such generalized dissension from the electoral process; and we discern no adequate basis for our requiring the State to provide and to finance a place on the ballot for recording protests against its constitutionally valid election laws.

"'No right is more precious in a free country than that of having a voice in the election of those who make the laws under which, as good citizens, we must live.' Wesberry v. Sanders, 376 U. S. 1, 17 (1964). But the right to vote is the right to participate in an electoral process that is necessarily structured to maintain the integrity of the democratic system. We think that Hawaii's prohibition on write-in voting, considered as part of an electoral scheme that provides constitutionally sufficient ballot access, does not impose an unconstitutional burden upon the First and Fourteenth Amendment rights of the State's voters."

Crawford v. Marion County Election Board (553 U.S. 181 {2008}). Decided 28 April 2008 by a vote of 6-3. Justice John Paul Stevens wrote the majority opinion; Justices David Souter, Ruth Bader Ginsburg, and Stephen Breyer dissented.

The Case: Following years of allegations of voter fraud in elections from coast to coast, a number of states moved in the first years of the 21st century to pass so-called "Voter ID" laws, which demanded that voters show stateor government-provided identification before casting a vote. Indiana was one of those states. William Crawford, an Indiana voter, sued the Marion County Election Board, claiming that the imposition of a "voter ID" to vote was akin to a poll tax, and demanded that it be struck down as volatile of the Twenty-fourth Amendment to the US Constitution. The district court in Indiana held that the Voter ID law was not in violation of the Twenty-fourth amendment; Crawford appealed to the United States Court of Appeals for the Seventh Circuit in Chicago. Holding for that court in upholding the law, Judge Richard Posner wrote, "The Indiana law is not like a poll tax, where on one side is the right to vote and on the other side the state's interest in defraying the cost of elections or in limiting the franchise to people who really care about voting or in excluding poor people or in discouraging people who are black. The purpose of the Indiana law is to reduce voting fraud, and voting fraud impairs the right of legitimate voters to vote by diluting their votesdilution being recognized to be an impairment of the right to vote." Crawford appealed to the US Supreme Court, which granted certiorari. Arguments were heard on 9 January 2008.

On 28 April 2008, the Court held, 6-3, that the Indiana law, and Voter ID laws in general, did not violate the Twenty-fourth amendment. Justice John Paul Stevens held for the Court, joined in part by Chief Justice John Roberts and Justice Anthony Kennedy; Justices Antonin Scalia, Clarence Thomas, and Samuel Alito concurred but agreed that the ID laws might "impose a burden" on some voters.

Justice Stevens wrote, "At issue in these cases is the constitutionality of an Indiana statute requiring citizens voting in person on election day, or casting a ballot in person at the office of the circuit court clerk prior to election day, to present photo identification issued by the government. Referred to as either the 'Voter ID Law' or 'SEA 483,' the statute applies to in-person voting at both primary and general elections. The requirement does not apply to absentee ballots submitted by mail, and the statute contains an exception for persons living and voting in a state-licensed facility such as a nursing home. A voter who is indigent or has a religious objection to being photographed may cast a provisional ballot that will be counted only if she executes an appropriate affidavit before the circuit court clerk within 10 days following the election. A voter who has photo identification but is unable to present that identification on election day may file a provisional ballot that will be counted if she brings her photo identification to the circuit county clerk's office within 10 days. No photo identification is required in order to register to vote, and the State offers free photo identification to qualified voters able to establish their residence and identity."

He then explained, "The complaints in the consolidated cases allege that the new law substantially burdens the right to vote in violation of the Fourteenth Amendment; that it is neither a necessary nor appropriate method of avoiding election fraud; and that it will arbitrarily disfranchise qualified voters who do not possess the required identification and will place an unjustified burden on those who cannot readily obtain such identification."

Stevens, a moderate who had become decidedly liberal over the years he spent on the Court, then went over the recent history of court decisions dealing with a poll tax:

"In *Harper v. Virginia State Board of Elections*, the Court held that Virginia could not condition the right to vote in a state election on the payment of a poll tax of $1.50. We rejected the dissenters' argument that the interest in promoting civic responsibility by weeding out those voters who did not care enough about public affairs to pay a small sum for the privilege of voting provided a rational basis for the tax. Applying a stricter standard, we concluded that a State 'violates the Equal Protection Clause of the Fourteenth Amendment whenever it makes the affluence of the voter or payment of any fee an electoral standard.' We used the term 'invidiously discriminate' to describe conduct prohibited under that standard, noting that we had previously held that while a State may obviously impose 'reasonable residence restrictions on the availability of the ballot,' it 'may not deny the opportunity to vote to a bona fide resident merely because he is a member of the armed services.' Although the State's justification for the tax was rational, it was invidious because it was irrelevant to the voter's qualifications. Thus, under the standard applied in *Harper*, even rational restrictions on the right to vote are invidious if they are unrelated to voter qualifications. In *Anderson v. Celebrezze*, 460 U. S. 780 (1983), however, we confirmed the general rule that 'evenhanded restrictions that protect the integrity and reliability of the electoral process itself' are not invidious and satisfy the standard set forth in *Harper*. Rather than applying any 'litmus test' that would neatly separate valid from invalid restrictions, we concluded that a court must identify and evaluate the interests put forward by the State as justifications for the burden imposed by its rule, and then make the 'hard judgment' that our adversary system demands."

Justice Stevens continued,

"The State has identified several state interests that arguably justify the burdens that SEA 483 imposes on voters and potential voters. While petitioners argue that the statute was actually motivated by partisan concerns and dispute both the significance of the State's interests and the magnitude of any real threat to those interests, they do not question the legitimacy of the interests the State has identified. Each is unquestionably relevant to the State's interest in protecting the integrity and reliability of the electoral process...Given the fact that petitioners have advanced a broad attack on the constitutionality of SEA 483, seeking relief that would invalidate the statute in all its applications, they bear a heavy burden of persuasion."

He concluded,

"In their briefs, petitioners stress the fact that all of the Republicans in the General Assembly voted in favor of SEA 483 and the Democrats were unanimous in opposing it. In her opinion rejecting petitioners' facial challenge, Judge Barker [the district judge who first heard the case] noted that the litigation was the result of a partisan dispute that had 'spilled out of the state house into the courts.' It is fair to infer that partisan considerations may have played a significant role in the decision to enact SEA 483. If such considerations had provided the only justification for a photo identification requirement, we may also assume that SEA 483 would suffer the same fate as the poll tax at issue in *Harper*. But if a nondiscriminatory law is supported by valid neutral justifications, those justifications should not be disregarded simply because partisan interests may have provided one motivation for the votes of individual legislators. The state interests identified as justifications for SEA 483 are both neutral and sufficiently strong to require us to reject petitioners' facial attack on the statute...The application of the statute to the vast majority of Indiana voters is amply justified by the valid interest in protecting 'the integrity and reliability of the electoral process.' The judgment of the Court of Appeals is affirmed."

WHO'S WHO

This section includes biographies of two individuals who played a significant part in drafting and passing the Twenty-fourth Amendment. They are both mentioned in earlier sections of this chapter.

Emanuel Celler (1888-1981)

During his 50-year career in the US House of Representatives, Emanuel Celler rose to become one of the most powerful lawmakers of his time. Serving as the chairman of the all-important Committee on the Judiciary, he was responsible in 1960 for the passage of the Twenty-third Amendment, which gave voting rights and electoral votes to the District of Columbia, and, in 1962, for the Twenty-fourth Amendment, which ended the poll tax in the United States regarding Federal elections.

Celler was born in Brooklyn, New York, on 6 May 1888, the son of Henry Celler, a whiskey seller, and his wife Josephine (née Müller) Celler. (Some sources on Celler's life report that he was the second child of his parents, while others say that he was the eldest.) The family was poor; the parents were born of German Jews who had come to America looking for a better life. When Henry Celler's whiskey business, which he ran out of his home under the brand "Echo Spring," failed, he earned his living selling goods door to door. Emanuel Celler attended local schools in Brooklyn and, in 1906, entered Columbia College (now Columbia University). Just as the younger Celler was entering Columbia, his father suddenly died, and his mother passed away five months later. In his 1953 autobiography, *You Never Leave Brooklyn: The Autobiography of Emanuel Celler*, Celler wrote, "I became the head of the household...I took up [his father's] wine route. I went to school in the morning and sold wines all afternoon until seven o'clock in the evening." Despite having to juggle his father's business with college studies, Manny, as he was known, graduated from Columbia in 1910 and, two years later, from the Columbia University Law School. That same year, 1912, he was admitted to the New York bar and opened a practice in New York City. In 1914, he married Stella Baar; together, the couple had two daughters, one of whom suffered from cerebral palsy.

A liberal Democrat, Celler began his upward climb in Democratic Party circles when, in 1917, as the United States entered the First World War, he was named as an appeal agent on a draft board in New York City, representing the US Government, ruling on the appeals of men who desired to be turned down for combat duty in Europe. In 1922, Celler was a delegate to the New York state Democratic convention. There, he was asked by officials at Tammany Hall (also known as the Society of St. Tammany, and the Democratic political organization that controlled New York City and New York State politics until the 1960s) to run for a seat in the US House of Representatives, representing the Tenth New York District, which had never before been represented by a Democrat. Celler agreed, and ran an unorthodox campaign, denouncing Prohibition and favoring American entry into the League of Nations. Despite the overwhelming Republican advantage in the district, he defeated his Republican opponent, Rep. Lester David Volk, by some 3,000+ votes, and, on 4 March 1923, took his seat in the US House of Representatives. He would remain in that seat for 49 years and 10 months, one of the longest periods of service in congressional history.

Almost from the start, Celler was a strong advocate for loosened immigration rules. He made his first speech on the floor of the US House in opposition to the Johnson-Reed Immigration Act of 1924, which set strict quotas limiting the number of immigrants from certain nations, based on the censuses of 1890, 1900, and 1910. The Act allowed more immigrants from Great Britain, Sweden, Ireland, and Germany, and limited the number of immigrants from Eastern European and Asian nations.

Celler was a consistent Democratic vote. Historians Louis Sandy Maisel, Ira N. Forman, Donald Altschiller wrote, "Beginning in his first term, Celler supported liberal causes, the whole gamut of New Deal legislation: prolabor laws, Social Security, the Tennessee Valley Authority, and so forth." However, they add, "From the age of twentyfive, when he first read [Theodor] Herzl's *Jewish State*, Celler, a Reform Jew, was an active and supporter of Jewish statehood. Time once termed him 'Zionist Celler.' During World War II, President Franklin D. Roosevelt confided in him about Churchill's support for a Jewish homeland in Palestine after the end of the war. Celler attended the United Nations sessions on the partition of Palestine and visited the country shortly before statehood was declared, meeting with David Ben-Gurion. While Celler supported President Harry S Truman's Marshall Plan and foreign aid, he opposed a loan to Great Britain because of its policy toward Palestine."

It was during the New Deal era that Celler was able to get his legislation passed. He voted regularly for legislation that regulated business practices, and he voted in favor of almost the entire range of governmental programs that President Franklin D. Roosevelt advocated, including Social Security, the Tennessee Valley Authority, and actions that aided labor unions. Celler was also a reliable vote for Roosevelt's foreign policy, even more so after the start of the Second World War. In 1940, he rose to become one of the key members of the House Judiciary Committee; at the start of the Eighty-first Congress (1949-51), he became the chairman of that important committee, where he played a leading role in the passage of some of the most important civil rights legislation of the 20th century.

Historian Catherine A. Barnes explained, "Celler played a key role in the development of civil rights legislation during the Kennedy Administration. He had prepared civil rights recommendations for Kennedy during his campaign for the presidency, and with Kennedy's backing, Celler sponsored the 24th Amendment, approved by Congress in August 1962 and ratified in 1964, which abolished the poll tax in federal elections. In February 1963 Kennedy sent Congress a modest civil rights bill limited largely to the protection of voting rights. Celler, who had proposed much stronger legislation in May 1961, urged Kennedy to broaden his bill to include public accommodations and employment. The rising tempo of the civil rights movement, in particular the April 1963 demonstrations in Birmingham, Alabama, finally brought Kennedy to support legislation of the type Celler advocated. After Kennedy presented an expanded bill to Congress in June, Celler and the Administration worked closely to secure its passage. His judiciary subcommittee held hearings on Kennedy's measure during the fall of 1963, reporting out a bill much stronger than the Administration's on October 21. Fearful that the subcommittee's proposal would fail in Congress, Kennedy worked out a compromise measure with Celler, who then shepherded it through the Judiciary Committee in late October. Celler also guided the bill, which became the landmark Civil Rights Act of 1964, through the full House in February 1964."

In 1960, Celler, with several Representatives and US Senators, worked to get a constitutional amendment through both houses of Congress that gave voting and electoral rights to the District of Columbia; at the same time, he tried to add to amendment language that would outlaw the poll tax in all federal elections in the United States. Because of the opposition of some Southern Democrats in the US Senate, the anti-poll tax portion of the amendment was stripped from the proposal, but the District of Columbia voting rights amendment passed through the Congress and was eventually ratified (in 1962) as the Twenty-third Amendment. Not giving up, Celler pushed to get amendment language through both houses to abolish the poll tax. Through the years of hard work of Senator Spessard Holland of Florida to end the poll tax, a proposed amendment was passed through the US Senate. In the US House, Celler, the chairman of the Judiciary Committee, adjusted some language and got the amendment past both houses of Congress and sent to the states, where it was ratified in 1964. In the history of the 27 constitutional amendments, Rep. Emanuel Celler is one of the few people who have been responsible for the passage of two amendments. Celler also worked behind the scenes to get enacted the Civil Rights Act of 1964 and the Voting

Rights Act of 1965 – two major pieces of civil rights legislation. In 1965, Celler, with Senator Philip Hart, Democrat of Michigan, co-authored the Hart-Celler Immigration Act, which eliminated the quota system imposed by the 1921 Reed Act and the 1924 Reed-Johnson Act, giving more allowances to peoples from the Eastern Hemisphere and fewer to those of the Western Hemisphere. President Lyndon Baines Johnson signed the bill into law on 3 October 1965 at the Statue of Liberty.

Despite his liberal bona fides, and his lengthy career of supporting liberal causes, Celler angered the liberal community on two major issues: his support, until the end of his congressional career in 1973, of the Vietnam War; and his lack of support for equal rights for women, despite being a strong advocate for civil rights. After he left the Congress, an Equal Rights Amendment did pass the Congress and was sent to the states, but it did not get the requisite number of state ratifications, and failed in 1982.

By 1972, Celler had angered many of his constituents by seeming aloof. He rarely visited the district, and did not have any connections to the people who sent him to Washington. Despite this, and his advanced age, in 1972, it appeared that he would easily win re-election. However, he was challenged in the Democratic primary – for the first time in his career – by a young female attorney named Elizabeth Holtzman. Despite Celler's long career and tremendous number of legislative successes, Holtzman won in a close race. When he left the House in January 1973, Celler was just two months shy of half a century of congressional service.

Celler returned to New York, where he practiced law and lived in Brooklyn. His wife died in 1976, and his health declined soon after. He died at home in Brooklyn on 15 January 1981, four months shy of his 93rd birthday. He was laid to rest in Mount Neboh Cemetery in Cypress Hills, New York.

Spessard Lindsey Holland (1892-1971)

Spessard Holland was a Southerner and a staunch segregationist, yet the key originator of the concept of a constitutional amendment to abolish the poll tax. Working to end the tax as a legislator in Florida, he rose to become that state's Governor, and then was elected to the US Senate, where he worked from 1949 until 1962 to have that amendment passed.

Spessard Holland was born in the small town of Bartow, Florida, on 10 July 1892, the son of Benjamin Franklin Holland, a farmer and citrus grove owner, and his wife, Fannie Virginia (née Spessard) Holland, a teacher at the Summerlin Institute in Bartow. Holland came from a long line of legislators: his paternal grandfather, Lindsay Holland, had served in the Georgia state legislature, and his maternal grandfather, Natural Spessard, had served in the Virginia state legislature. Holland attended the public schools in the Bartow area and went to Emory College (now Emory University) in Oxford, near Atlanta, Georgia, graduating in 1912. Returning to his home state, he entered the University of Florida College of Law at Gainesville, and graduated with a law degree in 1916. During his time at law school, Holland taught in the public schools of Warrenton, Georgia, from 1912 to 1914. In 1916, he was admitted to the Florida bar, and opened a law practice in his hometown of Bartow.

When the United States entered the First World War, Holland volunteered for service, was commissioned with the rank of second lieutenant, and was assigned first to the Coast (aka Coastal) Artillery Corps until 1918, when he was named to the Army Air Corps and sent to France until the end of the conflict. He was decorated with a Distinguished Service Cross. Returning home, in 1919 Holland was named the prosecuting attorney for Polk County,

Florida, where he served until 1920. The following year, he was elected a county judge for Polk County, serving until 1929. In 1919 he married Mary Agnes Groover, and together the couple had four children.

In the depths of the Depression, in 1932, Holland was elected to a seat in the Florida state Senate as a Democrat. Florida was run by the Democrats, and all statewide politicians were part of that party's machinery. While in the state Senate however, Holland bucked his party, which worked to deny black citizens the right to vote through every maneuver possible, and pushed to end the poll tax, a fee imposed on all voters, without which one could not vote. Holland's motives were not entirely pure, as he believed that the poll tax also harmed poor whites, who made up the backbone of the Democratic Party's voter rolls. The fact that blacks, who were rapidly moving towards the Democrats and away from the GOP, could vote for Democrats was an added bonus.

In 1940, Holland decided to run for governor. In the Democratic primary – which would be the general election because the state was run by Democrats – Holland defeated Francis P. Whitehair by more than 60,000 votes. During his single four-year term as Governor, Holland advocated the development of the Everglades as a national park, and began a massive program of road construction in the state. Holland decided not to run for re-election in 1944. Less than two years later, however, US Senator Charles Oscar Andrews, Democrat of Florida, decided against another term because of declining health. (Andrews would die on 18 September 1946, before his term ended.) Holland ran for the seat, and won against Republican Harry Schad, carrying 60.7% of the vote. For the remainder of Andrews' term, set to expire in January 1947, Florida Governor Millard Caldwell named Holland to serve the shortened term, so that in January 1947, Holland was sworn in for a full term of his own, with some degree of seniority over his fellow 1946-elected Senators.

Serving until 1971, Holland spent his first decade and a half trying to get a constitutional amendment to abolish the poll tax. He was initially named to the Committee on Rules and to the Committee on the District of Columbia, where he also pushed for an amendment for electoral and voting rights for the District. Holland, a staunch Democrat, strongly supported President Harry S Truman's foreign policy program, which included aid to Greece, known as the Truman Doctrine, aid to post-World War II Europe, known as the Marshall Plan, and joining the North Atlantic Treaty Organization, or NATO. In 1950, he backed Truman in sending American troops to southern Korea to keep that nation from falling into the hands of the Soviet-backed North Korean regime.

While a segregationist at heart, Holland believed that blacks and whites should be treated equally, demonstrated by his desire to end the poll tax. Holland, however, did not wholly embrace the burgeoning civil rights movement. In 1956, a document called The Southern Manifesto, signed by 19 US Senators and 77 members of the US House of Representatives, denounced the US Supreme Court's holding of separate but equal accommodations in education. Historian Tony Badger explained in 1999, "In Florida, Spessard Holland had sufficient doubts about the Manifesto and worked with [Senator James William] Fulbright [of Arkansas] and [Senator Marion] Price Daniel [of Texas] to tone it down, but he eventually signed and [Senator] George Smathers [of Florida] as a matter of reflex followed suit." In 1964, as both houses of Congress contemplated passing the landmark Civil Right Act of 1964, Holland told opponents of the bill, "We'll stand up and fight [it] as long as we can." Despite this historical stain on Holland's record, he did work to bring together badly divided parties to get the language for an anti-poll tax amendment through the US Senate in 1962, which became the Twenty-fourth Amendment to the US Constitution.

In 1970, after 24 years and four terms in the US Senate, Holland, in declining health, decided against running for re-election, and on 3 January 1971, he left the body he had spent a quarter of his life in. He returned to Florida, where he died at his home in Bartow on 6 November 1971, at the age of 79. He was laid to rest in the Holland family plot in the Wildwood Cemetery in Bartow. His widow, Mary Mathilda Groover, died of a stroke in March 1975 and was laid to rest next to her husband.

In a eulogy, Holland's fellow Democrat, US Senator Robert C. Byrd of West Virginia, said of him, "I never met a more fair-minded individual, one more dedicated or more conscientious in serving the people." In a eulogy delivered on the US Senate floor, Senator James Browning Allen, Democrat of Alabama, said, "Mr. President, with the retirement and subsequent death of the Honorable Spessard L. Holland, the Nation, as well as his native State of Florida, lost a great patriot and one of her most distinguished sons. The United States Senate, where Senator Holland made an outstanding record during an illustrious career of almost 25 years, lost some of its greatness and some of its luster on his retirement from the Senate; for, surely, it was Senator Holland and Senators of his type who earned for the US Senate the accolade of 'greatest deliberative body in the world.'"

FOOTNOTES, SOURCES, FURTHER READING

Footnotes

1 Williams, Frank B., Jr., "The Poll Tax as a Suffrage Requirement in the South, 1870-1901," *The Journal of Southern History*, XVIII:4 (November 1952), 469.

2 Crawford, Sidney Robert, "The Poll Tax" (Master's thesis, University of Arkansas, 1944), 6-7.

3 Chitwood, Oliver, "A History of Colonial America" (New York: Harper & Brothers, Publishers, 1931), 192

4 *The Civil Rights Cases* (109 US 3 {1883}), at 25.

5 Remarks of Senator John T. Morgan, 8 January 1900, in "The Congressional Record: Proceedings and Debates of the 56th Congress, 1st Session" (Washington: Government Printing Office, 1900), 33. See also Morgan, John Tyler, "Negro Suffrage in the South. Mr. Pritchard's Resolution. Speech in the Senate of the United States, January 8, 1900" (Washington: Government Printing Office, 1900).

6 [FN] Lewinson, Paul, "Race, Class, & Party: A History of Negro Suffrage and White Politics in the South" (New York: Russell & Russell, 1963), 46-97.

7 Brewer, William M., "The Poll Tax and Poll Taxers," *The Journal of Negro History*, XXIX:3 (July 1944), 264

8 Ibid., 265.

9 Binder, Sarah A.; and Steven S. Smith, "Politics or Principle? Filibustering in the United States Senate" (Washington, D.C.; The Brookings Institute, 1997), 140.

10 Ackerman, Bruce; and Jennifer Nou, "Canonizing the Civil Rights Revolution: The People and the Poll Tax," *Northwestern University Law Review*, CIII:1 (2009), 87.

11 North Carolina Conference of the NAACP et al. v. McCrory et al. (July 29, 2016), Fourth US Circuit Court of Appeals, Appeal 16-1468, 56.

12 Michael Joseph (Mike) Mansfield (1903-2001), Democrat of Montana, US Representative (1943-53), US Senator (1953-77), US Ambassador Extraordinary and Plenipotentiary to Japan (1977-88).

13 Richard Brevard Russell, Jr. (1897-1971), Democrat of Georgia, Member, Georgia state House of Representatives (1921-31), Governor of Georgia (1931-33), US Senator (1933-71).

14 Quentin Northrup Burdick (1908-1992), Democrat of North Dakota, US Representative (1959-60), US Senator (1960-92)

15 Jennings Randolph (1902-1998), Democrat of West Virginia, US Representative (1933-47), US Senator (1958-85).

16 Frank John Lausche (1895-1990), Democrat of Ohio, Judge, Municipal Court, Cleveland, Ohio (1932-37), Judge, Court of Common Pleas (1937-41), Mayor of Cleveland (1941-44), Governor of Ohio (1945-57), US Senator (1957-69).

17 Jacob Koppel Javits (1904-1986), Republican of New York, US Representative (1947-54), Attorney General, New York State (1954-57), US Senator (1957-81).

18 Prescott Sheldon Bush (1895-1972), Republican of Connecticut, US Senator (1952-63).

19 Emanuel Celler (1888-1981), Democrat of New York, US Representative (1923-73). See the comprehensive biography for Celler in the "influential biographies" section of the Twenty-fourth Amendment.

20 Thomas Gerstle Abernethy (1903-1998), Democrat of Mississippi, Mayor of Eupora, Mississippi (1927-29), District Attorney, Third Judicial District of Mississippi (1936-42), US Representative (1943-73).

21 John William McCormack (1891-1980), Democrat of Massachusetts, Member, Massachusetts state House of Representatives (1920-22), Member, state Senate (1923-26), US Representative (1928-71), Speaker of the House of Representatives (1961-71).

22 Edwin Edward Willis (1904-1972), Democrat of Louisiana, Member, Louisiana state Senate (1948-49), US Representative (1949-69)

23 Robert Thomas Ashmore (1904-1989), Democrat of South Carolina, Solicitor, Greenville, South Carolina, County Court (1930-34), Solicitor, Thirteenth Judicial Circuit of South Carolina (1936-53), US Representative (1953-69).

24 Elijah Lewis Forrester (1896-1970), Democrat of Georgia, Solicitor, City Court, Leesburg, Georgia (1920-33), Mayor, Leesburg, Georgia (1922-31), County Attorney, Lee County, Georgia (1928-37), Solicitor Gen., Southwestern Judicial Circuit (1937-50), US Representative (1951-55).

25 John Vernard Dowdy (1912-1995), Democrat of Texas, District Attorney, Third Judicial District of Texas (1945-52), US Representative (1952-73).

26 William Munford Tuck (1896-1983), Democrat of Virginia, Member, Virginia state House of Delegates (1924-32), Member, Virginia state Senate (1932-42), Lieutenant Governor of Virginia (1942-46), Governor of Virginia (1946-50), US Representative (1953-69)

27 Charles Abraham Halleck (1900-1986), Republican of Indiana, US Representative (1935-69).

28 William Moore McCulloch (1901-1980), Republican of Ohio, US Representative (1947-73).

29 Walter Edward Rogers (1908-2001), Democrat of Texas, City Attorney, Tampa, Texas (1938-40), District Attorney, Thirty-first Judicial Circuit of Texas (1943-47), US Representative (1951-67).

[30] John Vliet Lindsay (1921-2000), Republican (and, in 1971, Democrat) of New York, US Representative (1959-65), Mayor, New York City (1965-73).

[31] Howard Worth Smith (1883-1976), Democrat of Virginia, Commonwealth Attorney, Alexandria, Virginia (1918-22), Judge, Corporation Court, Alexandria (1922-28), Judge, Sixteenth Judicial Circuit of Virginia (1928-30), US Representative (1931-67).

[32] Byron Giles Rogers (1900-1983), Democrat of Colorado, City Attorney, Las Animas, Colorado (1929-33), Member, Colorado state House of Representatives (1932-35), Assistant United States Attorney for Colorado (1934-36), Attorney General for Colorado (1936-41), US Representative (1951-71).

[33] Seymour Halpern (1913-1997), Republican of New York, Member, New York state Senate (1941-54), US Representative (1959-73).

[34] Richard Harding Poff (1923-2011), Republican of Virginia, US Representative (1953-72), Justice, Virginia state Supreme Court (1972-2011).

[35] Charles Samuel Joelson (1916-1999), Democrat of New Jersey, City Counsel, Paterson, New Jersey (1949-52), Deputy Attorney General for New Jersey (1954-56), Member, Passaic County Prosecutor's Office (1956-58), Director of Criminal Investigation, State of New Jersey (1958-60), US Representative (1961-69).

[36] William Moore McCulloch (1901-1980), Republican of Ohio, US Representative (1947-73)

[37] C[ecil] Farris Bryant (1914-2002) was the 34th Governor of Florida (1961-65).

[38] John Vliet Lindsay (1921-2000), Republican (and, in 1971, Democrat) of New York, US Representative (1959-65), Mayor, New York City (1965-73).

[39] Emanuel Celler (1888-1981), Democrat of New York, US Representative (1923-73). See the comprehensive biography for Celler in the "Who's Who" section of this amendment.

[40] John Bell Williams (1918-1983), Democrat of Mississippi, Prosecuting Attorney, Hinds County, Mississippi (1944-46), US Representative (1947-68), Governor of Mississippi (1968-72).

[41] Howard Worth Smith (1883-1976), Democrat of Virginia, Commonwealth Attorney, Alexandria, Virginia (1918-22), Judge, Corporation Court, Alexandria (1922-28), Judge, Sixteenth Judicial Circuit of Virginia (1928-30), US Representative (1931-67).

[42] John William McCormack (1891-1980), Democrat of Massachusetts, Member, Massachusetts state House of Representatives (1920-22), Member, state Senate (1923-26), US Representative (1928-71), Speaker of the House of Representatives (1961-71).

[43] Byron Giles Rogers (1900-1983), Democrat of Colorado, City Attorney, Las Animas, Colorado (1929-33), Member, Colorado state House of Representatives (1932-35), Assistant United States Attorney for Colorado (1934-36), Attorney General for Colorado (1936-41), US Representative (1951-71).

[44] Spessard Lindsey Holland (1892-1971), Democrat of Florida, Prosecuting Attorney, Polk County, Florida (1919-20), County Judge, Polk County (1921-29), Member, Florida state Senate (1932-40), Governor of Florida (1941-45), US Senator (1946-71). See the comprehensive biography for Holland in the "influential biographies" section of this amendment.

[45] There is no such thing as the "General Services Agency"; what was meant was the General Services Administration, or the GSA, recently in a news in 2012 following a series of accounting scandals in that government department.

Sources Arranged by Chapter Sections

Debate in Congress

"The Congressional Record: Proceedings and Debates of the 87th Congress, Second Session. Volume 108 – Part 3. February 26, 1962, to March 15, 1962" (Washington: Government Printing Office, 1962), 5072-80.

"The Congressional Record: Proceedings and Debates of the 87th Congress, Second Session. Volume 108, Part 13. August 20, 1962, to August 30, 1962" (Washington: Government Printing Office, 1962), 17655-62.

Historical Background Documents

"Poll Tax and Enfranchisement of District of Columbia: Hearings Before a Subcommittee of the Committee on the Judiciary[,] United States Senate[,] Eighty-Sixth Congress[,] First Session, on S.J. Res. 126, Proposing an Amendment to the Constitution of the United States, Relating to the Qualifications of Electors[,] [and] S.J. Res. 60, Proposing an Amendment to the Constitution of the United States, Granting Representation in the House of Representatives and in the Electoral College to the District of Columbia, S.J. Res. 71, Proposing an Amendment to the Constitution to Provide That the People of the District of Columbia Shall be Entitled to Vote in Presidential Elections, [and] S.J. Res. 134, Proposing an Amendment to the Constitution to Provide That the People of the District of Columbia Shall be Entitled to Vote in Presidential Elections and for Delegates to the House of Representatives. August 17 and 27, 1959" (Washington: Government Printing Office, 1960), 2-9.

"Abolition of [the] Poll Tax in Federal Elections: Hearings Before Subcommittee No. 5 of the Committee on the Judiciary[,] House of Representatives[,] Eighty-Seventh Congress[,] Second Session[,] on H.J. Res. 404, 425, 434, 594, 601, 632, 655, 663, 670, S.J. Res. 29 [,] Amendments to the Constitution of the United States to Abolish Tax and Property Qualifications for Electors in Federal Elections. March 12, 1962, and May 14, 1962" (Washington: Government Printing Office, 1962), 1-20.

"Poll Tax Ban Action Completed," *St. Petersburg Times* [Florida], 28 August 1962, 1A.

Jet, XXV:17 (13 February 1964), 4.

"Anti-Poll Tax Amendment For US Elections Passed," *The Sun* [Baltimore, Maryland], 28 August 1962, 1,

"Poll Tax Receipt Needed To Vote in All Elections," *Big Spring Daily Herald* [Big Spring, Texas), 24 January 1964, 9.

"In Arkansas As Everywhere: Poll Tax Problem Old," *Northwest Arkansas Times* [Fayetteville, Arkansas, 25 January 1964, 8.

Original Primary Documents
"High Court Rules U.S. Free to Resume Aluminum Case; Georgia Poll Tax Law Upheld in Opinion by Justice Butler," *The Atlanta Constitution*, 7 December 1937, 22.

"Poll tax goes seen planning new move," *Baltimore Afro-American* [Maryland], 25 August 1962, 19.

"Poll Tax On Way Out," *St. Petersburg Times* [Florida], 28 August 1962, 8A.

Supreme Court Decisions
Breedlove v. Suttles (302 U.S. 277 {1937}).
Hall, Kermit L., The Oxford Companion to the Supreme Court of the United States, 2nd ed. (New York: Oxford University Press, 2005), 101-02.

Harman v. Forssenius (380 U.S. 528 {1965}).
Douglass, William E., "Constitutional Law: Poll Taxes," *Tulsa Law Review*, III:2 (1966), 216-20.

Harper v. Virginia State Board of Elections (363 U.S. 663 {1966}).
Karst, Kenneth L., "Harper v. Virginia Board of Elections 383 U.S. 663 (1966)," *Encyclopedia of the American Constitution*, edited Leonard W. Levy and Kenneth L. Karst, 2nd ed., Vol. 3 (Detroit: Macmillan Reference USA, 2000), 1271-72.

Burdick v. Takushi (504 U.S. 428 {1992}).
Deighton, Elizabeth E., "Burdick v. Takushi: Hawaii's Ban on Write-in Voting Is Constitutional," *Golden Gate University Law Review*, XXIII:3 (January 1993), 701-15.

Crawford v. Marion City Election Board (553 U.S. 181 {2008}).
Brilleaux, Kelly E., "The Right, the Test, and the Vote: Evaluating the Reasoning Employed in Crawford v. Marion County Election Board," *Louisiana Law Review*, LXX:3 (2010), 1023-60.

Who's Who
Emanuel Celler (1888-1981)
The guide to the Emanuel Celler Papers at the Brooklyn Public Library has a short biography; see it online at http://www.brooklynpubliclibrary.org/sites/default/files/files/pdf/bc/Emanuel%20Celler%20Collection.pdf; "Celler, Emanuel" official congressional biography, online at http://bioguide.congress.gov/scripts/biodisplay.pl?index=C000264; Celler, Emanuel, "You Never Leave Brooklyn: The Autobiography of Emanuel Celler" (New York: John Day Co., 1953), 6-7; Maisel, Louis Sandy; Ira N. Forman; and Donald Altschiller, "Jews in American Politics" (Lanham, Maryland: Rowman & Littlefield Publishers, Inc., 2001), 320; Barnes, Catherine A., "Celler, Emanuel" in Nelson Lichtenstein, ed., "Political Profiles: The Kennedy Years" (New York: Facts on File, 1976), 80-81; "Celler to Push Amendment on Literacy Tests," *The Washington Post*, 17 May 1962, A19; "Former Rep. Emanuel Celler Dies; Civil Rights Champion," *The Washington Post*, 16 January 1981, B5.

Spessard Lindsey Holland (1892-1971)
"Holland, Spessard Lindsey" official congressional biography, online at http://bioguide.congress.gov/scripts/biodisplay.pl?index=H000720; Wunsch, James L., 'Holland, Spessard Lindsey" in Nelson Lichtenstein, ed., "Political Profiles: The Kennedy Years" (New York: Facts on File, 1976), 230-31; Badger, Tony, "Southerners Who Refused to Sign the Southern Manifesto Southerners Who Refused to Sign the Southern Manifesto," *The Historical Journal*, XLII:2 (June 1999), 527; "Washng See-Saw," *The News Tribune* [Fort Pierce, Florida], 6 June 1962, 11; "Spessard Holland Dies," *News-Herald* [Panama City, Florida), 7 November 1971, 1; "Memorial Addresses and Other Tributes in the Congress of the United States on the Life and Contributions of Spessard L. Holland" (Washington: Government Printing Office, 1972); Remarks of Sen. James Browning Allen, 15 November 1971, in "*The Congressional Record*: Proceedings and Debates of the 92d Congress, First Session. Volume 117 – Part 31. November 9, 1971 to November 15, 1971" (Washington: Government Printing Office, 1971), 41251.

Further Reading

Ackerman, Bruce, and Jennifer Nou, "Canonizing the Civil Rights Revolution: The People and the Poll Tax," *Northwestern University Law Review*, CIII (2009), 1-86.

Friedman, Brendan F., "The Forgotten Amendment and Voter Identification: How the New Wave of Voter Identification Laws Violates the Twenty-Fourth Amendment," *Hofstra Law Review*, XLII:1 (2013), 343-82.

Mukherjee, Elora, "Abolishing the Time Tax on Voting," *Notre Dame Law Review*, LXXXV:1 (2009), 177-246.

Oppenheimer, Max Stul, "Return of the Poll Tax: Does Technological Progress Threaten 200 Years of Advances toward Electoral Equality," *Catholic University Law Review*, LVIII:4 (Summer 2009), 1027-70.

Schultz, David, and Sarah Clark, "Wealth v. Democracy: The Unfulfilled Promise of the Twenty-Fourth Amendment," *Quinnipiac Law Review*, XXIX:375 (2011), 375-432.

Speck, Sloan G. "'Failure to Pay Poll Tax or Any Other Tax': The Constitutionality of Tax Felon Disenfranchisement," *University of Chicago Law Review*, LXXIV:4 (2007), 1549-80.

Wilkerson-Freeman, Sarah, "The Second Battle for Woman Suffrage: Alabama White Women, the Poll Tax, and V. O. Key's Master Narrative of Southern Politics," *The Journal of Southern History*, LXVIII:2 (May 2002), 333-74.

Williams, Frank B., Jr., "The Poll Tax as a Suffrage Requirement in the South, 1870-1901," *The Journal of Southern History*, XVIII:4 (November 1952), 469-96

Wilson, Thomas, "The Poll Tax-Origin, Errors and Remedies," *The Economic Journal*, CI:406 (May 1991), 577-84.

AMERICA AT THAT TIME . . .

Although the material in this section may not be directly related to the adoption of the Twenty-fourth Amendment, it offers valuable insight into what was happening in America at the time the Amendment was adopted. Modeled after Grey House Publishing's Working American *series, whose author, Scott Derks, is responsible for its content, it includes a Historical Snapshot, Selected Prices, significant quotations, newspaper and magazine clips to give a sense of what was on the minds of Americans, and how it may have impacted the amendment process.*

HISTORICAL SNAPSHOT

1964

- In the first meeting between leaders of the Roman Catholic and Orthodox churches since the fifteenth century, Pope Paul VI and Patriarch Athenagoras I met in Jerusalem

- In his first State of the Union Address, President Lyndon Johnson declared a "War on Poverty"

- Surgeon General Luther Leonidas Terry reported that smoking may be hazardous to one's health (the first such statement from the US Government)

- Thirteen years after its proposal and nearly two years after its passage by the Senate, the Twenty-fourth Amendment to the Constitution, prohibiting the use of poll taxes in national elections, was ratified

- General Motors introduced the Oldsmobile Vista Cruiser and the Buick Sport Wagon

- The Beatles, having vaulted to the Number 1 spot on the U.S. singles charts for the first time with "I Want to Hold Your Hand," appeared on *The Ed Sullivan Show*, and were seen by an estimated 73 million viewers, launching the mid-1960s "British Invasion" of American popular music

- The Supreme Court ruled that congressional districts must be approximately equal in population

- Muhammad Ali beat Sonny Liston in Miami Beach, Florida, and was crowned the Heavyweight Champion of the World

- Teamsters President Jimmy Hoffa was convicted by a federal jury of tampering with a federal jury in 1962

- In *New York Times Co. v Sullivan*, the Supreme Court ruled that, under the First Amendment, speech criticizing political figures cannot be censored

- The first Ford Mustang rolled off the assembly line at Ford Motor Company

- A Dallas, Texas, jury found Jack Ruby guilty of killing John F. Kennedy assassin Lee Harvey Oswald

Voting Tax Repeal Hailed

WASHINGTON (AP) – President Johnson has hailed as a triumph of liberty a new amendment to the Constitution outlawing the poll tax as a requirement for voting in elections for federal office.

The 24th amendment was written into the law of the land this election year when South Dakota Thursday became the 38th state to approve it. Ratification by three-fourths of the 50 states was required.

Johnson said in a statement "it was a verification of the people's rights which are rooted so deeply in the mainstream of this nation's history."

"PROUD MOMENT"

"This triumph, now, of liberty over restriction is a grateful and proud moment for me," Johnson said.

"The tide of a strong national desire to bring about the broadest possible use of the voting process runs too strong to hold back," he said.

"In a free land where men move freely and act freely, the: right to vote freely must never be obstructed."

While certification ceremonies probably will be held here later, they are only a formality. Once South Dakota's Legislature completed its ratification, no further legal action was required.

THE PROVISIONS

The amendment provides that the right to vote in any primary or general election for president or vice president, or for senator or representative in the Congress, shall not be denied because of the failure to pay a poll tax or any other tax.

The poll tax, the payment of a fee as a requirement for voting, has long been caught up in controversy with civil rights defenders charging that it was used to keep Negroes from casting ballots.

Only five states — Alabama, Arkansas, Mississippi, Texas and Virginia—still have the poll tax.

The new amendment will not jar these states from continuing to require voters in state elections to pay a poll tax, since it applies only to elections for federal office.

Potomac Fever

Wholesale news: The way things are going in Washington, Bobby Baker probably won't take the fifth - unless they agree to give him a rake-off on the whole ease.

* * * *

Dick Nixon says Khrushchev is the "most able" world leader. Khrushchev owes it all to the secret ballot. He made the ballot so secret, no Russian can find one.

* * * *

The Senate refuses a tax break of families with college students. The idea is that if a kid is smart enough to get into college, he's smart enough to figure out his own tax loopholes.

* * * *

It was the third marriage for each, but the bride balked at the $2 marriage license counter: "Oh, dear, can't we go *first* class this time?"

* * * *

The space agency says it succeeded in 14 of 15 recent launch attempts. Final results of the 15th blast-off won't be known until election day in Ohio.

* * * *

A tax lawyer who's carefully inspected the new tax bill says it's anti-business. Not enough loop-holes to keep him in clients.

Cuba Exile Row Only Minor Incident, *The Salt Lake Tribune,* April 20, 1963

The Kennedy Administration appears determined not to get into a running fight with Dr. Jose Miro Cardona, who has just resigned as head of the Cuban exile organization in the United States.

That is the wise course. President Kennedy's Cuban policy is already deeply involved in domestic politics and every effort should be made to prevent more emotional fuel from being added to the fire as would be the case if the administration were to attempt a point-by-point reply to Miro's allegations.

YET THE ADMINISTRATION cannot escape the fact that the Cuban Revolutionary Council, which Miro used to head, was formed with U.S. government support and that the administration was therefore responsible for Miro and the council.

Weather the administration intended to support the council to the extent Miro alleges is another matter. Miro claims Mr. Kennedy told him, nearly a year after the Bay of Pigs fiasco, that the problem of Cuba was essentially a military one and that the exiles should contribute the major contingent of soldiers for another invasion. Now, says Miro, Mr. Kennedy has reneged on his implied promise to liberate Cuba—a promise which Mr. Kennedy categorically denies he ever made.

Since the Bay of Pigs, however, the administration has shown no sign of wanting such an invasion.

In fact, it was Mr. Kennedy's decision to crack down on hit-run raids on Cuba that precipitated Miro's resignation.

Mr. Kennedy could not have taken any other course.

The hit-run raids against Fidel Castro were totally ineffectual. If anything, they strengthened the dictator's position at home and afforded the Soviet Union an excuse for keeping troops in Cuba. And they might well have pushed the United States into war. . . .

Song of civil rights marchers as they entered Montgomery, Alabama, 1964:

Keep your eyes on the prize, hold on, hold on.
I've never been to heaven, but I think I'm right,
You won't find George Wallace anywhere in sigh . . . .

Computers May Enable Men To Farm By Phone

NEW YORK — "Farming by phone" may be the next big "brain" in his office or in the barn, which would automatically

---

"Computers May Enable Men to Farm by Phone," *The Greenville News* (South Carolina), November 25, 1963:

"Farming by phone" may be the next big innovation in agriculture, says a national farm magazine.

The phone would be used by farmers to take advantage of centralized computer installations, according to an article, "Livestock Feeding of the Future," in the November issue of *Electricity on the Farm* magazine.

The computers can help the farmer make the many business decisions he has to, such as how much of which ingredients to feed his animals for the best meat and milk, or production at the lowest cost. It's being done on a limited scale right now in Washington State, and the idea is expected to spread.

Here's the way it would work: the farmer could pick up the phone, call a number, and read off the type of animal he wants to feed, types of feed ingredients available, and other such information. This information would be fed into a computer at the state university or other centralized computer location.

The farmer would then be instructed to take a certain computer-type punch card from a file on his desk. He would place this card into an electronic "brain" in his office or in the barn, which would automatically instruct feed-making machinery how much of which ingredients to use for the most efficient feeding ration. Automatic equipment could then easily convey the feed to the cows, chickens, hogs, etc., in feeding areas around the farmstead.

Automation and computerization are fast becoming common to most large industries in the U.S., and agriculture, America's largest industry, will be no exception.

"Yeah! Yeah! Yeah! Music's Gold Bugs: The Beatles, They can't read music, their beat is corny and their voices are faint, but England's shaggy-maned exports manage to flip wigs on two continents," *The Saturday Evening Post,* March 21, 1964:

"So far Beatlemania has traveled over two continents. In Stockholm the arrival of the Beatles was greeted with teenage riots. In Paris another congregation held screeching services at the airport and the Beatles' performances at the Olympia Theater were sold out for three weeks. In the Beatles' native Liverpool 60 youngsters collapsed from exposure after standing all night in a mile-long line of 12,000 waiting to buy tickets to the Beatles' performance. When a foreman shut off the radio in the middle of a Beatles record at a textile mill in Lancashire, 200 girls went out on strike.

While the Beatles toured the United States, three of their singles were in the top six and their albums ranked one and two in the record popularity charts. Beatle wigs were selling at $3.00 a piece, high school boys were combing their forelocks forward and hairdressers were advertising Beatle cuts for women. Beatle hats, T-shirts, cookies, eggcups, ice cream, dolls, beach shirts, turtleneck pullovers, nighties, socks, and iridescent blue and green collarless suits were on the market, and a Beatle motor scooter for children and a Beatlemobile for adults were being readied for production. American bartenders were confronted by a sudden deluge of orders for scotch and Coke, the Beatles' favorite drink. 'I think everyone has gone *daft*,' says John Lennon. Adds Ringo, 'Anytime you spell beetle with an 'a' in it, we get the money.' In 1964, Beatle-licensed products stand to gross $50 million in America alone. As for the Beatles, their total 1964 income is expected to reach $14 million."

Kate Smith Breaks A Leg

MIAMI BEACH, Fla, (AP) — The veteran popular singer Kate Smith broke her leg Friday while rehearsing for her first night club appearance in 33 years of professional entertainment.

Six hours later, appearing on stage with her left leg in a cast up to her knee and carrying a cane for support, the 54-year-old songstress told a capacity crowd:

"You can't say I didn't fall for you."

If I had said that television is more popular than Jesus, I might have got away with it. It's a fact, in reference to England, we meant more to kids than Jesus did or religion at that time. I wasn't knocking it or putting it down. I was just saying it, as a fact and it's true, more for England than here. I'm not saying we're better or greater or comparing us with Jesus Christ as a person of God as a thing, or whatever it is, you know, I just said what I said and it was wrong, or was taken wrong,, and now it's all this!

—John Lennon

"The whole question of outlawing boxing is ridiculous-It's like outlawing war just because a few men get killed!"

Music, in performance, is a type of sculpture. The air in the performance is sculpted into something.

Personal Essay
Frank Zappa

Selected Prices

Baby Carrier..$14.00

Bean Bag Chair...$37.95

Beer, Stroh's Six Pack...$1.49

Briefcase, Leather $35.95

CB Radio...$39.88

Circular Saw..$22.88

Coffee Maker, Norelco..$23.88

Drive-in Movie Ticket, Carload $4.00

Turntable $199.95

Woman's Swimsuit, Bikini $13.00

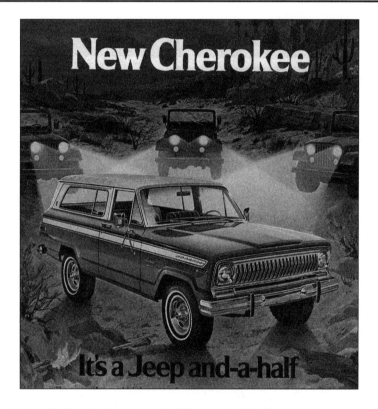

Year	Value of One Dollar in 2016 US Dollars
1960	$8.16
1961	$8.07
1962	$7.99
1963	$7.89
1964	$7.79
1965	$7.66

The Twenty-fifth Amendment

Chapter 16

S. J. Res. 1

Eighty-ninth Congress of the United States of America

AT THE FIRST SESSION

*Begun and held at the City of Washington on Monday, the fourth day of January,
one thousand nine hundred and sixty-five*

Joint Resolution

Proposing an amendment to the Constitution of the United States relating to succession to the Presidency and Vice Presidency and to cases where the President is unable to discharge the powers and duties of his office.

Resolved by the Senate and House of Representatives of the United States of America in Congress assembled (two-thirds of each House concurring therein), That the following article is proposed as an amendment to the Constitution of the United States, which shall be valid to all intents and purposes as part of the Constitution when ratified by the legislatures of three-fourths of the several States within seven years from the date of its submission by the Congress:

"ARTICLE —

"SECTION 1. In case of the removal of the President from office or of his death or resignation, the Vice President shall become President.

"SEC. 2. Whenever there is a vacancy in the office of the Vice President, the President shall nominate a Vice President who shall take office upon confirmation by a majority vote of both Houses of Congress.

"SEC. 3. Whenever the President transmits to the President pro tempore of the Senate and the Speaker of the House of Representatives his written declaration that he is unable to discharge the powers and duties of his office, and until he transmits to them a written declaration to the contrary, such powers and duties shall be discharged by the Vice President as Acting President.

"SEC. 4. Whenever the Vice President and a majority of either the principal officers of the executive departments or of such other body as Congress may by law provide, transmit to the President pro tempore of the Senate and the Speaker of the House of Representatives their written declaration that the President is unable to discharge the powers and duties of his office, the Vice President shall immediately assume the powers and duties of the office as Acting President.

"Thereafter, when the President transmits to the President pro tempore of the Senate and the Speaker of the House of Representatives his written declaration that no inability exists, he shall resume the powers and duties of his office unless the Vice President and a majority of either the principal officers of the executive department or of such other body as Congress may by law provide, transmit within four days to the President pro tempore of the Senate and the Speaker of the House of Representatives their written declaration that the President is unable to discharge the powers and duties of his office. Thereupon Congress shall decide the issue, assembling within forty-eight hours for that purpose if not in session. If the Congress, within

S. J. Res. 1—2

twenty-one days after receipt of the latter written declaration, or, if Congress is not in session, within twenty-one days after Congress is required to assemble, determines by two-thirds vote of both Houses that the President is unable to discharge the powers and duties of his office, the Vice President shall continue to discharge the same as Acting President; otherwise, the President shall resume the powers and duties of his office."

Speaker of the House of Representatives.

Vice President of the United States and
President of the Senate.

Proposed in Congress:	**6 July 1965**
Sent to States:	**6 July 1965**
Ratified:	**10 February 1967**

Chapter 16

THE TWENTY-FIFTH AMENDMENT

Section 1.
In case of the removal of the President from office or of his death or resignation, the Vice President shall become President.

Section 2.
Whenever there is a vacancy in the office of the Vice President, the President shall nominate a Vice President who shall take office upon confirmation by a majority vote of both Houses of Congress.

Section 3.
Whenever the President transmits to the President pro tempore of the Senate and the Speaker of the House of Representatives his written declaration that he is unable to discharge the powers and duties of his office, and until he transmits to them a written declaration to the contrary, such powers and duties shall be discharged by the Vice President as Acting President.

Section 4.
Whenever the Vice President and a majority of either the principal officers of the executive departments or of such other body as Congress may by law provide, transmit to the President pro tempore of the Senate and the Speaker of the House of Representatives their written declaration that the President is unable to discharge the powers and duties of his office, the Vice President shall immediately assume the powers and duties of the office as Acting President.

Thereafter, when the President transmits to the President pro tempore of the Senate and the Speaker of the House of Representatives his written declaration that no inability exists, he shall resume the powers and duties of his office unless the Vice President and a majority of either the principal officers of the executive department or of such other body as Congress may by law provide, transmit within four days to the President pro tempore of the Senate and the Speaker of the House of Representatives their written declaration that the President is unable to discharge the powers and duties of his office. Thereupon Congress shall decide the issue, assembling within forty-eight hours for that purpose if not in session. If the Congress, within twenty-one days after receipt of the latter written declaration, or, if Congress is not in session, within twenty-one days after Congress is required to assemble, determines by two-thirds vote of both Houses that the President is unable to discharge the powers and duties of his office, the Vice President shall continue to discharge the same as Acting President; otherwise, the President shall resume the powers and duties of his office.

Note: Article II, section 1, of the Constitution was affected by the 25th amendment.

Brief Summary

The Twenty-fifth Amendment establishes procedures for filling the office of president and vice president in the event either office falls vacant. Section 1 states that on the death or removal from office of the president, the vice president is to assume the presidency. Section 2 says that when the office of vice president is vacant, the president is to appoint a vice president, who then is to be confirmed by majority votes in the Senate and House of Representatives. Section 3 specifies the procedures a president is to follow if he or she is unable to fulfill the duties of the office and wishes to delegate the duties of the office to the vice president. Section 4 provides guidance in the event that Congress or the officers of the executive branch – that is, the Cabinet – conclude that the president is unable to discharge the duties of the office and has to be temporarily replaced.

Timeline

18 July 1947	President Harry Truman signs into law the Presidential Succession Act of 1947.
19 February 1965	The US Senate passes a presidential succession amendment.
13 April 1965	The US House of Representatives approves a plan on presidential disability, modifying the Senate's bill. It was returned to the Senate with revisions.
30 June 1965	The House approves a conference report reconciling the Senate and House bills.
6 July 1965	The Senate passes the Twenty-fifth Amendment.
10 February 1967	The Twenty-fifth Amendment is ratified when Nevada becomes the thirty-eighth state to ratify it; three states never ratify the amendment.
6 December 1973	Gerald Ford is sworn in as vice president following the resignation of Vice President Spiro Agnew.
9 August 1974	Gerald Ford is sworn in as president following the resignation of President Richard Nixon.
19 December 1974	Nelson Rockefeller is sworn in as Gerald Ford's vice president. For the only time in American history, both the president and vice president are unelected.
13 July 1985	President Ronald Reagan invokes the Twenty-fifth Amendment prior to undergoing a medical procedure, temporarily turning power over to Vice President George H. W. Bush.
29 June 2002	President George W. Bush invokes the Twenty-fifth Amendment prior to undergoing a medical procedure, temporarily turning power over to Vice President Dick Cheney.
21 July 2007	President George W. Bush invokes the Twenty-fifth Amendment once again before undergoing a medical procedure.

Introduction

At issue in this chapter is the death or disability of the American President and the legal reaction to it. America has had four of its Chief Executives murdered during their terms: Abraham Lincoln; James A. Garfield; William McKinley; and John F. Kennedy. A number of other Presidents died suddenly while in office, including William Henry Harrison, Zachary Taylor, Warren G. Harding, and Franklin D. Roosevelt. Several other Presidents have been struck by illnesses – from debilitating strokes to heart attacks – while in office, including Woodrow Wilson, Dwight D. Eisenhower, and Lyndon Baines Johnson. Warren G. Harding died suddenly while on a trip to San Francisco in 1923. In March 1981, President Ronald Reagan was the subject of an assassination attempt in which he was shot and nearly died; under the Twenty-fifth Amendment, he passed, for a short time, the duties and powers of the Presidency to Vice President George H.W. Bush.

With such a record of presidential history, the question is not why this amendment happened at all, but what took so long? Historian John D. Feerick wrote in 2010, " [S]ince the Constitutional Convention of 1787 there has been uncertainty as to both the definition of inability as well as the critical question of who is to be its judge. In addition, prior to the ratification of the Twenty-fifth Amendment, it was unclear whether a succession event resulted in the Vice President succeeding to the Office of the President itself, or simply assuming the powers and duties of the Office."[1] Prior to 1967, there was no fundamental constitutional provision for the succession of a Vice President, or any other federal officer, to the presidency, so the nation had no true solace that all would be well if the President died suddenly, or if the office of Vice President had to be vacated for some reason.

The assassination of President John F. Kennedy on 22 November 1963 gave new impetus to the burgeoning movement to amend the Constitution to make sure that the succession of a Vice President, or, in the case of a Vice President who could not continue in office, Speaker of the House, was constitutionally covered. One of the amendment's co-authors, Senator Birch Bayh, wrote in 1974, "The Amendment sought to clarify the ambiguity of Article II, Section 1 of the Constitution as to Presidential disability and to provide for the first time a procedure for filling a vacancy in the office of the Vice President."[2]

From the Union's earliest days, the threat of presidential disability hung over the Presidency, and with each new administration, that threat seemed to grow. This realization that such a threat was possible began as early as the Constitutional Convention in 1787. Historian John R. Vile explained, "As early as June 18 [1787], the delegates to the Convention anticipated the possibility of the death, resignation, or removal of the president. The Committee of Detail attempted to provide for such contingencies by designating the president of the Senate to fill in until such time as another president was chosen, the president was acquitted (the Convention had anticipate that the president might step aside during impeachment hearings), or his disability was removed. On August 27, Pennsylvania's Gouverneur Morris stated that the chief justice should be the 'provincial successor to the President.' At a time before the Convention had established neither the Electoral College nor the vice presidency, Virginia's James Madison was also concerned that, if the head of the Senate were designated to fill in, the Senate might drag its feet in selecting a successor. Madison wanted the council to the president to administer the office during vacancies. Identifying an issue that would long bedevil discussions of the subject, John Dickinson, of Delaware, observed that the term 'disability' was ambiguous, and it was not clear who would make such a determination."[3]

As noted by eminent historian Max Farrand, who collected the papers, debates, and minutes of the Constitutional Convention in four volumes in 1911 (reprinted in 1937), the debate over the matter of presidential disability came to a head on 7 September 1787:

I was and seconded to insert the following clause after the words "throughout the United States" in the first sect. [section] of the report.

"The Legislature may declare by law what officer of the United States shall act as President in case of the death, resignation, or disability of the President and Vice President; and such Officer shall act accordingly, until such disability be removed, or a President shall be elected."

...which passed in the affirmative [Ayes – 6; noes – 4; divided 1.]

[...]

The mode of constituting the Executive being resumed, Mr. [Peyton] Randolph [of Virginia] moved (to insert in the first Section of the report made yesterday).

"The Legislature may declare by law what officer of the US shall act as President in case of the death, resignation, or disability of the President and Vice-President; and such officer shall act accordingly until the time of electing a President shall arrive."

Mr. Madison observed that this, as worded, would prevent a supply of the vacancy by an intermediate election of the President, and moved to substitute – "until such disability be removed, or a President shall be elected..." Mr. Governr. [sic] Morris [should be Gouverneur Morris] 2ded [seconded] the motion, which was agreed to.

It seemed to be an objection to the provision with some, that according to the process established for choosing the Executive, there would be difficulty in effecting it at other than the fixed periods; with others, that the Legislature was restrained in the temporary appointment to *'officers'* of the US: (They wished it to be at liberty to appoint others than such.)

On the motion of Mr. [Peyton] Randolph as amended, it passed in the affirmative."[4]

Ultimately, the issue was inserted into the final document that became the original, unamended Constitution: Article II, section 1, clause 6 goes right to the heart of the issue of presidential succession:

"In Case of the Removal of the President from Office, or of his Death, Resignation, or Inability to discharge the' Powers and Duties of the said Office, the Same shall devolve on the Vice President, and the Congress may by Law provide for the Case of Removal, Death, Resignation or Inability, both of the President and Vice President, declaring what Officer shall then act as President, and such Officer shall act accordingly, until the Disability be removed, or a President shall be elected."

And there the issue lay. Although there were close calls – the deaths of several Vice Presidents, and the near assassination of President Andrew Jackson in January 1835 (an insane house painter, Richard Lawrence, tried to shoot Jackson at the Capitol, but both pistols misfired) – there was no actual threat to the President's ability to govern.

That situation, however, could not go on forever, and finally reached a head in 1841. The previous year, General William Henry Harrison, the Whig candidate for president, was elected, despite being nearly 70 years old at a time when most people in America did not live anywhere near that long. The threat grew even worse when, on inauguration day, 4 March 1841, a horrific snowstorm struck the Nation's capital – despite this, Harrison stood in the snow, with a small jacket on, reading a lengthy two-hour inaugural address. The elderly Harrison, whose health had not been good to begin with, caught a cold. On 4 April, one short month after taking office, the new President died. The nation was thrown into a tumult, faced with a bitter quandary: who would be the President now? Would there be new elections? Would the entire system of government break down?

Vice President John Tyler (not a Whig, but a Democrat added to the Whig ticket to attract Democrat votes) took over as "Acting President." But, was Tyler really the president? Was it possible for a man not elected president to serve in that capacity? None of the nation's leaders, in Congress, in the Cabinet, in the courts, had the answers. Senator William Allen, Democrat of Ohio, went to the floor of the US Senate to object to Tyler being called "the

President of the United States." As *The Congressional Globe* noted, Allen asked that Tyler instead be called "the Vice President, on whom, by the death of the late President the powers and duties of the office of President have devolved."[5] Tyler muddled along for the remainder of what was Harrison's term, clashing with Whigs in the cabinet (many of whom resigned out of principle not to serve a man not elected to the presidency) and in the Congress. Finished after one "term" in office, Tyler went back to his native Virginia, where he turned against his country and served in the Confederate Congress. He died in shame and his name remains stained to this day.

The same question of presidential disability came to life again less than a decade after Harrison's death, involving another General and another President who would die in office. General Zachary Taylor, the hero of the Mexican War, was elected President in 1848. A Whig like his predecessor Harrison, Taylor appeared to be in good health. However, on 4 July 1850, Taylor took ill during a Fourth of July celebration in the White House, where no air conditioning was available to cool down the balmy Washington summer. The President ate cold cherries and drank ice cold milk for lunch, developing a stomach ache that eventually turned into an illness that killed him within days. Once again, the people turned to a man not elected President – in this case, Vice President Millard Fillmore – to serve as the nation's chief executive. The questions were raised again – was this "Acting President" really the President? Does he have all of the powers, all of the trappings, of the man actually elected as President? But as with the Harrison-Tyler succession in 1841, no one knew the answer.

The issue came back in 1865, when Abraham Lincoln was assassinated, and Andrew Jackson, a so-called "War Democrat" (one who remained a Democrat but sided with the Union as opposed to being a secessionist), succeeded to the presidency. Amid clashes between Lincoln's fellow Republicans in the Congress and Democrat Johnson, the "differences in policy" led to Johnson's impeachment and acquittal in the US Senate by one vote.

The story was repeated throughout history: President James A. Garfield was murdered in 1881, giving way to Vice President Chester A. Arthur; President William McKinley was slain in 1901, and replaced by Vice President Theodore Roosevelt; and, in 1963, President John F. Kennedy was shot down in Dallas, making Vice President Lyndon Baines Johnson the 36th President of the United States. Each time, the succession from Vice President to President was seamless, smooth, but critics asked: was it constitutional?

While the US lost four presidents to assassination, it also lost seven Vice Presidents to various illnesses: George Clinton (served 1805-12); Elbridge Gerry (served 1813-14); William Rufus de Vane King (served 1853); Henry Wilson (served 1873-75); Thomas A. Hendricks (served 1885); Garret A. Hobart (served 1897-99); and James S. Sherman (served 1909-12). In addition, two Vice Presidents resigned their office: John C. Calhoun (served 1825-32); and Spiro Agnew (served 1969-73). As of 2012, the office of Vice President has been vacant for a total of 37 years, 290 days – nearly a fifth of the nation's history. The last man to serve as Vice President who was not elected to that office was Nelson Rockefeller, the former Governor of New York, who served from 1974 until 1977 as Gerald R. Ford's Vice President.

The history of the deaths of Vice Presidents is little studied; few of these men, despite being "one heartbeat away" from the presidency, merited any specific attention at the time that they served, much less even now. For instance, William McKinley's number two, Garret Augustus Hobart, was a lawyer from Paterson, New Jersey, served in the New Jersey state Assembly, rising to Speaker of that body, then in the state Senate, rising to President there. A banker and member of the Republican National Committee from 1884 to 1896, he was plucked from anonymity as William McKinley's Vice President at the party's national convention in St. Louis in 1896 and elected as Vice President of the United States. In an age when there was no television, with most speeches delivered in Romanstyle oratory, Hobart appeared to be the perfect number two during his tenure as President of the US Senate, where he cast a single vote: rejection of a resolution calling for the US to disclaim any intention of taking over Spanish protectorates in Cuba and the Philippines. When he took office on 4 March 1897, few knew that he was suffering from advanced heart disease. Long hours of work in the campaign and as Vice President – some historians call Hobart the "first modern Vice President" – took their toll on his delicate health. In spring 1899, following a Senate adjournment, Hobart collapsed and was taken by train to Long Branch, New Jersey, to recuperate. When McKinley, concerned about his friend, visited him, Hobart did not let on how ill he was. On 21 November 1899, he suffered a heart attack and died at the age of 55. Widely mourned, Hobart's passing threw the McKinley administration into a tailspin in an attempt to fill the vacuum left by his death. Secretary of State John Hay became the "Acting Vice President," while Senator William P. Frye, Republican of Maine and the Senate President pro tempore, served in the Vice President role in the upper body of the US Congress. It was not until the following year, when New York Governor Theodore Roosevelt was named as McKinley's running mate for the 1900 election, that an actual Vice President put into place.[6]

But not even the deaths of a myriad of Vice Presidents and the murder of three Presidents – McKinley was murdered by an anarchist in September 1901 – could lodge enough of a movement to change the Constitution as the nation entered the Twentieth century. Many historians believe that Congress was loath to tackle the subject because of a widespread fear that if an "ambitious" Vice President got into the presidency, nothing – not even the full recovery of a disabled President – could get him out of the office he did not belong in. As English politician James Bramston wrote in *Art of Politics*, commenting on intrigue in the British Parliament,

"But Titus said, with his uncommon sense,
When the Exclusion Bill was in suspense:
'I hear a lion in the lobby roar...
Say, Mr. Speaker, shall we shut the door
And keep him there, or shall we let him in
To try if we can turn him out again?'"[7]

Perhaps the most egregious case of presidential disability, and the inability of anyone to do anything about it, came during the last two years of the administration of President Woodrow Wilson. In trying to get the Congress to agree to American entry into the League of Nations, Wilson began a nationwide train tour to convince the American people to force Congress to go along with the President's views on the treaty that had ended the First World War. On 2 October 1919, following one speech in Pueblo, Colorado, after which he quickly returned to Washington, Wilson, who had been in ill health for many years,[8] suffered a massive stroke which, according to any standards of decency, necessitated his immediately removal as President. The attack, as historians James F. Toole and Robert J. Joynt explain, "came at one of the most critical periods of our nation's history. The Senate, at the very time of Wilons's stroke and total disability, was locked in a battle of the Treaty of Versailles, ratification of which would have made the United States a member of the League of Nations. Wilson's physician, Admiral Cary T. Grayson, and his chief consultant, Dr. Francis X. Dercum of the Jefferson Medical College, an eminent neurologist, wanted to make a full disclosure of Wilson's condition but were stopped from doing so by Mrs. Wilson. The treaty went down to defeat in the Senate because Wilson could not accept even mild reservations concerning the covenant, or constitution, of the League of Nations."[9] For the next 18 months, the time left in his second and final term as President, Wilson was an invalid; daily business was carried out by his Secretary, Joseph Tumulty, and important papers of state were signed in his name by Wilson's wife, Edith Bolling Galt Wilson. Working as a team, Mrs. Wilson and Tumulty kept the White House moving along, although there were few cabinet meetings, and Vice President Thomas Marshall was kept out of the loop of the affairs of the US government. When Secretary of State Robert Lansing pushed to either see the obvious unconscious President or have him removed from the office of the Presidency, Mrs. Wilson engineered Lansing's dismissal to keep the entire affair hushed up. To this day, many historians truly doubt the impact that Mrs. Wilson had, while others consider her "the first female President of the United States."

Despite this horrific example, Congress did not do anything to remedy the situation. The sudden – and, some would say, unexplained – death in August 1923 of President Warren G. Harding, which led to the succession of Vice President Calvin Coolidge, was also met with an inability – or a lack of desire – to do anything. President Franklin D. Roosevelt, who hid his paralysis from the nation, also hid, in his third term in office (1941-45) growing heart disease that sapped his strength and allowed him to be taken advantage of by Soviet dictator Josef Stalin at the peace meetings in Yalta, on the Black Sea. Roosevelt ran for a fourth term in 1945, despite his doctors' telling him that he would not live to see its end; nevertheless, he chose as his running mate a barely experienced former haberdasher from Missouri, Senator Harry S Truman, and then told Truman almost nothing about the affairs of government, the running of the Second World War, or the secret program to build an atomic bomb. When Roosevelt collapsed and died of a cerebral hemorrhage, brought on by years of poor health and a weak heart, in April 1945, just three months into his fourth term, the neophyte Truman became President, a job he was woefully unprepared for.

What may have finally tipped the scales was the shocking assassination of President John F. Kennedy in the Dallas, Texas, on 22 November 1963. As the mortally wounded President lay dying in Parkland Hospital, Vice President Lyndon Baines Johnson seemed to be in shock while considering what would happen next. Eventually, after Kennedy was pronounced dead, his body loaded into a casket and taken back to Air Force One to be returned to Washington, Johnson arranged to have as smooth a transition as possible. A federal judge, Sarah T. Hughes, gave Johnson the oath of office, making him the new President. While the nation had awoken to President John F. Kennedy, its 35th President, it went to sleep that night with President Lyndon Baines Johnson, the 36th.

For many years, several members of Congress had foreseen the need for some congressional action to change the succession for a dead or dying President, or a dead, dying, or resigned Vice President. One of these leaders was Senator Birch Bayh, Democrat of Indiana. Elected to the US Senate in 1962, the year before Kennedy's assassination, he set to work to draft a constitutional amendment to set the succession of both executive branch officials into the concrete of the US Constitution. Professor Herbert L. Abrams wrote in 1994, "Senator Birch Bayh, the architect of the Twenty-fifth Amendment, has himself deplored the fact that sections 3 and 4 have not worked as the framers intended. The amendment's central problem is threefold. First, the issue is deeply embedded in a political culture where those who surround the president and are closest to his aberrant behavior or disabling illness are dependent for their positions and prestige on keeping him in office. Second, a political judgment of disability by the vice president and the Cabinet must be based on a sound medical determination of impairment of such a degree that it impedes the president's ability to discharge some or all of the duties of office. Third, a mechanism for providing this type of unbiased, accurate information on the president's health never has been formally addressed. (To the extent that it has been considered, primary responsibility has been placed on the White House physician, who is enmeshed in a profound conflict of interest.)"[10]

Another Congressional leader in getting the amendment through was Rep. Emanuel Celler, Democrat of New York, whose name is associated with drafting the Twenty-third, Twenty-fourth, and Twenty-fifth Amendments. Celler had, as the chairman of the House Committee on the Judiciary, held hearings in the late 1950s and early 1960s on the potential of just such an amendment.

Despite Kennedy's assassination, it took more than 18 months after his death to get the precise language and enough support to get a proposed amendment through both houses of Congress. The US Senate passed its own amendment on 19 February 1965. The House approved its own plan on presidential disability on 13 April 1965 by a vote of 368-29, but it had made several changes to the Senate language. The two disparate proposed amendments now went to conference to be ironed out into one, simple amendment. Once that was accomplished, the House okayed the conference report on 30 June 1965 by a voice vote, which supporters said was more than a two-thirds vote necessary for passage. In the Senate, however, the conference report hit a roadblock when Senator Albert Gore, Democrat of Tennessee, objected to its language, stating, as *The Washington Post* said the next day, that "he was unsatisfied with some provisions of the plan and said he favored sending it back to House-Senate conferees for further consideration."[11] Gore stated that he would not allow the proposal to go any further, towards a full floor vote, until these concerns were addressed. The proposed amendment then hit another roadblock when Gore was joined by Senator Eugene McCarthy, Democrat of Minnesota, in blocking the amendment until their concerns were addressed.[12]

But they weren't addressed. Senator Robert F. Kennedy, Democrat of New York and brother of President John F. Kennedy, who was assassinated a year and a half earlier, was also not happy with the language, stating on the floor of the Senate that a potential arose, under the language of the proposed amendment, of a "specter of rival claimants" to the presidency, each supported by his own cabinet members. Ultimately, on 6 July 1965, Kennedy voted for the passage of the amendment.

Gore remained a steadfast opponent to the amendment's passage, and his arguments against its passage – demonstrated in the excerpts of the Senate debate highlighted in this chapter's debate section – attracted the support from fellow Democrats Frank J. Lausche of Ohio, Eugene McCarthy of Minnesota, and Walter Mondale of Minnesota, and Republican John Tower of Texas. Ironically, Gore's son, Albert A. Gore, Jr., would eventually serve as Vice President (1993-2001), as would Mondale (1977-81). Gore cautioned the Senate that a "venal Vice President would be in a position to ship around, so to speak, for support of his view" amongst the Cabinet members asked to decide on the President's ability and/or disability. The main author of the amendment, Senator Birch Bayh of Indiana, rejected Gore's argument, stating that bringing up "what-ifs" could only "muddy the waters." Ultimately, enough Senators stayed with Bayh to give the amendment enough support, and to pass it on 6 July 1965 by a vote of 68 to 5. It then went on to the states, and took until 10 February 1967 to gain enough states to be ratified and become part of the US Constitution.

Since its ratification in 1967, the Twenty-fifth Amendment has been put into use a few times. In 1973, when Vice President Spiro T. Agnew, former Governor of Maryland, was forced to resign when he was about to be indicted for taking kickbacks, President Richard M. Nixon invoked the Twenty-fifth Amendment to allow the Congress to vote on a "nominee" for Vice President. Ultimately, Nixon named Rep. Gerald R. Ford, Republican of Michigan and House Minority Leader, to replace Agnew, and Ford had to go through confirmation hearings and passage in both houses of Congress. The following year, when Nixon was wholly implicated in the cover-up of the crimes of Watergate, the President himself had to resign, and Ford, not elected as Vice President, became the President, and he named New York Governor Nelson Rockefeller as his own Vice President (the first time in the history of the United States that the two men controlling the executive branch of the US government had not been elected to either post). Undergoing medical procedures, President Ronald Reagan and President George W. Bush "temporarily" handed over power to their vice presidents while they were under sedation. Other recent presidents have secretly and prospectively prepared the necessary documents to relinquish power to the vice president, to be used in extraordinary circumstances.

One of the problems of the amendment, which to this day has not been cleared up, is the impact of medical testimony from "outside authorities" not directly involved in the process of determining presidential disability or inability. In widespread hearings before the House Committee on the Judiciary, one member of the committee, Rep. Durward Hall, Republican of Missouri, himself a physician (he had served in the US Army Office of the Surgeon General), lamented the lack of medical testimony from authorities in the field:

"I see no evidence in the hearings of any statement by either any White House physician, past or present, or any of the surgeons general of our civilian or uniformed branches, or civilian consultants available to the government, such as the American Medical Association...I wonder if those who ordinarily determine inability or disability were consulted or called for hearings or if they were excluded purposely."[13]

Other representatives agreed with Hall: Rep. Richard Poff, Republican of Virginia, stated that " [s]urely, the decision makers, whoever they may be, would not undertake so critical a decision without first consulting the experts in the field, namely the gentlemen of the medical profession."[14] Rep. Clark MacGregor also said, "I believe that the members of the Cabinet would not take the step jointly with the vice president to certify the president's inability to the appropriate officers of the Congress without a consultation with the very finest medical brains which were available to them."[15] In 1988, 23 years after the amendment was passage, Bayh wrote in a history of the amendment's impact that " [w]e might have been in error there. We were willing to accept the worst-case situation from a medical standpoint."[16] Bayh admitted that the amendment's chief weakness is that it has no statement forcing the President or Vice President to get a medical examination before disability or inability is confirmed; there is a mere "hope" that medical doctors, quite possibly with "no skin in the game," would be called in to make a final diagnosis on which the fate of the nation rests. In 1988, Dr. Bert Park, a Missouri physician, wrote, "[T]he Twenty-fifth Amendment, as presently worded, does not sufficiently protect the public. Today, as in the past, we remain beholden to the presidential physician for opinions that may not afford an unbiased and unrestricted revelation of the medical facts should the question of disability arise. Certainly our past experience with such cases is cause for grave concern. Whether by statute or joint resolution, it still remains for Congress to delineate more specifically how presidential inability is determined."[17] In 1995, in an update, Park urged the establishment of a "Presidential Impairment Panel" which, he said would be "staffed in part by physicians skilled in defining impairment, selected before the inception of an incoming administration, and divided equally by party would afford the vice president an unbiased second opinion apart from the presidential physician should the president's health be called into question. The panel would be advisory only, and could neither initiate proceedings against the chief executive nor depose him. Insofar as the amendment already designates 'such other body as Congress shall by law provide' to participate in this process, no burdensome revision of its wording would be necessary."[18]

Debate in Congress

The debate over the proposed language in the Twenty-fifth Amendment to the US Constitution was long and complicated. Approved by the US Senate on 19 February 1965, the amendment was sent to the House, where, after hearings in the House Judiciary Committee, an amended version was passed on 13 April 1965. Because the two houses now had to have a single bill to agree on, the proposed amendment was sent to a House-Senate conference. The conference report was agreed to by the House on 30 June 1965. Even though many of the House changes were in the final language and were opposed by many Senators, the conference report was agreed to in the Senate on 6 July 1965, sending the amendment to the states for ratification. Excerpts of all four House and Senate debates appear below.

The proposed disability amendment began with Senate language, debated here in the upper body of the Congress, 19 February 1965.

PRESIDENTIAL AND VICE PRESIDENTIAL
SUCCESSION – PRESIDENTIAL DISABILITY

Mr. MANSFIELD.[19] Mr. President, I ask unanimous consent that the unfinished business be laid down and may the pending business and that the morning hour be concluded.

The VICE PRESIDENT. Without objection, the Chair lays before the Senate the unfinished business.

The CHIEF CLERK. A joint representative (S.J. Res. 1) proposing an amendment to the Constitution of the United States relating to [the] succession to the Presidency and Vice-Presidency and to cases where the President is unable to discharge the powers and duties of his office.

The Senate resumed the consideration of the joint resolution (S.J. Res. 1) proposing an amendment to the Constitution of the United States relating to [the] succession to the Presidency and Vice-Presidency and to cases where the President is unable to discharge the powers and duties of his office.

Mr. MANSFIELD. Mr. President, I suggest the absence of a quorum.

The VICE PRESIDENT. The clerk will call the roll.

The Chief Clerk proceeded to call the roll.

Mr. MANSFIELD. Mr. President, I ask unanimous consent that the order for the quorum be rescinded.

The VICE PRESIDENT. Without objection, it is so ordered.

[The Senate then moved to Executive Session, to consider other business, including that dealing with the Department of Defense. We pick up the debate several hours later.]

The Senate resumed the consideration of the joint representative (S.J. Res. 1) proposing an amendment to the Constitution of the United States relating to [the] succession to the Presidency and Vice-Presidency and to cases where the President is unable to discharge the powers and duties of his office.

Mr. BAYH.[20] Mr. President, I as unanimous consent that the committee amendment be considered and agreed to en bloc, an that the bill as thus amended be considered as [the] original text for the purpose of further amendment, not prejudicing the rights of any Senator to further amend the bill.

The PRESIDING OFFICER. Is there objection? The Chair hears none, and it is so ordered.

[The Presiding Officer then read out a series of corrections, line by line, which were to be added to the Senate floor language.]

Mr. BAYH. Mr. President, I send to the desk an amendment to section 5 of the bill and ask that it be stated. I feel that this was the intention of the committee. It is a change of wording that needs to be made in order to have the bill conform to the intention of the committee. It does not change the bill in any way at all.

The PRESIDING OFFICER. The clerk will state the amendments.

The LEGISLATIVE CLERK. On page 3, in line 17, strike the following: "with the written concurrence of" and insert in lieu thereof: "and."

On page 3, line 20, strike the following: "transmits within two days to the Congress his" and insert in lieu thereof: "transmit within two days to with the President of the Senate and the Speaker of the House of Representatives their."

The PRESIDING OFFICER. The question is on agreeing to the amendments of the Senator from Indiana.

The amendments were agreed to.

Mr. BAYH. Mr. President, and Members of the Senate, on December 1, 1964, the President of the United States had a small growth removed from his hand. The Nation wondered. On January 23, 1965, Americans awoke to learn that during the night the President had entered the hospital with a cold. The Nation, and, indeed, much of the world worried. But we were fortunate on each of those occasions.

Today we have a strong, forthright, and vigorous President of the United States. I might also add that we are fortunate today because we have an able-bodied and vigorous Vice President of the United States. This was not the case in the sad months following November 22, 1963.

We have not been so fortunate in the past to have had able-bodied, vigorous Presidents and Vice Presidents.

Sixteen times in the history of our country we have been without a Vice President. All Americans can recall the eight Presidents who have died in office, but our memories fail us in remembering that seven Vice Presidents died in office; and one Vice President, John Calhoun, resigned to become a US Senator.

The total span during which this Nation has not had a Vice President has been in excess of 37 years. There have been serious presidential disabilities over various periods of the history of our country. I should like to review them briefly. President Garfield lay disabled for 80 days after being struck by the bullet of an assassin.

Ruth Silva, in her book "Presidential Succession," described that period in these words:

During these 80 days a great deal of urgent business demanded the President's immediate attention: there were postal frauds; officers did not perform their duties because they had not been commissioned; the country's foreign relations were deteriorating...Nearly every day the newspapers mentioned some important matter which was ignored because it required the President's personal attention.

And still there was no one to perform the functions that only the disabled President could perform.

President Wilson had a serious illness lasting 16 months. To all intents and purposes, history shows that his wife and his physician conducted the Government of the United States. None member of the Cabinet was permitted to see the President for a minute. No one could see or hear a word he said or wrote.

Presidential Assistant Joseph Tumulty was not allowed to see the President. However, in good conscience, he felt he was compelled to give Mrs. Wilson a list of business which he felt needed Presidential action.

I quote from Eugene Smith's "When the Cheering Stopped," relating to that time:

The railways taken over during the war still awaited return to their owners, the Costa Rican recognition matter was still up in the air, a commission to deal with the mining strike situation should be appointed, the Secretaries of the Treasury and the Interior and the Assistant Secretary of Agriculture needed replacements, there were vacancies in the Civil Service Commission, Shipping Board, Tariff Committee and other agencies, and that diplomatic appointments were needed for Bulgaria, China, Costa Rica (if recognized), Italy, the Netherlands, Salvador, Siam, and Switzerland. Also, the Democratic leadership in the Senate desperately wanted an expression of Wilson's policy in dealing with the Lodge amendments to US entry into the League of Nations.

Subsequently, without Presidential advice, America's entry, and later the League of Nations itself, failed.

President Cleveland underwent a major operation, in complete secrecy, aboard a private yacht cruising off Long Island.

More recently, in the memory of all of us, President. Eisenhower had three serious illnesses. The Vice President, Mr. Richard Nixon, in his book *Six Crises*, describes the period surrounding the presidential heart attack on September 24, 1955, as a period of "government lull."

However, if it was a period of government lull, I wonder what a period of government crisis would have been. I quote from the *New York Times* of September 27, 1955, to the times in which we lived:

Top-level decisions were pending on disarmament policy, budgetary problems, military force levels, certain politico strategic questions, withdrawal of troops from Korea, future military policy toward Formosa,[21] and [the] reduction of forces in Japan.

For some 2 months after President Eisenhower's heart attack the Government was directed, for all intents and purposes, by a six-man committee, comprised of Vice President Nixon, Presidential Assistant Sherman Adams, Mr. Dulles, Secretary of State, Attorney General [Herbert] Brownell, Secretary of the Treasury [George M.] Humphrey, and General [John W.] Persons.

Vice President Nixon wrote of this period in his *Six Crises*:

Although it was hardly mentioned, I am certain that many of us realized our team-government would be inadequate to handle an international crisis, such as a brush-fire war or an internal uprising in a friendly country or a crisis of any ally. The ever-present possibility of an attack on the United States was always hanging over us. Would the President be well enough to make the decision? If not, who had the authority to push the button?

Vice President Nixon, after President Eisenhower's second illness, which was a 30-minute operation for an attack of ileitis[22] on June 8, 1956, says, in his book *Six Crises*:

On several occasions afterward he (Eisenhower) pointed out to me that for the 2 hours he was under anesthesia, the Armed Forces was without a Commander-in-Chief. In the event of a national emergency during those 2 hours, who would have had the undisputed authority to act for a completely disabled President?

Again, Vice President Nixon, on President Eisenhower's third illness, which was a stroke on November 27, 1957, stated in his book:

It was a time of international tensions. Only a month before the Soviet Union had put its first Sputnik in orbit...The most immediate problem was a scheduled meeting of NATO only 3 weeks away...On the domestic front, the first signs of the 1958 economic recession were becoming obvious...We were having serious budget problems.

So wrote the former Vice President, who was forced to serve during three serious Presidential illnesses.

Former Attorney General Brownell, who was one of the committee of six during the illness mentioned, wrote of the half hour when President Eisenhower was unconscious during his ileitis operation that:

It was realized that the announced intention of the President to undergo a serious operation might entice a hostile foreign power to make some drastic move in the expectation of finding, at the critical moment, confused and uncertain leadership in the United States.

Senate Joint Resolution 1 is an effort to guarantee continuity within the executive branch of the Government. It is designed to provide that we shall always have a President or Acting President physically and mentally alert. Second, and of equal importance, it is to assure that whoever the man may be, there will be no question as to the legality of his authority to carry out the powers and duties of the office.

Mr. LONG of Louisiana.[23] Mr. President, will the Senator yield?

Mr. BAYH. I am glad to yield.

Mr. LONG of Louisiana. I commend the Senator for the fine work he has done both in studying the background and problem and also in bringing the measure before the Senate at this very early date. The Senator has labored long in the vineyard on this matter. I believe he managed the measure in the previous Congress, which the Senate passed. Unfortunately, on that occasion, the House failed to act. I certainly hope that the efforts of the Senator will be crowned with success, and also the efforts of his committee; and that this measure, having passed the Senate, will be promptly acted upon by the House of Representatives in the first session of Congress.

Mr. BAYH. I am grateful to the Senator for his kind words. I know of his long interest in this subject and have discussed it with him. I know of his concern that this loophole in the Constitution of the United States should be filled.

(At this point Mr. PELL took the chair as Presiding Officer.)

Mr. BAYH. Mr. President, let me review for a moment what has gone on before, to establish and clarify the Executive authority of the US Government. First, I referred to article II, section 1 of the Constitution.

I believe we should refer to article II, section 1 of the Constitution on this particular question. The contents of article II deal with the responsibility of the Executive authority in our country.

Section 1 specifies:

The executive Power shall be vested in a President of the United States of America. He shall hold his Office during the Term of four Years, and, together with the Vice President, chosen for the same Term, be elected, as follows...

In addition, article II, following the Executive powers, or executive contingencies, deals with the selection of electors, it deals with the manner in which the President and Vice President shall be elected. This, let me point out, has subsequently been amended in the 12th amendment. It deals with the qualifications which are prescribed for the President and Vice President. It deals with presidential compensation. It deals with the oath of office which the President is required to take. It deals, most important of all, with the powers and duties which are given to the President. It deals with messages – the state of the Union message, and others – which the President may make to the Congress. It also provides for the event of removal, death, resignation, or inability of the President.

I should like to read this last provision, because it is this provision with which we are dealing specifically in Senate Joint Resolution 1.

The clause reads as follows:

In case of the Removal of the President from Office, or of his Death, Resignation, or Inability to discharge the Powers and Duties of the said Office, the Same shall devolve on the Vice President, and the Congress may by Law provide for the Case of Removal, Death, Resignation or Inability, both of the President and Vice President, declaring what Officer shall then act as President, and such Officer shall act accordingly, until the Disability be removed, or a President shall be elected.

Senate Joint Resolution 1 is designed to clarify the ambiguity, and remove the uncertainty and doubt which has been raised over the years by this clause.

[Senator Bayh then read the entire language of Senate Joint Resolution 1 into the Record, which has been excised here for space.]

Mr. BAYH. Mr. President, Senate Joint Resolution 1 removes all doubt about the Vice President succeeding to the office of President.

There may be some Senators who might believe it rather foolish to deal with a problem of this kind when all America takes it for granted. All America does not take it for granted. There is significant constitutional authority, and constitutional scholars are concerned about the fact that there still is a scintilla of doubt as to whether the President, upon dying, is succeeded by the Vice President who succeeds to the office as President, or merely assumes the powers and duties of the office as Acting President.

I ask Senators to recall with me the first tragedy which occurred when President William Henry Harrison was lost, and he was succeeded by the then Vice President Tyler. The first papers which were given to the new President to sign contained under his name the words "Acting President." Subsequently, a close analysis of what our constitutional forefathers discussed in the Constitutional Convention leads us to believe that there was good reason for including the words "Acting President."

Inasmuch as Vice President Tyler decided that he did not wish to be acting President, he wished to be President, he struck the word "acting." Ever since that time, it has become so entrenched in the laws of the land that it is indeed the law of the land today.

We feel that we should remove any doubt whatsoever about this issue.

The point is not so ridiculous as it seems because on December 10, 1963, following the tragedy in Dallas, Tex., the *New York Times* published an article concerning a New Mexico lawyer named Leonard Jones, who had forwarded a brief to the Attorney General challenging the right of President Johnson to take the oath of office as President, rather than the oath as Acting President.

I also point out that the 22d amendment to the Constitution which is a relatively recent amendments, reads in part as follows:

SECTION 1. No person shall be elected to the office of President more than twice, and no person who has held the office of President, or acted as President...

I emphasize the word "acted":

...for more than two years of a term to which some other person was elected President shall be elected to the office of the President more than once.

Therefore, in the recent history of amending the Constitution, we have referred to the possibility of the Vice President perhaps being Acting President instead being President. This can be remedied and should be, I feel – and will be – by specifying, as we do, in section 1 of Senate Joint Resolution 1, that upon the death of the President, the Vice President shall become the President.

It also provides that in the event there is a vice-presidential vacancy either because of death, resignation, or removal – of either the Vice President or President, both cases of which would result in a vacancy – the President would be nominated by a majority vote in both Houses of Congress, and subsequently a new Vice President would be elected, who would, in fact, be the Vice President.

This formula provides, first, that there would be a Vice President at all times; second, that there would be a Vice President who would be acceptable to the President, a Vice President with whom the President could work.

I hope all Senators will agree with me that at the time of international crisis, such as the death of a President in the United States, the last thing we would need would be a Vice President with whom the President could not get along.

Third, it would provide for a Vice President who would have received a vote of confidence in would have been, in fact, elected by the Members of both Houses who have the responsibility for being close to the people and knowing what they desire and expressing their wishes in Congress.

I should like to emphasize briefly for the RECORD the importance of having a Vice President at all times.

I do not believe that there is any office in existence which has been subjected to more puns and ridicule at one time or another in a history of our country than the office of VP. This might have been well directed toward some Vice Presidents at an earlier time in the development of the country, but today we have seen a rapid development in the office of Vice President to the point where he is now a full-time officeholder.

Today, the Vice President is not a figurehead. He is the chief ambassador of our country, traveling all over the world carrying the flag and the good will of America with him. He sits in Cabinet meetings. He is a member of the National Security Council. He is Chairman of the National Aeronautic and Space Administration.[24] He is Chairman of the President's Committee on Equal Employment Opportunity. He presides over the Senate. He has the opportunity – and I feel that he should – two relieve the President of many of the social obligations which rest upon the Chief of State.

In addition, the Vice President is only one heartbeat away from the most powerful office in the world.

Therefore, I believe that it is abundantly clear that we need provisions in the Constitution to enable the United States to have a Vice President at all times.

Let me hastily pointed out that in the area of succession Congress has dealt with the problem on three occasions – in 1792, 1886, and 1894. On all three occasions it did not deal with replacing a Vice President or with the necessity of finding someone to serve as President when the President was unable to perform the powers and duties of his office, but only with the contingency that would arise when both the President and Vice President were removed.

Let us pass quickly to sections 3, 4, and 5 of the joint resolution, which deal with the inability of the President to carry out the powers and duties of his office.

Searching high and low for the intent of our Founding Fathers for a reference to which I referred earlier, first, inability and, second, disability, we find little solace in the notes on the Constitutional Convention. Only one question was raised on this point, and that was raised by John Dickinson of Delaware, when he rose on the floor and said:

What is meant by the term "disability," and who shall determine it?

To that question no answer was given. That is the only reference to this subject.

Mr. President, absent any direction by our Constitutional Fathers, we have been drifting on a sea of indecision for the best part of two centuries. We have not dealt with the admittedly complicated problem of Presidential inability.

Let us consider how Senate Joint Resolution 1 deals with the problem.

Section 3 specifies that the President may voluntarily declare his own disability, and, upon doing so, and upon transmitting to the Speaker of the House and the President of the Senate his written declaration, the Vice President shall assume the powers and duties of the office of Acting President for the duration of the President's illness or disability.

Let me emphasize two things. The Vice President assumes only the powers and duties of the office, not the office itself, and does not become President but, in fact, is only Acting President.

This, I think, is a reasonable assumption to make. It is an assumption which the Attorney General made in testifying before our committee. It is the assumption that Presidential power given up voluntarily may be assumed in the same manner in which it was given when the President desires to do so.

Mr. HRUSKA.[25] Mr. President, will the Senator yield, or would he prefer to finish his statement before yielding for a question?

Mr. BAYH. How extensively does the Senator wish to interrogate me?

Mr. HRUSKA. This deals with the Vice President assuming the powers and duties of the Presidency as Acting President. I should like to ask only a brief question on that point.

Mr. BAYH. I yield. I do not desire to avoid questions from my good friend from Nebraska, who I am sure has many penetrating questions to ask. However, I would like to complete my statement and not yield if the questioning is to be extensive.

Mr. HRUSKA. I have only a brief question.

Mr. BAYH. I yield.

Mr. HRUSKA. In regard to the question of the Vice President assuming the powers and duties of the President's office, may I ask whether there is any language in the joint resolution for creating the office of Acting President if the Vice President then in office is disabled and unable to act?

Mr. BAYH. There is not.

Mr. HRUSKA. There is not?

Mr. BAYH. No; not as long as there is a Vice President who is merely Acting President, and the President is alive.

Mr. HRUSKA. But if the President is disabled or is incompetent or for some other reason is not able to assume the duties and powers of the Presidency, under the joint resolution there will be no means by which a Vice President can be selected. Is that correct?

Mr. BAYH. The Senator is correct. I might elaborate on that point by giving the feeling of the sponsors as well as the members of the committee, by trying to incorporate very quickly some of the testimony which was brought before the committee. As the Senator knows well, and as I mentioned a moment ago, Congress has dealt with the problem of Presidential and Vice-Presidential deaths in three succession acts. Therefore, the Speaker of the House is next in line. We could become entangled in the question of separation of powers more than we have. Would the Speaker have to give up his office or resign from Congress? We have dealt with the two most important emergencies so far as the Executive is concerned, first, the need to have a Vice President at all times and, second, to have an able-bodied President. We feel that we should get this provision into the Constitution and then deal with some of the other eventualities and perhaps propose another constitutional amendment.

Mr. HRUSKA. That is one of the weaknesses in putting all these procedures into a constitutional amendment. There is no flexibility which would be called for in the event of a contingency which is not covered in a constitutional amendment. It would necessitate a long, extended, and rather tortuous course under another constitutional amendment.

Mr. BAYH. It depends on whether the Senator feels that the removal of the President from office even temporarily is of such significance that we should incorporate within the Constitution certain basic provisions that must be followed and the protections that must be given to the President, such as the protections already given, as in the case of impeachment, and such provisions as that under the 12th amendment so far as only the President is concerned.

Mr. HRUSKA. In the amendment which I understand will be offered by the Senator from Illinois [Mr. Dirksen],[26] provision is made for the contingency in this language:

The Congress may by law provide for other cases of removal, death, resignation, or inability of either the President or Vice President.

That contingency with respect to the Vice President is not contained in Senate Joint Resolution 1.

Mr. BAYH. The Senator is correct. It is not.

Mr. HRUSKA. I thank the Senator.

Mr. BAYH. I trust that we shall have the opportunity to discuss in some detail the relative merits of dealing with the question by statute compared with dealing with it by constitutional amendment, because I believe this is a question which should be discussed. I have certain strong feelings on the question, which are supported by a majority of the committee – though my friend from Nebr disagrees with them – that a statutory approach would be insufficient to deal with the problem. We have a difference of opinion, to be sure.

Mr. HRUSKA. I thank the Senator for his courtesy.

Mr. ELLENDER.[27] Mr. President, since the Senator from Indiana has yielded to my good friend from Nebraska, will he yield to me?

Mr. BAYH. I yield.

Mr. ELLENDER. Article II of the Constitution give to the Congress some rights to determine who shall succeed the President. Am I to understand that one of the main purposes of the amendment is to provide for the election of a Vice President in the event the President should die and the then Vice President should succeed him?

Mr. BAYH. That is correct.

Mr. ELLENDER. Does the Senator from Indiana concede that, other than providing for a method of selecting a Vice President, under the Constitution the Congress would have a right to do every other thing that is provided in the joint resolution?

Mr. BAYH. I am not certain that I understand the question. The proposed constitutional amendment would not in any way limit the powers which Congress already has to deal with the subject.

Mr. ELLENDER. I am not speaking of that, since the joint resolution relates to ways and means of electing a Vice President should a President die and be succeeded by the-then Vice President, could Congress now do everything except that part which relates to the selection of the Vice President?

Mr. BAYH. In other words, the Senator feels that Congress already has sufficient authority to deal with the question of disability.

Mr. ELLENDER. I am merely asking the question.

Mr. BAYH. It is my opinion that that is not the case.

Mr. ELLENDER. Will the Senator point out why? Article II of the Constitution seems very specific. It provides as follows:

In case of the removal of the President from office, or of his death, resignation, or inability to discharge the power and duties of the said office, the same shall devolve on the Vice President...

If that should happen, we would no longer have a Vice President, for he would have taken charge.

Continuing to read from article II:

...and the Congress may by law for the case of removal, death, resignation or inability, both of the President and Vice President, declaring what officer shall then act as President, and such officer shall act accordingly, until the disability be removed, or a President shall be elected.

The Congress has the right to do all those things now. I am wondering if Congress does not now have the authority to do everything that is proposed in the joint resolution we are now considering except providing for ways and means to select a Vice President.

Mr. BAYH. To be honest with the Senator from Louisiana, some Senators believe that Congress does have the authority. Others believe that Congress does not have the authority. The great weight of the evidence before our committee, including the message of the President of the United States and the testimony of various Attorneys General – including former Attorney General Brownell and former Attorney General Rogers[28] – is to the effect that now there is no power to do the things contained in the resolution.

I should like to point out the reason behind that attitude. The joint resolution is supported by the American Bar Association and many other similar associations. Two very small words in article II, section 1, which the Senator has read, are pointed out particularly. I should like to reread that portion of the article:

In case of the removal of the President from office, or of his death, resignation, or inability discharge the powers and duties of the said office, the same shall devolve...

What did our Constitutional Fathers mean when they use the word "same"? Did they mean the office or the powers and duties of the office? There is a great difference when we deal with disability.

Mr. ELLENDER. If a President should die and the Vice President should succeed him, the Vice President would certainly have the same powers as now devolve upon the President.

Mr. BAYH. Still the question of the President coming in remains. If the President is dead and cannot the powers and duties of the office, it does not make any whether he is Acting President or President. As Henry Clay said in discussing the subject when Tyler was making the decision, it is impossible to separate the powers and duties from the office. Once the Vice President has taken over from a sick President, it is impossible for the President to resume his office if that is true. During the illness of President Garfield the unanimous feeling among members of the Cabinet at that time was that Vice President [Chester Alan] Arthur should act, that he should take over. But it was the majority feeling, which was supported by the then Attorney General, that if he did – if he once assumed the powers and duties of the office – Garfield upon recovering could not take over the office again.

Mr. ELLENDER. As I interpret the language of the Constitution should the President be disabled, Congress could fix ways and means whereby the President could take over again after the disability was removed. The article states that Congress has the power to take certain action in the event of disability. The last part of the article states: "declaring what officer shall then act as President, and such officer shall act accordingly, until the disability be removed, or a President shall be elected."

That would indicate to me that if the disability were removed, Congress could certainly fix ways and means by which the President who might be disabled could resume the office.

[...]

Mr. ERVIN.[29] Mr. President, will the Senator yield?

Mr. BAYH. I yield.

Mr. ERVIN. In addition to the Aesop fable about the dog with the bone, a very apt adage is that "Too many cooks spoil the broth."

A multitude of amendments were offered along this line in seeking to take care of the situation. I introduced an amendment myself. I thought it was rather good. But I think the reason why we have progressed as far as we have in this matter is that the Senator from Indiana [Mr. BAYH] recognized that too many cooks can spoil the broth.

If we each try to get everything to accord with our own notion, we get nothing. The Senator has recognized the need for [the] clarification of a constitutional question. As a result of his fine example in that respect, other members of the Subcommittee on Constitutional Amendments and members the full Committee on the Judiciary have been influenced by his example and have sacrificed their individual views in an attempt to get some proposal that would recognize the problem, the necessity for a solution to the problem, and also that there must be a good deal of give and take.

I ask the Senator if one of the great problems which was before the committee – was not the question whether, in case of a vacancy, the Vice President would be appointed by the President for the sake of continuity in administration, or whether he should be elected by Congress for the sake of having some voice exercised by the representatives of the people in the selection of a Vice President.

Mr. BAYH. The Senator is correct. Those are two of the possibilities. As the Senator well recalls, two such proposals were before the Committee on Constitutional Amendments. It was the opinion of the subcommittee, plus that of the American Bar Association in their consensus group, and the full Committee on the Judiciary, that by combining both presidential and congressional action, we were dealing two things. We were guaranteeing that the President would have a man with whom he could work. We were also guaranteeing to the people their right to make that decision.

Mr. ERVIN. If my recollection serves me correctly – and if it does not, the Senator from Indiana can correct me because he has given great study to this measure – one of the things that former President Eisenhower emphasized the necessity having continuity of administration through a Vice President who was a member of the same party as the President. He laid more stress on that than on any other one thing in his advocacy of congressional action.

Mr. BAYH. The Senator is correct. As the Senator well knows, President Eisenhower who, more than any other living American, has had to deal with the problem of presidential inability, laid particular stress on the fact that this is a particular responsibility which the Vice President cannot escape.

Mr. ERVIN. The Senator from Indiana will recall that I introduced an amendment not only for the election of the Vice President by Congress, but also for the selection by Congress on the theory that Congress was comprised of representatives of the people.

Mr. BAYH. The Senator is correct. The Senator from Indiana felt it to be important that we should get a plan which would work, rather than any particular plan.

[...]

Mr. SIMPSON.[30] Mr. President, will the Senator from Indiana yield?

Mr. BAYH. I yield.

Mr. SIMPSON. Mr. President, let me first of all compliment the able and distinguished junior Senator from Indiana [Mr. BAYH] for a very fine presentation with respect to this all important subject.

Mr. President, as a cosponsor of this proposed legislation, the record has been filled with interesting materials on the history of this Nation which clearly shows the need for complete and adequate laws regulating the succession to the office of the President of the United States. Great many Members of Congress have made reference to the days of President Eisenhower's illnesses and the questions that arose during that time about the authority of the office of the President and the responsibilities of the Vice President.

In earlier history, the administrations of Presidents Garfield and Wilson were challenged by the same questions. Fortunately, the Nation was permitted to endure these times of crisis and has grown and prospered in spite of the inadequacies and doubts that we have concerning the highest office in the land.

Directly relating to the problem of Presidential inability is that of a vacancy in the office of Vice President. That office has been vacated 16 times in the Nation's history for a total period of 38 years.

In past years, the office of Vice President was subject to more ridicule than respect, but such is not a case today. Vice President Richard Nixon brought a new respect to the office because of the yeoman service that he gave to the Nation and to the world. The Vice President is the possible successor to the Nation's highest office. He has many responsibilities. I feel there is ample evidence that the United States needs a Vice President at all times.

I believe that the constitutional proposal we are discussing today sets forth a reasonable and complete plan for providing for Presidential inability and vacancies in the office of Vice President.

I am pleased to have been a cosponsor of this proposed constitutional amendment, both in the 88th and in the 89th Congresses. As indicated, the need for this type of action is long overdue. Unfortunately, it was not until the tragedy of November 1963, that we realized the possible consequences of not having a clear and adequate plan for succession to our executive offices.

Many of the great legal minds throughout the country have studied this proposed constitutional amendment and I believe, for the most part, are in full support of it. It is the simplicity of the proposal that gives it strength and, thus, makes it appealing.

The first section of the resolution provides that the Vice President will become President in the case of [the] death or resignation of the President. When there is a vacancy in the office of the Vice-Presidency, the President is to nominate a Vice President who will take office upon confirmation by a majority vote of both Houses of Congress.

Section 3 provides that if the President declares in writing that he is unable to discharge the powers and duties of his office, the Vice President shall act as President.

Under the terms of this proposed constitutional amendment, the Vice President and the majority of the Cabinet members can determine the President to be disabled. If the President disputes the decision of the Vice President and the Cabinet members, Congress will decide the issue.

Seldom does the Senate agree unanimously on a problem of such magnitude and importance as is this proposed constitutional amendment on presidential inability and vacancies in the office of Vice President, but last year when we considered the matter, there was not a dissenting vote.

It is my hope that this proposal will receive the approval of Congress and the necessary States so that the people of America can be assured that we will have a leader to deal with any crisis that may arise. I am proud to support this proposal.

Mr. BAYH. I thank my colleague, the distinguished Senator from Wyoming [Mr. SIMPSON], for his articulate presentation.

[...]

Mr. TYDINGS.[31] Mr. President, will the Senator from Indiana yield?

Mr. BAYH. I yield.

Mr. TYDINGS. One of the points made by the distinguished Senator from Louisiana [Mr. ELLENDER] questioned the language in section 4, which reads as follows:

Whenever the Vice President, and a majority of the principal officers of the executive department of such other body as Congress may by law provide...

This seems to be one of the phrases which was providing some concern to the Senator from Louisiana [Mr. ELLENDER].

My recollection of the committee hearings is that the reason for inserting the language "principal officers of the executive department or such other body as Congress may by law provide" was occasioned by the history of the development of our Cabinet. Originally the Cabinet consisted of four members. Subsequently, it was enlarged. Today the Cabinet consists of 10 members.[32]

It was felt that perhaps in another year or two Congress might create a new post in the Cabinet Congress might feel that the Chairman of the National Security Council or some other important official ought to be included in the Cabinet.

Therefore, we wanted to provide a little flexibility in the constitutional amendment, so that Congress could adjust the circumstances as it wished.

That is my recollection of the principal reason why this language was placed in the joint resolution.

The House took up the Senate's proposed amendment after a series of hearings in the House Committee on the Judiciary, the panel's chairman, Rep. Emanuel Celler, Democrat of New York, who had been a key member in the drafting and passage of the Twenty-third and Twentyfourth Amendments, took the lead in making major changes to the Senate language. Debate on these changes occurred in the House on 13 April 1965, excerpted below.

IN THE COMMITTEE OF THE WHOLE

Accordingly, the House resolved itself into the Committee of the Whole House on the State of the Union for the consideration of House Joint Resolution 1 with Mr. FASCELL[33] in the chair.

The Clerk read the title of the joint resolution.

By unanimous consent, the first reading of the joint resolution was dispensed with.

The CHAIRMAN. Under the rule, the gentleman from New York [Mr. CELLER][34] will be recognized for 2 hours and the gentleman from Ohio [Mr. McCULLOCH][35] will be recognized for 2 hours. The Chair recognizes the gentleman from New York [Mr. CELLER].

Mr. CELLER. Mr. Chairman, I yield myself such time as I may consume.

Mr. Chairman, this resolution, House Joint Resolution 1, has bipartisan support. I particularly offer praise to the gentleman from Ohio [Mr. McCULLOCH] and the gentleman from Virginia [Mr. POFF][36] who participated in the fashioning and polishing of this resolution. They did so most wisely and painstakingly. They immersed themselves into the intricacies of the legislation. Their help was immeasurable. By naming them, Mr. Chairman, I do not wish to detract from the constructive work done by most of the members of our committee, Democrats, and Republicans alike. I want to point out particularly likewise in that regard the gentleman from Colorado [Mr. ROGERS],[37] the gentleman from New Jersey [Mr. RODINO],[38] the gentleman from Texas [Mr. BROOKS],[39] the gentleman from Massachusetts [Mr. DONOHUE],[40] the gentleman from Wisconsin [Mr. KASTENMEIER],[41] the gentleman from California [Mr. CORMAN],[42] the gentleman from New York [Mr. LINDSAY],[43] and the gentleman from Florida [Mr. CRAMER].[44] To them I, indeed, offer an accolade of distinction for genuine service.

This is by no means, ladies and gentlemen, a perfect bill. No bill can be perfect. Even the sun has its spots. The world of actuality permits us to attain no perfection. Admirable as is our own Continue, it had to be amended 24 times. But nonetheless, this bill has a minimum of drawbacks. It is well-rounded, sensible, and [an] efficient approach toward a solution of a perplexing problem – a problem that has baffled us for over 100 years.

As to attaining perfection, let me call your attention to a very pertinent remark made by Walter Lippmann in the *New York Herald-Tribune* of June 9, 1964, when he referred to this proposed amendment. He said:

It is a great deal better than an endless search for the absolutely perfect solution, which will never be found and, indeed, is not necessary.

As was said by the distinguished former Attorney General of the United States, the honorable Herbert Brownell – I commend his words indeed to the gentleman from Ohio [Mr. BROWN][45] – speaking for himself and speaking for the American Bar Association:

Certainty and prompt action are...built into this proposal – namely, House Joint Resolution 1...During the 10-year debate on Presidential disability...many plans have been advanced to have the existence of disability decided by different types of commissions or medical experts, by the Supreme Court, or by other complicated and hoc procedures. But upon analysis...they all have the same fatal flaw...they would be time consuming and divisive.

We tried to avoid freighting down this amendment with too much detail. We leave that to supplementing, implementing legislation. We make the provisions as simple, yet as comprehensive as possible.

This is certain: we have trifled with fate long enough on this question of Presidential inability. We in the United States have been lucky, but luck down not last forever. The one sure thing about luck is that it is bound to change.

Sir Thomas Brown once said:

Court not felicity too far and weary not the favorable hand of fortune.

We can no longer delay. Delay is the art of keeping up with yesterday. We must keep abreast of tomorrow. Let us stop playing Presidential inability roulette. Let us pass this measure, which has the approval of the American Bar Association and the American Association of Law Schools. This measure has the approval of 36 State bar associations, including, incidentally, the bar association of the distinguished gentleman on the Rules Committee, the gentleman from Ohio [Mr. BROWN].

[...]

If I were perplexed and baffled over a legal question, I would not be likely to go to the gentleman from Ohio. More than likely I would go to a lawyer. The gentleman from Ohio is not a lawyer. This is a constitutional legal question. I would not go to Attorney General Brown; I would go to Attorney General Brownell. What did Mr. Brownell have to say on this subject, as to the need for a constitutional amendment and the fact that it would be dangerous to offer a mere statute? Mr. Brownell said:

The number of respected constitutional authorities have argued that there can be no temporary devolution of Presidential power on the Vice President during periods of Presidential inability.

And whatever we may think of that argument, I think a statute would not protect the Nation adequately the doubts that have been raised, which have been raised too persistently. As long as there is doubt, lingering doubt, concerning the constitutionality of the statute, as long as there is a question concerning the disabled President's constitutional stature after the recovery, I do not believe any inability, as a practical matter, however severe it may be, would be recognized lest recognition of that disability would oust the disabled President from office. Moreover, if the President's inability were severe and prolonged, you should note that devolution of the Presidential power on the Vice President would be somewhat of a crisis itself.

Beyond that, the present Attorney General, a very erudite scholar and a very practical Attorney General, similarly before the Committee on the Judiciary of the House and the Committee on the Judiciary of the Senate gave eloquent testimony as to the need for a constitutional amendment. I shall not burden you at this moment with his words but shall insert them in the RECORD.

[...]

Mr. HALL.[46] Mr. Chairman, will the gentleman yield?

Mr. CELLER. I yield to the gentleman.

Mr. HALL. Mr. Chairman, I appreciate your statement. I am one of those who I anxious to see correct and proper legislation enacted in order to fill this void. I notice in the hearings and in the committee report that the committee report that the distinguished committee which the gentleman chairs has had exhaustive hearings and has called on many people from many walks of life. I am addressing myself particularly to the question of Presidential inability or disability. I would say, sir, that in direct proportion to the complexity of life that you have so often and so well referred to today, there is also the difficulty of determining inability or disability of the human being to function. This strikes me as something, as a man who has practiced medicine, that is increasingly difficult in this complicated age to determine. I see no evidence in the hearings of any particular statement by either any White House physician, past or present, of any of the Surgeons General of our civilian or uniformed branches, or civilian consultants available to the Government, such as the American Medical Association; some or all of whom are usually called on in such extremes for [the] determination of these questions. I wonder, although fully realizing the need for a judicial determination – or a legislative determination – of the fact, if such opinion was sought. I am not able to find it here. I wonder if those ordinarily determine inability or disability were consulted or called for hearings; or if they were excluded purposely, or if it is simply presumed by the chairman that this type of advice will be sought in time of such exigency.

Mr. CELLER. For the very reason that the gentleman explained, which indicated a difficulty of definition, we did not specifically speak of medical experts or of a commission of those with expertise on subjects of this sort. But we did say the following: We said – "or such other body as Congress may by law provide." In other words, Congress may, by passing legislation implementing this, set up, if it wishes, some other body or some group of experts who would give advice and counsel instead of the members of the Cabinet. The members of the Cabinet, the members of the President's executive family, usually are the ones who are intimate with the President. They know his idiosyncrasies. They know a good deal about his health and they probably could tell a great deal concerning his physical condition. But if we in the Congress feel that more is desire, we could appoint another body.

Mr. HALL. I thank the chairman. I understand, and have no particular flaw to pick on the question of the President's Cabinet with the Vice President making the determination or seeking two-thirds of the votes of Congress in determining lack of ability. I am not quite sure that this Congress would ever, as a matter of practical procedure, set up, for example, the five Surgeons General to determine ability. At the same time, I am certainly not convinced that, wise as the members of the Cabinet may be about the President's personality traits and about deviation away from the norm thereof, that they could physically determine when association pathways of the human brain and mind, or even the emotions, were bereft of ordinary and expected continuity on the part of the President to the point of constituting disability.

[...]

Mr. POFF. Mr. Chairman, will my chairman yield so that I may respond to the gentleman's question?

Mr. CELLER. I yield to the gentleman from Virginia.

Mr. POFF. I appreciate the concern the gentleman expresses and I am in sympathy with the point he makes. I believe I can throw some light on this question by quoting from an opinion of Attorney General Kennedy, [on] August 2, 1961, in which he undertakes to describe what transpired when President. Eisenhower suffered a disability:

The problem of succession to the Presidency was considered immediately after former President Eisenhower's heart attack in September 1955. Congress was not in session, and there was no immediate international crisis. On the basis of medical opinions and a survey of the urgent problems demanding Presidential action immediately or in the near future, Attorney General Brownell orally advised the Cabinet and the Vice President that the existing situation did not require the Vice President to exercise the powers and duties of the President under article II of the Constitution.

I suggest that a similar thing could normally and reasonably be expected in the event this constitutional amendment is adopted, and ratified by the States. Surely, the decision makers, whoever they may be, would not undertake so critical a decision without first consulting the experts in the field, namely the gentlemen of the medical profession.

Mr. HALL...I certainly believe it is important, not necessarily that it be spelled out in this resolution we are considering today, but that a legislative record be made here today with respect to such a complex and difficultof-determination area. In the enabling legislation, which I understand will subsequently follow this amendment to the Constitution, we might indeed spell out what used to be involved.

[...]

Mr. MacGREGOR.[47] May I add to the very excellent answer given by the gentleman from Virginia, an historical note which may give further comfort to the gentleman from Missouri.

At the time of the severe stroke which occurred to Woodrow Wilson, the Secretary of State at the time suggested that the Vice President step in and exercise the powers and duties of the Presidency area this was not taken with good grace by the President, and when he recovered his ability, the Secretary of State soon found himself without a job. I believe with that historical precedent facing the Members of the Cabinet very would not take the step jointly with the Vice President to certify, in their judgment, the President's inability to the appropriate officers of the Congress without any consultation with the very finest medical brains which were available to them here in the Nation's Capital.

Mr. HALL. Mr. Chairman, will the gentleman yield further?

Mr. CELLER. I yield to the gentleman.

Mr. HALL. I appreciate that remark, and I think it is historically interesting. I would like to believe that the gentleman is adding to the legislative record which I am trying to establish to that ultimate end, but what we are trying to do here is to prevent historical precedents such as that from recurring. It is to that end that I rise and I think the point has been well made.

Mr. Chairman, I thank the gentleman from New York for yielding.

Mr. DUNCAN of Oregon.[48] Mr. Chairman, will the gentleman yield?

Mr. CELLER. I yield to the gentleman.

Mr. DUNCAN of Oregon. I have asked the chairman to yield in order to direct your attention to page 4, section 4, and ask a question about what seems to me to be an ambiguity and, if it is one that ought to be cleared up, I think, in a colloquy here on the floor of the House. The second paragraph of section 4 provides that if the President shall recover and he sends to the Congress a written declaration that no inability exists, "he shall resume the powers and duties of his office unless the Vice President and a majority of the principal officers of the executive departments, or such other body as Congress may by law provide, transmit within 2 days to the President pro tempore of the Senate and the Speaker of the House of Representatives their written declaration that the President is unable to discharge the powers and duties of his office."

My question, sir, is, is there not a 2-day period when we may be in a state of ambiguity, not knowing whether the President, having recovered, has the powers and duties of the office or whether the Vice President is the Acting President of the United States?

Mr. CELLER. It is the Acting President, that is, the Vice President, who is Acting President. He is in control unless the President, and so forth, does something or something happens. So, it is the Vice President that is in the saddle, but to make assurance doubly sure I will read [to] you a communication that I received from the Attorney General, dated April 13, 1965, which letter reads as follows:

Dear Mr. Chairman: The question has been raised as to whether, under section 5 of House Joint Resolution 1, as amended by the House Judiciary Committee on March 16 and 17, 1965, the Acting President would continue to discharge the powers and duties of the Office of President during the 2-day period within which the Vice President and a majority of the principal officers of the executive departments may transmit to the President pro tempore of the Senate and the Speaker of the House of Representatives their written declaration that the President is unable to discharge the powers and duties of his Office.

As I have previously indicated to you, it seems to me entirely clear that the Acting President would continue to exercise the powers and duties of the Office during this period. The same is true of the period of up to 10 days thereafter during which, under section 5 as it now stands, the Congress would be required to resolve the issue.

Mr. DUNCAN of Oregon. Mr. Chairman, will the gentleman yield for another question?

Mr. CELLER. Yes; I will.

Mr. DUNCAN of Oregon. In the event that the letter is not written by the Vice President and a majority of the principal officers of the executive departments, then who actually has the powers of the President during the 48-hour period following the transmittal by the President of his declaration to reassume the office?

Mr. CELLER. The Acting President would – and I used that term again – be in the saddle unless he agrees the President is fully restored.

Mr. DUNCAN of Oregon. So the intent of this section of this resolution is that the Acting President – and let us assume it is the Vice President – will continue to discharge the duties of that office until the expiration of all necessary time intervals or until the Congress shall take such action as may be necessary?

Mr. CELLER. The Vice President during that period could agree that the President is no longer disabled and the President will resume his powers.

Mr. DUNCAN of Oregon. He can then take affirmative action?

Mr. CELLER. Even within the period.

Mr. DUNCAN of Oregon. He could take affirmative action within the period and thereupon the President of the United States will reassume the duties and powers of his office?

Mr. CELLER. That is correct.

Mr. DUNCAN of Oregon. If he did not do that, he would continue as Acting President during all intervals of time necessary for the Cabinet and the President to transmit their letter and the Congress to take such action as may be necessary.

Mr. CELLER. It is interesting to note while the Senate did not do this, we put a time limit of 10 days on it. We insisted the Congress must act in 10 days. If it does not, the President goes back in.

After the Senate disagreed with changes made by the House and voted for different language, the two reports had to go to conference to iron out differences. The following introduction of the combined conference report occurred on 30 June 1965.

PRESIDENTIAL INABILITY AND VACANCIES IN THE OFFICE OF THE VICE PRESIDENT

Mr. CELLER submitted the following conference report and statement on the joint resolution (S.J. Res. 1) proposing an amendment to the Constitution of the United States relating to [the] succession to the Presidency and Vice Presidency and to cases where the President is unable to discharge the powers and duties of his office.

[Celler then had the clerk read the entire conference report, which is cut here for reasons of space.]

Mr. CELLER. Mr. Speaker, I ask unanimous consent for the immediate consideration of the conference report on the joint resolution (S.J. Res. 1) proposing an amendment to the Constitution of the United States relating to [the] succession to the Presidency and Vice Presidency and to cases where the President is unable to discharge the powers and duties of his office, and I ask unanimous consent that the statement of the managers on the part of the House be read in lieu of the report.

The Clerk read the title of the joint resolution.

The SPEAKER. Is there objection to the request of the gentleman from New York?

There was no objection.

The Clerk read the statement.

Mr. CELLER. Mr. Speaker, today we write on the tablets of history. We amend the Constitution, which Gladstone, speaking in 1898, hailed as the most wonderful work struck off at a given time by the brain and purpose of man.

The United States has two great symbols of her freedom and liberty. One is the Declaration of Independence and the other is the Constitution. The Declaration is the profession of faith, while the Constitution is its working instrument. It gives action to that faith.

There is no document in any country that can compare with our Constitution. It is the touchstone of our prowess and progress as a nation. Most countries envy us our Constitution.

The Constitution has such elasticity that it remains vital throughout the decades, but it is not immutable. It is not written in stone on Mount Sinai.

Associate Supreme Court Justice Oliver Wendell Holmes once said:

The Constitution is an experiment, as all life is an experiment. If new contingencies arise the Constitution must be made to fit them either by interpretation of fearless judges aware of historical perspective or by amendment.

Jefferson called the Constitution "the ark of our safety and grand palladium of our peace and happiness." He also said:

We must be content to accept of its good and to cure what is evil in it, hereafter (1788). Years later, in 1823, he said:

The States are now so numerous that I despair of ever seeing another amendment to the Constitution; although innovations of time will certainly call and now already call for some.

Note his prescience.

Let it be emphasized; we never should amend this charter for light or transient reasons. Only for just cause shown should we attempt any change. What we do today is epoch making. We offer an amendment for an overriding reason.

I would like to remind the Members that the House Committee on the Judiciary has been studying this problem since 1955 and has examined it from every conceivable angle. We have had the benefit of the testimony of political scientists, constitutional experts, the American Bar Association, and other groups who had no motive other than to serve this country by closing a gap which has existed since the adoption of the Constitution.

The Constitution was silent, too silent concerning presidential inability. Tragic events had cast ominous shadows which we dared no longer disregard. The assassin's bullet and possible nuclear holocaust forced action.

We, the conferees working dispassionately and with searching inquiry after both Houses had responded to the call for action. We met in numerous conclaves and finally rounded out differences. We labored hard and patiently. We accepted the pace of Nature, for is not patience her secret? We examined all contingencies and possibilities. We present a solution that is ample, wise, and practicable.

May I at this time pay tribute to the gentleman from Ohio [Mr. McCULLOCH] and the gentleman from Virginia [Mr. POFF], both on the Republican side, and to the gentleman from Colorado [Mr. ROGERS] and the gentleman from California [Mr. CORMAN] on the Democratic side – all conferees – who rendered painstaking and dedicated and wise services in the conference. They were of immeasurable help in the conference with the Senators. I am deeply grateful to them.

Mr. POFF. Mr. Speaker, the conference report represents a compromise. That word should be understood not as an apology for a concession but as a justification for an achievement, and achievement in the highest traditions of legislative and constitutional craftsmanship. It is an accommodation and an accord of viewpoints which once were widely divergent and now, happily, are concordant. The business of the Nation, left unattended for a century because [it was] too controversial, has been performed and the controversy has been resolved.

Aside from minor, relatively inconsequential language differences, the House version and the Senate version were substantially equivalent in all but four major particulars.

The first major difference was in section 3. That is the section under which the President can voluntarily vacate his office and vest the Vice President as Acting President with the powers and duties of his office. The difference was in the mechanics of [the] presumption of power by the President. Under the Senate version, the mechanics outlined in sections 4 and 5 would apply. Those mechanics involved first, a declaration of restoration by the President; second, an opportunity for a challenge by the Vice President transmitted to the Congress; and third, the possibility of congressional approval of the Vice President's challenge should. The House version did not actuate the mechanics of sections 4 and 5. Rather, it was felt that a distinction should be made between section 3 authorizing voluntary withdrawal of the President and section 4 authorizing involuntary removal of the President by the Vice President. The House felt that the President would be reluctant to utilize section 3 if to do so exposed himself to the possibility of the Vice Presidential challenge and congressional action when he decided to resume the office. Accordingly, section 3 of the House version provided that the President who used the provisions of section 3 could promptly restore himself to his office simply by transmitting a written declaration to the two Houses of Congress.

The conference report – after adding two words of clarification – accepted the House version.

The second major difference between the two versions was in the mechanics of restoration in sections 4 and 5. In the Senate version, the Vice President as Acting President, was allowed 7 days in which to make a decision about challenging the President's declaration of restoration. The House version was 2 days. By way of compromise, the conference report recommends 4 days. The conferees intend that the 4-day period be interpreted as an outside limitation on the time in which the Vice President may consider making a challenge; it is not necessary that the President wait 4 days to resume his office if he and the Vice President mutually agree that he do so earlier.

The third major difference involved a procedural uncertainty which Speaker McCORMACK during House debate recognized might cause calamitous consequences. Under the Senate version, the Vice President's declaration of restoration had the effect of submitting the dispute between the two men to the Congress for settlement. However, it simply instructed Congress "to immediately proceed to decide the issue." This left unclear what delay might occur in the event the Congress was in recess when it received the Vice President's challenge Under the House version, though Congress, if not in session, is required to assemble "within 48 hours" to decide the issue.

The conference report accepts the House version.

The fourth major difference is a conceptual difference. Under the Senate version, the Congress having received the Vice President's challenge was empowered to act upon it and if it upheld the challenge by a two-thirds vote, the Vice President would continue to hold office as Acting President; otherwise, the President would resume his office. The House version was essentially the same except that it imposed a 10-day limitation upon congressional action. It said that if the Congress did challenge within 10 days after receipt, then the President would resume his office. The House approach guaranteed that any delay on the part of the Congress, whether accidental and unavoidable or intentional and purposeful would operate in favor of the President elected by the people.

The conference report adopts the concept of a time limitation but increases the time limit from 10 days to 21 days, and if that Congress is in recess when the Vice President's challenge is received, then the 21 days begin to run from the day Congress reconvenes.

No one should assume that House insistence upon a time limit was a criticism of the Senate. It is true that the rules of the other body permit unlimited debate and a small minority of Senators hostile to the President and loyal to the Vice President as Acting President could, in the absence of a time limit, make a great deal of public mischief at a most critical time in the life of the Nation. It is no less true that such mischief could be wrought by a small dedicated band of enemies of the President in the House. By tedious invocation of the technical rules of procedure, that little band could frustrate action on the Vice President's challenge for a protracted period of time, during which the Vice President would continue to serve as Acting Resident and the President, knocking on his own door for readmission, would be kept standing outside. If this little band happened to be one more than half the membership of the House, their task would be much easier, because they could simply meet and adjourn every third day without any action at all. Thus, more than half but less than two-thirds could effectively accomplish by inaction the same thing it would take two-thirds to accomplish by vote if there is no time limit in the Constitution. The conference committee understood this danger, and that is why the 21-day provision is in the conference report.

Several matters need to be clearly established by legislative history. First of all, the conferees unanimously intend that the 21-day period be considered an outside limitation and should in no wise be interpreted to encourage a delay longer than necessary. Indeed, in the face of such a crisis as the Nation would face that a time when section 4 would become operable, the conferees feel that both Houses of Congress should act with the least possible delay.

Secondly, the conferees unanimously intend that should one House of the Congress proceed to a vote on the Vice President's challenge and less than two-thirds of its Members vote to uphold the challenge, this action shall have the effect of restoring the President immediately to his office, even though the other House has not yet acted.

Mr. Speaker, I have no fear but that this conference report will be adopted by a two-thirds vote. But I am prompted to express the hope and the plea that it will be adopted by a unanimous vote, and with such a congressional blessing, the proposal would, I am confident, be ratified by three-fourths of the States before the end of next year.

[...]

Mr. ROYBAL. Mr. Speaker, I rise to urge prompt ratification by the legislatures of the several States of the proposed 25th amendment to the Constitution relating to [the] succession to the Presidency and Vice Presidency and to cases where the President is unable to discharge the powers and duties of his office.

This proposed, overwhelmingly adopted by both House and Senate, can be of vital importance in helping clear up some 175 years of constitutional uncertainty and in assuring the continuity of the legal Government of the United States whenever the questions of Presidential disability or succession arise, or a vacancy in the office of the Vice President occurs.

As cosponsor of the joint congressional resolution which proposed the amendment, I believe we have come to realize more fully than ever before, especially since the tragic assassination of our late beloved President John F. Kennedy, that we can no longer afford, in the nuclear space age, to gamble with the future stability of our Government by leaving its fate to the on certain whims of chance.

Nothing less than the safe and sure continuity of the legal Government of the United States is at stake. This essential continuity has been endangered many times in the past, and in some instances, only good fortune has prevented possible disaster.

For more than a year after Lyndon Johnson became President, our national luck held out, and we were all witnesses to an impressive demonstration of the true inner strength of America's democratic traditions.

The new President firmly and quickly took up the reins of leadership, to assure continuity of the Government in the midst of a great constitutional crisis, to begin to heal the Nation's wounds, and to reinstall in our people a sense of unity and brotherhood and faith in the future.

This experience has again focused attention on the critical issue of Presidential and Vice Presidential succession, as well as the related, and in some ways more difficult, problem of Presidential disability.

As a result, there has developed a strong national consensus in favor of resolving these issues in a positive way, so that there will be no doubt concerning the constitutional provisions for handling such problems in the future.

As an affirmative response to the need for a solution to these problems, the joint congressional resolution proposes to amend the Constitution in three respects: first, it confirms the established custom that a Vice President, succeeding to a vacancy in the office of the President, becomes President in his own right instead of merely Acting President; second, it establishes a procedure for filling a vacancy in the office of Vice President; and third, it deals with the problem of Presidential disability.

⋙⋙⋙⋙⋙⋙

Once the House-Senate conference report went to both houses, it had to be voted on as if it were original legislation. The House passed the conference report on 30 June, sending it to the Senate for final passage. This is the limited debate over the conference report, 6 July 1965.

PRESIDENTIAL INABILITY AND VACANCIES IN THE OFFICE OF THE OFFICE OF VICE PRESIDENT – CONFERENCE REPORT

The PRESIDING OFFICER. Under the unanimous-consent agreement, the Chair lays before the Senate the pending business, which the clerk will state.

The LEGISLATIVE CLERK. Report of the committee of conference on the disagreeing votes of the two Houses on the amendment of the House to the joint resolution (S.J. Res. 1) proposing an amendment to the Constitution of the United States relating to [the] succession to the Presidency and Vice Presidency and to cases where the President is unable to discharge the powers and duties of his office.

The Senate resumed the consideration of the report.

The PRESIDING OFFICER. Who yields time?

Mr. BAYH. Mr. President, a parliamentary inquiry.

The PRESIDING OFFICER. The Senator will state it.

Mr. BAYH. It is my understanding that under the unanimous-consent agreement adopted by the Senate earlier, the time is to be controlled, 1 hour by the distinguished Senator from Tennessee [Mr. GORE][49] and 1 hour by me.

The PRESIDING OFFICER. Under the agreement, there is a limitation of 2 hours, 1 hour on each side.

Who yields time?

Mr. BAYH. Mr. President, the Senator from Tennessee [Mr. GORE] as a prepared speech. I do not desire to engage in colloquy.

I will yield myself just 2 minutes to say that this has been a much discussed subject over the past 187 years of our history. The past 187 years is replete with studies by the Congress, the Senate, and individuals concerned.

The purpose of the constitutional amendment, the conference report on which we are now called to approve, is to provide a means which we have devised by which the Vice President will be able to perform the powers and duties of the office of the President if the President is unable to do so.

Mr. President, in my estimation, it is impossible to devise a bill or a constitutional amendment which can cover all the contingencies and this particular, complicated field, but this Congress has gone further than any of his predecessors toward meeting the problem.

[...]

Mr. GORE. Mr. President, I yield 15 minutes to the senior Senator from Minnesota.

Mr. McCARTHY.[50] Mr. President, I believe that the Senate acted wisely in putting off action on the conference report for a few days so that we could carefully examine the language in the proposed amendment and so that all Senators, rather than the four or five who participated in the discussion last week might be fully aware and informed as to the committee interpretation and what would then be the congressional interpretation of what the proposed amendment to the Constitution would actually mean.

I note again that we are not enacting a statute, something which we could change in this Congress or in any subsequent Congress. We are acting on a constitutional amendment which would establish the procedure for the indefinite future.

I have serious reservations about more than the language of the amendment. I have very serious reservations about the substance of the amendment itself. It was my view when the question of presidential disability and vice-presidential succession was raised that there was sufficient authority in the Constitution to permit Congress to proceed by statute.

Paragraph 6, section 1, of article II of the Constitution gives Congress power to legislate in the area of presidential disability and of succession of a Vice President. This section of the Constitution reads:

In case of the removal of the President from office, or of his death, resignation, or inability to discharge the powers and duties of the said office, the same shall devolve on the Vice President, and the Congress may by law provide for the case of removal, death, resignation, or inability, both of the President and Vice President, declaring what officer shall then act as President and such officer shall act accordingly, until the disability be removed, or a President shall be elected.

It is my judgment that we could act by statute to meet both the problem of succession and disability. There are constitutional authorities who feel that we have power to act in case of a vacancy in the vice-presidency. However, there is some question as to our ability to act in case of disability.

I am willing to abide by the judgment of those who thought we needed a constitutional amendment. It was my opinion that the amendment should be a simple one and should make clear the right and authority of Congress to act by statute.

This was the opinion of Deputy Attorney General Katzenbach when he testified before the committee in 1963 and in his statement submitted to the committee in 1964. He asked for a simple constitutional amendment; and, following that, for action on the part of Congress to spell out the procedures by which inability might be determined and also by which the commencement and termination of any inability would be determined.

This is not the issue involved today. Congressional committees, in both the Senate and House, have considered, I am sure, the possibility of a simple amendment to leave the way open to proceed under statute but they have not approved this method.

At the same time, we are preparing to take what will probably be final action on, at least, the last chance to review the proposed amendment.

It has been argued that State legislatures would give a thorough review to the matter. We were informed last week that one State legislature was holding up action until after Congress had acted on the matter so that it would be the first State legislature to ratify the measure. It may be that the State legislature studied the matter and is fully informed as to the amendment. However, I have very grave doubts that this is so. I believe that after Congress acts on the matter, ratification by the States will be almost routine.

Mr. GORE. Mr. President, will the Senator yield?

Mr. McCARTHY. I yield.

Mr. GORE. Mr. President, I wonder if the able Senator believes that the members of the legislature which was awaiting the adoption of the conference report by the Senate in order to be the first State to ratified the amendment could have had an opportunity to read the conference report and determine that the conferees had added certain words to the language. Two of the words were "pro tempore." Another was "either," and the other word was "of."

The conference report did relate that minor changes in language had been made. However, I wonder if the Senator believes that the insertion of the word "either" in the Constitution of the United States, having to do with two bodies, either of which, under the terms of the pending amendment, would play a part in the declaration of presidential disability is a minor matter, and if the State legislature to which the Senator referred was aware of this fact.

Mr. McCARTHY. Mr. President, I believe that it could well be a most serious matter. Certainly, the language of the amendment as sent to conference would be preferable to this language.

I know that the Senator from Tennessee has given much study to the meaning of the words and the application of the disjunctive alternative of "either/or" in this case.

[...]

Mr. BAYH. Mr. President, will the Senator yield? Mr. McCARTHY. I yield.

Mr. BAYH. Mr. President, I do not want the record to be incorrect in expressing the present position of the Attorney General. Is the senior Senator from Minnesota aware of the testimony by the Attorney General before the committee in 1965?

Mr. McCARTHY. I knew the Attorney General was supporting the amendment.

Mr. BAYH. I thank the Chair.

Mr. McCARTHY. I was referring to what was his preferred position when as Deputy Attorney General he testified on the constitutional amendment dealing with Presidential inability. I believe his original position was sound, although, as in the case of many other people, he is willing to support the proposed amendment because of the urgency of the situation.

Mr. BAYH. But the Attorney General did say, before the Subcommittee on Constitutional Amendments of the Committee on the Judiciary, that he believed the proposed amendment was the best alternative that has been conceived.

Mr. McCARTHY. I do not know whether he said it was the best alternative that has been conceived. He said it was the only possible course of action rather than no action at all, not that it was better than any alternative that was ever conceived. He conceived one which he thought was the best he could conceive.

[...]

Mr. GORE. Mr. President...

The PRESIDING OFFICER. How much time does the Senator from Tennessee yield to himself?

Mr. GORE. Such time as I may desire.

This is the last opportunity for any group of men in any body politic to revise or clarify the language of the proposed amendment. The House has already adopted the conference report. Should the Senate adopt the conference report in its present form, the proposed amendment would then go to the States for ratification. If the amendment is ratified by three-fourths of the State legislatures, it will then become a part of the US Constitution.

The States will have no choice except to ratify or reject the amendment in the form submitted. That is why I say this is an important action on the part of the Senate.

The charter of our Republic is a precious document. Amendment of it should be approached with the greatest gravity.

In the beginning of our Republic the candidate for President who received the second largest vote became Vice President. The country's experience under that provision soon led to trouble, so much so that in 1804, I believe, the Constitution was amended so that the Vice President would be elected to a separate office by separate vote. Thus, it was sought to minimize the possibility of conflict between a President and a Vice President.

In July 1965 the US Senate is again undertaking to deal with the question of the President and the Vice President of the United States.

On last Wednesday, when the conference report on Senate Joint Resolution 1 was before the Senate, I was one of those who urged that the vote on the conference report be delayed to permit additional time for Senators to examine the language of the proposed constitutional amendment before taking the final congressional action on what would be one of the more important amendments ever adopted to our Constitution.

I wish to make it clear that I did not then, nor do I now, seek either to block action on or otherwise defeat an amendment which would fill an existing procedural void in the area of presidential succession and presidential disability. The tragic events of November 1963 have served to call to the attention of the American people that failure to act on this matter might, at some time in the future, pose serious consequences to our Republic. Indeed, we should regard ourselves as most fortunate that we have not already, at some time in our history, experienced a grave constitutional crisis for want of a procedure for determining with certainty the fact of presidential disability. Charity and certainty are the essential characteristics of any constitutional provision dealing with the subject.

The basic objective of an amendment such as we now consider should be the provision of a procedure certain for the declaration of disability of a President of the United States, but I submit that the provision now before the Senate provides an uncertain procedure.

In my opinion, the language of section 4 of the proposed amendment, which deals with the determination of the fact of Presidential disability by means other than the voluntary act of the President himself, lacks the degree of clarity and certainty required if the objective of this section of the amendment is to be achieved. If the fact of Presidential disability should ever become a matter upon which a President and other authorities designated in the amendment are in disagreement, the most essential requirement is that the procedure for making the determination be clear and precise, with the identity of those charged with responsibility for making the determination beyond question. Should the procedure not be clearly and precisely defined, or if the identity of the determining authority should be subject to conflicting interpretations, this Nation could undergo the potentially disastrous spectacle of competing claims to the power of the Presidency of the United States. This is precisely the risk which this section of the amendment is designed to avoid, but which, Mr. President, may be the result if this amendment should be adopted in its present form.

In my opinion, the language of section 4, if unchanged, is subject to conflicting interpretation – to say the least – and might create a situation in which a serious question could arise as to whether Presidential disability had been constitutionally determined.

I invite attention to the reports of the Senate Judiciary Committee, on page 11:

We must not gamble with the constitutional legitimacy of our Nation's executive branch. When a President or a Vice President of the United States assumes office, the entire Nation and the world must know without doubt that he does so as a matter of right.

I submit that under the proposed amendment one might assume or claim the power of the Presidency, not without doubt but under a cloud of doubt.

Let me read the first sentence of section 4:

Whenever the Vice President and a majority of either the principal officers of the executive departments or of such other body as Congress may by law provide, transmit to the President pro tempore of the Senate and the Speaker of the House of Representatives their written declaration that the President is unable to discharge the powers and duties of his of office, the Vice President shall immediately assume the powers and duties of the office as Acting President.

I invite attention to four words in the above sentence – all four of which were added in conference. This is not the same language as the fact upon which the Senate previously voted. The words added in conference are "either," "of," and "pro tempore."

These words do not appear in the section as it was approved unanimously by the Senate. The addition of the words "pro tempore" effected a change in the Senate version to conform to the language of the House version so as to provide that a declaration of presidential disability should be transmitted to the President pro tempore of the Senate rather than the "President of the Senate."

I raise no question about that.

The statement filed by the managers on the part of the House, referring to the addition of the words "either" and "of," states that "minor change in language was made for purposes of clarification." The addition of these two words was, in my opinion, more than a minor change in language. This is a change in language which is proposed to be written into the Constitution dealing with one of the most sensitive events of our Republic; namely, the possible declaration of disability of a President of the United States.

In the absence of implementing action by Congress, it is clear that a declaration of presidential disability may be transmitted to the Congress by the Vice President acting in concert with a majority of "the principal officers of the executive departments." Here after I shall refer to the principal officers of the executive departments as members of the Cabinet.

To me, it also seems clear, under the language of the provision, that if Congress should "by law provide" some "other body," the Vice President might then be authorized to act in concert with either the Cabinet or such other body.

How can any other meaning be read into the words "either" and "or"?

[...]

I should not like to indulge in the assumption that at any future time some diabolical person would be Vice President of the United States. However, the Constitution is the charter for the public. Rights must be safeguarded; so must constitutional procedure.

Let me repeat that we seek by this proposed amendment to provide a procedure certain for a declaration of disability of the President of the United States. I submit that the language of the conference report creates uncertainty, rather than certainty. This uncertainty cannot be eliminated by a statement of legislative intent, particularly so when the stated intent is not supported by the precise language of the amendment.

Historical Background Documents

Upon the death of President William Henry Harrison after just a month in office, the US Senate introduced a resolution to form a committee to "wait on the President" and receive any communications he may have. In this portion of the debate that then broke out, covered in depth in The Congressional Globe, *1 June 1841, Senator William Allen, Democrat of Ohio, argues that Vice President John Tyler, who became President upon the death of President William Henry Harrison, should not be called "President."*

Mr. ALLEN of Ohio[51] moved to amend it [the joint resolution] by striking out the words "President of the United States," and inserting in lieu thereof the words "the Vice President, on whom, by the death of the late President the powers and duties of the office of President have devolved."

In support of the motion, Mr. ALLEN proceeded to observe that it must be obvious to all men that, in offering the amendment, he could have been actuated by no personal or petty consideration having reference to the individual now at the head of the Executive Government, but that his sole and simple object was to obtain an expression of the sense of the Senate on an important question in the interpretation of the Constitution now arising for the first time. If it should be held that the present incumbent of the Presidential chair is Vice President, and not President of the United States, Mr. A. had no doubt that Congress would, notwithstanding, in consideration of his discharging all the duties of President, vote him the full salary assigned to the President. Mr. A. had not the least desire or design to cripple or in any way embarrass the present incumbent. He could not be suspected of so poor and petty an object as this. His sole object, he reported as to obtain a declaration of the sense of the Senate in the case. Mr. A. said that, in the Constitution, he found the following words:

"In case of the removal of the President from office, or of his death, resignation, or inability to discharge the powers and duties of the said office, the same shall devolve on the Vice President, and the Congress may by law provide for the case of removal, death, resignation, or inability, both of the President and Vice President, declaring what officer shall then act as President, and such officer shall act accordingly, until the disability be removed, of a President shall be elected."

The first clause in the portion of the Constitution classified all the contingencies; under which the Vice President shall discharge the duties and exercise the powers of President, and it made no distinction whatever between removal by death and removal by temporary inability to discharge the functions of the Presidential office. If, therefore, the late President had been afflicted with a disease producing, for time, a state of mental alienation, he would on his recovery have been reinstated in all the powers of that high office to which the People had elected him. But a contingency of that kind was provided 'for in the Constitution in the very same words as the case of the President's death. It might, perhaps, be said that the question was an unimportant one, inasmuch as it had reference mainly to the title to be applied to a public officer. Now Mr. A. had not raised it with the remotest desire to withhold the dignity of the title of President from the present incumbent of the chair. His anxiety in the matter arose from this: if the Presidential office was indeed now held by the Vice President, that fact recognized the existence of a case where the highest office in the Republic may be held otherwise than by an election of the People. The consequences of establishing such a principle might hereafter become very serious; but if the powers and duties of the Presidential office attached, in consequence of the death of the President, to the Vice President, he still remaining Vice President, then he continued to hold only the office to which the people had elected him, and thus the beautiful symmetry of our system of free and popular Government was preserved.

Having wished only to call the attention of the Senate to the question that it might make an official expression of its views of the case, Mr. A. would be content with expressing his own opinion in regard to it, however it might differ from that of other gentlemen.

Mr. TAPPAN[52] observed that the view just taken of the interpretation of the Constitution was much strengthened by reference to the 5th clause of the 3d section of the 1st article:

"The Senate shall choose their other officers, and also a President *pro tem.* in the absence of the Vice President, or when he shall exercise the office of President of the United States."

Mr. T. observed that it would be found, from an examination of the Constitution as originally adopted and as subsequently amended, that there was but one mode provided in that instrument by which a President of the United States could be created. It was very true that the Vice President, under certain contingencies, was required to exercise the powers and perform the duties of the office of President, but it was no way are declared that he thereby became the President of the United States. The President of the United States, as such, existed and could exist only by an election of the people.

All analogy went to confirm the view which had been taken by his colleague. In our courts of justice, if it happened that the Chief Justice was for a time absent from the bench, the oldest judge presided in his place. But when this took place in the Court of King's Bench, although he exercised for a time the powers and performed the duties of that officer. The same thing was true in this country. When a President of one of our courts of justice was for a time absent, or unable to discharge the duties of the bench his place was filled by the senior judge; yet the latter officer, though by courtesy and in common parlance he might be called President, was not legally entitled either to the style or the salary of the President of the court. In Mr. T's own State the President of the Court of Common Pleas was allowed a salary, to which the other judges of that court were not entitled. When in his absence one of these judges filled his place, he did not thereby become a salaried officer, nor did the law confer upon him the title of President of the Court.

The same analogy held in military affairs. If a colonel was shot in battle, the next officer in rank took command of the regiment, but he did not thereby become a colonel; nor was he entitled to a colonel's pay unless there was a special provision of law providing for the case. Mr. T. said he had seen a letter from a late Senator from the State of Mississippi, addressed to the other officer now presiding over the Senate, the object of which seemed to be two prove that the latter was at present the Vice President of the United States, and that his place as a Senator from New Jersey became vacant thereby. But this was too foolish and nonsensical to deserve any notice. The people only could make a public officer like the Vice President. The people had elected John Tyler as Vice President of the United States, and an election by the people alone could make the present President of the Senate their Vice President; he was at present a Senator, as others in the body and he voted on every question as such.

There was, then, nothing in the Constitution or in analogical cases to warrant the position that John Tyler is now the President of the United States. He might, indeed, be justly entitled to the salary attached to the Presidential office, inasmuch as he was in the discharge of all its duties. Mr. T. had nothing against that. But when the Senate officially addressed him, it ought to give him his true constitutional title. In personal conversation he might be addressed as President, but not when officially addressed by a Department of the Government; in their official language, none but the proper legal title ought to be applied to the individual exercising the powers of the Presidential office.

Mr. HUNTINGTON[53] said was opposed to this amendment; but he did not intend to enter into any discussion on the subject. He presumed every member of the Senate had made up his mind, and was prepared to vote without considering discussion necessary.

Mr. ALLEN called for the ayes and noes on his amendment.

Mr. WALKER[54] said, he was wholly unconscious that any movement would be made on this question in the Senate, until he heard the motion of his friend from Ohio [Mr. ALLEN.]. The motion, however, was made, and he was called upon to record his vote on the subject. The clause in the Constitution is, "In case of the removal of the President from office, or his death, resignation, or inability to discharge the powers and duties of the said office, the *same* shall devolve on the Vice President, and the Congress may, by law, provide for the case of removal, death, resignation, or inability, both of the President and Vice President, declaring what officer shall then *act as President*, and such officer shall act accordingly, until the disability be removed, or a President shall be elected." Now here are separate and distinct contingencies; first, the death of the President, or, secondly, the death of the President and Vice President. In the first case, the *office* of President devolves on the Vice President: in the other case, there is to be an acting President designated by law. Congress is to appoint by law some officer to "act as President until the disability be removed, or a President shall be elected." In the last case, then, there is to be an *acting* President, not for the expired term of the deceased President, but until an *actual* President shall be chosen. In the case, then, of the death of the President and Vice President, an officer designated by law is merely to *act as President*, until the *actual* President shall be chosen. But in the case of the death of the President, "the said office shall devolve on the Vice President." The language is, "*the same* shall devolve." What shall devolve? The immediate antecedent is "the said office, and it is a rule of grammatical construction, as well as of common sense, that the immediate antecedent is connected with the adjective which follows. It is then the office that devolves on the Vice President. He is not the Vice President acting as President, as in the contingency of the death of the President and Vice President; but he ceases to be the Vice President; he is no longer the Vice President, and he office of President is devolved upon him. Is Mr. Tyler still the Vice President discharging additional duties? If so, why is he not here performing the duties of Vice President? Could he come here and act as Vice President for a single moment? Surely not, because he has ceased to be the Vice President, for the reason that the Constitution has devolved on him the office of President, which office he holds for the entire term for which the President was chosen. This is the language and meaning of the Constitution, and when in the one case, that of the death of the President and Vice President, Constitution calls the officer *acting President*, who, for a brief period, discharges the duties of the station, and in the other case devolves the *office* of President for the entire unexpired term on the Vice President. Can there he any doubt on the subject? As to the case of [a] Colonel, acting as General, in case of the death in battle of the latter, the Colonel only *acts* as General for the temporary emergency: another person may be appointed General, and the Colonel returns to his former station, when the emergency has terminated during which he was *acting* as General.

Mr. ALLEN replied. His friend from Mississippi had asked, if Mr. Tyler was still Vice President, why was he not here presiding in the Senate? He would answer the question. Mr. Tyler was not here, because the Constitution had assigned to him duties which required his presence elsewhere, viz: the duties of the Presidential office. He was now an executive, not a legislative official. Mr. A. would put to his friend this question; and he put it with a view to illustrate the fearful consequence which might be apprehended as likely to ensue from the establishment of he position taken by that Senator. Suppose a President of the United States should be of one political party, and at the same time a Vice President of another political party; suppose the country to be equally divided between the two, and both parties mutually and highly incensed against each other; and under these circumstances, the President should be seized with a temporary illness, producing, for a time, such an alienation of mind as unfitted him for the discharge of his official duties, in consequence of which, those duties were discharged by the Vice President. After a time the President completely recovered. The question would then arise, which of the two officers should continue in the chair. And might we not justly fear, under such a state of things, a renewal of those fearful struggles for supreme power which had so often compassed the Old World with civil war and deluged it in blood? The question of succession had oftener than any other destroyed the peace of nations. Here was a Vice President armed with a purse and the sword, in actual possession, standing against the claims of the President, now restored to health and reason; and not only so, but with half the citizens of the Republic at his back. What would become of the office? Was it to vibrate between the two claimants? In what manner could a President of the United States – unimpeached, sane, and alive – cease to be President? There was none known to the Constitution. If John Tyler were now President of the United States, nothing but impeachment, removal, mental alienation, or death, would expel him from the office. According to the Senator's doctrine, though a President should be restored, a Vice President once discharging his duties might hold out, and the President chosen by the people must take his place as a private citizen. No. The office of a public officer was fixed until one of the contingencies occurred which were designated in the Constitution. And if a Vice President became President, none could remove him.

꒰ᘒ꒱꒰ᘒ꒱꒰ᘒ꒱꒰ᘒ꒱꒰ᘒ꒱

The following article in The North American Review, *November 1881, written by Senator Lyman Trumbull of Illinois following the assassination of President James A. Garfield, is very similar to the debates held in Congress in 1965 over the proposed language for the Twenty-fifth Amendment – despite the fact that they occurred 80 years apart.*

The protracted illness of President Garfield led to much discussion and a variety of opinions as to what constitutes a disability in the Presidential office which will justify the Vice-president in assuming its duties.

President Garfield's death renders unnecessary a practical decision of the question in his case; but the time may come when it will have to be decided, and it is of importance that, before that time arrives, the Constitution in that regard should, if possible, receive a definite and fixed construction, so that when it does arrive, the people of this Republic may be spared controversy as to the person entitled to the chief magistracy – a controversy which among other peoples has brought upon mankind more wars and greater desolation then any other cause. The provisions of the Constitution bearing upon this subject are the following:

"In case of the removal of the President from office, or his death, resignation, or inability to discharge the powers and duties of the said office, the same shall devolve on the Vice-president." "...No person except a natural born citizen, or a citizen of the United States at the time of the adoption of this Constitution, shall be eligible to the office of President." "...The Vice-president of the United States shall be president of the Senate." "...The Senate shall choose their other officers, and also a president pro tempore, in the absence of the Vice-president, or when he shall exercise the office of President of the United States."

The Twelfth Amendment, adopted in 1804, declares:

"If the House of Representatives shall not choose a President whenever the right of choice shall devolve upon them, before the fourth day of March, next following, then the Vice-president shall act as President, as in the case of the death or other constitutional disability of the President." "...No person constitutionally ineligible to the office of President shall be eligible to that of Vice-president."

Preliminary to a discussion of what constitutes Presidential inability, it is important to determine the position of a Vice-president, who, in the language of the Constitution, "shall exercise the office of President," or "shall act as President." That is, whether in such case he becomes "the President" or remains Vice-president, exercise and the powers and duties of President. In 1841, when, on the death of President Harrison, the first vacancy occurred in the Presidential office, and the question arose in Congress whether, in appointing a committee to inform the person then exercising the office of President, of the organization of the two Houses, he should be styled "President," or "Vice-president now exercising the office of President," Mr. Wise,[55] of Virginia, exclaimed that "he knew the fact, that the president incumbent [Mr. Tyler] claim the position that he was by the Constitution, by election, and by the act of God, President of the United States." The subject received but little consideration at the time in either House of Congress, and as the case then presented was one of death, both Houses decided to give the title President to the person exercising the duties of the office, in their communications with him – Mr. Calhoun[56] remarking at the time that, as none of those circumstances existed which might arise in the case of inability, "there could be no special occasion for discussing the subject." From that time till the present, whenever the Vice-president has acted as President, which has never been except in the case of the death of the President, he has been styled [as] President. The practice adopted under the circumstances, though entitled to consideration, is not decisive as to the true construction of the Constitution, even in case of death, and by no means settles it in a case of inability. As an original question, it would seem clear, from the language of the Constitution, that its framers never intended any person to be President except the person whom the people elected to that office. They provided that, in certain specified cases, another officer might perform the duties of the President, without regard to his eligibility to the office.

The original Constitution did not prescribe the qualifications of age and citizenship of [the] Vice-president as it did the President. Hence a Vice-President not eligible to the Presidency might, under the Constitution as it existed prior to 1804, have had devolved upon him the powers and duties of the Presidential office; but how could he become President? Even now the Constitution does not prescribe the qualifications of the officer who is to act as President in case of the death both of the President and Vice-president. He may be a person not eligible to the Presidency. The Constitution must be so construed as to be consistent with itself, which would be impossible if a person not eligible to the office of President could in any case become President. That instrument contains no provision declaring that the Vice-president shall under any circumstances become President. On the contrary, it in terms declares that in certain specified cases "the powers and duties of the said office" shall devolve on the Vice-presidential; that "he shall exercise the office of President" and "shall act as President." On whom is it that the Constitution in certain cases devolves the duties of the Presidential office? Is it on another President or on the Vice-president? Had the framers of the Constitution intended the Vice-president in certain contingencies to become President, they would have so said, instead of saying as they did, "he shall exercise the office of President," or "he shall act as President."

Assuming, as the language of the Constitution imports, that the Vice-president can in no event become President, there is less practical difficulty in determining what is meant by Presidential inability. If, in such a case, the Vice-president becomes President, the person whom the people elected to that office, though laboring under a mere temporary inability, would be ousted from the office whenever the Vice-president assumed its duties, as there could not be two Presidents at the same time, and the person elected Vicepresident, having ceased to be such by becoming President, would continue [as] President till the end of the term. Whereas, if the Vice-president in such case simply exercises the office of, or acts as President, there could be no reason why the President, when the inability ceased, should not resume the duties of his office; and the Vice-president, having ceased to act as President, would again become president of the Senate. The word "inability," as used in the Constitution, doubtless means both physical and mental inability, or either. Whenever the President, whether from physical causes, as in case of capture by the enemy in time of war, or from sickness, or from mental disease, is unable to discharge the duties of his office, the Constitution devolves them on the Vice-president. Before he can properly act, there must be some occasion for his action – some urgent duty to perform to which the President is unable, from mental or physical causes, to give attention. The framers of the Constitution clearly intended to provide that the Republic should suffer no detriment from the want of an executive head. If, during the illness of President Garfield, circumstances had arisen requiring of him the performance of important duties, such as the negotiation of treaties, the defense of the country, or, indeed, any act to delay which would be fraught with serious injury to the contrary, and he had been unable to act, that case of inability contemplated by the Constitution would seem to have arisen. The presumption is that no such circumstances existed. But how is the Vice-president to know of their existence in any case? In the absence of legislation he can only know, so as to act upon them, when they become so open, notorious, and indisputable as to be recognized by all as existing. When such a case arises, who will question the right or the duty of the Vice-president to act as President till the disability is removed? The Constitution has provided no tribunal to determine what shall constitute inability, or the evidence of it, and it will be difficult for Congress to do so. It would be dangerous to vest the power of thus superseding the President in a petit jury, or any judicial tribunal. The people who elect him have said that he can only be removed on impeachment, and Congress cannot provide for his removal directly or indirectly in any other way. They can prevent neither his death, his resignation, nor his inability, and they have never attempted to declare what shall be the evidence of his death, though they have passed a law of questionable constitutionality, declaring that the only evidence of his resignation shall be an instrument in writing declaring the same, subscribed by him, and delivered into the office of the Secretary of State. Four Presidents have died in office, and it required no statute to define in advance what should constitute the evidence of their death, nor any jury of inquest or other tribunal to determine when they died. To have required such proof would have been unreasonable and absurd. The whole people and all their officials took notice of the sad events, and the Vice-president in each case proceeded to exercise the powers and duties of the Presidential office without question from a human being. There are some things of which everybody takes notice, in which it is never necessary to prove.

Appearing before the Senate Special Subcommittee to Study Presidential Inability, author and journalist Sidney Hyman delivered the following testimony on 12 April 1956.

Every Constitutional system must pay some price in weakness for the elements of strength it has. Not everything is soluble. Not everything can be controlled by law. Some things, as a matter of course, have to be lived with in the full knowledge that they embrace built-in risks of the gravest sort. Some things which are in need of solution must be entrusted to the discretion of duly elected officials – whose constitutional morality must be taken on faith. For though is true enough on doctrinal grounds, that our aim is to have a government of laws and not of men, experience supports Edmund Burke's observation that 'the laws reach but a very little. Constitute the government however you will, infinitely the greater part of it must depend on the uprightness and wisdom of the chief ministers of state.'

One must first decide which of two alternatives contain the greater or lesser risk to constitutional government.

The alternatives we face are these: Is it to live with a constitutional ambiguity on the question of disability as it has stood for the past 169 years, knowing that the same time that it might explode in a crisis form at some future date? Or is it to risk distorting a general picture of constitutional strength and balance, in order to right one of its admittedly defective details?

If I rightly sense the current of thinking that runs through this committee, it has already decided between these alternative risks – and has decided in favor of the second one. That decision, I feel, is correct – though I held an opposite view in the interval immediately after President Eisenhower's heart attack. When it was widely thought that the end of his term would see him voluntarily stepping down from the Presidency, it seemed that as between risks, the lesser one was to do nothing about the question of disability and to gamble, instead, on the health of his duly elected successor in the Presidency. Or to turn the order around, it seemed that the greater risk was to introduce some sort of new mechanism into our constitutional system on the theory that it would end the fevered question of Presidential disability, but which might, in practice, lead to political deliriums far more menacing in their tendencies and effects.

On principle, it is, of course, both bad taste and bad practice to tailor a momentous constitutional question to the uncertain physical condition in which a specific President finds himself.

Under emergency circumstances – and in commonsense terms, the question of Presidential disability acquires its real cutting edge only in time of a pressing crisis – the Vice President, on a plea of doubt about his constitutional rights in the matter, could chain his hands with a self-denying ordinance. Fearing the charge of usurpation, he could refuse to act for the disabled President, when in point of fact, the very survival of the nation could depend on his so acting; and when the real charge to level against him would be his failure to so act at a time when the President had been felled.

Concerns of this sort – and they could crop up in any Presidency beyond Eisenhower's, should a President be felled and the nation hit hard by an atomic attack – have changed my own thinking from one to the other side of the risk scale. It has changed from the side that would let the constitutional ambiguity about Presidential disability stand as it is, while gambling on the future, to the side that would clarify the grounds on which a Vice President can, under a color of legal or moral rights, act for a disabled President.

However, a number of men of high repute for their constitutional wisdom in both the House and the Senate, are still of the mind that it is either impossible or undesirable to propose any specific answer to the disability question as it now stands. Their position – it should be said – is altogether divorced from any narrow motive of partisan politics, and for that reason, is all the more commanding of attention. Indeed, the heart of their argument is the hurdle that must be scaled by any specific proposal if it is to muster majority strength in both Chambers. The heart of their argument, if I may presume to sketch it beyond a previous allusion, is this:

The setting up of a new mechanism to determine the fact of Presidential disability, opens the way to the use of that same mechanism against the President when he is in excellent physical health, but in bad political health in one or another potent quarter. More specifically, it could become a concealed impeachment weapon to be used against the President on the pretext of his disability – a concealed weapon that might come into play when the open, constitutional weapon of an impeachment on the grounds of a President's misconduct, lacked the firepower to blast him from office. If the use of that concealed weapon won its aim, it would destroy a root principle that has done so much for the strength and stability of the American Government in the long historical haul. That principle is the duration of the President in office for a fixed term of years – an arrangement that permits him to conceive, execute, and prevail in sound policies that may be met at the outset by wild outcries, but whose solid merit comes to be seen when tempers cool, and calmer counsels gain ascendancy in the national mind. And the argument concludes: Even if the use of that concealed weapon failed in its ultimate objective, the bringing of it into action would split the Government, foster bitter dissentions, lower the dignity of the Presidency, weaken its authority, distract the public mind, and by this means, produce a toxic effect throughout our whole system of responsible power.

First, I would deny to a body like the Cabinet, much less a part of such body, a right of initiative or any role whatever in a disability proceedings. I would deny this to them on the ground that the Cabinet is not an elective body whose members can be tried individually in a polling booth. For the Cabinet, viewed in the general scheme of representative government, is not responsible directly to the people. It owes its place in the Government to the President's appointive power, and it is only as the President in his own person stands or falls in the judgment of the people, that Cabinet officers can be called to account by them for what they do.

Beyond this, the Cabinet has the form of a committee, however much it reaches its unity in the person of the President. As a committee, it can shift responsibility so dexterously from one member to another, as to make the onlooker dizzy, then bewildered, then indifferent, and at the deadly end of the chain, cynical about government as a whole. Yet a further ground for denying the Cabinet any role on a disability proceeding arises in connection with two common circumstances. One is when the Cabinet is heart and soul with the President, but has strained relations with the Vice President. Under this state of affairs, it is on likely that Cabinet members would step forward with information about a real disability. Rather, every inducement of loyalty and gratitude, not to mention self-interest, would work to the end of concealment. Under the second of the common circumstances, Cabinet members involved in a row with the President would be under the strongest temptations to settle their scores with him by declaring him mad. Even if the charge was not supported by such auxiliary government bodies as might be part of the disability proceedings, the fact that the highest officers of an administration had leveled such a charge against their Chief, would not only weaken his authority inside America – it would expose the whole nation to the suspicions or ridicule of a not altogether loving world.

On similar grounds, except for its unassailable right to be informed, I would not have the Congress initiate or share directly in a disability proceeding, regardless of the number of additional organs of Government that were called into play before the final yes or no was arrived at. For though the Congress is an elective body, and thus is responsible to the people for what it does, it remains an amorphous committee in which blame for what is done often has a habit of wandering around like a displaced person looking for a place to settle.

Moreover, as a committee, the Congress has a split personality. Part of it, the House, is formed on the basis of population. The other part, the Senate, is formed on the basis of the sovereign equality of the States. But whereas the whole House, if it was up to mischief in the case of a disability question could be reached by the people within 2 years at the most, only a third of the Senate could be so reached, while the remaining two-thirds could enjoy an immunity of between 4 and 6 years for the consequences of its actions.

In any case, there have been all too many instances in our history when one or both Houses of the Congress were under the control of a political party or faction bitterly hostile to the President. Why then endow such future Congress with a new tool for tumult, when parties or factions can even now cut down a President by the route of the congressional investigating committees?

Finally, except as to the question of a President's recovery from a previous disability might arise in connection with a suit between two claimants to the Presidential station, I would most emphatically deny to the Supreme Court or to any portion of its membership any part whatever in a disability proceedings. Not that I suspect the motives of the Court. Far from it. Rather, because I revere its traditional self-restraint, I would not have the Court forced into a position where the subtleties that make for its unarmed but massive moral authority in our society, would be needlessly subject did to political disruption.

In this short selection, Representative Emanuel Celler of New York writes in 1958 (seven years before the passage of the Twenty-fifth Amendment) of the growing movement to pass a constitutional amendment outlining the steps to the succession of a disabled President or Vice President, or the potential need to fill a vacancy in either executive office. It appears that while Celler was pushing for a constitutional amendment, he felt that the Constitution already laid out a pathway for the succession to either office.

"[Paragraph 6 of section 1 of Article II of the Constitution] shows, in the first instance, what action is limited to the Vice President and, in the second, limited to the Congress.

There is the clear indication in my mind that it was the Vice President who was to raise the question and the Vice President was to resolve the question.

History shows there was a reluctance on the part of [Vice President Thomas] Marshall and [Vice President Chester Alan] Arthur to take over. They were not usurpers. They were fearful that they might be called usurpers. Therefore, it is not the danger of [the] usurpation of power. It is the danger they won't use the power that the Constitution gives them. Surely, if they had the power to do that in 1881 and 1919, they have a right to do it now without a constitutional amendment. Would not that will reluctance be dissipated if Congress would simply make the declaration that the Vice President shall, in the case of the disability, as a result of the question which he raised and resolved, step in, and take over the duties? The fact that Congress so stated would be encouragement for him to come to that conclusion.

I am sure public opinion would determine if he was wrong. There is always the power of impeachment in case he was wrong. If he was intemperate and was not taking proper action, impeachment would curb any kind of excess, any kind of usurpation.

I think this resolution would be sufficient to do away with a reluctance to assume the power.

I have come to the conclusion, after a short the liberation, there is some law and precedence, after reading all the history, that all that is necessary is for the Vice President to act.

This very statement that the Attorney General read: 'It is a well-established rule of law that in contingent grants of power the one to whom the power is granted is to decide when the emergency has arisen...' leads me to the inevitable conclusion that, since the grant of power is to the Vice President, he determines the contingency upon which he exercises the power.

I find in my study of the matter there is no perfect answer to this, that every answer has its imperfections, and what we must try to do is to reach the least objectionable solution."

≈≫≈≫≈≫≈≫≈≫

Following the resignation of Vice President Spiro Agnew, President Nixon, as demanded by the Twenty-fifth Amendment, asked Congress, 11 October 1973, for the names of potential successors to Agnew. The following letter completed that process, and was sent by Minority Leader Gerald R. Ford, who, within weeks of this date, was chosen as the new Vice President. Less than a year later, in August 1974, Ford would become president upon Nixon's resignation.

HOUSE OF REPRESENTATIVES
WASHINGTON, D.C. 20515

GERALD R. FORD
MINORITY LEADER

October 11, 1973

Dear Mr. President:

On the basis of the criteria outlined by you at the meeting in your office I am recommending the following in the order of my preference:

1. John Connolly
2. Mel Laird
3. Nelson Rockefeller or Ronald Reagan

I will not go into the reasons for my views as I'm sure you are familiar with reasons in each instance. You can rest assured that I will fully cooperate and assist in this and all other problems in the months ahead.

Warmest personal regards.

Sincerely,

Gerald R. Ford, M.C.

The President
The White House

As Submitted to the States

Section 1. In case of the removal of the President from office or of his death or resignation, the Vice President shall become President.

Section 2. Whenever there is a vacancy in the office of the Vice President, the President shall nominate a Vice President who shall take office upon confirmation by a majority vote of both Houses of Congress.

Section 3. Whenever the President transmits to the President pro tempore of the Senate and the Speaker of the House of Representatives his written declaration that he is unable to discharge the powers and duties of his office, and until he transmits to them a written declaration to the contrary, such powers and duties shall be discharged by the Vice President as Acting President.

Section 4. Whenever the Vice President and a majority of either the principal officers of the executive departments or of such other body as Congress may by law provide, transmit to the President pro tempore of the Senate and the Speaker of the House of Representatives their written declaration that the President is unable to discharge the powers and duties of his office, the Vice President shall immediately assume the powers and duties of the office as Acting President.

Thereafter, when the President transmits to the President pro tempore of the Senate and the Speaker of the House of Representatives his written declaration that no inability exists, he shall resume the powers and duties of his office unless the Vice President and a majority of either the principal officers of the executive department or of such other body as Congress may by law provide, transmit within four days to the President pro tempore of the Senate and the Speaker of the House of Representatives their written declaration that the President is unable to discharge the powers and duties of his office. Thereupon Congress shall decide the issue, assembling within forty-eight hours for that purpose if not in session. If the Congress within twenty-one days after receipt of the latter written declaration, or, if Congress is not in session within twenty-one days after Congress is required to assemble, determines by two-thirds vote of both Houses that the President is unable to discharge the powers and duties of his office, the Vice President shall continue to discharge the same as Acting President; otherwise, the President shall resume the powers and duties of his office.

State Ratifications of the Twenty-fifth Amendment*

State	Date
Nebraska	12 July 1965
Wisconsin	13 July 1965
Oklahoma	16 July 1965
Massachusetts	9 August 1965
Pennsylvania	18 August 1965
Kentucky	15 September 1965
Arizona	22 September 1965
Michigan	5 October 1965
Indiana	20 October 1965
California	21 October 1965
Arkansas	4 November 1965
New Jersey	29 November 1965
Delaware	7 December 1965
Utah	17 January 1966
West Virginia	20 January 1966
Maine	24 January 1966
Rhode Island	28 January 1966

Colorado	3 February 1966
New Mexico	3 February 1966
Kansas	8 February 1966
Vermont	10 February 1966
Alaska	18 February 1966
Idaho	2 March 1966
Hawaii	3 March 1966
Virginia	8 March 1966
Mississippi	10 March 1966
New York	14 March 1966
Maryland	20 March 1966
Missouri	30 March 1966
New Hampshire	13 June 1966
Louisiana	5 July 1966
Tennessee	12 January 1967
Wyoming	25 January 1967
Washington State	26 January 1967
Iowa	26 January 1967
Oregon	2 February 1967
Minnesota	10 February 1967
Nevada	10 February 1967**
Connecticut	14 February 1967
Montana	15 February 1967
South Dakota	6 March 1967
Ohio	7 March 1967
Alabama	14 March 1967
North Carolina	22 March 1967
Illinois	22 March 1967
Texas	25 April 1967
Florida	25 May 1967

* *The amendment was ratified 584 days after it was submitted to the states.*

** *Nevada's ratification gave the amendment the requisite number of states needed to make it a part of the US Constitution.*

ORIGINAL PRIMARY DOCUMENTS

The US House of Representatives passed the proposed disability amendment, but it stalled in the US Senate because Senator Albert Gore, Sr. (D-Tennessee) demanded that the upper body slow down debate for more study. Here is how the roadblock was reported in The Washington Post, *1 July 1965.*

Disability Measure Sails Past in House But Stalls in Senate

———

By William Theis
United Press International

A constitution amendment to meet the twin dangers of serious Presidential disability and between-election void in the Vice Presidency was approved by the House yesterday but struck an unexpected snag in the Senate.

The House passed the amendment by an overwhelming voice vote. The follow up Senate action which would have sent the amendment to the states for ratification was postponed, however, when Sen. Albert Gore (D-Tenn.) objected.

Gore said he was dissatisfied with some provisions of the plan and said he favored sending it back to HouseSenate conferees for further consideration. The Senate leadership then put off final debate on the proposal until Tuesday, so that Gore could study the matter further.

Established Methods

The purpose of the amendment is to set up a system for Vice President to take over should a President become disabled and to establish a method of naming a Vice President should that office become vacant between Presidential elections.

The legislatures of three-fourths of the states must approve the amendment before it becomes part of the US Constitution. Because many of the state legislatures have finished their sessions this year, final ratification probably will not come until early 1967.

The necessary two-thirds approval of the Senate was predicted even though Gore and others questioned some of the machinery.

Kennedy Asks Study

Senator Robert F. Kennedy (D-NY) said that further study should be made of the entire problem although he favored passing the amendment without further delay.

He raised the question of possible pressures that might be brought upon a Cabinet should there be a dispute between a President and Vice President on disability. The New York Senator recalled that President Woodrow Wilson fired his Secretary of State for having sought to conduct a Cabinet meeting while Wilson as incapacitated by a stroke.

Sen. Eugene McCarthy (D-Wis.) also suggested that the proposed amendment wasn't the perfect answer to a perplexing problem.

ುಲ್ಯಾೋುಲ್ಯಾೋುಲ್ಯಾೋುಲ್ಯಾೋ

We get this perspective of the congressional passage of the presidential disability amendment from the Los Angeles Times, *7 July 1965.*

States to Get Amendment on Presidency

BY DON IRWIN
Times Staff Writer

WASHINGTON – The Senate Tuesday gave final congressional approval to a proposed constitutional amendment which would insure continuity in the Presidency.

A 68-5 roll call easily surpassed the required two-thirds majority for the amendment, which provides machinery for filling vacancies in the Vice Presidency and for the delegation of Presidential power if a President is disabled.

Must Be Ratified

The proposed 25th Amendment, which passed the House last Wednesday on a voice vote, cannot become effective until it is ratified by three-fourths, or 38, of the state legislatures. Present scheduling of legislative sessions makes it almost certain that ratification will not become final before mid-1967.

Although Senate approval was not doubted, it as preceded by two hours of debate on a question first raised last Wednesday by Sen. Albert Gore (D-Tenn.). He saw possible chaos in the final form of the resolution as worked out by Senate-House conferees and urged that it be sent back once more to conference.

With only the five exceptions, the Senate appeared to agree with the resolution's backers that Gore's fears were unjustified. They said the legislative record makes it clear that it is the intent of Congress that of any "other body" is created, it would supercede the Cabinet on the questions of determining inability.

An Alternative

Authority for formation of an "other body" was included in the resolution, Bayh emphasized, only to leave open an alternative method in the event future circumstances should make it desirable.

Bayh readily conceded from the start of the debate that the judiciary committees of both houses had found it "impossible to find an amendment that would cover all contingencies." He said they did their best to develop a formula that would provide flexibility to deal with unforeseen events.

He received full support from the minority leader, Sen. Everett M. Dirksen (R-Ill.), who saw "a hundred possibilities" that could come up under the amendment. As for Gore's feas, he said, they assume a "a venal Vice President" and Cabinet members "so wanting in fidelity to the republic that they will not do their duty."

Gore received principal support in the debate from Sen. Eugene McCarthy (D-Minn.), who said he felt the amendment was too complex and should have stopped with a grant of authority to Congress to deal with Presidential inability. McCarthy voted with Gore against the amendment, along with Sens. Frank J. Lausche (D-Ohio), Walter F. Mondale (D-Minn.) and John G. Tower (R-Tex.).

Provisions Listed

Following are the amendment's principal provisions:

1. In the event of a vacancy in the President, the Vice President shall succeed to the office. This provision gives constitutional backing to established practice.

2. If there is a vacancy in the Vice Presidency, the President shall nominate a new Vice President subject to confirmation by majorities of both houses of Congress.

3. The President can temporarily surrender his powers to the Vice President if he transmits to the speaker of the House and the president pro tem of the Senate a written declaration that he is "unable to discharge the powers and duties of his office."

4. The President may be replaced by the Vice President, serving as acting President if the Vice President and a "majority of either the principal officers of the executive department or such other body as Congress may by law provide" notify the speaker and the Senate's president pro tem that the President is unable to fulfill his duties.

5. The President may return to power upon transmission to the same officials of a written declaration that his inability is ended unless a majority of the cabinet or the "other body" challenge his finding in a statement sent within four days to the Congressional leaders.

6. In the event of such a challenge, Congress is to be convened within 48 hours if it is not in session. Congress would have 21 days to sustain the challenge and a two-thirds vote of both houses would be required. Failing such a vote, the President would return immediately to office.

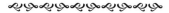

This editorial from The Evening News *of Newburgh, New York, 8 July 1965 offers its perspective on the passage, and potential ratification, of the presidential disability amendment.*

Disability Amendment

At long last Congress has approved a presidential disability plan and it now goes to the states. If 38 of the 50 states ratify it within seven years, it will become the 25th Amendment to our Constitution.

The plan looks like a sound one. Certainly, it is the best which has been advanced so far to meet what must always be a puzzling problem.

It's easy enough to say the Vice President will succeed in the event of the death of the President. But, what if there is no Vice President? What if the President is not dead, but disabled because of a major physical illness or injury? What if he is mentally incompetent?

These are questions which should have been answered long ago, but the nation always seemed to lack political leaders in the White House and con who were big enough to accept any limitation of power.

The disability plan, the text of which is reproduced elsewhere on the editorial page, is written with restraint, and it does leave to Congress the ultimate determination of the President's competence, should an ambitious Vice President and a cooperating Cabinet majority ever attempt to displace him on questionable grounds.

The proposal should be approved by our on New York legislature as soon as possible. And, we hope, by enough other states to make it effective.

The Independent of Pasadena, California, 22 October 1965, reported that California became the 10th state to ratify the presidential disability amendment.

State 10th To Ratify Succession

SACRAMENTO (AP) – The Senate put California on record Thursday as the 10th state to ratify a US constitutional amendment detailing succession to the presidency if the chief executive is disabled.

With little opposition, the measure sponsored by Assembly Speaker Jesse M. Unruh, D-Inglewood, was adopted 32 to 5.

The lower house-adopted resolution needed only 21 votes and doesn't require the signature of Gov. Brown. Thirty-eight states – three-fourths approval – is required within seven years before it can become the Twenty-fifth

Amendment to the US constitution. The amendment would:

–Allow the president to inform the president pro tem of the US Senate and the speaker of the House of Representatives that he is unable to discharge the duties of his office. The vice president would then take over as acting president until the president could declare himself able to resume office.

–Allow the vice president "and a majority of either the principal officers of the executive departments or such other body as Congress may by law provide," to declare the president disabled. The vice president would then again assume the powers of the president until the president declared himself fit to resume them.

If a dispute arises over whether the president can assume his office, Congress would decide the matter with a two-thirds vote needed to keep the vice president as chief executive.

–Allow the president to fill a vacancy in the vice presidency through the nomination of a candidate with the approval of a majority of Congress. This covers the situation which arose when President Johnson took office on the death of President Kennedy, leaving the nation without a vice president.

On 6 December 1973, Minority Leader in the US House of Representatives Gerald R. Ford was sworn in as the new Vice President to fill the vacancy left by the resignation of Spiro T. Agnew. Ford was thus on his way to becoming the first person to advance to the top two offices in the Executive Branch under the Twenty-fifth Amendment, which was ratified six years earlier. This groundbreaking news was reported in The New York Times.

FORD SWORN AS VICE PRESIDENT AFTER HOUSE APPROVES, 387-35; HE VOWS EQUAL JUSTICE FOR ALL

LOYALTY TO NIXON

1,500 Hear Ford Give His Full Support to President

By MARJORIE HUNTER
Special to *The New York Times*

WASHINGTON, Dec. 6 – Gerald R. Ford, pledging "equal justice for all Americans," took office just after dusk tonight as the 40th Vice President of the United States.

With President Nixon standing right behind him, he was sworn into office in the 116-year-old House chamber, which has been his political home for the last 25 years.

Only an hour earlier, the House completed action on his nomination by voting 387 to 35 for confirmation. He was confirmed Nov. 27 by the Senate by a vote of 92 to 3.

Mr. Ford, 60 years old, resigned his House seat before assuming the vice-presidency. He has been minority leader of the House since 1965.

Jerry Ford's Day

It was clearly Jerry Ford's day, and not even President Nixon's appearance overshadowed the new Vice President. The waves of applause and the smiles of his colleagues were seemingly beamed at him alone as he stood, in a trim navy blue suit, his right hand held high in recognition of old friends.

And, as he spoke, it was the Jerry Ford many of them had listened to through the years, speaking in a flat tone, declaring his love for his wife and his country and pledging his loyalty to his President.

The historic ceremony ended a vice-presidential vacancy that had existed since the resignation on Oct. 10 of Spiro T. Agnew just before he pleaded no contest to a charge of income tax invasion.

First Use of Amendment

The is the first time that a Vice President was chosen under the 25th Amendment to the Constitution. The amendment, ratified by the states in 1967, provides for Presidential Succession and for filling vice-presidential vacancies.

The 25th Amendment was adopted to deal with situations such as that which existed following the assassination of President Kennedy in 1963. At that time, the vice-presidency stood vacant 13 months after Vice President Johnson succeeded to the Presidency.

Mr. Ford heard none of today's five hours of House debate, nor did he vote. He arrived in the chamber just minutes after the final vote had been cast and was greeted by thunderous cheers and applause – the first of many such ovations that he received today.

He then went to the White House to inform President Nixon of the vote, and the two men returned to the Capitol an hour later for the official swearing-in.

They were greeted by tumultuous applause as they entered the House chamber together.

A capacity crowd of 1,500 persons – Senators, Representatives, members of the Cabinet and of the Supreme Court, ambassadors and other foreign dignitaries and visitors – witnessed the brief ceremony.

Mrs. Nixon, accompanied by White House aides, sat with the four Ford children in the executive gallery.

As Chief Justice Warren E. Burger administered the oath, Mr. Ford rested his left hand on a Bible held by his wife, who wore a tangerine wool crepe dress. The Bible was purchased for the occasion by their son Michael, a theological student.

Later, in a brief speech, Mr. Ford drew a burst of applause from the Republicans as he pledged his full "support and loyalty" to the President. He also bade a "fond good-bye" to his colleagues in the House.

"I am a Ford, not a Lincoln," he said, smiling. "My addresses will never be as eloquent as Lincoln's. But I will do my best to equal his brevity and plain speaking."

Mr. Ford pledged his dedication "to the rule of law and equal justice for all Americans" and declared, "I am not discouraged."

Later, he led the Senators across the Capitol to the Senate chamber where he will serve in the one job given to a Vice President under the Constitution – president of the Senate.

The vice-presidency has been vacant 17 times in this nation's history, due to death, resignation or succession to the Presidency.

Unexpected Development

It was just 57 days ago that a stunned nation learned of the abrupt resignation of Vice President Agnew. Two days later, on Oct. 12, President Union announced to Congressional leaders and others assembled in the East Room of the White House for a gala evening of champagne and laughter that he had chosen his old friend and fellow Republican, Mr. Ford, to be Vice President.

Earlier, there had been few surprises during the long hours of floor debate over the nomination. Democratic liberals, as expected, accused the nominee of lacking the qualities of leadership. Other Democrats and Republicans, also as expected, praised him as a man of honor, honesty, dedication and integrity.

The only unexpected development came as Representative Peter W. Rodino Jr. of New Jersey, chairman of the House Judiciary Committee, which handled the Ford hearings, announced that he would vote against confirmation.

"During the weeks that I spent reviewing Jerry's public and private life, I have only grown to respect his character and integrity more," Mr. Rodino told the hushed House.

Weeks of Hearings

However, asserting that his Newark district "typifies the plight which the cities of our nation face today," and accusing the Nixon Administration of failing to meet the needs of the poor and disadvantaged, Mr. Rodino said:

"I vote, not against Gerald Ford's worth as a man of great integrity, but in dissent with the present Administration'

indifference to the plight of so many Americans."

[...]

Mr. Ford's nomination reached the House floor this morning after weeks of hearings and exhaustive investigations by both the Senate and the House. The Federal Bureau of Investigation alone had detailed 359 agents to dig into his background, and the F.B.I. data covered 1,700 typewritten pages.

Thoroughness Praised

The nominee's tax records, personal finances, family connections, political campaigns and voting record were examined in detail.

Today, praising the thoroughness of the investigations and hearings, Representative Jack Brooks,[57] Democrat of Texas, told his colleagues, "We know more about Jerry Ford than I ever wanted to know."

While all other blacks present voted against the nomination, Representative Andrew Young,[58] Democrat of Georgia, said shortly before the five hours of debate ended that he would support the nominee.

Mr. Young said that he was troubled by Mr. Ford's efforts to weaken civil rights legislation but added that he also had doubts about the civil rights voting records of Presidents Kennedy and Johnson. He expressed hope that Mr. Ford would rise to his new job.

Pressure on Nixon

The debate was low key, even on the part of the nominee's severest critics, who had known from the start that they could not block the confirmation.

But the drama of the day was heightened by the realization of those present that with Mr. Ford installed as Vice President, sentiment for impeachment of Mr. Nixon – or pressure on him to resign – would intensify.

Many Democrats have openly called for impeachment, but until now most Republicans have spoken of it guardedly and usually only among themselves. Yet there are strong indications that many Republicans are becoming increasingly concerned over the tarnished image of their party because of the Watergate scandals, the Agnew affair and allegations of various political campaign misdeeds by the Nixon Administration.

The possibility that Mr. Nixon might not serve out his term was raised repeatedly by both Democrats and Republicans during the debate.

Speed Is Advised

Representative Clarence D. Long,[60] Democrat of Maryland, suggested that the Republicans would do well to take his advice by moving swiftly to make Mr. Ford the next President.

Declaring that the Republicans would have to take the lead in forcing Mr. Nixon out of office, he said:

"Any partisan Democrat would have to be out of his mind to take that millstone off the back of you Republicans. If you keep the present incumbent in for three more years, the Democrats could win with the Boston Strangler."

This was greeted by cheers and laughter from the Democrats and good-natured roars from the Republicans.

[...]

WHO'S WHO

This section includes a biography of one individual who played a significant part in drafting and passing the Twenty-fifth Amendment. He is mentioned earlier in this chapter.

Birch Evans Bayh, Jr. (1928–)

A longtime Indiana politician who rose to serve three terms in the US Senate, Birch Bayh was the leading supporter for an amendment to the US Constitution to provide for an orderly succession due to presidential disability or a potential vice presidential vacancy. It was through his machinations, as well as the work of Rep. Emanuel Celler, Democrat of New York, that the amendment ultimately passed through both houses of Congress.

Bayh was born on his family' farm in Terre Haute, in Vigo County, Indiana, on 22 January 1928, the son of Birch Evans Bayh, Sr. and his wife Leah Ward (née Hollingsworth Bayh), both schoolteachers. According to family history, Bayh's paternal relations began in England, emigrating to America and settling in Virginia, Missouri, and Indiana. Leah Bayh, who died in 1940 when her son was 12, was also descended from immigrants who settled in America's heartland. Birch Bayh, Jr., the subject of this biography, grew up with his maternal grandparents and attended local schools in Vigo County. At the end of the Second World War, he volunteered for service, and saw non-combat action as a Military Policeman (MP) with the United States Army in Allied-occupied Germany from 1946 to 1948. When he returned home, Bayh attended the Purdue University School of Agriculture, graduating in 1951. He later attended Indiana State University, earning a law degree from the Indiana University Maurer School of Law in 1960.

While he was attending school, Bayh was elected to a seat in the Indiana House of Representatives, where he served from 1954 to 1962. He rose to the speakership of that body; during his service, he was admitted in 1961 to the Indiana bar.

In 1962 Bayh decided to run for a seat in the US Senate. Senator Homer E. Capehart, a Republican who was widely respected on both sides of the aisle, was up for reelection. Capehart had been one of the Kennedy administration's harshest critics in the US Senate, opposing the President's foreign policy as well as his "New Frontier" domestic policy. Bayh, 31 years younger than Capehart, scored an upset victory of the long-term Senator, 50.3% to 49.7%. Bayh took his seat in the Eighty-eighth Congress (1963-65).

A member of the Senate Select Committee on Intelligence, Bayh was also a member of the Senate Judiciary Subcommittee on Constitutional Amendments. Interested in the subject of Presidential inability and/or disability, especially after the assassination of President Kennedy in November 1963, Bayh penned language that was the basis for what would become the Twenty-fifth Amendment.

In 1969, Bayh was asked about the potential impact of President Lyndon Baines Johnson on the ultimate passage of the Twenty-fifth Amendment:

"You are probably best known for your work with the Judiciary Committee and particularly with the Constitutional Amendments Subcommittee. And particularly, in light of your...book ["One Heartbeat Away" (1969)], with the Twenty-fifth Amendment. Did the White House play a significant role in the background initiative and so on of that particular amendment?"

"He certainly played a significant role in it. I talked to the President. In '64 I remember riding on a helicopter coming back from the UAW convention and approaching him on the subject, telling him what we were doing, of course telling him that his support would be very valuable to us. And he made the observation then which I think is accurate that in his judgment there would be no amendment until after the 1964 election, at a time in which there was a Vice President. This would make it look less like a slap at the Speaker and at the President Pro-tem of the Senate. I talked to him again after the election, informed him of our efforts, and in fact I worked closely with, I guess it was Ramsey Clark at that time who was helping put the State of the Union Message together."

In 1964, the US Senate, with the help of Bayh and other Senators from both sides of the political aisle, passed the historic Civil Rights Act of 1964. Bayh then joined fellow Democrat Ted Kennedy of Massachusetts on a plane back to Kennedy's home state. The way, the small plane crashed near Springfield, Massachusetts, and Bayh dragged the severely injured Kennedy to safety. Kennedy suffered a broken back, and suffered from his injury for the remainder of his life. Bayh had no long lasting injuries.

In 1971, Bayh also authored the language that became the Twenty-sixth Amendment, granting those 18 years old and older the right to vote.

In an interview in 2010, resulting in an article that called Bayh "a modern father of our Constitution," Bayh spoke of his role in the drafting of the Twenty-fifth Amendment:

"First of all, we were confronted with the stark reality that the President is human and life can be taken out rather quickly. It almost happened – it was a millimeter away with Reagan. We found out that – for the sixteenth time – the Vice President had become President and nobody died after the Vice President took office. But the significance of a President dying is deepened when there is a vacancy in the Vice Presidency. You get a real tragedy in the country when a President is assassinated or dies due to his health. To add to that the uncertainty about the authority of the person who takes over – as would be the case if the President who succeeds dies and you have the Speaker of the House take over – you may get someone who is of a different party. Although we like to believe that everybody knows who the Speaker of the House is, I'm not sure everybody equates Nancy Pelosi as being the next President of the United States.

"If I had to do this thing over, I'd try to find a way to placate my colleagues in the Senate, but back then it was a matter of deference. The President Pro Tern of the Senate, Robert C. Byrd, becoming President of the United States? The President Pro Temp of the Senate is not even the majority of the Senate. It's just whoever has been there the longest. One of the things that catalyzed this more than anything else and got people's interest was that joint session of Congress, with Lyndon Johnson addressing the Congress immediately after taking office. And there was this image of Carl Hayden and John McCormack at the ages of eighty-six, and seventy-one, respectively. Yet one or both of those people could end up being President of the United States. There needed to be steps taken to fill that vacancy.

"Why is it important to act? I think it's important to act so that you don't have the Succession Act take effect. The answer to many of the criticisms of the remaining gaps in the Twenty-Fifth Amendment is that it is essential to fill that vacancy quickly. Basically, it's one crisis at a time. The crisis of succession is bad enough. Let's not have a crisis of lacking confidence in the person who goes there, because that wasn't what was supposed to be done."

By 1980, Bayh's politics were out of sync with Indiana. He was challenged in the US Senate race that year by a little-known member of the US House of Representatives, James Danforth "Dan" Quayle. At a time when Bayh's name and lengthy career should have carried him even to a narrow victory, he was swept up in the defeat of many

Democrats nationwide. Quayle defeated him, 54% to 46%, setting up a career in the US Senate that culminated eight years later with his being elected Vice President of the United States. But in 1980, Bayh, after three terms, was ceremoniously voted out of office. He returned to the practice of law, which he continues as of this writing, remaining in the public arena speaking out on issues that matter to him. His son, Birch Evans "Evan" Bayh (1955), served as the US Senator from Indiana from 1999 to 2011.

FOOTNOTES, SOURCES, FURTHER READING

Footnotes

[1] Feerick, John D., "Presidential Succession and Inability: Before and After the Twenty-Fifth Amendment," *Fordham Law Review*, LXXIX:3 (December 2010), 911.

[2] Bayh, Birch, "Preface," in "Selected Materials on the Twenty-Fifth Amendment. Report of [the] Constitutional Amendments Subcommittee, by Senator Birch Bayh, Chairman, to the Committee on the Judiciary [,] United States Senate. October 1973" (Washington: Government Printing Office, 1974), v.

[3] "President, Disability," in John R. Vile, "The Constitutional Convention of 1787: A Comprehensive Encyclopedia of America's Founding" (Santa Barbara, California: ABC-Clio, 2005), 601.

[4] Farrand, Max, ed., "The Records of the Federal Convention of 1787" (New Haven, Connecticut: Yale University Press; four volumes, 1911), II:532-33, 535.

[5] Remarks of Senator William Allen of Ohio, 1 June 1841, in *Congressional Globe*, 27th Congress, 1st Session (1841), issue of 5 June 1841, 4. An extended version of the debate over Allen's remarks can be found in the "Background and history from sources both of the period and historical" section of this amendment. See also "William Allen" in Howard Carroll, "Twelve Americans: Their Lives and Times" (New York: Harper & Brothers, Franklin Square, 1883), 301-30.

[6] "Garret A. Hobart Dead. The Vice President Passes Away at His Home," *New-York Tribune*, 22 November 1899, 1, 2; "Hon. Garret A. Hobart," *The Washington Post*, 22 November 1899, 6.

[7] Wilmerding, Lucius, Jr., "Presidential Inability," *Political Science Quarterly*, LXXII:2 (June 1957), 165.

[8] George, Juliette L.; Michael F. Marmor, and Alexander L. George, "Issues in Wilson Scholarship: References to Early "Strokes" in the Papers of Woodrow Wilson," The *Journal of American History*, LXX:4 (March 1984), 845-53.

[9] Toole, James F.; and Robert J. Joynt, eds., "Presidential Disability: Papers, Discussions, and Recommendations on the Twenty-fifth Amendment and Issues of Inability and Disability in Presidents of the United States" (New York: The University of Rochester Press, 2001), xxi-xxii.

[10] Abrams, Herbert L., "Can the Twenty-Fifth Amendment Deal with a Disabled President? Preventing Future White House Cover-Ups," *Presidential Studies Quarterly*, XXIX:1 (March 1999), 116.

[11] "Disability Measure Sails Past in House But Stalls in Senate," *The Washington Post*, 1 July 1965, A2.

[12] "2 Senators Warn of Ambiguities in Bill on Presidential Disability," *The Washington Post*, 4 July 1965, A4.

[13] Hall remarks in "The Congressional Record: Proceedings and Debates of the 89th Congress, First Session. Volume III – Part 6. – 1965, to – 1965 (Pages – to –)" (Washington: Government Printing Office, 1965), 7938.

[14] ibid., 7938.

[15] ibid., 7938.

[16] Bayh, Birch, "The Twenty-fifth Amendment: Its History and Meaning" in Kenneth W. Thompson, ed., "Papers on Presidential Disability and the Twenty-fifth Amendment" (Lanham, Maryland: University Press of America, 1988), 29.

[17] Park, Bert E., "Presidental Disability: Past Experiences and Future Implications," *Politics and the Life Sciences*, VII:1 (August 1988), 50.

[18] Park, Bert E., "Resuscitating the 25th Amendment: A Second Opinion Regarding Presidential Disability," *Political Psychology*, XVI:4 (December 1995), 821.

[19] Michael Joseph (Mike) Mansfield (1903-2001), Democrat of Montana, US Representative (1943-53), US Senator (1953-77), US Ambassador Extraordinary and Plenipotentiary to Japan (1977-88).

[20] Birch Evans Bayh, Jr. (1928), Democrat of Indiana, Member, Indiana state House of Representatives (1954-62), US Senator (1963-81). See the "influential biographies" section for a biography of Bayh in this amendment.

[21] Formosa is now known as the island of Taiwan.

[22] Ileitis, now more commonly known as Crohn's Disease, is a form of inflammatory bowel syndrome (IBS), causing the inflammation of the ileum, a portion of the large intestine.

[23] Russell Billiu Long (1918-2003), Democrat of Louisiana, US Senator (1948-87).

[24] Actually, he meant the National Aeronautics and Space Administration, or NASA, then in its infancy.

[25] Roman Lee Hruska (1904-1999), Republican of Nebraska, US Representative (1953-54), US Senator (1954-76).

[26] Everett McKinley Dirksen (1896-1969), Republican of Illinois, US Representative (1933-49), US Senator (1951-69).

[27] Allen Joseph Ellender (1890-1972), Democrat of Louisiana, City Attorney, Houma, Louisiana (1913-15), District Attorney, Terrebonne Parish (1915-16), Member, Louisiana state House of Representatives (1924-36), US Senator (1937-72).

[28] William Pierce Rogers (1913-2001) served as the Attorney General (1957-61) in the second Dwight David Eisenhower administration, and later served as the Secretary of State (1969-73) in the first Richard M. Nixon administration.

[29] Samuel James Ervin, Jr. (1896-1985), Democrat of North Carolina, Member, North Carolina General Assembly (1923, 1925, 1931), Judge, Burke County (North Carolina) Criminal Court (1935-37), Judge, North Carolina Superior Court (1937-43), US Representative (1946-47), Associate Justice, North Carolina state Supreme Court (1948-54), US Senator (1954-74).

[30] Milward Lee Simpson (1897-1993), Republican of Wyoming, Member, Wyoming state House of Representatives (1926-27), Governor of Wyoming (1955-59), US Senator (1962-67).

[31] Joseph Davies Tydings (1928), Democrat of Maryland, Member, Maryland House of Delegates (1955-61), US Attorney for Maryland (1961-63), US Senator (1965-71).

[32] In 2012, there are now fourteen cabinet departments in the federal government.

[33] Dante Bruno Fascell (1917-1998), Democrat of Florida, Member, Florida state House of Representatives (1950-54), US Representative (1955-93).

[34] Emanuel Celler (1888-1981), Democrat of New York, US Representative (1923-73). See the comprehensive biography for Celler in the "influential biographies" section of the Twenty-fourth Amendment.

[35] William Moore McCulloch (1901-1980), Republican of Ohio, US Representative (1947-73).

[36] Richard Harding Poff (1923-2011), Republican of Virginia, US Representative (1953-72), Justice, Virginia state Supreme Court (1972-2011).

[37] Byron Giles Rogers (1900-1983), Democrat of Colorado, City Attorney, Las Animas, Colorado (1929-33), Member, Colorado state House of Representatives (1932-35), Assistant United States Attorney for Colorado (1934-36), Attorney General for Colorado (1936-41), US Representative (1951-71).

[38] Peter Wallace Rodino, Jr. (1909-2005), Democrat of New Jersey, US Representative (1949-89).

[39] Jack Bascom Brooks (1922), Democrat of Texas, US Representative (1953-95).

[40] Harold Daniel Donohue (1901-1984), Democrat of Massachusetts, Councilman and Alderman, Worcester, Massachusetts (1927-35), US Representative (1947-74).

[41] Robert William Kastenmeier (1924), Democrat of Wisconsin, Justice of the Peace, Jefferson and Dodge Counties, Wisconsin (1955-59), US Representative (1959-91).

[42] James Charles Corman (1920-2000), Democrat of California, Member, Los Angeles City Council (1957-60), US Representative (1961-81).

[43] John Vliet Lindsay (1921-2000), Republican (and, in 1971, Democrat) of New York, US Representative (1959-65), Mayor, New York City (1965-73).

[44] William Cato Cramer (1922-2003), Republican of Florida, Member, Florida state House of Representatives (1950-52), County Attorney, Pinellas County, Florida (1953-54), US Representative (1955-71).

[45] Clarence J. Brown (1893-1965), Republican of Ohio, Newspaper publisher (1917-19), Lieutenant Governor of Ohio (1919-23), Secretary of State of Ohio (1927-33), US Representative (1939-65).

[46] Dunward Gorham Hall (1910-2001), Republican of Missouri, US Representative (1961-73).

[47] Clark MacGregor (1922-2003), Republican of Minnesota, US Representative (1961-71).

[48] Robert Blackford Duncan (1920-2011), Democrat of Oregon, Member, Oregon House of Representatives (1956-62), US Representative (1963-67, 1975-81).

[49] Albert Arnold Gore (1907-1998), Democrat of Tennessee, Tennessee Commissioner of Labor (1936-37), US Representative (1939-44, 1945-53), US Senator (1953-71).

[50] Eugene Joseph McCarthy (1916-2005), Democrat of Minnesota, US Representative (1949-59), US Senator (1959-71).

[51] William Allen (1803-1879), Jacksonian and Democrat of Ohio, US Representative (1833-35), US Senator (1837-49), Governor of Ohio (1874-76).

[52] Benjamin Tappan (1773-1857), Democrat of Ohio, Judge, Fifth Ohio Circuit Court of Common Pleas (1816-23), Judge, United States District Court of Ohio (1833), US Senator (1839-45).

[53] Jabez Williams Huntington (1788-1847), Whig of Connecticut, Member, Connecticut state House of Representatives (1829), US Representative (1829-34), Judge, Connecticut state Supreme Court of Errors (1834), US Senator (1840-47).

[54] Robert John Walker (1801-1869), Democrat of Mississippi, US Senator (1835-45), Secretary of the Treasury (1845-49), Governor of Kansas Territory (1857).

[55] Henry Alexander Wise (1806-1876), Jacksonian and Whig of Virginia, US Representative (1833-44), US Minister to Brazil (1844-47), Governor of Virginia (1856-60), Delegate, Virginia Convention (1861).

[56] John Caldwell Calhoun (1782-1850), Democratic Republican, Nullifier, and Democrat of South Carolina, Member, South Carolina state House of Representatives (1808-09), US Representative (1811-17), Secretary of War (1817-25), Vice President of the United States (1825-32), US Senator (1832-43, 1845-50), Secretary of State (1844-45).

[57] Jack Bascom Brooks (1922), Democrat of Texas, US Representative (1953-95).

[58] Andrew Jackson Young, Jr. (1932), Democrat of Georgia, US Representative (1973-77), US Ambassador to the United Nations (1977-79), Mayor, Atlanta, Georgia (1982-90).

[59] Clarence Dickinson Long (1908-1994), Democrat of Maryland, US Representative (1963-85).

Sources Arranged by Chapter Sections

Debate in Congress
"The Congressional Record: Proceedings and Debates of the 89th Congress, First Session. Volume III – Part [-]. – 1965, to – 1965 (Pages – to -)" (Washington: Government Printing Office, 1965), 3200-86.

"The Congressional Record: Proceedings and Debates of the 89th Congress, First Session. Volume III – Part 6. – 1965, to – 1965 (Pages - to -)" (Washington: Government Printing Office, 1965), 7938-52.

"The Congressional Record: Proceedings and Debates of the 89th Congress, First Session.

Historical Background Documents
Remarks of Senators William Allen, Benjamin Tappan, Jabez Huntington, an Robert J. Walker, 1 June 1841, in *Congressional Globe*, 27th Congress, 1st Session (1841), issue of 5 June 1841, 4-5.

Trumbull, Lyman, "Presidential Inability," *The North American Review*, CCC (November 1881), 417-22.

Hyman, Sydney, "Is A Constitutional Amendment To Provide For Cases of President Disability Needed? Con," *Congressional Digest*, XXXVII:1 (January 1958), 17-21.

Celler, Emanuel, "Is A Constitutional Amendment To Provide For Case of President Disability Needed? Yes," *Congressional Digest*, XXXVII:1 (January 1958), 15-17.

Gerald R. Ford to Richard M. Nixon, 11 October 1973, Nixon Presidential Papers, White House Central Files, President's Personal Files (PPF), Box 169, Folder 7, Nixon Presidential Materials Project, National Archives, College Park, Maryland.

Original Primary Documents
"Disability Measure Sails Past in House But Stalls in Senate," *The Washington Post*, 1 July 1965, A2.

"States to Get Amendment on Presidency," *Los Angeles Times*, 7 July 1965, 1, 8.

"Disability Amendment," *The Evening News* [Newburgh, New York], 8 July 1965, 6A.

"State 10th To Ratify Succession," *The Independent* [Pasadena, California], 22 October 1965, 2.

Hunter, Marjorie, "Ford Sworn as Vice President After House Approves, 387-35; He Vows Equal Justice For All," *The New York Times*, 7 December 1973, 1, 27.

Who's Who
Birch Evans Bayh, Jr. (1928–)
"Bayh, Birch Evans, Jr.," official congressional biography, online at http://bioguide.congress.gov/scripts/biodisplay.pl?index=B000254; Transcript, Birch Bayh Oral History Interview I, 12 February 1969, by Paige E. Mulhollan, Lyndon Baines Johnson Library, Austin, Texas, 2; Bayh, Birch, "One Heartbeat Away: Presidential Disability and Succession" (Indianapolis: Bobbs-Merrill Co., 1968); "A Modern Father of our Constitution: An Interview with Former Senator Birch Bayh," *Fordham Law Review*, LXXIX:3 (December 2010), 788-89; Dewar, Helen, "Reagan Sweep to a Landslide Victory; Magnuson, McGovern, Bayh, Culver Lose," *The Washington Post*, 5 November 1980, A1.

Further Reading

Abrams, Herbert L., "Can the Twenty-Fifth Amendment deal with a Disabled President? Preventing Future White House Cover-Ups," *Presidential Studies Quarterly*, XXIX:1 (March 1999), 115-33.

Albert, Richard, "The Constitutional Politics of Presidential Succession," *Hofstra Law Review*, XXXIX:3 (2011), 497-576.

Amar, Akhil Reed, "Applications and Implications of the Twenty-Fifth Amendment," *Houston Law Review*, XLVII:1 (March 2010), 1-39.

Bellamy, Calvin, "Presidential Disability: The Twenty-Fifth Amendment Still an Untried Tool," *Boston University Public Interest Law Journal*, IX (Spring 2000), 373.

Feerick, John D., "The Twenty-Fifth Amendment: An Explanation and Defense," *Wake Forest Law Review*, XXX (1995), 481-503.

____, "A Response to Akhil Reed Amar's Address on Applications and Implications of the Twenty-Fifth Amendment," *Houston Law Review*, XLVII:1 (March 2010), 41-66.

____, *The Twenty-fifth Amendment: Its Complete History and Applications*, 3rd ed. (New York: Fordham University Press, 2014).

Gant, Scott E., "Presidential Inability and the Twenty-Fifth Amendment's Unexplored Removal Provisions," *Law Review of Michigan State University-Detroit College of Law* (Winter 1999), 791.

Gilbert, Robert E., ed. *Managing Crisis: Presidential Disability and the Twenty-Fifth Amendment* (New York: Fordham University Press, 2000).

Goldstein, Joel K., "Taking From the Twenty-Fifth Amendment: Lessons in Ensuring Presidential Continuity," *Fordham Law Review*, LXXIX:3 (December 2010), 959-1042.

Gustafson, Adam R. F., "Presidential Inability and Subjective Meaning," *Yale Law and Policy Review*, XXVII:2 (Spring 2009), 459-97.

Kassop, Nancy, "The Law: When Law and Politics Collide: Presidents and the Use of the Twenty-Fifth Amendment," *Presidential Studies Quarterly*, XXXV:1 (March 2005), 147-65.

McDermott, Rose, "Extensions on The Twenty-fifth amendment: The Influence of Biological Factors on Assessments of Impairment," *Fordham Law Review*, LXXIX:3 (December 2010) , 881-96.

Toole, James F., Robert J. Joynt, eds., *Presidential Disability: Papers, Discussions, and Recommendations on the Twenty-Fifth Amendment and Issues of Inability and Disability among Presidents of the United States* (Rochester, NY: University of Rochester Press, 2001).

AMERICA AT THAT TIME . . .

Although the material in this section may not be directly related to the adoption of the Twenty-fifth Amendment, it offers valuable insight into what was happening in America at the time the Amendment was adopted. Modeled after Grey House Publishing's Working American *series, whose author, Scott Derks, is responsible for its content, it includes a Historical Snapshot, Selected Prices, significant quotations, and newspaper and magazine clips to give a sense of what was on the minds of Americans, and how it may have impacted the amendment process.*

HISTORICAL SNAPSHOT

1967

- The connection between a cholesterol-lowering diet and a reduced incidence of heart disease was shown in a five-year study

- Both CBS and NBC televised the Super Bowl

- A reported 100,000 hippies lived in the San Francisco area, principally around Haight-Ashbury

- The first rock festival was held at Monterey, California, featuring the Grateful Dead and Big Brother and the Holding Company starring Janis Joplin

- Heavyweight boxer Muhammad Ali was denied conscientious objector status after refusing induction in the Army

- The United States revealed that an anti-ballistic missile defense plan had been developed against Chinese attack

- Hit songs included *Natural Woman, Soul Man, I Never Loved a Man, Penny Lane, By The Time I Get to Phoenix,* and *Can't Take My Eyes Off You*

- Bolivia confirmed the capture and death of Che Guevara

- When Army physician Captain Harold Levy refused to train Green Berets heading to Vietnam in the treatment of skin disease, he was court-martialed and sent to Fort Leavenworth prison

- Coed dorms opened at numerous colleges across the country for the first time

- *Sgt Pepper's Lonely Hearts Club Band* by the Beatles captured a Grammy award for best album

- U.S. troop levels in Vietnam reached 225,000; the U.S. death toll reached 15,997

- Thurgood Marshall became the first African American appointed to the U.S. Supreme Court

- Television premieres included *The Flying Nun, The Carol Burnett Show, Ironsides* and *The Phil Donahue Show*

Quiz Yourself

President Johnson's recent surgery provoked renewed interest and concern in the question of Presidential disability and succession. This quiz will test your knowledge of the proposed 25th Amendment to the Constitution and the issue of Presidential succession.

1. The 25th amendment, dealing with the problem of determining Presidential disability, was proposed by Congress July 7, 1965. To become effective, it — as is the case of any Constitutional amendment — must be ratified by: (a) 41 states; (b) 50 states; (c) 26 states; (d) 38 states.

2. To date, the amendment has been ratified by state legislatures in: (a) 31 states; (b) 19 states; (c) 5 states; (d) 50 states.

3. No further ratifications are expected in 1966 because: (a) the process of ratification is too time-consuming; (b) the only state legislatures currently in session oppose ratification; (c) no more state legislatures will be in session until 1967; (d) public opposition to the amendment is high.

4. President Johnson and Vice President Hubert H. Humphrey have an agreement under which the Vice President would become Acting President in the event of the President's disability. This type of agreement was made first by: (a) Roosevelt and Truman; (b) Kennedy and Johnson; (c) Eisenhower and Nixon; (d) Lincoln and Johnson.

5. Under the agreement with Mr. Johnson, Humphrey would become Acting President either on orders from the President or: (a) by an act of Congress; (b) after "appropriate" consultation; (c) confirmation by the Senate; (d) after approval from the Supreme Court.

6. Under the 25th Amendment, the Vice President becomes Acting President when the President informs Congress he is unable to perform his duties or when: (a) a majority of the Senate and House votes that the President is disabled; (b) the Vice President and a majority of the Cabinet or other body designated by Congress inform Congress the President is disabled; (c) a majority of the Democratic and Republican leaders in both chambers determines the President is disabled.

7. The President, after being disabled, resumes his powers after: (a) a two-thirds majority of Congress votes that the President is able to resume his duties; (b) the Cabinet informs Congress that the President is well; (c) the President informs Congress he is able to resume his power.

8. In addition to providing for an Acting President, the 25th Amendment also: (a) sets out the complete line of succession to the President's office; (b) provides that the Secretary of State would follow the Vice President in the line of Presidential succession; (c) provides for the filling of a vacancy in the office of the Vice President.

ANSWERS: 1. (d); 2. (a); 3. (c); 4. (c); 5. (b); 6. (b); 7. (c); 8. (c).

Copyright 1966, Congressional Quarterly Inc.

Ratify the 25th Amendment, *The New Mexican*, July 19, 1965

The proposed 25th amendment to the Constitution, on which congressional action has now been completed, will bring about one of the most vital structural changes ever made in the United States Government".

Most of the amendments in the past have been concerned with an expansion of individual rights. Several have sharply alerted Federal - state relations, but only four have brought about significant structural changes: the 12th altering the method of electing the President and Vice President; the 17th, providing for the direct election of Senators; the 20th, abolishing the lame-duck session of Congress; and the 22nd, limiting the President to two terms.

The proposed 25th would serve the important function of keeping the presidential power always in the hands of an able - bodied and competent person.

Here is editorial comment on the presidential succession amendment:

POST. WASHINGTON. D.C. — "The great improvements which the amendment will make in our system of government are to be found in Sections II and III. The first of these would permit the President to nominate a Vice President, whenever the office is vacant, with the approval of both houses of Congress. The second would permit the President to relinquish his duties and power to the Vice President during an illness, in a routine fashion, and to regain those powers without any questions being asked by simply announcing his recovery. These are the sections of the amendment that will be used to great advantage."

TIMES, Kansas City. Mo. — "It is unfortunate that the amendment was not approved by Congress early enough in the session to permit consideration by at least some of the states this year. But the measure did dangle in conference committee while the quibbling continued.

Nevertheless, it was approved and that is the fact of historical accomplishment. The responsibility now checks to the various states. The 25th amendment, should be given immediate priority whenever the legislatures next assemble."

SUN-TIMES, Chicago — "The proposed amendment requires the approval of 35, or three - fourths of the states, within the next seven years to become the 25th Amendment to the Constitution. It is hoped that such ratification can be achieved in as short a time as possible."

FREE PRESS. Detroit — "There is no foolproof way to insure an orderly succession to the White House in case a president dies or is incapacitated. Nor is there a perfect way to fill a vacancy in the vice-presidency. But the proposed 25th Amendment, which has now passed both houses of Congress and goes to the states f o r ratification, do as good a job as is feasible."

[. . .]

25th Amendment Begins Long Journey Towards Ratification, *Pharos Tribune*, July 7, 1965

WASHINGTON (UPI) The proposed 25th Constitutional Amendment, aimed at ending 176 years of confusion over the transition of power when a president becomes disabled, could begin its long journey to ratification as early as next week.

Approval by 38 of the 50 state legislatures is necessary before the amendment, given final congressional approval Tuesday by the Senate, can become a part of the U.S. Constitution.

The amendment would set procedures for the vice president to become acting president when a chief executive became disabled and also provide for filling vacancies in the vice presidency. It will be sent to the states in about a week or 10 days.

Considered likely to be among the first to give its approval was Wisconsin, whose legislature is till in session. Legislative leaders in Madison have already scheduled the amendment for possible action next week.

Other States

Other states with legislatures still in session include Alabama, Massachusetts, Ohio and Oklahoma. The outlook was favorable for early consideration in Ohio and Massachusetts.

Although many state legislatures are scheduled to come back into session later this year or early next year, final ratification is not expected for about two years. This is because not enough state legislatures will meet before January 1967 to make up the required total of 38.

Ratification of the 25th Amendment is considered virtually certain. Since the adoption of the Constitution on March 4, 1789, only three amendments proposed by Congress have been rejected by the states. All these dealt with controversial subjects.

The 25th Amendment deals with a potential source of confusion that was most recently brought home when former President Dwight D. Eisenhower had his heart attack in 1955. No objections were seen by the states to its adoption.

Senate approval of the measure came on a 68-5 vote, 19 more than the required two-thirds of the senators present and voting. The House approved the amendment last week.

What It Does

The amendment authorizes the vice president to take over as acting president immediately after he and a majority of the cabinet or such other body as Congress may create, have certified to Congress that the chief executive is unable to continue.

Continued

25th Amendment Begins . . . *(Continued)*

The President also could notify Congress on his own that he is unable to discharge his duties. The vice president then would become acting president.

A recovered president could resume his authority by a written declaration to Congress with this exception: if the vice president and a majority of the cabinet or new body created by Congress dispute his ability to perform his duties within four days. Congress would decide the issue within 21 days. A two-thirds vote of House and Senate would be needed to prevent a president from resuming office.

The amendment also permits a president to nominate his own choice when a vice presidential vacancy occurs. His nominee would have to be confirmed by majority vote of both House of Congress.

Year	Value of One Dollar in 2016 US Dollars
1963	$7.89
1964	$7.79
1965	$7.66
1966	$7.45
1967	$7.23
1968	$6.94
1969	$6.58

Selected Prices

Automobile, Datsun $2,196.00

Calculator, Electric Printing $1,495.00

Circular Saw $27.77

Electric Shaver $13.97

Guitar, Electric $199.95

Ketchup, Hunt's, 14 Ounces $0.22

Refrigerator, Frigidaire $208.00

Rider Mower $352.95

Router $34.95

Whiskey, Seagram's, Fifth $5.79

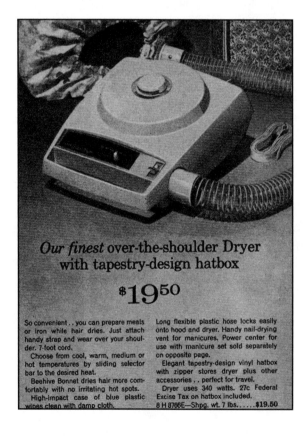

Seagram's Crown Royal is the finest Canadian whisky in the world. If it weren't, it wouldn't cost you what it does.

About nine dollars!
That's a lot to put out for a fifth of whisky.
But Seagram has put a lot into Crown Royal.
Smoothness you find hard to believe. And good taste that will spoil you for anything else.
In a way what you're paying for is inspiration.
And that doesn't grow on trees.

"A Shaky Start," *Time*, October 27, 1967:

Washington's scruffy Ambassador Theatre, normally a pad for psychedelic frolics, was the scene of an unscheduled scatological solo last week in support of the peace demonstrations. Its anti-star was author Norman Mailer, who proved even less prepared to explain Why Are We in Vietnam? than his current novel bearing that title.

Slurping liquor from a coffee mug, Mailer faced an audience of 600, most of them students, who had kicked in $1,900 for a bail fund against Saturday's capers. "I don't want to grandstand unduly," he said, grandly but barely standing.

It was one of his most coherent sentences. Mumbling and spewing obscenities as he staggered about the stage—which he commandeered by threatening to beat up the previous M.C.—Mailer described in detail his search for a usable privy on the premises. Excretion, in fact, was his preoccupation of the night. "I'm here because I'm like L.B.J.," was one of Mailer's milder observations. "He's as full of crap as I am." When hecklers mustered the temerity to shout, "Publicity hound!" at him, Mailer managed to pronounce flawlessly his all-purpose noun, verb and expletive: "**** you!"

"Chinaman's Chance," *Time*, September 8, 1967:

To sightseers tramping its cluttered avenues, San Francisco's Chinatown has always displayed a pungent blend of yang and yin. Those intertwined opposites—good and evil, sweet and sour, light and dark—describe not only Chinese philosophy but also the inner contradictions of a district whose neon signs and tourist bustle mask a swarming, sweatshop world of long hours, low pay, hard work and fear. For all its outward ambiance, the largest Chinese enclave outside Asia is one of America's most wretched slums.

Over 40,000 Chinese are jammed into the 42 blocks of Chinatown proper between Bush Street and Broadway, Kearny and Powell. About 30,000 have spilled north and west into adjacent residential districts; 10,000 more live throughout the Bay Area.

They first came by the thousands to California—Gum San, land of the Golden Mountains—when the gold fields and railroads beckoned, and in smaller streams when the U.S. set up immigration quotas and California passed its racial exclusion laws in 1892. Despite the restrictions, so many Chinese have entered the U.S. in the past seven decades that perhaps as many as half the people of Chinatown are there in violation of the immigration laws.

Since Mao Tse-tung took over the Chinese mainland, immigration via Hong Kong has swelled incrementally: more than 4,000 Chinese a year now settle in the Bay Area, creating a job shortage so severe that exploitation is the order of the day—and night. The traditional Chinese family fabric has visibly frayed. With mothers working, delinquency climbs. Tenement squalor sustains a tuberculosis rate double that of San Francisco as a whole.

Working conditions are no better. The major sources of jobs are restaurants, curio stores and the sewing shops, comprising 151 small, family-oriented contract clothing factories employing about 20 seamstresses apiece. Paid on a piecework basis, the women often labor from 8:30 a.m. until after midnight, seven days a week, fingers darting frenetically to make ends meet. Asked why she would work at least 12 hours a day for a net income of $26 a week, one mother of five said succinctly: "You have to in Chinatown."

Ever since one Chum Ming sailed east from his native Kwangtung in 1847 to grow up with the country, California's Chinese have been victimized by their language problems (even today, no more than 40 percent speak fluent English), their fear of deportation, and traditional kowtowing to fate and station. San Francisco's youngest, brightest Chinese Americans leave for the suburbs at a rate of up to 15,000 a year, and Chinatown has become a way station for immigrants and a ghetto of the old and unemployed poor.

Only recently has Chinese pride permitted a lowering of the all but impenetrable veil that shrouded their condition from the outside world. California's Labor Commission and the San Francisco Central Labor Council have heard depressing testimony from Chinatown residents about working conditions in the district. Last week, led by the International Ladies' Garment Workers Union, labor opened a campaign of pickets, sanctions and the threat of boycott against eight Chinatown sewing shops and a contracting firm. Although the goal is not immediate unionization, the 25,000-member culinary workers union is waiting in the wings, and a labor spokesman called the drive "the opening gun in a campaign we hope will eventually end substandard wages and conditions in Chinatown shops, stores, factories and bars."

"Patent Protects Inventor Rights," *Charleston Daily Mail*, November 16, 1967:

Suppose you invent something that you think can make a lot of money for you. You don't want anyone to "steal" your idea, that is, have the right to copy it exactly.

The government protects you from having this happen by granting you a "patent." A patent is an agreement between the government, representing the public, and the inventor.

The government agrees that no one but the inventor will be allowed to manufacture, use, or sell his invention for 17 years without the inventor's permission. In return, the inventor files his new discovery in the patent office so that everyone will profit from it when the 17 years are over.

Any person who has invented or discovered a new and useful art, machine, manufacture, or composition of matter may obtain a patent for it. This also includes any new or useful improvement.

Application for a patent must be made by the inventor, but he is usually represented by a patent lawyer or agent. A written description and drawings of the invention, together with an application fee, must be submitted to the Patent Office.

If the patent examiners (experts who work for the government's Patent Office) find the invention is actually new, a patent is granted after the payment of an additional fee. The patent now becomes the inventor's own property, and he may sell or assign it.

If anyone disregards a patent, the inventor can force him to stop using it or sue him for the profits made.

The present U.S. Patent system was started in 1836. It laid down the principle, then new, that patents should be given only after inventions had been carefully examined and compared with earlier ones. Two questions were asked: "Is the invention useful?" and "Is it new?" This system was copied by the rest of the civilized world.

"King Charges U.S. Stifled War Dissent," *Delaware County Daily Times* (Chester, Pennsylvania), June 1, 1967:

Dr. Martin Luther King has accused the Johnson administration of bringing the U.S. commander in Vietnam back to the United States to stifle antiwar dissent.

"It's a dark day in our nation when high-level authorities will seek to use every method to silence dissent," King declared Sunday.

Gen. William C. Westmoreland spoke before a joint session of Congress Friday.

In his sermon at the Ebenezer Baptist Church, where he is co-pastor with his father, the Rev. Martin Luther King, Sr., the civil rights leader said some "equate dissent with disloyalty."

King told the packed congregation he chose to preach in Vietnam "because conscience gives me no other choice."

Reiterating passages in a recent New York address, King deplored the downgrading of antipoverty programs which has coincided with increasing war expenditures, and charged that "a nation that continues year after year to spend more money on military defense than on programs of social uplift is approaching spiritual death."

In his impassioned sermon, King said America must repent from a "tragic, reckless adventure in Vietnam. This madness must stop. We must admit we've been wrong from the beginning of our adventure in Vietnam."

The Nobel Prize winner urged every young man who finds the war objectionable and unjust to file as a conscientious objector.

"It matters what you think of Mohammed Ali (heavyweight champion Cassius Clay's black Muslim name). You certainly have to admire his courage," King told the congregation, which included "Black Power" advocate Stokely Carmichael. Cries of "Amen" greeted the mention of Clay, who refused to be inducted into the Army last week and was stripped of his heavyweight title.

"Here is a young man willing to give up millions of dollars to do what conscience tells him is right," King said.

The Twenty-sixth Amendment

Chapter 17

S. J. Res. 7

Ninety-second Congress of the United States of America

AT THE FIRST SESSION

*Begun and held at the City of Washington on Thursday, the twenty-first day of January,
one thousand nine hundred and seventy-one*

Joint Resolution

Proposing an amendment to the Constitution of the United States extending the
right to vote to citizens eighteen years of age or older.

*Resolved by the Senate and House of Representatives of the United
States of America in Congress assembled (two-thirds of each House
concurring therein),* That the following article is proposed as an
amendment to the Constitution of the United States, which shall be
valid to all intents and purposes as part of the Constitution when
ratified by the legislatures of three-fourths of the several States within
seven years from the date of its submission by the Congress:

"ARTICLE —

"SECTION 1. The right of citizens of the United States, who are
eighteen years of age or older, to vote shall not be denied or abridged
by the United States or by any State on account of age.
"SEC. 2. The Congress shall have power to enforce this article by
appropriate legislation."

Carl Albert
Speaker of the House of Representatives.

Vice President of the United States and
President of the Senate. *Pro Tempore*

Proposed in Congress:	**23 March 1971**
Sent to States:	**23 March 1971**
Ratified:	**1 July 1971**

Chapter 17

THE TWENTY-SIXTH AMENDMENT

Section 1.
The right of citizens of the United States, who are eighteen years of age or older, to vote shall not be denied or abridged by the United States or by any State on account of age.

Section 2.
The Congress shall have power to enforce this article by appropriate legislation.

Note: Amendment 14, section 2, of the Constitution was modified by section 1 of the 26th amendment.

Brief Summary

The Twenty-sixth Amendment lowered the legal voting age in federal and state elections to eighteen by prohibiting the states from restricting the voting rights of citizens eighteen years old or older on the basis of age. Historically, only persons twenty-one years of age or older were eligible to vote in state and federal elections.

Timeline

1943	Georgia lowers the voting age to eighteen.
1955	Kentucky lowers the voting age to eighteen.
1963	The President's Commission on Registration and Voting Participation recommends lowering the voting age to eighteen.
1970	Senator Edward Kennedy proposes an amendment to the Voting Rights Act of 1965 to lower the voting age to eighteen.

22 June 1970	President Richard Nixon signs an extension to the Voting Rights Act of 1965, lowering the voting age in all federal, state, and local elections; Nixon expresses reservations about the constitutionality of the change, believing that a constitutional amendment is necessary.
21 December 1970	The US Supreme Court issues its decision in Oregon v. Mitchell.
10 March 1971	The US Senate passes the Twenty-sixth Amendment.
23 March 1971	The US House of Representatives passes the Twenty-sixth Amendment.
1 July 1971	The Twenty-sixth Amendment is ratified when Ohio and North Carolina ratify it; seven states took no action on the amendment.

Introduction

The last years of the 1960s, when young people protested against the Vietnam War, gave rise to the movement giving those same protestors, ages 18-21, the right to vote. Despite the positives results of this amendment – more voters, more voter participation – it was extremely controversial during its debate, passage, and the period leading up to ratification.

An historical look at how this amendment came to be added to the US Constitution shows that the expansion of the right to vote was a long road. This movement, if one could call it that, began in the years prior to the Civil War, leading to the ratification of the Fourteenth Amendment in 1868. That amendment specifically stated that "...when the right to vote...is being denied to any of the male inhabitants of such State, being twenty-one years or age, and citizens of the United States, or in any way abridged, except for participation in rebellion, or other crime..." Two years later, the Fifteenth Amendment, the second of the so-called "Reconstruction Amendments," also went to the heart of voting rights, explaining quite clearly: "The right of citizens of the United States to vote shall not be denied or abridged by the United States or by any state on account of race, color, or previous condition of servitude."

For a half century after that, the Congress passed additional amendments, none of which addressed voting rights. It was not until 1920, through the passage and ratification of the Nineteenth Amendment, that the issue once again took the notice of the Congress: "The right of citizens of the United States to vote shall not be denied or abridged by the United States or by any State on account of sex."

Four amendments – and nearly four decades -later, Congress again examined expanding voting rights in America, when, through the Twenty-third Amendment (ratified in 1961), it gave the right to the citizens of the District of Columbia, additionally giving the District three electoral votes in presidential elections. (Further legislation giving the District two US Senators and a voting US Representative has since gone nowhere.) The Congress quickly followed with the Twenty-fourth Amendment (ratified in 1964), which stated, "The right of citizens of the United States to vote in any primary or other election for President or Vice President, for electors for President or Vice President, or for Senator or Representative in Congress, shall not be denied or abridged by the United States or any State by reason of failure to pay any poll tax or other tax." While this amendment did not expand the reach of voting rights to any particular group, it did reaffirm the right to vote without using the failure to pay a poll tax to deny that right.

In 1970 America was in the midst of the Vietnam War; that year alone, some 6,100 American soldiers were killed in action, many of them between the ages of 18 to 21. In total, of the 58,202 Americans officially listed as killed in action -from the unofficial start of the war in 1956 to its end in 1975, including casualties from the Mayaguez incident in Cambodia in 1975, and deaths caused by war injuries of by exposure to Agent Orange -61% were 21 or younger.

While the Twenty-sixth Amendment was passed by Congress in 1971, it had been percolating for a long time. It was during the Second World War that the first legislative attempts to amend the Constitution to lower the voting age from 21 to 18 began in earnest. President Franklin D. Roosevelt lowered the military draft age to 18, popularizing the slogan "Old enough to fight, old enough to vote." The first serious proposal to change the Constitution regarding the age limitation came in 1942, when Rep. Victor Wickersham, Democrat of Oklahoma, introduced his proposed amendment on the same day, 17 October 1942, that the House voted to change the minimum draft age of men from 21 to 18. Two days later, similar and dual proposals were introduced: one in the House by Rep. (and later US Senator) Jennings Randolph, Democrat of West Virginia, and in the US Senate by Senator Arthur Vandenberg, Republican of Michigan. Although these initial steps received little notice and even less support, the states saw merit in the proposal. In 1943, Georgia lowered its own voting age to 18. Randolph continued to push Congress to enact such a constitutional amendment for the next 28 years; when it did, Randolph became known as "The Father of the Twenty-sixth Amendment."

Footnotes, Sources and Further Reading for this chapter appears on page 1095

From the end of the Second World War until the mid-1950s, fourteen proposals to lower the voting age were introduced in Congress, to no effect. During the single Congress in which the Republicans controlled the House, the Eightieth (1947-49), a combination of Republicans and Democrats nearly came together to get a constitutional amendment through, but in the end, nothing was done.

Historian Wendell W. Cultice, in his 1992 work on the movement, took note that during this same period, in the states, some 100 differing bills to lower the voting age were introduced.[1]

There was little direction from the White House – President Franklin D. Roosevelt never came out one way or another on the issue, while President Harry S Truman specifically asked that the voting age be *raised* to age 25. In his first State of the Union address in 1954, President Dwight Eisenhower called for the lowering of the voting age to 18. In that message, Eisenhower said, "We have three splendid opportunities to demonstrate the strength of our belief in the right of suffrage. First, I again urge that a Constitutional amendment be submitted to the States to reduce the voting age for Federal election. Second, I renew my request that the principle of self-government be extended and the right of suffrage granted to the citizens of the District of Columbia. Third, I again recommend that we work with the State to preserve the voting rights of citizens in the nation's service overseas."[2]

In 1952, in the midst of the Korean War, Senator Arthur Edson Blair Moody, Republican of Michigan, introduced Senate Joint Resolution 127, which proposed a constitutional amendment to lower the voting age. The following year, Senator William Langer, Republican of North Dakota, introduced his measure, titled Senate Joint Resolution 53, which also proposed a constitutional amendment lowering the voting age in all elections, federal, state, and local, to 18 from 21. After hearings and debate, Langer's proposal came to the floor of the US Senate on 21 May 1954, where it was voted down, 43-24, short of the two-thirds needed for passage. An examination of the votes shows that all positive votes came from Republicans, with Democrats split, and opposition coming mostly from Southern Democrats. Many of these, from the segregationist school of thought in the American South, believed that an expansion of voting rights could be used to give blacks additional rights, which they opposed. One of the leaders who denied any additional Senate floor votes on a proposed amendment was Senator Carl Hayden, Democrat of Arizona, who served as the Senate pro tempore from 1957 to 1967 and used his power to head off any votes. Hayden's argument, that states should be allowed to lower their voting ages if they so desired, was backed up by Hayden's own state of Arizona, a fact he used during Senate debates. Another Senator who opposed the movement was Spessard Holland of Florida, who backed the ending of the poll tax in federal, state, and local elections, which became the Twenty-fourth Amendment. Holland, during debate in 1954, stated that the Fourteenth Amendment specifically listed "twenty one years of age" as the cutoff date for voting, and felt that that amendment should not be altered. In fact, during the debate over the Twenty-fourth Amendment in 1961, Assistant Attorney General Nicholas de Katzenbach explained his support for ending the poll tax by citing the "twentyone years of age" citation. This argument led Senator Kenneth Keating, Republican of New York, who had both introduced potential amendment language and supported other proposals, to change his mind completely. During hearings on a potential amendment in 1961, he said, "I lean to the view that we should not interfere by constitutional amendment with the State's right to determine the qualifications for local officers in that State, and that our action should be limited to the President and Vice President."

After Eisenhower, there was little support from the White House. John F. Kennedy believed that state constitution, and not the federal constitution, should provide for lower-age voting. His successor, Lyndon Baines Johnson, was not known for support in such a measure; in 1954, as a US Senator from Texas, he had voted against a Republican resolution to lower the voting age. As President, Johnson did not speak out for or against the issue, holding off advocating for a constitutional amendment until after he had decided not to run for another election in March 1968, weighed down by the unpopularity of the Vietnam War. At a commencement address at Texas Christian University on 29 May 1968, Johnson said, "I believe we should extend the range of young people's participation in public life. I believe we should move forward – now – to grant the vote to 18-yr-olds. Several States have already done so. A majority of the people and many in Congress approve the idea. The great majority of young people in America have demonstrated their maturity, their desire to participate; their zeal for service." However, with his power all but gone, his word meant little, and his "recommendation," if one could call it that, was ignored.[3]

Ironically, from this period until the late 1960s, opposition to any statute or constitutional amendment expanding the voting rights of those aged 18 to 21 came not from Southern Democrats, but from one man, Rep. Emanuel Celler, Democrat of New York. A lifelong liberal who was at the forefront of the movement to give voting rights to the District of Columbia – embodied in the Twenty-fourth Amendment – and to offer a plan for the succession to the presidency in the event of disability or if the Vice Presidency becomes vacant – embodied in the Twenty-fifth Amendment – Celler nevertheless believed that any lowering of the voting age was unconstitutional, and that the US Constitution should not be changed to make it otherwise. And, as the chairman of the House Committee on the Judiciary from 1955 to 1972, Celler was in a position to stop all hearings and proposals from being considered in the US House of Representatives. With such an implacable foe blocking the way, it was impossible to get a constitutional amendment through the House. Celler was nothing if not consistent. He was also against expanding women's rights, and until his last days in office, he denounced and opposed the Equal Rights Amendment.

In an attempt to end the logjam, the Senate Judiciary Committee's Subcommittee on Constitutional Amendments held hearings in 1968 and again in 1970, listening to proposals on a constitutional amendment on lowering the voting age.[4] These hearings featured testimony from noted persons on both sides of the political aisle and demonstrated the desire, despite Celler's resistance, to amend the US Constitution.

By 1969, as Richard M. Nixon came into the White House, the focus had shifted from whether or not to have a constitutional amendment to how to do it. Under the leadership of Senator Birch Bayh, Democrat of Indiana, the US Senate Committee on the Judiciary's Subcommittee on Constitutional Amendments held a series of hearings on three specific legislative proposals: one jointly co-sponsored by Senator Michael Joseph "Mike" Mans, Democrat of Montana, then Senate Majority Leader, and Senator Everett M. Dirksen, Republican of Illinois; one sponsored by Senator Jennings Randolph, Democrat of West Virginia; and a third, sponsored by Senator Ruper Vance Hartke, Democrat of Indiana. In the subcommittee hearings, Chairman Bayh listed the extension of the vote to 18-year-olds as being akin to the DC vote amendment, and the amendment eliminating the poll tax, and that such work was "part of the fabric of our times." Bayh told his fellow senators that the proposed amendment was needed, as he said, because:

"This force, this energy, is going to continue to grow. The only question is whether we should ignore it, perhaps leaving this energy to dam up and burst and follow less-than-wholesome channels, or whether we should let this force be utilized by society through the pressure valve of the franchise."[5]

At the same time, both Democrats and Republicans on the House Committee on the Judiciary were pushing for hearings to be held there, but Chairman Celler refused to budge. Celler, and others who opposed the measure, pointed to the riots and violence on college campuses against the Vietnam War as evidence that people of that age group were unprepared to accept the right to vote. The power of images on televisions across the nation added weight to this argument – and the proposed amendment's supporters knew it. Senate debate then raged on the precise language of the proposal, or even if it should be left up to the individual states to add such amendment to their state constitutions. The one Senator behind the movement to get this specific amendment into the US Constitution, Senator Jennings Randolph, Democrat of West Virginia, stated that more than any other, his proposal, first introduced in 1943, had the best opportunity to pass both houses. Few Senators could argue with Randolph, a fixture of the US Senate who was widely respected on both sides of the aisle. Senator Mansfield backed Jennings' language, cited as Resolution 147. On 12 March 1970, a different resolution, numbered 545, which had some language differences and is known in some histories as the Mansfield resolution, passed the US Senate by a vote of 64-17, with 14 not voting. Among those in opposition were Senators James O. Eastland, Democrat of Mississippi, and the chairman of the Senate Committee on the Judiciary; Roman Hruska, Republican of Nebraska; Strom Thurmond, Democrat (and later Republican) of South Carolina; and Sam Ervin, Democrat of North Carolina.

The ball was now in the court of the US House of Representatives. Rep. Celler, still displaying his complete opposition to the measure, cautioned, "I will fight like hell against the inclusion of teen-age voting." Celler was even angrier because Mansfield had attached the proposed amendment to an extension of the Voting Rights Act for

1970, a measure he supported.[6] Celler realized that he wished to save the entire bill, so he even threatened to have the House vote on the voting age amendment separately.

In the midst of the Celler fight, President Nixon released a letter he sent to Speaker of the House John McCormack, Majority Leader Carl Albert, and Minority Leader Gerald R. Ford. In the correspondence, dated 27 April 1970, the President stated that he now opposed the extension of voting rights to those under 21 because such a move "represents an unconstitutional assertion of Congressional authority in an area specifically reserved to the States, and that it therefore would not stand the test of challenge in the courts." Nixon even visualized a scenario where the Congress would pass the amendment, the states would ratify it, and those between 18 and 21 would vote in the 1972 general election, only to have the US Supreme Court throw the amendment out as unconstitutional, potentially throwing the presidential election in the US House of Representatives. "The Nation could be confronted with a crisis of the first magnitude," Nixon forewarned.[7] He asked congressional leaders of both parties to pass the Voting Rights Act without the voting age constitutional amendment. Speaker McCormack refused, even though Minority Leader Ford called for a Senate-House conference that would strip out the voting age amendment. When McCormack refused Ford's request to have hearings in Celler's Judiciary Committee and extended debate on the House floor, this was also turned down. Ford was livid. "There have been no hearings held in the Committee on the Judiciary in the House of this proposition that Congress can, by a Federal legislative act, give the right to vote to 18-year-olds in local and State elections...We are asked, in less than one hour, to vote of this proposition. It is the most indefensible procedure I have ever seen."[8]

Extending debate dragged on, most notably because this was the first time a proposed amendment would be "attached" to another piece of legislation. However, because those who wanted a pure constitutional amendment were in the minority, they had to settle for a "rider" to the Voting Rights Act amendment. And, for a time, this appeared to work – states now had to comply with this non-constitutional congressional mandate.

In almost every case of amendments or legislation being passed by Congress and sent to the states, that is the last word anyone has on the matter, at least on the federal level. Everything then usually turns to the states, to see which states ratify the amendment. In case of the Twenty-sixth Amendment, however, an intervening action at the federal level gave new impetus to the movement encouraging rapid ratification.

On 21 December 1970, several months after Congress enacted the Voting Rights Act amendments with the attached language lowering the voting age, the US Supreme Court held, by a 5-4 decision, their opinion in *Oregon v. Mitchell* (400 US 112). The state of Oregon sued the United States government, in this case the personage of Attorney General John N. Mitchell, stating that as a state, it did not want to lower its voting age to 18 from 21, and that, under existing federal law, it did not have to do so. In the majority opinion, written by Justice Hugo Black, the court held that any law, short of a constitutional amendment, applied only to federal and not state and local elections, and upheld Oregon's challenge. Black wrote that Article I, section 4 of the US Constitution lays out the roadmap for voting requirements based on age; this specific article reads:

"The times, Places and Manner of holding Elections for Senators and Representatives, shall be prescribed in each state by the legislature there; but the Congress may at any time by Law make or alter such Regulations, except as to the Place of Senators."

Black wrote that the court's hands were tied; that "Congress has the final authority over federal elections." However, because the US Constitution only dealt with federal, and not state and local elections, it served as a check against an intrusion into the latter, because the federal government might "under the guise of insuring equal protection, blot out all state power, leaving the 50 States little more than impotent figurehead."[9]

In effect, the Court was saying we must uphold current law – but if you choose to change that current law via a constitutional amendment, it would make the decision in that specific case moot. Faced with the realization that only an amendment to the US Constitution could give voting rights to those 18 and older in state and local elections, the push to quickly ratify the proposed amendment gathered steam. By March 1971, opponents to the action were outnumbered, and a pure amendment passed the House on 23 March 1971 by a vote of 400 to 19.

Once the amendment was sent to the states, it took a mere 13 weeks to get the requisite number of states for ratification. Such progress was unheard of, demonstrated by the table below, which shows how long it took for the other amendments to be ratified:

Amendment	Ratification Period	
	Years	Months
1–10	2	3
11	11	
12	7.5	
13	10	
14	2	1
15	1	
16	3	7
17	1	
18	1	1.5
19	1	2.5
20	1	
21	9.5	
22	3	11
23	9	
24	1	5
25	1	7
26	3	
27	202	8*

*Note: *Originally a part of the package of 12 amendments sent to the states on 26 September 1789, it was rejected and only 10 – known as the Bill of Rights – were ratified in 1790. This amendment was initially adopted by only six states, while five others rejected it, well short of the requisite number needed. Over the years, states continued to ratify it, until 1992, when it received enough states to qualify it.*

On 1 July 1971, the Twenty-sixth Amendment was ratified after Ohio and North Carolina ratified it. A few days later, the head of the General Services Administration (GSA) and President Richard Nixon certified it as officially ratified.

Experts and others expected voting rates among the targeted group to rise, especially in the 1972 national election – and rise it did. While 63% of all voters participated, 55.4% of people in the 18-21 age group voted; this was a huge explosion from 1968, of which specific numbers are not available. Historian John Fetto, in a 1999 article examining the voting rates of young adults, wrote that many believed that the increased numbers of voters in this age group would tip the balance of the election to the Democrat, Senator George McGovern of South Dakota. Despite the Vietnam War and McGovern's appeal to the youth vote, a majority of the 18-21 votes went to Republican Richard Nixon, the incumbent. Fetto noted that while the 50% mark in 1972 was "not stellar by any measure" – especially considering that an amendment to the US Constitution had just been passed to extend this right to them -it was the "high-water mark" for that age group in national elections. The numbers of voters in this age bracket saw a slight increase in 1992 in the election of Bill Clinton to the presidency, but after that settled back to historic lows. In 2008, the election of Barack Obama saw an increase back to the 49% level.[10]

Regarding the impact of the lowering of the voting age, historians Nelson Polsby, Aaron Wildavsky, and Steven Schier wrote, "What of the voting habits of young people those under thirty years of age? Until 1972, they were not consistently a significant component of either party's coalition and their comparatively low turnout reduced any impact that their 18 percent share of the voting-age population might have given them. After the voting age was lowered in 1971 from 21 (in most states) to 18 nationwide, and because of the baby boom after World War II, the proportion of the voting-age population under the age of thirty increased to 28 percent, and in the 1970s there was much talk of young people as a separate, presumably more liberal, voting bloc. Since then, as the baby boomers have aged, young people have decreased as a proportion of all voters, representing 17 percent of the total electorate in 2004. Despite the much-touted appeal of the Obama candidacy to younger voters in 2008, their proportion of the electorate only increased slightly, to 18 percent."[11]

Debate in Congress

The debate in the US Senate centered on substitutes and amendments to the original language of the proposed amendment, known as the Mansfield Amendment. This debate was over not the amendment that later passed, but an attachment to the Voting Rights Act amendments, which the US Supreme Court would hold by the end of that year as applying only to federal and not state and local elections, The Congressional Record: 7082-92, 12 March 1970.

VOTING RIGHTS ACT AMENDMENTS OF 1969

The PRESIDING OFFICER. The Chair lays before the Senate the unfinished business which ill be stated by title.

The BILL CLERK. A bill (H.R. 4249) to extend the Voting Rights Act of 1965 respect to the discriminatory use of tests and devices.

The Senate resumed the consideration of the bill.

[...]

Mr. ALLEN.[12] Mr. President, I yield myself so much time as I may require out of the time allotted to me on the amendment.

The PRESIDING OFFICER. The Senator from Alabama is recognized.

Mr. ALLEN. Mr. President, I favor setting the voting age in the United States for all elections at the age of 18 years. I feel that our young people are better qualified they are more knowledgeable, and they are more interested in government and civic and public affairs than I as when I was that age.

I believe that it is only fair and right and proper that the voting age should be set at age 18. In the home State of the junior Sent from Alabama, by Act of Congress our registrars are required to register for voting every person in the State of the age of 21 years of age at the present time without literacy tests, without the ability to read or write and without any great degree of mental awareness.

That requirement has been placed on the people of Alabama by the Federal Government. And the Senator from Alabama feels that it is certainly not fair to require the registering of all people 21 years of age, no matter what the degree of their intelligence or mental awareness, and deny the right to vote to alert, knowledgeable, educated boys and girls of the age of 18 years. So, the junior Senator from Alabama strongly favors setting the voting age at 18 throughout the country.

To that end the junior Senator from Alabama is one of the cosponsors of Senate Joint Resolution 147 by the distinguished senior Senator from West Virginia [Mr. RANDOLPH],[13] which would submit to the States a constitutional amendment setting the voting age at 18 throughout the Nation.

The junior Senator from Alabama favors this method of changing our basis constitutional law. Any attempt to change this voting age by statute would run counter to four provisions of the US Constitution, which give to the State by necessary implication the right to set the qualifications of voters in the respective States.

Article I, section 2 and senate 1 of Article II of the Constitution, and amendments 10 and 17, place this right, this power, this obligation within the power of the respective States.

The States should have this power and this authority. It is a power and authority that has been recognized under our Constitution for over 180 years, since the adoption of the Constitution in 1789.

After the War Between the States,[14] a constitution amendment was submitted dealing with the franchising. When the women of the country were given the right to vote, that right was conferred by constitutional amendment.

When the poll tax was barred as a requirement for voting in Federal elections, that provision was put into our basic law by a constitutional amendment.

So the junior Senator from Alabama believes that such an important, such a basic, and such a fundamental right as the right to vote should be defined by the States.

This thought would be carried forward with a constitutional amendment because it would take ratification by three-fourths of the States and, if the States want to make that change, three-fourths of them favoring the proposal could ratify the amendment.

The 19th amendment, the woman suffrage amendment, as the distinguished Senator from West Virginia yesterday pointed out, was ratified by the necessary three-fourths of the States in 15 months. So this amendment setting the voting age at 18 could easily be submitted to the people and to the States. The method of submission would control whether it was submitted to conventions in the States or the respective legislatures; and the adoption could be easily had prior to the 1972 presidential election.

It is expressly provided in the Mansfield amendment that it does not become effective until January 1, 1971. Therefore, this right, supposedly conferred upon the young people by this statute, would not come into play until after the general elections of 1970.

It is unwise, in my judgment to handle this matter by statute. Not only is it an invasion of States rights, not only does it run roughshod over the Constitution which gives the States the power to set qualifications of voters; but also it is dangerous, and it is on very thin ice as far as the Constitution is concerned.

Let us assume that the statute is enacted. Let us assume that the Congress does pass this statute providing for the voting age to be set at age of 18. Let us assume that 5, 6, or 7 million young people of the age of 18, 19, or 20 go in and register and vote in the national election of 1972.

Let us assume that several days after that election the Supreme Court, in its great wisdom, declared this statute unconstitutional, and it found that 5 million young people have illegally voted in that election. Where would the presidential election be under there circumstances? What sort of confusion would that cause? Who would the President be? How would it be ascertained how many young people voted for one candidate and how many voted for another candidate?

On the other hand, if the pending amendment were adopted, it would set the effective date of this statute, this statutory method of changing the Constitution – and that is what it is, changing the Constitution by statute, and the junior Senator from Alabama submits that cannot be done.

What sort of confusion would reign in this country? Who would the President be? No, if the pending amendment were adopted, it would set the effective date of the amendment at January 1, 1973, after the next presidential election. This would give the Congress ample time to go ahead and handle this matter in the proper fashion of submitting a constitutional amendment. I dare say, in all sincerity, if that were one, the constitutional amendment would be submitted and ratified long before the effective date of this act and long before the 1972 presidential election.

What is the hurry? They could not vote in 1970 under the provisions of the statute itself. This would postpone the effective date until after January 1, 1973; and in all possibility the constitutional amendment would have been adopted long before that time.

Over 72 Members of the Senate – it was 72 at last count – are cosponsors of the constitutional amendment, and it takes only two-thirds of the Senate to pass a constitutional amendment. The amendment is now in the hands of a subcommittee headed by the distinguished Senator from Indiana [Mr. BAYH],[15] who stated on the floor of the Senate that he strongly favors the amendment – in addition, I might say, to favoring the statute, as well. He states a majority of the members of his subcommittee favor the proposal. The Senator from West Virginia states that a majority of the Committee on the Judiciary favors the amendment. The chairman of the committee states that, if the majority of the committee is for the amendment, he will not stand in the way and ill report it to the Senate.

When proposed legislation leaves the committee and is reported to the Senate, the distinguished majority leader sets the flow of consideration of legislation. I think we could very safely assume that the distinguished majority leader, favoring as he does the granting of the voting franchise to those who are 18 years of age, would give prior claim, prior standing to any such amendment, and the Senate would go ahead and vote to submit the amendment. So there is no hurry. There is no reason for a statute aside from the fact that it goes counter to the Constitution, in the judgment of the junior Senator from Alabama.

[...]

Mr. STENNIS.[16] Mr. President, will the Senator yield at this point?

Mr. ALLEN. Yes. I am delighted to yield to the distinguished Senator from Mississippi. [...]

Mr. STENNIS. As I understand it, the Senator is not attacking the entire amendment offered by the distinguished Senator from Montana, but the amendment would just move the provisions forward until January 1, 1973.

Mr. ALLEN. That is exactly right.

Mr. STENNIS. So as to put the provision beyond the forthcoming presidential election.

Mr. ALLEN. That is exactly correct, yes.

Mr. STENNIS. I think it is very timely. I do not agree, as the Senator from Alabama does not agree, with the amendment of the Senator from Montana in this respect. It seems clear to me that there is only one way to reach the end that the Senator from Montana has in mind, and that is through the constitutional amendment process; but there could be disagreement, and I know it is an honest disagreement, among the membership on that question. But, by all means, the matter should not be tied up. Its uncertainty, its constitutionality, and the survival of this provision, the change in the qualification of electors, should not be tied up and involved in the forthcoming presidential election.

That is the primary reason why the Senator has offered this proposal. Is it not?

Mr. ALLEN. That is exactly correct.

Mr. STENNIS. It is certain, it is just as clear as daylight, that this question will be contested. It is a great constitutional question. Is it not?

Mr. ALLEN. It is, indeed.

Mr. STENNIS. It will be challenged, and it should be passed on, should it become statutory law, by the Supreme Court of the United States. Does not the Senator agree with that?

Mr. ALLEN. Yes, that is correct.

[...]

Mr. MANSFIELD.[17] Mr. President, many ghosts and hobgoblins have been created in this Chamber. Many promises have been made. Some promises have not been kept.

From time to time illusions have been created, and one of the greatest illusions is what has been said turning down the amendment offered by the Senator from Montana. It is an amendment many others have joined in cosponsoring. The argument goes that the Judiciary Committee will forthwith report a proposed constitutional amendment seeking to lower the age for voting to 18. It is even suggested that there will be no trouble in obtaining House approval of such a proposal, even though the chairman of the appropriate House committee has indicated – and I recall press reports to this effect – that he is against 18-year-olds voting, regardless of how the ballot is extended to them. And low and behold, some time this year we will have a constitutional amendment which will have been approved by two-thirds of the membership of both Houses and within 2 years it will have been confirmed by threefourths of the legislature [sic] of the 50 States.

There is a good deal of talk of trips nowadays. But that is a pretty long trip. And the constitutional amendment process seeking to lower the voting age to 18 has been one of many pitfalls and has produced nothing in the way of actual achievement.

I recall the great furor in this country that was raised at the end of the last presidential election for a direct vote for the Presidency.

I have noticed since then that various other arguments have come up, that the possibility of getting this constitutional amendment out has been decreased somewhat and the possibility of getting it through both Houses during this session of Congress has become an unreality.

So I would not be taken away with the thoughts, promises, or encouragement of the moment. But I would like to stick to the facts, and I would like to see the Senate bite the bullet on the issue of allowing the 18-year-olds to vote.

There have been some questions raised about why these youngsters should be given this opportunity and this right to exercise the franchise; this conferring of a duty, so to speak. And I do not look at it in that way, because I think all Americans are born free – at least are supposed to be under the Constitution – and all Americans have equal rights. And as far as the age of 21 is concerned, it has been fully arbitrary and of no realistic value, in my opinion, in the light of the intelligence, the idealism, and the educational achievement of the youth of today.

[...]

Mr. KENNEDY.[18] Mr. President, will the Senator yield to me for 3 minutes?

Mr. MANSFIELD. I yield 3 minutes to the Senator from Massachusetts.

Mr. KENNEDY. Mr. President, I rise to second what the distinguished majority leader has suggested, with particular reference to his remarks on the question of whether the pending amendment will cause any delay or uncertainty in elections.

An obvious precedent is the history of the Voting Rights Act of 1965. Although the 1965 act made major changes in the election laws of many States, I am not aware that it caused any unreasonable delay or uncertainty in any elections that were held before its constitutionality was settled by the Supreme Court. Yet, we heard time and time again in the debate over the 1965 act that we would have mass confusion in the elections around the country. The argument was made that there would be thousands of voters whose participation in the election was uncertain. It was said that we would not know if that act was legal or illegal, and that countless elections would be held up. We hear these same arguments applied today. But the precedent of the 1965 act demonstrates that such arguments are unpersuasive. The act was passed in August 1965, and the constitutionality of its provisions was not settled until many months later, well into the spring of 1966. Yet, as I have said, there is no evidence that the status of any elections was clouded. Today, the amendment we are offering is even less likely to cloud the status of any elections. In 1965, the act was not passed until August in the non-Federal election year of 1965. The bill now on the floor will in all probability be passed several months in this year of 1970, but the effective date is January 1, 1971, for the voting age amendment, which is also a non-Federal election year. Thus, there was far more time allowed for a decision on the constitutionality of this amendment than there was on the 1965 act, before any elections would possibly be clouded by any uncertainty over it. I think we are meeting our responsibilities with respect to any possible unconstitutional uncertainty. We have gone far to insure that the electoral process will be secure and valid.

[...]

The PRESIDING OFFICER. All time having expired, the question is on agreeing to amendment No. 552 of the Senator from Alabama [Mr. ALLEN] to the amendment of the Senator from Montana [Mr. MANSFIELD]. On this question, the yeas and nays have been ordered, and the clerk will call the roll.

Author's note: The Senate then voted, with 15 yeas, 72 nays, and 13 not voting. Debate then shifted to a report on estuaries by the Department of the Interior, and resumed later.

VOTING RIGHTS ACT AMENDMENTS OF 1969

The Senate continued with the consideration of the bill (H.R. 4249) to extend the Voting Rights Act of 1965 with respect to the discriminatory use of tests and devices.

AMENDMENT NO. 551

Mr. MILLER. Mr. President, I call up by amendment No. 551, and ask that it be stated.

The PRESIDING OFFICER. The amendment will be stated.

The ASSISTANT LEGISLATIVE CLERK. The Senator from Iowa [Mr. MILLER] proposes an amendment as follows:

On page 2, strike from lines 7 and 8 the words "voting in any primary or in any election..." and in lieu thereof the following: "full rights and responsibilities of citizenship."

Mr. MILLER. Mr. President, I yield myself such time as I may require.

First, I would like to say in complete frankness that I think the author of the pending amendment, the distinguished majority leader, understands why there are a number of us who, in good conscience, cannot support a change in the voting eligibility rights by a statute.

I listened with great interest and considerable agreement to some of the arguments he has made, arguments which...

Mr. President, may we have order?

The PRESIDING OFFICER. The Senate will be in order.

Mr. MILLER. Arguments which I myself could make if I were a member of my State legislature; or which I myself could make if the pending measure were a proposed constitutional amendment.

There was one thing that particularly appealed to me about the arguments of the Senator from Montana. Over and over again, he has talked about the "responsibilities" that the young people should assume. I am offering this amendment, not for the purpose of doing any harm to his amendment at all, but, while with the understanding that I cannot in good conscience support the Mansfield amendment, with the objective of trying to make it into a better measure so that, if it is passed by Congress and it is upheld by the Supreme Court, we will have a better measure on the books.

Under my amendment, the declaration set forth in the Mansfield amendment would read as follows:

The Congress finds and declares that the imposition and application of the requirement that a citizen be twentyone years of age as a precondition to full rights and responsibilities of citizenship

"(1) denies and abridges...

And so on.

To me, this matter of 21 years or 18 years has to do, not just with voting, but with the full rights and responsibilities of citizenship. The Senator from Montana has, in his remarks, time after time called attention to responsibilities. I fully agree with that. But there is not a word about responsibilities in his amendment. If my amendment were agreed to, we would talk about full rights and responsibilities of citizenship in connection with this matter of age.

I suggest that probably the highest right and responsibility of citizenship is the right and responsibility of voting. However, there are other inherent features of full citizenship.

Paragraph 1, line 9 of the Mansfield amendment refers to the denial and abridgment of the inherent constitutional rights of citizens 18 years of age and over. I suggest that in addition to the voting right and responsibility there are other inherent rights and responsibilities, such as jury service. Unless there was something in the statutes that I am not familiar with, I believe that once a person is an eligible voter, that person then is eligible for not only the right but also the responsibility of jury service.

Marriage: It seems to me that if a person is old enough to vote, he is old enough to enter into a contract of marriage.

Inheriting property in their own name: In many States now, unless a person is 21, he cannot inherit property in his own name, and a Guardian or a trustee has to be established.

Legal and binding contracts: This is both a right and a responsibility. In many States, unless one is 21 years of age, a contract is not enforceable.

The jurisdiction of juvenile courts: In some States, juvenile courts have jurisdiction over people 18 years of age. It seems to me that if a person is old enough to vote, that person is old enough to get out of the jurisdiction of a juvenile court. I will say that most States, to my knowledge, do not go up as high as 18 years of age for juvenile court jurisdiction, but some do.

The coverage of State child labor laws: It is my understanding that in a few States child labor laws cover up through the age of 18, and possibly 19.

I suggest Mr. President that these rights and responsibilities are just as inherent – constitutional rights and responsibilities – as that of voting. They are just as much protected by the due process and equal protection of the laws guarantees under the 14th amendment as the right and responsibility of voting.

It seems to me that when Congress makes a declaration of policy having to do...

Mr. KENNEDY. Mr. President, will the Senator yield on that point?

Mr. MILLER. I yield.

Mr. KENNEDY. Is the Senator suggesting that the age to consume alcoholic beverages is equivalent to the Senate of the United States reducing the voting age to 18?

Mr. MILLER. No; I have not said anything about that. If the Senator from Massachusetts was listening to my arguments, I was pointing out such things as marriage, inheriting property, legal and binding contracts, jurisdiction of juvenile courts, and coverage of child labor laws.

I know that there are some who have argued this point. I do not make that argument.

Mr. KENNEDY. Is the Senator's proposal limited to the five categories he has mentioned?

Mr. MILLER. No; I am not limiting that, necessarily. As a matter of fact, I was going to mention another one – hunting and fishing permits. In some States, if one is 18 years of age or under, there is a special fee.

Mr. KENNEDY. The Senator is equating this with reducing the voting age to 18?

Mr. MILLER. I am pointing out that there are rights and responsibilities that are just as inherent in citizenship as voting. But this is my point. Voting is such a tremendously responsible and important right that if we are going to cover voting, a fortiori,[19] all these others ought to come along.

What I am trying to do is to point out is that when we make a declaration of policy in Congress, a national policy, regarding the deprivation of rights on account of age, it seems to me that, instead of confining it to voting rights, we ought to talk about full rights and responsibilities of citizenship.

Furthermore this declaration will fit with the rest of the amendment, because in paragraph (b) it says:

In order to secure the constitutional rights set forth in subsection (a).

Those rights are referred to win we talk about full rights and responsibilities of citizenship.

Mr. President, as I have said, I offer this for the purpose of improving the amendment. To me, this is a very awesome and historical declaration of policy by Congress. I do not leave that we ought to confine our attention only to the rights and responsibilities of 18-year-olds with respect to voting. We would have a better declaration of policy if we talked about full rights and responsibilities of citizenship.

Mr. President, I yield the floor.

Mr. MANSFIELD. Mr. President, I yield myself 5 minutes; thereafter it would be my intention to yield back the remainder of the time and bring this matter to a conclusion.

May I say to my distinguished colleague the Senator from Iowa that jury service and other responsibilities for 18-year-olds are propositions with which I think I might agree. So far as marriage for 18-year-olds is concerned, I am all for it. I do not know of a State in the Union in which people of that age cannot get married, and in some States matrimony is permitted at a younger age.

Mr. MILLER. Mr. President, will the Senator yield at that point?

Mr. MANSFIELD. I yield.

Mr. MILLER. I believe that in some States the consent of one or both parents is required.

Mr. MANSFIELD. If so, it is the case in very few States. But, by and large, I think it is a generally accepted tenet that young adults can be married at 18 on the basis of their own desires and wishes.

Contracts, I think, may fall in the same category.

As to juvenile and adult courts there may be differences; but, by and large, the age of 18 is the mark of differentiation between the jurisdiction of a juvenile court and courts that try adults. If one is 18 or over, he is considered an adult, he is tried as an adult and he must suffer the penalty of laws designed for adults.

I do not know too much about child labor laws, but I imagine that they do not apply to a person [of the age of] 18. One would have to be even younger, it is my guess, to be treated as a child under the child labor laws. Their application covers those anywhere up to 10 and 16, generally speaking.

The proposal to which the Senator seeks to offer his amendment, I would point out, deals with voting rights for 18-year-olds. The bill and the Scott substitute deal with voting rights. Therefore, I think that what the Senator from Iowa seeks should not be attempted in this bill; because, in my opinion, it would tend to becloud and befuddle the issue of the vote which is now clear-cut, straight, and understood by everyone, without any ifs, ands, or buts.

The amendment offered by the Senator from Iowa goes beyond the confines of voting, with which my amendment is concerned, and with which the bill and the Scott-Hart substitute our concerned. It deals with issues on which there has not been hearings, to my knowledge; whereas, on the question of voting rights, there have been ample hearings down through the years bringing us to today – when there is an opportunity for action for the first time, I hope that opportunity is not jeopardized.

In that respect I am not certain what the effect of the Senator's amendment would be, or what the words that would be added to the preamble of my amendment would accomplish, or whether even they would accomplish what the Senator from Iowa seeks to accomplish.

[...]

Mr. MANSFIELD. Mr. President, I ask unanimous consent that the Senator from West Virginia may proceed for 2 additional minutes.

The PRESIDING OFFICER. Is there objection? The Chair hears none, and it is so ordered.

Mr. RANDOLPH. Mr. President, I have said – and I repeat – that the arguments in this matter have been most persuasive on both sides of the approach. We are all seeking a common objective. I prefer the constitutional amendment route over the statute route. I believe it is sounder from a legal standpoint, and many of my Senate colleagues have joined me in urging a constitutional amendment.

Senate Joint Resolution 147 will be reported favorably, I believe, by the Judiciary Committee. I would expect that the measure when reported will be held on the Senate Calendar for action, so that if this amendment to the Voting Rights bill fails to achieve acceptance in the Senate-House conference, the Senate will be prepared to act immediately.

❧❧❧❧❧❧

Realizing that a statute lowering the voting age from 21 to 18 was unconstitutional, as held by the US Supreme Court, the House followed the Senate in passing an amendment to the US Constitution that was straightforward in its goal of lowering the voting age from 21 to 18. The argument here was how much support a proposed amendment would get in the lower house of Congress, Washington: Government Printing Office, 17 March 1971.

LOWERING THE VOTING AGE TO 18

[...]

The Chair recognizes the gentleman from New York [Mr. CELLER].

Mr. CELLER.[20] Mr. Chairman, I yield myself 10 minutes.

Mr. Chairman, this is a rather happy occasion for me to sponsor and cosponsor the so-called 26th amendment to the Constitution. It has been my privilege heretofore to cosponsor the 23d – extending the right to vote in presidential elections to residents of the District of Columbia – 24th abolishing the poll tax in Federal elections – and the 25th dealing with Presidential inability and succession – amendments, three constitutional amendments, and if this 26th amendment is ratified I will lay claim to sponsoring and cosponsoring four constitutional amendments. I say with all due modesty this is rather an achievement, and an achievement that I am extremely proud of.

Mr. Chairman, a government of, by, and for the people should be deeply interested in the right to vote. This right is the most basic of all.

The ballot box is the mechanism by which the will of the people shapes government. Democracy draws its strength and assures its survival through the exercise of the vote.

Throughout our history a continuing question has occupied the attention of Americans. Who, among our citizens is, shall be eligible to participate as voters? On at least four occasions our Constitution has been amended to enlarge or protect political participation. The 15th amendment – removing the test of color from the ballot box; the 19th amendment – woman's suffrage; the 23d amendment – District of Columbia vote for President and Vice President; and the 24th amendment – abolition of the poll tax. In recent years the Congress has vigorously acted to assure the free exercise of the right to vote. The proposed 26th amendment to the Constitution embodied in House Joint Resolution 223 represents another step in the American tradition of enlarging the franchise.

Members will recall that provisions of the Voting Rights Act Amendments of 1970 lowered the minimum voting age to 18 in Federal, State, and local primary and general elections. The measure was overwhelmingly approved in both Houses of Congress. Some of us expressed reservations about the constitutional authority of the Congress to modify voting age qualifications by statute. Nevertheless, we confidently expected a prompt resolution of the question by the Supreme Court. Six months after its enactment, the Supreme Court rendered its decision on the constitutionality of various provisions of the act. It upheld all provisions of the act save those reducing the minimum voting age in all elections. By a 5 to 4 decision the Court upheld the lower the voting age for national elections but invalidated the statute insofar as it attempted to lower the minimum voting age in State and local elections. As a result of the Court's decision, two sets of electoral machinery must be established in 47 States, which to date have not lowered the voting age to 18 for State and local elections. This dual voting age system is estimated by the Bureau of the Census to affect well over 10 million potential voters, or approximately 8.5 percent of the resident population 18 or over.

Although nine States today permit persons under 21 to vote in all elections, only three, Alaska, Georgia, and Kentucky, permit 18-year-olds to vote – Massachusetts, Minnesota, and Montana require at least 19 years of age; Hawaii, Maine, and Nebraska require at least 20 years of age. A dual-age voting system will be expensive and administratively burdensome to operate. A recent nationwide survey among election officials indicates that separate electoral facilities and procedures will have to be developed; separate Federal ballots would have to be prepared for each congressional district. Separate registration, separate voting and separate counting of the newly enfranchised present serious threats of uncertainty and delay in the tabulation of the election results in 1972. Additional voting machines may have to be purchased in order to accommodate the 18-to-20-year-old voter who at present is only permitted to vote in national elections. Alternatively, mechanisms to lock levers in voting machines under State and local offices may have to be installed, or separate paper ballots listing only Federal candidates may have to be used. Resort to one or more of these procedures would involve additional personnel, additional training, and additional expenses.

[...]

You know, youth wanes by increasing years, but the increase usually brings wisdom. Of course, I cannot be young again by any manner of means any more save in spirit. But maybe by offering this amendment I can at least wear, shall I say, the rose of youth.

The youth of America is our oldest tradition. That tradition has been in existence for over three centuries. Let us offer it our respect by a favorable vote.

I do not believe that youth will fail us if we offer our youth the privilege and responsibility of the ballot. It has been said that in the lexicon of youth there is no such word as "fail." They will not "fail" us. Some of our youth have disappointed us, but the preponderant majority are as sound of mind as they are strong in body. In the long run our voting youth will not betray their elders.

Indeed, eventually we all must resign ourselves to their care as we grow older. Thus, let us prepare them early by giving them the ballot.

The CHAIRMAN. The Chair recognizes the gentleman from Virginia [Mr. POFF].

Mr. POFF.[21] Mr. Chairman, I yield myself 5 minutes.

Last year when this issue came into focus I announced my support of a constitutional amendment. I reaffirm my position. It is too bad the Congress did not proceed initially on that course, because the result of the course that was chosen has been near disastrous. The Congress erred in failing to take the constitutional amendment route, and then in the drafting of the statute itself, the Congress erred in at least two particulars. The first error was in the language of the clause addressed to the 18-year-old franchise. That language limits its thrust and effect to primaries and elections. In doing so, it excludes from its impact other anterior steps in the voting process, including nomination, either by petition or by convention.

Finally the Congress erred in confining the impact of its statute to the denial of the right to vote, when, in fact, if the House intended to be thorough, it should have also proscribed the abridgment of that right.

Now in the shadow of the Court's decision,[22] we are confronted with what is called, in shorthand terminology, dual-age voting. As the chairman has indicated, we do face next year, unless this problem is promptly and effectively corrected, confusion, chaos, and possibly other difficulties at the polls.

We have three options as we choose a solution. We have only three. One would be to repeal the faulty statute we passed last year and thereby restandardize within each State the voting age in both State and Federal elections.

The second will be to allow the individual States individually to decide that they could live with the duality problem or should adjust their own laws to standardize the voting age at 18. And, finally, we can standardize the voting age at 18 by approving this constitutional amendment. The first of those alternatives, let us face it, is absolutely unlikely. The second is altogether unlikely. The third is the only reasonable, feasible, functional choice.

As responsible legislators we must make that decision today. We must propose this constitutional amendment promptly and allow the individual States, as the Constitution explicitly provides, to make their own decisions whether the Nation should attempt to live with this problem of dual voting or solve it by this change in our Federal Constitution.

Let me suggest that change in no way offends our federalism. On the contrary, it accords with it, because the States are given the opportunity in the amending process to make their own judgments. I repeat, it is the only mechanism by which the States can effectively resolve the dual age voting problem.

It is possible for them to so seasonably. It will not be long before the primaries are upon us and the State legislatures must act, if they are to do so effectively, sometime before early spring of 1972.

[...]

Mr. POFF. Mr. Chairman, I yield 5 minutes to the distinguished gentleman from Michigan [Mr. HUTCHINSON].

Mr. HUTCHINSON.[23] Mr. Chairman, I labor under no illusion that this proposition is in the least part in jeopardy before this House. I anticipate that it will be adopted by the requisite two-thirds vote of this House this afternoon and before the afternoon is very much older.

I may say that personally I have no fear of the 18-year-old franchise. I believe that in the two States which have had reasonably long experience with it, it has been demonstrated that the younger voters – the 18-, 19-, and the 20-year-old voters – are absorbed into the general pattern and there is no disruption that should cause anybody any trouble.

But, Mr. Chairman, I have decided in my best conscience that I must vote against this proposal this afternoon, because the people of Michigan so decisively in the last election voted it down.

In 1970, only 39 percent of the people of the State of Michigan voted in favor of amending our State constitution to extend the voting franchise to those 18 years of age and older. Only 39 percent were in favor. In my own district, only 37 percent of the people voted for it. In fact, the issue carried in only nine precincts out of 261 precinct in my district.

It occurs to me that if ever there was a mandate at the ballot box on an issue certainly here is that mandate.

I know the argument is made there has been an additional ingredient added into the situation, in that last December the Supreme Court in effect wrote a law different from that which the Congress voted and extended the right to vote in 18-year-olds only in national elections. Congress never passed any such law. The congressional act was intended to cover all elections. But the Supreme Court says what we did was to act only in national elections.

I know that additional ingredient has been added into this situation since the 1970 elections, but at the time the people of Michigan voted on this issue Congress had already spoken. The President had already signed into law the Voting Rights Act of 1970, which included title III, which purported to extend the right to vote in all elections across the board, State and local, as well as Federal.

Nevertheless, the people of my State resoundingly said "No" and the people of my district resoundingly said "No." So, under the circumstances, I feel myself mandated to represent them here.

So often I have people say to me "What good does it do to vote?" I say to you that if the decision of the people made at the ballot box is to be completely ignored, indeed that question becomes awfully hard to answer.

Mr. PUCINSKI.[24] Mr. Chairman, will the gentleman yield for a question?

Mr. HUTCHINSON. I yield to the gentleman from Illinois.

Mr. PUCINSKI. I appreciate the gentleman's statement that the people of Michigan have by a resounding vote turned down the vote for 18-year-olds. Would the gentleman venture a guess as to what the outcome might have been if indeed the 18-, 19-, and 20-year-olds had been permitted to vote on that proposition.

Mr. HUTCHINSON. I dare say that the result would not have been different in Michigan nor would it have been different in my district, for the reason it was so overwhelmingly defeated.

Mr. PUCINSKI. But the question is, was it defeated by those who are not directly involved in terms of permission to do so. If we had permitted 18-, 19-, or 20-year-olds to vote on this particular question as to whether or not they should be permitted hereafter to vote in elections, do you think the outcome would have been different?

Mr. HUTCHINSON. No; I think the outcome would have been the same.

Mr. CELLER. Mr. Chairman, I yield 5 minutes to the gentleman from Texas [Mr. POAGE].

Mr. POAGE.[25] Mr. Chairman, I do not have any mandate. It has been some years since the people of Texas voted on this question. They rejected it at that time. I do not know what they will do in the future. I am not trying to say what my State or any State should do within its own jurisdiction, nor am I trying to pass upon whether 18-, 19-, or 20-year-olds or 16-year-olds or 12-year-olds should vote. I am, however, of the opinion that we would do well to maintain our system of a federal union with the States having some voice in their own internal affairs, and certainly retaining the right to fix the qualifications of voters for local office.

I know that there has been a strong argument made that now the States must maintain two separate accounts to determine who may vote only for Federal officials and who may vote for State and local officials, such as for justices of the peace. True, as a result of legislation and of court decisions the State election officials have to keep two separate sets of ballots and it is expensive. I heard the argument made that in one of the States in the Northeast it cost them $700,000 to meet this double standard and the argument is made that to avoid that expense we should pass this constitutional amendment.

Why do we have to pass a constitutional amendment if, let us say, in Texas they want citizens to vote at 18? Congress does not have to submit to any kind of amendment. If Maine or Oklahoma wants to allow 18-year-olds to vote they can allow it without any action by this body. That can be determined by the home State as it should be. The legislators of any State can right now submit amendments to the State Constitution and if the people of the State involved want it, they can pass it. I have no quarrel with that. If Ohio wants to give the ballot to 16-year-olds that is their right but I do not want Ohio or any other State to tell Texas what we must do, nor do I want taxes to try to control the local affairs of any other State. I do not know why we should be dictated to by some other States, even though three-fourths of the other States want some other age limit.

I do not know why it should be our business here to deny the people of any State the right to determine who are the voters in their States for State offices. The Supreme Court held that is the privilege of the States at the present time. Now we propose to come along and say if a three-fourths majority of the States decide that they want to make some other State give the ballot in local elections to someone 18 years of age, that this majority is justified in imposing their will on the States which may have a different view. I do not believe anything of the kind. I think if Virginia wants to give the ballot to 12-year-olds, it is perfectly all right with me, but I do not want it in Texas, and I do not think the people of Texas want it.

[...]

Mr. POFF. Mr. Chairman, I yield 5 minutes to the distinguished gentleman from Illinois [Mr. McCLORY].

Mr. McCLORY.[26] Mr. Chairman, in urging overwhelming approval today of the proposed constitutional amendment extending voting rights to our young citizens 18, 19, and 20 years of age – I want to recall that I had sponsored and supported this measure in earlier Congresses.

It had been my hope that the shortcut route of extending voting rights to these younger citizens by way of legislation – in contrast to an amendment to the Federal Constitution – might satisfy the constitutional requirements.

It now appears that the constitutional requirement was satisfied by our action at the last session insofar as Federal elections are concerned. However, the US Supreme Court, in the case of Oregon against Mitchell, ruled on December 1, 1970, that an amendment to the Constitution would be essential to lower the voting age for State and local elections.

Our present dilemma results from the action which we took in the last Congress as construed by the Supreme Court. In other words, we will now have a dual system of voting – one applicable to State and local elections – and the other applicable to elections of Federal offices.

According to a report filed in the other body just a few weeks ago, it was shown that in my State of Illinois the Secretary of State, John W. Lewis, estimates that there could be a 40to 50-percent increase in election costs because of the need to keep two sets of registration books and two sets of ballots. The chairman of the Chicago Board of Election Commissioners estimated the additional cost for the city of Chicago as ranging from $150,000 to $200,000 at each general election.

By acting speedily here today and submitting that constitutional change to the States for ratification, the confusion, the threatened additional expense, and the distinct possibility of voting irregularities – and fraud – can be avoided.

[...]

Mr. CELLER. Mr. Chairman, I yield 5 minutes to the gentleman from New Jersey [Mr. Howard].

Mr. HOWARD.[27] Mr. Chairman, I am very, very happy that this legislation concerning a constitutional amendment for the 18-year-old vote is before the House of Representatives today.

In the 90th Congress I was the sponsor of House Joint Resolution 18 which would have provided for an 18-yearold vote in America.

In the 91st Congress I was the sponsor of House Joint Resolution 18 which, again, would have provided for an 18-year-old vote.

Mr. Chairman, we have seen the past history of this legislation. We are aware that we did pass legislation for an 18-year-old vote which the Supreme Court determined could only apply in Federal elections.

We are today going to pass I am sure a constitutional amendment which will provide for the 18-year-old vote throughout the Nation. I believe that this is fair, that this is just, that this is something that our country should do in order to recognize that our 18-year-olds, our 19-year-olds, and our 20-year-olds are adults in America.

But, Mr. Chairman, I believe that the most important thing that we should concern ourselves with today is to see that, in reality, our 20-, 19-, an 18-year-olds do actually vote in America in all elections.

As we all know, this legislation must be accepted by 38 State legislatures throughout the country. We also know that many, perhaps, two dozen States in past years have voted down on referendums [of the] the 18or 19-year-old vote proposal. I feel that unless we improve this legislation, unless we make it acceptable to people throughout the country, we will never get the 38 States to agree. Therefore, we will not have a truly 18-, 19-, and 20-year-old vote in this Nation.

Mr. Chairman, I shall offer at the proper time an amendment to this legislature which involves a bill I introduced several weeks ago to provide for a moving down from 21 to 18 the age of majority in this Nation under all law.

This is what Great Britain recently handled the 18-year-old vote. They said, yes, we will give all of the privileges of adults to people who are 20, 19, and 18, but we will also give them all the responsibilities of adults at ages 20, 19 and 18, and that means responsibility for signing contracts and many other things.

There is an indication that perhaps this amendment may be out of order; and a point of order may be made against this amendment because it is not germane. I feel that it is absolutely germane. In this legislation we are talking about privileges and responsibilities being given to people who are 20, 19, and 18. My amendment reducing the age of majority from 21 to 18 will do exactly the same thing – it will deal with privileges and responsibilities of people 20, 19, and 18 years of age.

I hope that this will be considered, because I feel many people in the House and perhaps many members of the Committee on the Judiciary who may not be in favor of an 18-year-old vote are well aware that we can pass this today. We can say we did it here in the House of Representatives, we got a two-thirds vote on it, and so we are in favor of reducing the voting age, knowing that many State legislatures will not bite the bullet, will not, in view of the recent referendum which they have had on this issue, agree, and in reality we will not have an across-the-board 18-, 19-, and 20-year-old vote in this country. But I feel if we add this amendment to the provision, if we say yes to the young people, we not only want to give you the vote, but we also think you are adult enough to be able to handle [the] responsibilities of majority in this Nation, then I feel that we will be able to see in a very short time 38 States agree with what the Senate did a short while ago, and what we are about to do here today, we may then really say to the young people, we believe that you are truly adult.

Historical Background Documents

In this letter from President Richard Nixon to the leaders of both Houses of Congress, the President goes on record as opposing the inclusion of language lowering the voting age in the Voting Rights Act of 1970, 27 April 1970.

A constitutional issue of great importance is currently before the House. As you know, the Senate has attached to the bill modifying and extending the Voting Rights Act of 1965 a rider that purports to enable Americans between the ages of 18 and 21 to vote in Federal, State and local elections.

I say "purports" because I believe it would not in fact confer the vote. I believe that it represents an unconstitutional assertion of Congressional authority in an area specifically reserved to the States, and that it therefore would not stand the test of challenge in the courts. This belief is shared by many of the Nation's leading constitutional scholars.

I strongly favor the 18-year-old vote. I strongly favor enactment of the Voting Rights Bill. But these are entirely separate issues, each of which deserves consideration on its own merits. More important, each needs to be dealt with in a way that is constitutionally permissible – and therefore, in a way that will work.

Because the issue is now before the House, I wish to invite the urgent attention of the Members to the grave constitutional questions involved in the 18-year-old vote rider, and to the possible consequences of ignoring those questions.

STATUTE VS. CONSTITUTIONAL AMENDMENT

The matter immediately at issue is not whether 18-year-olds should be given the vote, but how: by simple statute, or by constitutional amendment.

The argument for attempting it by statute is one of expediency. It appears easier and quicker.

The constitutional amendment route is admittedly more cumbersome, but it does appear that such an amendment could be readily approved. A resolution proposing such an amendment already has been introduced in the Senate, sponsored by two-thirds of the members, the same number required for passage. Sentiment in the House seems strongly in favor. Some contend that ratification would be a long and uncertain process. However, public support for the 18-year-old vote has been growing, and certainly the submission to the States of a constitutional amendment, passed by two-thirds of both Houses and endorsed by the President, would provide powerful additional momentum. An historical footnote is pertinent: When the women's suffrage amendment was proposed in 1919, many said the States would never go along – but ratification was completed in less than 15 months.

If the Senate provision is passed by the Congress, and if it is later declared unconstitutional by the courts, it will have immense and possibly disastrous effects.

At the very least, it will have raised false hopes among millions of young people – led by the Congress to believe they had been given the vote, only to discover later that what the Congress had purported to confer was not in its power to give.

It will have cost valuable time, during which a constitutional amendment could have been submitted to the States and the process of ratification gone forward. It would almost certainly mean that the 18-year-old vote could not be achieved before the 1972 election.

Beyond this, there looms the very real possibility that the outcome of thousands of State and local elections, and possibly even the next national election, could be thrown in doubt: because if those elections took place before the process of judicial review had been completed, no one could know for sure whether the votes of those under 21 had been legally cast. It takes little imagination to realize what this could mean. The Nation could be confronted with a crisis of the first magnitude. The possibility that a Presidential election, under our present system, could be thrown into the House of Representatives is widely regarded as dangerous; but suppose that a probably unconstitutional grant of the 18-year-old vote left the membership of the House unsettled as well?

The Senate measure contains a provision seeking an early test of its constitutionality, but there can be no guarantee that such a test would actually be completed before elections took place. And the risk of chaos, if it were not completed, is real.

THE CONSTITUTIONAL QUESTIONS

On many things the Constitution is ambiguous. On the power to set voting qualifications, however, the Constitution is clear and precise: within certain specified limits, this power belongs to the States. Three separate provisions vest this power with the States: Article I, Section 2 (election of members of the House of Representatives), the Tenth Amendment (reserved powers) and the Seventeenth Amendment (direct election of Senators) all lodge this power with the States. There are four provisions placing limitations on this power: the vote cannot be limited on grounds of race (the Fifteenth Amendment), sex (the Nineteenth Amendment), or failure to pay a poll tax (the Twenty-fourth Amendment); nor can States impose voting qualifications so arbitrary, invidious or irrational as to constitute a denial of equal protection of the laws (the Fourteenth Amendment).

Advocates of the proposal that passed the Senate rely on the power given Congress under the Fourteenth Amendment to enforce equal protection of the laws, and particularly on the Supreme Court's 1966 decision in the case of *Katzenbach v. Morgan*. This case upheld Federal legislation enfranchising residents of New York who had attended school in Puerto Rico, and who were literate in Spanish but not in English. However, I do not believe that the Court's decision in *Katzenbach v. Morgan* authorizes the power now asserted by the Senate to enfranchise young people. Neither do I believe it follows that because Congress has power to suspend literacy tests for voting throughout the Nation, as the new Voting Rights Act would do, it has power also to decide for the entire Nation what the proper age qualification should be.

Where Puerto Ricans were denied the right to vote, the Court could readily conclude that there had been discriminatory treatment of an ethnic minority. This was especially so because of the particular circumstances of those whose rights were at issue: US citizens by birth, literate in Spanish, but not literate in English because their schools, though under the American flag, had used Spanish as the language of instruction.

Similarly with literacy tests: the Court already has upheld the right of Congress to bar their use where there is presumptive evidence that they have been used in a discriminatory fashion. If Congress now finds that literacy tests everywhere impose a special burden on the poor and on large numbers of black Americans, and for this reason abolishes literacy tests everywhere, it is using the same power which was upheld when the Court sustained the Voting Rights Act of 1965.

To go on, however, and maintain that the 21-year voting age is discriminatory in a constitutional sense is a giant leap. This limitation—as I believe—may be no longer justified, but it certainly is neither capricious nor irrational. Even to set the limit at 18 is to recognize that it has to be set somewhere. A 21-year voting age treats all alike, working no invidious distinction among groups or classes. It has been the tradition in this country since the Constitution was adopted, and it was the standard even before; it still is maintained by 46 of the 50 states; and, indeed, it is explicitly recognized by Section 2 of the Fourteenth Amendment itself as the voting age.

If it is unconstitutional for a State to deny the vote to an 18-year-old, it would seem equally unconstitutional to deny it to a 17-year-old or a 16-year-old. As long as the question is simply one of judgment, the Constitution gives

Congress no power to substitute its judgment for that of the states in a matter such as age qualification to vote which the Supreme Court has recognized is one which the States may properly take into consideration.

ONE CONSTITUTION

A basic principle of constitutional law is that there are no trivial or less important provisions of the Constitution. There are no constitutional corners that may safely be cut in the service of a good cause. The Constitution is indivisible. It must be read as a whole. No provision of it, none of the great guarantees of the Bill of Rights is secure if we are willing to say that any provision can be dealt with lightly in order to achieve one or another immediate end. Neither high purpose nor expediency is a good excuse. We damage respect for law, we feed cynical attitudes toward law, whenever we ride roughshod over any law, let alone any constitutional provision, because we are impatient to achieve our purposes.

To pass a popular measure despite the Constitutional prohibition, and then to throw on the Court the burden of declaring it unconstitutional, is to place a greater strain and burden on the Court than the Founding Fathers intended, or than the Court should have to sustain. To enact the Senate proposal would be to challenge the Court to accept, or to reject, a fateful step in the redistribution of powers and functions, not only between the Federal Government and the States but also between itself and the Congress.

Historically, under the Fourteenth Amendment as well as under many other provisions of the Constitution, it has been the duty of the Court to define and enforce the division of powers between the Federal Government and the States. Section 5 of the Fourteenth Amendment gives Congress power to "enforce" Constitutionallyprotected rights against intrusion by the States; but the primary role in defining what those rights are belongs to the Court.

For the most part, the Court has acted with due deference and respect for the views of Congress, and for Congress' assessment of facts and conditions and the needs to which they give rise. But the Court has had the last word.

However, it is difficult to see how the Court could uphold the Senate proposal on the 18-year-vote without conceding that Congress now has the last word.

To present this challenge to the Court would thus raise equal and opposite dangers: on the one hand, if the Court acquiesced, its own power as the protector of our rights could be irreparably diminished; and on the other, if the Court rebuffed the challenge, the often valuable latitude Congress now has under broad readings of its Fourteenth Amendment power might in consequence be severely limited. Neither outcome, in my view, would be desirable.

THE PATH OF REASON

I have recently canvassed many of the Nation's leading constitutional scholars for their views on the Senate proposal. Some feel that, by a broad reading of *Katzenbach v. Morgan*, the proposal's constitutionality could be sustained. The great majority, however, regard it as unconstitutional—and they voice serious concern not only for the integrity of the Constitution but also for the authority of the Court, if it should be sustained.

At best, then, it would be enacted under a heavy constitutional cloud, with its validity in serious doubt. Even those who support the legislation most vigorously must concede the existence of a serious constitutional question.

At worst, it would throw the electoral process into turmoil during a protracted period of legal uncertainty, and finally leave our young people frustrated, embittered and voteless. I therefore urge:

That the 18-year-old vote rider be separated from the bill extending the Voting Rights Act.

That the Voting Rights Bill be approved.

That Congress proceed expeditiously to secure the vote for the Nation's 18-, 19-, and 90-year-olds in the one way that is plainly provided for in the Constitution, and the one way that will leave no doubt as to its validity: Constitutional amendment.

Sincerely,

RICHARD NIXON

❧❧❧❧❧❧❧❧

This 1971 report of the Senate Judiciary Committee's subcommittee on Constitutional Amendments did a complete examination of the issues surrounding the potential of lowering the voting age in federal, state, and local elections.

THE CASE FOR 18-YEAR-OLD VOTING

In recent years, we have achieved a nationwide political consensus favoring a lowering of the voting age to 18. In the extensive hearings of the Senate Subcommittee on Constitutional Amendments in the 91st Congress, the objective was agreed to by Senator Barry Goldwater and Senator Edward M. Kennedy, by Deputy Attorney General Richard Kleindienst and former Attorney General Ramsey Clark. This consensus has emerged from a solid series of arguments supporting an extension of the franchise to younger voters.

First, these younger citizens are fully mature enough to vote. There is no magic to the age of 21. The 21-year age of maturity is derived only from historical accident. In the eleventh century 21 was the age at which most males were physically capable of carrying armor. But the physical ability to carry armor in the eleventh century clearly has no relation to the intellectual and emotional qualifications to vote in twentieth century America. And even if physical maturity were the crucial determinant of the right to vote, 18-year-olds would deserve that right: Dr. Margaret Mead and others have shown that the age of physical maturity in American youth has dropped more than three years since the eighteenth century. As Vice President Agnew said recently in endorsing a lowered voting age, "young people today are better educated and they mature physically much sooner than they did even 50 years ago."

The simple fact is that our younger citizens today are mentally and emotionally capable of full participation in our democratic form of government. Today more than half of the 18 to 21-year olds are receiving some type of higher education. Today nearly 80 percent of these young people are high school graduates. It is interesting to compare these recent statistics with some from 1920, when less than 10 percent went to college and less than 20 percent of our youngsters actually graduated from high school.

Second, our 18-yr-old citizens have earned the right to vote because they bear all or most of an adult citizen's responsibilities. Of the nearly 11 million, 18-to-21-year-olds today, about half are married and more than 1 million of them are responsible for raising families. Another 1,400,000 are serving their country, serving all of us, in the Armed Forces. And tens of thousands of young people have paid the supreme sacrifice in the Indochina War over the past five years.

Today more than 3 million young people, ages 18 to 21, are full-time employees and taxpayers. As former Attorney General Ramsey Clark has pointed out:

We subject 10-12 million young citizens between 17 and 21 years of age to taxation without representation. This is four times the population of the Colonies the night the tea was dumped in Boston harbor...It exceeds the population of all but several of the States of the Union.

In 26 States, persons at the age of 18 can make wills. In 49 States, they are treated as adults in criminal courts of law. Can we justify holding a person to be legally responsible for his or her actions in a criminal court of law when we continue to refuse to consider that same person responsible enough to take action in a polling booth? Surely a citizen's rights in our society ought to be commensurate with his responsibilities.

As Submitted to the States

Section 1. The right of citizens of the United States, who are eighteen years of age or older, to vote shall not be denied or abridged by the United States or by any State on account of age.

Section 2. The Congress shall have power to enforce this article by appropriate legislation.

State Ratifications of the Twenty-sixth Amendment

State	Date
Connecticut	23 March 1971
Delaware	23 March 1971
Minnesota	23 March 1971
Tennessee	23 March 1971
Washington State	23 March 1971
Hawaii	24 March 1971
Massachusetts	24 March 1971
Montana	29 March 1971
Arkansas	30 March 1971
Idaho	30 March 1971
Iowa	30 March 1971
Nebraska	2 April 1971
New Jersey	3 April 1971
Kansas	7 April 1971
Michigan	7 April 1971
Alaska	8 April 1971
Maryland	8 April 1971
Indiana	8 April 1971
Maine	9 April 1971
Vermont	16 April 1971
Louisiana	17 April 1971
California	19 April 1971
Colorado	27 April 1971
Pennsylvania	27 April 1971
Texas	27 April 1971
South Carolina	28 April 1971
West Virginia	28 April 1971
New Hampshire	13 May 1971
Arizona	14 May 1971
Rhode Island	27 May 1971
New York	2 June 1971
Oregon	4 June 1971
Missouri	14 June 1971
Wisconsin	22 June 1971

Illinois	29 June 1971
Alabama	30 June 1971
Ohio	30 June 1971
North Carolina	1 July 1971
Oklahoma	1 July 1971
Virginia	8 July 1971
Wyoming	8 July 1971
Georgia	4 October 1971
South Dakota	4 March 2014

ORIGINAL PRIMARY DOCUMENTS

Here, The Tuscaloosa News *give us a perspective on the inner workings of Congress as the proposed voting age amendment comes to fruition, 8 March 1971.*

Amendment in Judiciary Works

The judiciary committee of the US House of Representatives took unprecedented action by reporting favorably a proposed amendment to the constitution extending the right to vote in all elections to any person 18 years or older Thursday.

The measure still must be approved by a third vote of both houses of Congress and three-fourths of the state legislatures.

Congressman Walter Flowers (D-Ala.), a member of the Judiciary Committee and supporter of the amendment, said "It is unfortunate that the recent narrow decision of the Supreme Court has put the election machinery of the whole nation in a real by bind. Unless some is done along these lines I am afraid a great many problems will arise in the 1972 elections."

He was speaking of the narrow 5-4 decision of December 21, which upheld a 1970 federal act insofar as voting in federal election is concerned but does not allow application in state and local elections.

"I shall support the bill on the house floor as I did in committee because I am convinced that responsible participation by young Americans in the electoral process is in the best interest of us all."

The Alabama congressman said, "I hope for early action by both the house and the senate so that this matter can ultimately be decided by the states, where the decision should he made, prior to the next election."

ورحيورحيورحيورحيورحي

An editorial in The Deseret News *of Salt Lake City, Utah, 22 March 1971, gives the local reaction to the potential of a lower voting age amendment, and the paper calls for the support for just such an amendment.*

Ratify This Amendment

The voting age should be lowered to 18 for state and local elections as it already has been for federal elections. Otherwise the states will have to go to the trouble and expense of setting up two separate ballots and registration lists. That's why the Legislature put on the ballot for the 1972 elections an amendment to Utah's Constitution allowing 18, 19, and 20-year olds to vote in state and local contests. The change, of course, couldn't take effect until after the 1972 elections.

But the voting age just might be lowered in time to permit the younger voters to participate in the 1972 elections if the US House of Representatives goes along with the Senate, as it is expected to do Tuesday, and authorizes an amendment to the United States Constitution along the same lines.

Consequently, the federal amendment should be made a special order of business when the Utah Legislature is called into special session later this year to deal with reapportionment.

In the legislatures of three-fourths of the states ratify the federal amendment, there will be no need for a vote on the Utah State amendment. On the average the ratification of the federal amendment takes 15 months. Conversely, if the federal amendment isn't ratified by November 1972, Utahns can still amend their state constitution.

The question is no longer whether or not the voting age should be lowered in state and local elections. Rather, the challenge now is to accomplish this change as expeditiously as possible.

৵৽৵৽৵৽৵৽৵৽

The Spokesman-Review *newspaper of Spokane, Washington, 24 March 1971, reports on the passage in the Congress of the proposed voting age amendment.*

Age 18 Vote Amendment Up to State Legislatures By Marjorie Hunter

WASHINGTON (NYT) – A proposed constitutional amendment to lower the voting age to 18 in all elections cleared Congress Tuesday after little more than token opposition.

If ratified by at least 38 of the 50 state legislatures, it would become the 26th amendment to the US constitution. Final approval came Tuesday in the house on a vote of 400 to 19. The senate had earlier approved the proposed amendment by a vote of 94 to 0. Unlike most legislation, it does not require the President's signature.

Certified copies of the amendment will be sent to all states. However, there is nothing to preclude state legislatures from ratifying the amendment before receiving the papers.

Calls Pour In

Even before the House vote had been tallied, telephone calls began pouring in from officials of a number of state legislatures anxious to be the first to ratify the amendment.

"The bandwagon's already rolling," said Rep. Emanuel Celler, D-N.Y., the dean of the house who managed the amendment on the floor.

Among those states whose legislatures were ready to ratify the amendment within seconds after congressional clearance were Massachusetts, Minnesota and Indiana. Washington State ratified the amendment Tuesday afternoon.

In moving quickly to submit the proposed amendment to the states, Congress has sought to provide the means of avoiding a costly and possibly chaotic situation in the 1972 general elections.

Court Limits Law

A law passed a year ago by Congress lowered the voting age to 18. But the Supreme Court ruled in December that the law would apply only to federal elections, not state and local elections.

Thus, unless the proposed amendment is ratified, most states will be faced with setting up dual registration and voting procedures costing up to $20 million nation-wide.

While a number of states in the past have rejected proposals to lower the voting age to 18 or 19, a *New York Times* survey indicates that a sufficient number of state legislatures will approve the amendment before the November general elections.

Otherwise, the young voters will find themselves able to vote for president but not for justice of the peace.

11 Million Affected

There are 11 million Americans between the ages of 18 and 21. Approximately a million of these already are allowed to vote in all elections in nine states.

The minimum voting age is 18 in Georgia, Kentucky and Alaska; 19 in Minnesota, Montana and Massachusetts; and 20 in Maine, Nebraska and Hawaii.

Celler remarked whimsically that "by offering this amendment, perhaps, I can again wear the robes of youth." He will be 83 years old in May.

If approved by the states, it would be the fourth constitutional amendment that Celler has sponsored and guided through the House. The others were the 25th, dealing with presidential succession; the 24th, abolishing the poll tax as a voting requisite; and the 23rd, giving residents of the District of Columbia the right to vote for president.

Although the amendment sped through the House, Rep. John G. Schmitz, R-Calif., suggested Congress should repeal 18-year-old voting in federal elections, instead of seeking to broaden their voting rights. Some argued that the states should decide individually on the matter.

But the only real threat to approval came when Rep. James Howard, D-N.J., sought to enlarge the resolution to grant full rights – such as the right to purchase and the right to enter contracts – to the 18 year olds.

As heralded in The Blade *of Toledo, Ohio, 4 July 1971, just 100 days after being submitted to the states, the new constitutional amendment is declared as ratified by the head of the General Services Administration.*

Amendment Giving Ballot To Youth To Be Certified

———

Nixon To Observe Ceremony, Desk Made
For Thomas Jefferson To Be Used

———

THURMONT, Md. (AP) – President Nixon worked today, beside the desk Thomas Jefferson may have used while drafting the Declaration of Independence, will witness a historic ceremony marking the extension of the ballot to 18-year-olds.

The Jefferson desk is being brought over from the State Department for the use of the administrator of the General Services Administration, Robert Kunzig, in officially certifying that the 26th Amendment to the Constitution has been ratified.

Ohio came through last Wednesday with the required approval of a 38th state.

Singing Group

Dignitaries will be on hand in the White House East Room, as well as the "Young Americans" – a singing group of about 500 15-to-20-year-olds who appeared in Constitution Hall in Washington Sunday and leave today on a 28-day tour of Europe.

Mr. Kunzig acts as the event because GSA is the repository for nearly every state document.

The Thomas Jefferson desk is on loan to the State Department for the formal reception room on the eighth floor from Georgia Parsons formerly from Philadelphia.

Made For Jefferson

White House assistant Bruce Whelihan after some historical research, reported that the desk was made to order for Jefferson, and he used it at his residence in Philadelphia while serving in the Continental Congress. It is a matter of speculation whether or not Jefferson sat at the desk while working on several drafts of the Declaration of Independence.

The President and Mrs. Nixon plan to return from Camp David to the White House about mid-day today.

They went there early Sunday after the President spoke at the National Archives in Washington at ceremonies launching a five-year bicentennial era in advance of the nation's 200th anniversary in 1976.

It was weather-perfect at the presidential mountaintop retreat.

And during the morning Mr. Nixon spent some time in sports coat and slacks beside the swimming pool working on the national budget. He got some help from John D.Ehrlichmann, his assistant for domestic affairs, H.R. Haldeman, chief of the White House staff, and Lawrence M. Higby, administrative assistant under Haldeman.

Supreme Court Cases

Oregon v. Mitchell *(400 U.S. 112 {1970}). Decided 21 December 1970 by a vote of 5-4. Justice Hugo Black delivered the opinion of the Court.*

The Case: After President Richard Nixon signed into law an amendment to the 1965 Voting Rights Act giving eighteen-year-olds the right to vote, Oregon and other states opposed the change and filed suit in federal court, arguing that the change was unconstitutional.

By a vote of 5-4, the Court held that Oregon had the right to set requirements for state elections but that Congress had the right to set them for federal elections. Therefore, the change in the law was constitutional, paving the way for the Twenty-sixth Amendment.

Justice Hugo Black wrote,

"The final question presented by these cases is the propriety of Title III of the 1970 Amendments, which forbids the States from disenfranchising persons over the age of 18 because of their age. Congress was of the view that this prohibition, embodied in § 302 of the Amendments, was necessary among other reasons in order to enforce the Equal Protection Clause of the Fourteenth Amendment. The States involved in the present litigation question the assertion of congressional power to make that judgment.

"It is important at the outset to recognize what is not involved in these cases. We are not faced with an assertion of congressional power to regulate any and all aspects of state and federal elections, or even to make general rules for the determination of voter qualifications. Nor are we faced with the assertion that Congress is possessed of plenary power to set minimum ages for voting throughout the States. Every State in the Union has conceded by statute that citizens 21 years of age and over are capable of intelligent and responsible exercise of the right to vote. The single, narrow question presented by these cases is whether Congress was empowered to conclude, as it did, that citizens 18 to 21 years of age are not substantially less able.

"We believe there is serious question whether a statute granting the franchise to citizens 21 and over while denying it to those between the ages of 18 and 21 could, in any event, withstand present scrutiny under the Equal Protection Clause. Regardless of the answer to this question, however, it is clear to us that proper regard for the special function of Congress in making determinations of legislative fact compels this Court to respect those determinations unless they are contradicted by evidence far stronger than anything that has been adduced in these cases. We would uphold § 302 as a valid exercise of congressional power under § 5 of the Fourteenth Amendment."

Justice Black added,

"There remains only the question whether Congress could rationally have concluded that denial of the franchise to citizens between the ages of 18 and 21 was unnecessary to promote any legitimate interests of the States in assuring intelligent and responsible voting. There is no need to set out the legislative history of Title III at any great length here. Proposals to lower the voting age to 18 had been before Congress at several times since 1942. The Senate Subcommittee on Constitutional Amendments conducted extensive hearings on the matter in 1968 and again in 1970, and the question was discussed at some length on the floor of both the House and the Senate.

"Congress was aware, of course, of the facts and state practices already discussed. It was aware of the opinion of many historians that choice of the age of 21 as the age of maturity was an outgrowth of medieval requirements of time for military training and development of a physique adequate to bear heavy armor. It knew that, whereas only six percent of 18-year-olds in 1900 had completed high school, 81 percent have done so today. Congress was aware that 18-year-olds today make up a not insubstantial proportion of the adult workforce; and it was entitled to draw upon its experience in supervising the federal establishment to determine the competence and responsibility with which 18-year-olds perform their assigned tasks. As Congress recognized, its judgment that 18-year-olds are capable of voting is consistent with its practice of entrusting them with the heavy responsibilities of military service. Finally, Congress was presented with evidence that the age of social and biological maturity in modern society has been consistently decreasing. Dr. Margaret Mead, an anthropologist, testified that, in the past century, the 'age of physical maturity has been dropping and has dropped over 3 years.' Many Senators and Representatives, including several involved in national campaigns, testified from personal experience that 18-year-olds of today appeared at least as mature and intelligent as 21-year-olds in the Congressmen's youth.

"Finally, and perhaps most important, Congress had before it information on the experience of two States, Georgia and Kentucky, which have allowed 18-year-olds to vote since 1943 and 1955, respectively. Every elected Representative from those States who spoke to the issue agreed that, as Senator Talmadge stated, 'young people [in these States] have made the sophisticated decisions and have assumed the mature responsibilities of voting. Their performance has exceeded the greatest hopes and expectations.'

"In sum, Congress had ample evidence upon which it could have based the conclusion that exclusion of citizens 18 to 21 years of age from the franchise is wholly unnecessary to promote any legitimate interest the States may have in assuring intelligent and responsible voting. If discrimination is unnecessary to promote any legitimate state interest, it is plainly unconstitutional under the Equal Protection Clause, and Congress has ample power to forbid it under § 5 of the Fourteenth Amendment. We would uphold § 302 of the 1970 Amendments as a legitimate exercise of congressional power."

WHO'S WHO

This section includes a biography of one individual who played a significant part in drafting and passing the Twenty-sixth Amendment. He is mentioned in earlier sections of this chapter.

Jennings Randolph (1902-1998)

This politician's years of work to lower the voting age from 21 to 18 finally came to fruition in 1971, with both the passage and ratification of the Twenty-sixth Amendment. Jennings Randolph sat in the US House of Representatives for nearly 14 years (1933-47) and the US Senate for more than 26 years (1958-85).

He was born in Salem, in Harrison County, West Virginia, on 8 March 1902, the son of Ernest Randolph, an attorney, and his wife Idell (née Bingman) Randolph. Both parents were admirers of the firebrand politician and perennial Democratic candidate for President, William Jennings Bryan, and they named their son in Bryan's honor. Randolph attended a local primary school, then graduated from Salem Academy in 1920, and entered Salem College (now Salem-Teikyo University). In his senior year, Randolph worked as a member of the West Virginia Inter-Collegiate Press Association and, upon graduating in 1924, went to work for the *Clarksburg Daily Telegram* of West Virginia. In 1925 Randolph moved to the state capitol of Charleston to work for the *West Virginia Review* and as a professor in journalism and public speaking at Davis and Elkins College, which was affiliated with the Presbyterian Church.

In 1930, in the midst of the Depression, Randolph, a liberal Democrat, ran for a seat in the US House of Representatives, challenging the incumbent, Rep. Frank L. Bowman, a Republican, but was defeated. Two years later, Randolph ran with New York Governor Franklin D. Roosevelt at the top of the ticket, easily defeating Bowman and, on 4 March 1933, Randolph entered the Seventy-third Congress (1933-35) as a freshman member. Earlier that same year, he married Mary Katherine Babb, also a West Virginia native; the couple had two sons.

During his tenure in the House, which lasted until 3 January 1947, Randolph was a reliable supporter of Roosevelt's New Deal economic program. He was also a firm backer of his state's number one resource, coal, and of every effort to get fewer regulations on coal mines and mining. He was a cosponsor of the Civil Aeronautics Act of 1938, which gave US government assistance for airmail networks to be established across the nation, and provided funds to train pilots to man the planes. He also predicted oil shortages on the world market, something not perceived at the start of the Second World War. "In the future, we will not be able to depend on the importation of oil from any foreign country," he said, "even though it may appear now to be a very friendly one," he said in a speech on the House floor in 1943.

Randolph became best known, however, for his introduction, from 1942 until 1971, of a resolution for a constitutional amendment to lower the voting age in the United States from 21 to 18. Years later, during arguments in the US Senate for the legislation, he said, "our young people posses a great social conscience, are perplexed by the injustices which exist in the world, and are ready to rectify these ills."

Footnotes, Sources and Further Reading for this chapter appears on page 1095

In 1946, Randolph was defeated in his re-election bid for a seventh term when Melvin C. Snyder, a veteran of the Second World War and prosecuting attorney in West Virginia, beat him in a Republican wave. Out of politics for the first time in more than a decade, Randolph took a position as the assistant to the president of Capital Airways, and later as the firm's director of public relations. In 1947, Randolph was named as the chairman of the Aviation Planning Commission in Washington, D.C., where he served for two years, and then in 1953 as the chairman of a panel sponsored by the US Department of Commerce that examined federal appropriations for airport construction in the United States. He also served as a professor in public speaking a Southeastern University in Washington, D.C., from 1935, during his time in Congress; in 1952, he was named as that school's dean of the school of Business Administration.

On 18 January 1958, US Senator Matthew Mansfield Neely, Democrat of West Virginia, died. Republican Gov. Cecil H. Underwood felt that continuity in the makeup of the state's US Senate delegation was important, and he named Randolph, a Democrat, to the vacancy. That November Randolph won a special election to fill the remainder of Neely's term, and, in 1960, won election to a full 6-year term. Randolph was ultimately re-elected for four terms, serving from 5 November 1958 until his retirement on 3 January 1985. He served as the chairman of the Senate Committee on Public Works from the Eighty-ninth through the Ninety-fifth Congresses, and as the chairman of the Senate Committee on Environment and Public Works from the Ninety-fifth through the Ninety-sixth Congresses.

While in the Senate, Randolph continued to gather support for the constitutional amendment to lower the voting age from 21 to 18. He introduced the legislation eleven times, in both the US House of Representatives and the US Senate. It was due to his persistence that in 1971 the Congress passed a constitutional amendment to do just that, and Randolph has become known as "The Father of the Twenty-sixth Amendment."

Randolph prided himself during his congressional career in "bringing home the pork" – making sure that West Virginia got its fair share of federal appropriations. Randolph not only brought federal dollars back to his home state, but also helped to fund programs that aided people in the economically depressed area known as Appalachia. He voted for the Civil Rights Act of 1964 and the Voting Rights Act of 1965. He was an enthusiastic supporter of President Lyndon B. Johnson's domestic economic program, The Great Society.

Despite allegations that he had accepted illegal campaign contributions from an oil company, Randolph won his final Senate term in 1978. Following his wife's death from cancer in 1981, Randolph decided not to run for reelection in 1984. He spent his last decade in a long-term nursing facility in St. Louis, Missouri. On 8 May 1998, Randolph died at the St. John's Mercy Skilled Nursing Center in St. Louis, at the age of 96. His body was returned to his native West Virginia, and he was laid to rest in the Seventh Day Baptist Cemetery in Salem, in Harrison County, West Virginia. His gravestone reads simply: "Jennings Randolph. 1902-1998."

In a speech in front of the Chamber of Commerce in Clearwater, Florida, in May 1961, Randolph cautioned his listeners to make their voices heard on issues important to them. He said that "big government" should never intimidate people into silence. "[I]n this bigness the individual thinks that someone else has the duty to speak for him...All men in office, if not, should be gratified for the constituents back him who write their thoughts to him. But too often we are told merely to vote for or against, with never an argument for the benefit of the men who should hear it." He added, "Counsel and advise us – and we shall be helped if you do just that...there are more than two sides to any political question."

FOOTNOTES, SOURCES, FURTHER READING

Footnotes

[1] Cultice, Wendell W., "Youth's Battle for the Ballot: A History of Voting Age in America" (New York: Greenwood Press, 1992), 30-32.

[2] Eisenhower 1954 State of the Union in Robert L. Branyan and Lawrence Harold Larsen, "The Eisenhower Administration, 1953-1961: A Documentary History" (New York: Random House; two volumes, 1971), I:462.

[3] "Public Papers of the President of the United States. Lyndon Baines Johnson: 1968-69" (Government Printing Office; two volumes, 1970), I:669.

[4] Senate Judiciary Committee, Subcommittee on Constitutional Amendments, "Hearings Before the Subcommittee on Constitutional Amendments of the Committee of the Judiciary United States Senate, Ninetieth Congress, Second Session, on S.J. Res., 8, S.J. Res. 14, and S.J. Res. 78, Relating to Lowering the Voting Age to 18, May 14-16, 1968" (Washington: Government Printing Office, 1968), 1.

[5] ibid., 2.

[6] Finney, John W., "Senate Approves 18-Year-Old Vote in All Elections," *The New York Times*, 13 March 1970, 1, 22.

[7] "Letter to The Leaders Supporting a Constitutional Amendment to Lower the Voting age. April 27, 1970" in "Public Papers of the Presidents of the United States: Richard Nixon. Containing the Public Messages, Speeches, and Statements of the President. 1970" (Washington: Government Printing Office, 1971), 401-05.

[8] Ford remarks in "Congressional Record. Proceedings and Debates of the 91st Congress, Second Session. Volume 116 – Part —(17 June 1970), 20197.

[9] Black opinion in *Oregon v. Mitchell* (400 US 112 {1970}), at 126.

[10] Fetto, John, "Down for the Count: Voting Rates for Young Adults," American Demographics, XXI:11 (November 1999), 46-47.

[11] Polsby, Nelson W.; Aaron Wildavsky, Steven E. Schier, and David A. Hopkins, "Presidential Elections: Strategies and Structures of American Politics" (Lanham, Maryland: Rowman & Littlefield Publishers, Inc., 2012), 30.

[12] James Browning Allen (1912-1978), Democrat of Alabama, Member, Alabama state legislation (1938-42), Member, Alabama state Senate (1946-50), Lieutenant Governor of Alabama (1951-55, 1963-67), US Senator (1969-78).

[13] Jennings Randolph (1902-1998), Democrat of West Virginia, US Representative (1933-47), US Senator (1958-85)

[14] Southerners refer to the Civil War as "The War Between the States."

[15] Birch Evans Bayh, Jr. (1928), Democrat of Indiana, Member, Indiana state House of Representatives (1954-62), US Senator (1963-81). See the "influential biographies" section of the Twenty-fifth Amendment for a biography of Bayh.

[16] John Cornelius Stennis (1901-1995), Democrat of Mississippi, Member, Mississippi state House of Representatives (1928-32), District Prosecuting Attorney (1932-37), Circuit Judge (1937-47), US Senator (1947-89).

[17] Michael Joseph (Mike) Mansfield (1903-2001), Democrat of Montana, US Representative (1943-53), US Senator (1953-77), US Ambassador Extraordinary and Plenipotentiary to Japan (1977-88).

[18] Edward Moore Kennedy (1932-2009), Democrat of Massachusetts, Assistant District Attorney, Suffolk County, Massachusetts (1961), US Senator (1962-2009).

[19] A "fortiori argument," from the Latin "argumentum a fortiori," is one that is defined as "an argument with greater reason or more convincing force, used in drawing a conclusion that is inferred to be even more certain than another."

[20] Emanuel Celler (1888-1981), Democrat of New York, US Representative (1923-73). See the comprehensive biography for Celler in the "influential biographies" section of the Twenty-fourth Amendment.

[21] Richard Harding Poff (1923-2011), Republican of Virginia, US Representative (1953-72), Justice, Virginia state Supreme Court (1972-2011).

[22] The Supreme Court, in *Oregon v. Mitchell* (1970), held that under the US Constitution, the Congress only had jurisdiction over federal elections, and could not dictate an age limit for state and local elections, barring a constitutional amendment.

[23] J. Edward Hutchinson (1914-1985), Republican of Michigan, Member, Michigan state House of Representatives (1946, 1948), Member, Michigan state Senate (1951-60), US Representative (1963-77).

[24] Roman Conrad Pucinski (1919-2002), Democrat of Illinois, US Representative (1959-73).

[25] William Robert Poage (1899-1987), Democrat of Texas, Member, Texas state House of Representatives (1925-29), Member, Texas state Senate (1931-37), US Representative (1937-78).

[26] Robert McClory (1908-1988), Republican of Illinois, Member, Illinois state House of Representatives (1950), Member, Illinois state Senate (1952, 1956, 1960), US Representative (1963-83).

[27] James John Howard (1927-1988), Democrat of New Jersey, US Representative (1965-88).

Sources Arranged By Chapter Sections

Debate in Congress
"The Congressional Record: 7082-92.

"The Congressional Record: Proceedings and Debates of the 92nd Congress, First Session. Volume 117 – Part 6. March 17, 1971, to March 25, 1971" (Washington: Government Printing Office, 1971), 7532-37.

Historical Background Documents
"Letter to The Leaders Supporting a Constitutional Amendment to Lower the Voting age. April 27, 1970" in "Public Papers of the Presidents of the United States: Richard Nixon. Containing the Public Messages, Speeches, and Statements of the President. 1970" (Washington: Government Printing Office, 1971), 401-05.

US Senate, Committee on the Judiciary, Committee on Constitutional Amendments, "Lowering the Voting Age to 18: A Fifty-State Survey of the Costs and Other Problems of Dual-Age Voting" (Washington: Government Printing Office, 1971), —5-6.

Original Primary Documents
"Amendment in Judiciary Works," *The Tuscaloosa News* [Alabama], 8 March 1971, 16.

"Ratify This Amendment," *The Deseret News* [Salt Lake City, Utah], 22 March 1971, 10A.

"Age 18 Vote Amendment Up to State Legislatures," *The Spokesman-Review* [Spokane, Washington], 24 March 1971, 2A.

"Amendment Giving Ballot To Youth To Be Certified," *The Blade* [Toledo, Ohio], 4 July 1971, 2A.

Supreme Court Cases
Oregon v. Mitchell (400 U.S. 112 {1970}).
Greene, Richard S., "Congressional Power over the Elective Franchise: The Unconstitutional Phases of Oregon v. Mitchell," *Boston University Law Review*, LII (1972), 505.

Who's Who
Jennings Randloph (1902-1998)
"Randolph, Jennings" official congressional biography, online at http://bioguide.congress.gov/scripts/biodisplay.pl?index=R000046; "Randolph, Jennings" in Charles Moritz, ed., "Current Biography 1962" (New York: H.W. Wilson, 1963), 344-46; Le Vine, Steve, "Retiring Sen. Jennings Randolph to write for paper he left in 1926," *Pittsburgh Post-Gazette* [Pennsylvania], 1 January 1985, 18; US Congress, "Tributes to the Honorable Jennings Randolph of West Virginia in the United States Senate, Upon the Occasion of His Retirement from the Senate" (Washington: Government Printing Office, 1984); Stout, David, "Senator Jennings Randolph of West Virginia Dies at 96," *The New York Times*, 9 May 1998, A12; "Speaks in Clearwater. Sen. Randolph Cites Role of Individual," *St. Petersburg Times* [Florida], 27 May 1961, 1B.

Further Reading

Cheng, Jenny Diamond, "Uncovering the Twenty-sixth Amendment" (Ph.D. dissertation, The University of Michigan, 2008).

Engdahl, Sylvia, ed., *Amendment XXVI: Lowering the Voting Age* (Detroit: Greenhaven Press, 2010).

Fearon-Maradey, Sarah, "Disenfranchising America's Youth: How Current Voting Laws Are Contrary to the Intent of the Twenty-Sixth Amendment," *University of New Hampshire Law Review*, XII:2 (2014), 289-315.

Fish, Eric S., "The Twenty-Sixth Amendment Enforcement Power," *Yale Law Journal*. CXXI:5 (March 2012), 1168-1235.

____, "Originalism, Sex Discrimination, and Age Discrimination," *Texas Law Review*, XCI:1 (November 2012), 1-18.

Neale, Thomas H., "The Eighteen-Year-Old Vote: The Twenty-Sixth Amendment and Subsequent Voting Rates of Newly Enfranchised Age Groups," *Congressional Research Service Report* 83-103, 1983.

Sarabyn, Kelly, "The Twenty-Sixth Amendment: Resolving the Federal Circuit Split Over College Students' First Amendment Rights," *Texas Journal on Civil Liberties & Civil Rights*, XIV:1 (Fall 2008), 28-93.

Turner, Nancy, "The Young and the Restless: How the Twenty-Sixth Amendment Could Play a Role in the Current Debate over Voting Laws," *American University Law Review*, LXIV:6 (2015), 1503.

AMERICA AT THAT TIME . . .

Although the material in this section may not be directly related to the adoption of the Twenty-sixth Amendment, it offers valuable insight into what was happening in America at the time the Amendment was adopted. Modeled after Grey House Publishing's Working American *series, whose author, Scott Derks, is responsible for its content, it includes a Historical Snapshot, Selected Prices, significant quotations, and newspaper and magazine clips to give a sense of what was on the minds of Americans, and how it may have impacted the amendment process.*

HISTORICAL SNAPSHOT

1971

- Ohio agreed to pay $675,000 to relatives of Kent State victims

- *Masterpiece Theatre* premiered on PBS with host Alistair Cooke

- The situation comedy *All in the Family,* with Carroll O'Connor as Archie Bunker, began on CBS TV

- A federal grand jury indicted Rev. Philip Berrigan and five others on charges of plotting to kidnap Henry Kissinger

- The 1964 Gulf of Tonkin resolution, which amounted to a declaration of war against Vietnam, was repealed by Congress

- Charles Manson and three women followers were convicted in Los Angeles of murder in the 1969 slayings of seven people, including actress Sharon Tate

- OPEC decided to set oil prices without consulting buyers

- Two *Apollo 14* astronauts walked on the moon

- The U.S. Capitol building was bombed in protest of U.S. involvement in Laos

- Senator Edward Kennedy estimated that 25,000 Vietnamese civilians had been killed in the previous year

- Army Lt. William L. Calley, Jr. was convicted of murdering at least 22 Vietnamese civilians in the My Lai massacre

- President Nixon pledged a withdrawal of 100,000 more men from Vietnam by December

- The U.S. Supreme Court upheld the use of busing to achieve racial desegregation in schools

- Anti-war protesters calling themselves the Mayday Tribe began four days of demonstrations in Washington aimed at shutting down the nation's capital

- President Nixon ordered John Haldeman to do more wiretapping and political espionage against the Democrats

New Voters 'Anything But Republican', *The Hutchinson News*, September 24, 1971

Ohio, what have you done? One thing that becomes clear in a variety of recent political maneuverings, particularly in student communities, is that some early negative judgments pertaining to the impact of the 26th amendment were far more projective than realistic.

When, on June 30, the Ohio state legislature committed the nation to Constitutional enfranchisement of 11,300,00 citizens between the ages of 18 and 21, a sizable body of political opinionmakers hastened to dismiss the whole business as carrying small moment. Particularly among those noisy liberals ever anxious to secure the goodwill of the radical left, it was the popular cant that:

a) not enough young people would get involved to significantly affect it;

b) if they did, there would be no more unanimity among them than exists among their parents; and

c) even if they did somehow miraculously congeal into a voting bloc, they would possess no means to make themselves visible to the national leadership of either party prior to election time. Thus they would be unable to prevent durable party machines from providing them with no issue – choices in the candidates.

While there is some accuracy in all of the above, it did not and does not fully describe the situation. Crucially, certain important people didn't buy it.

By all accounts, the new voters are indeed going to affect the political scene, though not as most observers would have predicted, and, alas, not as the 26th amendment partisans have hoped.

To wit: the glumly cynical suggestion that apathy would cripple the new voters' leverage has so far proved false. As anxious to believe the myth of their own heightened political sensitivity as the media hypists who created it, young people are registering up a storm, particularly in college communities where their numbers are an eminently real force.

The nation that they would prove as politically heterogeneous a body as their parents, a nation counter to the myth at work in the high–registration phenomenon, has been shown to be incorrect also. It was essentially a puny effort by reactionaries to fuddle everybody's sense of identity, and as such it was five years too late. So far, the new registrations are either overwhelmingly Democratic or independent, which, in this case, probably means anything but Republican.

Political Power Source

All of this is hardly lost upon the big national political klaverns. Elements within both are moving to block what they view as a threat, or to exploit a potential power source.

The poor Republicans, they are not the establishment, they are not a centrist majority party. They have, since World War I, been a conservative elite; the Goldwater party. Operating from a perennially defensive position, any new enfranchise-disadvantages them. Richard Nixon supported the 26th amendment only to avoid a howling backlash from a petulant moderate center be desperately needs to coalesce for 1972. To the new voters, he's a bogeyman.

Thus, with the unanimity known only in shield-rings, the GOP has dedicated itself to blockbusting the youth vote. . . .

The 18-Year-Olds, *The News*, September 14, 1971

Ratification of the 26th amendment legalizing voting by 18-year-olds has raised almost as many questions as it has settled.

One surfaced this week when Attorney General Francis B. Burch ruled in response to an inquiry from Delegate Isiah Dixon Jr. (D. Baltimore City) that although all 18-year-olds in Maryland are now eligible to vote in all elections that they are barred from jury duty.

This, he said, is despite the fact that jurors for service in Maryland courts are selected from the lists of qualified voters assembled by the Supervisors of Elections.

Since the ratification of the required number of states of the new 26th amendment giving the vote to all between the ages of 18 and 21 years, election boards have been merely adding the names of the new registrants to the existing voting lists.

In other words, as of today, the new voters are not segregated.

There is no way in the world in which persons charged with the selection of persons for jury duty picked at random from the names of the lists of qualified voters can tell whether or not they are over 21 years of age.

Yet, according to the Attorney General, although Maryland's jury law states that all registered voters are eligible for jury duty in another clause it specifically says that all jurors must be at least 21 years of age.

"The new 26th amendment to the Federal Constitution," ruled the state's highest legal authority, "merely gives the right to vote to all persons 18 years of age or older.

"In no part of the amendment is the issue of age qualification for jury duty even mentioned."

As a result, rules Mr. Burch, the Annotated Statutes of the Free State of Maryland constitute the controlling law on the issue in the Free State.

And until such time as the General Assembly amends the existing 21-year-old requirement for jury duty and the lower age limit is approved by the Governor, no persons under the age of 21 years, regardless of the fact that his or her name appears on a voting list, may be drawn for jury duty or enter a jury box of any court in the State.

While President Nixon has advocated lowering the age for jury duty to 18 years, the proposal has fallen like a lead balloon in Congress and there is no indication that such legislation will be enacted during the present session.

This creates a costly and cumbersome situation for Supervisors of Elections throughout Maryland.

It not only means that from this time on they must maintain separate and distinct lists carefully segregating voters between the ages of 18 and 21 years from those voters over that age who are liable to being selected for jury duty.

But they will have to retrace their steps—at least as far back as June 30 when the 26th Amendment legalizing youth voting became nationally effective, carefully check the ages of all voters listed since that time and place those in the 18 to 25-year-old category onto the list of those ineligible for jury duty.

This is only one instance in which the new 26th Amendment opens a Pandora's box of unresolved issues which must eventually be settled by widespread revisions of the state's legal code.

No one knows, as of today, whether or not it is legal for an 18-year-old attending a college or preparatory school in a community either in Maryland or in some other part of the nation to register in the community where he is attending school or in his home community and later vote by absentee ballot.

Continued

The 18-Year-Olds . . . *(Continued)*

So far California and Pennsylvania, both of whose Legislatures are in session, have clarified this very important question by passing laws permitting students, if they wish, to register in the community in which their school or college is located, but nothing definitive has been done in Maryland.

This is, incidentally, a burning issue in many small college towns where the number of students attending the institution of higher learning located in their midst far exceeds the total of permanent residents.

Not unnaturally, taxpayers of these communities are fearful of college students participating heavily in local elections, although their residence is only temporary, passing costly bond issues for the permanent residents to pay for, and in extreme cases, by bloc voting taking over the political control of the municipal government although none of them plan to become permanent residents after graduation.

In Maryland, citizens of Prince Georges County are understandably concerned.

They have in their mist the University of Maryland with more than 26,000 newly eligible new voters.

Such a potential "bloc," if it could be manipulated by any political party or candidates into a solidified voting unit, might well upset the entire political balance of Prince Georges County.

We do not even infer that this is likely. The new youth voters will—in our opinion—vote as their conscience dictates.

But such a potentiality of a large group of young people all in the same age bracket either spontaneously or by manipulations of political parties or groups being welded into a cohesive political force cannot be dismissed as a phantasy.

Meanwhile, the General Assembly has other "antiquated" statutes to ponder over at its next session.

Now that 18-year-olds are placed on the same plane as adults by the 26th Amendment insofar as exercising their franchise is concerned, what are we going to do with the law barring them from being sold liquor until they attain the ripe old age of 21?

If they are old enough to fight for their country and vote, a strong argument could be made for the thesis that they are also of sufficient age to be legally served with liquor in restaurants, cafes, taverns and other outlets and make open purchases of bottled liquors at licensed stores.

Next issue to be faced is what the General Assembly is going to do if anything, to bring the new philosophy of the 26th Amendment making "adults" of all youths over the age of 18 with reference to purchasing automobiles in their own names without the endorsement of their parents or guardians, executing mortgages, purchasing real estate or any other property in their own name, borrowing money from lending institutions upon their unsupported signatures, and scores of other restrictions which have previously placed them in the status of being minors and required the acquiescence of their parents or guardians in all legal transactions.

These are vexatious and controversial questions and they must all be faced—together with many others—by the members of the General Assembly.

Predictably, the business community will look with some concern on divorcing from their safeguards the protective endorsements of the signatures of parents or guardians guaranteeing repayment of loans, mortgages, conditional automobile sales, and countless other items to those previously believed too young to obtain such financing upon their unsupported signatures.

Continued

The 18-Year-Olds . . . *(Continued)*

The law is indiscriminate. Once enacted it effects equally the youngster of high moral character and possessed of as much maturity of judgment as he will have achieved at the present arbitrary age limit of 21 years, and the under-developed juvenile of marked instability of judgment and character who is a notoriously poor credit risk.

But yesterday's lad and lass subject to parental controls have been suddenly been made by decision of Congress and a sufficient number of sovereign states "presidential electors."

We can only hope that they will measure up to the responsibilities inherent in the power placed in their hands by a trusting nation.

"Poll Reveals Significant Marijuana Use at Tulane," *The Tulane Hullabaloo*, November 3, 1967:

Thirty-one percent of the 200 students answering a HULLABALOO poll report they've used marijuana at one time, although only seven percent say they use it frequently.

But there was little difference noted in the poll between the percentages of male and female students who have tried marijuana; the poll showed a regular increase of use with age in both sexes. One out of six freshmen, six out of 10 juniors, and over 70 percent of graduate students responding to the poll said they had used marijuana at least once.

These figures are significantly higher than the national percentage of marijuana use by college students reported in a Gallup poll published in the November Reader's Digest. That poll, which covered 426 American colleges, indicated that only six percent of the nation's college students have ever used marijuana.

Of the students answering the Gallup poll, 51 percent said they did not even know a single student who had tried marijuana, and estimated that only four percent of those on the campus and 13 percent of all college students have tried marijuana or LSD.

The Gallup poll also showed that the majority of American college students were "reluctant" to try drugs and generally disapprove of those students who use marijuana or LSD.

On the Tulane campus, however, 59 percent of those responding to the poll felt that the use of marijuana should be legalized.

"Pot, according to scientific evidence, is less harmful to the body than tobacco and nicotine. Banning it is as ridiculous as the Prohibition laws in the 1920s, because of the increase in use of the drug," commented one student.

"California Reservists Speak Out Against War," WIN Peace and Freedom through Nonviolent Action, December 15, 1970:

In two separate actions, Northern California military Reservists recently demonstrated their opposition to the war.

On October 31, a contingent of Army, Marine and Coast Guard Reservists marched in a peace parade through downtown San Francisco.

The same week, 16 Marine Reservists in Marin County, just north of San Francisco, bought an advertisement in a local newspaper. Their ad supported a county ballot proposition calling for withdrawal of U.S. troops from all of Southeast Asia.

The Marines were all enlisted men of M Co., 23rd Marine Regiment, San Rafael. A Marine Corps spokesman made vague threats to the press that the men would be punished for their actions, but so far the Marine Corps has apparently been unable to find any regulation it can use against them.

Selected Prices, 1971

Apartment, NYC, Two-Bedroom, Month	$475.00
Coloring Book	$0.10
Condoms, Nine	$3.00
Jeans, Lady Wrangler	$15.00
Jewel Case, Gucci	$99.00
Pipe	$3.95
Potter's Wheel	$55.00
Puppy, Husky	$150.00
Slide Rule	$2.95
Wok	$17.50

Year	Value of One Dollar in 2016 US Dollars
1969	$6.58
1970	$6.22
1971	$5.96
1972	$5.78
1973	$5.44
1974	$4.90

"Sky Spies to Watch Pollution"

Air and water pollution can be monitored effectively and traced to the source by survey satellites being developed by the United States, researchers reported today.

Two teams of researchers who are testing camera and sensor systems for the satellites, the first of which will be launched in March 1972, made their report to an Earth Conference. . . .

The application with the broadest current user interest is detecting elements of water pollution, tracing them to their source, and measuring the dispersion and concentration of the pollutants.

To illustrate, the MIT-NASA team showed a picture of Massachusetts Bay, near Salem, and identified a plume-like image as the flow from a combined sanitary and storm sewer and a smaller plume as a surface slick created by a power plant coolant.

Seventy percent of the solid particles contaminating urban air have not been identified, and even if we had limitless resources we could not formulate really effective control programs because we know so little about the origin, nature and effects of most air pollutants.

—Dr. Rene Dubos of
Rockefeller University

The Twenty-seventh Amendment

Chapter 18

ARCHIVIST OF THE UNITED STATES
UNITED STATES OF AMERICA

TO ALL TO WHOM THESE PRESENTS SHALL COME,

GREETING:

KNOW YE, That the first Congress of the United States, at its first session, held in New York, New York, on the twenty-fifth day of September, in the year one thousand seven hundred and eighty-nine, passed the following resolution to amend the Constitution of the United States of America, in the following words and figures in part, to wit:

The Conventions of a number of the States having at the time of their adopting the Constitution, expressed a desire, in order to prevent misconstruction or abuse of its powers, that further declaratory and restrictive clauses should be added: And as extending the ground of public confidence in the Government will best ensure the benificent ends of its institution;

Resolved by the Senate and House of Representatives of the United States of America in Congress assembled, two thirds of both Houses concurring, that the following Articles be proposed to the Legislatures of the several States, as Amendments to the Constitution of the United States, all or any of which Articles, when ratified by three fourths of the said Legislatures, to be valid to all intents and purposes, as part of the said Constitution, viz.:

Articles in addition to, and amendment of, the
Constitution of the United States of America,
proposed by Congress and ratified by the
Legislatures of the several States, pursuant to the
fifth Article of the original Constitution.

*   *   *   *   *   *   *

Article the Second...No law, varying the
compensation for the services of the Senators and
Representatives, shall take effect, until an
election of Representatives shall have intervened.

*   *   *   *   *   *   *

And, further, that Section 106b, Title 1 of the United States Code provides
that whenever official notice is received at the National Archives and
Records Administration that any amendment proposed to the
Constitution of the United States has been adopted, according to the
provisions of the Constitution, the Archivist of the United States shall
forthwith cause the amendment to be published, with his certificate,
specifying the States by which the same may have been adopted, and that
the same has become valid, to all intents and purposes, as a part of the
Constitution of the United States.

And, further, that it appears from official documents on file in the
National Archives of the United States that the Amendment to the
Constitution of the United States proposed as aforesaid has been ratified
by the Legislatures of the States of Alabama, Alaska, Arizona, Arkansas,
Colorado, Connecticut, Delaware, Florida, Georgia, Idaho, Illinois,
Indiana, Iowa, Kansas, Louisiana, Maine, Maryland, Michigan,
Minnesota, Missouri, Montana, Nevada, New Hampshire, New Jersey,
New Mexico, North Carolina, North Dakota, Ohio, Oklahoma, Oregon,
South Carolina, South Dakota, Tennessee, Texas, Utah, Vermont, Virginia,
West Virginia, Wisconsin, and Wyoming.

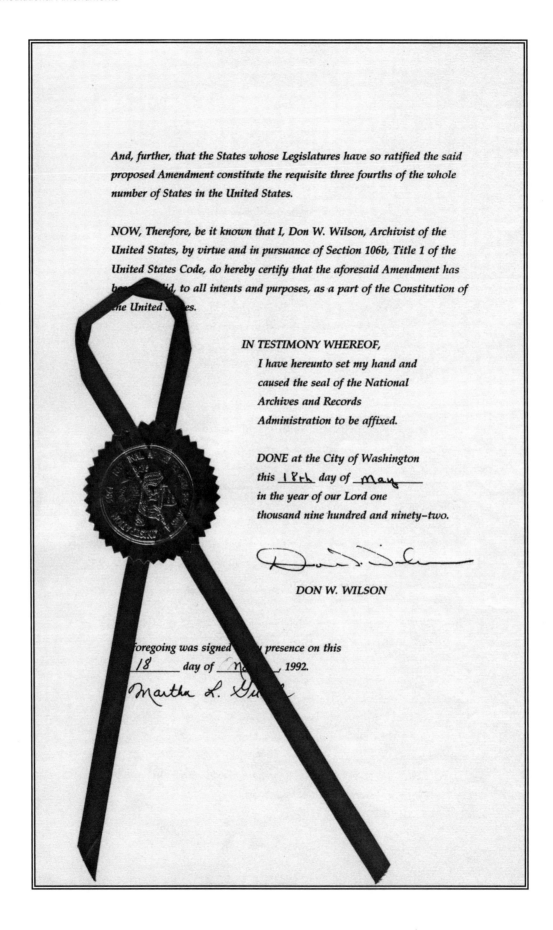

And, further, that the States whose Legislatures have so ratified the said proposed Amendment constitute the requisite three fourths of the whole number of States in the United States.

NOW, Therefore, be it known that I, Don W. Wilson, Archivist of the United States, by virtue and in pursuance of Section 106b, Title 1 of the United States Code, do hereby certify that the aforesaid Amendment has been valid, to all intents and purposes, as a part of the Constitution of the United States.

IN TESTIMONY WHEREOF,
I have hereunto set my hand and caused the seal of the National Archives and Records Administration to be affixed.

DONE at the City of Washington this 18th day of May in the year of our Lord one thousand nine hundred and ninety-two.

DON W. WILSON

foregoing was signed in my presence on this 18 day of No , 1992.

Martha L. Gu

Proposed in Congress:	**25 September 1789**
Sent to States:	**28 September 1789**
Ratified:	**7 May 1992**

Chapter 18

THE TWENTY-SEVENTH AMENDMENT

No law, varying the compensation for the services of the Senators and Representatives, shall take effect, until an election of representatives shall have intervened.

Brief Summary

The Twenty-seventh Amendment simply says that before any law that alters the salary of members of the US Congress can go into effect, the next term of office for congressional representatives has to begin. The purpose was to make it more difficult for members of Congress to enact pay raises for themselves and other government officials, particularly those that were retroactive. The amendment is unique in that nearly 203 years passed between its proposal and its ratification.

Timeline

8 June 1789	Representative James Madison proposes what would become the Twenty-seventh Amendment to the US House of Representatives.
24 August 1789	The House passes what would become the Twenty-seventh Amendment, along with other amendments that would become the Bill of Rights.
9 September 1789	The US Senate passes twelve articles of amendment, including what would become the Twenty-seventh Amendment.
24 September 1789	A joint House-Senate committee presents final versions of twelve proposed amendments; the House passes the committee's version.
25 September 1789	The Senate passes the committee's version of the twelve proposed amendments.
15 December 1791	The Bill of Rights is ratified. What would become the Twenty-seventh Amendment is not included among the ten amendments of the Bill of Rights; as of this date, only six states have ratified what would become the Twenty-seventh Amendment.

Footnotes, Sources and Further Reading for this chapter appears on page 1143

6 May 1873	Ohio ratifies the amendment; no time limit had been placed on ratification.
5 June 1939	The US Supreme Court issues its decision in Coleman v. Miller.
6 March 1978	Wyoming ratifies the Twenty-seventh Amendment.
1982	University of Texas at Austin student Gregory Watson begins researching the history of the amendment and launches a campaign for its final ratification.
7 May 1992	The Twenty-seventh Amendment is ratified when Michigan becomes the thirty-eighth state to ratify it.

Introduction

Two full centuries in the making, the congressional pay amendment was a small but vital part of the arguments over potential amendments to the US Constitution when it was first ratified in 1789. Professor Richard B. Bernstein wrote in 1992, "No provision of the United States Constitution has a more drawn-out, tortured history than the Twenty-seventh Amendment, which was ratified more than two centuries after Representative James Madison introduced it in the First Congress."[1]

Few people would have predicted that when James Madison was doing his utmost first to formulate the language for the original Constitution, and then to bring together in one large package the twelve ideas known eventually as the Bill of Rights, that one of the original twelve amendments submitted to the states for ratification in 1789 would be tossed aside for 203 years, which is how long it took to gain the requisite number of states required for ratification. I am sure that Madison himself, along with his contemporaries, would themselves have been shocked by such a story. Here's how it happened.

When formulating the model for a constitutional government that would take the place of the Articles of Confederation, the Founding Fathers looked to the same people and place they had just rejected: Mother England, and the parliamentary system. Of course, America has never had a Parliament like the British government has had, but the model based on democratic ideals was the one they sought to emulate. Prior to 1832 in England, one issue that took center stage was the fact that candidates paid all of their own expenses for running for office. Edward Porritt, who with his wife Annie Gertrude Porritt, wrote the fundamental work on the House of Commons prior to the 1832 period of legislative and other reforms which changed the British nation, explained, "Candidates paid all the expenses of the pre-reform period; but they paid most of them because it was customary to do so, not because there were laws which directed that all the returning officers' charges should be paid by candidates. But in the middle years of the eighteenth century enactments were passed which established the principle that expenses at elections were chargeable on candidates; and after the House of Commons had been reformed in 1832, it was made possible for returning officers to collect at law many charges upon candidates which in the earlier history of the representative system had had nothing but usage to support them."[2] Thus it was not until the Great Reform Bill of 1832 that members of the House of Commons had their expenses and salaries paid by the people. However, as the Porritts note, rank bribery and vote-buying soon came about, and they offer several examples, including a 1693 candidate who so desired a seat in Parliament – and the high rank and station that went with it – that he offered the town of Wigan to build "a conduit in the market place and bring water to it to supply it, at his own charge."[3]

Fears of such corruption gripped the men who cobbled together the first twelve amendments that were to be submitted to the states (only 10 of these were ratified as the Bill of Rights). During the years of the First and Second Continental Congress, colonial legislatures paid for the expenses of their members of Congress: their travel, their staying at inns, their food, even feed for their horses, and for their upkeep while they debated the new nation's fate in Philadelphia, then the home of the Continental Congress. As the war of independence against England persisted and grew ever longer, the economy in the thirteen colonies worsened, and delegates to the Continental Congresses found their expenses taking longer and longer to be refunded. Relations between the legislators and their colonial then state governments grew worse and worse.

During the original Constitutional Convention in 1788, three states requested language be put into the Constitution curbing the right of Congress to raise its own pay right after an election – when few, if any, of their constituents would be watching, and they would have two years to enjoy the pay raise without any threat to their re-election chances. Madison's original language regarding this matter was reflected in the so-called "Virginia Plan." Because it came from two Virginians – Madison and Gov. Edmund Randolph – and reflected the ideas and ideals of large states, it had the best chance of being the main structure of the Constitution. In short, the plan divided Congress into two houses – a Senate and a House of Representatives. The Lower House would be elected by the people, and the Upper House by state legislatures. (The Seventeenth Amendment, ratified in 1913, made the direct election of US Senators by the people part of the US Constitution.) Initially introduced on 29 May 1787, the plan called for members of the national legislature to "receive liberal stipends by which they may be compensated for the devotion of their time to public service." Delegate Elbridge Gerry of Massachusetts spoke out against this measure:

"The evils we experience flow from the excess of democracy. The people do not want virtue; but are the dupes of pretended patriots. In Massts. [Massachusetts] it has been fully confirmed by experience that they are daily misled into the most baneful measures and opinions by the false reports circulated by designing men, and which no one on the spot can refute. One principal evil arises from the want of due provision for those employed in the administration of Governnt [sic]. It would seem to be a maxim of democracy to starve the public servants. He mentioned the popular clamour in Massts. for the reduction of salaries and the attack made on that of the Govr. though secured by the spirit of the Constitution itself. He had he said been too republican heretofore; he was still however republican, but had been taught by experience the danger of the levilling [sic] spirit."[4] Despite the opposition of Gerry and others – delegate Benjamin Franklin even asked for a clause in the Constitution denying any compensation for members of the national legislature – on 26 July 1787, twenty-three resolutions were proposed to the Committee on Detail, including:

"*Resolved*, That the members of the first branch of the legislature ought to be elected by the people of the several states for the term of two years; to be paid out of the public treasury; to receive an adequate compensation for their services..."[5]

The motion to include the provision was eight states to three – Rhode Island had not sent delegates to the convention – and was added to language proposed by William Pierce of Georgia, who motioned that "the wages [of members of Congress] should be paid out of the National Treasury."[6]

Even though it appeared that Madison's thrust had carried the day, in fact it had not. Connecticut's Oliver Ellsworth opposed the inclusion of the provision, instead calling for the individual states to pay for their national legislators. He noted, "[T]he manners of different state were different in the Stile [sic] of living and in the profits accruing from the exercise of like talents. What would be deemed therefore a reasonable compensation in some States, in others would be very unpopular, and might impede the system of which it made a part."[7] Randolph, with Madison the originator of the Virginia Plan's main argument, countered Ellsworth. "[I]f the States were to pay the members of the Natl. Legislature," he said, "a dependence would be created that would vitiate the whole System." He added that "[t]he whole nation has an interest in the attendance & services of the members. The National Treasury therefore is the proper fund for supporting them."[8] Randolph received backing and support from Rufus King of Massachusetts; Farrand noted, "Mr. King, urged the danger of creating a dependence on the States by leavg. [sic] to them the payment of the members of the Natl. Legislature. He supposed it wd. [would] be best to be explicit as to the compensation to be allowed. A reserve on that point, or a reference to the Natl. Legislature of the quantum, would excite greater opposition than any sum that would be actually necessary or proper."[9]

Delegate James Wilson of Pennsylvania was against "fixing the compensation" amount, "as circumstances would change." Madison, wrote Farrand, "concurred in the necessity of preserving compensations for the national government independent on the state governments; but at the same time approved of *fixing* them by the Constitution, which might be done by taking a standard which would not vary with circumstances." When delegate Hugh Williamson of North Carolina defended the idea of states paying for their representation, Farrand noted about Madison that:

"He disliked particularly the policy suggested by Mr. Wiliamson [sic] of leaving the members from the poor States beyond the Mountains, to the precarious & parsimonious support of their constituents. If the Western States hereafter arising should be admitted into the Union, they ought to be considered as equals & as brethren. If their representatives were to be associated in the Common Councils, it was of common concern that such provisions should be made as would invite the most capable and respectable characters into the service."[10]

After much argument and debate, the first draft of the Constitution, revealed on 6 August, noted in Article VI, Section 10, that "[T]he members of each House shall receive a compensation for their services, to be ascertained and paid by the State, in which they shall be chosen."

So, it was apparently settled: the states, and not the federal government, would pay the salaries and expenses of members of Congress. Eight days later, delegate Oliver Ellsworth reported that he had changed his mind, and wanted the salaries paid by the federal government. His motion to reopen the debate ripped the bandage off a healing wound. Pierce Butler of South Carolina again renewed his argument that the Senate, of the two bodies, would have members elected directly by state officials rather than the people, and that the men who sat in this body, "who will be so long out of their respective States, that they will lose sight of their Constituents unless dependent on them for their support," needed to be paid directly by the people. John Langdon of New Hampshire opposed Butler, stating that Butler's stance would "oblige the distant States to bear the expence [sic] of their members travelling to and from the Seat of Govt."

A majority of the delegates then agreed that the federal government would pay salaries and expenses – but how much? In the end, no precise or exact number could be arrived at, and the phrase "to be ascertained by law" was included to allow future Congresses to set these limits.

When the Committee on Style and Arrangement presented the completed document to the delegates on 12 September for their perusal and, ultimately, their signatures, they found inserted into the Constitution the provision, embraced in Article I, Section 6, Clause 1:

"The Senators and Representatives shall receive a Compensation for their Services *to be ascertained by Law*, and paid out of the Treasury of the United States." [Author's italics]

Thus, through this portion of the Constitution, members of Congress were paid by the *federal* government, and not the *state* governments. That issue was settled.

Realizing, however, that the Constitution should be a blueprint of rights held by the people as well as checks and balances of the actions the federal government takes toward the states., the drafters of the original Constitution sought, once a House of Representatives was established, to include a prohibition on a congressional pay raise for a present Congress. In the House in that first Congress (1789-91) were four men who would play a key role in the formation of language for a proposed congressional pay amendment, embodied in what was later known as the Bill of Rights: Madison of Virginia, Elbridge Gerry of Massachusetts, John Vining of Delaware, and Theodore Sedgwick of Massachusetts. As he had at the Constitutional Convention, Madison supported the idea of a congressional salary and expenses, so he backed an amendment making sure that such a perk was not abused, speaking in a debate of the first Congress:

"I do not believe this is a power which, in the ordinary course of Government, is likely to be abused...Perhaps of all the powers granted, it is least likely to abuse; but there is a seeming improprietu in leaving...men without control to put their hand into the public coffers, to take out money to put in their pockets; there is a seeming indecorum in such power, which leads me to propose a change. We have a guide to this alteration in several of the amendments which the different conventions have proposed. I have gone, therefore, so far as to fix it, that no law varying compensation, shall operate until there is a change in the Legislature, in which case it cannot be for the particular benefit of those who are concerned in determining the value of the service."[11]

Sedgwick wholeheartedly opposed the amendment, stating that it could be used by wealthy landowners against those who didn't have the funds to run for Congress, which would prevent "men of shining and disinterested abilities, but of indigent circumstances."[12]

The first 12 proposed amendments submitted to the states made sure to include a prohibition of a congressional pay raise that would not go into effect until after another election. In fact, had the entire twelve been ratified as they were submitted, we would speak of the Second Amendment today not as a fundamental right to own and possess firearms, but as a limit on congressional salaries and expenses. The original amendment language stated, 'No law, varying the compensation for the services of senators and representatives, shall take effect until an election of representatives shall have intervened." Indeed, it took over 200 years to ratify. What was the difficulty of its passage?

In 1993, historian Ruth Ann Strickland explained, "The Twenty-seventh Amendment was not ratified due to generational rhythms or shifting political coalitions. More likely, it was triggered by the growing disenchantment with congressional perquisites and arrogance. The probable passage of the Twenty-seventh Amendment as further reinforced by the 'rubbergate' scandal on the Hill, as numerous members of the House of Representatives engaged in check kiting."[13]

When this amendment was first submitted to the states, there was no section of the amendment calling for ratification within a specified period – usually seven years – and within two years after its submission, six states, of the 14 total states in the Union at that time, approved it. It was not until 1873 that a seventh state ratified it. The lights went dark on this proposed congressional pay amendment until *1978*, when Wyoming ratified it. Again the amendment went quiet until 1989, when additional states ratified it. Finally, in 1992, 17 states ratified it, giving it two more than the requisite 38 states needed for ratification. The amendment received far more support, albeit over a longer period, than any of the 10 amendments it had been submitted with in 1789.[14]

On 14 May 1992, Don Wilson, the archivist of the United States, certified the ratification of the amendment as number 27, in accordance with Section 106b of Title I of the United States Code. Although their "approval" was not necessary, on 20 May 1992, the House, by a vote of 414-3, and the US Senate, by a vote of 99-0, confirmed the Twenty-seventh Amendment to the US Constitution.

Those who opposed giving the amendment "amendment status" look to the controlling US Supreme Court decision on the matter of constitutional amendments: the 1921 case of *Dillon v. Gloss* (256 US 358), in which a unanimous Court, in the voice of Justice Willis Van Devanter, held that amendments submitted to the states *must* have an "end date" in which ratification must be completed, or else the amendment would be dead. For instance, the Equal Rights Amendment, submitted to the states in 1975, had a seven-year time limit (which, perhaps unconstitutionally, was extended in 1982 for three additional years, which also ended without the amendment being ratified). In *Dillon*, Justice Van Devanter wrote that under Article V of the original US Constitution, in which the "amending power" of the federal government is lodged, there was no language "suggest[ing] that an amendment once proposed is to be open to ratification for all time, or that ratification in some of the States may be separated from that in others by many years and not effective."[15]

Noted constitutional attorney and legal scholar Laurence H. Tribe wrote in 2008, "Many copies of the Constitution that you're likely to come across don't include [the Twenty-seventh Amendment]; they end with the Twentysixth Amendment, which lowered the voting age to 18 in 1971. The Twenty-seventh Amendment was ratified 21 years later, in 1992. Some copies of the Constitution that exclude the Twenty-seventh Amendment do so for the simple reason that they were published before its ratification. Some exclude it because their publishers lazily *copied* the Constitution verbatim from something published years earlier. And some exclude it for a more complex and interesting reason: those are the publishers who don't regard the Twenty-seventh Amendment as ever having been validly ratified."[16]

Debate in Congress

The debate here was limited to arguments over whether the original Constitution should be amended at all, and to James Madison's lengthy speech supporting each of the twelve amendments that were submitted to the states in what was called the Bill of Rights, 8 June 1789.

AMENDMENTS TO THE CONSTITUTION.

Mr. Madison rose, and reminded the House that this was the day that he had theretofore named for bringing forward amendments to the constitution, as contemplated in the fifth article of the constitution, addressing the Speaker as follows: This day, Mr. Speaker, is the day assigned for taking into consideration the subject of amendments to the constitution. A I considered myself bound in honor and in duty to do what I have done on the subject, I shall proceed to bring the amendments before you as soon as possible, and advocate them until they shall be finally adopted or rejected by a constitutional majority of this House. With a view of drawing your attention to this important object, I shall move that this House do now resolve itself into a Committee of the whole on the state of the Union; by which an opportunity will be given, to bring forward with some propositions, which I have strong hopes will meet with the unanimous approbation of this House, after the fullest discussion and most serious regard. I therefore move you, that the House now go into a committee on this business.

Mr. SMITH[17] was not inclined to interrupt the measures which the public were so anxiously expecting, by going into a Committee of the whole at this time. He observed there were two modes of introducing this business to the House. One by appointing a select committee to take into consideration the several amendments proposed by the State conventions; this he thought the most likely way to shorten the business. The other was, that the gentleman should lay his propositions on the table, for the consideration of the members; that they should be printed, and taken up for discussion at a future day. Either of these modes would enable the House to enter upon business better prepared than could be the case by a sudden transition from other important concerns to which their minds were strongly bent. He therefore hoped that the honorable gentleman would consent to bring the subject forward in one of those ways, in preference to going into a Committee of the whole.

[...]

Mr. JACKSON.[18] – I am of opinion [sic] we ought not to be in a hurry with respect to altering the constitution. For my part, I have no idea of speculating in this serious manner on theory. If I agree to alterations in the mode of administering this Government, I shall like to stand on the sure ground of experience, and not be treading air. What experience have we had of the good or bad qualities of this constitution? Can any gentleman affirm to me one proposition that is a certain and absolute amendment? I deny that he can. Our constitution, sir, is like a vessel just launched, and lying at the wharf; she is untried, you can hardly discover any one of her properties. It is not known how she will answer her helm, or lay her course; whether she will bear with safety the precious freight to be deposited in her hold. But, in this state, will the prudent merchant attempt alterations? Will he employ workmen to tear off the planking and take asunder the frame? He certainly will not. Let us, gentlemen, fit out our vessel, set up her masts, and expand her sails, and be guided by the experiment in our alterations. If she sails upon an uneven keel, let us right her by adding weight where it is wanting. In this way, we may remedy her defects to the satisfaction of all concerned; but if we proceed now to make alterations, we may deface a beauty, or deform a well proportioned piece of workmanship. In short, Mr. Speaker, I am not for amendments at this time; but if gentlemen should think it a subject deserving of attention, they will surely not neglect the more important business which is now unfinished before them. Without [passing] the collection bill we can get no revenue, and without revenue the wheels of Government cannot move. I am against taking up the subject at present, and shall therefore be totally against the amendments, if the Government is not organized, that I may see whether it is grievous or not.

[...]

[Rep. James Madison then took to the floor to deliver a speech defending each of the twelve proposed amendments, which he felt should be embodied in the Bill of Rights and sent to the states for ratification.]

In the next place, I wish to see that part of the constitution revised which declares that the number of Representatives shall not exceed the proportion of one for every thirty thousand persons, and allows one Representative to every State which rates below that proposition. If we attend to the discussion of this subject, which has taken place in the State conventions, and even in the opinion of the friends to the constitution, an alteration here is proper. It is the sense of the people of America, that the number of Representatives ought to be increased, but particularly that it should not be left in the discretion of the Government to diminish them, below that proportion which certainly is in the power of the Legislature as the constitution now stands; and they may, as population of the country increases, increase the House of Representatives in a very unwieldy degree. I confess I always thought this part of the constitution defective, though not dangerous; and that it ought to be particularly attended to whenever Congress should go into the consideration of amendments.

There are several minor cases enumerated in my proposition, in which I wish also to see some alteration take place. That article which leaves it in the power of the Legislature to ascertain its own emolument, is one to which I allude. I do not believe this is a power which, in the ordinary course of Government, is likely to be abused. Perhaps of all the powers granted, it is least likely to abuse; but there is a seeming impropriety in leaving any set of men without control to put their hand into the public coffers, to take out money to put in their pockets; there is a seeming indecorum in such power, which leads me to propose a change. We have a guide to this alteration in several of the amendments which the different conventions have proposed. I have gone, therefore, so far as to fix it, that no law varying compensation, shall operate until there is a change in the Legislature, in which case it cannot be for the particular benefit of those who are concerned in determining the value of the service.

✺✺✺✺✺✺

Debate in the House of Representatives on the Potential Congressional Compensation Amendment, 14 August 1789.

The next proposition in the report was as follows:

Article I, Section 6. Between the words "United States," and "shall in all cases," strike out "they" and insert "but no law varying the compensation shall take effect, until an election of representatives shall have intervened. The members..."

Mr. SEDGWICK[19] thought much inconvenience and but very little good would result from this amendment; it might serve as a tool for designing men; they might reduce wages very low, much lower than it was possible for any gentleman to serve without injury to his private affairs, in order to procure popularity at home, provided a diminution of pay was looked upon as a desirable thing. It might also be done in order to prevent men of shining and disinterested abilities, but of indigent circumstances, from rendering their fellow-citizens those services they are well able to perform, and render a seat in this House less eligible than it ought to be.

Mr. VINING[20] thought every future Legislature would feel a degree of gratitude to the preceding one, which had performed so disagreeable a task for them. The committee, who had made this a part of their report, had been guided by a single reason, but which appeared to them a sufficient one. There was, to say the least of it, a disagreeable sensation, occasioned by leaving it in the breast of any man to set a value on his own work; it is true it is unavoidable in the present House, but it might, and ought to be avoided in [the] future; he therefore hoped it would obtain without any difficulty.

Mr. GERRY[21] would be in favor of this clause, if they could find means to secure an adequate representation; but he apprehended that it would be considerably endangered; he should therefore be against it.

Mr. MADISON thought the representation would be as well secured under this clause as it would be if it were omitted; and as it was desired by a great number of the people of America, he would consent to it, though he was not convinced it was absolutely necessary.

Mr. SEDGWICK remarked once more, that the proposition had two aspects which made it disagreeable to him; the one was to render a man popular to his constituents, the other to render the place ineligible to his competitor.

He thought there was very little danger of an abuse of power of laying their own wages; gentlemen were generally more inclined to make them moderate than excessive.

The question being put on the proposition, it was carried in the affirmative, twenty-seven for, and twenty against it.

The committee then rose and reported progress, and the House adjourned.

෴෴෴෴෴

Later elected Speaker of the House, Rep. Boehner of Ohio speaks on the ratification of the congressional compensation amendment, 7 May 1992.

RATIFICATION OF THE MADISON AMENDMENT

The SPEAKER pro tempore. Under a previous order of the House, the gentleman from Ohio [Mr. Boehner] is recognized for 5 minutes.

Mr. BOEHNER. Mr. Speaker, today is a very historic day in the United States. Today the State of Michigan became the 38th State to ratify the original Madison amendment. Therefore, today we have the 27th amendment to the U.S. Constitution.

The Madison amendment says simply that no law that varies the compensation for the services of Senators and Representatives can become effective until an election of Representatives has intervened.

The House in the 1989 Ethics in Government Act inserted that same language. The House followed the words of Madison when it gave itself its last pay raise. Madison proposed these words in September in 1789.

The necessary States to ratify this amendment did not occur in 1791. For all these years this amendment was laying there, proposed without a deadline.

Since 1978, 31 States have ratified this amendment, three this week.

The reason I am here today is to thank my colleagues in the freshman class on both sides of the aisle who participated in this project. This class has been heavily involved in the reform movement. We agreed early on that we needed a project to help bond our class around reform. This was our project and we have worked with those 15 remaining States that have not ratified this amendment. Earlier this week on Tuesday, the States of Alabama and Missouri ratified the amendment, setting up the historic day today when Michigan at 11:13 this morning was the 38th State to ratify the Madison amendment.

This is a long process that has endured, and the long process of reform is underway in America.

This is one small step that Congress and the American people have taken so that Congress will again become more accountable to the people in America. Nobody in America can give themselves a pay raise without getting the boss' vote. And what this amendment does is it gives the bosses, our bosses, the American voters, the right to judge whether we should have a pay increase or not.

Mr. Speaker, it is a responsible measure, and I hope and pray that it is certified by the Secretary of State and does in fact stay in effect.

෴෴෴෴෴

The leading historian on the Constitution and other facets of history in the Senate, Senator Robert Byrd, Democrat of West Virginia spoke out on the ratification of the Twenty-seventh Amendment, 19 May 1992.

THE PAY AMENDMENT.

Mr. BYRD. Mr. President, on May 12, I submitted, for myself and for the distinguished majority leader and the distinguished Republican leader, and the Senate agreed to, Senate Resolution 295, requesting the Archivist of the United States to communicate to the Senate a list of the States whose legislatures have voted to ratify the article of amendment to the Constitution of the United States proposed by the First Congress in 1789 to require a delay in the effective date of laws varying the compensation of Members of Congress.

The Archivist reported to the Senate on May 15 a list of ratifying States, indicating that 40 States had voted as of the report to ratify this amendment, beginning with Maryland on December 19, 1789, and concluding with Illinois on May 12, 1992. The number of States needed to ratify an amendment, which was 10, three-quarters of the original 13 States when the pay amendment was first sent to them, is now 38, three-fourths of our present 50 States.

According to the Archivist, Michigan became the 38th State to approve this amendment when its legislature ratified the amendment on May 7, 1992. As requested in Senate Resolution 295, the Archivist accompanied the list of ratifying States with copies of each of the resolutions adopted by the 40 ratifying States. Other States may ratify the pay amendment. Pursuant to Senate Resolution 295 the Archivist is requested to communicate to the Senate any further resolutions of ratification as he receives them.

Mr. President, as I described on submitting Senate Resolution 295, the reason for requesting the Archivist to forward these resolutions to the Senate is that the Congress, as the Supreme Court correctly interpreted article V of the Constitution in its most recent decision on the Constitution's amendment process, *Coleman v. Miller*, 307 U.S. 433 (1939), has the final responsibility to determine whether an article of amendment has been ratified by the requisite three-fourths of the States and has become a part of the Constitution.

In section 106(b) of title I of the United States Code, the Congress has provided by law that the Archivist of the United States shall have the ministerial task, '[w]henever official notice is received at the National Archives and Records Administration that any amendment proposed to the Constitution of the United States has been adopted, according to the provisions of the Constitution,' of publishing the amendment with a certificate of its ratification. The Archivist implements this responsibility by receiving ratifying resolutions from the States, comparing them with the text of the amendment which has been proposed by the Congress to assure that the States are ratifying what the Congress has proposed, counting the State ratifications, and, in the ordinary course, certifying an amendment once sufficient States have ratified.

In statutory form this procedure traces from 1818, when the Congress first enacted a law (Act of April 20, 1818, ch. 80, sec. 2, 3 Stat. 439) expressly giving this duty to the Secretary of State. It was last fully utilized in 1971 in the case of the 26th amendment, securing the right of 18-year-olds to vote, when the Administrator of General Services had the duty. The Congress had transferred the duty to the GSA Administrator in 1951 from the Secretary of State, and subsequently transferred it again to the Archivist in 1984.

The history of ratification procedures predates, of course, the act of April 20, 1818, and begins with the Bill of Rights, of which the congressional pay amendment originally had been part. The First Congress, upon agreeing to send amendments to the States, resolved to request the President to transmit the proposed amendments to the Executives of the original States. Then, beginning with the receipt of the first ratification, which was by Maryland, President Washington deposited the originals in the Office of Secretary of State Jefferson, and directed his Secretary, in the President's words, 'to lay a copy of the same before' the House and Senate (1 Annals of Cong. 939, 1077 (1790)). The same was done with each ratification of the Bill of Rights through that of Vermont, whose ratification Washington caused to be laid before the two Houses of Congress on January 18, 1792. After the requisite ratifications had been before the Congress for nearly 2 1/2 months, Jefferson provided to the States, by letters of March 1, 1792, official notice of the ratification of the first 10 amendments (2 Schwartz, Bill of Rights 1203 (1971)).

While in the ordinary course no question is presented about the efficacy of State ratifications, there has been a firm historical understanding, shared by the Congress and the Supreme Court, and until now by the executive branch, that the Executive's function with regard to certifying constitutional amendments is purely ministerial.

The Congress should have the opportunity to decide substantive questions, particularly when, as now, the Congress has asked that the ratifications be laid before it in order to permit the Congress to consider whether an amendment has been adopted in accordance with the Constitution.

In 1868 there was a question, which was novel at that time, about whether States could vote to rescind their ratifications of a constitutional amendment and whether such States should be counted toward ratification. On July 9, 1868, the Senate agreed to a resolution requesting the Secretary of State to report on the actions of States ratifying the proposed 14th amendment. Then, in a proclamation issued on July 20, 1868, the Secretary of State, acknowledging that no law authorized him to 'decide doubtful questions' about ratification, posed the question which needed to be answered; namely, whether the ratifications of rescinding States should be counted.

The following day, on July 21, the Congress answered the Secretary of State's question by adopting a concurrent resolution certifying the ratification of the 14th amendment and directing its promulgation by the Secretary of State. Only then, on July 28, 1868, did the Secretary of State certify the adoption and validity of the 14th amendment 'in conformance' to the July 21 concurrent resolution of the Congress.

In 1939, the Supreme Court, in Chief Justice Hughes' opinion for the Court in Coleman versus Miller, specifically recognized, to use the Court's words, the force of this 'historic precedent' (307 U.S. at 450). In that case, seven Justices were also of the view that only Congress is empowered to determine whether an amendment has lapsed. In Chief Justice Hughes' words, 'We think that the Congress in controlling the promulgation of the adoption of a constitutional amendment has the final determination of the question whether by lapse of time its proposal of the amendment has lost its vitality prior to the required ratifications.' Justice – and former Senator – Black's concurring opinion, joined in by Justices Roberts, Frankfurter, and Douglas, forcefully stated that 'Congress has sole and complete control over the amending process' (Id. at 459).

As I described in my statement a few days ago submitting Senate Resolution 295, the ratification of the congressional pay amendment presents a substantial and novel question of constitutional interpretation. That question is: 'Does an amendment proposed by Congress without a deadline for ratification remain open for ratification for more than 200 years?' Individuals may differ over the proper answer to that question. Indeed, over the past week or so, a number of distinguished constitutional scholars have offered widely differing views. No one can credibly dispute, however, that the question is an important one, and that by the prior precedent of the political branches, and by the Court's decision in Coleman versus Miller, it should be resolved by the Congress.

Indeed, a perusal of the resolutions of ratification which the Archivist has communicated to the Senate show that at least 12 States – Arkansas, Colorado, Iowa, Illinois, Kansas, Minnesota, Missouri, Montana, Nevada, North Dakota, Oregon, and Texas – expressly acknowledged the Supreme Court's holding, in Coleman versus Miller, that Congress, in the words of the Kansas Legislature, is 'the final arbiter' on whether too much time has elapsed between the original submission of an amendment and its ratification.

It is because of the importance of the constitutional question, and in appreciation of the role of the Congress under the Constitution in this regard, that I offered Senate Resolution 295 and requested the Archivist last week to defer taking any definitive action with regard to the ratification of this amendment for a brief period to permit the Congress an opportunity to fulfill its constitutional responsibilities. It is true that section 106(b) of title I of the United

States Code, which I referred to earlier, directs the Archivist to certify the adoption of an amendment 'forthwith' once he has received 'official notice' of its ratification in accordance with the provisions of the Constitution.

That law does not state, however, how the Archivist is to receive official notice of an amendment's ratification. When no constitutional questions are presented by an amendment's ratification, for example, with the amendment securing the right of 18 year olds to vote, it seems clear that the Archivist may consider direct notifications from ratifying States to be official notice. But in a case like the amendment presently before us, where a serious question exists about the efficacy of ratifications separated by more than 200 years, the resolutions of the ratifying States do not alone provide official notice of the amendment's ratification.

In such a case, the Archivist, as the Secretary of State before him, must appropriately look to Congress to resolve the constitutional questions and provide such official notice, providing him with a statutory basis upon which to act. All three branches of Government have previously construed this statute in this way, and I believe that it remains the correct reading today.

The Archivist would have fulfilled his obligation to act 'forthwith' by acting promptly to promulgate the pay amendment upon receiving a concurrent resolution of the Congress that ratification is complete, just as the Secretary of State, who had the same obligation to act 'forthwith,' issued a final proclamation on the adoption of the 14th amendment within just 1 week of the Congress' adoption of a concurrent resolution directing that amendment's promulgation.

Regrettably, the Archivist has not followed the historic precedent established by his predecessor in this area, the Secretary of State, but instead certified the ratification of the amendment without providing the Congress with the brief period which the Secretary of State understood that the Congress required to assess its constitutional responsibilities. Nevertheless, the Archivist's actions do not alter the fact that the decision about the time that has elapsed while the States have voted to ratify the congressional pay amendment is one for the Congress to make. Indeed, I have been assured that the Department of Justice understands that the Archivist's actions do not preclude Congress from exercising its proper role in the amendment process.

Last week, I submitted a second resolution, Senate Concurrent Resolution 117, which was referred to the Committee on the Judiciary, to certify the ratification of the congressional pay amendment. As I indicated in my statement, consideration of that resolution was at that time premature, because we had not yet received the official documentation of the State actions from the Archivist. The distinguished senior Senator from Iowa [Mr. GRASSLEY] also submitted a concurrent resolution, Senate Concurrent Resolution 118, to the same effect, which like mine was referred to the Committee on the Judiciary. It is my hope that the Senator from Iowa, whom I congratulate on his resolution, will join me in securing adoption of the resolutions which I will offer today, because there should be no partisan differences concerning them.

We have now received the Archivist's report and can appropriately consider the ratification question. It is apparent that the requisite number of States have ratified and that the text of the amendment that they agreed to is substantively identical, differing only in punctuation and capitalization.

The constitutional question is more difficult. All prior amendments have been ratified in a far shorter period, indeed, less than 4 years. Moreover, in this century, the Congress has seen fit to require amendments to be ratified in a short period of 7, or, in one case after an extension, 10 years.

I do not believe that the absence of any such deadline for this amendment is dispositive of the question. I believe that the norm should be that States should determine whether to ratify an amendment expeditiously, as has been the history for more than 200 years, whether a specific deadline is specified or not. I believe that contemporaneous action is preferable, because it better reveals the will of the people and is the most reasonable understanding of the intent of the Framers of our Constitution.

In most circumstances, I believe that a lapse of this length would be too great to sustain ratification of an amendment. This is true, I believe, for each of the other arguably outstanding amendments that had no specific deadline but were never ratified and are still out there floating around. The other amendment tracing from 1789, for example, addressing the size of the House of Representatives, has been superseded in my view by subsequent developments, the growth of the Nation and legislation fixing the size of the House. An amendment proposed in 1810, dealing with titles of nobility, has turned out not to address a problem of lasting significance.

An 1861 amendment addressing slavery, which was sent to the States on the eve of President Lincoln's inauguration and would have forever protected the institution of slavery from abolition, has been repudiated by history and by the adoption of the 13th amendment, which was timely ratified by the States in 1865 and has resolved that question for all time. Finally, the amendment proposed in 1924 dealing with child labor has been superseded by evolving decisions of the Supreme Court and by legislation. It, too, for a long time has ceased to respond to a lasting problem.

Additionally, the States have long had no interest in, and may be deemed finally and officially to have been abandoned, the size of the House, titles of nobility, slavery, and child labor amendments.

Although I have concluded that the congressional pay amendment should be found to have been properly ratified, I am equally firmly convinced that decisive action should be taken by the Congress to establish, for each of these other old proposed amendments, that no live interest has been expressed in these amendments by any State for decades, that the amendments failed of ratification in a timely fashion, and that they are no longer subject to being ratified.

The congressional pay amendment deserves a different fate. It responds to a concern, wisely identified by James Madison, about potential conflicts of interest and the appearance of conflicts of interest, that remains as valid today as it was the day that Madison drafted it. Consistent with Madison's concerns, the New Hampshire Legislature, on ratifying the amendment in 1985, identified the precise concern of the amendment in its resolution of ratification, to wit:

It is in the best interest of the taxpayer that this proposed amendment be ratified so that self-interest will not play a direct role in the decision of a United States Senator or Representative when voting on a law varying the compensation of Senators and Representatives.

The States, 40 of them in all, and 33 of them in a reasonably contemporaneous manner, have told us that they believe that this amendment deserves a place in our Constitution. There is strong support for the amendment among the public and in the Congress.

I do not believe that it would serve a useful purpose, or one necessitated to accommodate the intent of the Framers, in this unique situation, to begin the process of proposing this amendment for ratification anew. I believe that for the case of this amendment the purposes normally served by contemporaneous action have been fulfilled by the widespread, indeed almost universal, support for the amendment and the lack of any change in relevant conditions.

I do not intend our action with regard to this amendment to serve as a precedent or model for any other amendment, either one proposed in the past or one that may be proposed in the future. For all other such amendments, I believe that contemporaneous action, including reasonable proximity between proposal by the Congress and ratification by the States, is desirable and should be required, whether through a specific deadline or subsequent judgment.

For the reasons that I have outlined, however, I believe that it is appropriate and proper for the Congress finally to declare that the congressional pay amendment duly proposed by two-thirds of each House of the First Congress, and duly ratified by the legislatures of more than three-fourths of the States, has become a part of the Constitution of the United States to all intents and purposes.

I have prepared three resolutions to carry out these conclusions which I believe express the Senate's historic understanding of its responsibilities, and should merit the approbation of all my colleagues.

First, in keeping with the precedent established with regard to the 14th amendment, I have prepared a concurrent resolution, the form of resolution used by the Congress in declaring the ratification of that great amendment. It builds upon the concurrent resolutions which Senator Grassley and I offered separately last week – I offered a resolution on behalf of the two leaders – and which resolutions were referred to the Committee on the Judiciary. Now that we have received the report of the Archivist, it is appropriate, I believe, to begin the resolution by a reference to that report, as it is on the basis of that report we now have formal notice of the action of the ratifying States and also have the benefit of the Archivist's technical review of the ratifying documents.

I have also prepared a simple Senate resolution which puts the Senate directly and immediately on record as supporting the declaration of the validity and ratification of the pay amendment. Although I believe and hope that the House will act promptly on the concurrent resolution, I do not believe that the Senate should delay in expressing to the States, and to the Archivist, its conclusion that the pay amendment is now a valid part of the Constitution.

Finally, I have prepared a concurrent resolution to resolve that ratification periods for the size of House, titles of nobility, slavery, and child labor amendments, of the 1st, 11th, 36th, and 68th Congresses, have lapsed and that those amendments are no longer subject to ratification as part of the Constitution.

While we do not have a direct precedent, as in the case of the 14th amendment, for the form of the resolution, it is my considered judgment that the action should be taken also in the form of a concurrent resolution. Our action with respect to amendments which have lapsed, or which, additionally, have been repudiated by a subsequent ratified amendment as in the case of the slavery amendment draws equally from the power which the Supreme Court has recognized is constitutionally committed to Congress with respect to the amendment process. It is, therefore, appropriate that the Congress utilize the same instrument – namely, a concurrent resolution – both with respect to a declaration that an amendment has been ratified and with respect to a declaration that an amendment has lapsed.

Mr. President, I accordingly send to the desk a concurrent resolution on the ratification of the 27th amendment to the Constitution of the United States, a Senate resolution to the same effect, and a concurrent resolution on the lapse of the Nation's four other proposed but old and unratified amendments.

Mr. President, these resolutions will not be referred to any committee prior to the end of the day. I hope that during the day other Senators will want to cosponsor them and I will be happy to have them as cosponsors.

I ask unanimous consent that the report of the Archivist, together with the full text of the State ratifications and the texts of the four outstanding unratified amendments, be reprinted in the Record at the conclusion of my remarks.

Mr. President, I apologize for keeping Senators waiting. I yield the floor.

In reply to Byrd, Senator Charles Grassley, Republican of Kansas, spoke on the floor of the US Senate, 20 May 1992.

THE 27TH AMENDMENT TO THE CONSTITUTION.

Mr. GRASSLEY. Mr. President, I am a cosponsor of a resolution put forth by Senator Byrd, our distinguished President pro tempore, which deals with the subject of the 27th amendment to the Constitution. We are going to be voting on that issue this morning. I am glad that we are moving forward with this resolution.

Along the same line as what Senator Byrd is doing, I introduced a separate concurrent resolution last week that would declare the 27th amendment to be a part of our Constitution. That language of the 27th amendment has been floating around the country in reality for 202 years, since it was proposed by James Madison and adopted by the First Congress with the necessary two-thirds vote. It was ratified by a few States immediately, and recently by the several States, mostly since 1978. Finally, it was declared a part of our Constitution by the Archivist.

The Archivist has received the papers of certification from at least 38 ratifying States to this amendment. He has now notified the Senate concerning those papers. The Archivist made a decision that he has the constitutional power to make that the ratification, even after 202 years, and effectively make this a part of our Constitution.

So in an effort to make this crystal clear and in pursuit of the goal of clarity, I joined Senator Byrd in support of the resolution that we will be voting on, which puts the Senate on the record regarding this crucial amendment to the Constitution.

I do not think the importance of this day can be minimized at all. I have personally waged many battles in the past decade and a half, not only against congressional pay raises, but probably more often and more legitimately, against the various schemes of Congress—schemes to avoid accountability for pay raises—like having them without a vote.

Now, of course, this change in process is a part of the Constitution. As a result, a change will take place in the nature of any pay raise debate and all because of this long-awaited amendment that James Madison first proposed in the First Congress.

The text of the amendment that Madison proposed and which is now a part of our Constitution simply says:

No law varying the compensation for the services of Senators and Representatives shall take effect, until an election of Representatives shall have intervened.

It is as simple as saying Congress can vote itself a pay raise, but there must be an election by the people where, if the people want to make an issue out of the raise, they can do it and reject the very people who presumably voted for the pay raise.

Now the resolution that we are voting on today does not add anything to the ratification process. It simply affirms what I believe is already true: That this amendment became law when the 38th State voted in favor of its ratification. Since that 38th State ratified, 2 other States have also ratified, making the total number 40.

However, I think there is a reason that the Senate needs to act by this resolution and that reason is to ward off any legal attacks that might come on the issue of timeliness. The question is whether or not, after 202 years from its proposal to the Constitution by James Madison, the requisite three-fourths of the States ratification will be considered contemporaneous ratification. Since the 1920's, Congress has regularly put in proposed constitutional amendments a statement that they must be ratified by the three-fourths of the States within 7 years.

However, the Supreme Court made clear in 1939 in the Coleman decision that Congress has the authority to say whether the timeliness standard has been met. So I believe the constitutional standard has been met by the 38th State ratification, and the Senate is acting to go on record in support of the timeliness of this ratification.

I think many of us in this body are pleased to be able to follow in the steps of Madison as supporters of what is a very good idea, and an idea that is part of the Constitution of the State of Iowa, in which State legislators cannot raise their pay without an intervening election.

I believe this is the will of the people. I believe it will require more responsible governance on our part. I also believe that it will result in a more measured response on the part of Members who might otherwise be hasty on this issue. So I am pleased that the Senate will act on this resolution with the promptness that it deserves.

I yield back the remainder of my time.

Historical Background Documents

In this short selection, we see an argument between famed orator Patrick Henry and James Madison over the idea – not included in the original Constitution – of an amendment regarding congressional compensation and expenses. Because of the lack of such a provision, those who backed the original Constitution promised to add an amendment addressing the matter in a set of amendments, to be known as the Bill of Rights, June 1788.

Mr. HENRY. Mr. Chairman, our burden should, if possible, be rendered more light. I was in hopes some other gentleman would have objected to this part. The pay of the members is, by the Constitution, to be fixed by themselves, without limitation or restraint. They may therefore indulge themselves in the fullest extent. They may make their compensation as high as they please. I suppose, if they be good men, their own delicacy will lead them to be satisfied with moderate salaries. But there is no security for this, should they be otherwise inclined. I really believe that, if the state legislatures were to fix their pay, no inconvenience would result from it, and the public mind would be better satisfied. But in the same section there is a defect of a much greater consequence. There is no restraint on corruption. They may be appointed to offices without any material restriction, and the principal source of corruption in representatives is the hope or expectation of offices and emoluments. After the first organization of offices, and the government is put in motion, they may be appointed to any existing offices which become vacant, and they may create a multiplicity of offices, in order thereafter to be appointed to them. What says the clause? "No senator or representative shall, during the time for which he was elected, be appointed to any civil office, under the authority of the United States, which shall have been created, or the emoluments whereof shall have been increased, during such time." This is an idea strangely expressed.

He shall not accept of any office created during the time he is elected for, or of any office whereof the emoluments have been increased in that time. Does not this plainly say that, if an office be not created during the time for which he is elected, or if its emoluments be not increased during such time, he may accept of it? I can see it in no other light. If we wish to preclude the enticement to getting offices, there is a clear way of expressing it. If it be better that Congress should go out of their representative offices by accepting other offices, then it ought to be so. If not, we require an amendment in the clause, that it shall not be so. I may be wrong. Perhaps the honorable member may be able to give a satisfactory answer on this subject.

Mr. MADISON. Mr. Chairman, I most sincerely wish to give a proper explanation on this subject, in such a manner as may be to the satisfaction of every one. I shall suggest such considerations as led the Convention to approve of this clause. With respect to the right of ascertaining their own pay, I will acknowledge that their compensations, if practicable, should be fixed in the Constitution itself, so as not to be dependent on Congress itself, or on the state legislatures. The various vicissitudes, or rather the gradual diminution, of the value of all coins and circulating medium, is one reason against ascertaining them immutably; as what may be now an adequate compensation, might, by the progressive reduction of the value of our circulating medium, be extremely inadequate at a period not far distant.

It was thought improper to leave it to the state legislatures, because it is improper that one government should be dependent on another; and the great inconveniences experienced under the old Confederation show the states would be operated upon by local considerations, as contra distinguished from general and national interests. Experience shows us that they have been governed by such heretofore, and reason instructs us that they would be influenced by them again. This theoretic inconvenience of leaving to Congress the fixing their compensations is more than counterbalanced by this in the Confederation – that the state legislatures had a right to determine the pay of the members of Congress, which enabled the states to destroy the general government. There is no instance where this power has been abused. In America, legislative bodies have reduced their own wages lower, rather than augmented them. This is a power which cannot be abused without rousing universal attention and indignation. What would be the consequence of the Virginian legislature raising their pay to four or five pounds per day? The universal indignation of the people. Should the general Congress annex wages disproportionate to their service, or repugnant to the sense of the community, they would be universally execrated. The certainty of incurring the general detestation of the people will prevent abuse.

It was conceived that the great danger was in creating new offices, which would increase the burdens of the people; and not in a uniform admission of all meritorious characters to serve their country in the old offices. There is no instance of any state constitution which goes as far as this. It was thought to be a mean between two extremes. It guards against abuse by taking away the inducement to create new offices, or increase the emolument of old offices; and it gives them an opportunity of enjoying, in common with other citizens, any of the existing offices which they may be capable of executing. To have precluded them from this, would have been to exclude them from a common privilege to which every citizen is entitled, and to prevent those who had served their country with the greatest fidelity and ability from being on a par with their fellow-citizens. I think it as well guarded as reason requires; more so than the constitution of any other nation.

James Madison writes to James Monroe on the inclusion of a congressional compensation amendment to the Bill of Rights, 9 August 1789.

New York, August 9, 1789.

Dear Sir,

Your ideas on the proposed discrimination between foreign Nations coincide, I perceive, exactly with those which have governed me. The Senate did not allow that no effort should be made for vindicating our commercial interests, but argued that a more effectual mode should be substituted. A committee was appointed in that branch to report such a mode. The report made is founded on something like a retort of her restrictions in the West India channels. It is now said that as the measure would involve an imposition of extraordinary duties, the Senate cannot proceed in it. Mr. Gerry, alluding to these circumstances, moved two days ago for a bill giving further encouragement to trade and navigation, and obtained a committee for the purpose. What will be the result is uncertain. If the attempt, added to what has passed, should, as it probably will, be made known abroad, it may lead to apprehensions that may be salutary.

The attention of the House of Representatives for some days has been confined to the subject of compensations. The bill is at length brought into its final shape. Much discussion took place on the quantum for the members of Congress, and the question whether it should be the same for both Houses. My own opinion was in favor of a difference, founded on a reduction of the sum proposed with regard to the House of Representatives and an augmentation as to the Senate. As no difference took place, the case of the Senate, and of the members from S. Carolina and Georgia, had real weight against a lesser sum than 6 dollars, which I own is lighter than I had contemplated for the House of Representatives, and which I fear may excite criticisms not to be desired at the present moment.

Yesterday as spent on a Message from the President relative to Indian affairs, and the Militia Bills are ordered, providing for a Treaty with the hostile Tribes, and for regulating the Militia. The latter is an arduous task, and will probably not be compleated [sic] at this Session.

As Submitted to the States

No law, varying the compensation for the services of the Senators and Representatives, shall take effect, until an election of Representatives shall have intervened.

State Ratifications of the Twenty-seventh Amendment

State	Date
Maryland	19 December 1789
North Carolina	22 December 1789
South Carolina	19 January 1790
Delaware	28 January 1790
Vermont	3 November 1791
Virginia	15 December 1791
Ohio	6 May 1873
Wyoming	6 March 1978
Maine	27 April 1983
Colorado	2 April 1984
South Dakota	21 February 1985
New Hampshire	7 March 1985
Arizona	3 April 1985
Tennessee	23 May 1985
Oklahoma	10 July 1985
New Mexico	14 February 1986
Indiana	24 February 1986
Utah	25 February 1986
Arkansas	6 March 1987
Montana	17 March 1987
Connecticut	13 May 1987
Wisconsin	15 July 1987
Georgia	2 February 1988
West Virginia	10 March 1988
Louisiana	7 July 1988
Iowa	9 February 1989
Idaho	23 March 1989
Nevada	26 April 1989
Alaska	6 May 1989
Oregon	19 May 1989
Minnesota	22 May 1989
Texas	25 May 1989
Kansas	5 April 1990
Florida	31 May 1990
North Dakota	25 March 1991
Alabama	5 May 1992
Missouri	5 May 1992

Michigan	7 May 1992
New Jersey	7 May 1992
Illinois	12 May 1992
California	26 June 1992
Rhode Island	10 June 1993
Hawaii	29 April 1994
Washington	6 April 1995
Nebraska	1 April 2016

Note: The amendment was ratified 74,003 days after it was submitted to the states.

ORIGINAL PRIMARY DOCUMENTS

"A Founder Updates the Constitution": A Look at the Twenty-seventh Amendment, 203 years after its passage, in The Washington Post, *14 May 1992. The role of Madison is remembered in this article, published just as the Twenty-seventh Amendment was being considered as ratified.*

Across Two Centuries, A Founder Updates the Constitution

By Bill McAllister

James Madison's 202-year-old proposal for a constitutional amendment to prevent members of Congress from voting themselves a midterm pay raise is an idea whose time has come, the archivist of the United States declared yesterday.

With that endorsement, Archivist Don W. Wilson effectively proclaimed the one-sentence, 24-word measure the 27th Amendment to the Constitution. The amendment states, "No law, varying the compensation for the services of the senators and representatives, shall take effect, until an election of representatives shall have intervened."

Wilson's decision appeared to undercut suggestions by members of the Senate and House that Congress can block the measure from being added to the Constitution because it took so long for the required three-fourths of the states to ratify the proposal. Two leading constitutional scholars suggested yesterday that Congress may not have such power.

Congress submitted the amendment to the states on Sept. 25, 1789, as part of a package of 12 initial amendments. Ten of these were ratified by 1791 and became the Bill of Rights, but the pay raise prohibition found relatively little support. By 1800, only six states had endorsed the idea.

The amendment languished until the 1980s when a state legislative aide in Texas discovered the proposal and orchestrated a campaign that led to its approval last Thursday morning by the Michigan legislature, an action that gave it approval by the required three-fourths of the states.

Some members of Congress including House Speaker Thomas S. Foley (D-Wash.) and Sen. Robert C. Byrd (D-W. Va.), have expressed reservations over the viability of Madison's idea, insisting that the Founding Fathers wanted state approval of constitutional amendments to be contemporaneous with their submission by Congress. The Supreme Court made a similar suggestion in 1921 and 1939 rulings, but congressional supporters of the Madison amendment, noting that Congress imposed no time limit when it sent the measure to the states, argued that the Michigan action added it to the Constitution.

Yesterday, Wilson, 49, a Reagan administration appointee who holds a Ph.D. in history, sided with the supporters. "Upon receipt of formal notification of ratification of the congressional pay amendment by three-fourths of the states, I will, in accordance with 1 USC 106b, certify the adoption of the amendment," he said in a written statement.

His action ended any question over whether the archivist would grant conditional approval to the amendment or await further action by Congress or do nothing, options that his staff had suggested last week were possibilities following the Michigan vote.

As head of the National Archives and Records Administration, Wilson is the custodian of the Constitution. As such, he has the authority to declare when an amendment has been adopted. His publication of such a notice is likely in "the next day or two," said Susan Cooper, an Archives spokeswoman, noting that Wilson is still awaiting receipt of formal ratification papers from one of the last of the required 38 states.

Constitutional scholars seemed to agree that Congress's time to act on Madison's amendment had passed. "It is not Congress's role to declare Michigan's 1992 ratification too recent or Maryland's 1789 ratification too ancient," said Laurence H. Tribe, Harvard Law School professor of constitutional law, in an article in yesterday's *Wall Street Journal*.

Duke University law professor Walter Dellinger said he, too, considered the process completed. "My own view is that Congress has no formal role to play," he said. "The amendment process is completed by act of the last necessary state."

He did say that a congressional resolution backing the amendment would do "no harm" and might end the dispute. The founders were wary, he noted, of giving Congress the sole power to determine amendments.

Members of Congress seemed determined to press for congressional review. 'Congress – not the courts and not the executive – has the final say over whether an amendment has received the required votes for ratification in a reasonable time,' said Byrd.

Rep. Don Edwards (D-Calif.), chairman of the House Judiciary subcommittee on civil and constitutional rights, accused Wilson of usurping "ministerial" powers he holds by an act of Congress. "I don't see how Congress could give up such an important function to a political appointee," he said, disputing suggestions that congressional action is unnecessary.

"On its face it's a dangerous precedent," he said. Even so, Edwards said he had no doubt that Madison's proposal "is going to be made part of the Constitution. But it's going to be done right."

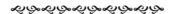

A statement from the Speaker of the US House of Representatives, as reported in the Wisconsin State Journal *[Madison], 15 May 1992.*

Foley Accepts Pay Amendment

By Katherine Rizzo
Associated Press

WASHINGTON – House Speaker Thomas Foley said Thursday he's changed his mind and doesn't think Congress needs to endorse a constitutional amendment banning instant raises for legislators.

"I now recognize it as an amendment," Foley told reporters a day after US Archivist Don Wilson announced plans to publish the 27th Amendment in the Federal Register.

"He saw the light. It's tremendous," said Rep. John Boehner, R-Ohio, who helped organize a drive to spur the last few state votes on the provision. "The amendment is ratified."

Foley's decision ended plans for House hearings into whether the long-dormant amendment became defunct sometime between 1789, when James Madison wrote it and last week, when Michigan became the 38th and deciding state to ratify it.

Modern-day amendments have gone to the states with seven-year limits, but the pay-raise amendment, drafted in the first Congress, didn't have a deadline.

The 202 1/2-year ratification period concerned a Congress reluctant to tamper with the Constitution and less than keen on pay-raise talk in an election year.

Foley said he saw no reason for any congressional action. "I do not think that that would serve any purpose," he said Thursday.

The chairman of the panel that had been gearing up for hearings said he still wants Congress to officially express its view.

"It would certainly serve a very useful purpose to have both the House and the Senate examine the papers and declare that they're in order and that the constitutional requirements have been met," said Rep. Don Edwards, D-Calif., who heads the civil and constitutional law subcommittee.

Boehner, too, wants a House vote to "affirm that we accept 38 ratifications."

Wilson, the archivist, says he'll certify the 27th Amendment as soon as the "instruments of ratification" for the states have been verified.

Foley said he's not worried about the precedent of states getting two centuries to consider changing the democracy's written foundation.

And he said he doesn't think the 27th Amendment will stop Congress from getting an automatic pay raise in January.

A 1989 law set up a system that gives Congress automatic, yearly cost-of-living raises.

The amendment wouldn't stop the COLA, he said, "because that is not a variation of law."

Boehner disagreed, saying, "I don't think the COLA can be paid. The Constitution supersedes any statutes passed by Congress."

Source: "Foley accepts pay amendment," *Wisconsin State Journal* [Madison], 15 May 1992, 3A.

An editorial in the Syracuse Herald-Journal *of New York, 30 May 1992.*

What Other Papers Are Saying

———

Milwaukee Sentinel on Congressional Pay Raises (May 23):

———

Congress apparently has come to the conclusion that what was good enough for the country 203 years ago is good enough now.

The Senate, by a 99-0 vote, and the House, by a margin of 414-3, gave their blessings to an amendment barring midterm raises for congressmen, even though it took from 1789 until early this month to get the mandatory approval from three-fourths of the states.

House Speaker Thomas S. Foley, D-Wash., had suggested the long delay might taint the legality of what is now the 27th Amendment, but said lawmakers didn't want the electorate to get the idea that Congress might try to undo the documented will of the people.

Certainly, few legislators would want to stand for re-election with that on their records.

One thing is sure. Any member of Congress who did not vote for the amendment, and is not among this year's lengthy list who have announced their retirements, may be in for trouble.

Bet your boots that prospective opponents are already taking names of those who voted "No" or who declined to vote.

SUPREME COURT CASES

Dillon v. Gloss *(256 U.S. 368 {1921}). Decided 16 May 1921 by a unanimous vote. Justice Willis Van Devanter delivered the opinion of the Court.*

The Case: The case arose in the wake of Prohibition. The petitioner, Dillon, was arrested and charged with violation of the National Prohibition Act. He petitioned for a writ of habeas corpus, arguing that in setting a time limit (seven years) for the ratification of the Eighteenth Amendment, Congress exceeded its authority under Article V of the Constitution and that therefore the amendment was invalid.

The Court held that Congress, if chooses, can set a reasonable time for the ratification process and that seven years is reasonable.

Justice Van Devanter wrote,

"We do not find anything in [Article V of the Constitution] which suggests that an amendment once proposed is to be open to ratification for all time, or that ratification in some of the states may be separated from that in others by many years and yet be effective. We do find that which strongly suggests the contrary. First, proposal and ratification are not treated as unrelated acts, but as succeeding steps in a single endeavor, the natural inference being that they are not to be widely separated in time. Secondly, it is only when there is deemed to be a necessity therefore that amendments are to be proposed, the reasonable implication being that when proposed they are to be considered and disposed of presently. Thirdly, as ratification is but the expression of the approbation of the people and is to be effective when had in threefourths of the states, there is a fair implication that it must be sufficiently contemporaneous in that number of states to reflect the will of the people in all sections at relatively the same period, which of course ratification scattered through a long series of years would not do. These considerations and the general purport and spirit of the article lead to the conclusion expressed by Judge Jameson 'that an alteration of the Constitution proposed to-day has relation to the sentiment and the felt needs of to-day, and that, if not ratified early while that sentiment may fairly be supposed to exist, it ought to be regarded as waived, and not again to be voted upon, unless a second time proposed by Congress.' That this is the better conclusion becomes even more manifest when what is comprehended in the other view is considered; for, according to it, four amendments proposed long ago – two in 1789, one in 1810 and one in 1861 – are still pending and in a situation where their ratification in some of the states many years since by representatives of generations now largely forgotten may be effectively supplemented in enough more states to make three-fourths by representatives of the present or some future generation. To that view few would be able to subscribe, and in our opinion it is quite untenable. We conclude that the fair inference or implication from article 5 is that the ratification must be within some reasonable time after the proposal."

Coleman v. Miller *(307 U.S. 433 {1939}). Decided 5 June 1939 by a vote of 7-2. Chief Justice Charles Hughes delivered the opinion of the Court.*

The Case: The case arose in Kansas as a result of the unratified Child Labor Amendment (1924). Kansas had rejected the amendment in 1925. When it came up for a vote again in 1937, a group of state senators voted against it, but they were overridden by one vote when the lieutenant governor, the presiding officer of the senate, cast the deciding vote in favor of the amendment. Later, the state's lower chamber ratified the amendment. The senators challenged the right of the lieutenant governor to cast the deciding vote, arguing that the amendment had lost its vitality by virtue of having previously been rejected and by the passage of time.

The Court, modifying its decision in *Dillon v. Gloss*, held that Congress has the final say in determining whether, by the passage of time, a proposed amendment has lost its vitality before being ratified by the required number of state legislatures. It further held that this was a political issue and hence one not with the purview of the judiciary. This decision would put to rest any questions about the validity of the Twenty-seventh Amendment, given the nearly 203 years between its proposal and its ratification.

Chief Justice Hughes wrote,

"The more serious question is whether the proposal by the Congress of the Amendment had lost its vitality through lapse of time, and hence it could not be ratified by the Kansas legislature in 1937. The argument of petitioners stresses the fact that nearly thirteen years elapsed between the proposal in 1924 and the ratification in question. It is said that, when the amendment was proposed, there was a definitely adverse popular sentiment, and that, at the end of 1925 there had been rejection by both houses of the legislatures of sixteen States, and ratification by only four States, and that it was not until about 1933 that an aggressive campaign was started in favor of the amendment. In reply, it is urged that Congress did not fix a limit of time for ratification, and that an unreasonably long time had not elapsed since the submission; that the conditions which gave rise to the amendment had not been eliminated; that the prevalence of child labor, the diversity of state laws, and the disparity in their administration, with the resulting competitive inequalities, continued to exist. Reference is also made to the fact that a number of the States have treated the amendment as still pending, and that, in the proceedings of the national government, there have been indications of the same view. It is said that there were fourteen ratifications in 1933, four in 1935, one in 1936, and three in 1937.

"We have held that the Congress, in proposing an amendment, may fix a reasonable time for ratification. *Dillon v. Gloss*, 256 U. S. 368. There, we sustained the action of the Congress in providing in the proposed Eighteenth Amendment that it should be inoperative unless ratified within seven years. No limitation of time for ratification is provided in the instant case, either in the proposed amendment or in the resolution of submission. But petitioners contend that, in the absence of a limitation by the Congress, the Court can and should decide what is a reasonable period within which ratification may be had. We are unable to agree with that contention.

"It is true that, in *Dillon v. Gloss*, supra, the Court said that nothing was found in Article V which suggested that an amendment, once proposed, was to be open to ratification for all time, or that ratification in some States might be separated from that in others by many years, and yet be effective; that there was a strong suggestion to the contrary in that proposal and ratification were but succeeding steps in a single endeavor; that, as amendments were deemed to be prompted by necessity, they should be considered and disposed of presently, and that there is a fair implication that ratification must be sufficiently contemporaneous in the required number of States to reflect the will of the people in all sections at relatively the same period, and hence that ratification must be within some reasonable time after the proposal. These considerations were cogent reasons for the decision in *Dillon v. Gloss*, supra, that the Congress had the power to fix a reasonable time for ratification. But it does not follow that, whenever Congress has not exercised that power, the Court should take upon itself the responsibility of deciding what constitutes a reasonable time and determine accordingly the validity of ratifications. That question was not involved in *Dillon v. Gloss*, supra, and, in accordance with familiar principle, what was there said must be read in the light of the point decided."

Chief Justice Hughes concluded,

"For the reasons we have stated, which we think to be as compelling as those which underlay the cited decisions, we think that the Congress, in controlling the promulgation of the adoption of a constitutional amendment, has the final determination of the question whether, by lapse of time, its proposal of the amendment had lost its vitality prior to the required ratifications. The state officials should not be restrained from certifying to the Secretary of State the adoption by the legislature of Kansas of the resolution of ratification."

WHO'S WHO

This section includes biographies of two individuals who played a significant part in drafting and passing the Twenty-seventh Amendment. They are both mentioned in earlier sections of this chapter.

Elbridge Gerry (1744-1814)

He served as a member of the Continental Congress, of the first congresses, and as Vice President of the United States. But it is the use of his name to mock the use of local power to engineer a congressional district favorable to one side of the political aisle or the other – now known as "gerrymandering" – for which Elbridge Gerry is best known. He did play an important role in the formation of the American nation, including the Constitutional Convention, and in the debate over the proposed amendment that, 203 years after its initial passage, became the Twenty-seventh Amendment to the US Constitution.

The third of twelve children of Thomas Gerry and his wife Elizabeth (née Greenleaf) Gerry, Elbridge was born in Marblehead, Massachusetts, on 17 July 1744. Thomas Gerry, a seaman and merchant, had been born in Devonshire, England, in 1713, and immigrated to New England in 1740 on a merchant ship that docked in Boston. Making his way to Marblehead, Gerry met Elizabeth Greenleaf, the daughter of a Marblehead merchant, and the two soon married. Their son, El-bridge, appeared almost from the beginning of his life to be headed for greater things; in 1758 he entered Harvard College (now Harvard University), and, although his grades were not spectacular, graduated in the upper portion of this class in 1762. He then went to work for Gerry & Company, run by his father. Gerry became more and more politically involved in the leading matter on the minds of people at the time: the growing dispute between England and the American colonies. He naturally found himself on the side of the colonists and, in 1765, returned to Harvard to complete his education, and submitted a thesis that argued it was wholly lawful for the colonists to defy those commercial laws passed by the English Parliament that went against colonial business rights. Radicalized by the Boston Massacre – the shooting of unarmed colonial protestors by British troops in Boston in 1772 – Gerry was elected to the General Court, also known as the Massachusetts colonial assembly.

Working with fellow Massachusetts politician Samuel Adams, brother of John Adams, Gerry helped form the Committee of Correspondence, in which messages opposing the government in London were secretly passed around to raise opposition to Parliament's policies. In 1773, Gerry drafted the letter that was sent to other colonies establishing a support network of colonial committees of correspondence. The following year, when he pushed for a program in Marblehead to inoculate people for small pox, Gerry was attacked by those who feared the shots; the hospital he helped to construct was burned down. In protest over the action, he resigned his membership in the Committee of Correspondence and returned home. It was not until the British government passed a series of legislative laws, known in the colonies as the Intolerable Acts or the Coercive Acts, in 1774 (including the socalled "Quartering Act," which allowed British troops to be "quartered" in the homes of colonists, against their will if necessary) that Gerry felt compelled to return to the political field. He was elected to the Massachusetts Provincial Congress, a body considered illegal by the British authorities, and he served on the congress' Committee of Supply and its Executive Committee of Safety. When fighting broke out between colonial militiamen and British troops in April 1775 at Lexington and Concord, both in Massachusetts, it was Gerry, utilizing his merchant supply routes and experience, who aided the colonial troops with arms and other materiel. The following year, as the war plunged the colonies into a conflict that rapidly sapped its economic strength, Gerry was elected to a seat in the First Continental Congress, which met in Philadelphia. He was an early and enthusiastic supporter of American independence, going further in his beliefs and statements that some of the most ardent supporters of independence. John Adams, also elected to the First Continental Congress, wrote of his fellow Massachusetts delegate, "If every man here was a Gerry, the Liberties of America would be safe against the Gates of Earth and Hell." In July 1776, Gerry signed his name to the Declaration of Independence, in effect marking him as either a Founding Father or one slated for death for treason against the King of England. During his two tenures in the First and Second Continental Congress, 1776-81 and 1783-85, Gerry used his expertise in business and merchant matters to aid the newborn American nation in the area of finance.

Gerry did not play a role in the military side of the war; instead, by 1783, he realized, alongside many other politicians, that the governing document of the-then colonial government, the Articles of Confederation, were leaving the "central" government weak and unable to properly fight the war, or formulate a plan for a future government under a single nation if the colonies defeated the British. The Articles left the Continental Congress unable to properly regulate commerce amongst the colonies that would aid in raising revenue to fund a central government. Gerry had initially believed that any dictates from a central government over trade infringed on the rights of the separate colonies to conduct business on their own terms. Peace settled with England did not immediately change his attitude. What did was the 1785 passage of a law in Massachusetts that laid a heavy import duty on British goods into that state, as well as a similar duty on American goods shipped to England on British ships. Seeing trade impacted on a local basis changed Gerry's mind on the need for a national, rather than a state-bystate, standard. Gerry wrote to Rufus King, "I am sorry [that] the states have not adopted the Recommendation of the last year, respecting Commerce. They were the best that could then be obtained, but would prove vastly inadequate to the Exigency of our affairs at this Time. If Congress and the legislatures have not sense sufficient to rectify the commercial *Evils*, they will rectify *themselves*." That September, Gerry wrote to Samuel Adams, "I am happy to find that We unite in Sentiment in the Necessity of vesting Congress with more commercial powers: and flatter myself We shall not differ in making them in the first Instance temporary, and in opposing a general Revision of the Confederation. [I]t is difficult to determine on a good Expedient, to remedy our present Evils, but We shall attempt it, if Time will permit..." In 1786, Gerry married for the first time, at age 41, to 20-year-old Ann Thompson of New York.

Troubled by the uprising, led by farmer Daniel Shays, against the power of the federal government under the Articles of Confederation, Gerry decided to take up an invitation and attend the so-called Constitutional Convention, held in Philadelphia in the summer of 1787. While there were arguments over whether or not to have a strong central government with weak state governments, or a weak central government with stronger state governments, Gerry felt that a weak central government, led by men of intelligence, should lead over weak state governments. Such a scheme, he believed, could forestall any attempts to use power against the people, while at the same time holding back and defending against anarchy, which Gerry saw giving way to Shays' Rebellion. One man that Gerry feared was George Washington, who, as the head of the Continental Army during the Revolutionary War, was now being considered as the leading candidate to be the first chief executive of the nation under a new Constitution. Gerry believed that once given the reins of power, Washington could well seize them and style himself into a dictator. Gerry found himself during much of the convention at odds with James Madison, the leading proponent of a document that would have three separate branches in the federal government, including a Congress with an upper and lower body. When Madison resisted, and included a specific listing of rights in the main body of the document, Gerry denounced it. He strongly called for a proviso in the Constitution in which citizen legislators would not be paid for their service. He said during one debate, "It would seem to be a maxim of democracy to starve the public servants." Despite his and others' opposition, including that of delegate Benjamin Franklin, the payment through the federal treasury was established in the original Constitution. Even though Gerry's work to rescue the document over objections between large state representation and small state representation was important to ultimately saving the Convention from collapsing, in September, when the document was completed, Gerry refused to sign, objecting to, most notably, the lack of a bill of rights. Madison refused to listen to Gerry's argument that states would resist ratifying the document if a bill of rights was not involved. Gerry was half right; once Madison realized that the states would not ratify, he promised that a bill of rights would be drafted immediately in the new US Congress and sent to the states quickly. Even though Gerry demanded that his state not ratify the Constitution, it did with the proviso that a bill of rights would soon follow.

Gerry was elected to a seat in the US House of Representatives, where he sat in the First (1789-91) and Second Congress (1791-93). He was instrumental in helping to draft the twelve amendments sent to the states for ratification – ultimately, only 10 of the 12 were ratified at that time. Of the two that were not ratified, the one that went to the heart of Gerry's objections to the Constitution itself was the one that allowed legislators in the Federal Congress to grant themselves increases in salary. This amendment, had it been ratified at that time, would have outlawed any rise in congressional compensation until after an election for a seat in the US House of Representatives or the US Senate had occurred. Unknown to Gerry, the amendment would not be ratified as the Twentyseventh Amendment until 1992, 203 years after Gerry first helped to draft it.

Gerry had been close to Samuel Adams and John Adams in Massachusetts; in 1797, John Adams, now the second President of the United States, named Gerry, along with John Marshall and Charles Cotesworth Pinckney, as envoys extraordinary to France to discuss and conclude differences between the two nations. When the French Foreign Minister, Charles Maurice de Talleyrand-Périgord, 1st Prince de Bénévent, mistreated the three diplomats and then demanded bribes (in the sum of $250,000) in return for meeting his agents, who had been branded as "X, Y, and Z" by the Americans, the envoys stormed out in protest. This so-called "XYZ Affair" outraged the American nation. While Marshall and Pinckney sailed from France back to the United States, Gerry, in contravention of his instructions, remained in Paris, fearing that if he left there was a possibility of war between the US and France. In the end, Gerry worked through the outrageous behavior of the French and concluded the talks on a firm footing that left his name in good stead. President Adams later said, "He [Gerry] was nominated and approved and finally saved the peace of the nation; he alone discovered and furnished the evidence that X, Y, and Z, were employed by Talleyrand; and he alone brought home the direct formal official assurances, upon which the subsequent commission proceeded and peace was made."

Returning to America, in October 1798, Gerry was approached by the Republican Party of Massachusetts (not the Republican Party as we know it today) to run as their candidate for Governor of the state. He was defeated. In 1801, Gerry was again defeated. In 1810, he ran a third time, and was elected, serving until 1812. He ran a fourth time in 1812, but was defeated. Although he had begun his career as a member of the loose coalition known as the "anti-Administration" party – those in opposition to the administration of President George Washington – by the time he had served as Governor, he was a firm anti-Federalist, committed to fighting a strong central government. Despite his hatred of strong-willed political power, it was during his tenure as Governor that an electoral bill came through the legislature that had his support; it was an action that set aside areas of Federalist support into narrower and narrower districts, in effect diluting that party's strength. Critics dubbed his bill a "gerrymander," and saluted the governor with cartoons of a salamander named Elbridge Gerry. Even today, two centuries later, we can still hear the term "gerrymander" used in political parlance, as in "they tried to gerrymander that district."

In 1812, James Madison, who had grown into an anti-Federalist himself, ran for President, and Gerry was named as his running mate. Elected as Vice President of the United States, Elbridge Gerry reached a political plateau few could have predicted, even as he railed against the federal government and centralized power. The War of 1812 began just prior to their administration, but during Gerry's short time in office, both Madison and Gerry were ill, and there were fears that an antiwar Senator could take over if one or more of the men died in office.

Gerry did not need to worry about the fate of the nation, although his own fate was sealed. Chest pains were followed by heaviness in his lungs, which led to his death, perhaps from dropsy (now called edema), on 23 November 1814 at the age of 70. He had served as Vice President for a little more than 20 months. He was laid to rest not in his native Massachusetts but in the Congressional Cemetery in Washington, DC.

In a 1955 dissertation on Gerry's life, Eugene Kramer wrote, "Elbridge Gerry was short in stature and slight in build. His fashionable dress was neat and dapper without being foppish or ornate. A rather high pitched nasal twang marred his speaking voice, making it unpleasing in private conversation and public address. This handicap combined with a long, laboring and repetitious writing and speaking style, did not help his public career. Such a lack of facility in communicating ideas may have been caused by an interest in dry economic affairs or by his training in the Continental Congress where policy decisions were rarely reached in open debate." And from historian Samuel Morison in 1929, "Gerry was an important figure in his day and generation; signer of the Declaration of Independence, member of the Federal Convention, minister to France, governor of Massachusetts, vice-president of the United States. It seems worthwhile to search for the key to its character and career."

Theodore Sedgwick (1746-1813)

Examination of the work of the First Congress (1789-91), of which Theodore Sedgwick was a member, shows that during the raucous debate over the eventual twelve amendments sent to the states for ratification (of which only ten were ratified), Sedgwick played a key role in shaping the language over one of the two amendments not ratified at that time – the one that took 203 years to ratify, ultimately becoming the Twenty-seventh Amendment to the US Constitution. Sedgwick later served as Speaker of the House during the Sixth Congress (1799-1801).

Sedgwick was born in Hartford, Connecticut, on 9 May 1746, the son of Benjamin Sedgwick, a farmer and the owner of a store in Hartford, and his wife Ann (née Thompson) Sedgwick. The Sedgwick family can be traced back to the Sedgwickes of Dent, Yorkshire, during the reign of Henry VI, who was the King of England from 1422 to 1461. According to "A Genealogical Register of the first Settlers of New-England," published in 1829, Theodore was descended from Robert Sedgwick, who "went to England...and was employed by [Oliver] Cromwell in 1654. He was engaged in the great expedition against the Spanish West-Indies, when Jamaica was taken. There he d[ied]" 24 May 1656.

Benjamin Sedgwick moved his family to Cornwall, Connecticut, soon after the birth of his son Theodore, but died suddenly in 1757 when the younger Sedgwick was just 11. His older brother, John, served as the family's new source of revenue, working, as his father did, as a farmer and innkeeper. Theodore Sedgwick attended a local academy, then entered Yale College (now Yale University) in 1761. Although he was thrown out of the institution for allegedly breaking the rules, in 1772, he was given a degree for the years that he did his work there.

Sedgwick studied the law in the offices of a local attorney in Great Barrington, Massachusetts, was admitted to the Massachusetts bar in 1766, and then opened a law office there. The following year, he relocated to Sheffield, Massachusetts and, in 1768, married Elizabeth Mason of that town. The couple had no children, and Elizabeth Sedgwick died of the smallpox in 1771. In 1774, Sedgwick married Pamela Dwight, the daughter of Joseph Dwight (1703-1765), a noted judge in colonial Massachusetts, and Abigail Williams, the daughter of the Christian preacher Jonathan Williams. Sedgwick and his second wife had ten children, most notably Catharine Maria Sedgwick, a well-known 19th century writer, and Theodore Sedgwick, Jr., a leading Jacksonian politician.

In 1773, Theodore Sedgwick penned the so-called "Sheffield Resolves," a list of grievances that colonists lodged against the British crown and government. The following year, when a Berkshire Provincial Congress was held to address these concerns, Sedgwick was elected as one of two delegates to the conference to represent Sheffield. A series of British actions, culminating in the so-called Intolerable Acts – including the quartering of British troops in the homes of colonists against their will – gave rise to a desire for a boycott in Massachusetts of British goods and, ultimately, a call for colonial independence from Britain.

Sedgwick was named to the Continental Army with the rank of Major, and he saw action in the unsuccessful American invasion of Canada as well as at the battle of White Plains, New York, in 1776. After his military career ended, Sedgwick served as a commissioner of supply to purchase needed goods for the Continental Army. In 1780, he was elected to represent Sheffield in the newly-instituted Massachusetts state House of Representatives, established under a new state constitution enacted that same year. After three years of service in the House, in 1783, Sedgwick was elected to the Massachusetts state Senate to represent Berkshire County; he sat in this body from 1784 to 1785, after which he resigned. Those in Sheffield, however, desired his leadership, and they elected him again to the state House, where he served from 1787 until 1789, rising to become Speaker of that body in 1788. During this same period, Sedgwick served as a commissioner to try to settle a border dispute with New York; he also served three terms (1785, 1787-88) as a delegate to the Confederation Congress, where he initially opposed any changes to the Articles of Confederation, then the governing document of the US government. However, the outbreak of a rebellion of farmers in western Massachusetts, led by farmer Daniel Shays, convinced Sedgwick that a new founding document, establishing a strong central government, was needed to stave off anarchy in the states.

Although he did not serve as a delegate to the Constitutional Convention in Philadelphia in 1787, Sedgwick was there to support the document, but only with the promise that a comprehensive list of personal rights, called the Bill of Rights, would be immediately sent to the states for ratification as amendments to the new Constitution. Sedgwick sat on a committee that drafted the language of proposed amendments; once the promise of their being submitted to the states came about, Massachusetts narrowly ratified the original Constitution. This document created a US Congress, with a lower house – a House of Representatives – and an upper house – a Senate. In 1788, in elections for seats in the First Congress (1789-91), Sedgwick was elected to represent Berkshire and Hampshire counties. It was in this first Congress that Sedgwick rose to oppose an amendment that would curb any raises in congressional compensation from taking effect until after a new election had taken place. In the floor debate, Sedgwick noted that rich landowners could use the amendment to take power, and that the amendment would protect "men of shining and disinterested abilities, but of indigent circumstances." Although there was dissension over the matter, it was included as one of 12 amendments submitted to the states, although only 10 of these were ratified at the time.

A staunch Federalist, Sedgwick was a close confidante of President George Washington, and in 1795, when Alexander Hamilton resigned as Secretary of the Treasury, Washington offered the vacant post to Sedgwick, who declined the honor.

Having served from the First Congress (1789-91) into the Fourth Congress (1795-97), Sedgwick resigned his seat in 1796, when the Massachusetts General Court elected him to the US Senate to fill the vacancy caused by the resignation of Caleb Strong. Remaining a true Federalist, Sedgwick backed President John Adams, although he broke with Adams in 1798, when Sedgwick was refused a nomination to the US Supreme Court to succeed the deceased Justice James Wilson. Sedgwick was a supporter of the controversial Alien and Sedition Acts of 1798.

In 1798, as his Senate term was ending, Sedgwick ran for his old seat in the US House, and he was elected. In this, the Sixth Congress (1799-1801), Sedgwick was elected as the Speaker of the House. During his single two-year term as Speaker, he argued with President Adams, eventually working to deny him a second term in 1800. He disliked Thomas Jefferson, and was forced to back Aaron Burr for President. When Burr came in second – prior to the Eleventh Amendment, the Vice President was the candidate who received the second highest number of electoral votes – it was Sedgwick as the Speaker who had to announce Jefferson's election as President.

Sedgwick did not seek another term, but stepped down in 1801. In what the *Connecticut Courant* of Hartford called "Mr. Sedgewick's [sic] Farewell Address," the retiring Speaker told the House, "Accept, gentlemen, my thanks for the respectful terms in which you have been pleased to express the opinion you entertain of the manner in which I have discharged the arduous duties of the station to which I was raised by your kind regard... Although I am conscious of having intended faithfully to execute the trust confided to this chair; yet I am sensible, that whatever success may have attended my endeavors, is justly attributable to the candid, and honorable, and firm support which you have constantly afforded: I cannot law the least claim to any thing that I have done, because the generous confidence which you had reposed in me, demanded, that I should devote all my feeble talents to your service."

Sedgwick appeared to retire from politics at the end of his House service, but two years later, he did accept an appointment as an associate justice of the Massachusetts Supreme Judicial Court, on which he served until his death. While on this court, he denounced slavery, declaring that all men were "born free and equal" in the first decade of the 19th century.

Sedgwick's second wife died in 1807, and the following year, he married his third wife, Penelope Russell. Sedgwick died in Boston on 24 January 1813, at the age of 66. He was laid to rest in the Sedgwick family cemetery in Stockbridge, Massachusetts. His grave reads, "Beneath this stone are deposited the remains of the Hon. THEODORE SEDGWICK, who died in Boston, Jan. 24 A.D. 1813. Aged 66."

FOOTNOTES, SOURCES, FURTHER READING

Footnotes

[1] Bernstein, Richard B., "The Sleeper Wakes: The History and Legacy of the Twenty-Seventh Amendment," *Fordham Law Review*, LXI:3 (1992), 497-557.

[2] Porritt, Edward; and Annie Gertrude Porritt, "The Unreformed House of Commons: Parliamentary Representation Before 1832" (Cambridge: At the University Press; two volumes, 1903), I:153.

[3] Ibid., I:159.

[4] Farrand, Max, ed., "The Records of the Federal Convention of 1787" (New Haven, Connecticut: Yale University Press; two volumes, 1911), I:48.

[5] "The Twenty-Three Resolutions Referred to the Committee of Detail[,] July 26," in Hannis Taylor, "The Origin and Growth of the American Constitution. An Historical Treatise in Which the Documentary Evidence as to the Making Embodied in the Existing Constitution of the United States is, for the First Time, Set Forth as a Complete and Consistent Whole" (Boston: Houghton Mifflin Company, 1911), 583.

[6] Farrand, I:216

[7] Ibid., I:371-72

[8] Ibid., I:372.

[9] Ibid., I:372

[10] Ibid., I:373.

[11] "The Debates and Proceedings in the Congress of the United States; With an Appendix, Containing Important State Papers and Public Documents, and the Laws of a Public Nature; With a Copious Index. Volume 1, Comprising (with Volume II) the Period from March 3, 1789, to March 3, 1791, Inclusive. Compiled from Authentic Materials, by Joseph Gales, Senior" (Washington: Printed and Published by Gales and Seaton, 1834), 457.

[12] Ibid., I:755.

[13] Strickland, Ruth Ann, "The Twenty-Seventh Amendment and Constitutional Change by Stealth," *PS: Political Science and Politics*, XXVI:4 (December 1993), 718.

[14] Rhode Island never ratified the original Constitution, and as such could not vote on the original 12 amendments; thus, because at the time only 11 of the 12 states could vote on the first amendments to the Constitution, only 9, and not 10, were needed for ratification of the amendments. Rhode Island finally ratified the Constitution in 1790, but by that time the Bill of Rights had already received the sufficient number of states for ratification.

[15] Van Devanter decision in *Dillon v. Gloss* (256 US 358 {1921}), at 374.

[16] Tribe, Laurence H., "The Invisible Constitution" (New York: Oxford University Press 2008), 3.

[17] William Loughton Smith (1728-1814), Pro-Administration of South Carolina, Member, South Carolina Privy Council (1784), Member, South Carolina state House of Representatives (1787-88), US Representative (1789-97), US Minister to Portugal and Spain (1797-1801), US Minister to the Ottoman Porte (1799), Member, South Carolina state House of Representatives (1808).

[18] James Jackson (1757-1806), Republican of Georgia, US Representative (1789-91), US Senator (1793-95, 1801-06), Governor of Georgia (1798-1801).

[19] Theodore Sedgwick (1746-1813), Federalist of Massachusetts, Member, Massachusetts state House of Representatives (1780, 1782-83, 1787-88), Member, state Senate (1784-85), Delegate, Continental Congress (1785, 1786, 1788), US Representative (1789-96, 1799-1801), US Senator (1796-99), Judge, Supreme Judicial Court of Massachusetts (1802-13).

[20] John Vining (1758-1802), No Affiliated Party, Delaware, Member, Continental Congress (1784-85), Member, Delaware state House of Representatives (1787-88), US Representative (1789-93), Member, Delaware state Senate (1793), US Senator (1793-98).

[21] Elbridge Gerry (1744-1814), Anti-Administration of Massachusetts, Member, Massachusetts colonial House of Representatives (1772-75), Member, Continental Congress (1776-80, 1783-85), Signer, Declaration of Independence (1776), delegate, Constitutional Convention (1787), US Representative (1789-93), Governor of Massachusetts (1810-12), Vice President of the United States (1813-14).

Sources Arranged by Chapter Sections

Debate in Congress

"The Debates and Proceedings in the Congress of the United States; With an Appendix, Containing Important State Papers and Public Documents, and the Laws of a Public Nature; With a Copious Index. Volume 1, Comprising (with Volume II) the Period from March 3, 1789, to

March 3, 1791, Inclusive. Compiled from Authentic Materials, by Joseph Gales, Senior" (Washington: Printed and Published by Gales and Seaton, 1834), 440-58, 755-65.

"The Congressional Record: Proceedings and Debates of the 102nd Congress, Second Session. Volume 138 – Part 9" (Washington, D.C.: Government Printing Office, 1992), H3075, S6828-30, S6939.

Historical Background Documents
Elliott, Jonathan, "The Debates in the Several State Conventions, on the Adoption of the Federal Constitution, as Recommended by the General Convention at Philadelphia, in 1787. Together with the Journal of the Federal Convention, Luther Martin's Letter, Yates's Minutes, Congressional Opinions, Virginia and Kentucky Resolutions of '98-'99, and Other Illustrations of the Constitution. In Five Volumes. Second Edition, With Considerable Additions" (Philadelphia: J.B. Lippincott & Co.; five volumes, 1891), III:368-70.

Madison to James Monroe, 9 August 1789, in "Letters and Other Writings of James Madison, Fourth President of the United States. In Four Volumes. Published by Order of Congress" (Philadelphia: J.B. Lippincott & Co.; four volumes, 1865), I:489-90.

Original Primary Documents
McAllister, Bill, "Across Two Centuries, A Founder Updates the Constitution," *The Washington Post*, 14 May 1992, —.

"What Other Papers are Saying," *Syracuse Herald-Journal* [New York], 30 May 1992, 5.

Supreme Court Cases
Dillon v. Gloss (256 U.S. 368 {1921}).
Dillon v. Gloss U.S. Supreme Court Transcript of Record with Supporting Pleadings (Farmington Hills, MI: Gale, 2011).

Coleman v. Miller (307 U.S. 433 {1939}).
Stone, Robert, ed., *Coleman v. Miller U.S. Supreme Court Transcript of Record with Supporting Pleadings* (Farmington Hills, MI, 2011).

Who's Who
Elbridge Gerry (1744-1814)
"Gerry, Elbridge," official congressional biography, online at http://bioguide.congress.gov/scripts/biodisplay.pl?index=G000139; Billias, George Athan, "Elbridge Gerry, Founding Father and Republican Statesman" (New York: McGraw-Hill, 1976); Gerry to Rufus King, 27 May 1785, mentioned in Edmund C. Burnett, ed., "Letters of Members of the Continental Congress" (Washington, D.C.: Published by The Carnegie Institution of Washington; eight volumes, 1936), VIII:121; Gerry to Samuel Adams, 30 September 1785, in ibid., VIII:224; Adams' remark on Gerry's mission in Paris in James Trecothick Austin, "The Life of Elbridge Gerry: With Contemporary Letters. To the Close of the American Revolution" (Boston: Wells and Lilly – Court-Street; two volumes, 1828-29), II:276; Kramer, Eugene, "The Public Career of Elbridge Gerry" (Ph.D. dissertation, Ohio State University, 1955), 2; Morison, Samuel E., "Elbridge Gerry: Gentleman-Democrat,' *The New England Quarterly*, II:1 (January 1929), 7.

Theodore Sedgwick (1746-1813)
"Sedgwick, Theodore," official congressional biography, online at http://bioguide.congress.gov/scripts/biodisplay.pl?index=S000222; Farmer, John, "A Genealogical Register of the First Settles of New-England" (Lancaster, Massachusetts: Published by Carter, Andrews, & Co., 1829), 258; Welch, Richard E., Jr., "Theodore Sedgwick, Federalist: A Political Portrait" (Middletown, Connecticut: Wesleyan University Press, 1965); "Mr. Sedgewick's Farewell Address," *Connecticut Courant* [Hartford], 16 March 1801, 3.

Further Reading

Berstein, Richard B., "The Sleeper Wakes: The History and Legacy of the Twenty-Seventh Amendment," *Fordham Law Review*, LXI (1992), 497-557.

Dalzell, Stewart, and Eric J. Beste, "Is the Twenty-Seventh Amendment 200 Years Too Late?," *George Washington Law Review*, LXII (April 1994), 502.

Paulsen, Michael Stokes, "A General Theory of Article V: The Constitutional Lessons of the Twenty-Seventh Amendment," *The Yale Law Journal*, CIII:3 (December 1993), 677-789.

Spotts, JoAnne D., "The Twenty-seventh Amendment: A Late Bloomer or a Dead Horse?," *Georgia State University Law Review*, X (1993), 337-65.

Van Alstyne, William W., "The Proposed Twenty-Seventh Amendment: A Brief, Supportive Comment," *Washington University Law Review*, MCMLXXIX:1 (1979), 189-204.

AMERICA AT THAT TIME . . .

Although the material in this section may not be directly related to the adoption of the Twenty-seventh Amendment, it offers valuable insight into what was happening in America at the time the Amendment was adopted. Modeled after Grey House Publishing's Working American *series, whose author, Scott Derks, is responsible for its content, it includes a Historical Snapshot, Selected Prices, significant quotations, and newspaper and magazine clips to give a sense of what was on the minds of Americans, and how it may have impacted the amendment process.*

HISTORICAL SNAPSHOT

1992

- Unemployment topped 7.1 percent, the highest in five years

- U.S. bombed Iraq for its failure to comply with United Nations-sponsored inspections

- David Letterman was offered $16 million to move to CBS opposite late-night host Jay Leno; Johnny Carson's last night as host of *The Tonight Show* drew a record 55 million viewers

- Bestsellers included Rush Limbaugh's *The Way Things Ought to Be*, H. Norman Schwarzkopf's *It Doesn't Take a Hero,* John Grisham's *The Pelican Brief* and Anne Rice's *The Tale of the Body Thief*

- The Supreme Court ruled that cross-burning is protected under the First Amendment, and that prayer at public school graduations is unconstitutional

- More than 20,000 people in California bought guns after the Los Angeles riots, which erupted when the men accused of beating Rodney King were acquitted

- In Kenya, Meave Leakey discovered the oldest hominid fossil to date, estimated to be 25 million years old and believed to be from the period of the ape-human divergence

- Movie openings included *Unforgiven, The Crying Game, Scent of a Woman, Malcolm X, Aladdin, Sister Act, Basic Instinct, The Last of the Mohicans, A River Runs Through It* and *White Men Can't Jump*

- Rudolph Marcus won the Nobel Prize in chemistry for his theory of electron-transfer reactions

- Eric Clapton won a Grammy award for his record "Tears in Heaven" and his album, "Unplugged"

- Poverty rose to 14.2 percent, the highest level since 1983

- At the Olympic Summer Games in Barcelona, the U.S. basketball team included Larry Bird, Magic Johnson and Michael Jordan

Selected Prices

Automobile, 1992 Miata $14.978.00

Bath Towel, J.C. Penney $4.90

Bed, Cherrywood, Full-Size $399.88

Christmas Tree, 7' Artificial. $124.99

Crackers, Nabisco Ritz-Bits. $1.69

Cruise Ticket, Alaska, per Person $2,395.00

Dishwasher, Whirlpool. $299.00

Fax Machine. $353.43

Festival Ticket, New Orleans Jazz $25.00

Flashlight, First Alert, Rechargeable $7.99

Hose, 3-Gauge Sprinkler, 50' $7.99

Shirt, Man's Spalding Golf Shirt $14.98

Turkey, per Pound $0.69

Weed Killer, Monsanto Round-Up, 24 Ounces $16.99

Vodka, Absolute, 750 ml $12.29

Year	Value of One Dollar in 2016 US Dollars
1990	$1.85
1991	$1.77
1992	$1.72
1993	$1.67
1994	$1.63
1995	$1.58

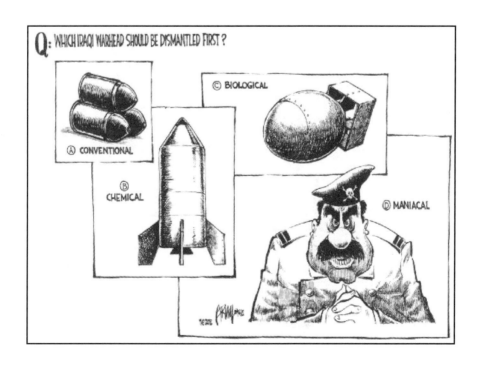

"Kneeboarding," *National Geographic World,* August 1992:

Bank out, mule kick, or flare . . . whatever you call it, this jump makes a splash. So does Zachary Rohner whenever he hits the water. Zack, who lives in Davie, Florida, set records in the junior boys' division for kneeboarding for four years. He graduated from that 12-and under group as Number One. Now at 14 he hopes to spin and flip his way to the top of the 18-and-under boys' division. . . .

"You have to love to compete and love to crash." That's Zack's prescription for kneeboarding success. He's a veteran of more than 30 competitions with a long string of titles—and a long string of practice crashes (falls) that helped him earn those titles.

"If you can't do something at first, just keep trying," says Zack. He practices every weekend on Lake Red Water in Florida, near his home.

Kneeboarding behind a motorboat started in California in 1975 as a spin-off from surfing. Zack discovered the sport when he was eight. "A neighbor showed me how to do it," he says. "I liked it right away so I just kept going."

"It's so easy to learn; 95 percent of the people who try it slide right off the beach and get a good ride the first time," says Mario Fassa, the reigning world champion.

Once you get beyond the first ride, what keeps you coming back for more? Zack, Mario, and others say it's the variety (you can do more tricks than you can on water skis) and the fun of flipping the board into the air. There's even a competition category called flip-out. The goal is to do 10 flips as fast as possible.

Kneeboarders also compete in slalom and trick events. Each trick earns a set number of points. Two of Zack's favorites are the wake O front (a complete turn while jumping the boat's wake) and the barrel roll.

Americans with Disabilities Timeline

1817
The American School for the Deaf was founded in Hartford, Connecticut, the first school for disabled children anywhere in the United States.

1848
The Perkins Institution in Boston, Massachusetts, became the first residential institution for people with mental retardation.

1864
The Columbia Institution for the Deaf and Dumb and Blind was authorized by the U.S. Congress to grant college degrees.

1927
The Supreme Court decision ruled that forced sterilization of people with disabilities was not a violation of their constitutional rights; nationally, 27 states began wholesale sterilization of "undesirables."

1935
The League for the Physically Handicapped in New York City was formed to protest discrimination by the Works Progress Administration.

The Social Security Act established federally funded old-age benefits and funds to states for assistance to blind individuals and disabled children.

1943
The LaFollette-Barden Vocational Rehabilitation Act added physical rehabilitation to the goals of federally funded vocational rehabilitation programs and provided funding for certain health care services.

1945
President Harry Truman created an annual national "Employ the Handicapped Week."

1948
The National Paraplegia Foundation, founded by members of the Paralyzed Veterans of America as the civilian arm of their growing movement, began advocating for disability rights.

1956
Social Security Amendments created the Social Security Disability Insurance program for disabled workers aged 50 to 64.

1961
President John Kennedy appointed a special President's Panel on Mental Retardation.

Continued

Timeline . . .

1963
The Mental Retardation Facilities and Community Health Centers Construction Act authorized federal grants for the construction of public and private nonprofit community mental health centers.

1965
Medicare and Medicaid were established providing federally subsidized health care to disabled and elderly Americans covered by the Social Security program.

1968
The Architectural Barriers Act prohibited architectural barriers in all federally owned or leased buildings.

1973
The Rehabilitation Act prohibited discrimination in federal programs and services and all other programs or services receiving federal funds.

1974
A suit filed in Pennsylvania on behalf of the residents of the Pennhurst State School and Hospital became a precedent in the battle for de-institutionalization of the mentally handicapped.

1975
The Individuals with Disabilities Education Act required free, appropriate public education in the least restrictive setting.

1977
Demonstrations by disability advocates took place in 10 American cities after Joseph Califano, U.S. Secretary of Health, Education and Welfare, refused to sign meaningful regulations.

1978
The American Disabled for Public Transit staged a year-long civil disobedience campaign to force the Denver, Colorado Transit Authority to purchase wheelchair lift-equipped buses.

1981–1984
Disability Rights advocates generated more than 40,000 cards and letters to Congress to halt attempts by the Reagan Administration to amend regulations implementing the Rehabilitation Act of 1973 and the Education for All Handicapped Children Act of 1975.

The Reagan Administration terminated the Social Security benefits of hundreds of thousands of disabled recipients.

Continued

Timeline . . .

1985
The Mental Illness Bill of Rights Act required states to provide protection and advocacy services for people with psychological disabilities.

1986
Toward Independence, a report of the National Council on the Handicapped, outlined the legal status of Americans with disabilities and documented the existence of discrimination.

1988
The Air Carrier Access Act prohibited airlines from refusing to serve people simply because they were disabled and from charging people with disabilities more than non-disabled travelers for airfare.

1990
The Americans with Disabilities Act provided comprehensive civil rights protection for people with disabilities; it mandated that local, state and federal governments and programs be accessible, and that businesses with more than 15 employees make "reasonable accommodations" for disabled workers.

No otherwise qualified handicapped individual in the United States, shall, solely by reason of his handicap, be excluded from the participation in, be denied the benefits of, or be subjected to discrimination under any program or activity receiving federal financial assistance.

—The Rehabilitation Act of 1973, Section 504

Congress adds its OK to 27th Amendment, May 21, 1992

By Jim Drinkard
Associated Press

WASHINGTON — Congress on Wednesday jumped aboard the already-ratified 27th Amendment to the Constitution, a day after the change became the law of the land.

Without debate, the Senate voted 99-0 for a resolution giving its blessing to the amendment, which forbids any pay raise Congress gives itself from taking effect until after the next congressional election.

The House followed suit a few hours later after delaying its vote until more lawmakers could return to Washington to vote in favor of what was seen as a politically popular, if symbolic, measure. The vote there was 414-3.

No action by Congress was needed, since the amendment had taken effect Tuesday, when it was published in the Federal Register. But House Speaker Thomas Foley, D-Wash., said lawmakers wanted to dispel any notion that they wanted to preserve the right to vote themselves an immediate pay raise.

The amendment was the first change in the Constitution since 1971, when the 26th Amendment granted 18-year-olds the right to vote.

Written by James Madison, the latest amendment was among the first ever sent to the states by the first Congress in 1789. Unlike the quickly ratified Bill of Rights, however, the proposal languished without ratification until Michigan put it over the top earlier this month.

Some had questioned its validity because of the 202-year lapse.

But the issue of whether the proposal was too old quickly withered in a political atmosphere in which Congress is under fire for pay raises, perquisites and ethical lapses and any reform measure is seen as a shield against an angry public.

Four amendments proposed long ago remain pending before the states; Byrd has introduced a resolution to declare them dead.

One, an amendment that would protect slavery from being banned by the Constitution, already is seen as moot because the 13th Amendment outlawed slavery. The others would limit each House member to representing 50,000 people, allow regulation of child labor and bar acceptance by American citizens of foreign titles of nobility.

All senators voted for the amendment except Sen. Lloyd Bentsen, D-Texas, who did not vote. In the House, only Reps. Neal Smith, D-Iowa; Craig Washington, D-Texas; and Chris Perkins, D-Ky., voted against it.

Making strides
Even small contributions help
in the fight against cancer

The American Cancer Society needs your help.

The Galveston chapter is holding a fund-raiser from 5 p.m. to 7 p.m. Sunday at Kempner Park, 28th Street and Avenue O. It's called Making Strides Against Cancer, and you don't have to contribute much to feel good about the event.

It's a celebration of how far mankind has come in the fight against cancer. Today, more than half the patients who are diagnosed with cancer fight it and beat it. It wasn't that long ago that there really wasn't much of a fight at all. Victory was out of the question.

Survival rates are better these days because a lot of people with the society have worked hard to educate the public about the importance of preventive measures and early detection. The rates also are better because the society has been successful in raising money for cancer research.

You can contribute to both types of success by attending the festival Sunday.

You can learn a thing or two about cancer risks and spread the word. And you can make a donation — either directly to the society or by a pledge to one of the walkers, runners or wheelchair riders in Sunday's Move-Along-AThon.

Whatever you do Sunday, try to drop by for a few minutes to help make the event a success.

People who have contributed time—whether it be a few minutes or years of service—have made the difference in survival rates that are the point of this celebration. The best contribution you could make would be your presence Sunday.

Written by Heber Taylor, assistant managing editor of The Galveston Daily News, *June 5, 1992.*

The 27ᵗʰ Amendment

An Editorial from *The Richmond Times-Dispatch*

House Speaker Tom Foley, who at first vowed to fight ratification of the 27ᵗʰ Amendment, seems to have recovered his political and constitutional senses. He now says that he "recognizes" the amendment written by James Madison 203 years ago as legitimate. James Madison foresaw that Congress would be tempted to give itself hefty compensation. His amendment requires a congressional election to take place between the time Congress voles itself a raise and the time it takes effect. This is a handy check against the sort of greedy midnight pay grabs we've seen in recent years.

Since the Constitution places no time limits on the ratification of amendments, Mr. Foley and other recent opponents of the 27ᵗʰ Amendment really had no constitutional grounds on which to challenge it. . .

The 27ᵗʰ Amendment may be tested as soon as the next round of federal cost-of-living salary increases. Under a 1989 law, Congress gave itself automatic cost-of-living raises, a mechanism clearly intended to dodge the furor that has accompanied Congress' recent pay raise votes. Some say the new amendment invalidates those automatic raises. Some say it doesn't. Mr. Madison would be amused.

Appendix A

THE CONSTITUTIONAL AMENDMENT PROCESS

The authority to amend the Constitution of the United States is derived from Article V of the Constitution. After Congress proposes an amendment, **the Archivist of the United States**, who heads the National Archives and Records Administration (NARA), is charged with responsibility for administering the ratification process under the provisions of 1 U.S.C. 106b. The Archivist has delegated many of the ministerial duties associated with this function to the Director of the Federal Register. Neither Article V of the Constitution nor section 106b describe the ratification process in detail. The Archivist and the Director of the Federal Register follow procedures and customs established by the Secretary of State, who performed these duties until 1950, and the Administrator of General Services, who served in this capacity until NARA assumed responsibility as an independent agency in 1985.

The Constitution provides that **an amendment may be proposed either by the Congress** with a two-thirds majority vote in both the House of Representatives and the Senate **or by a constitutional convention** called for by two-thirds of the State legislatures. None of the 27 amendments to the Constitution have been proposed by constitutional convention. The Congress proposes an amendment in the form of a joint resolution. Since the President does not have a constitutional role in the amendment process, the joint resolution does not go to the White House for signature or approval. The original document is **forwarded directly to NARA's Office of the Federal Register (OFR)** for processing and publication. The OFR adds legislative history notes to the joint resolution and publishes it in slip law format. The OFR also assembles an information package for the States which includes formal "redline" copies of the joint resolution, copies of the joint resolution in slip law format, and the statutory procedure for ratification under 1 U.S.C. 106b.

The Archivist submits the proposed amendment to the States for their consideration by sending a letter of **notification to each Governor** along with the informational material prepared by the OFR. The Governors then formally submit the amendment to their State legislatures. In the past, some State legislatures have not waited to receive official notice before taking action on a proposed amendment. When a State ratifies a proposed amendment, it sends the Archivist an original or certified copy of the State action, which is immediately conveyed to the Director of the Federal Register. The OFR examines ratification documents for facial legal sufficiency and an authenticating signature. If the documents are found to be in good order, the Director acknowledges receipt and maintains custody of them. The OFR retains these documents until an amendment is adopted or fails, and then transfers the records to the National Archives for preservation.

A proposed amendment **becomes part of the Constitution as soon as it is ratified by three-fourths of the States** (38 of 50 States). When the OFR verifies that it has received the required number of authenticated ratification documents, it drafts a **formal proclamation for the Archivist** to certify that the amendment is valid and has become part of the Constitution. This certification is published in the Federal Register and U.S. Statutes at Large and serves as official notice to the Congress and to the Nation that the amendment process has been completed.

In a few instances, States have sent official documents to NARA to record the rejection of an amendment or the rescission of a prior ratification. The Archivist does not make any substantive determinations as to the validity of State ratification actions, but it has been established that the Archivist's certification of the facial legal sufficiency of ratification documents is final and conclusive.

In recent history, the signing of the certification has become a ceremonial function attended by various dignitaries, which may include the President. President Johnson signed the certifications for the 24th and 25th Amendments as a witness, and President Nixon similarly witnessed the certification of the 26th Amendment along with three young scholars. On May 18, 1992, the Archivist performed the duties of the certifying official for the first time to recognize the ratification of the 27th Amendment, and the Director of the Federal Register signed the certification as a witness.

Source: The U.S. National Archives and Records Administration

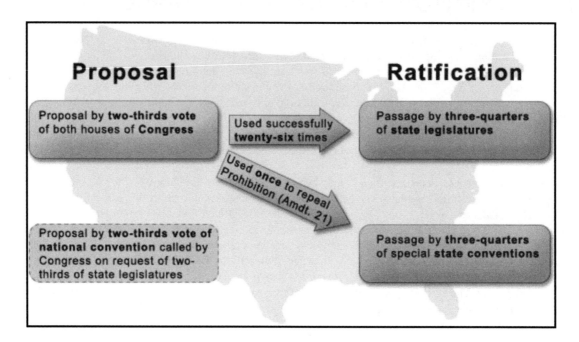

Source: utexas.edu

Appendix B

RATIFICATION OF AMENDMENTS TO THE U.S. CONSTITUTION

David C. Huckabee
Specialist in American National Government
Government Division

Congressional Research Service ♦ *The Library of Congress*

Summary

Article V of the U.S. Constitution provides two ways to propose amendments to the document and two ways to ratify them. Amendments may be proposed either by the Congress, by two-thirds votes of the House and the Senate (of those present and voting, provided a quorum is present), or by a convention called by Congress in response to applications from the legislatures of two-thirds (34) or more of the states.

Amendments must be ratified by three-quarters (38) or more of the states. The Congress can choose to refer proposed amendments either to state legislatures, or to special conventions called in the states to consider ratification. Only the 21st Amendment (repeal of Prohibition) has been ratified by conventions held in the states.

In the period beginning with the First Congress, through September 30, 1997 (105th Congress, 1st Session), a total of 10,980 proposals had been introduced to amend the Constitution. Thirty-three of these were proposed by Congress to the states, and 27 have been ratified. Excluding the 27th Amendment (Congressional Pay), which took more than 202 years, the longest pending proposed amendment that was successfully ratified was the 22nd Amendment (Presidential Tenure), which took three years, nine months, and four days. The 26th Amendment (18-year-old vote) was ratified in the shortest time: three months and 10 days. The average ratification time was one year, eight months, and seven days.

Ratification Deadlines

The practice of limiting the time available to the states to ratify proposed amendments began in 1917 with the 18th Amendment (Prohibition). All amendments proposed since then, with the exception of the 19th (Women's Suffrage) and the proposed child labor amendment, have included a deadline either in the body of the amendment proposed to the states, or in the joint resolution transmitting the amendment to the states to be ratified.

The 20th through 22nd Amendments incorporated the ratification deadline in the body of the amendment, so these amendments' deadlines are now part of the Constitution. Beginning with the 23rd Amendment, Congress began imposing the seven-year deadline in the joint resolutions transmitting the amendments to the state legislatures in order to avoid including extraneous language in the Constitution.[1]

---

[1] See: Walter Dellinger, "The Legitimacy of Constitutional Change: Rethinking the Amendment Process," *Harvard Law Review*, vol. 97, Dec. 1983, p. 408. Two exceptions to this practice were the 27th Amendment, because it was proposed in 1789, and the proposed District of Columbia voting representation amendment, where a seven-year time limit was included in the body of it.

The ratification deadline "clock" begins running on the day final action is completed in Congress (presidential approval of proposed amendments is not necessary). The amendment may be ratified at any time after final congressional action, even though the states have not been officially notified. The Archivist of the United States officially notifies the states (by registered letters to the governors) that an amendment has been proposed. The Archivist also keeps track of state ratifications and issues a proclamation when ratification is completed.[2]

The rules governing the consideration of proposed amendments vary among the states. Many legislatures require proposed amendments to be approved by "constitutional majorities"—a majority of the membership of the legislature (rather than a quorum for doing other legislative business). Some states require amendments to be ratified by the same margin as a proposed amendment to their state constitutions; others only require a majority of the legislators present and voting (provided a quorum is present). At least seven states require a "supermajority"[3] vote in one or more "chamber, either by rule, statute, or state constitution."[4]

The unprecedented time period of the 27th Amendment's successful ratification, and the decision by the 95th Congress to extend the seven-year deadline for the proposed Equal Rights Amendment (ERA) for an additional two years, 10 months, and 16 days,[5] has prompted speculation that Congress might have the power to revive other amendments proposed without ratification deadlines (in the body of the amendment) by enacting new ratification deadlines. At this writing, this matter is unresolved, but constitutional scholars distinguish the Equal Rights Amendment extension from efforts to revive amendments whose deadlines have expired because the ERA deadline was extended before the original deadline had expired.

The following tables list information about amendments that were proposed by Congress. Table 1 lists the dates of proposal and ratification, and the number of days each successful amendment was pending before the states before ratification. Table 2 provides summary statistics about amendments, and Table 3 lists the amendments Congress proposed that were not ratified by the states. Table 3 provides the date the amendment was proposed, its ratification deadline (if it had any) and the number of states that ratified it.

---

[2] Pursuant to 1 U.S.C. 106b.

[3] A "supermajority" requires more than a simple majority (one half, plus one). A supermajority ratification requirement for proposed amendments has been recognized by a federal District Court. In *Dyer v. Blair*, 390 F. Supp. 1291 (N.D. Ill. 1975), a federal District Court upheld an Illinois supermajority requirement for ratification of a proposed amendment to the U.S. Constitution.

[4] The seven States requiring "supermajority" votes to ratify amendments are Alabama, Colorado, Delaware, Georgia, Idaho, Illinois, and Kansas. See Scott Mackey and Brenda Erickson, The *Balanced Budget Amendment: The Road to Ratification: A Preliminary Report*, (Washington: National Conference of State Legislatures, 1995), p. 4.

[5] The Equal Rights Amendment was proposed on March 22, 1972. The original ratification deadline of March 21, 1979 was extended until January 30, 1982, with the adoption of H.J.Res. 638 on October 11, 1978.

Table 1. Time Required to Ratify Constitutional Amendments

Amendment	Date Proposed	Date Ratified	No. of days
1—Religion, speech, assembly	25-Sep-1789	15-Dec-1791	811
2—Bear arms	"	"	811
3—Quartering soldiers	"	"	811
4—Searches and seizures	"	"	811
5—Rights of persons	"	"	811
6—Rights of accused	"	"	811
7—Civil trials	"	"	811
8—Punishment for crime	"	"	811
9—Unenumerated rights	"	"	811
10—Reserved powers	"	"	811
11—Suits against states	04-Mar-1794	07-Feb-1795	340
12—Election of Pres. & Vice Pres.	09-Dec-1803	15-Jun-1804	189
13—Slavery	31-Jan-1865	06-Dec-1865	309
14—Rights guaranteed	13-Jun-1866	09-Jul-1868	757
15—Right to vote	26-Feb-1869	03-Feb-1870	342
16—Income tax	12-Jul-1909	03-Feb-1913	1,302
17—Pop. election of Senators	13-May-1912	08-Apr-1913	330
18—Prohibition	18-Dec-1917	16-Jan-1919	394
19—Women's suffrage	04-Jun-1919	18-Aug-1920	441
20—Commencement of terms	02-Mar-1932	23-Jan-1933	327
21—Repeal of prohibition	20-Feb-1933	05-Dec-1933	288
22—Presidential tenure	21-Mar-1947	27-Feb-1951	1,439
23—Pres. electors for D.C.	17-Jun-1960	29-Mar-1961	285
24—Abolition of poll taxes	27-Aug-1962	23-Jan-1964	514
25—Pres. vacancy, disability	06-Jul-1965	10-Feb-1967	584
26—18-year-old vote	23-Mar-1971	01-Jul-1971	100
27—Congressional salaries	25-Sep-1789	07-May-1992	74,003

Source: For dates proposed and ratified: U.S. Congress, House. *The Constitution of the United States of America, As Amended*, H. Doc. 102-188, 102nd Cong., 2nd sess., (Washington: GPO, 1992). Time to ratify calculated by CRS.

Table 2. Range, Mean, and Median Values for Ratifying Ratifying Constitutional Amendments

(Excluding 27th Amendment)

Maximum time to ratify	22nd amend.	1,439 days
Minimum time to ratify	26th amend.	100 days
Mean and median times to ratify	Median	Mean
18th & 19th centuries	811 days	670 days
20th century	394 days	546 days
18th – 20th centuries	670 days	617 days

Table 3. Unratified Amendments

Subject	Date proposed	Ratification deadline	No. of states ratifying
APPORTIONMENT—Regulates the apportionment of Representatives among the states.	25-Sep-1789	None	10
TITLES OF NOBILITY—Revokes citizenship of people accepting titles of nobility or "any present, pension, office or emolument of any kind whatever, from any emperor, king, prince or foreign power."	1-May-1810	None	12
SLAVERY—Prohibits constitutional amendments that will authorize Congress to "abolish or interfere, within any State, with the domestic institutions thereof, including that of persons held to labor or service by the laws of said State."	2-Mar-1861	None	2
CHILD LABOR—Gives Congress the "power to limit, regulate, and prohibit the labor of persons under 18 years of age."	2-Jun-1924	None	28
EQUAL RIGHTS—"Equality of rights under the law shall not be denied or abridged by the United States or by any State on account of sex."	22-Mar-1972 (proposed) 11-Oct-1978 (extended)	21-Mar-1979 (original) 30-Jan-1982 (extension)	35
D.C. REPRESENTATION—Treats the District of Columbia "as a State ... for the purposes of representation in the Congress, election of the President and Vice President, and article V of this Constitution."	22-Aug-1978	21-Aug-1985	16

Sources: U.S. Congress, House, *The Constitution of the United States of America As Amended,* H. Doc. No. 102-188, 102nd Cong., 2nd sess, (Washington: GPO, 1992); U.S. Library of Congress, Congressional Research Service, *Proposed Amendments to the Constitution of United States of America Introduced in Congress from the 91st Congress, 1st Session, Through the 98th Congress, 2nd Session, January 1969–December 1984,* by Richard A. Davis, CRS Report 85-36 GOV, (Washington: Feb. 1, 1985.)

Appendix C

PROPOSED AMENDMENTS TO THE US CONSTITUTION

Following this Introduction, each of these proposed amendments is defined and discussed in detailed sections. These sections include, as available, reprinted documents that help put the amendment into historical context, such as political debates, government reports, newspaper articles and Supreme Court cases.

Introduction

In 1897, historian Herman Ames published a massive historical work that documented the amendments of the US Constitution. He covered in detail the process of creating an amendment, examining the issues behind those that passed through Congress and were ratified by the states. He wrote, "The 'fathers' of the Constitution were not sanguine enough to suppose that the organic law which they had framed was so perfect that it would never need to be altered. The experience of the Government under the 'Articles of Confederation' had produced the conviction that there was need of system of [amendment] by which the Constitution could be made to conform to the requirements of future times. The specific provisions of Article V, which defines the manner of securing amendments to the Constitution, were not so much the result of institutional growth – as is true of so many of the provisions of the Constitution – as of mature deliberation and the spirit of compromise which characterized the work of the Constitution." **[1]** It is Ames' examination of the amending power of the Constitution that gives us a road map to the amending process.

In addition to the 27 amendments that have been ratified by the states – the main body of this work – a number of other amendments came close, but were never ratified. These proposed amendments are covered here. Why were they proposed? Why didn't they get ratified? Will they get ratified in the future? There have also been approximately 10,000 proposed amendments to the Constitution that did not come close to being ratified, many of these being the same amendment, proposed over and over again.

A recurring theme regarding proposed amendments has revolved around making the Constitution "religion friendly." In 1869, a constitutional amendment was introduced that acknowledged God "as the source of all authority and power in civil government, [and] the Lord Jesus Christ as the ruler among nations, and His will, revealed in the Holy Scriptures, as of supreme authority, in order to constitute a Christian government..." **[3]** Since 1880 numerous proposals were introduced in Congress to have a religious or Christian religious amendment added to the Constitution. In recent decades, an amendment that would protect school prayer or a moment of silence has been proposed, with little national support.

Other potential amendments dealt with the inability – or lack of desire – of the US government to properly safeguard the rights of blacks as granted under the Thirteenth, Fourteenth, and Fifteenth Amendments. In 1904, historian Charles W. Thomas, in an article for *The North American Review*, called on Congress to pass and submit to the states a "Sixteenth Amendment" which stated "[t]he Fifteenth Amendment to the Constitution of the United States and sections 2 and 3 of the Fourteenth Amendment thereto are hereby repealed and abrogated." [4]

In recent years, with the influx into the United States of non-English speaking persons, specifically from Spanish-speaking countries, there have been increased efforts to get a "national language" amendment added to the US Constitution. There has been little national support for such an amendment.

Time Limits

The amendment that eventually became the Twenty-seventh, ratified in 1992, was submitted to the states in 1789, a 203-year process. The Equal Rights Amendment, sent to the states in 1972 was given an additional three years past the typical seven-year limit, and expired in 1982. Why was one amendment allowed such a long time for passage, while the other fizzled out after a decade?

The answer is that since the submission of the Eighteenth Amendment, the US Supreme Court ordered Congress to place time limits on the ratification of constitutional amendments which, in most cases, is seven years. The 17 amendments that came before this decision were not held to that ruling.

The Supreme Court in *Coleman v. Miller*, 307 U.S. 433 (1939), declared that the question of the reasonableness of the time within which a sufficient number of states must act is a political question to be determined by the Congress. Justice Willis Van Devanter, writing the majority opinion, explained, "That this is the better conclusion becomes even more manifest when what is comprehended in the other view is considered; for, according to it, four amendments proposed long ago – two in 1789, one in 1810 and one in 1861 – are still pending and in a situation where their ratification in some of the States many years since by representatives of generations now largely forgotten may be effectively supplemented in enough States to make three-fourths by representatives of the present or some future generation. To that view few would be able to subscribe, and in our opinion it is quite untenable." [2]

[1] Ames, Herman V., "The Proposed Amendments to the Constitution of the United States During the First Century of Its History" in "Annual Report of the American Historical Association for the Year 1896 in Two Volumes" (Washington: Government Printing Office; two volumes, 1897), II:13.

[2] Van Devanter decision in *Dillon v. Gloss* (256 US 368 {1921}, at 375.

[3] "Proposed Amendment to Constitution of the United States" in Edward McPherson, "A Political Manual for 1869, Including a Classified Summary of the Important Executive, Legislative, Judicial, Politico-Military and General Facts of the Period. From July 15, 1868, to July 15, 1869" (Washington City: Philp & Solomons, 1869), 506.

[4] Thomas, Charles W., "A Sixteenth Amendment," The North American Review, CLXXIX; 574 (September 1904), 407.

THE APPORTIONMENT AMENDMENT, 1789

Text of the Proposed Amendment

After the first enumeration required by the first article of the Constitution, there shall be one Representative for every thirty thousand, until the number shall amount to one hundred, after which the proportion shall be so regulated by Congress, that there shall be not less than one hundred Representatives, nor less than one Representative for every forty thousand persons, until the number of Representatives shall amount to two hundred; after which the proportion shall be so regulated by Congress, that there shall not be less than two hundred Representatives, nor more than one Representative for every fifty thousand persons.

Discussion

In discussing the first twelve proposals sent to the states in 1789, historian Herman V. Ames wrote in 1897, "The House of Representatives, as the most numerous of the two constituent elements of Congress, and as the branch which springs most directly from the people, has been the object of many propositions for amendment. Some 150 amendments have been proposed to the provisions of the Constitution relative to this branch of Congress. Many attempts have been made to alter the qualifications of its members, to change their number and apportionment, and to control their election." [1]

Of the first proposed twelve amendments to the US Constitution sent to the states in 1789, only one has never been ratified. That single amendment is known as the Apportionment (or Enumeration) Amendment, and its main purpose was to set the apportionment for members of Congress.

The issue is not terribly exciting, and doesn't deal with giving additional or expanded rights to a certain group of persons. There is little historical evidence behind the so-called Apportionment Amendment, only that it was passed by the First Congress in 1789 as a potential "first" amendment, ahead of the freedom of speech and the freedom to own a firearm. Whatever the reason, many states simply ignored it, and it remains one of two of the original twelve not ratified at the time. The second of these two was ratified in 1992 as the Twenty-seventh Amendment. Historian Paul Rodgers wrote "The Congressional Apportionment Amendment was not ratified and now exists in limbo because no deadline for ratification was specified. However, the Amendment is unnecessary because the phrase `The number of Representatives shall not exceed one for every thirty Thousand' (Article I, Section 2, Clause 3) is interpreted to mean that there shall be at least thirty thousand persons for each Representative. To avoid the House leadership's becoming unwieldy, the Congress passed a law in 1911 that fixed the House membership at 435." [2]

[1] Ames, Herman V., "The Proposed Amendments to the Constitution of the United States During the First Century of Its History" in "Annual Report of the American Historical Association for the Year 1896 in Two Volumes" (Washington: Government Printing Office; two volumes, 1897), II:40.

[2] Rodgers, Paul, "United States Constitutional Law: An Introduction" (Jefferson, North Carolina: McFarland & Company, Inc., Publishers, 2011), 238.

ORIGINAL DOCUMENTS REGARDING THE APPORTIONMENT AMENDMENT

The Apportionment (Enumeration) Amendment is sent to the Senate for passage, 24 August 1789.

Monday, August 24.

Mr. FITZSIMONS, from the committee appointed, according to order, presented a bill establishing the salaries of the executive officers of Government, with their assistants and clerks, which was received and read the first time.

Mr. BENSON, from the committee appointed for the purpose, reported an arrangement of the articles of amendment to the constitution of the United States, as agreed to by the House on Friday last; also, a resolution prefixed to the same, which resolution was twice read and agreed to by the House, as follows:

Resolved by the Senate and House of Representatives of the United States of America in Congress assembled, (two thirds of both Houses deeming it necessary,) that the following Articles be proposed to the Legislatures of the several States, as Amendments to the constitution of the United States, all or any of which Articles, when ratified by three fourths of the said Legislatures, to be valid to all intents and purposes as part of the said constitution.

ARTICLES in addition to, and amendment of, the Constitution of the United States of America, proposed by Congress, and ratified by the Legislatures of the several States, pursuant to the fifth Article of the original Constitution.

ARTICLE THE FIRST.

After the first enumeration, required by the first Article of the Constitution, there shall be one Representative for every thirty thousand, until the number shall amount to one hundred, after which the proportion shall be so regulated by Congress, that there shall be not less than one hundred Representatives, nor less than one Representative for every forty thousand persons, until the number of Representatives shall amount to two hundred, after which the proportion shall be so regulated by Congress, that there shall not be less than two hundred Representatives, nor less than one Representative for every fifty thousand persons.

Source: "The Debates and Proceedings in the Congress of the United States; with an Appendix, Containing Important State Papers and Public Documents, and All the Laws of a Public Nature; with a Copious Index. Volume I, Comprising (with Volume II) The Period from March 3, 1789, to March 3, 1791, Inclusive. Compiled from Authentic Sources, by Joseph Gales, Senior" (Washington: Printed and Published by Gales and Seaton, 1834), I:808-14.

References

Amar, Akhil Reed "The Bill of Rights as a Constitution," *The Yale Law Journal*, C (1991), 1131-1210.

"The Debates and Proceedings in the Congress of the United States; with an Appendix, Containing Important State Papers and Public Documents, and All the Laws of a Public Nature; with a Copious Index. Volume I, Comprising (with Volume II) The Period from March 3, 1789, to March 3, 1791, Inclusive. Compiled from Authentic Sources, by Joseph Gales, Senior" (Washington: Printed and Published by Gales and Seaton, 1834).Volume I contains a vast sea of debate on the first twelve amendment sent to the states as the Bill of Rights, including the so-called "apportionment amendment."

Additional reading

Levy, Leonard W., "Origins of the Bill of Rights" (New Haven, Connecticut: Yale University Press, 1999), 287-88.

THE ANTI-NOBILITY TITLE AMENDMENT

Text of the Proposed Amendment

If any citizen of the United States shall accept, claim, receive or retain any title of nobility or honour, or shall, without the consent of Congress, accept and retain any present, pension, office or emolument of any kind whatever, from any emperor, king, prince or foreign power, such person shall cease to be a citizen of the United States, and shall be incapable of holding any office of trust or profit under them, or either of them.

Discussion

In 1810, members of Congress moved to amend the Constitution for the first time since the Twelfth Amendment was ratified in 1804. This amendment stated simply that any American citizen who accepted or received a title of nobility from any foreign power – even an ally of the United States – without the ascent of Congress, would be stripped of their American citizenship. Some historians call this proposed amendment "the missing Thirteenth Amendment," because they believe that it was actually ratified by the states. But it has never received the requisite number of states for ratification, and as such cannot be counted as a part of the US Constitution. Its identification with a "thirteenth amendment" was due to the fact that, had it been ratified, it would have been the 13th amendment.

Concerns had begun rather early in America's history on the usage of titles of nobility to gain favor with wavering citizens. In Federalist 84, Alexander Hamilton explained, "Nothing need be said to illustrate the importance of the prohibition of titles of nobility. This may truly be denominated the corner stone of republican government; for so long as they are excluded, there can never be serious danger that the government will be any other than that of the people." [1]

On 18 January 1810, Senator Philip Reed (1760-1829), Democratic-Republican (not a modern Republican, but a post-revolutionary Republican) of Maryland, introduced in the US Senate a proposed constitutional amendment that would ban any acceptance by an American citizen of a title of nobility from a foreign land or government. Sent to a committee of three, and then a committee of five, Reed's amendment was brought to the US Senate floor and quickly received the support it needed to get out of the Senate and sent to the US House for consideration. The US Senate approved Reed's amendment by a vote of 19-5 on 27 April 1810, just three months after it was introduced, and the US House of Representatives followed with a vote of 87-3 on 1 May 1810. One of the US Senators who voted against the amendment was Nicholas Gilman of New Hampshire, the only member of the Constitutional Convention of 1787 still in Congress. [2] There was little controversy in the debate, as at the time its necessity was seen as a strike against England and France and their attempt to "bore in" to the citizens of the new American nation through the issuances of titles of nobility from their nations. Two years after the amendment was passed by Congress, the United States was at war with Great Britain, and English troops eventually marched on the capital city of Washington and burned nearly every government structure to the ground.

True speculation as to the reasons behind the passage of the so-called "Titles of Nobility Amendment" (TONA) are mired in historical details. Jol A. Silversmith, who wrote about the "Missing Thirteenth Amendment," explained, "No debates about the amendment are recorded in the *Annals of Congress* or contemporary newspapers, so the reasons for its proposal are a matter of some speculation. One theory is that TONA was a reflection of the general animosity to foreigners evident in the United States before the War of 1812. This animosity manifested itself in a number of fashions. Henry Clay, for example, only with difficulty succeeded in limiting a Kentucky bill prohibiting the citation of British court decisions or treatises to works written after July 4, 1776. A similar bill was passed in Pennsylvania in 1810. Georgia's constitution of 1777, in force until 1789, excluded any person who held or claimed a title of nobility from voting or holding office. It is therefore understandable, Ames states, that in addition to finding nearly unanimous support in Congress, TONA found strong support in some states, for example passing both houses of the Pennsylvania legislature unanimously." [3]

Congressional research shows that the amendment was ratified by twelve states:

State	Date
Maryland	25 December 1810
Kentucky	31 January 1811
Ohio	31 January 1811
Delaware	2 February 1811
Pennsylvania	6 February 1811
New Jersey	13 February 1811
Vermont	24 October 1811
Tennessee	21 November 1811
North Carolina	23 December 1811
Georgia	31 December 1811
Massachusetts	27 February 1812
New Hampshire	9 December 1812

Three states voted the proposed amendment down:

New York	12 March 1812
Connecticut	13 May 1813
Rhode Island	15 September 1814

When war came between the United States and Britain, the matter of titles of nobility quickly became unimportant, and the amendment could not gather additional support before it was shelved (this was a time before a US Supreme Court dictate held that Congress had to impose firm deadlines for the ratification, or lack thereof, of a constitutional amendment). Historian John R. Vile wrote in 1994, "In 1810, Congress proposed another still unratified amendment whose history and motivation are still fairly obscure. This amendment would have made it illegal for any US citizen, and not for those who hold office, to accept titles of nobility from abroad…although this changed the text of the Constitution, support for this amendment may have reflected some of the concerns initially expressed by anti-Federalists that the new Constitution was establishing an aristocracy." [4]

[1] Hamilton, Alexander; John Jay, and James Madison (John C. Hamilton, ed.), "The Federalist. A Commentary on the Constitution of the United States. A Collect of Essays, by Alexander Hamilton, Jay and Madison. Also Continentalist and Other Papers, by Hamilton" (Philadelphia: J.B. Lippincott & Co., 1880), 629.

[2] Thorpe, Francis Newton, "The Constitutional History of the United States" (Chicago: Callaghan & Company; three volumes, 1901), 332.

[3] Silversmith, Jol A., "The `Missing Thirteenth Amendment': Constitutional Nonsense and Titles of Nobility," *Southern California Interdisciplinary Law Journal*, VIII (April 1999), 579.

[4] Vile, John R., "Constitutional Change in the United States: A Comparative Study of the Role of Constitutional Amendments, Judicial Legislative and Executive Actions" (Westport, Connecticut: Praeger Publishers, 1994), 24-25

References

"The Debates and Proceedings in the Congress of the United States; with an Appendix, Containing Important State Papers and Public Documents, and All the Laws of a Public Nature; with a Copious Index. Eleventh Congress – First and Second Sessions. Comprising the Period from May 22, 1809, to May 1, 1810, Inclusive. Compiled from Authentic Materials" (Washington: Printed and Published by Gales and Seaton, 1853). The few points of debate, which are few and far between, in this volume of the Annals of Congress, begin on page 530.

Silversmith, Jol A., "The `Missing Thirteenth Amendment': Constitutional Nonsense and Titles of Nobility," *Southern California Interdisciplinary Law Journal*, VIII (April 1999), 577-617.

Additional reading

"Constitution of the United States of America: Analysis and Interpretation" (Washington, D.C.: Government Printing Office, 2005), 47.

Vile, John R., "Constitutional Change in the United States: A Comparative Study of the Role of Constitutional Amendments, Judicial Legislative and Executive Actions" (Westport, Connecticut: Praeger Publishers, 1994), 24.

THE CORWIN SLAVERY AMENDMENT

Text of the Proposed Amendment

No amendment shall be made to the Constitution which will authorize or give to Congress the power to abolish or interfere, within any State, with the domestic institutions thereof, including that of persons held to labor or service by the laws of said State.'

Discussion

Of the proposed articles to the Constitution that made it to the states but did not get ratified is the Corwin Amendment, perhaps the most controversial. It proposed to save the Union as it rushed towards civil war, encapsulating slavery as a protected right in the US Constitution. Had it passed, it would have become the 13th amendment; instead, the amendment that became the actual Thirteenth Amendment outlawed slavery. [1]

In the period before the Civil War broke out, in November 1861, Republican Abraham Lincoln was elected the 16th President of the United States. At almost that same moment, southern slave-holding states began their march towards secession, their exit from the Union that consisted of the United States. This movement began in December 1861, when South Carolina became the first state to secede.

In February 1861, the administration of President James Buchanan was spending its last days doing nothing about the attempts by the southern states to seize federal property, including armories holding vast numbers of arms and similar materiel and ammunition which would eventually be turned against Union troops. The ultimate step towards war came when South Carolina troops fired on Fort Sumter; war had been declared between the North and the South.

In the Congress, however, and in official circles in Washington, talks were going on behind the scenes to try to head off this onrushing national disaster. A "peace convention" involving leading politicians from both sections met in Washington, with little success. The proposal that seemed to have the best chance of avoiding war came from a rather inconspicuous member of the House of Representatives, Representative Thomas Corwin, Democrat of Ohio. Corwin realized that the incoming administration of Abraham Lincoln did not have the political, nor the military, strength to fight a massive ground war to keep the slave states in the Union. So, in opposition to the political beliefs of most if not all of his Republican colleagues in the House and the Senate, Corwin introduced a potential amendment to the US Constitution which would cement the right to own slaves. Today, just the thought of such a proposal seems ludicrous. But Corwin was serious, believing that the preservation of the Union was far more important than freeing the slaves held in the country. To this end, he introduced his amendment which read:

"No Amendment shall be made to the Constitution which will authorize or give to Congress the power to abolish or interfere, within any state, with the domestic institutions thereof, including that of persons held to labor or service by the laws of said State."

On 2 March 1861, both houses of Congress passed this amendment with the requisite two-thirds vote in the affirmative. What was perhaps not fully realized at the time, was that Corwin's amendment, given its power to amend the Constitution by Article V, would have prohibited future congresses from using Article V from amending that constitutional amendment – in effect, Corwin's amendment would have been unconstitutional according to the original Constitution. At the same time, the language of the amendment did not preclude it being changed itself later on. But in the desire to do anything to put a halt to the growing threat of war, thoughts of what the amendment meant to the future were put aside. The vote in the House was 128 in favor with 65 against; in the Senate, the vote was 24 in favor and 12 against. [3]

President Buchanan, two days before he left office, signed the potential amendment. When the amendment outlawing slavery eventually became the actual Thirteenth Amendment, it too was signed by a President, Abraham Lincoln. These two instances are the only times in American history where potential constitutional amendments were signed by the president, even though his signature was not needed. Since this time, Congress has found that a president does not need to sign, and cannot veto, a potential constitutional amendment. **[4]**

The motion by Corwin did nothing to stop the war. Only three states ratified it, and by the time the third and final state voted in favor of it, Americans, fighting on both sides of the slavery and the Union issue, were dying on the battlefields that would litter the American landscape.

[1] Vile, John R., "Constitutional Change in the United States: A Comparative Study of the Role of Constitutional Amendments, Judicial Legislative and Executive Actions" (Westport, Connecticut: Praeger Publishers, 1994), 24-25.

[2] Kyvig, David E., "Ohio and the Shaping of the US Constitution" in Michael Les Benedict and John F. Winkler, "The History of Ohio Law" (Athens: Ohio University Press, 2004), 346-47.

[3] Holzer, Harold, "Lincoln, President-Elect: Abraham Lincoln and the Great Secession Winter 1860-1861" (New York: Simon & Schuster, 2008), 429.

[4] Tsesis, Alexander, "The Thirteenth Amendment and American Freedom: A Legal History" (New York: New York University Press, 2004), 2.

ORIGINAL DOCUMENTS REGARDING THE CORWIN SLAVERY AMENDMENT

Emboldened by the secession of several southern states and the movement in Congress led by action on the Corwin Amendment, the southern states laid down a series of demands which appeared to be a call for the surrender of the Northern states in their fight to end slavery. "National Difficulties: A Resolution of the Legislature of Tennessee" asking for a Constitutional Amendment to preserve slavery in the US Constitution, 28 January 1861, demonstrates the lengths to which these states were prepared to go to remain in the Union while making sure that slavery was constitutionally protected.

NATIONAL DIFFICULTIES: RESOLUTIONS OF THE LEGISLATURE OF THE STATE OF TENNESSEE RELATIVE TO

The present condition of national affairs, and suggesting certain amendments to the Constitution.

January 28, 1861. – Laid upon the table, and ordered to be printed.

1. *Resolved by the general assembly of Tennessee*, That a convention of delegates from all the slaveholding States should assemble at Nashville, Tennessee, or such other place as a majority of the States co-operating may designate, on the 4th day of February, to digest and define bases upon which, if possible, the federal Union and the constitutional rights of the slave States may be preserved and perpetuated.

2. *Resolved*, That the general assembly of Tennessee appoint a number of delegates to said convention, of our ablest and wisest men, equal to our whole delegation in Congress; and that the governor of Tennessee immediately furnish copies of these resolutions to the governors of the slaveholding States, and urge the participation of such States in said convention.

3. *Resolved*, That in the opinion of the general assembly of Tennessee, such plan of adjustment should embrace the following propositions as amendments to the Constitution of the United States:

First. A declaratory amendment that African slaves, as held under the institutions of the slaveholding States, shall be recognized as property, and entitled to the *status* of other property in the States where slavery exists, in all places within the exclusive jurisdiction of Congress in the slave States, in all the Territories south of 36 30', in the District of Columbia, in transit, and while temporarily sojourning with the owner in the non-slaveholding States and Territories north of 36 30'; and, when fugitives from the owner, in the several places above named, as well as in all places, in the exclusive jurisdiction of Congress in the non-slaveholding States.

Second. That in all the territory now owned, or which may be hereafter acquired by the United States, south of the parallel of 36 30', African slavery shall be recognized as existing, and be protected by all the departments of the federal and territorial government; and in all north of that line, now owned or to be acquired, it shall not be recognized as existing. And whenever States formed out any of said territory South of said line, having a population equal to that of congressional district, shall apply for admission into the Union, the same shall be admitted as slave States; while States north of the line, formed out of said territory and having a population equal to a congressional district, shall be admitted without slavery. But the States formed out of said territory, north and south, having been admitted as members of the Union, shall have all the powers over the institution of slavery possessed by the other States of the Union.

Third. Congress shall have no power to abolish slavery in places under its exclusive jurisdiction, and situate within the limits of States that permit the holding of slaves.

Fourth. Congress shall have no power to abolish slavery within the District of Columbia as long as it exists in the adjoining States of Virginia and Maryland, or either, nor without the consent of the inhabitants, nor without just compensation made to such owners of slaves as do not consent to such abolishment. Nor shall Congress at any time prohibit officers of the federal government, or members of Congress, whose duties required them to be in said District, from bringing with them their slaves, and holding them as such, during the time their duties may required them to remain there, and afterwards taking them from the District.

Fifth. Congress shall have no power to prohibit or hinder the transportation of slaves from one State to another, or to a Territory in which slaves are by law permitted to be held, whether that transportation be by land, navigable rivers, or by the sea.

Sixth. In addition to the fugitive slave clause, provide that when a slave has been demanded of the executive authority of the State to which he has fled, if he is not delivered, and the owner permitted to carry him out of the State in peace, that the State so failing to deliver, shall pay to the owner the value of such slave, and such damages as he might have sustained in attempting to reclaim his slave, and secure his right of action in the Supreme Court of the United States, with execution against the property of such State, and of the individual members thereof.

Seventh. No further amendment of the Constitution shall affect the five preceding articles, nor the third paragraph of the second section of the first article of the Constitution, nor the third paragraph of the second section of the fourth article of said Constitution; and no amendments shall be made to the Constitution which will authorize or give to Congress any power to abolish or interfere with slavery in any of the States by whose laws it is or may be allowed or permitted.

Eighth. That slave property shall be rendered secure in transit through, or while temporarily sojourning in the non-slaveholding States or Territories, or in the District of Columbia.

Ninth. An amendment to the effect that all fugitives are to be deemed those offending the laws within the jurisdiction of the State, and who escape therefrom to other States; and that it is the duty of each State to suppress armed invasions of another State.

4. *Resolved*, That said convention of the slaveholding States, having agreed upon a basis of adjustment satisfactory to themselves, showed, in the opinion of this general assembly, refer it to a convention of all the States, slaveholding and non-slaveholding, in the manner following: It should invite all the States friendly to such plan of adjustment to elect delegates in such manner as to reflect the popular will, to assemble in a constitutional convention of all the States, north and south, to be held at Richmond, Virginia, on the ___ day of February, 1861, to revise and perfect said plan of adjustment for its reference for final ratification and adoption by conventions of the States respectively.

5. *Resolved*, That should a plan of adjustment satisfactory to the south not be acceded to by the requisite number of States to perfect amendments to the Constitution of the United States, it is the opinion of this general assembly that the slaveholding States should adopt for themselves the Constitution of the United States, with such amendments as may be satisfactory to the slaveholding States; and that they should invite into a union with them all States of the north which are willing to abide such amended Constitution and frame of govern-ment, severing at once all connexion with States refusing such reasonable guarantees to our future safety – such renewed conditions of federal union being first submitted for ratification to conventions of all the States respectively.

6. *Resolved*, That the governor of Tennessee furnish copies of these resolutions immediately to the governors of the slaveholding and non-slaveholding States.

Source: "National Difficulties. Resolutions of the Legislature of the State of Tennessee, Relative to the Present Condition of National Affairs, and Suggesting Certain Amendments to the Constitution" House of Representatives Miscellaneous Document No. 27, 36th Congress, 2d Session (Washington: Government Printing Office, 1861), 1-3.

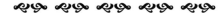

An update on the Corwin's amendment sees little movement towards passage.

TELEGRAPHIC.
MATTERS AT WASHINGTON.

The Vote on Mr. Corwin's Report.
Feeling among the Members.

———————

Special Despatch to the Commercial Advertiser. Washington, Thursday, Feb. 7.

Mr. Corwin, in the House to-day, said he would postpone the call for the question on his proposition until one week from to-day, when he hoped that the debate on the report of the committee of thirty-three would come to an end.

There is considerable animation manifest in the House to-day, and the members begin their work with good feeling.

The political barometer is so fluctuating, that little can be predicated from any single observation. The wisest have erred after much close study of the signs.

Source: "Telegraphic: Matters at Washington," *New York Commercial Advertiser*, 7 February 1861, 3.

"Amendments to the Constitution," a perspective from Pennsylvania, 21 February 1861 with a viewpoint from a small town newspaper on the goings-on in Washington, DC, arguing against the hasty submission of any pro-slavery amendment, including the ones introduced by Senator John Jordan Crittenden and Representative Thomas Corwin.

AMENDMENTS TO THE CONSTITUTION.

The friends of the Crittenden proposition have sought by every act to force that measure of adjustment to a final result with indecent haste. In a matter of such grave importance as the material amendment of the fundamental law of the land, one would suppose that a decent respect for the opinions of its illustrious originators, not less than those great public interests which are to be affected thereby, demands that such contemplated amendment or departure from established principles should be weighed with the utmost caution, deliberation and calmness, ere it should pass into the finality of established law. No possible exigency in the affairs of the government can justify a departure from such a policy. Under a constitution that has worked uniformly well for seventy-two years, dispensing happiness and prosperity among millions of people, there cannot spring up in a day such grievances and wrongs as require an immediate and hasty overhauling of the machinery, and the instant substitution of some new and untried contrivance, for the old, well balanced and time-tested machine, or for any part of it. To say that this political machine which we call a constitution, should, after moving smoothly along for seventy-two years, suddenly cause to perform some of its functions, or as suddenly commence to perform new functions, never contemplated by those who put it in motion, thereby causing intolerable and unendurable wrong to a great many people; and that therefore the machinery must be immediately readjusted with a new safety valve, or something of that sort, to save it from smashing incontinently to pieces, is so ansurd as not to be entitled to the dignity even of respectful consideration.

The Constitution, the bulwark of the personal rights and liberties of the American people, was the work of many years of deep and earnest thought. The most sagacious and comprehensive minds of the century which that chart of human rights illustrates, brought it from their closets in fragments, and framed the noble structure at Philadelphia, after many months of laborious effort. It is now proposed to approach it with Vandal hand, as if the structure was in a blaze, and tear away, here a rafter and there a joint, to despoil it of its grand old-fashioned columns, and supply their places with a new style of architecture, improvised by restless and daring men who feel no longer at home in the hospitable house of our Fathers.

If we are to do this thing, let us at least not do it in a hurry. We love the Union, because the Constitution is the Union. We love the Constitution because "justice" and "liberty" are established perpetually under its protecting roof. Let us have a care lest we put injustice and slavery in their places.

But we have another objection to this *post haste* style of amending the organic law. For six years past a political and moral doctrine known as Republicanism has been under quiet, searching, unintermitting examination in this country. It was no new doctrine; but so far had it been departed from and ignored by the then existing parties, that its very origin was in obscurity, and demanded equally with its spirit and tendency, the most minute investigation. After two years of calm discussion and inquiry, this doctrine was put upon trial at a Presidential election, and was declared constitutional and wise by some thirteen hundred thousand American citizens. The constitutional majority, however, was against it. Still, Massachusetts did not secede; neither did Pennsylvania, a *border State*, standing between the New England and the successful Slave States, demand that this Republican doctrine should be adopted, and the constitution amended in accordance with it, as the condition upon which she would remain in the Union. The defeated States did something better than this. They submitted uncomplainingly to the decree of the majority, and immediately recommenced the process of convincing that majority that it was in error. For four years this process went on as before, and in all those States where free, constitutional discussion was permitted, the rejected doctrine of 1856 was accepted by the people, and the candidate representing it was elected to the highest office in the government. The popular vote in its favor, even though its discussion was forbidden in 15 of the 33 States, rose from one million three hundred thousand to nearly two millions.

This judgment of the people, therefore, was not formed upon impulse or in a moment. It was the result of calm discussion and sober reflection. If it is to be overcome, let it be done in the same calm, deliberate and rational manner. There is an unspeakable *meanness* in the attempt which is now being persistently made to excite the fears of the people, and under the pressure of this thought-disabling influence, under the effects of intense excitement formented for the occasion, under the whip and spur of a gallop that knows no cooling time, lest the people should pause to think, to wrest from them those principles which are the result of mature and earnest reflection, and crush them under the heel of an irrepealable constitutional amendment.

Source: "Amendments to the Constitution," *The Reporter and Tribune* (Washington, Pennsylvania), 21 February 1861, 2.

"The National Crisis" as Reported in the Daily Dispatch *of Richmond, Virginia, 2 March 1861. Here is a southern perspective as the Congress prepared to pass the Corwin Amendment.*

SATURDAY MORNING....MARCH 2, 1861.
THE NATIONAL CRISIS.

_____

The Debate in Congress on the Corwin Amendment – Interview between Senator Douglas and Mr. Lincoln – The Southern Confederacy – A Northern Senator on Record – The Lincoln Conspiracy, &c.

_____

THE DEBATE IN CONGRESS ON THE CORWIN AMENDMENT.

When the motion to reconsider the vote respecting Mr. Corwin's amendment in the report of the Committee of Thirty-Three, was made in the House of Representatives, Thursday –

Mr. Kilgore [1], who moved the motion, called the attention of his Republican friends to the importance of the vote they were now called upon to give. But a few days ago they all emphatically declared, by sustaining the resolution unanimously adopted, that they had no desire or disposition to interfere with slavery in the States where it exists.

Yesterday, however, they seemed to have forgotten this declaration, carried away by wild fanaticism, and also the peculiar condition of the country requiring some action. If they had changed their grounds since the occasion which he had referred, and were now disposed to invade the sovereignty of the States, then he was no Republican.

In repeated speeches he had said those who blessed the Republicans of such design uttered a slander. Should they say to the world, when they are about to possess the power of the Government, that they are for using it to break down the sovereign rights of the United States, and invade their privileges. If that was the doctrine, he should not subscribe to it.

They should bear in mind that they were not the masters, but the mere servants of the people. The proposition to amend the Constitution should be taken to their masters, and the latter should be asked whether they will approve or reject it.

He appealed to them for the sake of the peace and quiet of the country, and for the good of the Republican party, to come forward to-day, and, with the same unanimity they voted for the resolution to which he had referred, declare the same thing in the pending proposition as an amendment to the Constitution. If you fail to give peace you wrong yourselves and not the people, and on your head will fall the responsibility.

Mr. Stanton [2] said that while there were fifteen slaveholding States acknowledging allegiance to the Federal Government, and therefore having in their hands the power to protect themselves against an invasion of their rights, it was a matter of little consequence whether such an amendment to the Constitution should be inaugurated or not.

But the state of the country is now essentially and radically changed. Seven or eight States now deny allegiance to the Government, and have proceeded to organize a separate Confederacy, independent of the Federal Government. Whether it will be recognized or not is a question for the future.

If these State maintain their position for a year or two, and it should appear that nothing but war or subjugation can bring them back, he would be disposed to recognize their independence. In this state of things, if the remaining slaveholding States remain in the Union, they are entitled to additional guarantees. – [Exclamation on Democratic side – "Good, that is right."]

There are now seven slaveholding and nineteen free States. In ten years hence Delaware will, for all practical purposes, be free. This will make twenty free and six slaveholding States, and in a few years more we will have five more free States. There would then be the requisite three-fourths of States to change the Constitution, and confer on the Federal Government power to interfere with slavery in the States.

He held that this was a power which should never be invested in Congress, even if there were only one slaveholding State. Slavery was a matter of local and State concern. If he were a citizen of a slaveholding State, desiring the emancipation of slavery, he would resist interference by the Federal Government. If it the purpose to afford constitutional protection to the slaveholding States, which the altered condition of the country demands, it was incumbent upon them to submit the proposition to the people to say at least how they will recognize it.

It ought not to be said that the Constitution which our fathers made is sufficient. At the time of its adoption there was only one free State, all the others slaveholding. Therefore there was no necessity for such guarantees then.

He was in earnest when he said that he did not desire to interfere with slavery in the States, and apprehended that his associates did not. If the Border Slave States remain in the Union he apprehended they have the right to demand such guarantees, and, so far as he is concerned, they shall have them. – [Applause from the Southern side.]

His friends on the Republican side were making a mistake. He would tell them that public opinion in the States they represent will not warrant their refusal. At all events, it was ungenerous to refuse the people an opportunity to express their opinion. Their position would not be sustained. He would say to his Southern friends, if this guarantee be now refused, let them forego any act of secession until there shall be an opportunity to appeal to the people of the free States. [Applause.]

Mr. Lovejoy [3], amid the greatest confusion and excitement, appealed to Mr. Stanton to withdraw his demand for the previous question, which Mr. Stanton most emphatically refused to do.

Several gentlemen complained of the confusion, as it was impossible to know what was going on. Some said that the noise was owing to the large number of strangers on the floor, whilst others charged the disorder to members themselves.

The Speaker directed and the Doorkeeper to perform his duty.

The question was then taken, and the vote rejecting Mr. Corwin's proposed amendment to the Constitution reconsidered – yeas 128, nays 65.

[1] David Kilgore (1804-1879), Republican of Indiana, Member, Indiana state House of Representatives (1833-36, 1838, 1839, 1855), Presiding Judge, Yorktown Circuit (1839-46), US Representative (1857-61).

[2] Benjamin Stanton (1809-1872), Republican of Ohio, Member, Ohio state Senate (1841, 1843), US Representative (1851-53, 1855-61), Lieutenant Governor of Ohio (1862).

[3] Owen Lovejoy (1811-64), Republican of Illinois, Member, Illinois state House of Representatives (1854), US Representative (1857-64).

Source: "The National Crisis," Richmond *Daily Dispatch*, 2 March 1861, 1.

৵৽ ৵৽ ৵৽ ৵৽ ৵৽

"The Corwin Amendment Passed!" as announced by The Sun *of New York, 4 March 1861. Mixed amongst the stories highlighting the inauguration of Abraham Lincoln as President is the notice that the pro-slavery amendment by Rep. Corwin has passed both houses of Congress.*

EXTRA SUN

———

MONDAY, March 4, 1861.

———

COMPLETE ACCOUNT OF THE INAUGURATION OF ABRAHAM LINCOLN, AS SIXTEENTH PRESIDENT OF THE UNITED STATES

———

PROCEEDINGS OF CONGRESS.

———

MR. CORWIN'S AMENDMENT PASSED! ! !

[…]

THE HOUSE CONSTITUTIONAL AMENDMENT PASSED! ! !

The question was then taken on the original resolution, as it came from the house.

The following was the vote:

YEAS – Messrs. Anthony, Baker, Bigler, Bright, Crittenden, Dixon, Douglas, Foster, Grimes, Gwin, Harlan, Hunter, Johnson, (of Tenn.,) Kennedy, Lawthaan, Mason, Morrill, Nicholson, Polk, Pugh, Rice, Sebastian, Ten Eyck, Thompson.

NAYS – Messrs. Bingham, Chandler, Clark, Doolittle, Durkee, Foot, King, Sumner, Trumbull, Wade, Wilkinson, Wilson – 12.

Senator Polk was in the Chair, and decided that it was carried, two-thirds having voted in the affirmative.

5:20 A.M. – Mr. TRUMBULL appealed from the decision of the chair, on the ground that it required two-thirds of the whole vote of the Senate.

The decision was sustained – Yeas, 33; Nays, 1.

Messrs. WADE and MASON moved to take up the Crittenden resolutions. Agreed to.

The question was then on Mr. CLARK'S amendment which was disagreed to by Yeas, 15; Nays, 22.

Mr. CRITTENDEN then to a substitute the resolutions of the Peace Conference.

Motion lost by yeas, 7, nays 28.

The question was then on the adoption of the Crittenden compromise resolutions. Lost by the following vote:

YEAS – Messrs. Bayard, Bigler, Bright, Crittenden, Douglas, Gwin, Hunter, Johnson of Tennessee, Kennedy, Lane, Latham, Mason, Nicholson, Polk, Pugh, Rice, Sebastian, Thompson and Wigfall – 14.

NAYS – Messrs. Anthony, Bingham, Chandler, Clark, Dixon, Doolittle, Durkee, Fessenden, Foote, Foster, Grimes, Harlan, King, Morrill, Sumner, Ten Eyck, Trumbull, Wade, Wilkinson and Wilson – 20.

Mr. BRIGHT moved an executive session. Lost.

At 7 A.M., the Senate took a recess till ten o'clock.

Mr. PUGH said that he wanted a test vote, and therefore moved to lay the whole subject on the table. He wanted to stop discussion.

A vote was then taken on the amendment, which was lost by yeas 14, nays 25. Messrs. BIGLER, DOUGLAS, CRITTENDEN, JOHNSON of Tennessee, LATHAM, RICE and SEBASTIAN voting with the Republicans against it.

Mr. BINGHAM then offered an amendment, which is the CLARK amendment.

The amendment was lost by yeas 13; nays 24, Messrs. ANTHONY, BAKER, DIXON, FOSTER, HARLAN, and TEN EYCK voting in the negative. Mr. GRIMES offered as an amendment the substitute offered by Mr. SE-WARD. Lost by yeas 14; nays 25, Messrs. ANTHONY, BAKER, DURKEE, FOSTER, TEN EYCK, and WADE voting in the negative.

Mr. JOHNSON of Arkansas, offered as an amendment the proposition of the Peace Conference. Lost by yeas 3; nays 34.

The Senate reassembled at ten o'clock. The President called the Senate to order. A large number of enrolled bills were announced signed.

The joint resolution to correct certain clerical errors in the Tariff bill was passed.

Several reports were made, and the bill to incorporate the Metropolitan Gas Light Company was taken up and debated, Mr. BRIGHT opposing its passage.

At half past eleven, a message was received from the House, that having finished business, it was ready to adjourn.

Mr. BRIGHT proceeded:

Mr. CLARK said it was a struggle of an overgrown company to see how powerful it could get. The Senate has come here to talk a bill down a the close of the session.

Twelve o'clock arrived, and the Vice President called the Senate to order, and said:

Senators: – In taking final leave of this position, I shall ask a few moments in which to tender to you my grateful it acknowledgments for the resolution declaring your approval of the manner in which I have discharged my duties, and to express my deep sense of the uniform courtesy which as the presiding officer I have received from the members of this body. If I have committed errors your generous forbearance refused to rebuke them, and during the whole period of my service I have never appealed in vain to your justice or charity.

Source: "Mr. Corwin's Amendment Passed," *The Sun* [New York], 4 March 1861, 1.

✽ ✽ ✽ ✽ ✽

"Secessionism On The Rise," 7 March 1861 gives an update on the Corwin Amendment. Excerpted from the New York Journal, *it predicts the amendment's chances of passing in the legislature of Maryland, a pro-slavery state.*

FROM MARYLAND

THE INAUGURAL IN BALTIMORE

SECESSIONISM ON THE RISE – THE CORWIN AMENDMENT.

From Our Own Correspondent.

BALTIMORE, March 5, 1861.

The 4th of March has gone, and left behind it a cold, raw, and snow-like day, contrasting quite as sharply with yesterday's invigorating temperature as Mr. Buchanan's treasonable reign stands in bleak contrast with the beneficent opening of Mr. Lincoln's assumption of the reins of Government.

The rush for the Inaugural, yesterday, that the newspaper offices, was unexampled, and the general feeling was favorable, so far as it obtained utterance. The telegraph made sad work of it, but enough could be gathered to give a pretty clear idea of the tone of the address, and the opinion, even of some of the fire-eaters, was, it would do.

[…]

The last and the first of the traitor Presidents is to arrive in town to-day, on his winding way from Washington to Wheatland, and is to be entertained by "mine host" of Barnum's Hotel, at his private residence. The *Exchange* newspaper, by the by, salutes him this morning with a raking fire of denunciation, for failing to stand by and complete the treason that was to consign the Federal Government over to the keeping of the slaveholder aristocracy of the Cotton States. Nothing that Republicans have ever said of the Sage of Wheatland, in their most angry moments, can equal the violence of this his quondam supporter [1].

Several of our prominent Secessionist merchants, or rather sympathizers with Secessionism, are said to have expressed themselves perfectly satisfied with the Inaugural. Among them, I hear with pleasure the name of William T. Walters, esq., one of the wealthiest and most influential members of our mercantile community, and a beneficent patron of the fine arts.

It is hardly probable that Gov. Hicks [2] will call together the existing Legislature, to pass upon the Corwin amendment to the Constitution. There is no need for hurry in the premises, now that it has been voted by Congress. Besides, it would be quite as well to let the people speak their views on the subject next Fall, when the new Legislature is to be chosen. The Democracy [3] are urgent, however, to get the Legislature together, for the purpose of impeaching the Governor and making capital for the next Fall elections. They owe the Governor no love, but will certainly depose him for refusing to execute their orders in the matter of the election of Controller [4]. They have also other charges of mal-administration in office against him, which they profess are sufficient to break him, if they can get at him.

[1] "Quondam," Latin for "former," i.e., a former friend or a former lover.

[2] Thomas Holliday Hicks (1798-1865), Governor of Maryland (1858-62), US Senator (1862-65).

[3] The Democratic Party during the 19th century was sometimes referred to as "The Democracy."

[4] This word is usually spelled "Comptroller," but appears here as it is spelled in the article.

Source: "From Maryland: The Corwin Amendment," *New York Journal*, 7 March 1861, 6.

"The Constitutional Amendment" as editorialized in the Lowell Daily Citizen & News *of Massachusetts, 5 April 1861. Here is local reaction to the slavery amendment.*

DAILY CITIZEN & NEWS.

Lowell, Friday, April 5, 1861.

CONSTITUTIONAL AMENDMENT. The majority of the committee on federal relations in the legislature have recommended a reference of the constitutional amendment to the next legislature. Though not dissenting, in direct terms, from the amendment, they think it may be best be considered by a national convention of the several states, and conclude by reporting a resolution in favor of that measure. The minority take exceptions to the amendment itself, as unnecessary, inexpedient and objectionable in its terms. It is especially objected that the term "domestic institutions" is of doubtful interpretation, and might hereafter be claimed to shield the worst forms of barbarism. Various other objections are raised, and finally it is urged that no such compromise, if adopted would operate to bring back the recusant states, and would therefore be inefficient for the purpose for which it is intended. The majority report is signed by Wm. D. Northend of the senate, G.T. Davis, J.F. Phillips and R.H. Burnham of the house; while the minority report bears the names of Wm. Whiting of the senate and Messrs. Albee and Robbins of the house.

Source: "Constitutional Amendment," *Lowell Daily Citizen* [Massachusetts], 5 April 1861, 2.

THE CHILD LABOR AMENDMENT, 1926

Text of the Proposed Amendment

Section 1. The Congress shall have the power to limit, regulate, and prohibit the labor of persons under eighteen years of age.

Section 2. The power of the several States is unimpaired by this article, except that the operation of State laws shall be suspended to the extent necessary to give effect to legislation enacted by the Congress

Discussion

The Industrial Revolution changed the way that work was done in the United States. Prior to this period, most people lived and worked on farms. One of the ways that family-run farms could compete was to have the children work the fields, although labor was backbreaking, and many children suffered serious injuries. During the early part of the 20th century, one of major league baseball's greatest pitchers was Mordecai "Three Finger" Brown, who earned his nickname when he lost two fingers on his right hand working machinery as a child, an experience matched by many. Children not only worked on farms, but in mills, factories, and any place they could get a job to help support their families. This gave rise to a movement in the first years of the 20th century to ban all child labor under the age of 18. Many of the same reformers who pushed for a federal income tax, for the direct election of US Senators, for giving women the right to vote, and for banning the sale and manufacture of intoxicating liquors, made their names known in the movement to ban child labor.

The first national legislative action to end child labor in the United States was introduced by Senator Albert Beveridge, Republican of Indiana, in 1906. Beveridge, a so-called "Progressive Republican," felt that it was government's role to outlaw such practices. However, when the proposal was sent to the respective judiciary committees of both houses of Congress, they concluded that Congress did not have the power under the Constitution to outlaw the practice across the nation. The Beveridge proposal died a quick death.

Despite this, progressives in both parties kept trying to get ban child labor. In September 1916, they succeeded, when Congress enacted a child labor law as part of Congress' power to regulate interstate commerce. This legislation banned the sale or distribution across state lines of products produced by minors – those 18 and under. The act struck the American South hardest of all, as many of its mills and farms employed children from the age of 14 and up, and a ban on its products would destroy the economy there. It was through this threat of the destruction of the economy that legal maneuvers began against the 1916 act which eventually made their way to the US Supreme Court. In June 1918, the Court, in *Hammer v. Dagenhart* (247 US 251), declared the 1916 act as unconstitutional.

Those in both political parties who wished to end child labor kept up their fight. A new piece of legislation, called the Child Labor Tax Act, was passed on 24 February 1919. This action attacked the profits of those who employed children for labor, hitting those persons with 10% tax on mills, mines, quarries, farms, and manufacturing concerns where children covered by the previous act worked. Again, those effected by this law sued in court; in 1922, in *Bailey v. Drexel Furniture Co.* (259 US 20), struck down this law as unconstitutional as well.

Undeterred, Representative Israel Moore Foster, Republican of Ohio, introduced in February 1923 a resolution for a child labor amendment to the Constitution, and submitted it to the Committee on the Judiciary of the House of Representatives. Speaking to the two prior acts which had been struck down by the US Supreme Court, Representative Foster explained, "The two acts held unconstitutional operated as a minimum national standard. State laws were still operative and were enforced by State machinery. Only in a relatively few communities was Federal enforcing machinery necessary. State officials charged with enforcement of State child labor laws very generally testify that the Federal act increased the respect for the State laws. Agreement has been general that the amendment approved should (1) reserve to the individual States the right to adopt higher standards than those which Congress may enact from time to time, so that the Federal law will in effect establish a minimum national standard, and (2) be general in terms so that provision can be made for future as well as present needs." [1]

At the same time, Senator Samuel Morgan Shortridge, Republican of California, introduced in the US Senate a similar resolution, calling for the passage of a Child Labor Amendment to the Constitution. Shortridge took note of the several previous attempts to pass a child labor amendment, but that specific language embodied in these pieces of legislation had been twice struck down by the US Supreme Court. Shortridge noted in his resolution, which accompanied the report which he sent to the Committee on the Judiciary of the US Senate, "Inasmuch as the Congress has twice considered it necessary and wise to enact a law for the protection of the child life of our Nation it would seem to be the mature and deliberate judgment of the people that such a law would be beneficial. We must assume that the Congress considered that it had the power to enact such laws and thought it for the welfare of the Nation to exercise that power." [2]

The work of Foster and Shortridge went nowhere, as many members of the US Congress did not want to pass another piece of legislation that they felt the US Supreme Court would ultimately strike down again. However, in 1926, those who kept trying got enough votes in both houses to pass the amendment and submit it to the states. As of this writing, 28 states have ratified this amendment, which is still 10 states shy of the requisite number needed for ratification. Opposition to its ratification was fierce, as many Progressives, who had supported all of the reforms of the last 30 years backed off when Prohibition, the so-called "Grand Experiment," failed dismally. Clarence E. Martin, the President of the American Bar Association, called the proposed amendment "[A] communistic effort to nationalize children, making them primarily responsible to the government instead of to their parents. It strikes at the home. It appears to be a definite positive plan to destroy the Republic and substitute a social democracy." [3] Nicholas Murray Butler, the President of Columbia University and a leading Progressive voice in the first half of the twentieth century, wrote in an open letter to *The New York Times*, 28 December 1933, that he considered the potential amendment as an "equally serious attack upon the fundamental principles of our government and social order," equating the potential amendment with prohibition. He denounced those who would "send federal agents and inspectors into every home, every family, every school and every church in the land to see what anyone under 18 years of age was dealing." [4] Even such a notable of the time as A. Lawrence Lowell, the president emeritus of Harvard University, said on a radio show, 16 February 1934, that while he was in firm opposition to the use of child labor, he could not stand to allow the US government used its unfettered power to pry into the lives of families who may need their children to help them survive, especially during the time of the Great Depression. [5]

Today, the Child Labor Amendment is considered a dead issue, with no calls for any additional state legislatures to ratify it. If, however, those who continue to favor the passage of this amendment can muster ten more states, the proposed Child Labor Amendment would become the Twenty-eighth Amendment to the US Constitution.

[1] "Proposing [a] Child Labor Amendment to the Constitution of the United States" House Report No. 1694, 67th Congress, 4th Session (Washington: Government Printing Office, 1923), 2.

[2] "Child-Labor Amendment to the Constitution of the United States" Senate Report No. 1185, 67th Congress, 4th Session (Washington: Government Printing Office, 1923), 17.

[3] Trattner, Walter I., "Crusade for the Children" (Chicago: Quadrangle Books, 1970), 199.

[4] "The Child Labor Amendment. Dr. Butler Calls on Organizations and Individuals to Act Promptly to Secure Its Defeat," *The New York Times*, 28 December 1933, 18.

[5] Cadwalader, Thomas F., "The Defeat of the Twentieth Amendment," *Annals of the American Academy of Political and Social Science*, CXXIX (January 1927), 65-69.

ORIGINAL DOCUMENTS REGARDING THE CHILD LABOR AMENDMENT

"An Examination of the Proposed Twentieth Amendment to the Constitution," reported by the National Association of Manufacturers. Written by James A. Emery, the General Counsel of the National Association of Manufacturers, this report was released in August 1924 in opposition to a potential Child Labor Amendment to the US Constitution.

An amendment to the national Constitution is presumed to be urged only by "overwhelming necessity." The pending proposal, through its designation as the "Child Labor" amendment, makes a peculiarly sympathetic and disarming appeal. History indicates representative institutions were often imperiled by popular rulers before whom the people's vigilance relaxed. So, too, power is likely to be recklessly bestowed in response to a plausible appeal to the heart which dims the reason. Those who analyze and reflect will find lurking beneath a touching sentiment a determined endeavor to obtain a grant of power from the people, revolutionary in its effect upon their private life and government, and entirely unnecessary to accomplish an object which all desire.

Analysis of the proposed amendment demonstrates that it is not a "child labor" amendment, but an exclusive grant of power to the Congress, which directly and by implication confers control over the labor and education of all persons under eighteen to an extent not now possessed by any State of the Union.

It proposes a revolutionary transformation of the traditional relation and respective function of local and federal government and the primary control of parents over the training and occupation of their children.

It is unnecessary, since the nature and extent of the work done by children is grossly exaggerated. It is plainly evident that the protection of child life from exploitation is being more effectively and rapidly met by the States than perhaps any other like social question.

The legislation flowing from this amendment will inevitably be bureaucratic, increasingly expensive, and superparental in its control of minor life.

It will impair the sense of local responsibility for the remedy of community conditions, and substitute for that natural respect for local law the distrust and constant irritation aroused by the imposition and administration of remote, inaccessible and irresponsible bureaucratic authority.

The proposal is socialistic in its origin, philosophy and associations.

It will overwhelm the central government with administrative detail. Finally the very nature of the debate upon the amendment indicates that it will continually excite sectional dissensions and open the way to Congressional regulation of production especially novel in its application to agriculture.

[…]

The first section of the proposed amendment would grant to Congress the power to "limit, regulate and prohibit the labor of persons under 18 years of age." It will thus be observed that the word "children" is not employed, and the age limit of 18 includes plainly not merely all who may be described as children, but all who are commonly regarded as youths. This age limit, it may be observed, is two years in excess of that fixed in either of the "Child Labor" statutes which were invalidated. Neither is this grant of power confined to regulation, but it includes the right to "prohibit" the labor of any person under 18. It is commonly said by the proponents of the proposal that it is intended merely to give Congress the power which the States presently possess over the same subject. It is not open to dispute that no State possesses the power to prohibit the labor of all persons under 17, much less 18 years of age.

Can it even be doubted that if any State prohibited any person under 17, much less 18, from engaging in farm work, that such prohibition would not be judicially sustained? It may likewise be asked, would the people of any State grant such power of prohibition to their own Legislature? Yet they are asked to grant to the Congress a greater power than any State possesses or would be likely to be granted.

"What is the highest standard now? Is it more than 18 years?" asked Congressman Montague of the chief of the Children's Bureau.

"They are prohibited up to 18 years in no country, nor in the United States," she replied.

The power to prohibit carries much more than the right to prevent the acceptance of employment. It includes of necessity the authority to fix the conditions under which any person under eighteen may be permitted to engage in any occupation. It necessarily includes the power to say to such persons what hours they may work and at what employment, the wages which must be paid, the education or training preliminary to work.

Moreover, the power to prohibit employment may include the authority to appropriate wholly or partly for the support of those who are not permitted to support themselves. Nor does the power of prohibition merely run against unrelated employers. It includes the power to forbid any person under eighteen from working for the parent, or guardian, either in the home or around their premises, or farms or for them in any occupation.

Source: Emery, James A., "An Examination of the Proposed Twentieth Amendment to the Constitution of the United States (Being the so-called Child Labor Amendment)" (New York: Secretary's Office, The National Association of Manufacturers, 1924), 1-7.

ও৩৯১ ও৩৯১ ও৩৯১ ও৩৯১ ও৩৯১

US Supreme Court decisions regarding this proposed amendment

Hammer v. Dagenhart (247 US 251 {1918}). Decided 3 June 1918 by a vote of 5-4. Justice William Rufus Day wrote the majority opinion.

The case: To put an end to child labor across the United States, the US Congress passed a law on 1 September 1916 (39 Stat. 675) which intended to prevent the interstate commerce of products made with the use of child labor. Roland Dagenhart, who owned a cotton mill in Charlotte North Carolina, sued in federal court, arguing that the law was an unconstitutional infringment of the Commerce Clause of the US Constitution. A district court in North Carolina, after a hearing, struck down the 1916 act. United States Attorney W.C. Hammer, the attorney for the western district of North Carolina, appealed the decision directly to the US Supreme Court, which granted certiorari, or, the right to hear the case. Arguments were heard on 15 and 16 April 1918.

Six weeks later, on 3 June, Justice William Rufus Day held for a 5-4 court (he was joined in the majority by Chief Justice Edward Douglass White, and Justices Willis Van Devanter, James C. McReynolds, and Mahlon Pitney) that the 1916 act was unconstitutional. Justice Day explained, "In interpreting the Constitution it must never be forgotten that the Nation is made up of States to which are entrusted the powers of local government. And to them and to the people the powers not expressly delegated to the National Government are reserved... The power of the States to regulate their purely internal affairs by such laws as seem wise to the local authority is inherent and has never been surrendered to the general government...To sustain this statute would not be in our judgment a recognition of the lawful exertion of congressional authority over interstate commerce, but would sanction an invasion by the federal power of the control of a matter purely local in its character, and over which no authority has been delegated to Congress in conferring the power to regulate commerce among the States."

He continued,

"We have neither authority nor disposition to question the motives of Congress in enacting this legislation. The purposes intended must be attained consistently with constitutional limitations and not by an invasion of the powers of the States. This court has no more important function than that which devolves upon it the obligation to preserve inviolate the constitutional limitations upon the exercise of authority, federal and state, to the end that each may continue to discharge, harmoniously with the other, the duties entrusted to it by the Constitution."

He concluded,

"In our view the necessary effect of this act is, by means of a prohibition against the movement in interstate commerce of ordinary commercial commodities, to regulate the hours of labor of children in factories and mines within the States, a purely state authority. Thus the act in a twofold sense is repugnant to the Constitution. It not only transcends the authority delegated to Congress over commerce but also exerts a power as to a purely local matter to which the federal authority does not extend. The far reaching result of upholding the act cannot be more plainly indicated than by pointing out that if Congress can thus regulate matters entrusted to local authority by prohibition of the movement of commodities in interstate commerce, all freedom of commerce will be at an end, and the power of the States over local matters may be eliminated, and thus our system of government be practically destroyed. For these reasons we hold that this law exceeds the constitutional authority of Congress. It follows that the decree of the District Court must be *affirmed*."

Justice Oliver Wendell Holmes, Jr., was joined in dissent by Justice Louis D. Brandeis and John Hessin Clarke, bitterly argued that the Congress did have the right to regulate child labor laws under an expansive Commerce Clause, writing,

"The single question in this case is whether Congress has power to prohibit the shipment in interstate or foreign commerce of any product of a cotton mill situated in the United States, in which within thirty days before the removal of the product children under fourteen have been employed, or children between fourteen and sixteen have been employed more than eight hours in a day, or more than six days in any week, or between seven in the evening and six in the morning. The objection urged against the power is that the States have exclusive control over their methods of production and that Congress cannot meddle with them, and taking the proposition in the sense of direct intermeddling I agree to it and suppose that no one denies it. But if an act is within the powers specifically conferred upon Congress, it seems to me that it is not made any less constitutional because of the indirect effects that it may have, however obvious it may be that it will have those effects, and that we are not at liberty upon such grounds to hold it void."

He concluded,

"The act does not meddle with anything belonging to the States. They may regulate their internal affairs and their domestic commerce as they like. But when they seek to send their products across the state line they are no longer within their rights. If there were no Constitution and no Congress their power to cross the line would depend upon their neighbors. Under the Constitution such commerce belongs not to the States but to Congress to regulate. It may carry out its views of public policy whatever indirect effect they may have upon the activities of the States. Instead of being encountered by a prohibitive tariff at her boundaries the State encounters the public policy of the United States which it is for Congress to express. The public policy of the United States is shaped with a view to the benefit of the nation as a whole. If, as has been the case within the memory of men still living, a State should take a different view of the propriety of sustaining a lottery from that which generally prevails, I cannot believe that the fact would require a different decision from that reached in [another decision]. Yet in that case it would be said with quite as much force as in this that Congress was attempting to intermeddle with the State's domestic affairs. The national welfare as understood by Congress may require a different attitude within its sphere from that of some self-seeking State. It seems to me entirely constitutional for Congress to enforce its understanding by all the means at its command."

Source: Biklé, Henry Wolf, "The Commerce Power and *Hammer v. Dagenhart*," *University of Pennsylvania Law Review and American Law Register*, LXVII:1 (January 1919), 21-36.

❧❧ ❧❧ ❧❧ ❧❧ ❧❧

Bailey v. Drexel Furniture Co. (259 US 20 {1922}). Decided 15 May 1922 by a vote of 8-1. Chief Justice William Howard Taft wrote the majority opinion, while Justice John Hessin Clarke was the sole dissenter.

The case: Those who wished to end child labor kept up their fight after the US Supreme Court struck down federal laws against interstate commerce in *Hammer v. Dagenhart*. A new piece of legislation, called the Child Labor Tax Act, was passed in both houses of Congress on 24 February 1919. This action, with the 1918 *Hammer* ruling in mind, instead attacked the profits of those who employed children for labor, hitting those persons with 10% tax on mills, mines, quarries, farms, and manufacturing concerns where children covered by the previous act worked. Again, those effected by this law were forced to go to court. One of these was Drexel (his first name does not appear in the case files), the owner of Drexel Furniture, a manufacturing concern in the wetn district of North Carolina, was, because of the new congressional action, sent a tax bill in September 1921 of $6,312.79 for having a single male worker under the age of 14. Drexel sued for relief in the district court of the Western District of North Carolina. He argued that, like thedecn in *Hammer*, the Congress had unconstitutionally placed a burden on interstate commerce as well as the regulation of business. The district court, as it had in *Hammer*, held that the congressional action was unconstitutional. The US government sued directly to the US Supreme Court, and arguments were held before the high court on 7 and 8 March 1922.

On 15 May 1922, Chief Justice William Howard Taft, a former President of the United States, held for a solid 8-1 Court that the 1919 act, like the 1916 act which had been struck down in *Hammer* in 1918, was unconstitutional. Taft spent much of the majority opinion explaining that the Court regularly upholds tax laws passed by Congress. He explained,

"It is the high duty and function of this court in cases regularly brought to its bar to decline to recognize or enforce seeming laws of Congress, dealing with subjects not intrusted to Congress, but left or committed by the supreme law of the land to the control of the states. We cannot avoid the duty, even though it require us to refuse to give effect to legislation designed to promote the highest good. The good sought in unconstitutional legislation is an insidious feature, because it leads citizens and legislators of good purpose to promote it, without thought of the serious breach it will make in the ark of our covenant, or the harm which will come from breaking down recognized standards. In the maintenance of local self-government, on the one hand, and the national power, on the other, our country has been able to endure and prosper for near a century and a half.

"Out of a proper respect for the acts of a co-ordinate branch of the government, this court has gone far to sustain taxing acts as such, even though there has been ground for suspecting, from the weight of the tax, it was intended to destroy its subject. But in the act before us the presumption of validity cannot prevail, because the proof of the contrary is found on the very face of its provisions. Grant the validity of this law, and all that Congress would need to do, hereafter, in seeking to take over to its control any one of the great number of subjects of public interest, jurisdiction of which the states have never parted with, and which are reserved to them by the Tenth Amendment, would be to enact a detailed measure of complete regulation of the subject and enforce it by a socalled tax upon departures from it. To give such magic to the word 'tax' would be to break down all constitutional limitation of the powers of Congress and completely wipe out the sovereignty of the states...

"Taxes are occasionally imposed in the discretion of the Legislature on proper subjects with the primary motive of obtaining revenue from them and with the incidental motive of discouraging them by making their continuance onerous. They do not lose their character as taxes because of the incidental motive."

Then, Taft discussed the Court's finding in this specific case: "But there comes a time in the extension of the penalizing features of the so-called tax when it loses its character as such and becomes a mere penalty, with the characteristics of regulation and punishment. Such is the case in the law before us...[t]he case before us cannot be distinguished from that of *Hammer v. Dagenhart*. Congress there enacted a law to prohibit transportation in interstate commerce of goods made at a factory in which there was employment of children within the same ages and for the same number of hours a day and days in a week as are penalized by the act in this case. This court held the law in that case to be void. In the case at the bar, Congress in the name of a tax which on the face of the act is penalty seeks to do the same thing, and the effort must be equally futile."

He concluded,

"The analogy of the *Dagenhart* Case is clear. The congressional power over interstate commerce is, within its proper scope, just as complete and unlimited as the congressional power to tax, and the legislative motive in its exercise is just as free from judicial suspicion and inquiry. Yet when Congress threatened to stop interstate commerce in ordinary and necessary commodities, unobjectionable as subjects of transportation, and to deny the same to the people of a state in order to coerce them into compliance with Congress' regulation of state concerns, the court said this was not in fact regulation of interstate commerce, but rather that of state concerns and was invalid. So here the so-called tax is a penalty to coerce people of a state to act as Congress wishes them to act in respect of a matter completely the business of the state government under the federal Constitution."

Note: In a 1922 law article, Joseph R. Long wrote, "The recent decision of the Supreme Court that the Child Labor Tax Law of 1919 is unconstitutional will probably stand out as one of the landmarks in our constitutional history. It brings to a halt the attempt to use the federal taxing power as a substitute for a general police power, an attempt which, if successful, would have revolutionized our constitutional system by practically wiping out the sovereignty of the States. This decision should go far toward clearing the air, so to speak, of the fogs that were fast obscuring some of the most fundamental principles of constitutional law."

Sources: Long, Joseph R., "Federal Police Regulation by Taxation," *Virginia Law Review*, IX:2 (December 1922), 81-97; Whittaker, William G., "Child Labor in America: History, Policy, and Legislative Issues," *CRS Report for Congress*, 9 February 2005.

References

Biklé, Henry Wolf, "The Commerce Power and *Hammer v. Dagenhart*," *University of Pennsylvania Law Review and American Law Register*, LXVII:1 (January 1919), 21-36.

Long, Joseph R., "Federal Police Regulation by Taxation," *Virginia Law Review*, IX:2 (December 1922), 81-97.

Whittaker, William G., "Child Labor in America: History, Policy, and Legislative Issues," *CRS Report for Congress*, 9 February 2005.

Additional reading

Levine, Marvin J., "Children for Hire: The Perils of Child Labor in the United States" (Westport, Connecticut: Greenwood Press, 2003).

Loughran, Miriam E., "The Historical Development of Child-Labor Legislation in the United States" (Ph.D. dissertation, Catholic University of America, 1921).

THE EQUAL RIGHTS AMENDMENT

Text of Proposed Amendment

Section 1. Equality of rights under the law shall not be denied or abridged by the United States or by any State on account of sex.

Section 2. The Congress shall have the power to enforce, by appropriate legislation, the provisions of this article.

Section 3. This amendment shall take effect two years after the date of ratification.*

Note: *Because of the US Supreme Court decision in *Coleman v. Miller* (307 U.S. 433 {1939}), the authors of the amendment had to expand the deadline for ratification to seven years, ending in 1979, which, in 1978, was extended a second time to June 1982.

Discussion

The push for an Equal Rights Amendment began in the 1920s. The earlier history of the movement for the voting and other rights for women, from the nation's birth until the end of the First World War, is covered in the chapter on the Nineteenth Amendment.

Since the time that women won the right to vote, as embodied in the Nineteenth Amendment that was ratified in 1920, there has been movement toward an Equal Rights Amendment. In 1923, Alice Paul, one of the leaders of the suffrage movement, drafted a Equal Rights Amendment that was introduced in the Congress as "The Lucretia Mott Amendment," named after an early advocate for women's rights. Until 1972, such an amendment was introduced on a regular basis, always receiving little support. Consistently voted to be tabled, or sent back to committee, it did not get an actual floor vote until 1946, when the US Senate voted for its passage, 38-35. Although this was far short of the two-thirds needed for passage, it was the closest it ever came. In 1950, a modified Equal Rights Amendment was again passed by the US Senate, but again did not get the required votes. [1]

In 1967, a new group, the National Organization for Women (NOW), made as its top legislative action the passage of an Equal Rights Amendment. Three years later, during hearings before the US Senate's Committee on the Judiciary's Subcommittee on Constitutional Amendments on such a proposal, members of NOW barged into the hearing room and disrupted the hearing, demanding that an Equal Rights Amendment bill be brought before both houses of Congress. The chairman of the subcommittee, Senator Birch Bayh, Democrat of Indiana, agreed to the protestors' demands, and, in May 1970, opened hearings on the potential language for an Equal Rights Amendment. A month later, through the machinations of Rep. Martha Wright Griffiths (1912-2003), Democrat of Michigan, who filed a discharge petition in the House Judiciary Committee, a proposed Equal Rights Amendment was brought to the floor of the US House of Representatives. A similar proposal was brought to the floor of the US Senate, but died in the 1970 session.

However, on 12 October 1971, the House voted 354-23 for what was called House Joint Resolution 208 (aka Equal Rights Amendment), sending it to the Senate for a vote. One of the amendment's leading opponents was Rep. Emanuel Celler, Democrat of New York, and the chairman of the House Committee on the Judiciary, who told a packed House during the final debate, with his voice shaking with emotion, that women "represented motherhood and creation" and that this amendment would force women to be sent into battle alongside men. Women, Celler said, "in the carnage and slaughter of battle, on the land, on the sea and in the air, is unthinkable." He finished his statement with the question, "Can you imagine women being trained by a drill sergeant or, with fixed bayonets, charging the enemy? Why, the family structure, in one fell swoop, would be torn asunder." One of the amendment's supporters, Rep. Bella Abzug, Democrat of New York, answered Celler by saying, "We don't want men or women in the trenches, but the brutality of war is not more upsetting to women than it is to men." [2]

Immediately, foes of the House action, especially those in the US Senate, declared their readiness to frustrate any attempt to pass the amendment. Senator Sam Ervin, Democrat of North Carolina, who had led the fight in 1970 to scuttle the bill in the upper house, told reporters that he was again prepared to either lead a filibuster against the amendment, or would offer amendments to change the House-approved bill, sending it to a House-Senate committee where he and Rep. Celler could kill it. **[3]**

However, groups such as NOW and others mobilized, forcing the US Senators to go on the record for or against the amendment. This strategy worked, by peeling off one Senator at a time until the requisite number was in their camp. After long and raucous debate, on 21 March 1972, the Senate passed the House bill by a vote of 84 to 8, and sent it to the states for ratification. **[4]** The vote got bipartisan support, while Ervin as joined by Senators George S. McGovern (D-South Dakota) and Henry M. "Scoop" Jackson (D-Washington State), as well as Barry Goldwater (R-Arizona) and John C. Stennis (D-Mississippi) in opposition. Ervin led the debate with impassioned pleas for it to be defeated. He said that the amendment would "repeal the handiwork of God" who had created men and women differently. "Sadly," he said, "the women who have been pressing for this are like the majority of the members of the Senate and House in their lack of knowledge about what this would do." Amendments proposed by Ervin were all voted down, leading to the final vote.

Two hours after the amendment cleared its Senate hurdle, Hawaii became the first state to ratify it. At the same time, women who argued against the amendment's passage, led by conservative activist Phyllis Schafly, formed the National Committee to Stop ERA.

With a ratification deadline of seven years, those pushing for the amendment went to work, and by 1977 had gotten 35 states to vote in the affirmative for the amendment. However, in the remaining states there was wide resistance to the potential amendment, and those who backed it, including NOW, asked Congress in March 1977 for an extension of the ratification deadline. In October 1977, Rep. Elizabeth Holtzman, Democrat of New York, who had defeated Rep. Emanuel Celler in 1972 over the issue of the Equal Rights Amendment, introduced a bill in Congress asking for the amendment to be extended past its 22 March 1979 deadline. On 15 August 1978, the US House voted 233-189 to extend the deadline for an additional three years and three months; the Senate voted for the new deadline of 30 March 1982 on 6 October 1978 by a vote of 60-36.

In May 1979, a number of states, led by Arizona, Idaho, and Washington State, filed suit in federal court to find the extension given to the amendment unconstitutional. In December 1981, a federal judge held that the deadline was constitutional. Appealed to the US Supreme Court, this opinion was upheld in January 1982.

In the final months of the ratification movement, NOW and ERA supporters pushed to find three additional states to ratify the amendment to no avail. On 30 June 1982, the process ended three states shy of ratification. In four of the states targeted near the end, including Florida, Illinois, and North Carolina, all were shown to have less than 50% support from white men, most of whom made up the membership of these states' legislatures.

In July 1982, the Equal Rights Amendment was reintroduced in Congress. In 1982, the US House of Representatives, controlled by Democrats, voted 278-147 to approve the amendment, 6 votes shy of the two-thirds needed. Since 1985, supporters of the original proposed amendment have reintroduced it in numerous congresses, but each time since it has been tabled and sent back to committee. While the National Organization for Women remains the amendment's most steadfast supporter, it does not have the legislative strength, nor the strength in Congress, that it once had.

[1] Brown, Barbara A.; Thomas I. Emerson, Gail Falk, and Ann E. Freedman, "The Equal Rights Amendment: A Constitutional Basis for Equal Rights for Women," *The Yale Law Journal*, LXXX:5 (April 1971), 871-985.

[2] "House Okays Equal Rights Bill; Wrought Fight Expected in Senate," *The Pittsburgh Press* [Pennsylvania], 13 October 1971, 32.

[3] "Goes Plan fight on Lib Voting," *The Deseret News* [Salt Lake City, Utah], 13 October 1971, 2A.

[4] "Senate approved equal rights for women amendment," *The Wilmington News* [North Carolina], 23 March 1972, 1.

ORIGINAL DOCUMENTS REGARDING THE EQUAL RIGHTS AMENDMENT

"Amend the Constitution Relative to Equal Rights for Men and Women": A House Judiciary Committee Report, 1945. The following is a report on hearings for an Equal Rights Amendment to be submitted to the House for debate and a vote. This did not happen in 1945, and has remained so for the next 27 years. Note the language regarding women working outside the home.

Text of Equal-Rights Amendment As Now Before Congress

"Equality of rights under the law shall not be denied or abridged by the United States or by any State on account of sex.

"Congress and the several States shall have power, within their respective jurisdictions, to enforce this article by appropriate legislation.

"This amendment shall take effect 8 years after the date of ratification."

[…]

Equality Legislation in the United States Today

(Submitted by the research department of the National Woman's Party, Helena Hill Weed, chairman)

The Judiciary Committee,
House of Representatives, Washington, DC:

The research department of the National Woman's Party presents herewith to the Judiciary Committee a résumé of the progress already made in equalizing laws which formally applied to one sex only.

We do this in order to show that the position of women word not be jeopardized by the incorporation of the equal-rights amendment into the Constitution of the United States.

All the laws which have been cited by the opposition as either impossible to equalize or as socially undesirable have already been equalized in one State or another, without detriment to women. On the other hand, these changes to equality have greatly benefited women, enhanced the dignity of family life, and improved general social conditions for both men and women.

This résumé covers only the laws of the 48 States and the District of Columbia, and does not cover those of other jurisdictions subject to the authority of the United States. It is also confined to those laws which are most frequently cited as "beneficial laws which would be jeopardized by enforcement of the equal-rights amendment."

The equal laws cited in this résumé have been taken from two codifications of the laws affecting the legal status of women which have already been published by the United States Government.

[…]

While complete State records showing the progress toward equalization of the laws are not now available, the trend toward complete equalization of the laws is unmistakable.

Adoption of the equal-rights amendment would require all the States to carry this equalization to completion with respect to all laws that still discriminate against either men or women, and would make these reforms permanent.

Impermanence of Existing Equal Laws

There is no permanent security for women in existing equal laws. As long as women remain outside the protection of the fourteenth amendment and are denied that equality of human rights which the Constitution declares are inalienable, any or all of these equal laws may be repealed at any time by a mere majority vote of the legislature "at its will or whom," as the Supreme Court has declared (*Berthoff v. O'Reilly*, 14 N.Y. 509, 30 Am. Rep. 823; *Munn v. Illinois*, 94 US 113).

In the absence of such constitutional limitations, the women of any State could again be subjected to the indignities and degradation of the English common law as it existed at the time the Constitution was written in 1787, while there would be no limit to the establishment of future discriminations against women if organized groups exerted political pressure for their enactment.

Present and Proposed Social Security Laws are a Perfect Example of the In-Security of Working Women Who Lack Constitutional Protection of Rights

The present Social Security Act and the proposed Wagner-Murray-Dingell bill are dedicated to be measures for the protection of the individual, the home, and the general welfare. Working men and women contribute equally, in proportion to age and earnings, toward the social-security fund from which benefits are paid, but both measures contain gross discriminations against women with regard to benefits accrued.

Both measures were planned with reference to "an ideal family," in which the husband provides the cash income while the wife and children remain in the home, making no cash contribution to the support of the family. Neither measure takes into consideration the present status of women, particularly of married women, in industry, nor of existing economic conditions which compel married women to augment the family income by work outside the home. Nor is consideration given to unmarried women who support dependents – women who are often denied marriage because they cannot shirk these obligations.

Source: "Amend the Constitution Relative to Equal Rights for Men and Women. Statements Presented to Subcommittee No. 2 of the Committee on the Judiciary[,] House of Representatives[,] Seventy-Ninth Congress[,] First Session on H.J. Res. 1, H.J. Res. 5, H.J. Res. 30, H.J. Res. 42, H.J. Res. 49, H.J. Res. 66, H.J. Res. 71, H.J. Res. 80, H.J. Res. 82, and H.J. Res. 96[,] Proposing an Amendment to the Constitution of the United States Relative to Equal Rights for Men and Women" (Washington: Government Printing Office, 1945), 1-4.

The Equal Rights Amendment passes the US House of Representatives, as reported here in The Washington Post, *13 October 1971.*

Equal Rights for Women Clears House, 354-23

By Richard L. Lyons
    Washington Post Staff Writer

The House approved the women's rights constitutional amendment yesterday after striking out a section that women said would have made it meaningless. No Senate action is expected until next year.

The purpose of the amendment, pushed by women's groups for half a century, is to give women equal legal rights with men. Sponsors said it also would strike down laws that favor women over men, as in child custody suits.

A provision to exempt women from the military draft and to let stand laws protecting the health nd safety of women workers was defeated, 265 to 87.

Rep. Martha Griffiths (D-Mich.), chief sponsor of the equal rights amendment, said women want full equality under the law and would prefer that the resolution be killed if the exemptions were approved.

The amendment was endorsed and sent to the Senate by a vote of 354 to 23, far more than the two-thirds required. It will become part of the Constitution only if approved by a two-thirds vote of the Senate and by the legislatures of 38 states.

The House passed a similar resolution last year, but it died in the Senate. An amendment has passed the Senate three times over the years, but always with the exemption attached. The Senate Judiciary Committee has taken no action this year.

A resolution like Mrs. Griffiths' has been placed on the Senate calendar, bypassing the committee. But the press of other business as Congress seeks to adjourn and the preoccupation of the amendment's chief sponsor, Sen. Birch Bayh (D-Ind.), with his wife's illness [1] is expected to delay Senate consideration until next year.

Mrs. Griffiths and her allies argued that the "protective" work laws are more often used to discriminate against employment or promotion of women than to protect them. Rep. Bella Abzug (D-N.Y.) observed that women are permitted to scrub office building floors at night "while our protectors are asleep."

Rep. Emanuel Celler (D-N.Y.), Judiciary Committee chairman and an opponent of the amendment, said it would be "unthinkable for women to be integrated into the carnage of war." Rep. David W. Dennis (R-Ind.), said that if fathers were drafted during war-time then mothers would have to be drafted too.

Others conjured up pictures of male and female soldiers in the same foxholes. But Mrs. Griffiths replied that the Amendment only required that women be equally subject to the draft, not that they be assigned to the front lines. They could do office work and release men for combat, she said.

To arguments that drafting women would weaken the national defense, Rep. Thomas P. O'Neill (D-Mass.) responded that this has not been the case in Israel.

Supporters of the amendment said women are discriminated against in a host of ways, from the rights to buy and sell property to the right to an equal education. Opponents said the amendment would cause much litigation and confusion, and that equality not provided by the 14th Amendment and civil rights laws should be given by specific legislation.

Rep. Fletcher Thompson (R-Ga.) tried to add a provision Forbidding busing of school students to achieve racial balance. It was ruled out of order as not germane.

Source: "Equal Rights for Women Clears House, 354-23," *The Washington Post*, 13 March 1971, A1, A12.

A year after passing the US House of Representatives, the Equal Rights Amendment passes the US Senate, and is sent to the states for ratification, as reported in The Washington Post, *23 March 1972.*

FEMALE RIGHTS CLEARS SENATE, GOES TO STATES

By Spencer Rich
    Washington Post Staff Writer

Sweeping aside all proposed language changes by overwhelming margins, the Senate approved the women's equal rights amendment yesterday, 84 to 8, and sent it to the states for ratification.

The historic vote ended a 49-year struggle by both men's and women's organizations to win congressional endorsement of a constitutional amendment specifying that women are to receive absolute equality with men before the law. The House approved the measure last Oct. 12 by a 354-to-23 vote. A two-thirds vote was required in both chambers.

Hawaii ratified the proposed constitutional amendment less than two hours after it was passed by the Senate. Final approval by the state senate and house came at 5:10 p.m. (EST), putting the island state in contention to be the first to ratify the amendment.

If ratified within seven years by three quarters of the state legislatures (38 states), the proposal will become the 27th amendment to the Constitution. It would go into effect two years after ratification.

The key paragraph reads:

"Equality of rights under the law shall not be denied or abridged by the United States or by any state on account of sex."

Sponsors of the amendment led in the Senate by Birch Bayh (D-Ind.) and Marlow W. Cook (R-Ky.) and in the House by Martha W. Griffiths (D-Mich.) said it would wipe out a broad spectrum of archaic state and federal laws and regulations which, though in some case ostensibly designed to protect women, actually lock them into a subordinate role and limit their legal and economic rights.

They said the amendment will:

- Wipe out state laws limiting the types of jobs women may take and the number of hours they may work.

- Eliminate laws restricting women's rights in some states to handle property and start businesses on an equal basis with men.

- End discriminatory admissions practices by state colleges and some graduate schools, and discrimination in hiring and promotions in public schools and colleges.

- Forbid discrimination against women in state and local government jobs.

- End laws treating women more harshly in a number of criminal situations – for example, one state statute which permits women to be jailed for three years for habitual drunkenness but men for only 30 days, and two state laws which permit a wronged husband but not a wronged wife to plead "passion killing."

- Abolish state laws that give women less favorable treatment than men in the handling of their children's property, and more favorable treatment in cases of child support, child custody, and alimony.

- End the present exemption of women from the military draft.

Opponents of the amendment, led in the Senate by Sam J. Ervin Jr. (D-N.C.), argued that making women subject to the draft and wiping out their presumptive rights to alimony, child support and child custmoy, as well as special labor protective laws, would take away protections far more valuable than they would gain.

But women's groups said they would be willing to accept liability to the draft in order to establish the principle of equality as part of the Constitution. In repeated responses to Ervin, Bayh told the senate than wome were unlikely to be assigned to combat roles if drafted because they would still have to meet tests of strength and physical skill for combat which only men were likely to pass.

Bayh also said the amendment wouldn't wipe out all alimony, child-support and child-custody laws, but only force them to be interpreted or rewritten so as to give completely equal treatment to men and women, allowing the court to use its judgment.

The senator said this might mean that a judge would compel a wife to pay alimony if her income was far higher than her husband's. But if the husband's were higher, he would continue to have the primary responsibility for family support.

Ervin also contended that the amendment would prohibit separate sleeping and toilet facilities for men and women in the Army, public buildings, prisons and other public facilities, and might force repeal of laws against rape, white slavery and sexual crimes against young girls.

But Bayh said the amendment definitely would continue to permit separate sleeping and toilet facilities, and wouldn't bar laws against rape, homosexual cohabitation or molestation of minors provided they applied generally to both sexes.

Ervin's attempts to write in specific assurances on these and similar points were rejected in a series of roll calls. Though both Virginia and both Maryland senators voted for the constitutional amendment on final passage, Virginia's Harry Byrd supported Ervin on these votes.

On the final vote, voting "no" were Ervin, Wallace F. Bennett (R-Utah), James L. Buckley (Cons.-R-N.Y.), Norris H. Cotton (R-N.H.), Paul J. Fannin (R-Ariz.), Barry Gold-water (R-Ariz.), Clifford P. Hansen (R-Wyo.), and John Stennis (D-Miss.). James East-land (D-Miss.) was present and paired against passage.

Democratic presidential candidates Edmund S. Muskie (Maine) and Hubert H. Humphrey (Minn.) voted for passage, but both George S. McGovern (S.D.) and Henry M. Jackson (Wash.) were absent.

The Maryland Senate last night allowed the introduction of a resolution that would have Maryland ratify the proposed equal rights amendment. The resolution, drafted by Sen. Edward T. Conroy (D-Prince George's), was referred to a committee.

The chief reason for passage of the amendment this year was a substantially improved lobbying effort by such groups as the National Organization of Women, National Women's Political Caucus, National Federation of Business and Professional Women's clubs and many others.

Source: "Female Rights Clear Senate, Goes to States," *The Washington Post*, 23 March 1972, A1, A9.

References

Baldez, Lisa; Lee Epstein, and Andrew D. Martin, "Does the US Constitution Need an Equal Rights Amendment?," *The Journal of Legal Studies*, XXXV:1 (January 2006), 243-83.

Emerson, Thomas I., "In Support of the Equal Rights Amendment," *Harvard Civil Rights – Civil Liberties Law Review*, VI (1971), 225-33.

Soule, Sarah A; and Susan Olzak, "When Do Movements Matter? The Politics of Contingency and the Equal Rights Amendment," *American Sociological Review*, LXIX:4 (August 2004), 473-97.

BALANCED BUDGET AMENDMENT

Text of the Proposed Amendment

Section 1. Total outlays for any fiscal year shall not exceed total receipts for that fiscal year, unless two-thirds of the duly chosen and sworn Members of each House of Congress shall provide by law for a specific excess of outlays over receipts by a roll call vote.

Section 2. Total outlays for any fiscal year shall not exceed 18 percent of the gross domestic product of the United States for the calendar year ending before the beginning of such fiscal year, unless two-thirds of the duly chosen and sworn Members of each House of Congress shall provide by law for a specific amount in excess of such 18 percent by a roll call vote.

Section 3. Prior to each fiscal year, the President shall transmit to the Congress a proposed budget for the United States Government for that fiscal year in which
  (1) total outlays do not exceed total receipts; and
  (2) total outlays do not exceed 18 percent of the gross domestic product of the United States for the calendar year ending before the beginning of such fiscal year.

Section 4. Any bill that imposes a new tax or increases the statutory rate of any tax or the aggregate amount of revenue may pass only by a two-thirds majority of the duly chosen and sworn Members of each House of Congress by a roll call vote. For the purpose of determining any increase in revenue under this section, there shall be excluded any increase resulting from the lowering of the statutory rate of any tax.

Section 5. The limit on the debt of the United States shall not be increased, unless three-fifths of the duly chosen and sworn Members of each House of Congress shall provide for such an increase by a roll call vote.

Section 6. The Congress may waive the provisions of sections 1, 2, 3, and 5 of this article for any fiscal year in which a declaration of war against a nation-state is in effect and in which a majority of the duly chosen and sworn Members of each House of Congress shall provide for a specific excess by a roll call vote.

Section 7. The Congress may waive the provisions of sections 1, 2, 3, and 5 of this article in any fiscal year in which the United States is engaged in a military conflict that causes an imminent and serious military threat to national security and is so declared by three-fifths of the duly chosen and sworn Members of each House of Congress by a roll call vote. Such suspension must identify and be limited to the specific excess of outlays for that fiscal year made necessary by the identified military conflict.

Section 8. No court of the United States or of any State shall order any increase in revenue to enforce this article.

Section 9. Total receipts shall include all receipts of the United States Government except those derived from borrowing. Total outlays shall include all outlays of the United States Government except those for repayment of debt principal.

Section 10. The Congress shall have power to enforce and implement this article by appropriate legislation, which may rely on estimates of outlays, receipts, and gross domestic product.

Section 11. This article shall take effect beginning with the fifth fiscal year beginning after its ratification.'

Discussion

That the United States is in financial trouble, evidenced by the chart below, is not up for debate. What is up for debate, however, is what should be done to solve it. Do we raise taxes...do we cut spending...do we do both?

Do we do little more of one and a little less of the other? What would a hike in personal income taxes do the US economy during these slow economic times? What would severe cuts do to the fabric of the social safety nets that aids the poor and disadvantaged?

The first time a call was made in the Congress to enact an amendment specifically aimed to forcing the US government to balance its accounts was in 1935, when Senator Millard Tydings, Democrat of Maryland, introduced Senate Joint Resolution 36, which, if enacted, would have banned the US government from appropriating even one dollar to pay for expenditures that resulted in deficit spending, and that previous government debt must be paid for within 15 years of the amendment's ratification. The following year, Rep. Harold Knutson, Republican of Minnesota, introduced House Joint Resolution 579, which allowed for deficit spending during times of war or crisis, but forced the government to spend what it brought in during peacetime.

These early attempts at a Balanced Budget Amendment went nowhere, but in 1947 the Senate Committee on Appropriations held hearings on a potential amendment. It reported the measure out of committee, but since the Committee on the Judiciary did not follow up, the proposal died. It has been brought up, on occasion, in numerous Congresses, with detractors using every resource at their hands to end debate. The potential for a balanced budget has attracted presidential support. Ronald Reagan and George H.W. Bush both supported a constitutional amendment, while Bill Clinton backed the idea short of amending the Constitution.

ORIGINAL DOCUMENTS REGARDING THE BALANCED BUDGET AMENDMENT

Senator John C. Stennis, Democrat of Mississippi, speaks in support of a Balanced Budget Amendment, 12 March 1979, delivered before the US Senate Committee on the Judiciary's Subcommittee on the Constitution.

I am acutely conscious of the lasting and enduring nature of our Constitution and I certainly recognize that it should not be tinkered with or amended except for [the] most compelling reasons. However, the financial history of this nation for the past 25 years and my strong sense of fiscal responsibility compel me to propose the amendment embodied in Senate Joint Resolution 6. I believe that it is an idea whose time has come.

Let me briefly explain the proposed amendment. It's basic purpose is to seek to assure that the total outlays of the government during any fiscal year do not exceed the total receipts available to the government during such fiscal year.

For this purpose the proposed amendment provides that no later than the twentieth day after the close of each fiscal year the President shall ascertain the total receipts of the government during such fiscal year, not including receipts derived from the issuance of bonds, notes, or other obligations of the United States. Likewise, during the same twenty day period, the President shall ascertain the total outlays of the government during such fiscal year, not including any outlays for the redemption of bonds, notes, or other obligations of the United States.

If the total receipts are determined to be less than the total outlays, then under the amendment the President would be required to determine the percentage rate of income surtax which would be necessary to raise enough additional taxes to eliminate the deficit and transmit it to the Congress by a special message. The income tax surtax would be levied and effective for the calendar year following the close of the fiscal year with respect to which the Presidential determination was made, and would be an additional income tax upon all individual and corporate incomes.

It can be seen that the proposed amendment is clear and simple. It would require that any Federal deficit be offset by a surtax to be levied in the calendar year following the year in which the deficit was incurred. No exercise of judgment or discretion on the part of anyone would be involved. If expenditures exceeded revenues during a fiscal year a surtax would have to be levied during the following calendar year to bring the budget into balance. The rate of surtax would be determined by the President purely as a mathematical calculation and, as I have said, this would not require any exercise of judgment or discretion.

There is an essential and necessary escape valve in the proposed amendment, however. Under this safety valve the requirement for a balanced budget could be waived and set aside by a three-fourths vote of all members of each House in the case of a grave national emergency such as a war or serious depression. This would be the sole exception to the requirement that the budget be balanced.

I believe that the Congress should make a start now – at this very moment – to advance towards a pay-as-you-go constitutional amendment. At best it will take several years to get the constitutionally-required two-thirds vote in each House and have the amendment ratified by three-fourths of the States. This means that even if the Senate passes the amendment at this session, its effective date would still be several years down the road, so that the Congress would have the time to bring the budget in balance. In addition, as a further protection, the amendment itself provides that it should not become operative until the first fiscal year beginning after the amendment is ratified.

I do think it is pertinent to refer to the unhappy fiscal history which makes this amendment so necessary. I will recapitulate it briefly at this point.

It took us 173 years – from 1789 to fiscal year 1962 – before the Federal budget reached $100 billion. In the 18 years since fiscal year 1962 the budget has skyrocketed to $531 billion. Thus, even with anticipated receipts of $502 billion, the estimated deficit for fiscal 1980 is $29 billion.

In fiscal year 1970 the national debt was $382 billion. The estimated national debt at the end of fiscal year 1980 is $898 billion. Therefore, we find that in ten years the national debt will have increased by $516 billion, an average of more than $51 billion a year. The estimated interest on the national debt for fiscal year 1980 of $57 billion is more than the entire Federal budget for fiscal year 1951.

Give the record of the Federal deficits over the past quarter of a century, it is clear that the Executive and Legislative branches, acting in a permissive legislative situation without constitutional compulsion or restriction have utterly failed to bring Federal spending under control. This is why I believe we need a strong, mandatory constitutional amendment with real teerh and action-enforcing provisions.

Source: Stennis, John A. "Should A Constitutional Amendment Be Adopted To Require Balanced Federal Budget? Pro," *The Congressional Digest*, LVIII:5 (May 1979), 138-40.

Senator Edmund Muskie, Democrat of Maine, speaks in opposition to a Balanced Budget Amendment, 12 March 1979, delivered before the US Senate Committee on the Judiciary's Subcommittee on the Constitution.

In almost two hundred years, our nation had held just one Constitutional Convention; and the timeless brilliance of that assembly's work is enhanced with the passing of each new decade.

A new Constitutional Convention should be rejected out of hand.

But the anger and frustration which gave rise to the idea in the first place is another matter entirely. That is a very serious thing indeed. We as legislatures must respond – but with leadership, poise, and responsible solutions.

The public's frustration with seemingly endless inflation is genuine. It is centainly understandable. Inflation can destroy the fruits of a lifetime's labor and undermine and entire social order.

But Federal deficits, harmful though they sometimes are, are not the root of the problem. More importantly, changing the fundamental law of the land to mandate an unworkable Federal balance in good times and bad is not the solution. On the contrary, it could provike an even deeper dilemma. And the array of varying approaches is anything but simple.

Almost 50 bills, resolutions, and state petitions regarding a balanced Federal budget and now under consideration by Senate committees. For analytical purposes, we have broken all the proposals into several basic categories.

The first category encomps what might be called the basis formula – a simple requirement that the Federal budget be in balance except in specified emergencies.

The defects of this approach are as simple as its language. It limits or even eliminates the Federal government's ability to respond quickly and flexibly to changing economic conditions.

Moreover, a balanced Federal budget may be flatly impossible to achieve in times of severe recession.

Finally, since we are given no definition of a state of "emergency," we could anticipate prolonged debate and confusion just when prompt, effective action might be most necessary. And the end of that debate might well come too late to allow for meaningful responses to economic conditions.

Of course, since most of these proposals require a two-thirds vote of Congress to open the escape hatch, we might never have to concern ourselves with responding at all. A two-thirds vote is difficult to obtain on any issue. That's why the cloture rule now calls for a three-fifths vote instead of the traditional two-thirds.

Source: Muskie, Edmund S., "Should A Constitutional Amendment Be Adopted To Require Balanced Federal Budget? Con," *The Congressional Digest*, LVIII:5 (May 1979), 139-41.

Congress moves to pass a Balanced Budget Amendment, as reported in the Los Angeles Times, *14 November 2011. The massive climb in deficit spending since 2009 has led to more calls for the passage of a balanced budget constitutional amendment.*

Congress' week: Supercommittee scramble, balanced budget pitch, gun debate

By Lisa Mascaro, November 14, 2011

The House and Senate are both in session this week, but the main focus on Capitol Hill will be the workings of the secret supercommittee on deficit reduction that is approaching its final days to cut a deal to reduce the nation's deficit by $1.5 trillion.

The committee technically has until Nov. 23 to vote on a proposal, but it must post it 48 hours ahead of time, which is one week from today. Expect long days and nights under the Capitol dome as lawmakers on the 12-member panel shuttle proposals back and forth to strike a deal.

"The 23rd of November is going to be an historic day in this country – historic because we found a solution and began a process, or historic because we, as Americans, for the first time looked the other way," said Sen. Johnny Isakson (R-Ga.), who is not on the panel, as he implored his colleagues from the Senate floor to find consensus.

The House returns for a one-week stint with a full agenda before recess for a long Thanksgiving holiday, with the top priority being passing a funding bill to keep the government running past Friday.

Congress has forced the federal government to operate with stop-gap funding this year, almost shutting down the government as debates have raged over spending cuts.

This week's vote is expected to cool to a more measured agreement to simply keep government open. The proposal is expected to be a hybrid: funding some agencies through the end of the 2012 fiscal year while funding others only until December when the next stop-gap will be needed.

The House will take up the government funding bill first, by midweek, sending it later to the Senate for final passage, likely by Friday.

Jobs have been the stated focus of both Democrats and Republicans as the unemployment rate remains a top issue for voters. At the same time, the GOP-led House will take up another measure designed to appeal to its conservative base – a long-fought 2nd Amendment provision that would allow conceal-carry permits to be recognized across state lines.

The House will also take up a proposed balanced budget amendment – a perennial conservative favorite that was promised as part of the summer debt ceiling debate. Balanced budget amendments to the Constitution have been attempted before, but never cleared the long hurdle of passing both chambers of Congress and being ratified by the states.

The Senate will continue to make its way through a package of fiscal 2012 spending bills, including funding for the State Department and foreign aid, areas that are being targeted for cuts.

Then again, those battles could pale in comparison to the days ahead for the final push of the supercommittee.

Source: Mascaro, Lisa, "Congress' week: Supercommittee scramble, balanced budget pitch, gun debate," *Los Angeles Times*, 14 November 2011, online at http://articles.latimes.com/2011/nov/14/news/la-pn-congress-week-ahead-debate-20111114.

ॐ ॐ ॐ ॐ ॐ

The Balanced Budget Amendment Fails in the US House of Representatives, as Reported in the Los Angeles Times, *18 November 2011. One of the negative votes came from Rep. Paul Ryan (R-Wisconsin), chairman of the House Committee on the Budget, and the 2012 Republican vice presidential candidate. His reason was that it did not go far enough to combat the growing federal deficit and debt.*

The Balanced Budget Amendment Fails in the US House of Representatives

House rejects balanced-budget amendment The vote on a cherished but elusive GOP goal comes 16 years after a similar measure fell short by one vote in the Senate.

By Kathleen Hennessey, Washington Bureau
November 18, 2011

Reporting from Washington — The House of Representatives rejected a balanced-budget amendment to the Constitution on Friday, failing to revive a long-held and elusive goal for the GOP.

The vote came 16 years after an amendment failed to pass Congress by 1 vote in the Senate, but the intervening years have put the amendment further out of reach.

In a largely partisan 261-165 vote, the measure fell well short of 284 votes needed to pass. President Obama has said he opposes the amendment. The Senate, which also is required to vote on the amendment as part of the August deal to raise the debt ceiling, is not expected to pass it.

That's in part because the bipartisan cooperation needed to amass a two-thirds vote on any fiscal measure seems something of a pipe dream in today's political climate. Congress has locked horns all year on the best way to reduce the deficit and revive the sluggish economy.

Even as lawmakers voted on the budget amendment, the 12-member congressional "super committee" charged with reducing the deficit appeared deadlocked.

Friday's vote offered few signs of hope. Republicans watched Democrats turn away from the amendment — even those who voted for it in the past.

House Minority Whip Steny H. Hoyer (D-Md.) noted that when he voted for the amendment in 1995 he had confidence that Congress could come together to vote for spending increases in an emergency as allowed.

"Regrettably, over the 16 years, I've lost that confidence," Hoyer said.

The amendment was essentially identical to the one voted on in 1995. It would have required the government to balance its books within two years of ratification, but no sooner than 2017. A three-fifths vote of each chamber would be required before Congress could add to the debt or raise taxes. The president would be required to submit a balanced budget and the restrictions could be waived in wartime.

The debate played out as the federal debt hit the $15-trillion mark, a milestone Republicans used to bolster their case.

"We need the discipline that a balanced-budget amendment provides," said Rep. Robert W. Goodlatte (R-Va.).

Republicans vowed to continue pushing for the amendment and are certain to use its popularity with the public to attack opponents in campaigns next year.

While the GOP has embraced the amendment and its goals, few have lined up behind specific policies that would make it happen in short order.

The budget the House approved this year, which included major changes to Medicare that Democrats criticized as extreme, still would not have yielded a budget surplus until 2040, according to the nonpartisan Congressional Budget Office.

Eliminating the annual deficit — now roughly $1.3 trillion — would require such drastic and painful cuts that some conservatives are convinced politicians would instead be inclined to raise taxes. Those advocates and lawmakers pushed Republican leaders to propose an amendment that included a strict spending cap and mandated a larger majority vote before Congress could raise new revenue.

Leadership chose to return to the 1995 version in hopes of wooing fiscally conservative Democrats with a record of support. But the votes were not there. The amendment won support from 25 Democrats.

Four Republicans voted against it: Reps. Justin Amash (R-Mich.), Louie Gohmert (R-Texas), David Dreier (R-San Dimas) and House Budget Committee Chairman Paul D. Ryan (R-Wis.). Ryan said he worried that this version "makes it more likely taxes will be raised, government will grow, and economic freedom will be diminished."

Dreier, who voted for the amendment in 1995, said he had changed his mind. Two years after his vote, Congress balanced the budget for several years, he noted.

"I found we were able to balance the federal budget without touching that inspired document, the U.S. Constitution," Dreier said.

Several Democrats made a similar argument, saying an amendment was not needed to address a lack of political will.

Some pointed to California, among the 49 states required to balance its budget, as the cautionary tale, setting up an odd debate over who had it worse, Sacramento or Washington.

Rep. Linda T. Sanchez (D-Lakewood) had no doubt. "California has tried this flawed plan, and guess what? It hasn't worked."

Source: Hennessey, Kathleen," House rejects balanced-budget amendment," *Los Angeles Times*, 18 November 2011, online at http://articles. latimes.com/2011/nov/18/nation/la-na-congress-budget-20111119.

"Sleepy Balanced-Budget Amendment Debate Continues in US Senate," as reported in The Hill *newspaper, 13 December 2011.*

Sleepy balanced-budget amendment debate continues in the Senate

By Josiah Ryan
The Hill, 12/13/11

The Senate meandered through a sleepy afternoon of debate over the rival balanced-budget amendment bills that will hit the floor for votes on Wednesday afternoon, with senators mostly repeating floor speeches already delivered earlier in the year.

Republicans of every stripe, from Tea Party favorite Sen. Rand Paul (Ky.) to centrist Sen. Olympia Snowe (Maine), came to the floor in unison to express their support for Sen. Orrin Hatch's (R-Utah) version of the bill that would also place restrictions on raising taxes. All 47 Republicans are co-sponsors of that bill.

Democrats, meanwhile, were split, with some, like Senate Judiciary Committee Chairman Patrick Leahy (Vt.) and Sen. Kent Conrad (N.D.) arguing that the Congress should not tamper with the Constitution but balance the budget annually on its own volition. Other senators like Sen. Mark Udall (D-Colo.), however, expressed support for a limited version of the amendment expressed in S.J.Res 24.

That Democratic version would prevent Congress from lowering taxes on millionaires and also exempt the Social Security trust funds from the amendment's accounting.

The Senate spent hours in a break and in quorum calls on Tuesday afternoon.

Source: Ryan, Josiah, "Sleepy balanced-budget amendment debate continues in the Senate," *The Hill*, 13 December 2011, online at http://thehill.com/blogs/floor-action/senate/199187-sleepy-balanced-budget-amendment-debate-in-the-senate.

References

Muskie, Edmund S., "Should A Constitutional Amendment Be Adopted To Require Balanced Federal Budget? Con," *The Congressional Digest*, LVIII:5 (May 1979), 139-41.

Stennis, John A. "Should A Constitutional Amendment Be Adopted To Require Balanced Federal Budget? Pro," *The Congressional Digest*, LVIII:5 (May 1979), 138-40.

Wildavsky, Aaron B., "How to Limit Government Spending; Or, How a Constitution Amendment Tying Public Spending to Economic Growth Will Decrease Taxes and Lessen Inflation" (Berkeley: University of California Press, 1980).

Additional reading

Buchanan, James M., "Clarifying Confusion About the Balanced Budget Amendment," *National Tax Journal*, XLVIII:3 (September 1995), 347-55.

Tabellini, Guido; and Albert Alesina, "Voting on the Budget Deficit" (National Bureau of Economic Research Working Paper No. 2759, November 1988).

Appendix D

LIST OF SUPREME COURT CASES BY AMENDMENT

First Amendment
Schenck v. United States, 3 March 1919
Everson v. Board of Education, 10 February 1947
New York Times Co. v. United States, 30 June 1971
Hazelwood School District v. Kuhlmeier, 13 January 1988

Second Amendment
United States v. Miller, 15 May 1939
District of Columbia v. Heller, 26 June 2008
McDonald v. Chicago, 28 June 2010

Fourth Amendment
Silverman v. United States, 6 March 1961
Beck v. Ohio, 23 November 1964
Katz v. United States, 18 December 1967
Terry v. Ohio, 10 June 1968
Arizona v. Gant, 21 April 2009

Fifth Amendment
Miranda v. Arizona, 13 June 1966
Ohio v. Reiner, 19 March 2001

Sixth Amendment
Powell v. Alabama, 7 November 1932
Sheppard v. Maxwell, 6 June 1966
Barker v. Wingo, 22 June 1972

Eighth Amendment
Trop v. Dulles, 31 March 1958
Furman v. Georgia, 29 June 1972
Gregg v. Georgia, 2 July 1976
Roper v. Simmons, 1 March 2005

Ninth Amendment
Griswold v. Connecticut, 7 June 1965
Roe v. Wade, 22 January 1973

Tenth Amendment
New York v. United States, 19 June 1992
Printz v. United States, 27 June 1997

Eleventh Amendment
Van Stophorst v. Maryland, 1791
Chisholm v. Georgia, 18 February 1793
Cohens v. Virginia, 3 March 1821
Osborn v. Bank of the United States, 19 March 1824
Bank of the United States v. Planters' Bank of Georgia, 20 March 1824

Edelman v. Jordan, 25 March 1974
Fitzpatrick v. Bitzer, 28 June 1976
Florida Department of State v. Treasure Salvors, Inc., 1 July 1982
Seminole Tribe of Florida v. Florida, 27 March 1996
Kimel v. Florida Board of Regents, 11 January 2000

Twelfth Amendment
Ray v. Blair, 3 April 1952

Thirteenth Amendment
Bailey v. Alabama, 3 January 1911
Jones v. Alfred H. Mayer Co., 17 June 1968
United States v. Kozminski, 29 June 1988

Fourteenth Amendment
The Slaughter-House Cases, 14 April 1873
The Civil Rights Cases, 15 October 1883
Elk v. Wilkins, 3 November 1884
Yick Wo v. Hopkins, 10 May 1886
Plessy v. Ferguson, 18 May 1896
Brown v. Board of Education of Topeka, 17 May 1954
Mapp v. Ohio, 19 June 1961
Gideon v. Wainwright, 18 March 1963
Afroyim v. Rusk, 29 May 1967
Loving v. Virginia, 12 June 1967
Regents of the University of California v. Bakke, 28 June 1978
Adarand Constructors, Inc. v. Peña, 12 June 1995
Obergefell v. Hodges, 26 June 2015

Fifteenth Amendment
United States v. Cruikshank, 27 March 1876
Guinn v. United States, 21 June 1915
Grovey v.Townsend, 1 April 1935
Smith v. Allwright, 3 April 1944
Gomillion v. Lightfoot, 14 November 1960
South Carolina v. Katzenbach, 7 March 1966
Rice v. Cayetano, 23 February 2000
Shelby County v. Holder, 25 June 2013

Sixteenth Amendment
Hylton v. United States, 8 March 1796
Pollock v. Farmers, 8 April 1895
Brushaber v. Union Pacific Railroad Co., 24 January 1916
Bowers v. Kerbaugh-Empire Co., 3 May 1926
Commissioner of Internal Revenue v. Glenshaw Glass Co., 28 March 1955

Seventeenth Amendment
MacDougall v. Green, 21 October 1948
Trinsey v. Commonwealth of Pennsylvania, 6 August 1991

Eighteenth Amendment
Crane v. Campbell, 10 December 1917
National Prohibition Cases, 7 June 1920
Dillon v. Gloss, 16 May 1921

James Everard's Breweries v. Day, Prohibition Director of New York, et al. Edward & John Burke, Limited, v. Blair, Commissioner of Internal Revenue, et al., 9 June 1924
Olmstead v. United States, 4 June 1928

Nineteenth Amendment
Bradwell v. Illinois, 15 April 1873
Minor v. Happersett, 29 March 1875
Leser v. Garnett, 27 February 1922
Breedlove v. Suttles, 6 December 1937
Reed v. Reed, 22 November 1971
Frontiero v. Richardson, 14 May 1973
Cleveland Board of Education v. LaFleur, 21 January 1974
Stanton v. Stanton, 15 April 1975
Craig v. Boren, 20 December 1976

Twenty-first Amendment
State Board of Equalization v. Young's Market Co., 9 December 1936
Mahoney v. Joseph Triner Corp., 23 May 1938
Indianapolis Brewing Co. v. Liquor Commission, et al., 3 January 1939
Ziffrin, Inc. v. Reeves, 13 November 1939
Carter v. Virginia, 31 January 1944
Hostetter v. Idlewild Bon Voyage Liquor Corp., 1 June 1964
Joseph E. Seagram & Son, et. v. Hostetter, 19 April 1966
Craig v. Boren, 20 December 1976
California Retail Liquor Dealers Association v. Midcal Aluminum, Inc., 3 March 1980
Bacchus Imports, Ltd., v. Dias, 29 June 1984
Granholm v. Heald, 16 May 2005

Twenty-third Amendment
Hepburn & Dundas v. Ellzey, 1805
Loughborough v. Blake, 1820
National Mutual Insurance Co. v. Tidewater Transfer Co., Inc., 20 June 1949

Twenty-fourth Amendment
Breedlove v. Suttles, 6 December 1937
Harper v. Virginia State Board of Elections, 24 March 1966
Harman v. Forssenius, 27 April 1965
Burdick v. Takushi, 8 June 1992
Crawford v. Marion County Election Board, 28 April 2008

Twenty-sixth Amendment
Oregon v. Mitchell, 21 December 1970

Twenty-seventh Amendment
Dillon v. Gloss, 16 May 1921
Coleman v. Miller, 5 June 1939

Index

Credits

Grey House Publishing thanks the following for permission to reprint material:

Afro American (Baltimore)

Atlanta Constitution

Big Spring Daily Herald of Texas

The Blade (Toledo)

The Chicago Tribune

The Deseret News (Salt Lake City)

The Evening News

The Hill (Washington DC)

The Independent (Pasadena)

Los Angeles Times

The New York Times

Northwest Arkansas Times

Northwestern University Law Review

St. Petersburg Times

The Spokesman-Review (Spokane)

The Sun (Baltimore)

Syracuse Herald-Journal, Milwaukee Sentinel

The Tuscaloosa News

The Washington Post

Wisconsin State Journal

Grey House
Publishing

2016 Title List
Visit www.GreyHouse.com for Product Information, Table of Contents, and Sample Pages.

Grey House
Publishing

General Reference
An African Biographical Dictionary
America's College Museums
American Environmental Leaders: From Colonial Times to the Present
Encyclopedia of African-American Writing
Encyclopedia of Constitutional Amendments
Encyclopedia of Gun Control & Gun Rights
An Encyclopedia of Human Rights in the United States
Encyclopedia of Invasions & Conquests
Encyclopedia of Prisoners of War & Internment
Encyclopedia of Religion & Law in America
Encyclopedia of Rural America
Encyclopedia of the Continental Congress
Encyclopedia of the United States Cabinet, 1789-2010
Encyclopedia of War Journalism
Encyclopedia of Warrior Peoples & Fighting Groups
The Environmental Debate: A Documentary History
The Evolution Wars: A Guide to the Debates
From Suffrage to the Senate: America's Political Women
Global Terror & Political Risk Assessment
Nations of the World
Political Corruption in America
Privacy Rights in the Digital Era
The Religious Right: A Reference Handbook
Speakers of the House of Representatives, 1789-2009
This is Who We Were: 1880-1900
This is Who We Were: A Companion to the 1940 Census
This is Who We Were: In the 1910s
This is Who We Were: In the 1920s
This is Who We Were: In the 1940s
This is Who We Were: In the 1950s
This is Who We Were: In the 1960s
This is Who We Were: In the 1970s
U.S. Land & Natural Resource Policy
The Value of a Dollar 1600-1865: Colonial Era to the Civil War
The Value of a Dollar: 1860-2014
Working Americans 1770-1869 Vol. IX: Revolutionary War to the Civil War
Working Americans 1880-1999 Vol. I: The Working Class
Working Americans 1880-1999 Vol. II: The Middle Class
Working Americans 1880-1999 Vol. III: The Upper Class
Working Americans 1880-1999 Vol. IV: Their Children
Working Americans 1880-2015 Vol. V: Americans At War
Working Americans 1880-2005 Vol. VI: Women at Work
Working Americans 1880-2006 Vol. VII: Social Movements
Working Americans 1880-2007 Vol. VIII: Immigrants
Working Americans 1880-2009 Vol. X: Sports & Recreation
Working Americans 1880-2010 Vol. XI: Inventors & Entrepreneurs
Working Americans 1880-2011 Vol. XII: Our History through Music
Working Americans 1880-2012 Vol. XIII: Education & Educators
World Cultural Leaders of the 20th & 21st Centuries

Education Information
Charter School Movement
Comparative Guide to American Elementary & Secondary Schools
Complete Learning Disabilities Directory
Educators Resource Directory
Special Education: A Reference Book for Policy and Curriculum Development

Health Information
Comparative Guide to American Hospitals
Complete Directory for Pediatric Disorders
Complete Directory for People with Chronic Illness
Complete Directory for People with Disabilities
Complete Mental Health Directory
Diabetes in America: Analysis of an Epidemic
Directory of Drug & Alcohol Residential Rehab Facilities
Directory of Health Care Group Purchasing Organizations
Directory of Hospital Personnel
HMO/PPO Directory
Medical Device Register
Older Americans Information Directory

Business Information
Complete Television, Radio & Cable Industry Directory
Directory of Business Information Resources
Directory of Mail Order Catalogs
Directory of Venture Capital & Private Equity Firms
Environmental Resource Handbook
Food & Beverage Market Place
Grey House Homeland Security Directory
Grey House Performing Arts Directory
Grey House Safety & Security Directory
Grey House Transportation Security Directory
Hudson's Washington News Media Contacts Directory
New York State Directory
Rauch Market Research Guides
Sports Market Place Directory

Statistics & Demographics
American Tally
America's Top-Rated Cities
America's Top-Rated Smaller Cities
America's Top-Rated Small Towns & Cities
Ancestry & Ethnicity in America
The Asian Databook
Comparative Guide to American Suburbs
The Hispanic Databook
Profiles of America
"Profiles of" Series – State Handbooks
Weather America

Financial Ratings Series
TheStreet Ratings' Guide to Bond & Money Market Mutual Funds
TheStreet Ratings' Guide to Common Stocks
TheStreet Ratings' Guide to Exchange-Traded Funds
TheStreet Ratings' Guide to Stock Mutual Funds
TheStreet Ratings' Ultimate Guided Tour of Stock Investing
Weiss Ratings' Consumer Guides
Weiss Ratings' Guide to Banks
Weiss Ratings' Guide to Credit Unions
Weiss Ratings' Guide to Health Insurers
Weiss Ratings' Guide to Life & Annuity Insurers
Weiss Ratings' Guide to Property & Casualty Insurers

Bowker's Books In Print® Titles
American Book Publishing Record® Annual
American Book Publishing Record® Monthly
Books In Print®
Books In Print® Supplement
Books Out Loud™
Bowker's Complete Video Directory™
Children's Books In Print®
El-Hi Textbooks & Serials In Print®
Forthcoming Books®
Large Print Books & Serials™
Law Books & Serials In Print™
Medical & Health Care Books In Print™
Publishers, Distributors & Wholesalers of the US™
Subject Guide to Books In Print®
Subject Guide to Children's Books In Print®

Canadian General Reference
Associations Canada
Canadian Almanac & Directory
Canadian Environmental Resource Guide
Canadian Parliamentary Guide
Canadian Venture Capital & Private Equity Firms
Financial Post Directory of Directors
Financial Services Canada
Governments Canada
Health Guide Canada
The History of Canada
Libraries Canada
Major Canadian Cities

Grey House Publishing | Salem Press | H.W. Wilson | 4919 Route, 22 PO Box 56, Amenia NY 12501-0056

2016 Title List

Visit www.SalemPress.com for Product Information, Table of Contents, and Sample Pages.

Science, Careers & Mathematics

Ancient Creatures
Applied Science
Applied Science: Engineering & Mathematics
Applied Science: Science & Medicine
Applied Science: Technology
Biomes and Ecosystems
Careers in Building Construction
Careers in Business
Careers in Chemistry
Careers in Communications & Media
Careers in Environment & Conservation
Careers in Healthcare
Careers in Hospitality & Tourism
Careers in Human Services
Careers in Law, Criminal Justice & Emergency Services
Careers in Manufacturing
Careers in Physics
Careers in Sales, Insurance & Real Estate
Careers in Science & Engineering
Careers in Technology Services & Repair
Computer Technology Innovators
Contemporary Biographies in Business
Contemporary Biographies in Chemistry
Contemporary Biographies in Communications & Media
Contemporary Biographies in Environment & Conservation
Contemporary Biographies in Healthcare
Contemporary Biographies in Hospitality & Tourism
Contemporary Biographies in Law & Criminal Justice
Contemporary Biographies in Physics
Earth Science
Earth Science: Earth Materials & Resources
Earth Science: Earth's Surface and History
Earth Science: Physics & Chemistry of the Earth
Earth Science: Weather, Water & Atmosphere
Encyclopedia of Energy
Encyclopedia of Environmental Issues
Encyclopedia of Environmental Issues: Atmosphere and Air Pollution
Encyclopedia of Environmental Issues: Ecology and Ecosystems
Encyclopedia of Environmental Issues: Energy and Energy Use
Encyclopedia of Environmental Issues: Policy and Activism
Encyclopedia of Environmental Issues: Preservation/Wilderness Issues
Encyclopedia of Environmental Issues: Water and Water Pollution
Encyclopedia of Global Resources
Encyclopedia of Global Warming
Encyclopedia of Mathematics & Society
Encyclopedia of Mathematics & Society: Engineering, Tech, Medicine
Encyclopedia of Mathematics & Society: Great Mathematicians
Encyclopedia of Mathematics & Society: Math & Social Sciences
Encyclopedia of Mathematics & Society: Math Development/Concepts
Encyclopedia of Mathematics & Society: Math in Culture & Society
Encyclopedia of Mathematics & Society: Space, Science, Environment
Encyclopedia of the Ancient World
Forensic Science
Geography Basics
Internet Innovators
Inventions and Inventors
Magill's Encyclopedia of Science: Animal Life
Magill's Encyclopedia of Science: Plant life
Notable Natural Disasters
Principles of Astronomy
Principles of Chemistry
Principles of Physics
Science and Scientists
Solar System
Solar System: Great Astronomers
Solar System: Study of the Universe
Solar System: The Inner Planets
Solar System: The Moon and Other Small Bodies
Solar System: The Outer Planets
Solar System: The Sun and Other Stars
World Geography

Literature

American Ethnic Writers
Classics of Science Fiction & Fantasy Literature
Critical Insights: Authors
Critical Insights: Film
Critical Insights: Literary Collection Bundles
Critical Insights: Themes
Critical Insights: Works
Critical Survey of Drama
Critical Survey of Graphic Novels: Heroes & Super Heroes
Critical Survey of Graphic Novels: History, Theme & Technique
Critical Survey of Graphic Novels: Independents/Underground Classics
Critical Survey of Graphic Novels: Manga
Critical Survey of Long Fiction
Critical Survey of Mystery & Detective Fiction
Critical Survey of Mythology and Folklore: Heroes and Heroines
Critical Survey of Mythology and Folklore: Love, Sexuality & Desire
Critical Survey of Mythology and Folklore: World Mythology
Critical Survey of Poetry
Critical Survey of Poetry: American Poets
Critical Survey of Poetry: British, Irish & Commonwealth Poets
Critical Survey of Poetry: Cumulative Index
Critical Survey of Poetry: European Poets
Critical Survey of Poetry: Topical Essays
Critical Survey of Poetry: World Poets
Critical Survey of Shakespeare's Plays
Critical Survey of Shakespeare's Sonnets
Critical Survey of Short Fiction
Critical Survey of Short Fiction: American Writers
Critical Survey of Short Fiction: British, Irish, Commonwealth Writers
Critical Survey of Short Fiction: Cumulative Index
Critical Survey of Short Fiction: European Writers
Critical Survey of Short Fiction: Topical Essays
Critical Survey of Short Fiction: World Writers
Critical Survey of Young Adult Literature
Cyclopedia of Literary Characters
Cyclopedia of Literary Places
Holocaust Literature
Introduction to Literary Context: American Poetry of the 20th Century
Introduction to Literary Context: American Post-Modernist Novels
Introduction to Literary Context: American Short Fiction
Introduction to Literary Context: English Literature
Introduction to Literary Context: Plays
Introduction to Literary Context: World Literature
Magill's Literary Annual 2015
Magill's Survey of American Literature
Magill's Survey of World Literature
Masterplots
Masterplots II: African American Literature
Masterplots II: American Fiction Series
Masterplots II: British & Commonwealth Fiction Series
Masterplots II: Christian Literature
Masterplots II: Drama Series
Masterplots II: Juvenile & Young Adult Literature, Supplement
Masterplots II: Nonfiction Series
Masterplots II: Poetry Series
Masterplots II: Short Story Series
Masterplots II: Women's Literature Series
Notable African American Writers
Notable American Novelists
Notable Playwrights
Notable Poets
Recommended Reading: 600 Classics Reviewed
Short Story Writers

2016 Title List

Visit www.SalemPress.com for Product Information, Table of Contents, and Sample Pages.

History and Social Science

The 2000s in America
50 States
African American History
Agriculture in History
American First Ladies
American Heroes
American Indian Culture
American Indian History
American Indian Tribes
American Presidents
American Villains
America's Historic Sites
Ancient Greece
The Bill of Rights
The Civil Rights Movement
The Cold War
Countries, Peoples & Cultures
Countries, Peoples & Cultures: Central & South America
Countries, Peoples & Cultures: Central, South & Southeast Asia
Countries, Peoples & Cultures: East & South Africa
Countries, Peoples & Cultures: East Asia & the Pacific
Countries, Peoples & Cultures: Eastern Europe
Countries, Peoples & Cultures: Middle East & North Africa
Countries, Peoples & Cultures: North America & the Caribbean
Countries, Peoples & Cultures: West & Central Africa
Countries, Peoples & Cultures: Western Europe
Defining Documents: American Revolution
Defining Documents: Civil Rights
Defining Documents: Civil War
Defining Documents: Emergence of Modern America
Defining Documents: Exploration & Colonial America
Defining Documents: Manifest Destiny
Defining Documents: Postwar 1940s
Defining Documents: Reconstruction
Defining Documents: 1920s
Defining Documents: 1930s
Defining Documents: 1950s
Defining Documents: 1960s
Defining Documents: 1970s
Defining Documents: American West
Defining Documents: Ancient World
Defining Documents: Middle Ages
Defining Documents: Vietnam War
Defining Documents: World War I
Defining Documents: World War II
The Eighties in America
Encyclopedia of American Immigration
Encyclopedia of Flight
Encyclopedia of the Ancient World
Fashion Innovators
The Fifties in America
The Forties in America
Great Athletes
Great Athletes: Baseball
Great Athletes: Basketball
Great Athletes: Boxing & Soccer
Great Athletes: Cumulative Index
Great Athletes: Football
Great Athletes: Golf & Tennis
Great Athletes: Olympics
Great Athletes: Racing & Individual Sports
Great Events from History: 17th Century
Great Events from History: 18th Century
Great Events from History: 19th Century
Great Events from History: 20th Century (1901-1940)
Great Events from History: 20th Century (1941-1970)
Great Events from History: 20th Century (1971-2000)
Great Events from History: Ancient World
Great Events from History: Cumulative Indexes
Great Events from History: Gay, Lesbian, Bisexual, Transgender Events

Great Events from History: Middle Ages
Great Events from History: Modern Scandals
Great Events from History: Renaissance & Early Modern Era
Great Lives from History: 17th Century
Great Lives from History: 18th Century
Great Lives from History: 19th Century
Great Lives from History: 20th Century
Great Lives from History: African Americans
Great Lives from History: American Women
Great Lives from History: Ancient World
Great Lives from History: Asian & Pacific Islander Americans
Great Lives from History: Cumulative Indexes
Great Lives from History: Incredibly Wealthy
Great Lives from History: Inventors & Inventions
Great Lives from History: Jewish Americans
Great Lives from History: Latinos
Great Lives from History: Middle Ages
Great Lives from History: Notorious Lives
Great Lives from History: Renaissance & Early Modern Era
Great Lives from History: Scientists & Science
Historical Encyclopedia of American Business
Issues in U.S. Immigration
Magill's Guide to Military History
Milestone Documents in African American History
Milestone Documents in American History
Milestone Documents in World History
Milestone Documents of American Leaders
Milestone Documents of World Religions
Music Innovators
Musicians & Composers 20th Century
The Nineties in America
The Seventies in America
The Sixties in America
Survey of American Industry and Careers
The Thirties in America
The Twenties in America
United States at War
U.S.A. in Space
U.S. Court Cases
U.S. Government Leaders
U.S. Laws, Acts, and Treaties
U.S. Legal System
U.S. Supreme Court
Weapons and Warfare
World Conflicts: Asia and the Middle East
World Political Yearbook

Health

Addictions & Substance Abuse
Adolescent Health & Wellness
Cancer
Complementary & Alternative Medicine
Genetics & Inherited Conditions
Health Issues
Infectious Diseases & Conditions
Magill's Medical Guide
Psychology & Behavioral Health
Psychology Basics

2016 Title List

Visit www.HWWilsonInPrint.com for Product Information, Table of Contents and Sample Pages

Current Biography
Current Biography Cumulative Index 1946-2013
Current Biography Monthly Magazine
Current Biography Yearbook: 2003
Current Biography Yearbook: 2004
Current Biography Yearbook: 2005
Current Biography Yearbook: 2006
Current Biography Yearbook: 2007
Current Biography Yearbook: 2008
Current Biography Yearbook: 2009
Current Biography Yearbook: 2010
Current Biography Yearbook: 2011
Current Biography Yearbook: 2012
Current Biography Yearbook: 2013
Current Biography Yearbook: 2014
Current Biography Yearbook: 2015

Core Collections
Children's Core Collection
Fiction Core Collection
Graphic Novels Core Collection
Middle & Junior High School Core
Public Library Core Collection: Nonfiction
Senior High Core Collection
Young Adult Fiction Core Collection

The Reference Shelf
Aging in America
American Military Presence Overseas
The Arab Spring
The Brain
The Business of Food
Campaign Trends & Election Law
Conspiracy Theories
The Digital Age
Dinosaurs
Embracing New Paradigms in Education
Faith & Science
Families: Traditional and New Structures
The Future of U.S. Economic Relations: Mexico, Cuba, and Venezuela
Global Climate Change
Graphic Novels and Comic Books
Immigration
Immigration in the U.S.
Internet Safety
Marijuana Reform
The News and its Future
The Paranormal
Politics of the Ocean
Racial Tension in a "Postracial" Age
Reality Television
Representative American Speeches: 2008-2009
Representative American Speeches: 2009-2010
Representative American Speeches: 2010-2011
Representative American Speeches: 2011-2012
Representative American Speeches: 2012-2013
Representative American Speeches: 2013-2014
Representative American Speeches: 2014-2015
Representative American Speeches: 2015-2016
Rethinking Work
Revisiting Gender
Robotics
Russia
Social Networking
Social Services for the Poor
Space Exploration & Development
Sports in America
The Supreme Court
The Transformation of American Cities

U.S. Infrastructure
U.S. National Debate Topic: Surveillance
U.S. National Debate Topic: The Ocean
U.S. National Debate Topic: Transportation Infrastructure
Whistleblowers

Readers' Guide
Abridged Readers' Guide to Periodical Literature
Readers' Guide to Periodical Literature

Indexes
Index to Legal Periodicals & Books
Short Story Index
Book Review Digest

Sears List
Sears List of Subject Headings
Sears: Lista de Encabezamientos de Materia

Facts About Series
Facts About American Immigration
Facts About China
Facts About the 20th Century
Facts About the Presidents
Facts About the World's Languages

Nobel Prize Winners
Nobel Prize Winners: 1901-1986
Nobel Prize Winners: 1987-1991
Nobel Prize Winners: 1992-1996
Nobel Prize Winners: 1997-2001

World Authors
World Authors: 1995-2000
World Authors: 2000-2005

Famous First Facts
Famous First Facts
Famous First Facts About American Politics
Famous First Facts About Sports
Famous First Facts About the Environment
Famous First Facts: International Edition

American Book of Days
The American Book of Days
The International Book of Days

Junior Authors & Illustrators
Eleventh Book of Junior Authors & Illustrations

Monographs
The Barnhart Dictionary of Etymology
Celebrate the World
Guide to the Ancient World
Indexing from A to Z
The Poetry Break
Radical Change: Books for Youth in a Digital Age

Wilson Chronology
Wilson Chronology of Asia and the Pacific
Wilson Chronology of Human Rights
Wilson Chronology of Ideas
Wilson Chronology of the Arts
Wilson Chronology of the World's Religions
Wilson Chronology of Women's Achievements

Grey House Publishing | Salem Press | H.W. Wilson | 4919 Route, 22 PO Box 56, Amenia NY 12501-0056

DATE DUE